2021-2022
SEPTEMBER–AUGUST
NIV®

Standard Lesson
COMMENTARY®

NEW INTERNATIONAL VERSION®

EDITORIAL TEAM

Jane Ann Kenney
Ronald L. Nickelson
Taylor Z. Stamps
Margaret K. Williams

Volume 28

Standard®
PUBLISHING
part of the David C Cook family

IN THIS VOLUME

Standard Lesson Commentary is published annually by Standard Publishing, www.standardpub.com. Copyright © 2021 by Standard Publishing, part of the David C Cook family, Colorado Springs, CO 80918. All rights reserved. Printed in the United States of America. All Scripture quotations, unless otherwise indicated, are taken from the Holy Bible, New International Version®, NIV®. Copyright ©1973, 1978, 1984, 2011 by Biblica, Inc.® Used by permission. All rights reserved worldwide. www.zondervan.com "NIV" and "New International Version" are trademarks registered in the United States Patent and Trademark Office by Biblica, Inc.® Lessons and/or readings based on *International Sunday School Lessons for Christian Teaching*; copyright © 2018, by the Committee on the Uniform Series. U.S.A. "Standard Lesson Commentary" is a registered trademark of Standard Publishing. No part of this book may be reproduced in any form, except for brief quotations in reviews, without the written permission of the publisher.

INDEX OF PRINTED TEXTS

The printed texts for 2021–2022 are arranged here in the order in which they appear in the Bible.

☞ *Don't forget the visuals!* ☜

The thumbnail visuals in the lessons are small reproductions of 18″ x 24″ full-color posters that are included in the *Adult Resources* packet for each quarter. Order numbers 1629121 (fall 2021), 2629122 (winter 2021–2022), 3629122 (spring 2022), and 4629122 (summer 2022) from either your supplier, by calling 1.800.323.7543, or at www.standardlesson.com.

CUMULATIVE INDEX

A cumulative index for Scripture passages used in the STANDARD LESSON COMMENTARY *for September 2016–August 2022 (the entire six-year cycle) is provided below.*

Standard Lesson Resources

Whether you use Standard Lesson Commentary® or Standard Lesson Quarterly®, you'll find a wealth of additional helps in the Standard Lesson Resources® line. These printed and digital products provide the most comprehensive resources for teaching the *ISSL/Uniform Series* available anywhere!

Adult Resources

This pack provides 12 full-color visuals to illustrate the lesson each week. Also included is a Presentation Tools CD that includes digital images of all the visuals and a PowerPoint® presentation for each lesson.

In the World

This online feature draws from a current event— something your students are probably talking about that very week— and helps you use it to illustrate the lesson theme.

Devotions®

Reflect on each Sunday's lesson outside of the classroom. Devotions® supplements the daily Bible readings recommended in Standard Lesson to challenge you to experience personal growth in Christ.

Standard®
PUBLISHING
part of the David C Cook family

Explore these resources and more at:
https://www.standardlesson.com/standard-lesson-resources/

CELEBRATING
GOD

Special Features

Lessons
Unit 1: God's People Offer Praise

Unit 2: Called to Praise God

Unit 3: Visions of Praise

QUARTERLY QUIZ

Use these questions as a pretest or as a review. The answers are on page iv of This Quarter in the Word.

Lesson 1

1. The inhabitants of which nation are said to melt away? (Edom, Moab, Canaan) *Exodus 15:15*

2. Miriam was the sister of Moses and _____. *Exodus 15:20*

Lesson 2

1. God was said to enthrone between the _____ on the ark. *2 Samuel 6:2*

2. When Michal saw David dancing before the ark, she cherished him in her heart. T/F. *2 Samuel 6:16*

Lesson 3

1. Bartimaeus called out to Jesus, saying, "Have _____ on me." *Mark 10:48*

2. After Bartimaeus received his vision, he returned home. T/F. *Mark 10:52*

Lesson 4

1. Peter charged his audience to repent and be _____. *Acts 2:38*

2. After the day of Pentecost, believers hoarded all their possessions. T/F. *Acts 2:45*

Lesson 5

1. The psalmist referred to the people of God as sheep. T/F. *Psalm 100:3*

2. The people were to "enter his gates with" what? (peace, love, thanksgiving) *Psalm 100:4*

Lesson 6

1. The psalmist declares that the Lord rules the world in _____. *Psalm 9:8*

2. The Lord does not forsake those who do what things? (Pick two: trust him, seek him, question him, understand him, doubt him) *Psalm 9:10*

Lesson 7

1. The psalmist says that people praised God, and he delivered them from distress. T/F. *Psalm 107:6*

2. What does the Lord pour out upon nobility? (love, shame, contempt) *Psalm 107:40*

Lesson 8

1. The psalmist noticed the special nature of the altar, in that even what creatures raised their young there? (bats, birds, bees) *Psalm 84:3*

2. The psalmist would rather be a _____ in God's house than dwell with the wicked. *Psalm 84:10*

Lesson 9

1. For the psalmist, songs of praise were to be accompanied by timbrel and _____. *Psalm 149:3*

2. God can be praised through dance. T/F. *Psalm 150:4*

Lesson 10

1. In Revelation's throne room scenes, angels occasionally sit on the throne. T/F. *Revelation 7:10*

2. The angels wipe away the tears of the saints. T/F. *Revelation 7:17*

Lesson 11

1. After the "angel sounded," how many elders worshipped God? (12; 12,000; 24) *Revelation 11:16*

2. The nations were _____ and God's wrath had come. *Revelation 11:18*

Lesson 12

1. The smoke from Babylon will rise for a thousand years. T/F. *Revelation 19:3*

2. What is the bride of the Lamb pictured as wearing? (fine linen, leather, wool) *Revelation 19:8*

Lesson 13

1. At Cornelius's house, Peter taught that God accepts people from every nation who convert to the Jewish faith. T/F. *Acts 10:35*

2. Peter taught that Jesus was appointed by God as what? (witness, judge, prosecutor) *Acts 10:42*

QUARTER AT A GLANCE

by Christopher Cotten

WHO AMONG THE GODS IS LIKE YOU, LORD? Who is like you—majestic in holiness, awesome in glory, working wonders" (Exodus 15:11). This quarter's lessons focus on the gift and privilege of worship, the acts of celebrating God for who he is and his work in our lives and in the world. Moses expressed amazement and awe through his worship, and these studies will explore worship that creates in us the same response.

People of Praise

The quarter begins under the heading "God's People Offer Praise." These first four lessons show us several individuals who praised God in different ways and in different circumstances. These lessons provide examples of praise-filled lives. They show us individuals who had serious flaws, or who faced great challenges in life, but who, nevertheless, rendered praise to God.

Moses, looking down on the corpses of the Egyptian charioteers, sang with confidence: "Your right hand, Lord, was majestic in power. Your right hand, Lord, shattered the enemy" (Exodus 15:6). King David, dancing with reckless abandon, reminds us to praise God for his great power, even when—or especially when—we might be worried about what others think or how they will see us. Bartimaeus, a man who had been blind for many years, shows us how trust and praise are connected, even in the midst of our difficulties.

Finally, this quarter includes the example of the first people who responded to Peter's preaching on the day of Pentecost. Luke records the ways in which lives changed because of obedience to the gospel. Reformed lives resulted in an orientation of praise and worship, daily breaking of bread, sharing of food, and worshipping "with glad and sincere hearts, praising God" (Acts 2:46-47a).

Praise in the Psalms

The central portion of the quarter, "Called to Praise God," brings us to the Psalter, the great hymnal of God's Old Testament people. These psalms can strengthen our prayer life and provide instruction for how to approach God in the face of injustice and sin. These psalms also show us how to celebrate God's goodness and mercy. For thousands of years, God's people have been writing poetry and songs for worship in that regard.

Many of us have a powerful tool for nurturing spirituality and devotion at our fingertips each week: our church hymnal or other Christian songbook. Do you have one on hand? Resolve to make use of it in your private devotionals. The psalms remind us that any believer can compose songs or poetry of worship; we do not have to leave these things to the "professionals." Our faith can be expressed in songs and poetry of our own.

> *Our faith can be expressed in songs and poetry of our own.*

Visions of Praise

Our final month will be spent in Revelation. In the throne room scenes, where the worship by the angels, the elders, and the multitudes is united, we see how worship can change our view of reality. It is easy, in our media-saturated lives, to take what we see around us—illness, poverty, political discord, war—as all there is. When we gather in worship, however, we are reminded of the true nature of reality.

No matter the suffering around us, God is on his throne watching over creation and moving us ever closer to the time when all things will be made new. On that great day he will be ultimately victorious and his justice and peace will rule over all.

GET THE SETTING

THE FOCUS for the fall 2021 quarter celebrates God through worship and praise. At the most basic level, worship is the act of attributing worth to God, and one way of doing so is through praising him. Praise is not a modern invention, nor is it limited to the Judeo-Christian tradition. Since the beginning of civilization, humans have offered praise and worship to fictitious gods.

Praise in the Ancient World

One such account in Ancient Near Eastern literature comes from the coronation of Sulgi, written over five thousand years ago. Sulgi praises his god in response to his own coronation as king. A similar account occurs years later in "The Tradition of the Seven Lean Years." Here Djoser, an Egyptian king, seeks to learn the extent of a famine through praises to Khnum, an imaginary god.

Praise is also used to motivate a god to act on behalf of the person praising. One such example is found in the Babylonian "Prayer of Lamentation to Ishtar." This prayer is an attempt to sway the god through flattery.

On the surface, these accounts may look similar to the biblical idea of praise. But the Christian should never resort to deceit or mere flattery (see Psalm 12:3; Proverbs 29:5). Instead, the Old and New Testaments present a different approach to praise and worship, one that is superior to its Ancient Near Eastern counterparts. Whereas these examples highlight a human-centered approach to praise, biblical praise is done in response to who God is and what he has done.

Biblical Praise: Direct

The biblical authors incorporated praise in two ways: direct praise and praise in narrative form. Direct praise includes the author's recorded words praising God. This method, found in poetry or direct speech, usually describes the proclamation of praise from the point of view of the person offering that praise. Often, these expressions of praise include particular words indicative of worship—words such as *praise, thanksgiving,* and *bless.*

Examples of direct praise are found in the lesson on the Song of Moses and Miriam (lesson 1), the lessons from the psalms (lessons 5–9), and those from Revelation (lessons 10–12). These passages highlight the focused nature of direct praise, expressions of worship to an active and caring God.

Biblical Praise: Narrative

A second way biblical authors demonstrate praise is through the use of narrative. These are biblical passages in which an author depicts a scene of praise. Such scenes present a picture of people praising God, often in response to God's work or intervention among his people. Examples of narrative praise can be found in the story of the healing of Bartimaeus (lesson 3), the events of the day of Pentecost (lesson 4), and the conversion of Cornelius (lesson 13).

Sometimes the biblical author describes people praising God after events that do not clearly indicate his direct intervention. In these cases, the praise may be for God's protection or his goodness. An example of this type of praise is found in the return of the ark to Jerusalem (lesson 2). Narrative praise shows that praising God can serve as an example to others.

Conclusion

Just as the Bible contains accounts of direct praise to God and narratives of people praising God, so it should be with the pages of our lives. We can and should praise God directly. And the narrative that creates for others can inspire them to praise God as well.

THIS QUARTER IN THE WORD

Mon, Aug. 30	God Hardens Pharaoh's Heart	Exodus 14:1-9
Tue, Aug. 31	Don't Just Do Something; Stand There!	Exodus 14:10-20
Wed, Sep. 1	Victory by the Sea	Exodus 14:21-31
Thu, Sep. 2	Blessed Be God Our Savior	Luke 1:67-75
Fri, Sep. 3	Victory in Jesus	1 Corinthians 15:51-58
Sat, Sep. 4	Moses Sings of God's Triumph	Exodus 15:1-10
Sun, Sep. 5	Moses and Miriam Praise God	Exodus 15:11-21
Mon, Sep. 6	David Prepares to Transport the Ark	2 Samuel 6:1-5
Tue, Sep. 7	The Holiness of the Sanctuary	Hebrews 9:1-7
Wed, Sep. 8	Uzzah Disregards the Ark's Holiness	2 Samuel 6:6-11
Thu, Sep. 9	The House of the Lord!	Psalm 122
Fri, Sep. 10	Go to God's Dwelling Place	Psalm 132:1-12
Sat, Sep. 11	The Ark in the Heavenly Temple	Revelation 11:15-19
Sun, Sep. 12	David Dances Before the Ark	2 Samuel 6:12-19
Mon, Sep. 13	Blind Eyes Shall Be Opened	Isaiah 35:1-6
Tue, Sep. 14	Declare God's Glory Among the Nations	Psalm 96
Wed, Sep. 15	Glory to God's Name Alone	Psalm 115:1-3, 9-18
Thu, Sep. 16	Only God Is Good	Mark 10:17-22
Fri, Sep. 17	Greatness Through Servanthood	Mark 10:42-45
Sat, Sep. 18	Praise the Lord, O My Soul!	Psalm 146
Sun, Sep. 19	Praise God for Healing!	Mark 10:46-52

Mon, Nov. 15	A Vision of Praise	Isaiah 6:1-8
Tue, Nov. 16	Let the Heavens Be Glad	1 Chronicles 16:23-34
Wed, Nov. 17	Let All God's Angels Worship Him	Hebrews 1:5-14
Thu, Nov. 18	King of Kings, Lord of Lords	Revelation 19:9-16
Fri, Nov. 19	God Judges the Wicked	Revelation 19:17-21
Sat, Nov. 20	The Lord Rejoices over You	Zephaniah 3:14-20
Sun, Nov. 21	The Lord Almighty Reigns	Revelation 19:1-8
Mon, Nov. 22	God Speaks to a Pagan King	Genesis 20:1-7, 14-16
Tue, Nov. 23	An Angel Speaks to Cornelius	Acts 10:1-8
Wed, Nov. 24	A Vision of Inclusion	Acts 10:9-22
Thu, Nov. 25	The Queen of Sheba Blesses God	1 Kings 10:1-9
Fri, Nov. 26	A Centurion Comes to Jesus	Luke 7:1-10
Sat, Nov. 27	Peter Enters Cornelius's House	Acts 10:23-33
Sun, Nov. 28	God Shows No Partiality	Acts 10:34-47

Answers to the Quarterly Quiz on page 2

Lesson 1—1. Canaan. 2. Aaron. **Lesson 2**—1. cherubim. 2. False. **Lesson 3**—1. mercy. 2. false. **Lesson 4**—1. baptized. 2. false. **Lesson 5**—1. true. 2. thanksgiving. **Lesson 6**—1. righteousness. 2. trust him/seek him. **Lesson 7**—1. false. 2. contempt. **Lesson 8**—1. birds. 2. doorkeeper. **Lesson 9**—1. harp. 2. true. **Lesson 10**—1. false. 2. false. **Lesson 11**—1. 24. 2. angry. **Lesson 12**—1. false. 2. fine linen. **Lesson 13**—1. false. 2. judge.

LESSON CYCLE CHART

International Sunday School Lesson Cycle, September 2016–August 2022

Year	Fall Quarter (Sep, Oct, Nov)	Winter Quarter (Dec, Jan, Feb)	Spring Quarter (Mar, Apr, May)	Summer Quarter (Jun, Jul, Aug)
2016–2017	**The Sovereignty of God** (Isaiah, Matthew, Hebrews, Revelation)	**Creation: A Divine Cycle** (Psalms, Luke, Galatians)	**God Loves Us** (Psalms, Joel, Jonah, John, Romans, Ephesians, 1 Peter, 1 John)	**God's Urgent Call** (Exodus, Judges, Prophets, Acts)
2017–2018	**Covenant with God** (Pentateuch, 1 & 2 Samuel, Nehemiah, Jeremiah, Ezekiel, 1 Corinthians, Hebrews)	**Faith in Action** (Daniel, Matthew, Acts, Ephesians, 1 Timothy, James)	**Acknowledging God** (Pentateuch, 2 Chronicles, Psalms, Luke, John, 2 Corinthians, Hebrews, Revelation)	**Justice in the New Testament** (Matthew, Luke, Romans, 2 Corinthians, Colossians)
2018–2019	**God's World and God's People** (Genesis)	**Our Love for God** (Deuteronomy, Joshua, Psalms, Matthew, Luke, Epistles)	**Discipleship and Mission** (Matthew, Mark, Luke, Acts, Romans)	**Covenant in God** (Ruth, 1 Samuel, Matthew, Mark, Ephesians, Colossians, Hebrews)
2019–2020	**Responding to God's Grace** (Pentateuch, 1 Samuel, 1 Kings, Luke, Epistles)	**Honoring God** (1 Kings, 1 Chronicles, Matthew, Luke)	**Justice and the Prophets** (Esther, Prophets, 1 Corinthians)	**Many Faces of Wisdom** (Proverbs, Ecclesiastes, Gospels, James)
2020–2021	**Love for One Another** (Genesis, 1 Samuel, Luke, John, Acts, Epistles)	**Call in the New Testament** (Gospels, Acts, Romans, 1 Corinthians, Hebrews)	**Prophets Faithful to God's Covenant** (Deuteronomy, Joshua, 1 & 2 Kings, Ezra, Nehemiah, Lamentations, Prophets)	**Confident Hope** (Leviticus, Matthew, Luke, Romans, 2 Corinthians, Hebrews, 1 John)
2021–2022	**Celebrating God** (Exodus, 2 Samuel, Psalms, Mark, Acts, Revelation)	**Justice, Law, History** (Pentateuch, 2 Samuel, Ezra, Job, Isaiah, Nahum)	**God Frees and Redeems** (Deuteronomy, Ezra, Matthew, John, Romans, Galatians)	**Partners in a New Creation** (Isaiah, John, Revelation)

Copyright © 2017 Standard Publishing, part of the David C Cook family, Colorado Springs, Colorado 80918.
Based on *International Sunday School Lessons for Christian Teaching*,
copyright © 2012 by the Committee on the Uniform Series.

TEACHING IS MORE THAN TALKING

Part 1: It Begins with You   *Teacher Tips by Mark A. Taylor*

WHAT DO teachers do? They talk, of course. Teachers prepare to know exactly what to say, and students come to class expecting to hear from the teacher.

But Bible students need more than wise words from well-prepared teachers. Bible students need not only to *know* what a passage means but also to *decide* how those verses should influence them daily.

Marching Orders

To help students make these decisions, teachers must first make the same decisions themselves. A teacher's preparation begins with personal reflection and prayer. What is God teaching you, the teacher, as you open his Word to prepare your lesson? How does this week's passage speak to your struggles, your problems, your questions, your temptations, and your answers to prayer? Before you prepare to *teach,* study the passage to *learn.* You won't lead your class to a place you haven't already been yourself.

I once heard a speaker say, "We should approach every Bible passage with this question: 'What are God's marching orders for me in these verses?'" Each week, this will be the most productive first step in your lesson preparation. Before you look at background commentary, before you examine the study notes in your Bible, before you read the lesson treatment in this book, look at the Scripture by itself. Read it repeatedly. Read it aloud. Read it several days in a row.

After you've read the Scripture several times, make two lists. The first list asks, "What must I do to obey this passage?" The second list asks, "What are my questions about this passage?" Keep the first list before you as you seek answers for the second list. After you've meditated on the Scripture, seeking God's voice as you read, you'll be ready to deepen your knowledge of the Scripture by studying commentary from others.

As you complete this process, discerning the meaning of the particular passage of Scripture, you will accumulate facts, background, and insight on the passage, which you'll be eager to share. You'll probably have enough material to fill every minute of your class session with your own voice, but you should resist the urge to do so. Remember, teaching is more than talking. Good teachers listen as much as they speak. The good teacher facilitates an environment safe for learners to ask questions and speak for themselves.

From Guru to Facilitator

Adults studying the Bible bring a wealth of experience and insight to every class session. As their teacher leads them to see a Scripture truth in light of real-life problems, these class members have plenty to talk about!

This means you're not the only teacher in your class. You will try not to present yourself as guru sharing expertise from behind a lectern but as a facilitator, a fellow student pursuing truth with everyone in the class. From time to time throughout the session, you will step away from your teaching notes to hear class members share their experiences and test their own conclusions about what the passage is teaching. When a class member asks a question, you won't rush to answer it first but will ask the class what they think. You're creating an environment for adult learners to lead their own learning.

It's fine to add your own experiences to the conversation. Feel free to tell them what you've been thinking as you've sought to apply the text to your life. It's necessary that you share information class members may not know: context, related passages, the meaning of Bible words in the original language. You owe them that. But above all, you owe them the chance to wrestle with the Scripture's demands on their lives by showing them the impact it has made on your life.

PRAISE WITH MUSIC

DEVOTIONAL READING: Exodus 15:11-21
BACKGROUND SCRIPTURE: Exodus 14:1–15:21

EXODUS 15:11-21

11 Who among the gods
is like you, LORD?
Who is like you—
majestic in holiness,
awesome in glory,
working wonders?

12 "You stretch out your right hand,
and the earth swallows your enemies.
13 In your unfailing love you will lead
the people you have redeemed.
In your strength you will guide them
to your holy dwelling.
14 The nations will hear and tremble;
anguish will grip the people of Philistia.
15 The chiefs of Edom will be terrified,
the leaders of Moab will be seized with
trembling,
the people of Canaan will melt away;
16 terror and dread will fall on them.
By the power of your arm
they will be as still as a stone—
until your people pass by, LORD,
until the people you bought pass by.

17 You will bring them in and plant them
on the mountain of your inheritance—
the place, LORD, you made for your
dwelling,
the sanctuary, Lord, your hands
established.

18 "The LORD reigns
for ever and ever."

19 When Pharaoh's horses, chariots and horsemen went into the sea, the LORD brought the waters of the sea back over them, but the Israelites walked through the sea on dry ground. 20 Then Miriam the prophet, Aaron's sister, took a timbrel in her hand, and all the women followed her, with timbrels and dancing. 21 Miriam sang to them:

"Sing to the LORD,
for he is highly exalted.
Both horse and driver
he has hurled into the sea."

KEY TEXT

Who among the gods is like you, LORD? Who is like you—majestic in holiness, awesome in glory, working wonders? —Exodus 15:11

CELEBRATING GOD

Unit 1: God's People Offer Praise

LESSON AIMS

After participating in this lesson, each learner will be able to:

1. Describe the events that caused the Israelites to burst into spontaneous praise.

2. Explain how the events fit on a time line of God's continued care for Israel.

3. List attributes and/or actions of God today that parallel those of the text.

LESSON OUTLINE

Introduction

A. Rescued in the Sequel

Once upon a time theaters had special movies for Saturdays. There was usually a feature film, followed by one episode of a serial movie. Each segment was designed to leave the hero or heroine in an impossible situation, the intended goal being that the viewer would return the following week to see the resolution of the cliffhanger.

Back before World War II, I went with my visiting uncle to see a feature film that was followed by a serial movie about Dick Tracy. As the episode ended, Tracy was in a diving bell, and the air hose was cut by the villain. There was no way Tracy could survive. My uncle's visit came to an end, and I never saw the sequel! I never found out how the famous Dick Tracy was rescued.

Moses led the Israelites into a similar cliffhanger situation (Exodus 14). Though freed from bondage, they found themselves trapped between the Egyptian army and the Red Sea. The Israelites seemed doomed—*except* for the fact that God was with them. Though I don't know what happened to Dick Tracy, I *do* know what happened to Israel. Today's lesson about a song in that regard teaches us important things even some 35 centuries later.

B. Lesson Context

Long before the exodus of 1447 BC, God had promised Canaan to Abraham, Isaac, and Jacob (Genesis 13:14-15; 26:3; 28:13). The fulfillment of the promise seemed to be in jeopardy when Jacob and his family moved to Egypt because of a famine in Canaan. Still, God worked through Joseph, a son of Jacob, so that the family could have all it needed during the years of famine (41:53-54).

Over the centuries, the Israelites witnessed significant leadership changes in Egypt, from native Egyptians, to foreign intruders, and then back to the Egyptians again. These intruders are sometimes called Hyksos or "shepherd kings," but the word more likely just means foreigners who ruled Egypt. This caused the Egyptians to develop an even greater dislike for shepherds (compare Genesis 46:34), something that became very significant in the history of the emerging nation of Israel.

Finally there came a new king to whom Joseph's reputation meant nothing (Exodus 1:8). The original favor Jacob (Israel) and his sons experienced changed into servitude and oppression. Measures were taken to subdue the people and slow their population growth. After the Israelites spent 430 years in Egypt (12:40-41), God was ready to act to fulfill the promises (2:23-25).

It was during this time that Moses was born. It is well-known that he was adopted by a princess of Egypt, but he had to flee Egypt at age 40 after killing an Egyptian (Exodus 2; the age factor for this event is found only in Acts 7:23). Forty years later Moses encountered the Lord at Sinai. God called Moses to lead his enslaved people away from Egypt, and the promise was repeated (Exodus 3:8). God worked through Moses and Aaron (Moses' brother) to bring about nine plagues that devastated Egypt. The tenth plague took the lives of all the firstborn except among the Israelites.

At that point Pharaoh expelled the Israelites from Egypt (Exodus 12:31-33). It had been 430 years to the day since Jacob and his family entered Egypt (12:40-41). As God's people left Egypt, they were reminded again that their destination was Canaan (13:5, 11).

Pharaoh, however, changed his mind and decided to bring his labor force back (Exodus 14:5-8). The Egyptians pursued Israel to the edge of the Red Sea. It seemed that the Israelites were blocked by the sea and victory for the Egyptians was assured. God had other plans.

The Israelites crossed the Red Sea safely after the waters parted, but the Egyptians drowned when they tried to follow. The God of Israel was superior to any of the fictitious gods of Pharaoh! The crossing of the Red Sea was pivotal in the history of ancient Israel. The slaves were free, beyond reach of Pharaoh. Moses and the people responded by bursting forth with joyous singing (Exodus 15:1-21).

The printed text for this lesson concerns their song. The first song in the history of this new nation is a song of rejoicing because of the victory that the Lord has obtained for the people. We note in passing that there is a minor difficulty in finding an appropriate designation for this song. It is sometimes called a Song of Moses and Miriam (compare Exodus 15:20-21) or a Song of Moses and Israel (15:1). A Song of Moses already exists in Deuteronomy 32; see 31:30, which introduces the chapter that follows as a "song" of Moses.

I. Song, Part 1
(EXODUS 15:11-19)
A. God's Preeminence (v. 11)

11. Who among the gods is like you, LORD? Who is like you—majestic in holiness, awesome in glory, working wonders?

These two rhetorical questions point to the uniqueness of God. The Egyptians had hundreds of *gods* and goddesses. Though some of the plagues might have been considered attacks on specific gods (like darkness explicitly challenging the sun god Ra; see Exodus 10:21-23), we know for sure that the plagues were a judgment on all the Egyptian gods (Exodus 12:12; Numbers 33:4). So-called gods that were conceived in human imaginations and created by human hands were no match for the *Lord*.

The second question builds on the first, focusing on the Lord's great attributes that set him apart from other "gods." Emphasis on God's *holiness* begins in the book of Exodus (see Exodus 3:5) and continues through Revelation (example: Revelation 15:4). In a way, to call God holy is to call him unique. He is totally unlike any false deity that has ever or could ever be imagined to exist. Because the Lord is holy, he also commands his people to be holy (Leviticus 11:44-45; compare 1 Peter 1:15-16). Only by being unique in ways similar to God's character can his people be a blessing to the nations (Genesis 12:1-3).

The final phrases of the verse declare that the

HOW TO SAY IT

Canaan	*Kay*-nun.
Edom	*Ee*-dum.
Megiddo	Muh-*gid*-doe.
Moab	*Mo*-ab.
Philistia	Fuh-*liss*-tee-uh.
Sinai	*Sigh*-nye or *Sigh*-nay-eye.

Lord is to be held in reverence for his praiseworthy deeds and for the *wonders* he has done.

B. God's Power (vv. 12-13)

12. "You stretch out your right hand, and the earth swallows your enemies.

The *right hand* of God often refers to his great power to deliver his people (examples: Psalms 17:7; 139:10). In this case, it celebrates God's victory over the Egyptians on Israel's behalf (Exodus 14:21-30). Given that *the earth swallows* their *enemies*, however, it seems that this verse is also pointing to future events. The Egyptian army was swallowed up by the sea, after all.

In the not-too-distant future, Israel would see Korah and 250 like-minded rebels swallowed up when "the earth opened its mouth" (Numbers 16:32). In that instance, as when the sea swallowed the Egyptians, it was a sign of God's judgment on wickedness and delivering his people. Deliverance was from the evil influence of Korah and others among the Israelites (16:1-31).

> *What Do You Think?*
> When a task needs doing, how do you know when the Lord wants you to do it rather than wait for him to do it himself, or vice versa?
> *Digging Deeper*
> What principles do you see in Exodus 4:13; Psalms 27:14; 37:7; Isaiah 6:8; and Ezekiel 22:30-31 that help frame your answer?

13. In your unfailing love you will lead the people you have redeemed. In your strength you will guide them to your holy dwelling.

The verbs in this verse and the next are past tense in the Hebrew, even though the thoughts in view are for the future. Speaking about a future action as though it has already happened makes the certainty of the coming event seem rock solid because it is already being spoken of as accomplished. When speaking about what God will do, those events really are assured of happening.

God's faithfulness to his promises prompted him to redeem *the people* of Israel from Egypt (Exodus 2:24). Although we often think of redemption in almost purely spiritual terms, Isra-

el's leaving Egypt is one prime physical example of the concept. God spoke of it to Moses as delivering Israel from Egypt (3:8). Our spiritual redemption mirrors this: we are God's people led out of sin and into new life (Colossians 1:9-14).

God was taking the people to the promised land. Canaan was the place God chose as his *holy dwelling* (see Genesis 28:16-22; Psalm 78:54). The tabernacle would travel through the wilderness with the people as a symbol of God's presence (Exodus 29:44-46). When they were settled in the land, God would allow Solomon to build the temple in Jerusalem as a permanent reminder that God chose to dwell with his people (2 Chronicles 6:1-11).

> *What Do You Think?*
> In what ways would (or should) your life change were you to spend more time reflecting on and emulating God's holiness?
> *Digging Deeper*
> Which of these three texts spurs you most to start doing so today: Ephesians 1:4; Hebrews 12:14; 1 Peter 1:15-16? Why?

C. The Nations' Fear (vv. 14-16)

14a. The nations will hear and tremble;

The emphasis changes from how God protects Israel to how others will respond when they *hear* of his power and mighty acts.

14b. anguish will grip the people of Philistia.

The Hebrew word translated *anguish* elsewhere describes the pain of childbirth (Psalm 48:6; Jeremiah 22:23; etc.). In this context, it probably reflects the magnitude and acuteness of the pain of *the people of Philistia*. Elsewhere these people are called simply Philistines (example: Joshua 13:2-3). The land is called Palestine today, located on the eastern shore of the Mediterranean Sea.

15a. The chiefs of Edom will be terrified, the leaders of Moab will be seized with trembling,

The land of *Edom* was south and southeast of the Dead Sea. Its inhabitants traced their lineage to Esau (Genesis 25:30; 36:1). *Moab* lay east of the Dead Sea. Genesis traces their parentage to Lot by his older daughter (19:36-37). As the Israelites were ending their 40 years in the wilderness, they were instructed not to provoke either Edom or Moab because of the inheritance God had given those nations' forefathers (Deuteronomy 2:5, 9).

The Israelites even went around Edom, for the Edomites refused to let them pass through the land (Numbers 20:21; 21:4). This was evidence of the fear of *the leaders* who led the nation. The amazement and *trembling* of the rulers of these two nations are emphasized; certainly their reactions to God's mighty works for Israel influenced both nations in their entirety.

15b. the people of Canaan will melt away;

Jericho was located in *Canaan* and is a prime example of the consuming terror *the people* felt. Forty years after singing this song (see Numbers 14:34), Joshua sent two spies to the city of Jericho (Joshua 2:1). Rahab, a Canaanite woman herself, reported that the people of the land were terrified of Israel. One reason that she gave was that they had heard about Israel's crossing of the Red Sea (2:9-11, 24).

16. terror and dread will fall on them. By the power of your arm they will be as still as a stone—until your people pass by, LORD, until the people you bought pass by.

Given that Moses and the Israelites had very recently escaped Egypt into an uncertain nomadic existence, it is not surprising that *terror and dread* of them did not spread immediately among the hostile nations. Nomads were not necessarily cause for concern, though a large group was worth keeping track of. Not even the Israelites themselves were convinced they would survive in their new unsettled existence (example: Numbers 20:3-5). But 40 years later, when Israel camped on the east side of the Jordan, opposite Jericho, the tides turned toward fear (Deuteronomy 2:25; 3:4).

Once again a metaphor, this time regarding God's *arm*, celebrates *the power* of the Lord in working on behalf of his chosen people (compare Exodus 15:12, above). Though the other nations would resist the Lord, their efforts would be as effective as if they stood *as still as a stone* (compare 1 Samuel 25:37). This state of affairs would last until the Lord had established in the land his *people,* whom he had *bought* (compare Exodus 15:13, above). This is consecration language, most

recently seen in God's declaration that the firstborn of animals and humans were his (with provisions for redeeming them; see Exodus 13:11-15).

What Do You Think?
 Should Christians ever base their praise on what they anticipate God will do to an earthly enemy in the future? Why, or why not?
Digging Deeper
 What passages in addition to Psalm 6:10 and Proverbs 25:21-22 influence your response?

D. Promises for Israel (vv. 17-19)

17. You will bring them in and plant them on the mountain of your inheritance—the place, LORD, you made for your dwelling, the sanctuary, Lord, your hands established.

Once again Moses spoke of God's settling the people in their promised land, this time referring specifically to *the mountain* Zion (Psalm 2:6; Daniel 9:16; etc.). *The sanctuary* refers specifically to the future temple, which would be built on Zion (2 Chronicles 5:2-7).

18. "The LORD reigns for ever and ever."

In the book of Numbers, some people challenged the Lord's reign by challenging his chosen leader Moses (compare 1 Samuel 8:6-9). As a result, some were swallowed by the earth; others were consumed with fire; and 14,700 died in a plague (Numbers 16:32, 35, 49). In another incident many died after being bitten by serpents (21:8-9; see John 3:14).

19. When Pharaoh's horses, chariots and horsemen went into the sea, the LORD brought the waters of the sea back over them, but the Israelites walked through the sea on dry ground.

Chariots had been introduced into Egypt as instruments of war by the Hyksos, who ruled Egypt for a time (see Lesson Context). Previously, chariots were used for ceremonial purposes. The Egyptians quickly discovered their military usefulness and added many chariots to their armies.

The Egyptians lost 600 chariots as a result (Exodus 14:7, 28). In a battle several years before,

WORSHIP WITH ABANDON

Visual for Lessons 1 & 2. *Start a discussion by pointing to this posted visual as you ask, "When was the last time you worshipped this way?"*

the Egyptians had captured hundreds of chariots from Canaanite forces at the Battle of Megiddo. Neither the destroyed chariots nor their drivers were easy to replace. We may also note the 900 iron chariots mentioned in Judges 4:3, which form the power by which the Canaanites oppress the Israelites roughly two centuries later. A song is also written about their defeat (Judges 5).

The verse before us summarizes the song of Exodus 15. It describes the contrast in the outcomes for the two groups. Both the Egyptians and *the Israelites* experienced the depths of *the sea*. For God's people, the depths were just *dry ground*. But those same depths became the final resting place for the Egyptians, who had been their taskmasters.

❧ UNINTENDED CONSEQUENCES ❧

Witty observers of the human condition sometimes declare "laws" to describe common human experiences. For instance, Murphy's Law states: "If anything *can* go wrong, it *will* go wrong!" There are two laws of mechanical repair. The first, for the repairman, says, "After your hands become coated with grease, your nose will begin to itch." The second, for car owners, "When the repairman tries to find the malfunction, the car will run perfectly."

And then there is the law of unintended consequences. Pharaoh finally had yielded to God after the tenth plague, but the man changed his mind and led his army in an intent to recapture

the freed Hebrews. Pharaoh and his army died in the process of discovering the unintended consequences of rebellion against God.

The law of unintended consequences is stated another way in Numbers 32:23: "Be sure that your sin will find you out." What more needs to happen for you to live in such a way that you don't experience the consequences of your sin?   —C. R. B.

II. Song, Part 2
(EXODUS 15:20-21)
A. Miriam's Example (v. 20)

20. Then Miriam the prophet, Aaron's sister, took a timbrel in her hand, and all the women followed her, with timbrels and dancing.

Miriam and both of her siblings are designated as prophets (see Exodus 7:1; Deuteronomy 18:15; 34:10; compare Micah 6:4). (The Hebrew word translated *prophet* has a feminine ending in this verse. Therefore, the use of *prophetess* would be appropriate when referring to Miriam.) She is one of several women in the Bible who are designated as prophetesses (Judges 4:4; 2 Kings 22:14; Nehemiah 6:14; Isaiah 8:3; Luke 2:36).

Based on Miriam's comments in Numbers 12:2, her role as a prophetess is appropriate, for she indicated that the Lord had also spoken through her (although at that time she was misusing the fact). Exodus 7:1-2 provides an illustration of the function of a prophet as one who gives voice to the commands of God.

This is the first reference to Miriam by name, and Moses identified her as a *sister* to Aaron, instead of to himself. Perhaps this is meant to remind the reader that, while Miriam and Aaron grew up in the same household together, Moses was raised in Pharaoh's house with limited access to his birth family (Exodus 2:8-10). Miriam is usually thought to be the older sister of Moses, whose task was to see what would happen to her baby brother when he was placed in a basket at the bank of the Nile River (2:3-4).

Miriam *and all the women* use their *timbrels* (small drums) and rhythmic dance to provide accompaniment to the song of Moses. How the second part of the song is worded is our next verse.

What Do You Think?
What are some occasions that would be appropriate to label as "a time to dance" (Ecclesiastes 3:4)?

Digging Deeper
Why did you, or did you not, include "a church worship service" as one of your responses?

B. The Exaltation of God (v. 21)

21. Miriam sang to them: "Sing to the LORD, for he is highly exalted. Both horse and driver he has hurled into the sea."

The refrain that *Miriam* and the women *sang* is very similar to how the song began (see Exodus 15:1, not in our printed text). The implication may be that Miriam is the one who leads the other women in a type of antiphonal rendition. (That's when one group answers another.) In any case, their words are a final reminder on how the most powerful nation in the world at that time was no match for the God of Israel.

❧ *WHOLE WORSHIP* ❧

One of my fellow professors in a Christian college offered a class for freshman students to help them get "plugged in" to a local church. One of the assignments required students to visit three churches unlike the one they were most familiar with. Each student was then to write and submit a report on each.

One student had attended only churches with contemporary worship services. The church services she reported on were more traditional. When this student wrote her report, she revealed an interesting difference between the two. Traditional worship services primarily extolled who God is and what he has done; the contemporary worship services focused on expressions of adoration for God.

Miriam and those who sang with her exulted in both expressing their feelings about God and proclaiming what he had done for them. The two are intricately connected. This week, what blessings might you experience if your worship embraced both types?
—C. R. B.

Conclusion

A. In Context

Our songs always come with context. For instance, the story behind "Amazing Grace" adds depth to the lyrics of the song itself. (Look it up online.) Its long history in England and especially in North America has shaped how we hear or sing it today. The situations in which we have heard it played or sung change how we process the lyrics. Different arrangements let us hear the song afresh.

Like the song that Moses, Miriam, and the people sang, our songs come from specific situations: of deliverance, of healing, of crossing from death into life. When we sing, with whom we sing—these things matter! Therefore, let us do as the psalmist challenged us and "sing to the Lord a new song, for he has done marvelous things" (Psalm 98:1). What song will you sing as a result of God's character and work in your life—in your family, church, and community?

What Do You Think?
Which concept or imperative in today's lesson do you have the most trouble coming to grips with? Why?

Digging Deeper
How will you resolve this problem?

B. Prayer

Almighty God, as we face trials this week, we commit ourselves to remember that in you we have victory. In Jesus' victorious name we thank you. Amen.

C. Thought to Remember

God always wins.

VISUALS FOR THESE LESSONS

The visual pictured in each lesson (example: page 14) is a small reproduction of a large, full-color poster included in the *Adult Resources* packet for the Fall 2021 Quarter. That packet also contains the very useful *Presentation Tools* CD for teacher use. Order No. 1629121 from your supplier.

INVOLVEMENT LEARNING

Enhance your lesson with NIV® Bible Student (from your curriculum supplier) and the reproducible activity page (at www.standardlesson.com or in the back of the NIV® Standard Lesson Commentary Deluxe Edition).

Into the Lesson

Ask a volunteer to research "top ten songs this week," including lyrics (or do this yourself as you prepare for class). Have the volunteer choose three or four of the songs and read the lyrics to the class. (*Option.* Play the songs for the class.)

After the lyrics are read to each song (and/or the songs are played), ask class members what the songs are praising or celebrating; jot responses on the board. Encourage class members to express their opinions about the messages of the songs.

Make a transition by saying, "Today we begin a four-lesson study around the theme of worshipful praise. The contrast we see between the praise in popular music and the examples of praise in our lessons may prove interesting!"

Into the Word

Make sure that class members understand the setting for the lesson by summarizing the Lesson Context for them. Then ask two class members to read aloud Exodus 15:11-21 (or the whole chapter), alternating with each verse. As they read, have class members listen for details that are new or surprising to them. Allow a few to share their items after the reading.

Distribute handouts (you prepare) that feature four columns headed *Attributes of God / Today / Actions of God / Today*. Have half the class divide into triads to complete the first column from today's text. Have the other half of the class divide into triads to complete the third column, listing the specific events mentioned in the text that led the Israelites to praise God. Class members should include one or more verse references for each item in their list.

Possible entries for Attributes of God: unique, unequaled, glorious, holy, (Exodus 15:11); unfailing, strong (v. 13); reigns forever (v. 18); worker of miracles (v. 19); victorious (v. 21). *Possible entries for Actions of God:* led his people (v. 13); caused

the earth to swallow enemies (v. 12); caused enemies to tremble (vv. 14-15); inspired fear among enemies (vv. 14-16); made it possible for the Israelites to pass by unharmed (v. 16); accomplished his purpose (vv. 16-17); brought the waters to overwhelm Pharaoh's armies, but the Israelites crossed the sea on dry land (vv. 19, 21).

After six or eight minutes, ask volunteers to share as you make an all-class master list on the board, using the same column headings. As each half of the class finishes, ask the other half what was missed. (Save the two *Today* columns for Into Life, below.)

Option. To expand the study beyond that of the printed text, distribute copies of "The Problems Before the Praise" exercise on the activity page, which you can download, to complete in study pairs as indicated. Since this section has both a Bible-study element and personal reflection segment, you may wish to save the latter for the end of your class time.

Into Life

Send class members back to their triads to complete the *Today* columns of the handout. Half the class is to list good Christian worship songs, both old and new, that include the attributes of God found in today's text. Those in the other half are to list great acts of God that have inspired or could inspire songs of praise. Be prepared to offer some examples where learners seem to be stuck.

Option 1. To close the session, distribute copies of the "His Love Lasts My Whole Life" exercise from the activity page, to complete as indicated. Allow individuals to share their compositions, but don't put anyone on the spot to do so.

Option 2. Close the class session with a responsive reading of Psalm 136. After a leader reads the first half of each of the 26 verses, the class responds with the second half: "His love endures forever."

PRAISE IN DANCE

DEVOTIONAL READING: 2 Samuel 6:12-19
BACKGROUND SCRIPTURE: 2 Samuel 6

2 SAMUEL 6:1-5, 14-19

¹ David again brought together all the able young men of Israel—thirty thousand. ² He and all his men went to Baalah in Judah to bring up from there the ark of God, which is called by the Name, the name of the LORD Almighty, who is enthroned between the cherubim on the ark. ³ They set the ark of God on a new cart and brought it from the house of Abinadab, which was on the hill. Uzzah and Ahio, sons of Abinadab, were guiding the new cart ⁴ with the ark of God on it, and Ahio was walking in front of it. ⁵ David and all Israel were celebrating with all their might before the LORD, with castanets, harps, lyres, timbrels, sistrums and cymbals.

· ·

¹⁴ Wearing a linen ephod, David was dancing before the LORD with all his might, ¹⁵ while he and all Israel were bringing up the ark of the LORD with shouts and the sound of trumpets.

¹⁶ As the ark of the LORD was entering the City of David, Michal daughter of Saul watched from a window. And when she saw King David leaping and dancing before the LORD, she despised him in her heart.

¹⁷ They brought the ark of the LORD and set it in its place inside the tent that David had pitched for it, and David sacrificed burnt offerings and fellowship offerings before the LORD. ¹⁸ After he had finished sacrificing the burnt offerings and fellowship offerings, he blessed the people in the name of the LORD Almighty. ¹⁹ Then he gave a loaf of bread, a cake of dates and a cake of raisins to each person in the whole crowd of Israelites, both men and women. And all the people went to their homes.

KEY TEXT

David and all Israel were celebrating with all their might before the LORD, with castanets, harps, lyres, timbrels, sistrums and cymbals. —2 Samuel 6:5

Photo © Getty Images

CELEBRATING GOD

Unit 1: God's People Offer Praise

LESSONS 1–4

LESSON AIMS

After participating in this lesson, each learner will be able to:

1. Describe the events surrounding the ark's entrance into Jerusalem.

2. Evaluate David's intentions.

3. Evaluate his or her preferred style of worship to consider needed change, if any.

LESSON OUTLINE

Introduction

A. If at First . . .

Failure is difficult to deal with, especially for dreamers with big plans. Many youths dream of the perfect job and end up settling for one that simply pays the bills. Some couples dream of the perfect outdoor wedding and end up making the best of a rainy day. Parents often dream of having the perfect family but end up struggling to hold together the fragile unity that remains after years of conflict and tragedy.

When it comes to preparing for the perfect job, wedding, or family, we are seldom granted a redo. Some dreams simply don't pan out and never will. But we thank the Lord that such is not always the case! Some failures allow for second chances. Hence the proverb "If at first you don't succeed, try, try again."

It takes grit, determination, and a good dose of vulnerability to recover from a failure—especially a public failure—and then attempt the same feat again. King David suffered a highly visible public failure. Yet we learn in today's lesson that he refused to let it define him. And God was gracious to grant him success on his second try. But would the people come together to celebrate with David?

B. Lesson Context

Today's lesson focuses on the relocation of the ark of the covenant to David's new capital city, Jerusalem (see the parallel account in 1 Chronicles 15). The ark of the covenant was Israel's most sacred object. It was an ornate chest constructed to God's specifications in about 1446 BC.

The lid of the ark was called the atonement cover. That lid featured two winged cherubim facing each other from opposite ends; that's where God said he would meet with Moses (Exodus 25:10-22). One detail of the ark's construction is especially important for today's lesson: the gold rings and wooden poles (see 2 Samuel 6:3, below). The ark itself contained the Ten Commandments, Aaron's staff, and manna from Israel's wilderness wanderings (Hebrews 9:4; compare Exodus 40:20). These were reminders of deliverance from Egypt and provisions on the way to the promised land.

The ark was housed in the innermost part of the tabernacle, "the Most Holy Place" (Leviticus 16:2). Only the high priest was ever allowed to enter, and that only once a year after extensive acts of ritual cleansing (16:3-25). That ark was so holy that those responsible for its upkeep and transportation were not allowed to touch it, lest they die (Numbers 4:15, 20; see 2 Samuel 6:5, below).

After God led the Israelites into the promised land, they forsook the covenant during the period of the judges (about 1380–1050 BC). Repeated numerous times was the dreary cycle of *rebellion, retribution, repentance,* and *restoration.*

As that period drew to a close in the days of Samuel, the Philistines captured the ark of the covenant and took it to Ashdod (about 1070 BC). That was a city near the Mediterranean coast and about 45 miles west of Jerusalem. But God inflicted health problems on the Philistines, so they sent the ark back to Israel (1 Samuel 5:6–6:12).

The cart transporting the ark made its way to the Israelite city of Beth Shemesh (1 Samuel 6:13-15). Unfortunately, the people there disrespected the ark by gazing on its contents, and 70 people died as a result (6:19). So residents sent it to Kiriath Jearim, where it stayed for 20 years (1 Samuel 7:1-2) until the days of King David.

The first seven and a half years of David's reign was a time of distraction as he was occupied with securing his position as king (2 Samuel 1:1–5:5). Having successfully done so, and having secured Jerusalem as his capital as well as defeating the Philistines again (5:6-25), David turned his attention to the ark.

I. A Hopeful Gesture
(2 SAMUEL 6:1-5)
A. Gathering the People (vv. 1-2)

1. David again brought together all the able young men of Israel—thirty thousand.

Again refers to David's reassembling the *men* of his army. They had conquered Jerusalem (2 Samuel 5:6) and defeated Philistine armies (5:20-25). When it came to defeating the Jebusites of Jerusalem, David as their leader appears to have done

so on his own accord, though God gave him success (5:6-10). Regarding defeat of the Philistines, David twice inquired of the Lord (5:19, 23). It may be significant, then, that there is no record of David's consulting the Lord regarding what he (David) had in mind next.

The number *thirty thousand* is interesting in that it is also the number of men who died when the Philistines defeated the Israelites and captured the ark in 1 Samuel 4:10. This parallelism suggests that readers should view today's passage in light of that earlier encounter with the ark.

What Do You Think?
What will be your best area of service the next time a celebration at your church calls for inviting "a cast of thousands"?
Digging Deeper
In that regard, what passages in addition to Matthew 22:9; Mark 6:42-44; Colossians 4:12b; and 3 John 8 might speak to this issue?

2a. He and all his men went to Baalah in Judah to bring up from there the ark of God,

Baalah in Judah is another name for Kiriath Jearim (see Lesson Context plus Joshua 15:9 and 1 Chronicles 13:6). That town is only about eight miles west of Jerusalem, so a walking trip can be made from Jerusalem to there and back in one day. The ark had been resting there for some 20 years since its recovery from the Philistines (see Lesson Context).

2b. which is called by the Name, the name of the LORD Almighty, who is enthroned between the cherubim on the ark.

Every aspect of God's designation is significant in this verse. *Lord* (indicated by small capital letters within the text to show the name *Yahweh* was used) refers to the personal name of Israel's God (compare Genesis 4:26; Exodus 3:14). The word translated *Almighty* is translated "hosts" in older versions of the Bible and may refer to angelic beings who serve the Lord as he directs (see Psalm 148:2; compare Hebrews 1:13-14). It also may refer to stars, planets, and other heavenly bodies that he had created (Nehemiah 9:6). The word speaks to God's fighting on behalf of

WORSHIP WITH ABANDON

Visual for Lessons 1 & 2. *Follow last week's discussion of this visual by asking learners to state the implied opposite of worshipping "with abandon."*

his chosen people (example: Isaiah 1:24; see also on Psalm 84:1 in lesson 8). The bottom line is that this designation celebrates the Lord's power in various contexts (examples: 1 Samuel 17:45; Isaiah 1:24).

On the phrase *enthroned between the cherubim,* see the Lesson Context (compare Psalms 80:1 and 99:1).

B. Acquiring the Ark (vv. 3-4)

3a. They set the ark of God on a new cart and brought it from the house of Abinadab, which was on the hill.

Had David consulted the Levites, whom God appointed to care for the ark (see Numbers 1:50-51; 1 Chronicles 6:48), he would have learned that the ark must be carried by only two long wooden poles through rings affixed to the ark (Exodus 25:12-15; 37:5). This method both (1) kept the ark a safe distance from human contact and (2) kept the top-heavy ark stable.

Why David chose instead to *set the ark of God on a new cart* isn't revealed in the text. Perhaps it is evidence of David's ignorance of the law, or maybe it betrays a flippancy toward God's presence. Or he could have thought that if a cart safely brought the ark back from the Philistines, it could surely take the ark safely to Jerusalem (see Lesson Context).

Older versions of the Bible include the town name "Gibeah" instead of *hill*. This is because the Hebrew word can refer to either a hill or a specific town. If the latter, it likely was Gibeah, located about four miles north of Jerusalem and nine miles east of Kiriath Jearim. Elsewhere, the underlying Hebrew word is translated "hill" (1 Samuel 26:3), and that may be the sense here. This would suggest that *the house of Abinadab* was located on a small hill (see 1 Samuel 7:1).

3b-4. Uzzah and Ahio, sons of Abinadab, were guiding the new cart with the ark of God on it, and Ahio was walking in front of it.

A common assumption today is that *Abinadab* was a Levite, an assumption also held by the first-century Jewish historian Josephus (*Antiquities of the Jews,* 6.1.4). However, we should conclude that Abinadab was *not* a Levite since 1 Chronicles 15:12-13 has David's later statement that Levites were not involved in transporting *the ark of God* on this occasion.

Four Levites (specifically Kohathites; see Numbers 4:1-15) were to carry the ark by means of the two poles that were kept in the gold rings (Exodus 25:14-15). Two branches of the Levites did indeed use carts for transportation of various tabernacle items, but not the branch that was charged with transporting the ark (Numbers 7:4-9). The use of a cart in this regard is reckless in that it indicates David's failure in not inquiring of the Lord regarding procedure.

C. Celebrating the Occasion (v. 5)

5. David and all Israel were celebrating with all their might before the LORD, with castanets, harps, lyres, timbrels, sistrums and cymbals.

King *David* and the Israelites celebrated in grand style the consecration of David's capital city. He spared no expense with wood, string, and percussion instruments. On the distinctions among the various kinds of instruments, see the commentary on Psalm 150:3-5 in lesson 9.

The celebration was cut short, however, by tragedy: when the cart tipped, the ark slid, and Uzzah lost his life trying to stabilize it (2 Samuel 6:6-7, not in today's text). The party ended, and David left the ark in the house of Obed-Edom, where it remained until David tried again (6:6-13). When David sent for the ark a second time, he had greater respect for God's holy presence. God must be honored and his instructions obeyed. Having learned his lesson, David picked up his celebration where it left off and welcomed the ark into his city the right way—our next verse.

II. A Hope Fulfilled
(2 SAMUEL 6:14-16)
A. The Dancing King (v. 14)
14a. Wearing a linen ephod,

The *ephod* was one of six pieces of clothing traditionally worn by priests (see Exodus 28). In terms of construction, ephods were to be made "of gold, and of blue, purple and scarlet yarn, and of finely twisted *linen*" with "two shoulder pieces attached to two of its corners" (28:6-7). As part of a larger ensemble, the ephod's holy intent was to communicate "dignity and honor" (28:2).

Given all that, it is unclear what we should make of King David's wearing of a priest's garment since the Old Testament offices of prophet, priest, and king were normally distinct from one another (compare 1 Kings 1:32-45). Perhaps the safest conclusion is that David wore the ephod in the same sense that young Samuel did in 1 Samuel 2:18: a waistcoat suitable for worship. That would lead us to understand the garment as having religious significance apart from the priesthood.

There's also the possibility that David's taking on a priestly role could foreshadow Jesus, who would come as both king and high priest (Hebrews 7). Normally only priests offered sacrifices, but we see an exception to that in 2 Samuel 6:13, 17 (below; compare 1 Kings 8:5, 62; 1 Samuel 10:9-13).

14b. David was dancing before the LORD with all his might,

Dancing was a common form of celebration in Israel, especially for women. Israelite women danced with Miriam to celebrate God's victory over Pharaoh's army at the Red Sea (Exodus 15:20; see lesson 1). During the era of the judges (see Lesson Context), a daughter danced to celebrate her father's triumphant return from war (Judges 11:34), and the women of Shiloh danced in celebration of an unspecified festival (21:21-23;

see further discussion of dance in commentary on Psalms 149:3 and 150:4 in lesson 9). To dance is the opposite of mourning (Psalm 30:11; Lamentations 5:15).

During the time of David, women danced to celebrate the return of Saul's army after David's defeat of Goliath and a successful campaign against the Philistines (1 Samuel 18:6-7). Dancing has a negative connotation in Exodus 32:19.

> **What Do You Think?**
> What can you do to help ensure that your church's worship services communicate a spirit of joy?
> *Digging Deeper*
> Under what circumstances, if any, should a worship service *not* communicate a spirit of joy? Why?

❧ *IMPORTANCE OF BEING FULLY DRESSED* ❧

My father once told me about being the guest preacher for a revival meeting and staying in the host minister's home. For breakfast on Monday morning, Dad wore a dress shirt and casual pants to breakfast. The minister appeared minutes later in a suit and tie. Dad asked, "Do you have a funeral today?" The minister's wife answered, "No, he never comes to breakfast less than fully dressed."

HOW TO SAY IT

Abinadab	Uh-*bin*-uh-dab.
Ahio	Ah-*yo*.
Baalah	Bay-ul-*eh*.
Beth Shemesh	Beth *She*-mesh.
cherubim	*chair*-uh-bim.
ephod	*ee*-fod.
Josephus	Jo-*see*-fus.
Kiriath Jearim	*Kir*-iath **Jee**-uh-rim or Jee-*a*-rim.
Leviticus	Leh-*vit*-ih-kus.
Michal	*My*-kal.
Obed-Edom	O-bed *Ee*-dum.
Philistines	Fuh-*liss*-teenz or *Fill*-us-teenz.
Uzzah	*Uz*-zuh.

David's attire when the ark came to Jerusalem was certainly not equivalent to a suit and tie. As king, he may never have come to breakfast less than fully dressed. But when celebrating the Lord, he clothed himself in a way that might make us cringe today. Even so, should we not think twice before voicing criticism of the clothing of our fellow worshippers?　　　　　—C. R. B.

B. The Shouting People (v. 15)

15. while he and all Israel were bringing up the ark of the LORD with shouts and the sound of trumpets.

As *all Israel* joined David, no other instrumental *sound* other than that of the *trumpets* is mentioned as accompanying the *shouts*. It's hard to hear stringed instruments over loud trumpets! Trumpets are associated with priests dozens of times in the Old Testament (example: Joshua 6:4-13, 20) and with the presence of the Lord (examples: Exodus 19:16-19; 20:18; compare Matthew 24:31; 1 Corinthians 15:52; Revelation 1:10). In the case of the latter, trumpets were linked to fear of God. Once again we see evidence that David took on a role associated more with priests than with kings. But only one person seems to have objected—our next verse.

C. The Disgruntled Queen (v. 16)

16. As the ark of the LORD was entering the City of David, Michal daughter of Saul watched from a window. And when she saw King David leaping and dancing before the LORD, she despised him in her heart.

Michal was David's first wife, and they had a rough history together (see 1 Samuel 18:20-29; 19:11-17; 25:43-44; 2 Samuel 3:13-16). Her reasons for despising David aren't completely clear. But there may be a clue in the fact that she was not celebrating with the crowds, choosing instead to stay inside and watch *from a window*. Perhaps she did this to model what she considered to be royal behavior—behavior that kept herself apart from the common people in their revelry.

We are told in 2 Samuel 6:20 (not in our printed text) that Michal accused David of acting in an undignified and inappropriate way in front

of other women who served him. David rebuffed her by claiming that he danced *before the Lord* (6:21-22).

> **What Do You Think?**
> What are some appropriate ways to respond to a spirit of negativity regarding worship and leadership practices in a church?
> *Digging Deeper*
> Categorize your responses in two ways: (1) opposition based on doctrinal conviction and (2) opposition based on personal preferences.

III. A Hope Shared
(2 SAMUEL 6:17-19)
A. God Grants Success (v. 17)

17a. They brought the ark of the LORD and set it in its place inside the tent that David had pitched for it,

David appeared at this point to have completed his mission now that *the ark of the Lord* was in *the tent that David had pitched for it*. But this raises a question: Given the cause of the tragedy in 2 Samuel 6:6-7, discussed above, did David's preparations at this point conform to instructions in Numbers 1:51 for moving the tabernacle? The parallel account in 1 Chronicles 15:12-13 indicates not.

17b. and David sacrificed burnt offerings and fellowship offerings before the LORD.

Burnt offerings (Leviticus 1) were prescribed for specific occasions (examples: Exodus 29:38-42; Numbers 28:9-10). But they were also appropriate as freewill offerings (Leviticus 22:18). *Fellowship offerings* (Leviticus 3) could express thanks or obligation to God (7:11-16).

Both kinds of sacrifices indicated the joy of the occasion and the felt need to praise God for bringing it about. Regarding the possibility of David's exercising a priestly role, see commentary on 2 Samuel 6:14b, above.

B. David Blesses the People (v. 18)

18a. After he had finished sacrificing the burnt offerings and fellowship offerings,

David's son Solomon will later follow in his

father's footsteps by sacrificing *burnt offerings* and *fellowship offerings* in dedicating the newly finished temple; the massive numbers of Solomon's sacrifice recorded in 1 Kings 8:62-63 make an interesting contrast to the "seven bulls and seven rams" offered on this occasion (1 Chronicles 15:26).

18b. he blessed the people in the name of the Lord Almighty.

On pronouncing blessing on *the people,* compare Leviticus 9:23; Joshua 8:33; 1 Chronicles 16:2; and 2 Chronicles 31:8. Regarding *the name of the Lord Almighty,* compare 1 Samuel 17:45; 2 Samuel 6:2 (above); and Isaiah 18:7.

What Do You Think?
▶ What procedures can you help your church implement to convey that the offering time is itself a significant act of corporate worship?
Digging Deeper
What's the single most important thing your church can do to honor both monetary and nonmonetary sacrifices appropriately?

C. Israel Shares the Bounty (v. 19)

19. Then he gave a loaf of bread, a cake of dates and a cake of raisins to each person in the whole crowd of Israelites, both men and women. And all the people went to their homes.

The language here is inclusive: David shared this celebration with *all the people*—not just his fighting *men* or the priests or those of his own tribe. God's presence among his people was a momentous occasion for *the whole crowd of Israelites*. A full meal for the assembled celebrants was a massive and extravagant undertaking (compare Nehemiah 8:10).

❧ *A Meal That Unites* ❧

While in Bible college, I was part of a male quartet. On weekends, we often accompanied a professor who preached at one of the college's supporting churches. These Sunday ventures typically included a song or two by the quartet and a sermon by the professor, followed by a fellowship dinner. We post-adolescent boys had hearty appetites and never let our upcoming quartet concert dampen our enthusiasm for good cooking.

When David hosted a giant fellowship meal for all gathered, he continued a practice we see throughout Scripture. Sharing a meal brings people together in more than just a physical sense. Do your own meals foster unity among God's people?
—C. R. B.

Conclusion

A. The End and the Means

We Christians get excited when we see God at work in our midst. We are then tempted to respond in ways that come naturally to us; we are inclined to do what our culture has conditioned us to do when things are going our way.

Yet David learned that not any and all responses are appropriate to our holy God. In every believer's life, the *end* and the *means* are all tangled together. How a thing is accomplished matters to the Lord.

We must consult God's Word to learn the right means to the ends we seek as we honor the Lord. We must not rush to do what seems right in our own eyes, even when we are trying to do right by God. Let us not assume we know God's will until we have carefully tested it against his Word.

What Do You Think?
▶ In what ways does this lesson require you to modify your response to the question associated with Exodus 15:20 in lesson 1, if at all?
Digging Deeper
What other passages are relevant here?

B. Prayer

Holy God, teach us to love you like David did when he was at his best. May our excitement take no heed to reactions around us as we seek only to glorify you. In Jesus' name we pray. Amen.

C. Thought to Remember

Praise God
with all your might.

INVOLVEMENT LEARNING

Enhance your lesson with NIV® Bible Student (from your curriculum supplier) and the reproducible activity page (at www.standardlesson.com or in the back of the NIV® Standard Lesson Commentary Deluxe Edition).

Into the Lesson

Ask participants to share stories of the best news they ever received. Discuss various ways people react to good news, both privately and publicly. (If your class is large, you may wish to conserve time by putting participants in small groups for the sharing of stories.)

Lead into Bible study in one of two ways. If no one mentions praying to or worshipping God in thanks as reactions to good news, ask why and discuss. If praying or worshipping *was* mentioned, ask how often those are usual or primary reactions. After either, say, "Today's lesson allows us to see how some reacted exuberantly to the blessing of God's presence, giving us an opportunity to compare their expressions with the way we react to God's blessings."

Into the Word

Spend a few minutes explaining the context for today's lesson. Do so by first inviting a class member (recruited in advance) to present a three-minute summary of the ark of the covenant by using *what, where, when,* and *why* categories, as those aspects form the lesson's backdrop.

Have two participants read aloud 2 Samuel 6:1-5, alternating with every verse. Have two other participants do the same with verses 14-19. Then divide the class into groups of three to list elements of worship they detect in these passages.

After five minutes, call the groups together to compare lists. List findings on the board by group. After all are listed, focus on elements discerned by only one group. Invite class discussion on whether those are viable for inclusion.

Into Life

Send participants back to their groups of three to make a second list alongside their first: for each element on the first list, challenge groups to name a similar element seen in worship today. After five

minutes, allow the whole class to reflect on group discoveries.

Option. To have your class dig deeper into worship in the New Testament era, distribute copies of the "New Testament Worship" exercise from the activity page, which you can download. Have small groups complete it as indicated. After groups complete the listing, reconvene for whole-class discussion. Pay particular attention to "other" texts that groups saw fit to enter.

Move the discussion to a more personal consideration of worship as you distribute handouts (you prepare) that feature the following continuum:

Observer-----Participant-----Celebrant

Have listed below the continuum the following definitions:

- **Observer:** one who watches performances at a worship service
- **Participant:** one who does what the worship leader asks (stands, sits, claps hands, sings, etc.)
- **Celebrant:** one whose expressions of worship are spontaneous (lifts hands, speaks "amens," etc.)

Ask class members to place a mark along the continuum that best indicates their personal style while engaging in corporate worship. As learners take a minute to consider this choice, write the same continuum on the board.

Allow volunteers to share why they marked the continuum as they did. Discuss why this is so—is it a matter of personality, upbringing, or something else? Press the discussion deeper by asking if worship style becomes "better" by moving along the continuum to the right.

Ask three individuals to close with prayer. The first begins with the sentence "Thank you, Lord, for those who plan worship experiences for our church." The second begins with "Help us, Lord, to worship you from the heart." The third begins with the sentence "We worship you just now, Lord, because there is no other god but you."

PRAISE BY EXPECTING AND FOLLOWING

DEVOTIONAL READING: Mark 10:46-52
BACKGROUND SCRIPTURE: Mark 10:46-52; Luke 18:35-43

MARK 10:46-52

46 Then they came to Jericho. As Jesus and his disciples, together with a large crowd, were leaving the city, a blind man, Bartimaeus (which means "son of Timaeus"), was sitting by the roadside begging. 47 When he heard that it was Jesus of Nazareth, he began to shout, "Jesus, Son of David, have mercy on me!"

48 Many rebuked him and told him to be quiet, but he shouted all the more, "Son of David, have mercy on me!"

49 Jesus stopped and said, "Call him."

So they called to the blind man, "Cheer up! On your feet! He's calling you." 50 Throwing his cloak aside, he jumped to his feet and came to Jesus.

51 "What do you want me to do for you?" Jesus asked him.

The blind man said, "Rabbi, I want to see."

52 "Go," said Jesus, "your faith has healed you." Immediately he received his sight and followed Jesus along the road.

KEY TEXT

"What do you want me to do for you?" Jesus asked him. The blind man said, "Rabbi, I want to see."
—**Mark 10:51**

Photo © Getty Images

Celebrating God

Unit 1: God's People Offer Praise

Lessons 1–4

Lesson Aims

After participating in this lesson, each learner will be able to:

1. Describe the life situation of a blind person in the time of Jesus.

2. Explain the biblical connection between physical blindness and spiritual blindness.

3. Acknowledge the dangers of spiritual blindness.

Lesson Outline

Introduction

A. Mercy

We define *mercy* as "an act of compassion toward someone who is in need." Mercy by definition is not earned; it is freely given, without compulsion. We may ask for mercy in a stressful situation, but true mercy is not compelled. It is granted.

My city has a Mercy Hospital and a Mercy High School, both the work of a religious order known as the Sisters of Mercy. This group began in nineteenth-century Ireland to provide relief to poverty-stricken girls and women. Since its beginning, the Sisters of Mercy have founded schools, universities, and hospitals all over the world. Most of these feature the word *Mercy* prominently, not allowing this foundational Christian purpose to become neglected.

Today's lesson features a man whose life was wretched. But when he knew the Son of God was nearby, he immediately asked for mercy. He understood his need, his helplessness, and his possible healing through Jesus.

B. Lesson Context

Blindness was a familiar condition in the ancient world, with the Bible itself using some form of the word *blind* dozens of times. *The Papyrus Ebers,* an Egyptian medical text of about 1500 BC, identifies various diseases of the eyes and suggests numerous remedies. These take the form of potions—ingredients of which are decidedly *not* prescribed today! In some cases, Egyptian physicians were advised to paint the mixture on the eyes of the patient, using a bird's feather.

As with many supposed remedies, healing may have occurred in spite of the treatment and therefore given the impression of effectiveness. But from our current vantage point, there was no reliable cure for blindness in Jesus' day and little understanding of its causes.

Many believed that blindness was a curse from God for some type of sinful behavior. The sins of the parents were thought to affect their children, causing them to be born blind (see John 9:1-2). The ancients knew that some diseases could leave a sufferer with damaged vision or blindness (see

Leviticus 26:16). Such outcomes we now know may result from diseases like malaria or measles. In other cases, blindness might be the result of injury or could be progressive with age (such as cataracts or macular degeneration; the last line of Ecclesiastes 12:3 uses figurative language to describe failing eyesight).

In all cases, blindness was economically and socially debilitating. For example, blind men could not serve as priests (Leviticus 21:16-18). Those afflicted with blindness had little opportunity for employment and were reduced to begging or depending on family support to survive. The Jewish law forbade taking advantage of the blind (Leviticus 19:14; see Deuteronomy 27:18), but no amount of legal protection could restore sight. The parable of the great banquet includes blind people as among the most unfortunate (Luke 14:21; see also 14:13).

Blindness and sight in a spiritual sense are important themes in the book of Mark. When questioned on the meaning of the sower parable (Mark 4:1-20), Jesus revealed that there would be people who saw what Jesus did but would not understand the good news he brought (4:12). Later, when Jesus was in a boat with the Twelve, he chastised them for their failure to understand his person and mission, saying, "Do you have eyes but fail to see" (8:18). Mark, the author, left the question open-ended so that his readers might answer it too. In essence Mark asks: "Have you read about Jesus this far and still don't see who he is or understand the spiritual lessons he is teaching?"

I. The Blind Beggar
(Mark 10:46-48)
A. Daily Pleading (v. 46)
46a. Then they came to Jericho.

Jesus' encounter with the blind Bartimaeus took place during Jesus' final journey to Jerusalem for Passover. He left Galilee (Mark 9:30) and crossed the Jordan River to the east side (10:1), a region now referred to as Transjordan.

Moving south, down the valley, Jesus and his disciples re-crossed the river near *Jericho*. From

there they were poised to begin the uphill trek to Jerusalem (Mark 10:32), a trip of about 15 miles with a rise in elevation exceeding 3,300 feet.

Jericho shows up a few times in the New Testament, primarily in the parallel Gospel accounts of Matthew 20:29-34 and Luke 18:35-43. The city is mentioned much more frequently in the Old Testament (examples: Deuteronomy 34:1; 2 Kings 2:4; Jeremiah 39:5). This is especially true of the days when Israel's wanderings in the desert were ending. While the Israelites were camped across from Jericho, King Balak of Moab called Balaam to curse the people. This backfired spectacularly (Numbers 22–24). The walls of Jericho fell gloriously because of God's help (Joshua 6:2-25).

The city wasn't rebuilt until the time of Ahab's reign (874–853 BC). And in fulfillment of the curse that Joshua pronounced (Joshua 6:26), King Hiel's firstborn and youngest sons died when the king rebuilt the city (1 Kings 16:34).

46b. As Jesus and his disciples, together with a large crowd, were leaving the city, a blind man, Bartimaeus (which means "son of Timaeus"), was sitting by the roadside begging.

As usual, *Jesus* was accompanied by *his disciples*. The *large crowd* consisted of Jewish residents of Galilee making the annual pilgrimage to Jerusalem to celebrate the Passover (Mark 10:32). Perhaps some intentionally accompanied Jesus while others were just making their trip as usual.

All would leave Jericho via the western road. This made for a high-traffic area that was an ideal site for someone *begging* for money. Matthew's tell-

HOW TO SAY IT

Aramaic	*Air*-uh-**may**-ik.
Balaam	*Bay*-lum.
Balak	*Bay*-lack.
Bartimaeus	*Bar*-tih-**me**-us.
Bethlehem	*Beth*-lih-hem.
Galilee	*Gal*-uh-lee.
Hiel	*High*-el.
Jericho	*Jair*-ih-co.
Moab	*Mo*-ab.
Nazareth	*Naz*-uh-reth.
Rabboni	Rab-*o*-nye.

ing of this encounter features two unnamed blind men *sitting by the roadside* (Matthew 20:30). Mark focuses on the one whose identity is known, *Bartimaeus*. *Bar* is Aramaic for *son of* (example: Barnabas means "son of consolation"; Acts 4:36).

At least one Bible concordance translates the word *Bartimaeus* as "Son of the Unclean," but the verse before us simply clarifies that his father's name was in fact *Timaeus*. It would make some sense to translate that name in terms of uncleanness, given the restrictions on blind men in Israel (see Lesson Context). Even so, the name Timaeus is closely related to the concept of "honor" (Mark 7:10).

> **What Do You Think?**
> When seeing someone in need, what are some ways to ensure that your actions don't do more harm than good?
> *Digging Deeper*
> Which Bible passages are most informative to you in this regard? Why?

B. Disturbing the Peace (vv. 47-48)

47a. When he heard that it was Jesus of Nazareth,

Jesus' reputation clearly had preceded him; Bartimaeus was aware of Jesus' reputation as a miracle worker and healer (examples: Mark 6:54-56; 7:36-37). Hearing that this was *Jesus of Nazareth* made a difference, since the name Jesus (Hebrew: Joshua) was not uncommon. Though Jesus had been born in Bethlehem (Matthew 2:1; Luke 2:4-7), his parents lived in Nazareth and had returned to that town when Jesus was very young (Matthew 2:22-23; Luke 2:39). Throughout his life, therefore, Jesus was known as "Jesus of Nazareth" (Mark 1:24; 10:47; etc.).

47b. he began to shout, "Jesus, Son of David, have mercy on me!"

Bartimaeus was not concerned with social decorum, for he knew this opportunity may never come again. Rather than be quietly content with the city's enjoyment of a celebrity rabbi passing through, Bartimaeus *began to shout*. As he did, he focused on a very different aspect of Jesus' heritage by using the phrase *Son of David*.

At its most generic, this address acknowledged *Jesus* to be a descendant of the greatest king in Israel's history (Matthew 1:1, 6). More importantly, this is a messianic title (example: Mark 12:35). The same acclamation was repeated few days later when Jesus entered the city of Jerusalem to the excitement of a great crowd (Matthew 21:9).

The words of Bartimaeus reveal a heart that entertained a glimmer of hope that the one who had *mercy* on other blind people, expressed in their healing, might choose to heal him also (example: Mark 8:22-25). Jesus' healing ministry had caused a sensation in Galilee (Matthew 11:1-5; etc.). It marked him as much more than a teacher.

Luke teaches that the capacity for restoring sight was a fulfillment of prophecy concerning the Messiah, marking Jesus as that person (see Luke 4:18-21). Furthermore, Luke singles out curing blindness specifically in his listing of the mighty works of Jesus, showing how impressive such a cure was considered to be (7:21).

> **What Do You Think?**
> Under what circumstances are you more likely to call on Jesus audibly rather than silently (example: Matthew 9:20-21)?
> *Digging Deeper*
> When is one choice just as good as the other?

❧ *BLINDED BY CULTURE* ❧

Our family served as missionaries in an African nation years ago. One day a 10-year-old child came by. His name was Aaron, and he asked for some food. Not only was he poor; he also was crippled by a congenital deformity, requiring that he walk with a homemade cane. As he ate, he listened to my children doing their lessons.

Aaron began coming daily for lunch. At some point, he wistfully expressed his desire to go to school. "My family is too poor, and I'm crippled, so they don't think I can learn." My son, Mark, asked Aaron if he knew how to read. He did not, and so began 13-year-old Mark's "career" as a reading teacher!

Although Aaron's culture was blind to the potential of a child with a disability, Aaron himself was not. Similarly, Bartimaeus was physically blind, but spiritually his vision was 20/20. He could "see" that the Son of David could meet his needs even though his culture ultimately rejected their Messiah. What cultural blindness do you need to overcome for the sake of the Aarons and Bartimaeuses of your community?   —C. R. B.

48. Many rebuked him and told him to be quiet, but he shouted all the more, "Son of David, have mercy on me!"

Not a few in the crowd thought Bartimaeus was rude, too aggressive, or otherwise socially inept. Perhaps they were embarrassed for him because of his bellowing.

But before we judge the crowd and put ourselves in a position of superiority, let us think about what we feel when an otherwise peaceful walk around the block is interrupted by a loud homeless person requesting help. The Passover pilgrims were on a spiritual high, perhaps ready to sing some of the joyous "psalms of ascent"—ancient songs that celebrated the long climb to the temple (example: Psalm 122).

But Bartimaeus would not *be quiet* as *many* thought he should. Rather than accommodate his scolders, he yelled even louder, shouting directly at Jesus. He didn't change his plea but repeated exactly what he'd already been shouting, as though he was never interrupted: *Son of David, have mercy on me!* The scolding of the crowd resulted in the opposite of its intended effect!

> *What Do You Think?*
> In what circumstances are you most likely to raise your voice when the majority desires otherwise?
> *Digging Deeper*
> When might it be wise to heed that desire? Why?

II. The Merciful Master
(Mark 10:49-52)
A. Jesus Calls (vv. 49-50)

49a. Jesus stopped and said, "Call him." So they called to the blind man, "Cheer up!

Visual for Lesson 3. *Have this visual on display as a backdrop to a discussion on how the form of our prayers (boldness, etc.) relates to their content.*

Jesus' actions and words quickly changed the tone of the crowd (see Mark 10:48, above). Rather than view *the blind man* as a nuisance to be silenced, *they* changed their reaction to him to one of kindness. They apparently realized that by the man's securing Jesus' attention, a potential blessing awaited him.

The Greek imperative translated *cheer up* occurs seven times in the New Testament, here and in Matthew 9:2, 22; 14:27; Mark 6:50; John 16:33; and Acts 23:11. A near synonym occurs an additional six times, in 2 Corinthians 5:6, 8; 7:16; 10:1-2; and Hebrews 13:6. The contexts are always those of boldness in terms of doing something.

49b. On your feet!

The first imperative is immediately followed by a second. Telling Bartimaeus to get *on your feet* reveals his seated or prone position as a beggar (compare Matthew 9:5-7; Mark 2:9-12; Acts 3:6-7). This detail adds drama to the incident. The man had not been standing and amplifying his voice. Rather, he had been sitting or lying on the ground, forcing his voice to cut upwards through the noise of the crowd walking past. His cry to Jesus must have been loud indeed!

49c. He's calling you."

This phrase wraps up a four-fold echo. First, Bartimaeus had called out to Jesus; then the crowd had called to Bartimaeus for silence; then Jesus called for a personal audience with Bartimaeus; and finally the crowd communicated Jesus' calling to Bartimaeus. Though at this point members of the crowd could have tried to impede not only the blind man but also Jesus, they chose instead to announce Jesus' calling as he commanded it (contrast Luke 18:15-17).

Similarly, we today are called to call others to Jesus (Matthew 28:18-20). Though we hope not to stand in the way of those who seek Jesus, sometimes we can be going along our contented way and lose sight of the lost around us. At those times, we must hear Jesus' command to issue the invitation to approach him.

50. Throwing his cloak aside, he jumped to his feet and came to Jesus.

The man's garment was his outer *cloak*, perhaps what he was sitting on. It would be his most valuable possession. For him to toss it aside showed his eagerness; every action in this verse indicated faith. Bartimaeus expected *Jesus* to grant him mercy and remove his blindness.

B. Jesus Makes Whole (vv. 51-52)

51a. "What do you want me to do for you?" Jesus asked him.

Jesus' question was not posed from lack of knowledge. Most likely, it would have been evident to everyone in the crowd that Bartimaeus, by appearance, was blind. Even if the crowd was unaware, it's impossible for *Jesus* not to have known since he had divine insight (compare Matthew 9:4; 12:25; Luke 6:8; 9:47). Jesus' question was intended to prompt Bartimaeus to verbalize his need and his faith.

51b. The blind man said, "Rabbi, I want to see."

Bartimaeus's answer was straightforward. In receiving his sight he would no longer be an object of pity, a blind man begging for small change, dependent on others to lead him.

Bartimaeus lacked physical sight but had spiritual eyes that saw clearly who Jesus was. For Bartimaeus, Jesus was the prophesied "Son of David" (Mark 10:47-48, above), the Messiah promised by God.

Bartimaeus's spiritual insight led him to believe that Jesus could heal him from his physical blindness. Others with perfect physical eyesight were spiritually blind to the true identity of Jesus (see Matthew 23:13-26).

We may note in passing that Jesus was addressed by various designations of respect in the pages of the New Testament. The most common of those was "Teacher" (example: John 11:28). Another common address of respect was "Lord" sometimes meaning no more than "sir" (example: John 5:7). But the translation *Rabbi* in the verse before us is not in the category of "sir"; rather, the underlying Greek is the word *Rabboni*. John 1:38 and 20:16 help us by explaining that both *Rabbi* and *Rabboni* mean "Teacher."

52a. "Go," said Jesus, "your faith has healed you."

To become *healed* may have more than physical implications, though that is often the primary sense of the word (examples: Mark 5:28, 34; 6:56). The underlying word in the original language can also be translated "saved" (example: 13:13). This saving can be from death (example: 15:30) to be given new life (example: Luke 9:24).

Jesus was more than a healer; he came as the Savior. He can save people from physical maladies, but more importantly he also saves souls from sin (Mark 8:35; etc.). In the Gospel of Mark, the mocking crowd at the crucifixion challenged Jesus to come down from the cross. When he remained nailed to the wood, they scornfully shouted, "He saved others . . . but he can't save himself" (15:31), thereby revealing a complete misunderstanding of what was happening.

The pattern for Jesus' healing miracles in Mark includes the requirement for a display of *faith*. Some men believed in Jesus so strongly that they dug a hole in a roof to bring their paralyzed friend to him (Mark 2:1-5). A desperate mother approached Jesus to heal her daughter (7:24-30). The father of the demon-possessed boy, confessing his faith as well as his doubts, brought his son to Jesus for healing (9:23-24). Faith was essential in all these accounts.

52b. Immediately he received his sight and followed Jesus along the road.

Although Jesus had just said "Go" (previous half verse), Mark ends the story of Bartimaeus by having him join *Jesus along the road*. An interesting contrast is Mark 5:18-20. There a man healed from demonization desired to accompany Jesus, but Jesus forbade him.

> **What Do You Think?**
> Which of the following "your faith has" pas-
> sages speaks comfort to you most powerful-
> ly and personally: Matthew 9:22; Mark 5:34;
> 10:52; Luke 7:50; 8:48; 17:19?
> **Digging Deeper**
> Which one most leads you to encourage others?

❧ FAITHFUL IN DEATH ❧

I worked for several years as a hospice chaplain. During that time, I enjoyed some of the most rewarding experiences in my 60-plus years of ministry. Many of my patients were devout followers of Jesus.

What intrigued me was how those faithful patients dealt with the process of dying. I think of one Christian patient who was typical of many to whom I ministered. He was dying of kidney failure, but he exhibited a sense of peacefulness from the first day I visited him.

As his kidneys continued to fail and his death inexorably drew closer, his conversations with me proved that, while his body could not be healed, his spirit was being made whole (compare 2 Corinthians 4:16). He faced death with acceptance, but more than that, with hope and even joy!

Eventually each of us will reach the point where there is no healing for our current bodies. But are we moving daily toward the wholeness that Jesus offers us?
—C. R. B.

Conclusion
A. Lord, Have Mercy

The restoration of a blind man's sight was a great and merciful miracle. But in the larger context of the Gospels, Jesus encountered many who were spiritually blind, having unresponsive hearts that refused to recognize or honor him. Our journey with Jesus begins when we realize we are blind and on the side of the road, sidelined and desper-ate. It's at that point when we allow Jesus to make us whole. Then we join him, joyfully walking and learning as we go. This is a timeless picture of discipleship (Matthew 16:24; John 14:6).

When we consider the necessity of faith, we learn some things about Jesus—and about ourselves. In the instance of today's text, as in those that came before, Jesus honored faith. The faith of Bartimaeus was very simple: he believed that Jesus was willing and able to help. The man was not questioned about what he knew or believed about the coming Messiah. Neither was he queried regarding exactly what he meant when he called Jesus "Son of David" (Mark 10:47-48) or "Rabbi" (10:51). Neither his doctrines nor motives were called into account (contrast Mark 10:17-18; John 6:25-26; James 4:3).

When we are in crisis and see no relief, we may say "Lord, have mercy" without thinking about the import of these words. Yet this is a prayer, imploring God to notice our pitiful situation and provide relief. In that regard may we take a lesson from Bartimaeus, being willing to call on the Lord when the crowd has a different agenda. May the eyes of our hearts be opened to see Jesus clearly and obey him fully (see Ephesians 1:18).

> **What Do You Think?**
> Which concept or imperative in today's lesson
> do you have the most trouble coming to grips
> with? Why?
> **Digging Deeper**
> How will you resolve this problem?

B. Prayer

Father, reveal to us our own blindnesses so that we might be spiritually whole. As you extend that mercy to us, may we do likewise to others. Open our eyes, Lord, and let us see you clearly so that we may follow your Son as he would have us to. In Jesus' name, the one who cures blindness, we pray. Amen.

C. Thought to Remember

Physical blindness is temporary;
spiritual blindness is eternal.

INVOLVEMENT LEARNING

Enhance your lesson with NIV® Bible Student (from your curriculum supplier) and the reproducible activity page (at www.standardlesson.com or in the back of the NIV® Standard Lesson Commentary Deluxe Edition).

Into the Lesson

Choose a blindfold game to play with your class. Here are some possibilities:

• **What Is It?** Recruit six or eight to be blindfolded while everyone else watches. Give one unblindfolded class member a box of simple objects. He or she must describe each object without telling what it is. Blindfolded players must guess the object from the description.

• **Voice in the Dark.** Blindfold one participant. Class members disguise their voices as they repeat a sentence to the blindfolded person. The blindfolded person must guess who is speaking. If he guesses correctly, the person identified must wear the blindfold. Repeat.

Alternative. Ask volunteers to tell a story about a time they experienced a harrowing "lights out" event.

Use either of the above to lead into Bible study by saying, "It is difficult for sighted people to appreciate fully the disability of blindness. Today's lesson gives us a sense of the desperation of one person in that regard."

Into the Word

Have three participants read aloud the words of the narrator, Bartimaeus, and Jesus in today's lesson text. Then distribute handouts (you prepare) that reproduce these sentences:

1–Jesus was in Jerusalem when he met Bartimaeus, the man who was blind.

2–Jesus found Bartimaeus in the temple courts.

3–Bartimaeus quietly asked a friend to contact Jesus on his behalf.

4–When the crowd saw Jesus passing by and knew he could help Bartimaeus, they moved in unison to put the two in touch with one another.

5–When Jesus hesitated, the disciples convinced him to talk with Bartimaeus.

6–Jesus said to Bartimaeus, "I'm healing you."

7–Jesus knew Bartimaeus's need and healed him without further conversation.

8–Jesus said to Bartimaeus, "The disciples will heal you."

9–Jesus told Bartimaeus to wait 10 days to prove his faith, and then he would be healed.

Have participants work together in study pairs or triads to (1) determine whether each statement is true or false, (2) jot a verse reference beside each statement to indicate where in the narrative the answer is found, and (3) write a few words that would make false statements become true statements, without simply adding the word *not*. (*Expected conclusions*: all statements are false.)

Option 1. Use the handout as a closed-Bible true/false pretest. Delay reading of the text until after learners enter their answers. After no more than an announced time limit of one minute, have learners score their own answers as you read aloud the lesson text.

Option 2. For a deeper dive into this healing miracle, distribute to study pairs copies of the "One Story, Three Versions" exercise from the activity page, which you can download. You will also need to give to each study pair a set of five colored pencils: one each of brown, blue, green, red, and either yellow or orange. Complete and discuss results as indicated.

Into Life

Distribute handouts (you create) titled "Eyes Wide Open" to study pairs or triads. On it have listed the following passages down the left-hand side: Proverbs 4:19; Matthew 6:22-23; 15:12-14; John 3:19-21; 2 Corinthians 4:4; Ephesians 4:17-19; 1 Thessalonians 5:1-5; and 1 John 2:9-11. (You can list either all the actual wording of the passages or only the book, chapter, and verse references.)

Include instructions to circle the passage that learners find most convicting in warning of the dangers of spiritual blindness. Discuss.

PRAISE FOR SALVATION

DEVOTIONAL READING: Acts 2:37-47
BACKGROUND SCRIPTURE: Acts 2:32-33, 37-47

ACTS 2:32-33, 37-47

[32] God has raised this Jesus to life, and we are all witnesses of it. [33] Exalted to the right hand of God, he has received from the Father the promised Holy Spirit and has poured out what you now see and hear.

· ·

[37] When the people heard this, they were cut to the heart and said to Peter and the other apostles, "Brothers, what shall we do?"

[38] Peter replied, "Repent and be baptized, every one of you, in the name of Jesus Christ for the forgiveness of your sins. And you will receive the gift of the Holy Spirit. [39] The promise is for you and your children and for all who are far off—for all whom the Lord our God will call."

[40] With many other words he warned them; and he pleaded with them, "Save yourselves from this corrupt generation." [41] Those who accepted his message were baptized, and about three thousand were added to their number that day.

[42] They devoted themselves to the apostles' teaching and to fellowship, to the breaking of bread and to prayer. [43] Everyone was filled with awe at the many wonders and signs performed by the apostles. [44] All the believers were together and had everything in common. [45] They sold property and possessions to give to anyone who had need. [46] Every day they continued to meet together in the temple courts. They broke bread in their homes and ate together with glad and sincere hearts, [47] praising God and enjoying the favor of all the people. And the Lord added to their number daily those who were being saved.

KEY TEXT

They devoted themselves to the apostles' teaching and to fellowship, to the breaking of bread and to prayer.
—**Acts 2:42**

Photo © Getty Images

CELEBRATING GOD

Unit 1: God's People Offer Praise

Lessons 1–4

LESSON AIMS

After participating in this lesson, each learner will be able to:

1. Identify the transformation from sinful to saved.

2. Distinguish between elements related to *justification* (things that happen in order to be saved) and elements related to *sanctification* (things that happen for growth in holiness after one has been saved).

3. Brainstorm ways to enhance practices of the first-century church that should be continued in his or her church today.

LESSON OUTLINE

Introduction
    A. No Longer Endangered
    B. Lesson Context
I. A Divine Plan (Acts 2:32-33, 37-40)
    A. Promises Fulfilled (vv. 32-33)
    B. Promises Offered (vv. 37-40)
      God's Plan or Mine?
II. A Divine Change (Acts 2:41-47)
    A. Added to the Church (v. 41)
      Changing Perspectives
    B. The Active Church (vv. 42-46)
    C. A Growing Group (v. 47)
Conclusion
    A. Transformation
    B. Prayer
    C. Thought to Remember

Introduction

A. No Longer Endangered

News about the endangered species list is rarely uplifting. Of the 719 animal species that have been listed for the US, at least 11 are extinct on the continent, and many more remain endangered. Only 27 animals have been taken off the list, due to species recovery. In December 2019, the latest three joined the list of recovered species: the Monito gecko, the Kirtland's warbler, and the Foskett's speckled dace. Removal from the endangered list requires evidence that the species can survive and flourish on its own in its natural environment. Many factors come into play to make sure that such recovery can be expected to continue. When all criteria are met, we can celebrate a successful recovery.

As new life can be breathed into dying species, God can breathe new life into endangered people. Today's lesson gives us a dramatic example in this regard.

B. Lesson Context

The Gospel of Luke and the book of Acts were both written by Luke, a Gentile disciple and physician (Colossians 4:14). The Gospel is like a Part 1, while Acts is Part 2. Luke addressed both of his books to a certain Theophilus (Luke 1:3; Acts 1:1). Acts 1:8 anticipated the spread of the gospel message from Jerusalem to Samaria and on to the remotest parts of the earth. The contents of the book of Acts span about 30 years, beginning in AD 30. The time frame of our lesson is 50 days after Jesus' resurrection.

The apostle Peter was the one speaking in today's text (see Acts 2:14). There's a very good chance that many or most of his audience had been in the city during Jesus' trials, crucifixion, and resurrection; it was natural for those making the annual pilgrimage to Jerusalem for observances of Passover and the Festival of Unleavened Bread (Leviticus 23:5-6; Luke 22:1) to stay for the Festival of Weeks (Deuteronomy 16:9-12). The latter came to be known as Pentecost.

The people who heard Peter preach were from various locations (Acts 2:8-11). Imagine the nonstop talking in the streets about the events surrounding the crucifixion of Jesus of Nazareth! There would have been rumors, questions, and doubts about the identity of Jesus. *Did he really rise from the dead? Was he really the Christ?*

At first glance, we may be surprised that Peter exhibited the boldness we see in today's text. After all, he had denied Jesus three times before the crucifixion (Luke 22:54-62) and had cowered afterward in a locked room (John 20:19). But having been reinstated by Jesus himself after the resurrection (21:15-19), Peter became a different man.

I. A Divine Plan
(ACTS 2:32-33, 37-40)
A. Promises Fulfilled (vv. 32-33)

32. God has raised this Jesus to life, and we are all witnesses of it.

The Jewish people were expecting a king in the likeness of David (Matthew 12:23), not *this Jesus*. The people expected their Messiah to deliver them from Roman rule and "restore the kingdom to Israel" (Acts 1:6). Instead, Jesus was a humble servant who had no palace (compare Isaiah 53:1-3; Luke 9:58). He came to provide forgiveness of sins and a better kingdom (John 18:36).

The people might not have recognized the arrival of the Messiah, but that was all in the plan of *God* from the beginning (Acts 2:22-23; Galatians 1:4). The death of Christ was no accident or unforeseen wrinkle; it was the perfectly executed plan from God. From the Garden of Eden, in which God promised to strike the serpent (Gene-

HOW TO SAY IT

Corinthians	Ko-*rin*-thee-unz (*th* as in *thin*).
Deuteronomy	Due-ter-*ahn*-uh-me.
diaspora	dee-*as*-puh-ruh.
koinonia *(Greek)*	koy-no-*nee*-uh.
Leviticus	Leh-*vit*-ih-kus.
Messiah	Meh-*sigh*-uh.
Nazareth	*Naz*-uh-reth.
Pentecost	*Pent*-ih-kost.
Samaria	Suh-*mare*-ee-uh.
Theophilus	Thee-*ahf*-ih-luss (*th* as in *thin*).

sis 3:15; compare Romans 16:20), to the promise to Abraham, wherein his seed would be a blessing to all nations (Genesis 12:1-3), God worked his plan (compare Galatians 3:16-18).

That plan included raising Jesus from the dead just as the Scriptures had predicted (Acts 2:23-35). The apostles were *witnesses*. They had seen Jesus alive again and had watched him ascend to Heaven to sit at God's right hand (see next verse; also Luke 24 and Acts 1).

> *What Do You Think?*
> How can Colossians 3:1, etc., help you guard against actions that would serve to damage your Christian witness?
> *Digging Deeper*
> How much difference does it make to your answer that our witness is not that of the text's eyewitnesses? Why?

33a. Exalted to the right hand of God,

To be at *the right hand* of someone is to be in the position of honor or preeminence (Genesis 48:13-20; Psalm 80:17; Acts 7:56; Ephesians 1:20; etc.). Peter expanded on this a bit by quoting Psalm 110:1 in Acts 2:34 (not in today's text).

33b. he has received from the Father the promised Holy Spirit and has poured out what you now see and hear.

Just before returning to Heaven, Jesus reminded the disciples of his Father's plan to send them *the promised Holy Spirit* (Luke 24:49; compare John 14:16-17; 15:26). God began to fulfill this promise as he poured out his Spirit in Acts 2:1-4.

The phrase *what you now see and hear* points back to the evidence of the audible and visual phenomena of Acts 2:2-4. To correct a misinterpretation seen in Acts 2:13, Peter quoted from Joel 2:28-32 in Acts 2:16-21. That prophet had pronounced one of the greatest of all prophecies of Christ's church. Joel foresaw Judah devastated by a terrifying locust plague (Joel 2:1-11). Yet God promised to remove the plague and pour out his blessings if the people repented (2:12-27). In looking into the distant future, Joel also said that God planned to do more than restore crops: he also promised to pour out his Spirit (2:28-29).

Praise the Lord Who Saves

Visual for Lesson 4. *Start a discussion by pointing to this posted visual and asking, "What's the connection between the image and the imperative?"*

In Acts 2:34-36 (not in today's text), Peter concluded his sermon with convicting words. His message is often called the first complete gospel sermon because it was the first public announcement of the significance of Jesus' death, burial, resurrection, and ascension. The Scriptures had predicted that all this would happen to the Messiah (examples: Psalms 2, 16, 22; Isaiah 53; Luke 24:25-27).

B. Promises Offered (vv. 37-40)

37. When the people heard this, they were cut to the heart and said to Peter and the other apostles, "Brothers, what shall we do?"

This gospel message penetrated like a sword (Hebrews 4:12) as the people were called to account. Many came to the painful realization that God sent Jesus out of love for them (see John 3:16) but they had rejected him (Mark 10:32-34). Even though they had not personally driven the nails into his hands and feet, they had either agreed with those who did (Luke 23:21) or they had approved of the crucifixion by their silence.

Though we probably think of the reaction of being *cut to the heart* as little more than a gut feeling, certainly many in the crowd had their hearts prepared to receive correction from the Lord. A heart that is willing to ask *what shall we do* is prepared to discover the rich blessings of God. In this case, the people were asking the *apostles* for immediate help with their realized need.

A few years ago, I was comfortable. Semi-retirement suited me, especially as I remarried after my first wife's death. Everything was working according to *my* plan—until my new wife and I were approached by a ministry that served at risk youth. The ministry was seeking a short-term leader who could effect some needed changes. The ministry leaders asked if we were interested. Our answer was essentially, "Not really. Life is going according to our plan."

But soon came a request for a résumé and an interview. God's plan was at work, and we engaged the new ministry. It turned out to be my most satisfying two years in a lifetime of ministry.

Israel's plan for the type of Messiah they wanted and expected wasn't working. That was because God had other plans. With the Spirit's guidance, Peter was able to show the people how God was at work in ways they never expected! Are you alert to the possibility that *your* plan may not be *God's* plan?

—C. R. B.

38a. Peter replied, "Repent

The words *repent* and *repentance* occur more than 50 times in the New Testament. To repent is to turn away from sin and toward God in heart, mind, and lifestyle (compare Ezekiel 14:6; 18:30; Acts 3:19; 26:20). Throughout history there have been moments of truth in which people were faced with the stark choice of either walking away from God or toward him (Joshua 24:14-15; 2 Chronicles 7:14; etc.). A hard-hearted, prideful individual will not admit wrongdoing. But through repentance, that person can find peace with God. Instead of denying, excusing, or justifying sin, people must admit it and turn from it.

38b. and be baptized, every one of you, in the name of Jesus Christ

The apostle Paul later explained that to *be baptized* was to be "buried with [Christ Jesus] . . . into death in order that, just as Christ was raised from the dead . . . we too may live a new life" (Romans 6:4; see also Colossians 2:12). He further noted that "all of you who were baptized into Christ have clothed yourselves with Christ" (Galatians 3:27).

There is nothing magical about the waters of baptism; rather, baptism is God's chosen time when regeneration and renewal happen (Titus 3:5; 1 Peter 3:21). As such, baptism is not a human work of merit (compare Ephesians 2:8-9); rather, it is a work of God.

38c. for the forgiveness of your sins.

The most important thing anyone can do when reaching the age of knowing that they have sinned against God is to have those sins forgiven. The wonderful thing is that God is willing to forgive us *and* to help us resist future sin. The former (known as justification) happens through Christ; the latter (known as sanctification) happens through the Holy Spirit (see 1 Corinthians 6:11; also see next).

38d. And you will receive the gift of the Holy Spirit.

With *the gift of the Holy Spirit*, Christians have the power to put off the works of the flesh and to bear the fruit of the Spirit (Galatians 5:22-25). In this regard, Peter's sermon foreshadows the church's submission to the leading of the Spirit in the book of Acts and beyond.

39. The promise is for you and your children and for all who are far off—for all whom the Lord our God will call."

Those who heard this sermon likely understood *all who are far off* to refer to Jews who had left Israel in the diaspora (the dispersion of Jews beyond Israel). That dispersion was not limited to the exiles of 2 Kings 17:6 and 25:21. The reality of the diaspora is a context of the first century AD, with Jews living all over the Roman Empire (see Acts 2:9-11; James 1:1).

In both Acts 8 and 10, there was confusion and questioning about the nature of God's *call*. Christians of Jewish background initially believed that Jesus had come to redeem only Israel (compare Luke 24:21; Acts 11:18). But throughout the book of Acts, the Spirit led messengers to take the gospel to Gentiles as well.

40. With many other words he warned them; and he pleaded with them, "Save yourselves from this corrupt generation."

The word translated *corrupt* is also translated "crooked" in Luke 3:5. That's the idea in Deu-

teronomy 32:5, which refers to "a warped and crooked generation." Christians must shine like stars in a sin-darkened world and keep themselves "from being polluted by the world" (James 1:27).

> **What Do You Think?**
> Looking at 1 Peter 1:15-16, what is one way to increase your distance from the surrounding unholiness?
> **Digging Deeper**
> How does your status of being "in" but not "of" the world (John 17:13-19) speak to this?

II. A Divine Change
(Acts 2:41-47)
A. Added to the Church (v. 41)

41. Those who accepted his message were baptized, and about three thousand were added to their number that day.

Modern estimates suggest that Jerusalem's population was 60,000–80,000 at the time. With the annual observance of Pentecost, however, the number would have been temporarily much higher. The *three thousand* who *accepted* Peter's *message* were therefore a small fraction of those who could have. Even so, their influence in Jerusalem and their hometowns located in the regions listed in Acts 2:9-11 could be enormous (compare Luke 13:20-21).

❧ *Changing Perspectives* ❧

I accepted Christ and was baptized at a young age. In middle age, I visited Israel. At a spot in the Jordan River, I watched as several in our tour group were baptized. Most also had been Christians from their youth.

As a teacher of Christianity, I focused on biblical truth. In that light, I knew of no precedent for rebaptism in the New Testament except in the case of John's baptism (Acts 19:1-5). Since that didn't apply to me, and since I had already been baptized, I decided not to join them.

Years later, I went to Israel again. I approached that trip from a different perspective. I had begun to look at faith less academically. I reflected on how abundantly God had blessed me since I had been baptized. Standing again at the Jordan River, I decided to be baptized again.

That decision was not necessary in God's eyes since there is "one baptism" (Ephesians 4:5). But I did it as an act of personal spiritual and emotional renewal. How has your perspective on spiritual life changed with maturing faith?   —C. R. B.

B. The Active Church (vv. 42-46)

42a. They devoted themselves to the apostles' teaching

Decisions changed lives—and eternal destinies. The new Christians *devoted themselves* to things they had not done before.

For one thing, they heeded *the apostles' teaching*. Jesus had promised that the Holy Spirit would guide the apostles "into all the truth" (John 16:13). They passed those truths along as they taught about Jesus. That life-changing message, preserved in the pages of the New Testament, remains the very center of the Christian faith. True teaching is important!

42b. and to fellowship,

The new Christians' steadfastness in *fellowship* is still a model for today. We have the privilege of belonging to the greatest family on earth as we work together to spread the good news. The Greek word being translated is *koinonia,* and many churches use that word as the name of one of their Bible study classes: Koinonia Class. When Christians pool their time, talent, and treasure into the gospel task, we can say they are "fellowshipping" in the gospel (Galatians 2:9; 1 John 1:3-7).

42c. to the breaking of bread

Breaking of bread could refer either to an ordinary meal or to the Lord's Supper (compare and contrast Luke 9:16; 24:30; Acts 20:7; 27:33-36; 1 Corinthians 10:16; 11:23-24). Just which is in view here is a matter of some debate. At the very least, we should think that these meals involved close fellowship, since that was just noted.

42d. and to prayer.

Although *prayer* is mentioned fourth, that doesn't mean it's the least important! Whether prayer was offered by an individual (Acts 26:29) or by a group (12:5), these earliest believers real-

ized how important prayer was to their new relationship with God. And so it is today.

> **What Do You Think?**
> What plan for change do you have for strengthening your weakest area of the four mentioned in this verse?
> *Digging Deeper*
> What kind of help will you accept to do so?

43a. Everyone was filled with awe

Upon hearing the words of Peter and seeing the transformed lives, many present in the Pentecost crowd seemed to have been *filled with awe.* When the crowd realized they had rejected and killed the Messiah, they may have even been filled with fear, respect, and reverence.

43b. at the many wonders and signs performed by the apostles.

God continued to shake Jerusalem by empowering *the apostles* to do miracles, which is what *wonders and signs* are (see also Acts 2:19; 2:22; 4:30; 5:12; 6:8; 7:36; 14:3; 15:12). The miracles were wonders because those who witnessed them were amazed. They were signs because they pointed people to the truth about Jesus (compare John 14:11).

44-45. All the believers were together and had everything in common. They sold property and possessions to give to anyone who had need.

One of the most important characteristics of Christians is generosity. The fact that these earliest Christians *had everything in common* indicates that they shared their possessions, going so far as to sell property and give as anyone *had need* (example: Acts 4:32-37). There would have been a pressing need during this time because of those who had stayed in Jerusalem following Pentecost. These new Christians seemed to have lingered in town to continue in fellowship. Provisions would have likely run out for some, given the extension of the originally planned length of the trip.

God helps the needy, and Christians must be like-minded (Galatians 6:10; 1 John 3:17-18). This is one of the first lessons that the earliest Christians learned, and they learned it quite well.

46. Every day they continued to meet together in the temple courts. They broke bread in their homes and ate together with glad and sincere hearts,

These earliest Christians found strength in getting together *every day*. Larger groups could meet *in the temple courts,* while smaller gatherings could meet *in their homes.*

Temple gatherings occurred specifically "in Solomon's Colonnade" (Acts 5:12), along the east side of the outer court. Jesus had been here (John 10:23), and it became the site of a miracle that resulted in another sermon by Peter (Acts 3:11-26) and sharp confrontation with opponents (chapter 4).

Meeting in one another's homes was more conducive to sharing meals and personal interactions. The *sincere hearts* that led to or resulted from such gatherings set them apart from the rest of the world (see also Acts 5:42; 20:7). This happened as a natural outflowing of love, helping bind together those of "faith as precious as ours" (2 Peter 1:1).

In modern US society, Christians can allow themselves to become too busy to engage in this kind of fellowship. We may get home after work, shut the garage door, and "cocoon" for the rest of the evening. What a tragedy to miss out on opportunities that can bind the church together!

> *What Do You Think?*
> How do the attitudes and practices in Acts 2:46 aid you in answering the questions associated with Acts 2:42, above?
>
> *Digging Deeper*
> Which of the areas does your church need to promote most to avoid the divisions of Romans 16:17 and 1 Corinthians 1:10; 11:18?

C. A Growing Group (v. 47)

47. praising God and enjoying the favor of all the people. And the Lord added to their number daily those who were being saved.

Public meetings in the temple meant that the earliest Christians were not huddling together in secret. Instead, their public witness gained them *favor of all the people.* To have a good reputation with outsiders is important for attracting them to Jesus (Colossians 4:5; 1 Thessalonians 4:10-12;

1 Timothy 3:7). And that seemed to be what was happening here as *their number* continued to grow *daily.* As the first Christians succeeded in being a strong, loving witness to the community, they also had God's approval. After all, he is the one who ultimately saves (compare Romans 3:24-26 and Titus 3:4-7).

Conclusion
A. Transformation

The most powerful realization from today's text is that Christ is still good news for a dying world —he has been since the day of Pentecost, and he will continue to be so until he returns. Until then, we must share Jesus with everyone we can.

Foundational to this effort is a sense of awe, which is often missing in the church today. Sometimes our worship services feel stale. Our prayer lives may dry up. We allow the urgent to distract us from the important. But in those times, we can ask for transformation as we cry for God to "restore to me the joy of your salvation" (Psalm 51:12).

God still works in and through his people. May we be aware of his movement in our lives, our churches, and our communities so that we too may see the church growing daily.

> *What Do You Think?*
> Which concept or imperative in today's lesson do you have the most trouble coming to grips with? Why?
>
> *Digging Deeper*
> How will you resolve this problem?

B. Prayer

Lord, thank you for being the God of transformation! As you have been merciful, patient, and forgiving to us in that regard, may we be so to others who need to hear of your Son. In Jesus' name we pray. Amen.

C. Thought to Remember

God can transform those
who have ready hearts.

INVOLVEMENT LEARNING

Enhance your lesson with NIV® Bible Student (from your curriculum supplier) and the reproducible activity page (at www.standardlesson.com or in the back of the NIV® Standard Lesson Commentary Deluxe Edition).

Into the Lesson

Before class, prepare four slips of paper with the following prompts, one per slip:

A church service I'll always remember was . . .
The most exciting crowd I was ever in was . . .
A surprising experience I can't forget was . . .
The best concert I ever attended was . . .

As the class convenes, put the four slips into an opaque container. Then put into the same container enough blank slips of paper so that the total number of slips exactly equals the number of learners who are present. Pass the container around for each participant to draw one slip.

Ask each person who received a prompt to tell a story to complete it. For those who can't think of a response, be prepared to complete the prompt yourself.

Lead into Bible study by saying, "Today we're going to look at an experience that was unprecedented. How people reacted is informative some 2,000 years later."

Into the Word

Announce a closed-Bible pretest regarding today's lesson. As you do, give each learner a handout (you create) that features the following descriptive statements:

Committed to what the apostles taught
Constant in fellowship with one another
Convicted by God's presence among them
Concerned about the needs in their group
Continued daily to meet with each other
Claimed favor with everyone around them
Connected with new members daily

Have the following instructions printed at the bottom of the handouts: "Each statement above concerns one facet regarding the birth of the church as recorded in Acts 2:32-33, 37-47, but they're in the wrong order of occurrence. In

less than one minute, rearrange them so that the order of occurrence is correct." (***Important note:*** For teacher convenience, the order given here is the correct order. Be sure to mix them up on the handouts!)

After calling time when the minute is up, read the text aloud as participants check their own work. (The checking process will be easier if verse numbers are written beside the correct statements as they are encountered.)

Write the following outline on the board and summarize each point to reinforce what has been learned:

1–Why the Jews were in Jerusalem.
2–What happened to get their attention.
3–What Peter told his Jewish audience.

Option. For a deeper look at New Testament teaching on baptism, distribute copies of the "More on Baptism" exercise on the activity page, which you can download. Have study pairs complete it as indicated. (Since it can be time-consuming for all pairs to study every entry on the activity handout, you can assign fewer passages to each group.) Reconvene for whole-class discussion.

Into Life

Ask students to look again at the seven statements on the first handout. In groups, have learners compare and contrast the experience of the church initially established with the experiences of your congregation. (You may decide to assign just one statement to each of seven groups, etc.)

After five minutes, ask groups to share conclusions in whole-class discussion. Brainstorm ways to enhance the practice of those activities that should be continued today. If possible, agree on first steps for following through on this. Appoint a volunteer to speak with someone in congregational leadership about one or more ideas your class can help with in this regard.

PRAISE GOD WITH JOY

DEVOTIONAL READING: Psalm 100

BACKGROUND SCRIPTURE: Psalm 100

PSALM 100

A psalm. For giving grateful praise.
1 Shout for joy to the LORD, all the earth.
2   Worship the LORD with gladness;
     come before him with joyful songs.
3 <u>Know that the LORD is God.</u>

It is he who made us, and we are his;
     we are his people, the sheep of his
         pasture.
4 Enter his gates with thanksgiving
     and his courts with praise;
     give thanks to him and praise his name.
5 For the LORD is good and his love endures
         forever;
     his faithfulness continues through all
         generations.

Sabei que o Senhor é Deus!

Sachez que L'eternel est Dieu!

Erkennet, daß Jehova Gott ist!

γνῶτε ὅτι κύριος, αὐτός ἐστιν ὁ θεός,

דְּעוּ כִּי־יְהוָה הוּא אֱלֹהִים

Reconoced que Jehová es Dios

KEY TEXT

Know that the LORD is God. It is he who made us, and we are his; we are his people, the sheep of his pasture. —**Psalm 100:3**

CELEBRATING GOD

Unit 2: Called to Praise God

LESSONS 5–9

LESSON AIMS

After participating in this lesson, each learner will be able to:

1. Describe the structure of a psalm of praise.

2. Evaluate the basis for joyous praise.

3. List ways he or she can live that honor God as king.

LESSON OUTLINE

Introduction
  A. Worthy of Song
  B. Lesson Context: The Book(s) of Psalms
  C. Lesson Context: Psalm 100
 I. A Call to All (Psalm 100:1-2)
  A. Come with Joy (v. 1)
  B. Come with Gladness (v. 2)
    Get To
 II. A Call to Know (Psalm 100:3)
  A. Who God Is (v. 3a)
  B. Who We Are (v. 3b)
 III. A Call to Thanksgiving (Psalm 100:4-5)
  A. In God's Presence (v. 4)
    Check the Gate
  B. For God's Greatness (v. 5)
Conclusion
  A. Because the Lord Is Good
  B. Prayer
  C. Thought to Remember

Introduction

A. Worthy of Song

One database of hymns and hymnals on the internet lists over 240 hymns and songs whose lyrics reflect phrases from Psalm 100. Among these are "All People Who on Earth Do Dwell," Isaac Watts's "Before Jehovah's Awesome Throne," and Mozart's "Jubilate Deo." An arrangement of "Old Hundredth" was composed by Ralph Vaughn Williams to be performed in 1953 as the processional hymn for the coronation of Queen Elizabeth II of England. The attraction of Psalm 100 no doubt derives from its concise yet robust summons to joyful praise to God and its eloquent rationale for doing so.

B. Lesson Context: The Book(s) of Psalms

The book of Psalms is actually a collection of five books or sections. Most Bibles note these book divisions (often with Roman numerals) at the beginnings of Psalms 1, 42, 73, 90, and 107. Altogether these five books feature 150 poems.

Psalm 100, today's text, is found in the fourth of these five books. Many scholars consider this section of Psalms (that is, Psalms 90–106) to be the answer to the problem presented in the first three books: the Davidic dynasty established (Psalm 2; see lesson 6 on Psalm 9); the flourishing of that dynasty (Psalm 72); and the failure of that dynasty (Psalm 89; see also lesson 8 on Psalm 84). The emphasis in Book IV of Psalms is simply *God reigns!* (see Psalms 93, 96–99).

Here, finally, the problem presented in the first three books is stated. Human kings may disappoint us, but God is our ultimate king, and he reigns forever. He is the king who, through Moses, led the Israelites out of Egyptian bondage.

In this light, Book IV of Psalms has something of a Mosaic flavor (notice that the superscription of Psalm 90 attributes it to Moses). Book IV ends with two views of the wilderness wandering: God's viewpoint (Psalm 105) and Israel's viewpoint (Psalm 106). The former is about God's faithfulness to the covenant promises, while the latter is about Israel's sinfulness and failure to obey God and keep the covenant.

C. Lesson Context: Psalm 100

Psalm 100 is a brief poem that speaks to the proper response of the people of God to him. The ancient Israelites may have sung this psalm during the Festival of Ingathering (Exodus 23:16b; 34:22b), also called the Festival of Tabernacles (example: Deuteronomy 31:10). This annual seven-day observance celebrated the fall harvest and the completion of the agricultural year. It had historical significance as well, in that it commemorated the Lord's protection during Israel's sojourn in the wilderness (Leviticus 23:33-36, 39-43; Deuteronomy 16:13-15; Nehemiah 8:13-18).

The organization of Psalm 100 is a variation on the standard psalm structure known as the hymn, or praise, psalm. The standard structure consists of a summons to praise the Lord followed by reasons for that praise. This type of psalm first appears in Exodus 15:21 as Miriam and the women of Israel sang (see lesson 1). The author of Psalm 100 varied this pattern by using two invitations to praise (100:1-2, 4), each followed by a motivation for praise (100:3, 5). Conspicuous in Psalm 100's design are seven commands. The fourth command occupies the central position in the psalm (see Psalm 100:3a, below).

And although Psalm 100 does not explicitly celebrate God as king, it nevertheless shares some affinity with another type of psalm known as divine kingship psalms. Such psalms speak of the Lord's rule over the cosmos or nations.

Many psalms have superscriptions. These often include information regarding the historical circumstances of the psalm, the name of the writer, etc. The superscription of Psalm 100 does not indicate the author's identity. The date of its composition is also unclear. Alluding to temple structures would be appropriate in both the pre-exilic era (that is, before the destruction of Solomon's temple in 586 BC) and in the post-exilic era after the temple was rebuilt (515 BC; see Psalm 100:4, below).

However, given the context of Book IV, in which Psalm 100 is located, we can surmise that this particular poem was meant to be associated more closely with Moses than with other writers or prophets (see the superscription of Psalm 90; compare Psalm 100:2, below). Psalm 100 is the only psalm with a superscription that reads, "A psalm. For giving grateful praise."

I. A Call to All
(PSALM 100:1-2)
A. Come with Joy (v. 1)
1a. Shout for joy to the LORD,

The command to *shout for joy* appears in exactly the same Hebrew phrasing in only two places: here and in Psalm 98:4. To these we can compare Psalms 66:1; 81:1; and 95:1, which are similar. This is a call to unhindered praise.

The Hebrew word behind the translation *shout* is translated as "extol" in Psalm 95:2, and both senses are present here. This attests that the psalmist expects volume and excitement (compare also translations of triumphal cries in Psalms 41:11; 60:8; and 108:9). Such shouts could be accompanied by the clapping of hands (47:1), singing (98:4), and instruments (98:5-6).

The Lord is never referred to with explicitly royal language in the psalm we are studying. Even so, the call matches the worshipful equivalent of making fanfare for a king (compare Psalm 98:6; see 100:2, below). This is the first of four appearances (in a psalm of only five verses!) of the divine name Yahweh, identified in English translations as "LORD" in small caps (see 100:2-3, 5, below). This could just be the writer's preferred method of referring to God. Or it could be that the psalmist uses this designation specifically to show that all people will know God by name and have greater knowledge of him because of it.

1b. all the earth.

The word *earth* in this context refers to the world in its entirety (compare Psalms 8:1; 24:1; etc.). This word can also refer to specific nations or territories when used with parallel terms that speak of such groups (example: 74:8). Sometimes a doubled usage will refer to both in poetic

HOW TO SAY IT

Davidic	Duh-*vid*-ick.
Mosaic	Mo-*zay*-ik.
Yahweh *(Hebrew)*	*Yah*-weh.

parallelism (example: 67:6-7). This flexibility results at times in ambiguity as to whether the narrower or the wider sense is intended.

Assuming that this address is for people everywhere, we see God's concern for all humanity. The psalmist anticipated the day when all nations would come to know the Lord and would offer their praise to him—a theme that appears frequently in the psalms (examples: Psalms 22:27; 117:1). This theme complements the motifs of Israel proclaiming the Lord's name among the nations (examples: 96:3; 108:3) and of his reign over the nations (example: 47:7-9).

> **What Do You Think?**
> What are some ways you can manifest more joy on a daily basis?
> *Digging Deeper*
> What passages of Scripture offer examples of the kind of joy envisioned by the psalmist?

B. Come with Gladness (v. 2)

2a. Worship the LORD with gladness;

Given that this psalm is associated with Psalm 90 (see Lesson Context), we can surmise that the writer alludes to the exodus here. Serving *the Lord* therefore suggests a contrast between Israel's service to God and the nation's service to Pharaoh (Exodus 1:11-14; 5:17-18). Whereas their labors for Pharaoh caused the people to cry out to God in distress (2:23-24), service to God is accompanied by *gladness* (Numbers 10:10; 2 Chronicles 30:21; etc.). David expressed a similar thought in Psalm 68:3.

2b. come before him with joyful songs.

If this verse alludes to the exodus, then coming *before him* can very easily be an allusion to the ark of the covenant (Exodus 25:22). This brings to mind the ark's location in the tabernacle and later in the temple (Exodus 25:8-9; 2 Chronicles 6:1-2, 11).

Throughout the centuries, the people of God had experiences worthy of song. Israel sang in celebration of their rescue at the Red Sea (Exodus 15; see lesson 1). David had issued instructions for leading Israel in praising God for "all his wonderful acts" (1 Chronicles 16:7-9). Paul directed

Christians to sing to one another (Ephesians 5:19; Colossians 3:16). In all these instances, the people of God could declare with David, "[God] put a new song in my mouth" (Psalm 40:3).

> **What Do You Think?**
> As we see "gladness" connected with singing, what place should you allow for mournful songs in worship, if any? Why?
> *Digging Deeper*
> Thinking of mournful hymns such as "Abide with Me" and "Almost Persuaded," what additional examples can you offer?

❧ GET TO ❧

A friend of mine grew up in a communist country. Life changed dramatically when she attended a Christian college in the United States. When other students complained, "Do I *have* to go to chapel?" my friend would exclaim, "I'm so glad I *get* to go to chapel!"

"Get to" is better than "have to." The former nurtures gratitude; the latter generates grumpiness. Crawling out of bed on Monday morning, it's tempting to mutter, "I wish I didn't have to go to work." But considering the alternatives of being sick, injured, unemployed, or forbidden to go, isn't it better to say, "Thank you, Lord, that I get to go to work today"?

The same principle applies when one has a relationship with God. Do we have to pray? Yes, but even better, we get to. Do we have to sing? Yes, but we get to, and God gives us joyful reason to do so! It helps us serve the Lord with gladness when we remember that we don't just have to worship God. We get to!

—D. F.

II. A Call to Know

(PSALM 100:3)

A. Who God Is (vv. 3a)

3a. Know that the LORD is God.

This, the fourth command of this psalm, occupies the central position. It provides a rationale for all the other commands. The word *know* in this context suggests a profound awareness beyond mere intellectual perception (Deuteronomy 34:10; 1 Samuel 3:7; Psalm 139:2).

The Lord is God is a central affirmation of Old Testament faith (examples: Deuteronomy 4:35, 39; 1 Kings 8:60; Psalm 118:27). Its parallel of Jesus as Lord is a central affirmation of the New Testament (Romans 10:9; 1 Corinthians 12:3). In both instances, the proclamation sets apart the one who is confessing from those who will not confess the same. In the first-century church and throughout its early history in Rome, declaring Jesus to be Lord—the only Lord—was tantamount to denying the deity of a caesar or any other so-called god. It was a scandal. Yet any saving faith in the Lord must begin by confessing that he alone is God.

B. Who We Are (v. 3b)

3b. It is he who made us, and we are his; we are his people, the sheep of his pasture.

It would be easy to think of the first part of this half-verse's declarations in terms of the creation of humanity in Genesis 1:26-27. But pausing to look at the second part may lead us to a different conclusion: *his people* and *the sheep of his pasture* may be intended to refer primarily to God's creation of the nation of Israel. Psalm 95:6-7 is quite similar in this regard: "Let us kneel before the Lord our Maker; for he is our God and we are the people of his pasture, the flock under his care." Another close parallel is Psalm 79:13.

The metaphor of the nation of Israel as the Lord's sheep draws on ancient imagery. Kings were depicted as shepherds and their subjects as the monarch's sheep (example: 1 Kings 22:17). God is often referred or alluded to as shepherd as well (see Genesis 49:24; Psalm 23:1-3; Jeremiah 31:10; Ezekiel 34:11-12).

Being God's sheep suggested that the people of Israel could feel confident in their relationship to God but should be humble concerning their own abilities. Like sheep, Israel was weak, vulnerable, and needing care. However, they belonged to and were valued by the Lord God, the true and ultimate shepherd-king (Genesis 49:24; Psalm 80:1; Ezekiel 34:31). It was he who would guide, protect, and provide for them.

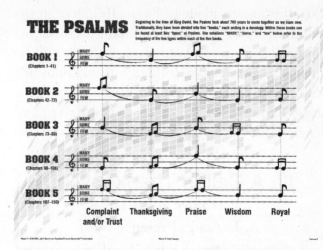

Visual for Lesson 5. *With this chart on display, note how the quantitative elements* many/some/few *serve to define the five types along the bottom.*

Whether referring to humanity in general or Old Testament Israel in particular, the text before us highlights both God's identity as Creator and the worshipper's identity as created being. The implications are profound: it effectively negates any notions of human self-sufficiency. Neither humanity in general nor Old Testament Israel in particular came into being by self-sufficient effort (see Acts 17:28). We do well to remember that it is Christ who has created the church (Matthew 16:18; Acts 2:47; 20:28). And the one who created the church is also the Creator of everything (John 1:1-3; Colossians 1:16).

> *What Do You Think?*
> How can you help your church balance its praise to God with regard to his three roles as Creator, Ruler, and Redeemer?
> *Digging Deeper*
> What examples from Scripture can you think of regarding praise for his three roles?

The shepherd-sheep imagery carries over into the New Testament. We recall that Jesus referred to himself as the shepherd who cares for his sheep to the point of giving his life for them (John 10:11, 15). The church is God's flock, and its elders are called to care for and to protect it as does Christ (Acts 20:28; 1 Peter 5:1-4; compare John 21:15-17).

Before moving on, we should pause to note that

the affirmations made in Psalm 100:3b echo the two halves of a standard covenant-promise formula: "I will . . . be your God, and you will be my people" (Leviticus 26:12; see also Exodus 6:7; Psalm 95:6-7). This formula's final appearance is associated with the promise of "a new heaven and a new earth" (Revelation 21:1-3).

III. A Call to Thanksgiving
(Psalm 100:4-5)
A. In God's Presence (v. 4)

4. Enter his gates with thanksgiving and his courts with praise; give thanks to him and praise his name.

The dedication of Solomon's temple took place during the Festival of Tabernacles (1 Kings 8:2, 65; see Lesson Context). The association of the dedication with that feast may provide context for allusions to the temple grounds here. Furthermore, *gates*, *courts*, and courtyards are mentioned together dozens of times in the Old Testament in that regard (examples: Jeremiah 36:10; 2 Chronicles 23:5; Nehemiah 8:16).

The gates refer to the entrances to the temple grounds, and courts are the areas in proximity. The complex included two temple courts: an "inner courtyard" (1 Kings 6:36) and a "great courtyard" (7:12). The chronicler designated the inner court as "the courtyard of the priests" (2 Chronicles 4:9). The "great courtyard" was evidently an outer court surrounding the entire temple complex. It is into this larger, outer court the psalmist envisioned the congregation entering (contrast Hebrews 10:19-22).

Those approaching God in the temple courts needed to bring appropriate offerings (examples: Deuteronomy 16:16-17; Psalm 96:8). What better than *thanksgiving* and *praise* (compare Micah 6:6-8; Hebrews 13:15)? The terms *thanksgiving* and *give thanks* refer to a proclamation or confession of what God had done (compare Leviticus 7:12-15). Joyful noise and psalms would accompany this thanksgiving (Psalm 95:2). Praise consisted of boasting about and exalting the Lord—to recognize the great things he had done and to admire his characteristics (examples: Psalms 18:1-3; 96:2-

3; 1 Chronicles 16:23-29). To *praise* the Lord's *name* is to acclaim his power and reputation with all due respect.

The Hebrew term translated *praise* is used in a variety of ways by Old Testament writers. These included proclamation or confession of what God had done (example: Psalm 26:7).

What Do You Think?
With Thanksgiving rapidly approaching (dates of October 11 in Canada and November 25 in the US), what are some creative ways you can use Psalm 100:4 in your observance?
Digging Deeper
What about Psalms 69:30 and 95:2 as well?

❧ CHECK THE GATE ❧

"Check the gate, son." After all these years, I can still hear Dad's voice.

Opening and closing gates was one of the first jobs I learned on the farm in southern Ohio where I grew up. Swinging on rusty hinges, our gates were made of wood that was weathered by years of exposure to the elements. Twisted pieces of baling wire fastened the gates shut, allowing us access to the field while keeping our Holstein cattle corralled inside. I would untwist the wire and push the gate open so Dad could drive his tractor into the field.

Later I learned about a different gate. In non-digital filmmaking, it referred to the window on the camera where light from the lens passed through to expose the film. It was important to "check the gate" or else a speck of dust could ruin the shot.

When you join other believers for prayer and worship, do you first "check the gate" of your heart? When it comes to such times with the Lord, this gate should always be open.　　　—D. F.

B. For God's Greatness (v. 5)

5a. For the Lord is good and his love endures forever;

This verse offers motivations for praising God. The simple affirmation that *the Lord is good* is used four times in the book of Psalms (here, and in Psalms 34:8; 135:3; and 145:9). To these can be added Psalms 106:1; 107:1; 118:1, 29; and 136:1, which all feature the sentence "Give thanks to the Lord, for he is good; his love endures forever" or a slight variation of it. The word translated *love* is elsewhere translated "kindness" (1 Samuel 15:6) and "approval" (Esther 2:17). God's mercy endures through the failures and sins of his people (Psalms 86:5; 89:33; 103:8). It is everlasting (103:17), and the Lord delights to show it (Micah 7:18). It is rooted and expressed primarily in covenant relationships (Deuteronomy 7:9, 12).

5b. his faithfulness continues through all generations.

The Hebrew word translated *faithfulness* here derives from the verbal root from which we get the word *amen,* an affirmative response to what has just been said. It refers to firmness, steadfastness, reliability, and consistency (Psalms 96:13; 98:3; 143:1). The congregation of Israel could expect their children, grandchildren, and succeeding *generations* to experience the same goodness from the Lord's hand that they had received.

God's long-standing relationship with his people demonstrates his reliable goodness, mercifulness, and truthfulness. Pairings of the words translated "love" and "faithfulness" occur frequently in the psalms (example: Psalm 57:3). These echo one of the Old Testament's foundational descriptions of the Lord God of Israel, as seen in Exodus 34:6-7.

The Lord's dealings with Israel proved to be more than sentimental impulses that could easily dissipate. The people could rely on God because he had been faithful to the covenants he made with their ancestors (examples: Exodus 2:24-25; 6:8; Joshua 23:14-15; 1 Kings 8:23-24). Israel had experienced the Lord's reliability and faithfulness for a long time, and the people could move into their future assured of his continued presence. They could know that God's acts of grace were not the product of a divine whim. We can trust in the Lord because he is constant, and his gracious purposes for us are reliable (1 Thessalonians 5:23-24; 2 Thessalonians 3:3; Hebrews 10:23; 1 John 1:9). Indeed, Jesus is called "Faithful and True" (Revelation 19:11).

Conclusion
A. Because the Lord Is Good

Enthusiastic joy is fitting for those who have come to experience God as described in Psalm 100. Here the psalmist calls the reader to a life of joyous thanksgiving and praise in the presence of our Lord. When we ponder who God is and who we are, then praise and thanksgiving are called for. The call to worship in this regard is a call away from the mundane distractions of life and toward the holy and loving God. The concerns of the preceding week should fade as the congregation at worship focuses minds and affections on the ever-present Lord.

The Lord is God, he is the Creator, he is our shepherd. He is good and faithful. We are his people, the sheep for whom he cares. Generations before us have experienced his goodness. And until our Lord Jesus returns, all generations who follow us are invited to experience his steadfast mercy and kindness as well.

How can we not join the psalmist in singing, rendering thanks and praise to the good and faithful God who calls us his own?

What Do You Think?
Which imperative in today's lesson will you have the most trouble implementing? Why?
Digging Deeper
Should you wait until your next blessing before making Psalm 100 your own expression, or should you first make the psalm your own in anticipation of blessings to come? Why?

B. Prayer

Our Father, we rejoice knowing that we belong to you! We praise you for your constant faithfulness. When we are tempted to drop our gaze to the troubles of this life, remind us again to lift our focus and our praise back to you. In Jesus' name we pray. Amen.

C. Thought to Remember
Be joyful! The Lord is good, and we belong to him.

INVOLVEMENT LEARNING

Enhance your lesson with NIV® Bible Student *(from your curriculum supplier) and the reproducible activity page (at www.standardlesson.com or in the back of the* NIV® *Standard Lesson Commentary Deluxe Edition).*

Into the Lesson

Play a segment of a song about being devoted to another person. (*Possibilities:* "Only You," "Hopelessly Devoted," and "Dedicated to the One I Love.") Follow with discussion about what might be problematic about the kinds of devotion such songs proclaim.

Alternative. Ask class members, formed in pairs or triads, to think of an example of one of the following two prompts (half the class discusses each), which you write on the board:

1–Parents' devotion to their children
2–Children's devotion to their parents

After a few minutes, allow volunteers to share. Discuss what is good about these devotions and what is dangerous. (Be prepared to discuss Matthew 10:37 and/or Luke 14:26 if mentioned.)

After either activity, lead into Bible study by saying, "Today we're beginning a five-week study from the psalms, some of which can surprise us regarding what they imply on this topic."

Into the Word

After reading today's lesson text aloud, distribute handouts (you create) of the following rendition of Psalm 100, which comes from the 1650 Scottish Metrical Psalter.

All people that on earth do dwell
Sing to the Lord with cheerful voice.
Him serve with mirth; His praise forth tell;
Come ye before Him and rejoice.

Know that the Lord is God indeed;
Without our aid, He did us make.
We are His flock; He doth us feed,
And for His sheep He doth us take.

O enter then His gates with praise;
Approach with joy His courts unto.
Praise, laud, and bless His name always,
For it is seemly so to do.

For why? The Lord our God is good;
His mercy is forever sure.
His truth at all times firmly stood,
And shall from age to age endure.

Ask class members, again working in their pairs or triads, to put verse numbers from Psalm 100 beside the phrases to which they refer. Another option would be for them to write in the margins the words from Scripture that match the words in this poem. Correct matches should be obvious either way.

Write the words *What* and *Why* across the top of the board. As you do, pose this question: "Which verses in Psalm 100 tell us *what* we are to do in our relationship with God, and which verses tell us *why* to do it?" After three or four minutes, make a composite list under each heading on the board during whole-class discussion.

Option. To add breadth this study, distribute copies of the "God Is King" exercise from the activity page, which you can download. Have learners work in pairs or triads to complete as indicated. Reconvene for whole-class discussion of findings.

Into Life

Write the word *KING* in a vertical line on your board or on poster paper. Brainstorm with the class to create an acrostic: for each letter, they should suggest a phrase or word to indicatze how to conduct life with awareness that God is king. Dig deeper by asking the class which idea is the most challenging to actually act on and why.

Close the class session by having the class sing a hymn or praise chorus that is based on Psalm 100, easily discovered with an internet search in advance.

Option. Distribute copies of the word-search puzzle "Important Ideas from Psalm 100" from the activity page as a take-home exercise as students depart.

Praise for God's Ultimate Justice

Devotional Reading: Psalm 9:1-12
Background Scripture: Psalm 9; Ecclesiastes 3:16-22

Psalm 9:1-12

For the director of music. To the tune of "The Death of the Son." A psalm of David.

1 I will give thanks to you, LORD, with all my heart;
I will tell of all your wonderful deeds.

2 I will be glad and rejoice in you;
I will sing the praises of your name,
O Most High.

3 My enemies turn back;
they stumble and perish before you.

4 For you have upheld my right and my cause,
sitting enthroned as the righteous judge.

5 You have rebuked the nations and destroyed the wicked;
you have blotted out their name for ever and ever.

6 Endless ruin has overtaken my enemies,
you have uprooted their cities;
even the memory of them has perished.

7 The LORD reigns forever;
he has established his throne for judgment.

8 He rules the world in righteousness
and judges the peoples with equity.

9 The LORD is a refuge for the oppressed,
a stronghold in times of trouble.

10 Those who know your name trust in you,
for you, LORD, have never forsaken those who seek you.

11 Sing the praises of the LORD, enthroned in Zion;
proclaim among the nations what he has done.

12 For he who avenges blood remembers;
he does not ignore the cries of the afflicted.

KEY TEXT

He rules the world in righteousness and judges the peoples with equity. —**Psalm 9:8**

Photo © Getty Images

49

CELEBRATING GOD

Unit 2: Called to Praise God

LESSONS 5–9

LESSON AIMS

After participating in this lesson, each learner will be able to:

1. Identify different types or aspects of justice in Psalm 9.

2. Compare and contrast those differences.

3. State a conviction to better demonstrate God's concern for justice.

LESSON OUTLINE

Introduction

A. Thanks to God

Do you like to read? An affirmative answer to this question often leads directly to a second: What do you like to read? Biography, science fiction, travel journals, devotionals, scholarly journals . . . The types you enjoy are probably informed by where and how you grew up, what you enjoyed studying in school, family and friendships, etc.

One type of literature that is often overlooked, however, is poetry. Reading a poem is a daunting thing for some. Why is the grammar so strange? Why are words repeated? Why don't the lines rhyme? What does this figurative language point to? The fact is that poems can be difficult to interpret! But the Academy of American Poets has some tips that can help you delve into poetry with more confidence.

First, they say to read it out loud. This can slow you down so you can hear the inflections of your own voice. Second, pay attention to where the lines or phrases break. Third, be curious and ask questions of the poem: Who wrote it? When? Why? And finally, be OK with the fact that you won't always understand a particular poem. Sometimes it will dance outside of your grasp.

These tips can help us not only understand but also enjoy the psalms.

B. Lesson Context: Psalms 9–10

Found in Book I of the Psalter (see Lesson Context of lesson 5), Psalm 9 is one of several alphabetic acrostics scattered throughout the psalms (other examples: Psalms 119; 145). An alphabetic acrostic is one in which each verse, stanza, or other pattern of lines begins with a successive letter of the alphabet. In English, this would look like:

Line 1 begins with a word that starts with A,
Line 2 begins with a word that starts with B,
Line 3 begins with a word that starts with C, etc.

This technique helps with memorization. But sadly, that help is usually "lost in translation" as alphabets vary among languages.

The acrostic format that begins in Psalm 9:2, below, continues into Psalm 10. This suggests that these two poems were originally one. From the standpoint of content, this makes perfect sense: Psalm 9 focuses on God's deliverance of the righteous, whereas Psalm 10 dwells on God's judgment on the wicked. For the psalmist and throughout much of Scripture, these two concepts go hand in hand. God's justice entails both lifting the oppressed and lowering their oppressors (example: Proverbs 10:30).

Two other factors further suggest that these two psalms were originally one: (1) Psalm 9 has a beginning superscript that introduces the psalm, whereas Psalm 10 lacks such a feature, which all other psalms in Book I have except for Psalms 1 and 2; and (2) Psalm 9 ends with the term "Selah." That term does not appear in the text of the 2011 *NIV*, although its presence may be indicated by a footnote. The word is likely a musical notation that indicates a pause in the recitation of a song. As a result, the old Greek translation of the book of Psalms combines Psalms 9 and 10 into one psalm. (This further results in the numbering of subsequent psalms to differ from that of our English translations until Psalm 147.)

C. Lesson Context: Superscription

Dozens of psalms begin like this one in being addressed "For the director of music."

"A psalm of David" identifies the author. The Psalter attributes 73 of its 150 psalms to him, "the hero of Israel's songs" (2 Samuel 23:1). The New Testament increases this tally (see Acts 1:16-20; 2:25-28; 4:25-26; Romans 4:6-8; 11:9-10).

I. Against the Wicked
(Psalm 9:1-6)
A. Praise the Lord (vv. 1-2)

1a. I will give thanks to you, Lord, with all my heart;

The word translated *give thanks* is rendered in terms of praise elsewhere, and there is much overlap in their meanings (compare Psalm 100:4, lesson 5; also see 2 Samuel 22:50). Ancient Hebrews associated the *heart* with one's intellect—the center of moral decision-making. So this psalm is not so much stressing an emotional reaction (the way

we would if singing "from the heart") as much as emphasizing the deliberate choice to praise God with the totality of the psalmist's being (compare Deuteronomy 4:29).

> *What Do You Think?*
> What needs to happen for you to shift from distracted, half-hearted praise to focused, wholehearted praise?
> *Digging Deeper*
> Does your answer change depending on whether it's corporate rather than individual worship? If so, why?

1b. I will tell of all your wonderful deeds.

To the upreach action of "will give thanks" in the previous half-verse, the psalmist adds one of outreach: *will tell of* indicates his intention to bear public witness. The sweeping basis of *all your wonderful deeds* undoubtedly includes the facts of creation (Genesis 1) and providential favor on Israel (example: Deuteronomy 4:34).

Though we often use words such as *wonderful* and *awesome* in exaggerated or overstated ways, it's quite difficult to do so with regard to God's acts! Think of the scientific laws he created to keep our world functioning and habitable. We take these for granted in daily life. But if we stop to ponder them, we will be stunned to realize (again!) what God has done for us—both for humanity in general and us in particular.

2a. I will be glad and rejoice in you;

Be glad and *rejoice* are parallel terms; the underlying Hebrew words are also found together in 1 Samuel 2:1; Psalms 5:11; 68:3. Such repetition made it easier to remember songs. That was especially important in a culture where the average person may not have been able to read and write. Such repetition therefore was not mere redundancy.

2b. I will sing the praises of your name, O Most High.

Using the word *name* as the psalmist does here was often a respectful way of referring to God himself (examples: 2 Samuel 22:50; Psalm 92:1). The name that God revealed to Moses and to Israel was Yahweh (Exodus 3:14), which is behind the designation "Lord" in Psalm 9:1a, above. This name tells us something about God: he is unchanging. What he has revealed about himself is who he is (compare Mark 12:26-27; 1 John 4:8).

By calling God *Most High*, David acknowledged that this God is above all other so-called gods, earthly kings, and whatever threat may confront God's people. Melchizedek, king of Salem, was the first recorded to use this honorific for God (Genesis 14:18-20). This same Melchizedek was honored as a precursor to Christ (Hebrews 7:1, 11, 17; compare Psalm 110:4). Only this God could enact the plan of salvation that is the source of our greatest joy and hope.

B. Fall of Enemies (vv. 3-6)

3. My enemies turn back; they stumble and perish before you.

The psalmist now introduces battle imagery. Given the psalm's attribution to David (see Lesson Context: Superscription), the *enemies* we are meant to think of were likely David's own, of which there were plenty. The Amalekites (example: 1 Samuel 30), the Jebusites (2 Samuel 5:6-7), and the Philistines (example: 5:17-25) all suffered defeats because God was with David.

Those idolatrous nations perished on account of God's interceding on Israel's behalf. This more literal translation of *you* makes obvious the respectful way David referred to God himself (see Psalm 9:2b, above). God directed mighty waters (Exodus 15:10), toppled walls (Joshua 6:16, 20), hurled hailstones (10:11), and extended daylight (10:1-15).

> ### What Do You Think?
> Placing this text alongside Proverbs 24:17, under what circumstances will you rejoice at the defeat of an enemy and under what circumstances will you not?
>
> ### Digging Deeper
> How, if at all, do Job 31:29-30 and Obadiah 12-13 help you answer this question?

4. For you have upheld my right and my cause, sitting enthroned as the righteous judge.

Whichever battles David referred to weren't about expanding his own power or padding his coffers. These are causes that no king should assume to be pleasing to God. God champions only a *right* and a *cause* if these things are pursued from right motives and with just action.

Proper verdicts must be rendered because God himself is a just *judge*. Though God sometimes maintains a person because he or she is righteous, it is more precise to say that God has achieved the good that the righteous person represents. In other words, because the accused represents God's cause in God's way, God is certain to judge in favor of that person for being in the right.

5. You have rebuked the nations and destroyed the wicked; you have blotted out their name for ever and ever.

The nations and *the wicked* are used as parallel terms here. The Hebrew words being translated occur together again in Psalm 9:17 (see also Jeremiah 25:31). This indicates that David was not writing about the Israelites' own sins. While it is good to keep in mind that unholy people can lead God's people astray, this must be balanced by remembering his concern for all peoples. Far from being a purely New Testament concern (example: Matthew 5:45; John 3:16), God's intention to bless all nations is embedded in the covenant he made with Abraham (Genesis 12:1-3).

David does not name his enemies, nor need he do so. When a person is in God's protective presence, the size, nature, and names of enemies are irrelevant. This fact lends this psalm a universal appeal. Future generations can apply it to their own worship experiences. It also suggests that the *name* of the enemy has already been forgotten.

6a. Endless ruin has overtaken my enemies, you have uprooted their cities;

HOW TO SAY IT

Amalekites	*Am*-uh-leh-kites or Uh-*mal*-ih-kites.
Jebusites	*Jeb*-yuh-sites.
Melchizedek	Mel-*kiz*-eh-dek.
Philistines	Fuh-*liss*-teenz or *Fill*-us-teenz.
Selah *(Hebrew)*	*See*-luh.

52

Praise for God's Ultimate Justice

Although David does not specify the *enemies* that are to suffer *endless ruin*, other texts suggest this might be a reference to the Amalekites (see Exodus 17:14; Deuteronomy 25:19). This marks a significant contrast between how God treats his people and how he treats the unrepentant of any nation. He makes no promise to save a remnant from nations like the Amalekites. When their wickedness reached a boiling point, God acted in righteous judgment.

God's people experience judgment differently, however. We undergo it as temporary discipline, meant to form us into the image of Christ (Hebrews 12:5-7, 11, quoting Proverbs 3:11-12; compare Psalm 94:12; Romans 14:10; 2 Corinthians 5:10).

6b. even the memory of them has perished.

The idea here is that destruction of enemies will be so complete that no one will even remember *them* (compare Psalm 34:16). Graves are normally indicated with some kind of marker as a monument of remembrance, or memorial. The wicked won't have even that.

❧ *MONUMENTS OF FAITH* ❧

After more than 40 years, construction of the Cathedral of Christ the Saviour was finally completed in Moscow, Russia, in 1883. The church was a huge, beautiful structure. But when the communist government took over, it began eradicating Christianity systematically. Soviet leader Joseph Stalin (ruling 1922–1952) ordered that the church be demolished, a plan carried out in 1931.

The cathedral's destruction was a symbol of the persecution Christians faced in communist Russia. After the fall of the communist government in the 1990s, the people of Moscow donated money for another church to be built on the site of the original. The cathedral, completed in 2000, again stands as a monument testifying to the faith of the people, a sign that the communist government failed to stamp out Christianity.

God foils the plans of those who oppose him. He works to use our difficult things for his glory. What "ruins" are you hoping will be rebuilt into a monument of faith in your life?   —L. M. W.

Visual for Lesson 6. *While discussing Psalm 9:9, have this posted as you ask for examples of places we seek safety instead of trusting God.*

II. For the Oppressed
(PSALM 9:7-12)

A. Celebrating God's Judgment (vv. 7-8)

7. The LORD reigns forever; he has established his throne for judgment.

In contrast to the wicked nations that are to be forgotten, *the Lord reigns forever. His throne* is the place from which he both judges and rules over all creation. God's people must cling to him. They must not ally themselves with evil. Doing so puts them in danger of experiencing the *judgment* meant for the nations.

8. He rules the world in righteousness and judges the peoples with equity.

Judgment without *righteousness* yields injustice (Amos 5:12; etc.). Such a state of affairs is all too common. But God always *judges* with perfect *equity* (compare Acts 10:34; Romans 2:11; Galatians 2:6), which is a model for us (Leviticus 19:15; 1 Timothy 5:21; James 2:1).

B. Seeking God's Refuge (vv. 9-10)

9. The LORD is a refuge for the oppressed, a stronghold in times of trouble.

This verse offers some interesting similarities to and differences from Psalm 10:1: "Why, Lord, do you stand far off? Why do you hide yourself in times of trouble?"

In Psalm 9:3-8, David was concerned with the fall of the unrighteous. Now in 9:9 the focus changes to address the reversal of fortune *for the oppressed* (compare 1 Samuel 2:8; Luke 1:52-55). The Hebrew word translated "oppressed" occurs only four times in the Old Testament: here and Psalms 10:18; 74:21; and Proverbs 26:28. But what kind of oppression is in view—or does it matter?

One way of exploring this question is to examine what words are used to translate those four instances in the Greek version of the Old Testament, then see how the New Testament uses those words. When we do so, we conclude that the idea is usually along the lines of one's lower-class status in life (compare Matthew 11:29; Luke 1:52; Romans 12:16; 2 Corinthians 7:6; 9:9; 10:1; James 1:9; 4:6; and 1 Peter 5:5).

The rich and powerful want to keep it that way! This implies that powerful persons are oppressing the weak. The oppression they inflict or allow parallels the phrase *in times of trouble* (compare Psalms 10:1; 41:1; 59:16). But the *refuge* available in God carries the imagery of elevated terrain (compare 2 Samuel 22:3), the safest place to build a city. This psalm draws on "protection themes" seen prominently in the Law of Moses (example: Deuteronomy 24:14-22) and the books of prophecy (example: Hosea 6:6). Such themes carry over into the New Testament (Matthew 5:1-12; James 1:27; etc.).

With such unified testimony across Scripture, Christians must be united in concern for the poor and oppressed. The church must not let political partisanship dictate its agenda. Instead, we must heed Scripture's specific testimony regarding God's concern for the poor, regardless of which directions the political winds are blowing.

> *What Do You Think?*
> In what one specific way can you serve as the Lord's hands and feet in being a "refuge for the oppressed" this week?
> *Digging Deeper*
> How do you know who is "oppressed"?

10. Those who know your name trust in you, for you, Lord, have never forsaken those who seek you.

Those who *know* the Lord—really know his character and have experienced his goodness—will put their *trust in* him. They make choices that are in line with God's will, not their own. To know in this sense is not a matter of mere belief in God's existence (see James 2:19). Rather, it's about making godly choices—choices that may seem foolish to the world (1 Corinthians 1:18-31). We follow a God whose ways are not those of humans (Isaiah 55:8-9). Such people actively *seek* God (Deuteronomy 4:29).

Seeking God is not some sort of "I'll know it when I see it" search for life's meaning. Rather, it asks the question, "What does God want from me in this situation?" To answer such questions involves searching the Scriptures, where God has revealed his will for people. It's about trusting the Spirit to aid in understanding and discernment. Seeking God means giving him control over the direction of our lives.

> *What Do You Think?*
> Without giving directive advice or immediately quoting Scripture, how would you counsel someone who feels forsaken by God?
> *Digging Deeper*
> How should Mark 15:34 and Hebrews 13:5 serve as a backdrop to your conclusion?

❧ *Exhaustion* ❧

My friend's sobs were so heavy that I could barely understand her. Hurrying to her house, I met her husband at the door. I found her sitting in the dark basement, tears running down her face.

She began telling me all the hard things: none of her home repair projects were done, Thanksgiving plans had fallen through, her kids did not respect her, her parents would visit for Christmas and cause stress . . .

Burdened by a load of anxiety and pain, she felt she could not make it through the upcoming holidays. "I'm just so tired, and I can't seem to do anything right," she told me.

And I understood. As a wife and mom, I sometimes feel I make more mistakes than not. The weight of spiritual and emotional burdens seems too heavy. In times like those, Psalm 9:9-10 serves as a reminder: God is my refuge. When my strength is gone, he carries my burden. How do you show your trust that he will do the same for you?

—L. M. W.

C. Praise Again (vv. 11-12)

11. Sing the praises of the LORD, enthroned in Zion; proclaim among the nations what he has done.

In response to God's overthrowing the unrighteous and upholding those who trust him, David appropriately called the people once again to *sing . . . praises*. David had been addressing his own thanks to God (see Psalm 9:1-2, above). But here he explicitly invited the people to join in the praise of thanksgiving.

Although the two imperatives here may sound quite generic, their application must have been in reaction to something specific. It doesn't seem adequate to say that God does wonderful things and stop there. As with David, we should *proclaim . . . what he has done.* For the original audience, this could have included celebrating work that God had done in founding their nation, delivering them from their wilderness wandering, and granting the promised land.

In the audience's more recent memory, it probably included David's military conquests. *Zion*, a synonym for Jerusalem, had been part of Jebusite territory until David captured it (2 Samuel 5:6-7). The mountain became associated with David's palace and later with the temple (1 Kings 8:1; Psalm 2:6). The latter association links Zion closely to the Lord (see Psalms 20:2; 74:2).

12. For he who avenges blood remembers; he does not ignore the cries of the afflicted.

In celebrating his deliverance, David did not lose sight of who brought it about: God did. In avenging *blood*, God proved his concern for justice. He is a God who so values life that he both offers abundant life through Jesus (John 10:10) and requires a reckoning from those who destroy life (Genesis 4:10; 9:5-6). God never grows deaf to *the cries of the afflicted.* He will administer justice. Just as God heard when the Israelites cried to him from their slavery in Egypt (Exodus 2:23-

25), so he hears all today who are held captive by violence, by injustice, by sin. But we must call on him in faith, trust, and repentance.

Conclusion

A. The Answer to Oppression

Oppression comes in all shapes and sizes; it is a global epidemic. The God of Israel did not ignore oppression, and neither should his people of any era. But we must not be lured by the fear-mongering ways of this world. Careful attention to Scripture is the answer. Only such study will yield a biblical view of oppression. Psalm 9 offers one small window in that regard. It shows us that those who know, trust, and seek the one true God have a powerful ally who fights for them.

For Christians, this energizes us to spread the gospel; the accounts of the person and work of Jesus are ever new. But we need not stop with the events of Scripture. What wonders has God worked in our lives? Have we grown tired of telling those stories? Are we even experienced in telling those stories?

May we boldly proclaim the God we know and trust so that our hope may indeed become the hope of this world.

> *What Do You Think?*
> Which concept or imperative in today's lesson do you have the most trouble coming to grips with? Why?
> *Digging Deeper*
> How will you resolve this problem?

B. Prayer

Lord, thank you for all the reasons we have to praise you! We thank you for hearing the cries of your oppressed people; open our ears that we may hear them as well. Embolden us to proclaim the gospel to others so all the world may join us in praising you. In Jesus' name we pray. Amen.

C. Thought to Remember

Seek, trust, and know
the righteous God of justice.

INVOLVEMENT LEARNING

Enhance your lesson with NIV® Bible Student (from your curriculum supplier) and the reproducible activity page (at www.standardlesson.com or in the back of the NIV® Standard Lesson Commentary Deluxe Edition).

Into the Lesson

Write the sentence *That's not fair!* on the board as class members are arriving. Begin with brainstorming as you ask class members to name situations in which they've made or heard that statement. Give them one minute to call out answers while you write them on the board.

When the minute is up, ask learners to decide which of the situations are serious (world hunger, etc.) and which are trivial (someone parked in my space, etc.) Put a [+] sign beside those deemed serious and a [−] sign beside the trivial choices. If the group has not named many serious injustices, prod them to think further and come up with a few to add to your list.

Say, "You may not have thought much about how God feels about those who take advantage of others. Today we'll see things from his point of view."

Into the Word

Explain how ancient Hebrew poetry uses parallelism to express and expand on the ideas it is presenting. Then demonstrate how this works by distributing handouts (you create) titled "Key Concepts" that have these instructions:

Write just one sentence to summarize the main thought in one (only) of these pairs of verses—your choice: Psalm 9:1-2, 3-4, 5-6, 7-8, 9-10, 11-12.

Allow exactly one minute to complete this activity; then ask learners to share their summaries.

Option 1. To ensure complete coverage of the six pairs of verses, assign each pair to a specific learner rather than allowing them to pick freely.

Option 2. Form groups of three or four to work on all six pairs, allowing 10 minutes.

Option 3. For deeper study, divide the class into smaller groups with at least two people in each group having smartphones. Have the groups use a Bible app or program to search on the words *oppressed* (Psalm 9:9) and *afflicted* (9:12) and make

notes about features of those passages. (*Option.* Since there will be at least 90 references total, you may wish to assign only one of the two words per group.) After groups finish, ask them to report their conclusions regarding God's outlook toward the oppressed and their oppressors.

Into Life

Lead class members to consider implications of today's text as you distribute a handout (you prepare) titled "Practical Examples." Have the following printed on each handout:

For each pair of verses in today's study, think of examples of the truth expressed in the statements below.

Verses 1-2: God does marvelous works throughout the ages and in my life.

Verses 3-4: The gospel prevails over attempts to squelch it.

Verses 5-6: God rebukes the nations.

Verses 7-8: God is righteous and his judgments will ultimately prevail.

Verses 9-10: God has been a refuge for the oppressed.

Verses 11-12: God's good news requires that I share the gospel.

This activity will go faster if only one or two verse-pairs are assigned per group of three or four participants. Reconvene for whole-class discussion.

Option. Use one or both of the exercises on the activity page, which you can download, to explore the subject of oppression as it may relate to poverty—the two topics often being associated in faith-based and secular discussion. There are many ways to use these exercises in that regard. You could have half the class divide into smaller groups for one exercise while the other half considers the other exercise.

Close by allowing volunteers to finish this sentence: "Based on today's study, here's how I could better demonstrate God's concern for justice."

PRAISE GOD FOR PAST DELIVERANCE

DEVOTIONAL READING: Psalm 107:33-43
BACKGROUND SCRIPTURE: Psalm 107

PSALM 107:1-9, 39-43

1 Give thanks to the LORD, for he is good;
    his love endures forever.
2 Let the redeemed of the LORD tell their
    story—
    those he redeemed from the hand of the
    foe,
3 those he gathered from the lands,
    from east and west, from north and
    south.
4 Some wandered in desert wastelands,
    finding no way to a city where they
    could settle.
5 They were hungry and thirsty,
    and their lives ebbed away.
6 Then they cried out to the LORD in their
    trouble,
    and he delivered them from their
    distress.
7 He led them by a straight way
    to a city where they could settle.
8 Let them give thanks to the LORD for his
    unfailing love
    and his wonderful deeds for mankind,
9 for he satisfies the thirsty
    and fills the hungry with good things.

39 Then their numbers decreased, and they
    were humbled
    by oppression, calamity and sorrow;
40 he who pours contempt on nobles
    made them wander in a trackless waste.
41 But he lifted the needy out of their
    affliction
    and increased their families like flocks.
42 The upright see and rejoice,
    but all the wicked shut their mouths.
43 Let the one who is wise heed these things
    and ponder the loving deeds of the LORD.

KEY TEXT

They cried out to the LORD in their trouble, and he delivered them from their distress.   —Psalm 107:6

Photo © Getty Images

CELEBRATING GOD

Unit 2: Called to Praise God

LESSONS 5–9

LESSON AIMS

After participating in this lesson, each learner will be able to:

1. State reasons for praising God.

2. Identify influences that hinder people's recall of God's faithfulness.

3. Prepare a journal that recounts personal experiences of the Lord's loving deeds.

LESSON OUTLINE

Introduction

A. Thinking and Thanking

A hymn for congregational singing was supposed to be listed in the church bulletin as "Come, Ye Thankful People, Come." But the word *Thankful* was misspelled and printed as *Thinkful*. Most of us are quite familiar with the bulletins we are handed as we enter a Sunday morning service. Typos may seem fewer these days because of computer spell-check features used to prepare bulletins. In the previous era, however, uncorrected typos could make for "interesting" reading!

When the minister noticed the error, he was not at all bothered or upset. Instead, he used the mistake to point out that thinking and thanking go hand in hand. A thankful person is "think-full"; such an individual is always mindful of the good things God provides daily. Ungrateful people, by contrast, tend to be those who are so caught up in the busyness of life that they do not stop to consider the role that gratitude should play in their lives. The thinking person will follow the admonition of Scripture to "remember the Lord" (Deuteronomy 8:18) and to "forget not all his benefits" (Psalm 103:2). Thinking will be followed by thanking.

The ancient book of Psalms has much to teach us yet in this regard.

B. Lesson Context

Psalm 107 opens Book V, which consists of chapters 107–150 (see Lesson Contexts of lessons 5 and 9). In its transitional role, Psalm 107 also wraps up a series of longer psalms, namely Psalms 104–106. These highlight the mighty works of God in the world he created (Psalm 104) and on behalf of his people through the centuries (105; 106). The latter includes various circumstances of great need through which the Lord had shown himself able to come to the rescue of those in distress (also 107). Psalms in this group are specific in affirming the greatness of the Lord and the wonders that demonstrate that greatness (examples: 104:1, 24; 105:2, 5; 106:2). A repeated refrain in Psalm 107 serves the same purpose (107:8, 15, 21, 31; see commentary on verse 8 below).

None of the psalms in this subgroup are attributed to a specific author. However, evidence within the psalms themselves suggests that they were written following the exiles' return from Babylon. The earliest possible writing then would be about 538 BC.

Lesson 5 spoke briefly of poetic parallelism, and some students see a certain parallelism in Psalm 107 in this manner (numerals are verse numbers):

Introduction: Call to Praise (1-3)

	Stanza One	Stanza Two	Stanza Three	Stanza Four
Situation (A¹):	4-5	10-12	17-18	23-27
Despair (B¹):	6a	13a	19a	28a
Rescue (C):	6b-7	13b-14	19b-20	28b-30
Thanks (B²):	8	15	21	31
Situation (A²):	9	16	22	32

Recap (33-42)

Conclusion: Call to Praise (43)

The saving actions attributed to God in Psalm 107 should be considered in light of the covenant God established with the nation of Israel. That covenant promised what he would do in response both to the people's obedience and disobedience. Blessings such as agricultural abundance and respect from surrounding nations would follow obedience (Deuteronomy 28:1-14). But curses such as disease, famine, and subjugation by enemies would come if the people abandoned the Lord for other gods (28:15-68).

I. God of the Redeemed
(PSALM 107:1-9)
A. Summons to Praise (v. 1)

1. Give thanks to the LORD, for he is good; his love endures forever.

This call to worship is found several places in the Old Testament (see 1 Chronicles 16:34; Psalms 106:1; 118:1, 29; 136:1). Variations of it are also noteworthy (see 1 Chronicles 16:41; Ezra 3:11; Psalms 30:4; 92:1; etc.). The text before us is in the imperative—the people must *give thanks to the Lord*! At other times, the idea summarizes the tasks of those who carried out the various daily duties associated with the people's worship (example: 1 Chronicles 16:37-42).

The theme of this verse was expressed earlier in Israel's history when the ark of the covenant was brought into the temple at Jerusalem following its completion (2 Chronicles 5:13) and again when the temple was dedicated (7:3).

This may imply that a psalm David had given to Asaph previously is a background to Psalm 107 (1 Chronicles 16:7-8). The same may be true of the song in Ezra 3:10-11, when the foundation of the second temple was dedicated by those who had traveled to Jerusalem from captivity in Babylon.

Within the Old Testament, the phrase *his love endures forever*—the reason for giving thanks—is found numerous times. Psalm 136 is especially notable in this regard.

> **What Do You Think?**
> What is a new way you could give thanks to God by your actions, not just in your words or thoughts?
> *Digging Deeper*
> When will you start?

B. Reasons for Praise (vv. 2-3)

2. Let the redeemed of the LORD tell their story—those he redeemed from the hand of the foe,

Christians often think of being *redeemed* as primarily spiritual in nature, something especially accomplished by Jesus (Ephesians 1:7). But redemption in earthly terms has a long history in Israel. The formative story of the exodus from Egypt is the account of God's redeeming the Hebrew slaves from their bondage (Exodus 6:6; 15:13; Psalm 106:9-10). The book of Ruth shows redemption in action on a smaller scale (Ruth 2:1; 4:1-6).

The redeemed come out of their dire situations because of God's intercession. This is obvious in the exodus example; in Ruth's case, God's work came long before, in the form of laws that gave her the opportunity to be redeemed by a relative of her dead husband. The exiles who returned from Babylon experienced God's restoration on a grand scale.

In these and all other situations, those who have been redeemed by *the Lord* must *tell their story—*

God Still Rescues!

Visual for Lesson 7. *While discussing verse 6, point to this visual as you ask learners for examples of situations from which the Lord rescued them.*

that is, they must bear witness to that fact. How could the nation be a light to all peoples (Isaiah 42:6) if they never told about the wonderful things God had done for them? Those who have been redeemed *from the hand of the foe—* any enemy—by God's intercession must give him the credit.

❧ REDEEMED ❧

When Aditi's husband became ill, she sought work from a brickmaker in their Indian hometown. He gave Aditi money for her husband's doctor bills in exchange for the woman's labor. However, he charged her such high interest rates that the longer she worked, the more she owed.

Eventually, her husband joined her in her work. But before they knew it, the entire family was enslaved to the brickmaker. This situation is known as peonage.

A woman approached Aditi and offered to pay off the loan and help her and her family escape the grip of the brickmaker. The woman was part of a ministry that worked to free enslaved people. Now Aditi and her family support themselves, free from the reach of their former boss, who used his power to control them.

God is ready to free us from the slavery of sin. He sent his Son to redeem us. Just as Psalm 107:2 says, he redeems us from our enemy. How often do you respond to that fact with rejoicing and thanks?
—L. M. W.

3. those he gathered from the lands, from east and west, from north and south.

Reading the curses in Deuteronomy 28:15-68, we notice that some of the same language is in our passage. These include being *gathered* from captivity in Psalm 107:2-3; and words such as "oppression," "calamity," and "sorrow" in 107:39 fit the circumstances described in the curses. The Lord had promised that his people would go into exile if they refused to obey him (example: Deuteronomy 28:64). But he also promised that if the people would return to him in their captivity, he would "gather [them] again from all the nations where he scattered [them]" (30:3).

Here the promised deliverance is celebrated; the Lord has indeed gathered his people from the four cardinal directions, bringing them home from exile (compare Isaiah 49:12). This reversal accomplishes what a previous psalm had hoped for (see Psalm 105:44). To this we can compare the future gathering of all God's redeemed (Luke 13:29-30).

C. Time of Despair (vv. 4-5)

4a. Some wandered in desert wastelands,

The reference to wandering *in desert wastelands* brings to mind the Israelites' 40-year punishment for failing to trust the Lord following the exodus of 1447 BC (Numbers 14:30-35). The immediate context in Psalm 107 should also remind the reader of the plight and peril of the journey into Babylonian exile of 586 BC. The words *desert* and *wastelands* are also translated "wilderness" in the Old Testament (see Psalms 78:40; 106:14). These synonyms serve to strengthen the image of desolation and hopelessness.

4b. finding no way to a city where they could settle.

No matter where they wandered, the people had found *no way to a city where they could settle* for refuge and permanency in terms of the 40-year punishment. During the later exile to Babylon, they traveled until their captors told them they had reached their destination (compare Psalm 137:1).

5. They were hungry and thirsty, and their lives ebbed away.

When one has insufficient food and water, the

impact is more than just physical. The results are felt deep within; despondency and hopelessness soon characterize one's very life.

D. Time of Deliverance (vv. 6-9)

6. Then they cried out to the LORD in their trouble, and he delivered them from their distress.

The turning point for those in *trouble* and *distress* wasn't the Lord's deliverance—the turning point was repentance. The people's cry *to the Lord* was one of faith that accompanied such change of heart (compare Ezekiel 14:6). The word *delivered* echoes the concept of redemption found in Psalm 107:2.

> **What Do You Think?**
> In what ways do you need to change your prayer life so that you don't call on the Lord only in times of distress?
> **Digging Deeper**
> What would be the likely result of not making such a change?

7. He led them by a straight way to a city where they could settle.

The people's wandering (Psalm 107:4, above) was replaced by a clear direction from the Lord. Whereas before they had nowhere to put down roots, they found *a city where they could settle,* perhaps a reference to returning to Jerusalem (compare and contrast Hebrews 11).

Of course, Jerusalem needed a lot of work before it was safe again, let alone functional (see Ezra 1:2-4; Nehemiah 2:5, 17). But if the Lord could bring them back to the city, he could certainly ensure that it was rebuilt and habitable (Ezra 6:13-18; Nehemiah 6:15).

❧ WHOSE CREDIT? ❧

Family members packed their things, gathered the children, and fled. They made their way across a national border, eventually settling on the other, "safe" side. There Ella was born. She was a toddler when violence again threatened her family.

The family moved to a refugee camp. Life there was safer. However, food and clothing were scarce.

And as a refugee, Ella had no citizenship. So when Ella got the chance to emigrate, she took it.

Ella met and married another refugee. They joined a church full of people who also had fled unrest and danger. Ella used her gifts to help start a children's program. And in addition to her citizenship in God's kingdom, Ella was granted citizenship in her new home country.

God led Ella throughout her life. You may never have been a person without a country, but there are times when you have felt alone and afraid. Do you take credit yourself for your rescue, or do you give credit to God?   —L. M. W.

8. Let them give thanks to the LORD for his unfailing love and his wonderful deeds for mankind,

The experiences recorded in the previous two verses are just a sample of countless examples of the Lord's *unfailing love.* The Lord's *wonderful deeds* are not and never have been limited to one generation or period of history.

9. for he satisfies the thirsty and fills the hungry with good things.

Older translations of the Bible have "longing" in place of *thirsty,* evoking a dire need for water. The verse before us recalls the lack of food and water described in Psalm 107:5, above. Lack was replaced with adequate means of sustaining life.

The message of the verse is clear: the Lord is willing and able to reverse peoples' circumstances (compare Nehemiah 1:9). Jesus' ministry was full of examples of his acting on behalf of suffering people (Matthew 4:23-25; etc). And in the first-century church, we see quite a surprising reversal: the acceptance of Gentiles into the kingdom of God (Acts 10:44-48; etc).

> **What Do You Think?**
> When the voiced prayers of gathered Christians are almost exclusively concerned with physical rather than spiritual needs, what should you do?
> **Digging Deeper**
> How do Colossians 1:9; 2 Thessalonians 3:1-2; and James 5:16 inform your response?

II. God of Reversals
(Psalm 107:39-43)

A. Humbling the Mighty (vv. 39-40)

39. Then their numbers decreased, and they were humbled by oppression, calamity and sorrow;

Psalm 107:33-38 (not in today's lesson text) further recounts the Lord's reversals of distress to blessing; see also the stanza layout in the Lesson Context. It is he who can bring about or allow a fruitful land to become barren as punishment for wickedness, which might manifest as spiritual apathy or outright idolatry (compare Psalm 107:33-34; Haggai 1:1-11).

Those who had once flourished under God's blessing didn't seem to learn the lessons of previous generations. So a cycle of *oppression, calamity, and sorrow* would begin anew; this is a major theme of the book of Judges. Though Israelite numbers had increased (see Psalm 107:38, not in our lesson text), disobedience resulted in their population being *decreased*.

It's tempting to do an in-depth study of the three words *oppression, calamity,* and *sorrow* individually to try to get at what specifically was involved with each one. But such an approach runs the danger of missing the bigger picture of the cumulative effect of those three (compare the same cumulative effect of "sword," "famine," and "plague" in Jeremiah 14:12 and numerous other passages).

HOW TO SAY IT

Asaph	*Ay*-saff.
Assyrian	Uh-*sear*-e-un.
Babylonian	Bab-ih-*low*-nee-un.
Deuteronomy	Due-ter-*ahn*-uh-me.
Ezra	*Ez*-ruh.
Herod Agrippa	Hair-ud Uh-grip-puh.
Isaiah	Eye-*zay*-uh.
Jeremiah	Jair-uh-*my*-uh.
Nebuchadnezzar	*Neb*-yuh-kud-*nez*-er.
peonage	*pea*-uh-nij.
Pharaoh	*Fair*-o or *Fay*-roe.
Sennacherib	Sen-*nack*-er-ib.

Reversals of life situations as seen throughout Psalm 107 served God's disciplinary purposes. But they were not his desire. What he desired all along was obedience. The sharpest examples of this discipline are the Assyrian and Babylonian exiles (2 Kings 17:6-23 and 2 Chronicles 36:15-21, respectively).

40. he who pours contempt on nobles made them wander in a trackless waste.

Nobles, referring to the royal line of rulers, are not exempt by their status from God's discipline (Luke 1:52). Humbling of the powerful and mighty is demonstrated throughout Scripture: consider Pharaoh (Exodus 14), Sennacherib (2 Kings 19:20-37), Nebuchadnezzar (Daniel 4), and Herod Agrippa I (Acts 12:20-23).

> ### What Do You Think?
> What specific practices can a Christian adopt to honor God's contempt for the powerful unrighteous while also honoring his desire for our obedience to authorities (Romans 13:1-6)?
> ### Digging Deeper
> What elements of Daniel 6:1-10 speak to this?

B. Honoring the Meek (v. 41)

41. But he lifted the needy out of their affliction and increased their families like flocks.

The humbling of nobles (above) stands in sharp contrast to the Lord's lifting of *the needy*. This language brings to mind the reversals described in the prayers of Hannah (1 Samuel 2:5-8) and Mary (Luke 1:46-55). In both Old and New Testaments, God's people celebrated his concern for the downtrodden. Though "Mary's Song" is usually considered during the Christmas season, we can and should celebrate by remembering her trust throughout the year: "He has helped his servant Israel, remembering to be merciful to Abraham and his descendants forever, just as he promised our ancestors" (Luke 1:54-55).

C. Heartening the Wise (vv. 42-43)

42. The upright see and rejoice, but all the wicked shut their mouths.

The upright are those who follow the Lord's ways and view people and situations as he does (examples: Genesis 6:9; 15:6; Deuteronomy 6:25). Such people *see* the series of circumstances described in the previous verses and *rejoice* to see such reversals take place (see expanded expression in Psalm 97:10-12). They know that these circumstances have not happened as the result of mere chance or luck. The Lord is the true ruler of the world, and he can reverse people's situations. *The wicked* are left speechless (compare Romans 3:19).

43. Let the one who is wise heed these things and ponder the loving deeds of the LORD.

Wise people get that way as they *heed* the *things* described in the previous verses and see in them manifestations of *the loving deeds of the Lord.* The Hebrew word translated as "loving deeds" is repeated throughout the psalm, a form of the word translated "love" in Psalm 107:1 and "unfailing love" in 107:8, 15, 21, 31. This indicates an obvious theme throughout Psalm 107, as the chapter is bookended with an emphasis on God's love and loving deeds.

Some of the Lord's actions described in this psalm (such as pouring contempt on nobles in 107:40, above) may not seem very loving. But they reflect a system of corrective justice and judgment that a loving, caring God set in motion to uphold his principles of righteous conduct. Human beings are not left to wonder what God's standards are. As Moses declared in Deuteronomy 29:29,

> The secret things belong to the Lord our God, but the things revealed belong to us and to our children forever, that we may follow all the words of this law.

God's love is demonstrated to all people (Matthew 5:45). But the wise have a greater understanding of and gratitude for how much God's loving deeds impact daily life.

Conclusion

A. Continue to Praise

God's consistently loving deeds and provision of care for those who faithfully honor and serve him must not be overlooked. Jesus spoke of blessings provided for those who seek first "[God's] kingdom and his righteousness" (Matthew 6:33). That must be tempered, however, by the awareness that even in times when such provisions are lacking, God's presence and grace have not been denied to the faithful. This too is consistently taught in Scripture (examples: 2 Corinthians 9:10-11; 12:7-10; Philippians 4:15-19).

God can and does still bring to pass the reversals found within this psalm, such as providing relief for the hungry (Psalm 107:9) and delivering the poor from their poverty (107:41). These are times to celebrate! But gratitude to God is *always* meant to be part of our spiritual demeanor (1 Thessalonians 5:18). It is not to hinge on whether material needs (or wants!) are supplied. The physical side of life does indeed matter, but it is not the only dimension of reality. Paul expressed the tension clearly: "Though outwardly we are wasting away, yet inwardly we are being renewed day by day" (2 Corinthians 4:16; compare Philippians 2:7-11).

For Christians, there is always the most important reason for giving thanks: our redemption in Jesus (Colossians 1:12-14; 1 Peter 1:3-5). Hope in our future resurrection gives us reason both to celebrate the work Jesus did on the cross and the work the Spirit continues to do in our lives, preparing us for an eternity of praise to God.

> **What Do You Think?**
> Which concept or imperative in today's lesson do you have the most trouble coming to grips with? Why?
> *Digging Deeper*
> How will you resolve this problem?

B. Prayer

Father, we thank you for the record in Scripture of your power to deliver your people. Help us, we pray, to deepen our understanding of your love toward us and model your ways to others. In Jesus' name we pray. Amen.

C. Thought to Remember

We can never praise the Lord too much!

INVOLVEMENT LEARNING

Enhance your lesson with NIV® Bible Student *(from your curriculum supplier) and the reproducible activity page (at www.standardlesson.com or in the back of the* NIV® *Standard Lesson Commentary Deluxe Edition).*

Into the Lesson

Ask a volunteer to come to the front of the room to have his or her hands bound. Use a scarf or length of rope to do so (only loosely—this is just a figurative binding for purposes of illustration). Give five class members index cards with these instructions, one per card:

1–Tell us your shoe size.
2–Hold your breath for 10 seconds.
3–Tell us what you had for dinner last night.
4–Make a snoring sound.
5–Using a falsetto voice, sing something.

Tell the person with bound hands that as five instructions are read, he or she must obey at least three of them without knowing in advance what the choices will be. The bound person then picks a number between one and five, and the participant with that card reads the direction. The bound person must then either obey it or "pass." Mention that only two passes are possible; when those are used up, the bound person must obey the remaining directives before being set free.

After three directives are obeyed, remove the binding. Ask the volunteer how it felt to be required to do things before being set free. Use his or her response to lead into Bible study by saying, "All of us have sought and received deliverance from something that bound us at one time or another. Let's see how the psalmist handled such an issue."

Into the Word

Begin by summarizing the likely historical setting for Psalm 107 (see Lesson Context). Then distribute to study pairs or triads the following questions on handouts (you create), with all questions on all handouts:

1–Why thank the Lord?
2–What trouble did the people experience?

3–What good things does the Lord do?

4–What punishments does God inflict on those who disobey him?

5–What blessing did God provide for those in need?

6–What should be the conclusion of those who consider what God has done?

Before pairs or triads begin work, have the 14 verses of the lesson text read aloud by two volunteers who alternate reading with each verse. Then allow several minutes for pairs or triads to work, after which they will share conclusions in whole-class discussion.

Option. For a deeper and broader look at Psalm 107, distribute copies of the "To Cry for Help" and/or "Psalm 107 Reflected in Scripture" exercises from the activity page, which you can download. Have participants work in groups to complete as indicated; follow with whole-class discussion of discoveries.

Into Life

Write this statement on the board:

A time I realized God's deliverance was . . .

Encourage the telling of personal experiences, experiences of their families, experiences of the mission field, or of your church. At an appropriate point, challenge participants by saying, "If we think carefully, we can see God's hand of deliverance in smaller experiences every day—experiences we may overlook." Ask students to think of ways this is true.

Distribute sheets of blank paper. Ask your learners to describe at the top of their sheets the most recent way they've seen God's loving hand at work in their lives. After one minute, ask volunteers to share, but don't put anyone on the spot to do so. Conclude by challenging learners to use the paper as a daily journal for the week ahead to remind them to remain aware of God's work.

PRAISE GOD FOR HIS PRESENCE

DEVOTIONAL READING: Psalm 84
BACKGROUND SCRIPTURE: Psalm 84

PSALM 84

For the director of music. According to *gittith*.
Of the Sons of Korah. A psalm.
1 How lovely is your dwelling place,
LORD Almighty!
2 My soul yearns, even faints,
for the courts of the LORD;
my heart and my flesh cry out
for the living God.
3 Even the sparrow has found a home,
and the swallow a nest for herself,
where she may have her young—
a place near your altar,
LORD Almighty, my King and my God.
4 Blessed are those who dwell in your
house;
they are ever praising you.
5 Blessed are those whose strength is in you,
whose hearts are set on pilgrimage.
6 As they pass through the Valley of Baka,
they make it a place of springs;
the autumn rains also cover it with
pools.
7 They go from strength to strength,
till each appears before God in Zion.
8 Hear my prayer, LORD God Almighty;

listen to me, God of Jacob.
9 Look on our shield, O God;
look with favor on your anointed one.
10 Better is one day in your courts
than a thousand elsewhere;
I would rather be a doorkeeper in the
house of my God
than dwell in the tents of the wicked.
11 For the LORD God is a sun and shield;
the LORD bestows favor and honor;
no good thing does he withhold
from those whose walk is blameless.
12 LORD Almighty, blessed is the one who
trusts in you.

KEY TEXT

Blessed are those who dwell in your house; they are ever praising you. —**Psalm 84:4**

Photo © Getty Images

CELEBRATING GOD

Unit 2: Called to Praise God

LESSONS 5–9

LESSON AIMS

After participating in this lesson, each learner will be able to:

1. Summarize the psalmist's desire.

2. Compare and contrast factors that can weaken desire for God's presence.

3. List ways that the Lord determines that a person does or does not desire his presence.

LESSON OUTLINE

Introduction

A. Longing for Home

One of my greatest earthly blessings is the home life that graced my upbringing. My family moved into a large house in the country in south-central Indiana when I was 4 (that was in 1957). I had no idea that this house would remain "home" until May 2018, when the house was sold about two and a half years after my mother's passing.

Over the years after going away to college, I made many trips back home, always with a great sense of anticipation. Eventually I brought my bride-to-be there, where we announced our engagement to my parents. Over the course of the years that followed, we brought our three children there for visits.

Thus more memories of home were added to those that I amassed while growing up. The sense of stability and security made home a very special place to visit. The question "Are we there yet?" was one asked by me, not by our children. Of course, the key to home being the place that it became was the people who lived there. My father and mother were very caring, godly individuals.

In today's text, the psalmist expresses his intense, fervent longing to be in a different kind of "home," which becomes instructive for us.

B. Lesson Context

Psalm 84 is one of the 17 psalms that constitute Book III of the Psalter (see the Lesson Context of lesson 5 for explanation of the psalms' arrangement in terms of five "books"). Expressions of praise characterize many of these psalms (see the visual for lesson 5). A total of 11 psalms are written "of the Sons of Korah," 4 of which are in Book III—namely, Psalms 84, 85, 87, and 88—according to their superscriptions (compare Lesson Context: Superscription in lesson 6). This could mean either that the songs were written *by* those descendants of Korah or that they were written *for* them to sing. In either case, the sons must have been musically gifted (2 Chronicles 20:19).

Regarding Korah himself, he was a descendant of Kohath, a son of Levi (Exodus 6:16-21). Korah, accompanied by members of the tribe of Reuben, had led a rebellion against the God-given authority of Moses and Aaron during the exodus. As a result, Korah was put to death along with 250 others (Numbers 16:1-2, 35).

Despite this blemish on the family line, Korah's descendants (Numbers 26:58) became prominent in the temple worship that King David arranged before his death, toward the day his son Solomon would complete the building of the temple. The record of the service of Korah's descendants as gatekeepers is found in 1 Chronicles 9:19; 26:1.

If Psalm 84 was written *for* rather than *by* the sons of Korah, one guess about its author is King David. This is based on the occurrence of the word translated "shield" in Psalm 84:9, 11 since this word occurs also in Psalms 3, 5, 144, and others—the superscriptions of which attribute them to David.

This would date the psalm's composition before David's death in 970 BC. But other psalms that are not attributed to David also have that word, so the conclusion is not ironclad.

The occasion of the composition may have been that of a pilgrimage to the temple, perhaps for a new-year festival. This, though speculative, is as good a guess as any (see on Psalm 84:5, below).

Regarding the superscription's "For the director of music," see discussion in Lesson Context: Superscription in lesson 6. The meaning of the phrase "According to gittith" is uncertain. The word *gittith* is likely a musical term, perhaps a musical instrument or a reference to a certain type of celebratory melody (see also Psalms 8 and 81).

I. Opening Appeal
(PSALM 84:1-3)

A. For God's Presence (vv. 1-2)

1. How lovely is your dwelling place, LORD Almighty!

In older translations of the Bible, the Hebrew adjective translated *lovely* (which might suggest a focus on beautiful appearance) is more commonly rendered "beloved", and that is the sense here (see Deuteronomy 33:12; Psalms 60:5; 108:6; etc.). The term suggests that this poem will focus on love or attachment—in this case the high degree

of fondness the writer has for the Lord's *dwelling place* (see Psalms 27:4; 43:3; 132:1-8). There is no place the psalmist would rather be!

The Hebrew word translated *dwelling place* is translated "tabernacles" (tents) in older versions of the Bible. The Israelites had constructed a tabernacle to be the portable home of the Lord's symbolic presence (Exodus 26). After the people had been established in the promised land for many generations, King David desired to build God a permanent dwelling in Jerusalem (2 Samuel 7:1-5). But the task fell instead to his son Solomon (2 Chronicles 3:1). It seems likely that the word "tabernacles" refers to courts or other divisions within the temple instead of multiple locations.

The designation *Lord Almighty* (appropriately translated "Lord of hosts" in other versions) is used over 200 times as a title for God in the Old Testament. We may find it surprising that only nine of those occur in the Psalter, with three of those nine in this psalm alone (Psalm 84:1, 3, 12). This designation celebrates the Lord's power in various contexts (examples: 1 Samuel 17:45; Isaiah 1:24). The word translated "hosts" in the older translations may refer to angelic beings who serve the Lord as he directs (see Psalm 148:2; compare Hebrews 1:13-14). It also may refer to stars, planets, and other heavenly bodies that he created (Nehemiah 9:6).

2a. My soul yearns, even faints, for the courts of the LORD;

The writer's absence from *the courts of the Lord* (understood as the temple courts) could be explained in one of several ways. More important

HOW TO SAY IT

Babylonian	Bab-ih-*low*-nee-un.
Baka	*Bay*-ka.
Kohath	*Ko*-hath.
Korah	*Ko*-rah.
Levi	*Lee*-vye.
Psalter	*Saul*-tur.
Reuben	*Roo*-ben.
Selah (Hebrew)	*See*-luh.
tabernacles	**tah**-burr-*nah*-kuls.
Zion	*Zi*-un.

Visual for Lesson 8. *Turn the question on this visual into a completion exercise as you write "My journey leads me toward God as I _____ daily."*

to this psalm, however, is not why he wasn't there, but the effect the absence had on the man. Such was his fervent desire that, even though he may have had no specific call to be there (annual pilgrimage feast, etc.), he *yearns* and *even faints* to be in God's presence nonetheless.

❧ *Your Fainting Heart* ❧

No one wants to faint on their wedding day! But the excitement of the big day can make the bride and groom light-headed. That's why, as a minister who has presided at many weddings over the years, I give the excited couple and their attendants two pieces of advice at the wedding rehearsal. First, hunger makes you faint, so eat something prior to the ceremony. Second, rigidity makes you faint, so bend your knees slightly instead of standing ramrod straight while in front of the audience.

Have you ever yearned so deeply for the presence of God that you felt like you were going to faint? Consider again my two pieces of advice. If your soul feels faint, maybe you're hungry and thirsty for righteousness (Matthew 5:6). Feast on God's Word. Or maybe you need to bend your knees—physically or spiritually—before the Lord in prayer. What will it take to revive your fainting heart?

—D. F.

2b. my heart and my flesh cry out for the living God.

We see parallelism here with the previous half-verse, with increasing intensity: *heart* and *flesh* are added to "soul" to indicate the man's entire being. A similar piling up of terms occurs in Deuteronomy 6:5: "Love the Lord your God with all your heart and with all your soul and with all your strength" (compare Matthew 22:37).

The temple, with its surrounding courts, was understood to be the dwelling place of God's glory (Psalm 26:8; compare 27:4). Thus to be able to be in those courts was to be as close to *the living God* as possible.

B. For a Place with God (v. 3)

3a. Even the sparrow has found a home, and the swallow a nest for herself, where she may have her young—a place near your altar,

We detect a note of jealousy for birds that were able to build nests within the Lord's *home*. As in some public buildings today, this was probably confined to the rafters or other high structures. The *altar* itself would be far too active for a bird nest. But the winged creatures could be present for every sacrifice without ever leaving home. The psalmist desired to be as intimately linked to the temple as the birds were.

3b. Lord Almighty, my King and my God.

The psalmist described his committed relationship with his sovereign. Yes, the psalmist affirmed, he is *Lord Almighty*; but he is also *my King and my God*. The possessive pronouns suggest closeness while the titles emphasize God's greatness. This is the great paradox of faith: the Creator of everything, seen and unseen, desires undivided relationships with those created in his image. Jesus was the one who demonstrated how close God wants to be to us (Matthew 1:23), as well as the great depths of love he was willing to go to in order to heal our relationship with him (John 3:16-17).

II. In God's Presence
(Psalm 84:4-7)
A. Constant Praise (v. 4)

4. Blessed are those who dwell in your house; they are ever praising you.

Because of their duties at the temple, priests and Levites were privileged to spend much of their time in those sacred surroundings. Their tasks gave them ample reasons and opportunities to offer praise to the Lord. When they honored the Lord by faithfully carrying out his work, the *house* was indeed a *blessed* place to be.

Though the temple of antiquity and church buildings today are very different in function and purpose, something similar can be said about our gathering places: when ministry through faithful preaching and teaching of God's Word and serving one another in love are carried out within the walls of the building, it is a blessed place to be. Why then shouldn't a person anticipate being in the place of worship as the psalmist did? If such good things are taking place, others will be attracted to what is happening.

Today, our bodies are temples of God's Holy Spirit (1 Corinthians 6:19). Even so, we should view our church buildings as tools to be used for the Lord's grace and glory. They are places to praise the Lord in corporate worship and where people should experience his love in the midst of his people.

> *What Do You Think?*
> What self-evaluation can you undertake to ensure that you are God's "house"?
> *Digging Deeper*
> Considering 2 Corinthians 13:5, what priority will you establish for doing so?

The word *Selah* at the end of this verse occurs 71 times in the psalms. ("Selah" is found in the 1984 edition of the *NIV* but not the 2011 edition, although it is sometimes found in a footnote.) The meaning is unknown, but most believe it to be a musical notation. It may direct the instruments to play more loudly while the singers are silent, or it may mark a pause for reflection since it usually comes after a significant or challenging statement has been made.

B. Continuing Strength (vv. 5-7)

5. Blessed are those whose strength is in you, whose hearts are set on pilgrimage.

This verse bolsters the possibility that this is a psalm of *pilgrimage* (see Lesson Context). Unlike the yearning and fainting of verse 2a, those who find themselves either physically on the way to the temple or at least determined to begin the journey find *strength* in the Lord.

6. As they pass through the Valley of Baka, they make it a place of springs; the autumn rains also cover it with pools.

This verse goes well with the description in the preceding verse of the pilgrimage to the place of worship. However, there is no place in recorded Scripture called *the Valley of Baka* in Israel; elsewhere, the Hebrew word behind the translation *Baka* refers to a certain kind of tree (2 Samuel 5:24; 1 Chronicles 14:14-15). Some think the reference is to a narrow valley near Jerusalem. Another idea is that this is a figurative description of the spiritual dryness that is relieved by arriving at the Lord's house.

7. They go from strength to strength, till each appears before God in Zion.

The Hebrew word translated *strength* twice here is different from the one translated "strength" in Psalm 84:5, above. Thus the psalmist piles up terms for emphasis. No matter the challenges one confronts on this pilgrimage, the strength available in the Lord can never be exhausted! Paradoxically, the longer the travelers walk, the stronger they become, upheld by *God* (see Isaiah 40:31). *Zion,* another name for Jerusalem (see Psalms 51:18; 102:21; etc.), is the location of the temple (2 Kings 21:4).

For Christians, the word *Zion* represents the blessings and privileges of "a new covenant" in Christ (Hebrews 12:22-24). This blessing will culminate in a residence for eternity in the new Jerusalem (Revelation 21:1-5). Whatever "dry spells" are encountered along the way, the one who draws strength from the Lord will find relief.

III. Closing Appeal
(PSALM 84:8-12)
A. For Self (v. 8)

8. Hear my prayer, LORD God Almighty; listen to me, God of Jacob.

This verse in Hebrew and older English translations shows us parallelism in an X-shaped format:

Lord God Almighty   Hear my prayer

listen to me   God of Jacob

Recognizing the *Lord . . . Almighty* (see commentary on Psalm 84:3, above) to be the same as the *God of Jacob* reminded the original reader that the Lord God had exercised his power to choose the family of Jacob to be the covenant people (Psalm 105:10; Acts 7:8). The repetition of sentiment found in *hear my prayer* and *listen to me* amplifies one's desire for God to hear and take notice. All these elements taken together emphasize the full range of God's power: his attending to an entire nation is set side by side with the psalmist's conviction that God is willing and able to hear the prayer of an individual.

> **What Do You Think?**
> What personal behaviors do you need to change to help ensure that God hears your prayers?
> *Digging Deeper*
> In what ways are Jeremiah 11:14; 14:12; and/or 1 Peter 3:7 relevant to your conclusion?

B. For the Lord's Anointed (v. 9)

9. Look on our shield, O God; look with favor on your anointed one.

It is possible that God is the one being designated as *our shield* as in Psalm 84:11, below (compare 59:11). But the parallelism that often characterizes Hebrew poetry (see above) suggests that the *anointed one* (that is, the king of Israel) is the shield—the one appointed by God to lead the people in faithfulness.

To *look with favor* is similar to the "listen to me" request in the previous verse. The psalmist desires God's attention in certain ways.

C. Statement of Trust (vv. 10-12)

10. Better is one day in your courts than a thousand elsewhere; I would rather be a doorkeeper in the house of my God than dwell in the tents of the wicked.

The psalmist now adds elements of time quantity (duration) and position status (role) to his preference for the *courts* of the Lord's *house*. The contrast between *one day* and *a thousand* (duration) is quite sharp. To *be a doorkeeper* in the temple is the position of a low-level attendant (2 Kings 23:4). The contrast with *the tents of the wicked* is seen in Psalm 83:5-7, where high-level leadership is in view.

> **What Do You Think?**
> Gauging your personal dedication to the Lord's "courts" on a scale of 1 to 10, what do you need to do to move one notch better?
> *Digging Deeper*
> Who could be a mentor to you in that regard?

❧ CALLED TO COME "CHOME" ❧

An acquaintance of mine purchased an old church building and transformed it into a private residence. Since it is a church/home, the owner nicknamed it his "chome."

Sometimes when loved ones die, friends say, "God called them home." But we don't have to wait till we die to be at home in the presence of God and his people. God calls us into community with him in the here and now. Like a magnet, his grace pulls us toward him and toward each other.

Come to think of it, the concept of "chome" is a good one in this regard. It starts with recognizing that people, not buildings, are the living church. Then when we add to that fact the practice of making our homes places where God is honored, prayers are common, worship is lifted up, and people are taught, we can say, "Be it ever so humble, there's no place like 'chome!'"—D. F.

11a. For the LORD God is a sun and shield;

Noteworthy here is the fact that the Hebrew noun being translated as *a sun* is *not* accompanied by a definite article, which, if present, would result in God's being "the sun." Thus there is no hint of sun worship here as was common in pagan practice at the time (Deuteronomy 4:19; 2 Kings 23:5, 11; Jeremiah 43:13; Ezekiel 8:16). Rather, the idea is one of spiritual light (Psalms 13:3; 18:28).

References to God as a *shield* and similar items

of protection are common in the Old Testament (example: Psalm 18:2).

11b. the LORD bestows favor and honor;

Other translations for *favor* and *honor* are "grace" and "glory" (examples: Zechariah 12:10; 2 Chronicles 7:1, respectively). These words together represent everything we should ultimately desire from *the Lord*. Echoing this is James 1:17:

> Every good and perfect gift is from above, coming down from the Father of the heavenly lights, who does not change like shifting shadows.

11c. no good thing does he withhold from those whose walk is blameless.

The idea of an upright *walk* is found several places in Scripture (see Genesis 6:9; 17:1; Psalms 15:2; 101:2, 6; 119:1; Proverbs 28:18). While God does indeed bless even those who do not do so (Matthew 5:45), special favor falls on those who seek his ways. *Blameless* implies integrity or wholeness, found particularly in Psalm 18:20-25. Next to salvation itself, the ultimate *good thing* God gives to Christians while we are on earth is the gift of the Holy Spirit, conferred at baptism (Acts 2:38).

> *What Do You Think?*
> What "good thing" you have received from God can and should you share with others?
> *Digging Deeper*
> What Scripture passages convict you most to get started *now* in this regard?

12. LORD Almighty, blessed is the one who trusts in you.

The final reference to being *blessed* in this psalm (previous ones were in Psalm 84:4-5, above) again acknowledges God as the *Lord Almighty* (see commentary on 84:1, above), who nonetheless is still concerned about the individual (*the one*). Anyone who *trusts in* him is blessed in the ways this psalm indicates and more.

This is heart of the psalm. While fervor for the Lord's temple and the annual pilgrimage feasts can indicate that a person's heart is yielded to God, such excitement itself is not enough. Yes, it is good to be in the house of the Lord, but that is not an end in itself. The key is trusting in the Lord of the house, living in daily fellowship with him.

Conclusion
A. Longing for God

While the psalmist was quite passionate about being in the Lord's house, readers today may wonder whether such passion is fitting for Christians. To this we can answer *yes* in terms of the need to gather with other Christians (Matthew 18:20; Hebrews 10:25) while at the same time remembering that church buildings of the New Testament era are not equivalent to the temple of the Old Testament era.

More than location, the psalmist's heart was set on spending time with God. It was God's presence that made the place of worship the sacred place that it was. While our houses of worship today bear little to no resemblance in form and function to the temple in Jerusalem, the psalmist's longing to be in God's presence still stands.

But how seriously do we take the truth that we are always in God's presence, given that *we* are the new-covenant temple? See 1 Corinthians 3:16-17; 2 Corinthians 6:16; and Ephesians 2:19-22. Christians long to be with Jesus and in his presence for eternity, and that is a good thing. But as we anticipate that great day, what a tragedy it would be to not draw on the good thing we have now: the indwelling of the Holy Spirit.

> *What Do You Think?*
> Which concept or imperative in today's lesson do you have the most trouble coming to grips with? Why?
> *Digging Deeper*
> How will you resolve this problem?

B. Prayer

Father, thank you for the presence of the Holy Spirit! We are humbled that you have promised to dwell with those who turn to you in simple trusting faith. We thank you for your presence with your people when we gather in worship. In Jesus' name we pray. Amen.

C. Thought to Remember

Remember the Lord's presence and be blessed!

INVOLVEMENT LEARNING

Enhance your lesson with NIV® Bible Student *(from your curriculum supplier) and the reproducible activity page (at www.standardlesson.com or in the back of the* NIV® Standard Lesson Commentary Deluxe Edition*).*

Into the Lesson

Distribute handouts (you prepare) that list the following prompts. Allow space for writing under each one:

1–A homecoming I'll always remember was . . .
2–When I think of "home," my first thought is . . .
3–Something special about my hometown is . . .
4–I most feel "at home" when . . .

Ask each learner to choose one of the prompts and jot their response under it, taking no more than one minute to do so. After calling time, ask class members to exchange sheets so they can jot their response to a prompt not chosen on the sheet they receive, again taking no more than one minute to do so. Do this once more. Then have volunteers read one of the responses on the sheet they're holding while the class tries to guess who wrote it.

Lead into Bible study by saying, "Clearly, the thought of 'home' can elicit powerful feelings. But 'home' can be interpreted in more ways than one, as today's lesson teaches."

Into the Word

After having Psalm 84 read aloud, distribute handouts (you prepare) that reproduce that text. Include the following instructions underneath:

1–Put a question mark [?] beside verses you don't understand.
2–Put an asterisk [*] beside verses that tell *why* the psalmist longed to be in the temple courts.
3–Circle the verse you'd most like to remember in the week ahead.
4–Make a list of all the emotions expressed by the psalmist.

Instruct students to answer just the first three, taking no more than one minute total. Then ask them to find a partner or two to compare how they marked the text and to brainstorm ideas for the fourth instruction.

Reconvene for whole-class discussion of responses to all four instructions. Add clarity by explaining the background and context for the psalm (see Lesson Context).

Option. For a broader and deeper consideration of God's presence and dwelling place, distribute copies of the "Where God Dwells" exercise on the activity page, which you can download. Allow study pairs or triads to complete it as indicated for ensuing whole-class discussion.

Into Life

Write this task on the board:

List ways that the Lord determines that a person [does/does not] want his presence.

Divide the class in half; then group students in each half into study pairs or triads. Those in one half of the class will make a "does" list; groups in the other half will make a "does not" list. After five minutes, let groups respond. Jot answers on the board.

With learners in the same two large groups, assign one to discuss the biggest threats to causing a person to switch from "does" to "does not." Have the other half discuss the opposite—what results in a person switching from "does not" to "does." Allow only a few minutes for this discussion before whole-class discussion.

Following that discussion, move the focus to another metaphor appropriate for this lesson: that of "home" being where one goes to be close to God. Discuss the situations, places, and/or times when they sense or have sensed closeness to God.

At an appropriate point, ask how such situations, places, and/or times can be repeated weekly or daily. *Option 1:* Close the class session with students quietly listening to a gentle rendition of "Softly and Tenderly." *Option 2:* Distribute copies of the "Heart Test" journal from the activity page as learners depart. Challenge them to log entries three times daily in the coming week. Promise to discuss results when the class meets again.

PRAISE GOD FOR HIS GREATNESS

DEVOTIONAL READING: Psalm 150
BACKGROUND SCRIPTURE: Psalms 147–150

PSALM 149:1-5

¹ Praise the LORD.

Sing to the LORD a new song,
   his praise in the assembly of his faithful people.
² Let Israel rejoice in their Maker;
   let the people of Zion be glad in their King.
³ Let them praise his name with dancing
   and make music to him with timbrel and harp.
⁴ For the LORD takes delight in his people;
   he crowns the humble with victory.
⁵ Let his faithful people rejoice in this honor
   and sing for joy on their beds.

PSALM 150

¹ Praise the LORD.
Praise God in his sanctuary;
   praise him in his mighty heavens.
² Praise him for his acts of power;
   praise him for his surpassing greatness.
³ Praise him with the sounding of the trumpet,
   praise him with the harp and lyre,
⁴ praise him with timbrel and dancing,
   praise him with the strings and pipe,
⁵ praise him with the clash of cymbals,
   praise him with resounding cymbals.

⁶ Let everything that has breath praise the LORD.
Praise the LORD.

Praise to the Lord, the Almighty

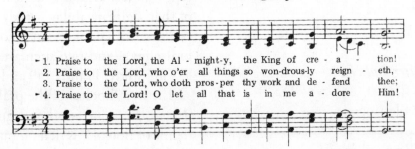

- 1. Praise to the Lord, the Al - might - y, the King of cre - a - tion!
- 2. Praise to the Lord, who o'er all things so won-drous-ly reign - eth,
- 3. Praise to the Lord, who doth pros - per thy work and de - fend thee;
- 4. Praise to the Lord! O let all that is in me a - dore Him!

KEY TEXT

Let everything that has breath praise the LORD. —**Psalm 150:6a**

CELEBRATING GOD

Unit 2: Called to Praise God

LESSONS 5–9

LESSON AIMS

After participating in this lesson, each learner will be able to:

1. List reasons for praising the Lord.

2. Explain the types and arrangement of the psalms.

3. Choose one verse from today's texts to use as a praise reminder for the week ahead.

LESSON OUTLINE

Introduction

A. Flash Mob

Food courts at shopping malls seem to be favorite targets of flash mobs. These are groups of people, usually well-rehearsed, who perform a song, dance, etc., from and for an unsuspecting crowd.

One such flash-mob appearance began in the typical way: a large crowd was eating amid the normal hubbub of a crowded food court and background music when different music began playing. The music was the "Hallelujah Chorus" from Händel's *Messiah.*

A young woman holding a cell phone in the crowd stood up, as is customary during that chorus. No surprise there. But then she began singing in a beautiful, operatic soprano. After her, a tenor sang a few bars. More singers joined in, then several more, and then more yet. Finally, an entire choir of professional singers, scattered throughout the court, was performing a magnificent version of that beautiful hymn of praise. Many diners recorded the unique scene on their phones.

The performance was so unexpected and so beautiful that it moved some to tears. But unexpected professional performances of stirring music aren't the only opportunities to wonder in awe in sensing the presence of God. Heartfelt prayers and personally sung hymns have their place too.

B. Lesson Context: Book V

Much of the material in the Lesson Contexts of lessons 5–8 applies here as well, so that information need not be repeated. What is different is that we are moving again into Book V of the Psalter. Whereas lesson 7 took us to the beginning of that segment, today's study takes us to its very end. The visual for lesson 5 notes many psalms of praise here, and two such are the subject of this lesson's study: Psalms 149 and 150.

The five "books" of the psalms are not disconnected from one another—quite the opposite! A theme of Book IV is that no matter what the problem, God is king (Psalms 96–99); Book V follows that with assurances that he will one day make all things right (Psalm 145). These facts called for praise on the part of the psalmists. The final psalm within each of the five books concludes with an extended doxology: an expression of joyful praise to the Lord.

C. Lesson Context: Praise Conclusion

Psalms 149 and 150 are two of the five psalms that are known collectively as "the praise conclusion" to the Psalter as a whole, namely Psalms 146–150. These five have three things in common in that all (1) are anonymous, (2) were likely composed after the rebuilding of Jerusalem's temple and walls (about 515 and 444 BC, respectively), and (3) begin and end with the phrase "Praise the Lord." That phrase unites them with a shared theme. Even given that unity, the five offer different emphases in regard to that praise.

Psalm	Praise Emphasis
146	The suffering have hope
147	God cares for his people
148	God's light is for everyone
149	God protects his people
150	Ways to praise

Set in the days of Ezra and Nehemiah, this was the time of Persian dominance (about 539–330 BC). Jewish life was difficult during this period (examples: Ezra 4:24; Nehemiah 4:10-11; Haggai 1:6). But despite the challenges, this new beginning and the thrill of restoration resulted naturally and appropriately in the need for new songs of praise. These five psalms—the last two of which are the subject of today's study—reveal some important things.

I. A New Song
(PSALM 149:1-5)
A. Call to Praise (vv. 1-3)

1a. Praise the LORD.

Praise the Lord, a plural command, is a translation of only two words in Hebrew; millions of people all over the world know this as the single, compounded word *hallelujah.* The first word, *hallelu,* is a command to praise. The *jah* that follows is a shortened version of Yahweh, the Hebrew name of God—the object of the praise.

The two words *hallelu* and *jah* occur adjacent to each other 24 times in the psalms, beginning in

Psalm 104:35 and ending in the last line of 150:6 —the final phrase of the Psalter. Scripture also has longer forms of this phrase in Isaiah 62:9; Jeremiah 20:13; and Psalms 117:1; 148:1b, 7.

In the New Testament, the Hebrew is transliterated (not translated) into Greek, so it sounds the same whether one is speaking Greek or Hebrew. The result is the four occurrences of our English "Hallelujah" (also a transliteration, not a translation) in Revelation 19:1, 3, 4, 6. So whether we say English "Praise the Lord" or the original Hebrew and adapted Greek "Hallelujah," we are saying the same thing!

1b. Sing to the LORD a new song,

Sing is also a plural command, occurring in that form 15 times in the Old Testament—10 of which are in the psalms (here and Psalms 33:3; 68:4, 32 [twice]; 96:1, 2; 98:1; 105:2; and 137:3). The last is in a context of oppression: captors requesting songs of the defeated who were in captivity (compare Romans 15:9; Ephesians 5:19; Hebrews 12:12; and James 5:13).

A new song suggests that circumstances have changed in such a way that the old songs are no longer sufficient (compare Psalms 33:3; 40:3; 96:1; 98:1; 144:9). In this case, the people have returned from their Babylonian captivity (see Lesson Context). Being something of a "second exodus," this return certainly called for new words of celebration! Isaiah speaks of the Messiah to come, and a new song is called for because of the new things God will do on the earth (Isaiah 42:10; 43:19). Similarly in Revelation, songs are composed because of the new circumstances of the saints in Heaven (see Revelation 4:9; 14:3).

> *What Do You Think?*
> What are some ways to help our fellow Christians embrace new songs of worship when they always want to sing old favorites?
> *Digging Deeper*
> What risks do we run by not trying?

❧ THE VALUE OF A TUNE ❧

In 1984 two music producers had an idea to bring famine relief to Ethiopia. Well-known

British musicians volunteered their talents, with the result that in a 24-hour recording session, the song "Do They Know It's Christmas?" came to be. It was an unexpected but tremendous success, earning millions of dollars in the first year. The message of the song resonated the world over, rousing people to action for the starving nation.

In some ways, Psalm 149 begins with a similar message to believers: it is a reminder of the praise that is due to God for all the things we may take for granted.

Perhaps a new song is called for because of what God is doing in your life. In what ways can your new song of praise give him the credit? Perhaps Revelation 5:9-10 can start your thinking on this.
—C. M. W.

1c. his praise in the assembly of his faithful people.

This clause applies the previous one by stating where the people are to offer *praise* to the Lord. *The assembly of his faithful people* sketches a setting of public, corporate worship. The faithful are those who demonstrate fidelity in their relationship with the Lord. They are not the ones who chase false gods or rebelliously disobey his commands.

2. Let Israel rejoice in their Maker; let the people of Zion be glad in their King.

Again, we see parallelism that often characterizes Hebrew poetry.

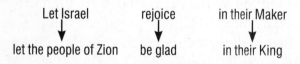

Such parallelism means that it's a mistake to see *Israel* and *the people of Zion* referring to different groups. In the same way, *rejoice* and *be glad* repeat one another.

Piling up phrases that have the same or very similar meanings emphasizes their importance. Though the English *let* may read like a suggestion or permission, it is actually a common way of translating Hebrew commands.

This verse also gives reasons for expressing joy. The two lines refer to the same being, namely God, but to different roles he has. First, the Lord

is not only the Creator of humans in general, but also the one who created the nation of Israel in particular. Second, the Lord is Israel's ruler (compare 1 Samuel 12:12; Isaiah 43:15). As subjects of his rule, the Israelites were beneficiaries of his protection. The Israelites are pointedly reminded that even though their earthly monarchy had come to an end, God was still their leader. He had made them a nation, and he could and would sustain them as such.

> **What Do You Think?**
> ▶ Thinking of the opposite of joy, what place should songs of a melancholy nature have in your church's Sunday worship, if any?
> *Digging Deeper*
> Consider as an example the lyrics and melody of the hymn "Almost Persuaded."

3. Let them praise his name with dancing and make music to him with timbrel and harp.

Here the psalmist provided means for expressing *praise* and joy. *Dancing* to the sound of musical instruments indicates boisterous, unrestrained worship. On the identities of the *timbrel and harp*, see Psalm 150:3-5, below.

B. Reasons for Praise (v. 4)

4. For the LORD takes delight in his people; he crowns the humble with victory.

Because this psalm was composed after the return from Babylonian exile (see Lesson Context), Ezra 7 forms a particularly fitting backdrop. In Ezra 7:27, the word here translated *crowns* is used for bringing honor to the temple under the approval of the Persian monarchy (see Ezra 6:1, 13-15).

In a similar way, *the Lord* was working on the hearts of *his people*. The *humble* are the afflicted, which is how the same word is translated in Psalms 9:12; 10:17; and elsewhere. This may include a spiritual sense—such people are aware of their low position before the Lord—or it may be meant in only a physical sense. The people experienced great uncertainty when they arrived back in Judah. They were certainly not wealthy or of high standing.

Victory (which can be translated "salvation") in the Old Testament often describes the deliverance from enemies (example: Exodus 14:13; 15:2). For the vulnerable population newly returned to Jerusalem and Judah, God's protection would indeed have been a comfort. The word translated *victory* can also be used of deliverance from sin, though this is much more prevalent in the New Testament as the word comes over from Hebrew into Greek (compare Psalm 3 with Revelation 7:10).

C. Another Call to Praise (v. 5)

5. Let his faithful people rejoice in this honor and sing for joy on their beds.

Psalm 149 can be divided into two stanzas. Whereas the first stanza (verses 1-4) invokes praise primarily looking back to the past acts of the Lord, the second stanza (verses 5-9) invokes praise looking forward to his future acts. The verse at hand again requires the people to praise the Lord, as the phrase *let his faithful people rejoice* echoes the command in 149:2.

Such celebrations are called for elsewhere: in anticipation of an enemy's defeat (Psalm 5:8-11), in sheer wonder at God's greatness (Psalm 95), and in instances of personification (96:12; 98:8), etc. *In . . . honor* refers to having been favored with a change of circumstance, from exiles to people living once again in their homeland. The Greek word used to translate the Hebrew is *doxa,* from which we get the word *doxology.*

On their beds sets up a contrast with Psalm 149:1, where the people are to offer praise "in the assembly of his faithful people." So both public and private praise are covered. A bed is not always a pleasant place to be (compare Job 7:13-

PRAISE GOD FOR HIS GREATNESS

Visual for Lesson 9. *Display this visual while learners ponder the praising-to-asking ratio in the discussion question associated with Psalm 150:2.*

15; Psalms 6:6; 41:3). There is also a time when silence is called for while lying in bed (4:4). We easily imagine that beds were tearful places during the exile. But in the verse before us, we see what should happen in private as a result of God's having transformed the situation of an entire nation (contrast Psalm 137).

II. The Setting of Praise
(PSALM 150)
A. Where (v. 1)

1a. Praise the LORD.

This imperative was treated above (see on Psalm 149:1a).

1b. Praise God in his sanctuary;

Here we see mention of a location where it is especially appropriate to *praise God.* The Hebrew word translated *sanctuary* occurs more than 500 times in the Old Testament. As a noun, it can take 20 different meanings, by one count, according to context. The big-picture idea is one of "sacredness" or "apartness." The context here seems to require that the sacred space in view is where God's people gather for worship (as in Psalms 68:24-26; 134:2; and 138:2).

1c. praise him in his mighty heavens.

The word *heavens* reflects the conception of people in Old Testament times, who considered the sky to be a vault over the earth. It is the place where the stars are located, the place that separates

HOW TO SAY IT

Babylonian	Bab-ih-*low*-nee-un.
Corinthians	Ko-*rin*-thee-unz (*th* as in *thin*).
Ezra	*Ez*-ruh.
Haggai	*Hag*-eye or *Hag*-ay-eye.
Judah	*Joo*-duh.
Nehemiah	*Nee*-huh-*my*-uh.
Persian	*Per*-zhun.
Titus	*Ty*-tus.
Yahweh (Hebrew)	*Yah*-weh.
Zion	*Zi*-un.

the earth from the abode of God beyond (see Ezekiel 1:22-26; Daniel 12:3; compare 2 Corinthians 12:2). The phrase *in his mighty* describes the magnificence of the heavens; the almighty God created it (Genesis 1:6-18; Psalm 19:1).

B. Why (v. 2)

2. Praise him for his acts of power; praise him for his surpassing greatness.

Two reasons for praising the Lord are given: his works and his character. *Acts of power* are things God has done in the past. Some psalms very clearly celebrate specific works God has done by recounting his deeds in Israel's history. For example, Psalm 136 recounts the acts of the Lord in creation (vv. 5-9), in delivering Israel from Egypt (vv. 10-16), in conquering enemies and giving Israel the land (vv. 17-24), and for providing food for all creatures (v. 25).

The phrase *his surpassing greatness* summarizes the Lord's character. God is perfect in his knowledge (Deuteronomy 29:29), in his ethics (Psalms 18:25; 92:15; Mark 10:18), in his works (Deuteronomy 32:4), and in his words (Numbers 23:19; Titus 1:2).

> *What Do You Think?*
> How can this psalm help you evaluate the ratio of "praising" to "asking for" in your personal prayer life?
> *Digging Deeper*
> How does correcting an imbalance start?

C. How (vv. 3-5)

3. Praise him with the sounding of the trumpet, praise him with the harp and lyre,

Here begins a three-verse list of several musical instruments the readers were encouraged to use to *praise him* (compare 1 Chronicles 15:28). Metal horns were known in the Old Testament world (example: Numbers 10:1-10), but *the sounding of the trumpet* signifies the blast of a ram's horn. These were used in worship (Leviticus 25:9), as a signal in war (Joshua 6:4-9, 20), to warn of danger (Joel 2:1), to express joyous celebration (2 Samuel 6:15), to herald news (1 Samuel 13:3), at the installation of a king (1 Kings 1:34), and to call to assembly (Jeremiah 4:5).

The harp and lyre are stringed instruments, mentioned together seven times in the psalms (here and Psalms 33:2; 57:8; 71:22; 81:2; 92:3; and 108:2). These two instruments therefore stand parallel with one another and indeed are essentially the same instrument. The main difference is that one was larger (and less portable) than the other. Evidence from ancient drawings indicates curved yokes and jar-shaped sounding boxes to be features.

4a. praise him with timbrel and dancing,

The timbrel is similar to a modern tambourine, being small enough to be held in the hand. Use of this rhythm percussion instrument is associated with dances of joy several times in the Old Testament (examples: Exodus 15:20; Psalm 149:3, above), even joy that has the wrong focus (Isaiah 5:11-12). An absence of timbrels is associated with a lack of joy (Isaiah 24:8).

4b. praise him with the strings and pipe,

The strings is a collective term for instruments such as the lyre and harp already mentioned. The designation may include a rather fixed collection of instruments, much like reference to "the strings" in an orchestra refers generally to violins, violas, cellos, etc.

Pipes are first mentioned in Genesis 4:21: "Jubal . . . was the father of all who play stringed instruments and pipes." It was probably a type of wind instrument; the 1984 *NIV* translated this word "flutes."

5. praise him with the clash of cymbals, praise him with resounding cymbals.

Cymbals, in the category of percussion instruments, would be struck together to make their sound. The Hebrew behind the translation *resounding* occurs five times in the psalms (here and Psalms 27:6; 33:3; 47:5; and 89:15). The translations in those other four instances are all in terms of volume, and that is the sense here. Thus *clash* and *resounding* are parallel terms. There's no holding back with these instruments!

The following two lists reveal that of the (at least) 14 named instruments or types of instruments recorded in the Old Testament, Psalms 149 and 150 feature the most frequently mentioned.

In Psalms 149–150		Not in Psalms 149–150	
Name	Times in OT	Name	Times in OT
trumpet	74	horn	14
harp	43	flute	4
harp	27	zither	4
timbrel	22	lyre	4
stringed instruments	4	harp	3
pipe	4	pipe	3
cymbals	3	lyres	1

Note: Although English designations are repeated in some cases above, the underlying words in the original language are all different. The repeated English designations reflect uncertainty in precise translation.

> **What Do You Think?**
> What can you do personally to help your church ensure an appropriately loud worship volume?
> *Digging Deeper*
> At what point, if any, does "loud" become "too loud"? Why?

D. Who (v. 6)

6. Let everything that has breath praise the LORD. Praise the LORD.

Breath was the first sign of life. At creation the Lord breathed into the man "the breath of life" (Genesis 2:7). Encouraging *everything that has breath* to *praise the Lord* is broader than a call to people only (see Psalm 103:22).

❧ *A LOT OF CLATTER AND NOISE* ❧

One day in elementary music class, the teacher divided us into sections to teach us a round. Each section was to sing its own words. To make our task more challenging, we were singing as if we were violins, clarinets, trumpets, and drums.

When we all sang simultaneously, it was *meant* to sound like the blending of instruments in an orchestra. Instead, we got distracted by the other parts, lost our places, and frequently dissolved into laughter. It was a noisy, happy mess.

As we grow up we can lose sight of the value of outright *doing* as that effort represents good intentions—a proper spirit and mind-set. Consider the instruments named in Psalm 150. There are certainly more types there than my class's

"orchestra song" had; we actually had only one—our voices. So in the resulting joyful noise, some within hearing distance may say that the emphasis is on *noise*!

But God wants to hear it. This is not to minimize the importance of quality and giving our best to God (Matthew 5:48; compare 1 Corinthians 13:1). It is, rather, to stress our need to praise him in all contexts of life. How can you match the psalmist's enthusiasm for doing so?   —C. M. W.

Conclusion

A. Count Your Blessings

When life becomes turbulent, it is easy to forget the Lord's might and character. That happens when we drop our gaze from him to focus on the problems themselves and nonbiblical solutions to them (compare Psalm 73:1-3). But when we return from that "exile," we realize our foolishness. In the process, we find new opportunities to sing for joy to the Lord, realizing that our old songs are inadequate in light of the Lord's new blessings.

No matter our situation, we should praise the Lord. We can do so by recalling past blessings—the great things he has done. We can praise him for future blessings—things God has promised when we are in his presence for all eternity. If celebrating the Lord's greatness will not give us joy and peace during the storms of life, what will?

> **What Do You Think?**
> Which concept or imperative in today's lesson do you have the most trouble coming to grips with? Why?
> *Digging Deeper*
> How will you resolve this problem?

B. Prayer

O Lord, our God, you are great, and you are good. In all circumstances, may we ever praise you for your care for us. In Jesus' name we pray. Amen.

C. Thought to Remember

Praise the Lord—always!

INVOLVEMENT LEARNING

Enhance your lesson with NIV® Bible Student (from your curriculum supplier) and the reproducible activity page (at www.standardlesson.com or in the back of the NIV® Standard Lesson Commentary Deluxe Edition).

Into Life

Write this sentence on the board and ask for volunteers to complete it:

The most exciting game I ever attended was . . .

After several have shared, ask what these stories have in common in terms of being memorable. Would the game have been as exciting if it had been watched by only one person? What if the crowd had been absolutely silent?

After this activity, lead into Bible study by saying, "God realizes the synergy of large crowds as they raise voices in praise. As we consider Psalms 149 and 150, be looking for ways biblical praise is like and unlike the expressions of celebration in the memorable games you've described."

Alternative. Play one or more praise songs or hymns that are based on a line of Psalm 149:1-5 and/or 150 (an easy internet search). As each is playing, ask who recognizes its scriptural basis. Use this to lead into the Scripture reading, next.

Into the Word

Have today's text read aloud several times. Recruit a different student for each reading ahead of time for advance practice. (*Option.* Use a professional recording for one of these readings of Psalms 146:1-5 and 150). Ask class members to sit silently as the text is read. Challenge them to imagine God's reaction as they listen.

Distribute handouts (you prepare) with the questions *Who? / What? / Where? / When? / Why? / How?* listed down the left-hand side as designations of six rows, one each. Across the top have printed *Psalm 149:1-5 / Psalm 150* as headers for two columns, one each.

Divide the class into groups of three or four to jot entries—as far as possible based on available information—in the 12 intersections of columns and rows. (Make sure to do this yourself ahead of time as part of necessary preparation to teach.)

After several minutes, reconvene for whole-class discussion of discoveries. Focus especially on entries that differ among groups. Distinguish between responses that have a factual basis and those that are speculative. Use information from the commentary to clarify, as far as possible, both the immediate contexts of the two psalms and how they fit into the Psalter as a whole. (See also the two expected responses below.)

Into Life

Write the following on the board and ask half the class to form pairs to brainstorm ways to complete it:

It's easiest to praise God when . . .

As those pairs work, write the following on the board and ask the other half of the class to form pairs to brainstorm ways to complete it:

It's most difficult to praise God when . . .

Call the class back together for sharing of insights. Follow those by asking these questions, allowing responses to each before posing the next:

1–How much mention of the worshippers' situations is included in these two psalms? (*Expected response:* none!)

2–What does this tell us about when or whether we should praise? (*Expected response:* Praise should be our practice regardless of what's happening to or around us.)

Give each participant an index card. Challenge class members to choose one verse from today's texts to write on the card as a praise reminder for the week ahead. Allow volunteers to read the verse they've chosen and share why. *Option.* As learners depart, give each a copy of the "Praise God Anyway!" exercise from the activity page, which you can download. To encourage its completion as a take-home exercise, promise to discuss results at the outset of next week's class.

UNITED IN PRAISE

DEVOTIONAL READING: Revelation 7:9-17
BACKGROUND SCRIPTURE: Revelation 7:9-17

REVELATION 7:9-17

⁹ After this I looked, and there before me was a great multitude that no one could count, from every nation, tribe, people and language, standing before the throne and before the Lamb. They were wearing white robes and were holding palm branches in their hands. ¹⁰ And they cried out in a loud voice:

"Salvation belongs to our God,
who sits on the throne,
and to the Lamb."

¹¹ All the angels were standing around the throne and around the elders and the four living creatures. They fell down on their faces before the throne and worshiped God, ¹² saying:

"Amen!
Praise and glory
and wisdom and thanks and honor
and power and strength
be to our God for ever and ever.
Amen!"

¹³ Then one of the elders asked me, "These in white robes—who are they, and where did they come from?"

¹⁴ I answered, "Sir, you know."

And he said, "These are they who have come out of the great tribulation; they have washed their robes and made them white in the blood of the Lamb. ¹⁵ Therefore,

"they are before the throne of God
and serve him day and night in his temple;
and he who sits on the throne
will shelter them with his presence.
¹⁶ 'Never again will they hunger;
never again will they thirst.
The sun will not beat down on them,'
nor any scorching heat.
¹⁷ For the Lamb at the center of the throne
will be their shepherd;
'he will lead them to springs of living
water.'
'And God will wipe away every tear from
their eyes.'"

KEY TEXT

I answered, "Sir, you know." And he said, "These are they who have come out of the great tribulation; they have washed their robes and made them white in the blood of the Lamb. —**Revelation 7:14**

CELEBRATING GOD

Unit 3: Visions of Praise

LESSONS 10–13

LESSON AIMS

After participating in this lesson, each learner will be able to:

1. Identify one or more examples of symbolic imagery.

2. Explain the significance of those images.

3. Evaluate his or her attitude toward the diverse nature of those who will be admitted before God's throne.

LESSON OUTLINE

Introduction

A. Diverse Harmony

Omonia Church of Christ in Athens, Greece, has developed a reputation for being diverse and harmonious. Greek, Arabic, Farsi, Russian, Bulgarian, Albanian, and Filipino are frequently spoken in the church. Some in attendance don headsets to hear worship services translated.

Omonia believes their diverse worship is not limited to times of formal services. The church started a ministry to serve refugees from Syria, Afghanistan, Iraq, and Iran. Victims displaced by war, violence, and oppression experience the love of Christ because of Omonia.

Appropriately, *omonia* means "harmony" in Greek; the word appears in the Greek version of the Old Testament (the Septuagint) in Psalm 55:14, in a context of remembered (but lost) fellowship. Different Greek words are used in the New Testament to convey this concept (see Philippians 1:27; 2:2; 1 Peter 3:8). One of those words is the source of our English word *symphony* (2 Corinthians 6:15). Like the wide range of instruments in a symphony orchestra, the diverse congregation of Omonia produces a beautifully unified harmony of worship and service to God. Omonia demonstrates the future realities of Revelation 7, today's text, in the here and now.

B. Lesson Context

Some Christians believe the book of Revelation speaks only of the future. Others believe the book speaks in coded language about the people and events of the first century AD. Still others believe the book is figurative or symbolic, using vivid imagery to teach spiritual lessons. Then there's the issue of separate approaches to sections consisting of chapters 1–3, 4–19, and 20–22!

No matter the interpretive perspective, three things should be observed by careful readers. First, Revelation combines elements of ancient letters, prophetic texts, and apocalyptic literature. It is considered partially a letter because of how the book opens with a greeting (Revelation 1:4-7) and is addressed to specific churches (see chapters 2 and 3). Revelation is considered a form of prophecy

(1:3), given to John in order that he might declare the "testimony of Jesus Christ" (1:9). Revelation is also considered an apocalyptic text. During the era in which John recorded his revelation, apocalyptic texts were commonplace. This was a highly stylized type of literature written to unveil God's plan for the world, both in the past and for the future.

Apocalyptic literature often presents this plan through vivid and cryptic imagery. A proper understanding of Revelation requires recognizing the imagery and language of apocalyptic literature (compare Matthew 24:29-31; Mark 13:24-27; Luke 21:25-28).

Second, the book of Revelation is loaded with allusions to the Old Testament and assumes the audience's familiarity with their source (compare Isaiah 6:1-3; Ezekiel 1:18, 22, 26-28; and Revelation 4). Revelation rests on the shoulders of Genesis (Genesis 1:1; see Revelation 21:1), Exodus (Exodus 19:6; see Revelation 1:5-6), Daniel (Daniel 7:13; see Revelation 1:7, 13; 14:14), and even Psalms (Psalm 2:9; see Revelation 2:27; 12:5; 19:15). The fullest understanding of Revelation recognizes its roots in the Old Testament.

Third, Revelation emphasizes worshipping God. The text is filled with poetic scenes of worship (see Revelation 4:8; 5:9-13; 7:10-17; 11:15-18; 12:10-12; 15:3-4; 16:5-7; 19:1-8). Each one makes claims about who is worthy to be worshipped in Heaven and on earth. Revelation calls the people to worship "our God, who sits on the throne" and "the Lamb" (7:10, below).

Today's passage continues John's vision of Heaven. Several startling events have occurred: the glorious entry of the Lamb into the throne room (Revelation 5:6) and the introduction of a sealed scroll and its opening (5:1; 6:1-17), leading to the dramatic gathering of the servants of God (7:1-8). John then turned his attention to the great multitude of people and witnessed their worship.

I. Uncountable Crowd
(REVELATION 7:9-10)
A. Every People Group Present (v. 9)
9a. After this I looked, and there before me was a great multitude that no one could count,

God will wipe away our tears.

Visual for Lesson 10. *While discussing verse 17, point to this visual as you ask for examples of global causes of tears that God will wipe away.*

We are given the impression this *great multitude* is far bigger than the large but countable number of those from Israel's tribes that John had just witnessed (Revelation 7:4-8). John's vision is similar to Daniel's vision of a throne room, where a crowd of "ten thousand times ten thousand" stands before the "Ancient of Days" (Daniel 7:9-10). This is not a mathematical formula but a way of saying this group is uncountable.

9b. from every nation, tribe, people and language,

The nature of this vast group is explained in the four ways seen here. The cumulative effect is to show that it is universally representative of all humanity. First, it includes people from *every nation*. This is the word for a national group, a political entity. It is also the word sometimes translated "Gentiles" when referring to any nation that is not Israel (Revelation 11:2).

One's *tribe* implies sharing ancestral bloodlines, as in the tribes of Israel (example: Revelation 7:4-8). Tribes transcend national borders. For example, a person's genetic "tribe" might be Irish, but this does not mean that person lives in Ireland.

A *people* is a group bound together by cultural identity. They would share many cultural markers that might transcend national or ethnic boundaries. One such marker may be their *language*. By one estimate, there are 6,500 distinct languages on earth today. There may have been a similar number in John's day. Languages are not confined to regional or national boundaries; they cross borders and can transcend political identities (see Acts 2:5-11; Revelation 13:7).

What Do You Think?
What is the best way you can help your church stay unified in its diversity?
Digging Deeper
Considering the ideas of unity and diversity, what could happen if one is stressed over the other? Or is that even possible? Explain.

9c. standing before the throne and before the Lamb. They were wearing white robes

The previous description reflects the worldwide penetration of the gospel. Regardless of one's heritage or cultural context of origin, any person can believe and share in God's salvation. The image of *wearing white robes* means that the person is cleansed from sin (Revelation 7:14).

The message to the church in Sardis commended those who had not soiled their garments (with sin) but instead had walked with Christ in white, "for they are worthy" (Revelation 3:4-5). Further, white robes are given as a reward to the martyrs of the church, those who have maintained their faith and witness even unto death (6:9-11).

9d. and were holding palm branches in their hands.

Use of *palm branches* reflects a practice of worship that began with the Festival of Tabernacles (Leviticus 23:33-36a, 39-43). This annual observance celebrated Israel's liberation from Egypt and God's faithfulness to his people during a time of need. The people were to "take branches from luxuriant trees—from palms . . . and rejoice before the Lord your God for seven days" (23:40).

The practice of associating palm branches with an event of victorious joy continued into the time between the Old and New Testaments (see the nonbiblical 1 Maccabees 13:51 regarding an incident of 141 BC). In the New Testament, crowds waved palm branches while shouting "Hosanna" (which means "save") during Jesus' triumphal entry (see John 12:13). The multitudes in John's vision stand in worship before the Lamb, who has indeed saved them (next verse).

The wind blew pleasantly in our faces as we chugged down the Keram River, Papua New Guinea, in a 30-foot-long dugout canoe. We could hear the cheers of Waran people lining the shore. They held palm branches as we came to celebrate the completion of the New Testament in their language.

Moving through the reception, we were surrounded by palm branches. People smiled and sang as they waved them. Some branches were placed horizontally across supports, forming a decorative doorway. A missionary who had lived among the Waran said most Westerners probably don't know much about palms, but the Waran use them extensively for a variety of things. He imagined that the "palm branch worshippers" of Revelation 7 will be led by the Waran, who know palm trees intimately.

Surrounded by the waving palms, I looked forward to the joyful celebration and worship that will surround the throne of God. How does the image speak to you?   —D. G.

B. Every Voice Lifting Praise (v. 10)

10. And they cried out in a loud voice: "Salvation belongs to our God, who sits on the throne, and to the Lamb."

The multitude acknowledges that their hope of *salvation* is realized. This implies God's victory over his enemies and deliverance for his people (see Revelation 12:10; 19:1). It is not any fictitious god that is being described, only *our God*. This also emphasizes the personal nature of God. His relationship with his people is fully demonstrated. The means of this deliverance is seen also in their worship of *the Lamb* (Revelation 5:13). Christ's death and resurrection as the Lamb of God (see John 1:29) enacts God's salvation.

What Do You Think?
In what ways does today's text inspire you to help your church improve an area of worship?
Digging Deeper
What aspects of worship in today's text, if any, should you *not* attempt to push—aspects that must wait until Jesus returns? Why?

II. Worshipful Circle
(Revelation 7:11-12)
A. Acts of Worship (v. 11)

11. All the angels were standing around the throne and around the elders and the four living creatures. They fell down on their faces before the throne and worshiped God,

The inner circle *around the throne* becomes the focus again (see Revelation 4:4, 6; 5:11). Their acts of worship involve their whole bodies. As they fall to their knees, their faces touch the ground, presumably in full view of the great multitude that worships by joyously waving palms.

B. Words of Acclamation (v. 12)

12a. saying: "Amen!

Saying could imply more than words merely spoken. As the words of worship from the inner circle are spoken in unison and have the structure of an ancient hymn, it is possible that these words were meant to be chanted or recited.

Those in the inner circle of worshippers voice their worship in powerful words directed to God for eternity. Similar worship is directed to the Lamb in the throne room (see Revelation 5:11-12).

The worship described here is bracketed on both sides with *Amen*, a Greek transliteration of a Hebrew word meaning "it is true." The word's usage by the worshippers recognizes and affirms what follows next.

12b. Praise and glory and wisdom and thanks and honor and power and strength

The first word of pronouncement of those around the throne is justified because they have experienced the Lord's goodness. *Glory* carries the image of being full of light—radiant like celestial bodies (see 1 Corinthians 15:41). The glory of

HOW TO SAY IT

apocalyptic	uh-*paw*-kuh-*lip*-tik.
Gentiles	*Jen*-tiles.
Maccabees	*Mack*-uh-bees.
Sardis	*Sar*-dis.
tabernacles	*tah*-burr-*nah*-kulz.
Zechariah	*Zek*-uh-*rye*-uh.

the Lord sometimes accompanies heavenly manifestations (Luke 2:9). A characteristic of God's presence in the tabernacle or the temple was a display of his glory (Exodus 40:34; compare Revelation 15:8).

The Bible often places *wisdom* in parallel with knowledge (example: Proverbs 14:6). God has absolute knowledge. He has determined what is right and wrong. God always does the right thing, having never-failing wisdom.

When recognizing God's salvation, a response of giving *thanks* is appropriate. It is an expression of gratitude to God for his care and his provision. *Honor* offers esteem for a person, based on the person's character and acts. God is worthy of ultimate honor for his great providential works of salvation and simply because he is God.

The word *power* is used frequently throughout the book of Revelation. It is tied to God's acts of creating and sustaining the universe (Revelation 4:11) and God's rule over the entire earth (11:17). It is impossible to imagine any greater power! The all-powerful one who created the universe also provides deliverance for his people. Related to power, *strength* describes the characteristic of a very strong person. As applied to God, this may be beyond our understanding. But we can say that God's strength is inexhaustible and without limits.

> **What Do You Think?**
> What are some ways you can incorporate the seven ascriptions of this verse into your own devotional and prayer life?
> **Digging Deeper**
> Were you to do more such ascribing and less "asking for," what could be the result?

12c. Be to our God for ever and ever.

This hymn ends on an important note that calls for the seven ascriptions to be recognized *for ever and ever*. This acknowledges the eternal nature of *God*. Even our best descriptions of his nature fail to account for the eternality of God—the one without beginning or end.

12d. Amen!"

The repetition of *Amen* brings a solemn sense of affirmation to these words of worship.

III. White-Robed Witnesses

(Revelation 7:13-17)

A. Robes Washed in Blood (vv. 13-14)

13. Then one of the elders asked me, "These in white robes—who are they, and where did they come from?"

In the midst of this worshipful vision, John is approached with a question from *one of the elders.* Prophetic literature is filled with examples of questions used as a method of teaching (example: Zechariah 4:2-6). The elder's question has the effect of asking, "Do you know the who, what, where, when, why, and how of what you see?"

14. I answered, "Sir, you know." And he said, "These are they who have come out of the great tribulation; they have washed their robes and made them white in the blood of the Lamb.

Whether out of respect or because of uncertainty, John allows the elder to answer his own question. In response, the elder points to two aspects of those in white robes. Regarding their emergence from *great tribulation,* we recall that Christians experience suffering and trials of body and faith. Jesus warned his followers that trouble and persecution were to be expected (Matthew 5:10-11; John 16:33; compare 2 Timothy 3:12).

To the audience of Revelation, this tribulation could have been related to persecution at the hands of the Roman Empire. To modern readers, this could also imply a future time of widespread suffering and persecution. For both ancient and modern audiences, John's vision affirms that following Jesus might result in suffering, even to the point of martyrdom.

Second, the *robes* have not always been *white;* they are so because they have been *washed . . . in the blood of the Lamb.* What the elder describes is not some sort of illusion; dipping a dirty garment in a red liquid and pulling it out as pure white is not a magic trick of chemical properties. Rather, the drama represents Christ's atonement and our forgiveness from sin based on his sacrificial death (see Hebrews 9:28; 1 John 1:7). The blood of the Lamb triumphs over sin and Satan (see Revelation 12:9-11). It is the fulfillment of John's earlier record of the words of John the Baptist: "Look, the Lamb of God, who takes away the sin of the world" (John 1:29). These words provide hope to suffering audiences of any era.

B. Servants Protected from Need (vv. 15-16)

15a. Therefore, "they are before the throne of God and serve him day and night in his temple;

Because they are pure, clothed in white robes, the multitude stands *before the throne of God.* They *serve him* without pause. The word translated *serve* can imply an act of worship; their acts of service are, in essence, acts of worship. Their service-worship occurs continually (*day and night*). This does not imply the existence of our current constructions of time; rather, it is an indication of ever-devoted service.

This vision pictures more than future heavenly bliss; it can also picture our existence now. Acts of worship can be our acknowledgment of a holy God and our submission to him. However, sin prevents us from practicing authentic worship in its entirety. We, like the white-robed multitude of John's vision, are free to worship in holiness, in purity, in sincerity, and in truth, for our sins have been washed in the blood of the Lamb. However, this worship will not be practiced fully and totally until God's final victory, an implication of the book of Revelation as a whole.

15b. and he who sits on the throne will shelter them with his presence.

This sincere, unfettered worship has another aspect: it occurs when God *will shelter* his people. This alludes to the pitching of a tent, a dwelling place to protect from the elements, undoubtedly echoing Old Testament tabernacle imagery of God's dwelling among his people in the tabernacle (see Exodus 40). John expresses this similarly when he speaks of Christ's first coming as the Word becoming flesh and dwelling among us (John 1:14). We await the day when the people of God are not separated from their Lord and can enter an eternal "Sabbath-rest" in the presence of God (Hebrews 4:9).

16. 'Never again will they hunger; never again will they thirst. The sun will not beat down on them,' nor any scorching heat.

Physical needs are satisfied in this perfect

relationship of continual worship in God's intimate presence. No one experiences *hunger* or *thirst*. No one experiences famine or other challenging weather phenomena such as oppressive *heat*. The saints are in the glorious presence of God, with his protection and blessing.

C. Tears Taken from the Faithful (v. 17)

17. For the Lamb at the center of the throne will be their shepherd; 'he will lead them to springs of living water.' 'And God will wipe away every tear from their eyes.'"

John's vision returns to the scene of heavenly worship and the source of all hope and salvation: *the Lamb.* Throughout John's writings, he presents Jesus as a good shepherd (see John 10:11-18; 21:15-17). Now John presents the good *shepherd* as the Lamb, leading his followers *to springs of living water.*

Undoubtedly John envisions more than the satiation of physical thirst. The Lamb will lead to "water welling up to eternal life" (John 4:14). In addition to providing eternal refreshment, the Lamb brings eternal peace and comfort, removing sorrow by wiping *every tear from their eyes.*

> **What Do You Think?**
> In what way can you be Jesus' hands and feet in comforting others until he returns?
>
> *Digging Deeper*
> In what situations will it be better for you to work individually in this regard rather than with a group? Why?

❧ *Every Tear* ❧

"George is in the hospital. He had a stroke."

The news hit me in the gut. We had supported one another, especially through our time serving as missionaries in Africa. It seemed like everyone suffered from war, famine, and disease. I remembered staying with a member of George's congregation, who revealed that she had lost a child decades before. Hearing of this, George reacted, with tears in his eyes, "There's so much hurt in this world."

We all shed tears. As the health of our loved ones fail, and as we face our own mortality, we all yearn for the day when God himself will wipe every tear from our eyes. Or do we?   —D. G.

Conclusion

A. Washed in the Blood

Suffering was no stranger to American poet Fanny Crosby (1820–1915). Blind since infancy, she undoubtedly experienced many trials and challenges. In spite of all those, she was able to proclaim, "Blessed assurance, Jesus is mine . . . Born of his Spirit, washed in his blood." A prolific writer of more than 8,000 songs, this is just one of Crosby's compositions that speak of Jesus' blood. In the midst of her suffering, Crosby was yet able to praise and worship God for salvation available through the blood of the Lamb.

Revelation 7 is a high point in the Bible concerning worship and praise. This passage is timely for all audiences. It acknowledges that although suffering occurs, confident hope is always called for because of the salvation bought and brought by the blood of the Lamb, Jesus. In times of joy or suffering, that fact should unite us in praise and worship. May we be a people who live in hope as we await the day when we will hunger and thirst no more, the day of no more tears. Until that day, may our lives be marked with praise and worship to the God who sits on his heavenly throne and to the Lamb who brings salvation.

> **What Do You Think?**
> Which concept or imperative in today's lesson do you have the most trouble coming to grips with? Why?
>
> *Digging Deeper*
> How will you resolve this problem?

B. Prayer

Dear God, may we ever offer praise and thanksgiving for your glory, wisdom, honor, power, and strength. In Jesus' name we pray. Amen.

C. Thought to Remember

Salvation comes through
the blood of the Lamb!

INVOLVEMENT LEARNING

Enhance your lesson with NIV® *Bible Student (from your curriculum supplier) and the reproducible activity page (at www.standardlesson.com or in the back of the* NIV® *Standard Lesson Commentary Deluxe Edition).*

Into the Lesson

Post four signs far apart in your learning space, one each reading *0%, 25%, 75%,* and *100%.* Ask class members to stand nearest to the sign that indicates the percentage of their typical week spent with people significantly different from themselves. Explain that such differences include racial, socioeconomic, and cultural aspects. After learners are so assembled, ask simply, "Why is this question important?"

After the discussion runs its course with no response by you, lead into Bible study by saying, "Someday all these differences will no longer cause divisions. Let's see how that will happen."

Into the Word

Open with the question, "What do you know about the book of Revelation?" Jot responses on the board. Use the Lesson Context as a basis to probe deeper when necessary to engage critical thinking skills. Then ask a volunteer to read today's text aloud, slowly. As class members listen, they should each raise a hand every time they hear something that encourages or excites them.

Divide the class into study pairs or triads. If possible have at least seven such groups. (If not possible, one or more groups will consider more than one of the topics in the following activities.)

Assign one of the following seven topics to each group: *nations, tribes, people, tongues, white robes, palms, throne.* Give all groups the same instructions: find notes in their study Bibles or online commentaries to explain the significance of the assigned term. After five minutes, let groups report; fill in any gaps in their explanations with results of your own study.

Before class prepare seven very large flashcards, each containing one of these seven words: *praise / glory / wisdom / thanks / honor / power / strength.* Shuffle the cards and distribute them randomly to seven students, one each. Have them stand in front of the class with their cards clearly visible. Ask the rest of the class, with Bibles closed, to call out instructions regarding the correct order of the words as used in Revelation 7:12 to praise God.

When the correct order occurs, ask students to return to their pairs or triads to research the significance of each word. Assign a different word to each group. After five minutes, let class members share, and, as before, you should be ready to fill in any gaps with information from your study.

Distribute handouts (you prepare) featuring two columns. Head the columns this way:

| *What Those in White Robes Received* | *What Each Blessing Might Mean* |

Ask students to work in their groups to make a list under each heading. Again, after four or five minutes, call for answers in whole-class discussion.

Option 1. Extend the Into the Word study by distributing copies of the "Power and Authority" exercise from the activity page, which you can download. Have groups complete it as indicated to contribute to ensuing whole-class discussion.

Option 2. Distribute copies of the "Nothing but the Blood" exercise from the activity page for one minute of individual work. Award a token prize to the first to finish correctly.

Into Life

Draw this continuum on the board:

Frantic---Troubled---Neutral---Positive---Ecstatic

Return to the differences you mentioned in the first activity. Distribute slips of paper and ask class members to write on them anonymously the word from the continuum that best describes how they think they will feel when being with people of all those differences before God's throne. Collect the slips and read them back to the class. Close with a prayer that is appropriate both to the nature of the lesson and what learners wrote on the slips.

GOD OF POWER

DEVOTIONAL READING: Revelation 11:11-19
BACKGROUND SCRIPTURE: Revelation 11

REVELATION 11:15-19

¹⁵ The seventh angel sounded his trumpet, and there were loud voices in heaven, which said:

"The kingdom of the world has become
the kingdom of our Lord and of his
Messiah,
and he will reign for ever and ever."

¹⁶ And the twenty-four elders, who were seated on their thrones before God, fell on their faces and worshiped God, ¹⁷ saying:

"We give thanks to you, Lord God
Almighty,
the One who is and who was,
because you have taken your great power
and have begun to reign.
¹⁸ The nations were angry,
and your wrath has come.
The time has come for judging the dead,
and for rewarding your servants the
prophets
and your people who revere your name,
both great and small—
and for destroying those who destroy the
earth."

¹⁹ Then God's temple in heaven was opened, and within his temple was seen the ark of his covenant. And there came flashes of lightning, rumblings, peals of thunder, an earthquake and a severe hailstorm.

KEY TEXT

The seventh angel sounded his trumpet, and there were loud voices in heaven, which said: "The kingdom of the world has become the kingdom of our Lord and of his Messiah, and he will reign for ever and ever."
—**Revelation 11:15**

Photo © Getty Images

CELEBRATING GOD

Unit 3: Visions of Praise

LESSONS 10–13

LESSON AIMS

After participating in this lesson, each learner will be able to:

1. Identify the purpose of the heavenly scene.

2. Relate a biblical perspective on the meaning of eternity.

3. Identify and correct a habit in light of the future described in Revelation.

LESSON OUTLINE

Introduction
  A. Hallelujah Chorus
  B. Lesson Context
I. Declaration of Truth (Revelation 11:15)
  A. Seventh Angel (v. 15a)
  B. Loud Voices (v. 15b)
II. Worship of God (Revelation 11:16-18)
  A. Position of Elders (v. 16)
  B. Recognition of Power (v. 17)
    The Audience of Our Worship
  C. Message of Judgment (v. 18)
III. Opening of Temple (Revelation 11:19)
  A. Contents (v. 19a)
  B. Weather (v. 19b)
    The Greatest Grand Opening
Conclusion
  A. Eternal Worship
  B. Prayer
  C. Thought to Remember

Introduction

A. Hallelujah Chorus

The Introduction for lesson 9 mentioned the "Hallelujah Chorus" as sung by a flash mob. That's intriguing in and of itself, but digging into the nature of the actual composition reveals some hidden treasures.

The "Hallelujah Chorus" is part of a much larger musical composition—an oratorio—titled *The Messiah,* by G. F. Händel (1685–1759). The composition as a whole falls into three main parts, which are further subdivided into some 16 scenes and 53 movements, depending on which arrangement is in view. A full performance can easily exceed two hours' duration—something quite foreign to the short attention spans of twenty-first century culture!

By one count, the oratorio includes some 60 references to Scripture, depending on how duplicates are counted. This fact should intrigue the Christian and make *The Messiah* worthy of devotional consideration. Among the Scripture references are Revelation 5:12-13; 11:15; and 19:6, 16. The "Hallelujah Chorus" is the movement that draws on the latter two—passages under consideration in this week's lesson and next's, respectively.

B. Lesson Context

Revelation has been traditionally understood to have been received by the churches in Asia Minor (modern-day Turkey) during the last decade of the first century AD. This likely dates its reception during the reign of the Roman Emperor Domitian (reigned AD 81–96). While scholars differ as to whether he persecuted Christians, it is widely accepted that one of his predecessors, Nero (reigned AD 54–68), instituted vast persecution of Christians across the empire. The audience of the apostle John (author of the book of Revelation) would have been familiar with such persecutions.

The key to understanding Revelation lies in recognizing the type of literature it is, known as "apocalyptic"; this type of writing can be found in other parts of Scripture (see the Lesson Context of lesson 10; compare and contrast Isaiah 13:10;

34:4; Daniel 8:9-10; Matthew 24:29-31; Mark 13:24-27; and Luke 21:25-28).

Apocalyptic literature features unveiling of a big-picture reality by a heavenly being (God or angels) to a human recipient. The reality that is revealed includes elements of both time (dealing with end-time salvation and judgment) and space (the reality of another, supernatural world).

In some instances, apocalyptic literature repeats a story several times with different details but the same ending. For example, the imagery of seals, trumpets, and bowls in Revelation depicts God's righteous judgment on rebellious and sinful earth. The final act in each series is accompanied by extraordinary weather phenomena that culminates in the worship of God for his righteous acts.

The central part of Revelation concerns three sets of seven events initiated in Heaven: the opening of seals (Revelation 6:1-17; 8:1-5), the sounding of trumpets (8:6-9), and the pouring out of bowls of judgment (16:1-21). The results on earth are cataclysmic. Each set of events ends with a time of worship and adoration. Today's lesson details the climax of the second of these three sets of events.

The immediate context for today's passage is that of seven angels who were ready to sound seven trumpets (Revelation 8:6). The results of the first four of the seven soundings find parallels with the 10 plagues poured out on Egypt (see Exodus 7:14–11:10).

- The first signals a bloody, fiery hailstorm that destroys one-third of the earth (Revelation 8:7).
- The second leads to something like the appearance of a burning mountain's being hurled into the sea; the sea turns to blood; sea creatures are killed; ships are destroyed (8:8-9).
- The third calls forth a fiery star from the heavens that pollutes many of the freshwater rivers and brings death (8:10-11).
- The fourth strikes parts of each of the great lights—the sun, moon, and stars (8:12).
- The fifth signals the opening of the Abyss, unleashing a hoard of locusts on humankind in the process (9:1-5).
- The sixth releases four mighty angels and their armies to kill one-third of sinful humanity (9:13-16).

These judgments, however intense, fail to stop the idolatry and sexual immorality in the world (see Revelation 9:20-21). Today's text focuses on the seventh and final angel.

I. Declaration of Truth
(REVELATION 11:15)
A. Seventh Angel (v. 15a)

15a. The seventh angel sounded his trumpet,

Various forms of the number seven occur hundreds of times in the Bible. Its occurrences often signal completeness (examples: Genesis 2:2; 2 Kings 5:10; Revelation 15:1, 8). Trumpets are blown at accessions of kings to their thrones (example: 1 Kings 1:34-41). The two concepts seem to combine here (see next).

B. Loud Voices (v. 15b)

15b. and there were loud voices in heaven, which said: "The kingdom of the world has become the kingdom of our Lord and of his Messiah, and he will reign for ever and ever."

Following, or perhaps accompanying, the sound of the trumpet are unidentified heavenly *voices* making the grand pronouncement we see here. Loudness in this book characterizes worship (see Revelation 5:12; 7:10). Should not God's victory be declared as loudly as possible?

What John saw speaks to the hope that the people of God have so longed to see: God has become the king over the whole earth. Old Testament prophets looked forward to a day when "the God of heaven" would "set up a kingdom that will never be destroyed . . . and it will itself endure forever" (Daniel 2:44).

In John's vision, the day when "the Lord will be king over the whole earth" (Zechariah 14:9) was foreseen as certain. The sin that separated the human realm from the heavenly realm will no longer be an obstacle. John later pictured this kingdom as the unified city of New Jerusalem; those who continue to sin are not allowed to enter the city (see Revelation 22:14-15).

The finality of this collective kingdom becomes clear as the voices' proclaim that God *will reign for ever and ever.* Whereas *the kingdom of the world* is temporary and filled with sin, the reign of God will be eternal, featuring everlasting life for the faithful.

God's eternal reign is shared with the Lord's *Messiah*, his Christ; these are Hebrew and Greek words that mean the same thing: "anointed one." As the heavenly chorus praises the one who sits on the throne and the Lamb (Revelation 7:10; see lesson 10), so do the heavenly voices here.

> **What Do You Think?**
>   What will you do the next time an expectation from an earthly kingdom contradicts an expectation of the heavenly kingdom?
>
> *Digging Deeper*
>   How do Mark 12:17; Acts 4:18-20; 5:29; Romans 13:1-7; and 1 Peter 2:13-17 help categorize your response?

II. Worship of God
(Revelation 11:16-18)
A. Position of Elders (v. 16)

16. And the twenty-four elders, who were seated on their thrones before God, fell on their faces and worshiped God,

A previous scene of worship reappears as *the twenty-four elders* fall *on their faces* (compare Revelation 4:10; 5:8, 14; 7:11; 19:4). More of what this implies is seen next.

> **What Do You Think?**
>   What are some ways you can "fall on your face" before God in a spiritual sense several times daily?
>
> *Digging Deeper*
>   What has to happen for this to be a priority?

B. Recognition of Power (v. 17)

17a. saying: "We give thanks to you, Lord God Almighty,

In their dramatic posture of worship and submission, the elders begin their *thanks* by addressing God in a certain way, using the respectful and reverential title *Lord God Almighty*. Each aspect of the designation bears significance; their collective effect is greater still.

The word translated *Lord* in and of itself can imply only a measure of respect, as with "sir" (examples: Matthew 13:27; 27:63). When combined with *God Almighty*, however, things change. The full, three-word use of this designation is found in the New Testament only in Revelation 4:8; 11:17; 15:3; 16:7; 19:6 (see lesson 12); and 21:22. It serves to relay the expansive power of God in the world.

The ancient Greek version of the Old Testament is the source of this phrase, primarily the book of Amos (10 times). God alone is almighty! John's use of this title reflected his confidence that God's redemptive plan would come to fruition, even in the midst of tribulation and suffering.

17b. the One who is and who was,

The elders describe God's eternal nature. This same description is used by the author himself, the apostle John, in Revelation 1:4; by the Lord God in 1:8; and by the four living creatures in 4:8. This description reflects and expands on God's self-designation "I AM" of Exodus 3:14 (compare John 8:58). As the description speaks of God's eternal, unchangeable nature it implies his sovereignty.

17c. because you have taken your great power and have begun to reign.

The elders' reasoning for giving thanks in Revelation 11:17a above is now stated. God's *power* is shown in its totality and fullness as his overthrow of evil results in an uncontested reign. God, by his actions, has answered the age-old question, "How long, Sovereign Lord?" (Revelation 6:10; see also Isaiah 6:11; Habakkuk 1:2). This part of John's prophetic vision will be the final move of God as he establishes "a new heaven and a new earth" (see Revelation 21; compare Isaiah 65:17; 2 Peter 3:13).

❧ THE AUDIENCE OF OUR WORSHIP ❧

I once sat in a church meeting where the attendees discussed improving the worship service. Different individuals shared what they wanted to add or remove from the service order. Some suggestions contradicted others. For example, one person wanted to sing more hymns, while another wanted more contemporary songs. A debate ensued over music styles.

I came to the conclusion that the biggest improvement we needed to make was to change our perspective on the audience of worship. We talked as if *we* were the recipients of the worship experience and that worship should reflect our personal preferences and sensibilities.

We were wrong. Instead, *God* should be at the center of our worship. And we should ask ourselves whether God is pleased with our worship!

John's vision of corporate worship in Heaven provides perspective. The elders surrounding the throne of God direct their full attention and acts of worship to him. How might we need to adjust our focus so that our worship mirrors that which takes place in Heaven?   —L. H.-P.

> **What Do You Think?**
> Which terms in verse 17 inspire you to address or think of God differently from now on? Why?
> *Digging Deeper*
> What further research should you do regarding this?

C. Message of Judgment (v. 18)

18a. The nations were angry, and your wrath has come.

The elders continue their pronouncement as they now describe reactions to God's exercise of his power. The word translated *nations* occurs some two dozen times in this book—sometimes in a positive sense (example: Revelation 5:9) and sometimes in a negative sense, as here. Nations frequently jostle against one another (Psalm 2:1), and now their anger is a result of having to face God's *wrath* (see Revelation 6:15-17). His wrath poured out on them does not result in repentance —quite the opposite! The "great day of the Lord" (Zephaniah 1:14), long prophesied, is at hand.

18b. The time has come for judging the dead,

The time of *judging the dead* is when all who have lived and died throughout history will be resurrected to face judgment (see Daniel 12:2). A fuller account of this brief description of the final judgment is found in Revelation 20:12-13.

18c. and for rewarding your servants the prophets

The reward to be given to the righteous also finds expression in Matthew 5:12; 16:27; 1 Corin-

thians 3:10-15; 2 John 8; Revelation 22:12; and elsewhere.

One of two categories to be rewarded is God's *servants the prophets* (compare Revelation 10:7). This can include those servants of God who spoke about the future as well as those servants who preached the message of God (compare Psalm 40:9; Acts 8:5; 1 Corinthians 9:16-18; etc.). Prophets can be both *fore*tellers and *forth*tellers. In both cases, the one proclaiming God's truth calls people to a faithful relationship with the Lord. The heart of this relationship is forsaking all other "gods" in remaining loyal to him alone (compare Galatians 4:8). Some in this group and the next experience martyrdom (Revelation 16:6; 18:24).

18d. and your people who revere your name, both great and small—

The second group to be rewarded are the *people* of God *who revere* God's *name*. They, like the prophets, were faithful—some even to the point of martyrdom in the service of the Lord. Some older translations call these reverential individuals "saints," drawing attention to the holiness of the body of Christ.

As if to stress the inclusive nature, *both great and small* are in view. Although 1 Corinthians 3:10-15 speaks of differing levels of reward, we should not separate these groups too much. Both are faithful to God, and they will be rewarded as such (see also Revelation 19:5).

18e. and for destroying those who destroy the earth."

The elders end their utterances by returning to the imagery of the angry mob, defeated and punished. Through a poetic use of parallelism, the elders describe God's visiting on *those who destroy the earth* the same thing in return.

We should be careful not to read twenty-first century concerns back into this statement. In this text, destroying the earth does not refer to environmental devastation, no matter how sinful such actions might be. The idea is in a broad context of biblical times. Jeremiah 51:25 uses the same wording in speaking of Babylon (compare 50:23). Sometimes Babylon is used figuratively (1 Peter 5:13; Revelation 14:8; 16:19; 17:5), so it may refer to evil entities in general.

The type of destruction that awaits those who destroy the earth is not specified here. To understand what that involves, one can turn to Matthew 5:22; 10:28; 13:41-42; 25:41; Luke 3:17; Revelation 19:20-21; 20:10, 15; etc. The bottom line is that the fulfillment of God's kingdom brings eternal retribution to those who oppose the people and purpose of God (see 2 Thessalonians 1:5-10).

> **What Do You Think?**
> Which should be your greater witness: expectation of Heaven or fear of judgment? Why?
> *Digging Deeper*
> Should your answer be the same for all Christians, or is it an individual thing? Why?

III. Opening of Temple
(REVELATION 11:19)
A. Contents (v. 19a)

19a. Then God's temple in heaven was opened, and within his temple was seen the ark of his covenant.

The vision expands to reveal the *temple*, which is the large sanctuary of *God* in *heaven* and the center of worship there (see also Revelation 3:12; 7:15; 15:5-8; 21:22). When it *opened*, John glanced into the innermost part of the heavenly temple and caught a glimpse of the greatest treasure of the temple: God's *ark of his covenant.*

For Israel, the ark was more than an ornate box containing various historical items (see Exodus 25:10-22). It symbolized God's presence with his people and his covenant mercy.

The ark was topped with a statuary representation of "two cherubim" with outstretched wings, forming the "atonement cover" (Hebrews 9:5), where God's presence could rule in mercy and covenant faithfulness. It was reserved for the Lord God alone and symbolized his presence with his people.

Instead of being seen only by the high priest once a year (Hebrews 9:7), the ark in Heaven fulfills its ultimate purpose. In this heavenly temple, God will rule his people, and his presence will be with them permanently (Revelation 21:3).

B. Weather (v. 19b)

19b. And there came flashes of lightning, rumblings, peals of thunder, an earthquake and a severe hailstorm.

The opening of the temple is accompanied by severe phenomena. As with the breaking of the seventh seal, there is *lightning, . . . thunder*, and *an earthquake* (see Revelation 8:5; compare 4:5).

Such imagery is characteristic of apocalyptic literature. It is intended to catch the reader's attention, perhaps to show the seriousness of God's judgment. Indeed, *a severe hailstorm* is often associated with such judgment (Exodus 9:22-27; Job 38:22-23; Psalm 78:48; Isaiah 28:17; Haggai 2:17; Revelation 8:7).

Additionally, such imagery would draw the audience to compare John's revelation with God's dramatic revelation to Moses (see Exodus 19:16-19). The God who revealed himself to Moses will, someday, reveal himself to all people as the judge and the one worthy of worship.

❧ *THE GREATEST GRAND OPENING* ❧

Several years ago, my father and uncle opened a construction business together. They had both been in the industry for years, although separately. In recent years, they started doing jobs together and landing increasingly larger contracts. Because business was going well, they decided to formalize their partnership.

Consequently, they became a registered company, hired employees, and worked out of my father's home. After a year in that temporary space, they bought a building and moved their operation there.

HOW TO SAY IT

apocalyptic	uh-*paw*-kuh-*lip*-tik.
cherubim	*chair*-uh-bim.
Domitian	Duh-*mish*-un.
Habakkuk	Huh-*back*-kuk.
Isaiah	Eye-*zay*-uh.
Jerusalem	Juh-*roo*-suh-lem.
Messiah	Meh-*sigh*-uh.
Nero	*Nee*-row.
Zephaniah	Zef-uh-*nye*-uh.

To celebrate the milestone, my dad and uncle planned a grand opening. They made renovations, giving the building a fresh, modern look. They invited city officials, family, friends, business associates, and clients. I watched my dad pour so much energy, time, and money into planning the event; he wanted it to be perfect.

God himself has been working on the greatest grand opening ever: that of the new heaven and earth. Invitations are going out all over the world. You already have yours: it's the gospel of Jesus. Presumably, you have accepted. Will you make sure others do so as well?   —L. H.-P.

Conclusion

A. Eternal Worship

A certain church closed its doors after 30 years of ministry. Hundreds once worshipped there each week. But in recent years, that number had dwindled to about 30.

Maintaining the property had become too burdensome. The decision to close this church and sell the property was difficult but necessary. The discussions surrounding the decision were very emotional. Church members had fond memories of weddings, baptisms, and other special moments shared in that building.

Although the congregants decided to close the doors of its place of worship, they leaned into discerning how best to continue to worship God and serve his people. Closing the church building did not mean that worship would cease. Instead, the group began to worship in local parks and with other congregations. They used the money from the sale of the church property to fund mission opportunities around the city. The people's worship and service continued . . . and that's the main thing.

Israel's center of worship, the temple, had been destroyed about 25 years before John wrote Revelation. But some 40 years before that destruction, the Jerusalem temple's importance had been superseded by Jesus' death and resurrection (Matthew 27:50-51; Hebrews 8:1–10:22). That resulted in a new understanding of "temple" (see 1 Corinthians 3:16-17; 6:19; 2 Corinthians 6:16; Ephe-

He reigns forever and ever.

Visual for Lesson 11. *Have this visual displayed prominently as a backdrop as you pose the discussion question associated with Revelation 11:15b.*

sians 2:21). John's vision saw an even better reality to come—that of God's heavenly temple where worship continues into eternity.

For the original audience that had experienced persecution, perhaps even being unable to worship communally, how encouraging this coming reality must have been! Today's passage invites us to anticipate a future where the kingdom of God is fully established everywhere, where injustice no longer prevails, and where we worship God for eternity.

> *What Do You Think?*
> Which concept or imperative in today's lesson do you have the most trouble coming to grips with? Why?
> *Digging Deeper*
> How will you resolve this problem?

B. Prayer

Lord, may we remember that you are everlasting and unchanging! You are worthy to receive every honor and praise. May we, like those in the book of Revelation, celebrate your reign forever and ever with an eternal "Hallelujah!" In Jesus' name we pray. Amen.

C. Thought to Remember

There is a future
when God's reign in Heaven
will join his reign on earth.

INVOLVEMENT LEARNING

Enhance your lesson with NIV® Bible Student (from your curriculum supplier) and the reproducible activity page (at www.standardlesson.com or in the back of the NIV® Standard Lesson Commentary Deluxe Edition).

Into the Lesson

Divide the class into groups of four and ask them to use smartphones to find headlines that could lead some to believe the world is out of control. After five or six minutes, ask a volunteer from each group to share the single most distressing headline they found. Discuss how people can function when bad news dominates.

Lead into Bible study by saying, "As we work through today's lesson, be thinking about how it can help you cope with our difficult world and how it could help you encourage someone else to cope as well."

Into the Word

Use the Lesson Context to prepare a brief lecture to establish the background for this week's Scripture study. Then distribute handouts (you prepare) that all feature the following four questions. Leave space below each one for writing.

What does Revelation 11:15-19 indicate about . . .
    God's power?
    God's justice?
    God's followers?
    God's sovereignty?

Send students back to their groups of four to complete this activity. (*Options.* All the groups can look for all four points, or you may assign a different one to each of the groups.) After several minutes, ask groups to report to the class. For discussion, focus especially where groups have different discoveries.

Option 1. Before doing the preceding activity, have learners gain a broader perspective on the book of Revelation by completing the "The Perfect Number" exercise from the activity page, which you can download. This is individual work; time limit of one minute. Give a token gift featuring the numeral *7* to learners who get all 14 correct answers.

Option 2. Follow either of the preceding two exercises by distributing copies of the "How Long?" exercise from the activity page. Assign to the same groups of four to prepare their conclusions for whole-class discussion.

Into Life

Distribute on handouts (you prepare) the following case studies. (*Options.* You can put all case studies on every handout or just one study per handout.) Send participants back to their groups to discuss how to respond to these statements, applying the truths of today's text.

- "Christianity is an interesting religion, like many other religions. Sincere followers of every religion will experience the same thing after death."
- "This world is such a mess—so much suffering, so much injustice, so much evil. I have trouble believing that a good God is in control."
- "I understand how the God of love works in the New Testament. But I don't see how that matches the descriptions of the God of wrath in the Old Testament."

Give the groups several minutes to discuss their case study (or studies) before reconvening for whole-class discussion. As they share, be sure to press to see how today's text speaks to each of the case studies.

Write the following words on the board:

Hopeful / Anxious / Happy / Joyful / [other]

Allow volunteers to share which word best describes their typical outlook and why. Encourage class members to consider specific ways their lives or views on life should change in light of the future described in the book of Revelation.

Option. Distribute copies of the "Today and Tomorrow" exercise from the activity page as a take-home project. To encourage completion, promise to discuss results at the beginning of next week's class.

MARRIAGE OF THE LAMB

DEVOTIONAL READING: Revelation 19:1-8
BACKGROUND SCRIPTURE: Revelation 19

REVELATION 19:1-8

¹ After this I heard what sounded like the roar of a great multitude in heaven shouting:

"Hallelujah!
Salvation and glory and power belong to
    our God,
²   for true and just are his judgments.
He has condemned the great prostitute
    who corrupted the earth by her
    adulteries.
He has avenged on her the blood of his
    servants."

³ And again they shouted:

"Hallelujah!
The smoke from her goes up for ever and
    ever."

⁴ The twenty-four elders and the four living creatures fell down and worshiped God, who was seated on the throne. And they cried:

"Amen, Hallelujah!"

⁵ Then a voice came from the throne, saying:

"Praise our God,
    all you his servants,
you who fear him,
    both great and small!"

⁶ Then I heard what sounded like a great multitude, like the roar of rushing waters and like loud peals of thunder, shouting:

"Hallelujah!
    For our Lord God Almighty reigns.
⁷ Let us rejoice and be glad
    and give him glory!
For the wedding of the Lamb has come,
    and his bride has made herself ready.
⁸ Fine linen, bright and clean,
    was given her to wear."

(Fine linen stands for the righteous acts of God's holy people.)

KEY TEXT

Let us rejoice and be glad and give him glory! For the wedding of the Lamb has come, and his bride has made herself ready. —**Revelation 19:7**

Photo © Getty Images

97

CELEBRATING GOD

Unit 3: Visions of Praise

LESSONS 10–13

LESSON AIMS

After participating in this lesson, each learner will be able to:

1. Identify the "bride of Christ."

2. Relate the word *hallelujah* to its Old Testament background.

3. Suggest one way to help his or her church overcome one unbride-like tendency.

LESSON OUTLINE

Introduction

A. Evidence and Justice

A few years ago, a popular television channel took the nation by storm when it released a "true crime" documentary. The documentary centered on a murder in a small midwestern town and the investigation that followed. The investigation resulted in what seemed to be the framing of an innocent man. The documentary pointed out how clues were overlooked, evidence planted, and the investigation otherwise mishandled. The man was convicted of the crime, and most who viewed the documentary came away with the impression that the wrong man had been convicted—a miscarriage of justice.

However, more evidence came to light many months after the documentary aired. That evidence showed that, in actuality, it was the *documentary* that was flawed, and justice *had* been served. It's a scary thought that our imperfect systems of justice can convict the innocent and acquit the guilty. Such error is impossible, however, when it comes to God. He is always just, acting in truth and righteousness. He stays true to his character, and we can be assured that he will always do what he says he will do. We can be sure that right will ultimately win out over wrong!

These facts are stressed repeatedly in the book of Revelation's figurative, apocalyptic language.

B. Lesson Context

A major figurative image throughout the book of Revelation is that of "Babylon" (see Revelation 14:8; 16:19; 17:5; 18:2, 10, 21; compare 1 Peter 5:13). John uses the image of Babylon to picture forces that oppose the will of God and oppose his people. We should note at the outset that the word *figurative* does not mean "not real" or "fictional"; rather, it means to express one thing in terms of another (examples: Matthew 16:5-21; John 16:25-30).

And so it is with the word *Babylon*. The actual city of ancient Babylon, so powerful during the sixth century BC, was a zero on the world stage of the first century AD. Apocalyptic literature (see Lesson Contexts of lessons 10 and 11) frequently uses vivid images to make a point, and the image of Babylon does just that. In John's vision, Babylon symbolizes worldly powers that oppose God and his people.

Some scholars propose that, for John's audience, Babylon was a code word for the city of Rome (compare 1 Peter 5:13). Both Rome and Babylon oppressed the people of God and opposed God's rule. Centuries before the time of John, the Babylonians (Chaldeans) had been God's instrument in punishing Judah (Jeremiah 40:1-3; Habakkuk 1:1-11; etc.). But the Babylonians went too far and ended up as objects of God's wrath in turn (Jeremiah 50; Habakkuk 2:6-17). Babylon experienced divine wrath for opposing God in both word and deed.

Similarly, the Roman Empire was insatiable in its conquests as it enslaved peoples across the Mediterranean world of the first century AD. Palestine had begun to experience Roman might in 63 BC, when Pompey besieged Jerusalem. The Jewish revolt of AD 66–70 resulted in the sacking of Jerusalem and the destruction of its temple. John wrote the book of Revelation some 25 years afterward.

Prior to today's passage, Revelation 18 sketches a lengthy celebration of the downfall of Babylon, rehearsing charges against it. That prophetic text guarantees, by extension, the ultimate downfall of all kingdoms and entities that oppose God. Today's passage takes us to what happens after the collapse of those foolish opponents.

I. Heaven's People
(REVELATION 19:1-3)
A. Praise to the Great God (v. 1)
1a. After this I heard what sounded like the roar of a great multitude in heaven shouting:

The phrase *after this* refers to the announcement of the judgment and destruction of Babylon (see Lesson Context regarding Revelation 18:2, 10, 21). *The roar of a great multitude* speaking in unison reminds us of the great crowds of the redeemed in previous visions of the throne room *in heaven* (Revelation 7:9; the same phrase [in Greek] is repeated in 19:6, below).

1b. "Hallelujah!

This word means "Praise God!" For further insight on this term, see commentary on Psalm 149:1a in lesson 9. In the entire New Testament, this word occurs only four times, and only in Revelation 19. It stresses the text's deep concern with proper worship of God (compare Revelation 19:3, 4, and [below] 6).

1c. Salvation and glory and power belong to our God,

What comes next is a now-familiar litany of divine action (*salvation;* see also Revelation 7:10; 12:10) and attributes (*glory and power;* see also 4:9-11; 5:12-13; 7:11-12).

This might serve as something of a model for our own prayer practices, either alone or in corporate worship. We too can praise God for his attributes and how he works out our salvation. He deserves all praise for all these and more.

> *What Do You Think?*
> What lifestyle changes might result from your focusing on these descriptions of God regularly in prayer?
> *Digging Deeper*
> What are some ways you can get and maintain momentum in this regard?

B. Honor to the Great Judge (v. 2)
2a. for true and just are his judgments. He has condemned the great prostitute who corrupted the earth by her adulteries.

The voice of the great chorus continues, focusing on God's victory over *the great prostitute* (Babylon) as stated in Revelation 18 (see the Lesson Context). *His judgments* on her have been *true and just*—as all have ever been and ever will be (see Psalm 119:160).

One of Babylon's two great sins is that she *corrupted the earth by her adulteries* (see also Revelation 17:2, 4; 18:3). This vivid figure of speech, as used by the prophets, describes idolatry (see Jeremiah 3:6-9; Ezekiel 23:36-37; etc.). This corrosive influence had affected "all the nations" (Revelation 14:8). John's original audience would have seen the connection to the Roman Empire.

2b. He has avenged on her the blood of his servants.”

This is the second of Babylon's two great sins: persecuting God's *servants* to the point of death. The question in Revelation 6:10—"How long, Sovereign Lord, holy and true, until you judge . . . and avenge our blood?"—has been put to rest (compare Psalms 13:1; 89:46).

If we remain faithful to God, then he will save us for all eternity. The multitudes of Heaven see the destruction of "the great prostitute" for what it really is: a magnification of the power of the God who is faithful to keep his promises to those who are faithful to him.

> *What Do You Think?*
> As you examine the content of your prayers in terms of *who God is* (his nature) and *what God does* (his works), what changes do you need to make?
> *Digging Deeper*
> Thinking back to lesson 9, how does Psalm 150:2 help frame your answer?

C. Justice for All Eternity (v. 3)

3. And again they shouted: "Hallelujah! The smoke from her goes up for ever and ever.”

The great crowd of heavenly voices cries out with the second of four occurrences of *hallelujah*. John uses this repetition to bring home the point: God is truly victorious and thus truly worthy of our praise! The crowd's desire for the wicked city's *smoke* to continue rising *up for ever and ever* acknowledges that *her* destruction is not temporary. It is permanent and final.

Although the words *for ever* are enough to assure that this punishment is everlasting, the extra *and ever* cements the certainty. The permanence of this judgment is ironclad. This judgment parallels the eternal reign of God and the eternal nature of his kingdom (see Revelation 11:15).

John's vision echoes similar language from the prophet Isaiah, where God's judgment on the land is described as "burning" and where "its smoke will rise forever" (Isaiah 34:9-10; compare Revelation 14:11).

II. The Throne
(Revelation 19:4-5)
A. Worship (v. 4)

4. The twenty-four elders and the four living creatures fell down and worshiped God, who was seated on the throne. And they cried: "Amen, Hallelujah!”

A second declaration of worship comes, this time from *the twenty-four elders* (see Revelation 4:10; 5:8, 14; 11:16). Together with *the four living creatures* (see 4:6-8; 5:6, 14; 7:11; 14:3), they surround God's *throne* as the inner circle of those in the presence of the Almighty.

But why the numbers 24 and 4? Some propose that 24 stands for the Old Testament's 12 tribes of Israel plus the New Testament's 12 apostles, while the other 4 reflect Ezekiel 1:5-14. The verse before us is the last time they are mentioned together (see also Revelation 5:6, 8, 11, 14; 7:11; 14:3).

Their united acclamation of worship consists of just two words: *Amen* and *Hallelujah*. Regarding the former, see on Revelation 7:12a in lesson 10; regarding the latter, see on 19:1b, above. The combined effect is to affirm the praise of the great crowd in 19:3 and repeat its central component: Praise the Lord!

B. Command (v. 5)

5a. Then a voice came from the throne, saying: "Praise our God,

Another *voice* joins the multitude, the elders, and the living creatures in worship. *The throne* itself always refers to the presence and authority of God (examples: Psalms 9:7; 11:4; 45:6; 47:8; Hebrews 1:8). Even so, the voice is likely not from God or from the Lamb, and it is uncertain whether it is from an angel herald or another entity. What is important is that the voice has divine authorization to call for worship.

When we understand the true nature of God, then we can praise him even in the midst of our deepest sorrow and toughest trials. We can do this because we understand that he is worthy. We also offer praise because we know that God's purposes are eternal, that his salvation is sure, and that his victory is guaranteed and complete.

The form of worship demonstrated here differs slightly from previous exclamations. Rather than the command "Praise the Lord," this version exclaims *Praise our God*. This echoes the commands of Psalm 66:8.

5b. all you his servants, you who fear him, both great and small!"

The type of *fear* in view is not that of the terror of those in Revelation 6:15-17. Rather, it refers to those who revere God (compare 11:18, last week's lesson).

> **What Do You Think?**
> How can you help your church improve its message on what it means to fear God?
> *Digging Deeper*
> What personal lifestyle change do you need to make first in this regard so that your practice matches your profession?

The phrasing *great and small* indicates the inclusive nature of the imperative (also Revelation 11:18). The status symbols considered important on earth no longer have the same impact, with regard to priority. As some have noted, the ground is level at the foot of the cross. And so it is before the throne.

❧ *ACCESS HEAVEN* ❧

I grew up in California, but in all my years there I never met a celebrity. The closest I ever came to crossing paths with one was in the late 1980s. I was visiting an art museum with some friends, when we heard that a well-known star was attending an art class with his son.

We made a beeline to the classroom, only to find the door blocked by security. We were so disappointed! To catch a glimpse of a star would have definitely been noteworthy.

Of course, when we finally arrive in Heaven, all that will cease to matter. In Revelation 19:5 a voice calls "all you his servants . . . both great and small" to praise God. In that moment, earthly distinctions among social classes, economic status, rank, or family background will be irrelevant. We won't be sequestered or segregated in front of the throne of God. No one will take a back seat. Together we

will enjoy the beauty of our Lord in Heaven. That future and eternal reality easily eclipses any five-second glimpse of a star here on earth!

We note that Revelation 6:15-17 also mentions people of the highest to lowest in earthly standing. That context concerns those who will be lost for eternity. Placing that passage alongside 19:5 has something to say about how we view and treat people in the here and now, doesn't it?   —P. L. M.

III. Unified Multitude
(REVELATION 19:6-8)
A. Tripled Voice (v. 6)

6a. Then I heard what sounded like a great multitude, like the roar of rushing waters and like loud peals of thunder, shouting:

John hears yet another voice, this time only described in similarity to *a great multitude*. This seems to be a different group, however, than the group mentioned in Revelation 19:1. The sound likened to *rushing waters* is not that of a soothing bubbling brook. Rather, the sound is more like that of a thunderous waterfall or the crashing of stormy waves on a beach.

The word translated *thunder* occurs 10 times in this book (here and Revelation 4:5; 6:1; 8:5; 10:3, 4 [twice]; 11:19; 14:2; and 16:18). The word is always associated with divine power, authority, and/or initiative (compare John 12:29). Its use in the verse at hand alongside the sound of water bears strong similarity to the prophet's visions in Ezekiel 1:24 and 43:2.

HOW TO SAY IT

apocalyptic	uh-*paw*-kuh-*lip*-tik.
Babylon	*Bab*-uh-lun.
Babylonians	Bab-ih-*low*-nee-unz.
Chaldeans	Kal-*dee*-unz.
Habakkuk	Huh-*back*-kuk.
Judah	*Joo*-duh.
Mediterranean	*Med*-uh-tuh-*ray*-nee-un.
omnipotent	ahm-*nih*-poh-tent.
omnipresent	*ahm*-nih-*prez*-ent.
omniscient	ahm-*nish*-unt.
Palestine	*Pah*-luh-*stein*.

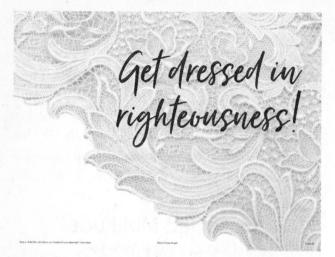

Visual for Lesson 12. *Use this visual as a backdrop as you discuss what a life dressed in righteousness should look like on earth.*

The description of this stupendous chorus of voices emphasizes the size of this crowd. If you have been in a football stadium and heard the noise of tens of thousands of voices at once, then you know how loud it can be. This may be similar to what John experienced.

6b. Hallelujah!

We come now to fourth and final *Hallelujah* in the book of Revelation. Again, see insight on this term in the commentary on Psalm 149:1a in lesson 9. This imperative to praise God (the word's meaning) is accompanied by a reason to do so (see next).

6c. For our Lord God Almighty reigns.

God's actions are often grouped under three headings: he creates, he rules, and he redeems. The text before us speaks to the second of those. In that light, the praise is for the universal kingship of *our Lord God*. There can be no rival to God, either in his rule or in our praise of him.

Older versions of the Bible include the word "omnipotent" instead of *Almighty*. This verse introduces us to one of what might be called "the three omnis." The word *omnipotent* means "all-powerful." The other two omni- words are *omnipresent* and *omniscient,* meaning "present in all places at all times" and "all-knowing," respectively.

God's power to reign is demonstrated by his overwhelming and permanent victory over enemies; now his all-powerful nature brings his promises to their completion. See also commentary on Revelation 11:17c in lesson 11.

B. Tripled Command (v. 7a)

7a. Let us rejoice and be glad and give him glory!

Three more imperatives are now added to the one ("hallelujah") above. This is unique, being the only place in the New Testament where the verbs *rejoice, be glad,* and *give* occur together in the same verse.

C. Reason (vv. 7b-8)

7b. For the wedding of the Lamb has come,

This is the reason for the unique triple command of the half-verse just considered. It is the moment the faithful had been waiting for: the time and occasion when the faithful servants of God see their eternal, heavenly fellowship with their Savior, Jesus Christ, finalized. Such joy! This is the moment when all God's work throughout history moves toward its magnificent conclusion.

The wedding language we see here was not unfamiliar to John's original audience. Old Testament prophets often used marriage as a figurative reference to describe the relationship between God and his people (examples: Isaiah 54:5-7; Hosea 2:19). Jesus, too, described the kingdom of heaven in terms of a marriage (see Matthew 22:1-14; 25:1-13).

A marriage requires two parties: a bride and a groom. The groom in view here is *the Lamb*. Various forms of the word *lamb* appear 35 times in the New Testament, and 29 of those are in the book of Revelation. In 28 of those 29 cases, the reference is to Jesus. (The single exception is in Revelation 13:11.)

Outside of the book of Revelation, John the Baptist referred to Jesus as "the Lamb of God" (John 1:29). Peter said that Jesus was "a lamb without blemish or defect" (1 Peter 1:19). The idea of Christ as the sacrificial lamb lies at the very heart of our redemption and salvation.

7c-8. and his bride has made herself ready. Fine linen, bright and clean, was given her to wear." (Fine linen stands for the righteous acts of God's holy people.)

The book of Revelation is loaded with figurative language; that is when an image of one thing is used to express another (see the Lesson Context). This is the great challenge in interpreting both Jesus' parables and the book of Revelation as a whole. A key difference between the parables and Revelation is that Jesus often identified the references in his parables later (examples: Matthew 13:18-23, 36-43), while the apostle John almost never does that in Revelation. A rare exception is in the verses before us when John explains that *fine linen stands for the righteous acts of God's holy people.*

This imagery reflects the holiness of the *bride,* having been redeemed by the Lamb (see Revelation 7:9, 14). Clothing imagery serves important figurative purposes in the Bible (see Job 29:14; Psalm 132:9; Isaiah 52:1; 61:10).

John's use of wedding imagery speaks to the relationship between God and his people. The bride of Christ is the church: holy ones sanctified by the work of the Holy Spirit. The bride has been redeemed because of the blood of the Lamb (see Revelation 5:9), the very same blood applied to those who "washed their robes and made them white" (7:14). The time for rejoicing is coming! Like a bride engaged to be married, the church awaits the return of Christ and the eternal marriage feast between the bride and the groom.

> *What Do You Think?*
> What changes do you need to make with regard to how your lifestyle could better reflect the holiness depicted in verse 8?
> *Digging Deeper*
> How do Isaiah 61:10; Ezekiel 44:17; and Zechariah 3:4 help frame your answer?

❧ SAY YES TO THE DRESS ❧

When I got married, I wore a white dress in spite of secular culture's trend to view the significance as quite old-fashioned. Recently I've seen a sharper turn in this regard, from brides wearing white to little significance in wearing white at all. In fact, a few years ago my friend wore a black satin outfit during her ceremony!

How differently we will feel about white clothing when our Lord returns! As the bride of the Lamb, the church will *want* to wear white, made that way by the groom, the Lord Jesus Christ. No other clothing will compare to it.

Don't forget what that groom-provided clothing stands for: holiness. And because holiness is necessary to "see the Lord" (Hebrews 12:14), don't let the world convince you that such thinking is just old-fashioned.   —P. L. M.

Conclusion
A. Got Your Clothing Ready?

Weddings are designed to create memories and ingrain those memories in the minds of those who attend. Therefore, the wedding party's clothes are normally chosen with great care and coordinated for maximum effect. The wedding party may take hours to get ready for the ceremony. Because the ceremony will be remembered for years—for its beauty as well as its glitches—everyone goes to great lengths to ensure that everything is "perfect."

The wedding ceremony between the Lamb and his bride culminates in the rescue of the bride from the power of sin and evil. When Jesus, the Lamb, receives his bride, the church, it will be the wedding for all time! The groom has done his part by paying the price for sin on the cross. But the bride has her part to do as well, considering John's statement that she has "made herself ready" (Revelation 19:7). Jesus has provided us with "garments of salvation" and a "robe of his righteousness" (Isaiah 61:10), but we must put them on.

> *What Do You Think?*
> Which concept or imperative in today's lesson do you have the most trouble coming to grips with? Why?
> *Digging Deeper*
> How will you resolve this problem?

B. Prayer

Praise to you, God most high! Glory to you, Lord of Heaven and earth! Thanks be to you for your gracious gift of Jesus, your Son and our Savior. May our hearts give praise to the King of kings and Lord of lords. In Jesus' name we pray. Amen.

C. Thought to Remember

Look for hallelujah moments in your life.

INVOLVEMENT LEARNING

Enhance your lesson with NIV® Bible Student (from your curriculum supplier) and the reproducible activity page (at www.standardlesson.com or in the back of the NIV® Standard Lesson Commentary Deluxe Edition).

Into the Lesson

Lead participants into reminiscing about a memorable wedding, either their own or one they attended. Ask how their expectations of wedding procedures and traditions differ from those of other cultures.

Alternative. Distribute copies of the "Weddings" icebreaker exercise from the activity page, which you can download. Award a token prize to the participant who collects the most affirmations.

After either activity, make a transition by noting that today's lesson may challenge our view of how weddings "should" be.

Into the Word

Have two volunteers read Revelation 19:1-8 aloud, alternating with every verse. Then start an agree/disagree discussion as you distribute handouts (you create) on which are printed definitions of, and credible differences between, "praise" and "worship" from your own research. (This can be either a discussion for small groups or the entire class, depending on the size and nature of your class.)

Option. Distribute copies of the "OT in NT" matching exercise from the activity page, which you can download. Announce a speed drill for individuals to complete the exercise as indicated, time limit of one minute. Have learners raise a hand when finished. After calling time, allow learners to correct their own work. Give a token prize suitable to the nature of the exercise to the participant who raised his or her hand first and has all answers correct. Discuss what significance learners see in the Old Testament allusions to the verses from Revelation 19.

Next, use the Lesson Context to ensure that learners understand the meaning and significance of "Babylon," which is mentioned several times in Revelation 18, the text that immediately precedes today's text from Revelation 19. Then write the following on the board as the focal point in the discussion to follow:

The Futures of . . .

| *Babylon* | *The Church* |

Encourage free discussion of the contrast. Jot participants' responses under the appropriate column heading. As learners offer an entry under either one, immediately press them to indicate the direct contrast that should go under the other column heading.

Depending on the nature of your class, you may wish to use one or both of these options: (1) instead of the designations *Babylon* and *The Church*, use *The Great Prostitute* and *The Bride*; (2) include the five row headings *What / Where / When / Why / How* down the left. This will focus learners on providing entries for each of the resulting 10 intersections of rows and columns.

Into Life

Continue the immediately preceding activity by writing *Unbride-Like Church* under the entries in the *Babylon* column and *Bride-Like Church* under the entries in the *The Church* column. Ask participants to voice distinguishing characteristics and qualities of each type of church; jot responses on the board.

Distribute blank index cards. Challenge learners to write on their cards one unbride-like quality or tendency that they can help their church overcome in the week ahead. Suggest that they place their cards somewhere at home to be seen often over the next few days. Promise to offer time in the next class session to discuss results.

Option. Ask learners how they would respond to someone who said, "Since we don't know when Jesus is coming back, if ever, I can just wait until then to repent." Encourage use of Scripture to justify their responses. (You can also have volunteers do this as a role play for the class.)

GOOD NEWS FOR ALL

DEVOTIONAL READING: Acts 10:34-47
BACKGROUND SCRIPTURE: Acts 10:34-47

ACTS 10:34-47

34 Then Peter began to speak: "I now realize how true it is that God does not show favoritism 35 but accepts from every nation the one who fears him and does what is right. 36 You know the message God sent to the people of Israel, announcing the good news of peace through Jesus Christ, who is Lord of all. 37 You know what has happened throughout the province of Judea, beginning in Galilee after the baptism that John preached— 38 how God anointed Jesus of Nazareth with the Holy Spirit and power, and how he went around doing good and healing all who were under the power of the devil, because God was with him.

39 "We are witnesses of everything he did in the country of the Jews and in Jerusalem. They killed him by hanging him on a cross, 40 but God raised him from the dead on the third day and caused him to be seen. 41 He was not seen by all the people, but by witnesses whom God had already chosen—by us who ate and drank with him after he rose from the dead. 42 He commanded us to preach to the people and to testify that he is the one whom God appointed as judge of the living and the dead.

43 All the prophets testify about him that everyone who believes in him receives forgiveness of sins through his name."

44 While Peter was still speaking these words, the Holy Spirit came on all who heard the message. 45 The circumcised believers who had come with Peter were astonished that the gift of the Holy Spirit had been poured out even on Gentiles. 46 For they heard them speaking in tongues and praising God.

Then Peter said, 47 "Surely no one can stand in the way of their being baptized with water. They have received the Holy Spirit just as we have."

KEY TEXT

Peter began to speak: "I now realize how true it is that God does not show favoritism but accepts from every nation the one who fears him and does what is right." —**Acts 10:34-35**

CELEBRATING GOD

Unit 3: Visions of Praise
LESSONS 10–13

LESSON AIMS

After participating in this lesson, each learner will be able to:

1. Summarize how God welcomed Gentiles into his kingdom.

2. Explain his or her identity with the Gentiles in that regard.

3. Role-play an evangelistic encounter with an unbeliever.

LESSON OUTLINE

Introduction

A. Still Waiting?

According to the Deaf Bible Society, only 2 percent of people who are deaf worldwide have been introduced to the gospel. As a result, the deaf constitute one of the largest and least-reached demographics. A man who was deaf recounted his story of attending church while he grew up, but never understanding what Jesus had done.

Although there are estimated to be several hundred sign languages in use worldwide, only recently has there been an effort to begin Bible translation among these communities. As of this writing, not a single sign language has a complete Bible translation, not even American Sign Language (ASL)!

But wait—since deafness is not a visual impairment, why do people who cannot hear need a Bible translation just for them? By one estimate, the great majority of children who are deaf cannot read. Thus having a video Bible translated into sign language overcomes a barrier.

We should not assume that everyone is aware of the good news of Jesus. That was the situation for many in the first century AD. And many or most Jews who *were* aware of the gospel thought that Gentiles didn't need to know because non-Jews were, by and large, excluded (see Acts 10:45; 11:1-18). But God had a different idea, as today's lesson demonstrates.

B. Lesson Context

Today's passage is an excerpt from a longer story that extends from Acts 10:1 to 11:18. The length of this account, which comprises more than 6 percent of the book of Acts, reflects its significance.

This turning point in history occurred after the day of Pentecost, when the apostle Peter had declared in his gospel message that "the promise is for you . . . and for all who are far off—for all whom the Lord our God will call" (Acts 2:39). Given Peter's surprise in today's passage, he may have presumed that "all who are far off" referred only to all *Jews* who were far off (compare addressees in James 1:1).

Our lesson text has Peter standing before a Gentile audience, poised to share the gospel. This was a huge step for Peter. To observant Jews, Gentiles were unclean pagans, who might endanger the apostles' own religious and moral purity. Any sharing of faith beliefs by Jews to Gentiles would have been "clean" ones testifying to "unclean" ones.

But God was changing that mind-set. The correction began with two visions that occurred about 21 hours apart: the first to a Roman centurion named Cornelius (Acts 10:1-6) and the second to the apostle Peter (10:9-16). The respective locations were the cities of Caesarea Maritima and Joppa, about 30 miles apart, on the coastline of the Mediterranean Sea.

Cornelius was no ordinary Gentile. He had a track record of praying to Israel's God and modeling generosity to his neighbors (Acts 10:2). There is no indication, however, that Cornelius had fully converted to Judaism. Luke (the author of Acts) refers to individuals like Cornelius as fearing God and/or being "devout" (10:2; 13:26; 17:4, 17). This was in contrast to "proselytes"—those who had converted to Judaism fully (6:5; 13:43). Even so, God, recognizing the sincerity of Cornelius's faith, chose this man to be the starting point for extending the gospel to Gentiles.

God reached out to Cornelius by means of an angel, who instructed him to send for Peter (Acts 10:3-8). Next, God gave Peter a vision in which the apostle was commanded repeatedly to eat food forbidden to Jews (10:9-16). This conveyed a message that what had been declared unclean was no longer so.

Immediately following Peter's vision, messengers from Cornelius arrived and invited Peter to the Gentile's house (Acts 10:17-23). Upon arriving, Cornelius and Peter shared their experiences (10:24-33). This takes us into today's text.

I. Peter's Message
(ACTS 10:34-43)

A. God's Invitation to Gentiles (vv. 34-35)

34. Then Peter began to speak: "I now realize how true it is that God does not show favoritism

Having evaluated the sequence of events, *Peter* realized that his own vision, disturbing as it was, had been timed to coincide perfectly with the vision to Cornelius. Peter therefore could draw no conclusion other than *that God does not show favoritism*—he is impartial in intending the gospel for everyone (see also Romans 2:11; Ephesians 6:9; Colossians 3:25; 1 Peter 1:17).

What Do You Think?
> What practice can you adopt to ensure that you are open to changing your mind when new evidence comes along?

Digging Deeper
> When was the last time the Bible changed your mind about anything?

---

35. but accepts from every nation the one who fears him and does what is right.

Here, the word *nation* does not refer to political identity but to ethnic and religious background. People everywhere who *fear* God and who demonstrate that fear by obeying him are welcome. If this seems obvious to us after 2,000 years of Christian history, it was shocking to Peter and his first-century Jewish compatriots (compare Acts 10:45; 11:17-18).

We can imagine Peter's surprise to hear these words coming from his own mouth! This occasion marked the first time that an Israelite offered Gentiles the opportunity of becoming full beneficiaries of God's covenant—a new covenant—without requiring circumcision (compare Acts 15:1-21; Galatians 2:2-5).

B. God's Invitation to Jews (vv. 36-37)

36. You know the message God sent to the people of Israel, announcing the good news of peace through Jesus Christ, who is Lord of all.

Despite the nature of his audience, Peter did not hide the fact that Jesus' ministry focused almost exclusively on *the people of Israel* (compare Matthew 15:24). But at the same time, Peter noted that *Jesus*, who was the anticipated *Christ*—meaning "anointed one" (see Acts 10:38, below)—of the Jews, to be the *Lord of all* people.

The *peace* Jesus preached referred primarily

to peace between God and sinners. But in the context of Peter's sermon, it also included peace between divided people groups (Gentiles and Jews) that becomes possible through common faith in Christ.

God had promised Abraham that his descendants would be a blessing to all nations (Genesis 12:2-3). As the messenger of God's *message*, Jesus came to fulfill that promise (see Luke 4:18-21). Old Testament prophets had looked forward to a day when God would bring peace to the whole world (see Isaiah 52:7); Peter understood Jesus as the fulfillment of that prophecy. Jesus is the only way to have full peace with both God (Romans 5:1) and fellow humans (Ephesians 2:14).

37. You know what has happened throughout the province of Judea, beginning in Galilee after the baptism that John preached—

The phrase *you know what has happened* indicates a certain level of prior knowledge on the part of Peter's Gentile audience (compare Acts 26:26). But there was still more to learn! So Peter framed his teaching by setting two reference points: one of geography (*throughout the province of Judea, beginning in Galilee*) and one of chronology (*after the baptism that John preached*).

Another way to say this is that the gospel of Jesus became a historical reality in both place and time (see Mark 1:9; Luke 4:14-20; 16:16; Galatians 4:4). His ministry was preceded by that of John the Baptist, who preached "a baptism of repentance for the forgiveness of sins" (Mark 1:4).

C. Jesus' Mission to the World (vv. 38-41)

38a. how God anointed Jesus of Nazareth with the Holy Spirit and power,

The designation *Jesus of Nazareth,* used often by Jesus' enemies, was well known by this time (John 18:5, 7; 19:19). Regarding *the Holy Spirit and power* by which Jesus began his ministry, see Luke 4:14-20.

38b. and how he went around doing good and healing all who were under the power of the devil, because God was with him.

The primary purpose of Jesus' miracles—whether they dealt with physical *healing* or spiritual relief from oppression by *the devil*—was

to provide evidence of his divine nature (John 14:11). Many people, sadly, didn't grasp that, choosing instead to focus on passing physical needs rather than enduring spiritual issues (John 6:26). And many who *did* see a connection between Jesus and the supernatural chose to identify him with the worst elements of the demonic realm (Luke 11:15). Even so, Jesus had authority to bring physical and spiritual liberation because *God was with him.*

39. "We are witnesses of everything he did in the country of the Jews and in Jerusalem. They killed him by hanging him on a cross,

Peter pressed to the heart of Jesus' ministry, having witnessed it firsthand. Indeed, to be *witnesses* was the task for which Jesus had chosen him and the other apostles (Luke 24:45-49; Acts 1:8). In this regard, Peter points a finger directly at *the Jews,* not the Romans, as being responsible for Jesus' death (see also Acts 5:29-30). Yet the testimony of Jesus' death doesn't end there.

> *What Do You Think?*
> Should you prepare your testimony before you share it with others, or just speak as the context dictates and the Holy Spirit leads?
> *Digging Deeper*
> Is Matthew 10:19 helpful in answering this question? Why, or why not?

40a. but God raised him from the dead on the third day

God's ultimate vindication of Jesus was the resurrection. It happened *on the third day* after Jesus was crucified, just as he had said would happen (Luke 9:22; 18:33; compare 24:7, 46). All Jesus' teachings and miraculous works led up to this point. All Jesus' teachings and miracles would have been for naught had the resurrection not occurred (1 Corinthians 15:13-19). It is the resurrection that confirms Jesus to be the Son of God (see Romans 1:4), who has the power over death (Revelation 1:18).

40b. and caused him to be seen.

We can be certain of the resurrection because God *caused* the resurrected Jesus *to be seen.* Peter and others actually saw the risen Christ themselves (see Matthew 28:16-20; Luke 24:36-53; John 20:11-29; 1 Corinthians 15:3-8).

41. He was not seen by all the people, but by witnesses whom God had already chosen—by us who ate and drank with him after he rose from the dead.

An interesting fact of the resurrection is that between that event and Jesus' ascension, Jesus is recorded to have been seen only by believers. They had seen the evidence of his miracles and had rejected him nonetheless. They had attributed his work to demonic power once before (Luke 11:15) and could be expected to do so again.

This underscores the unique role of Jesus' followers. God chose specific *witnesses* to encounter his resurrected Son (see Luke 24:45-48). For Peter, standing before Cornelius, this is where the gospel message became personal. God had put the stamp of approval on Peter and his message by means of the two visions mentioned earlier. That message was crucial to bringing Jesus to the Gentiles, starting with this household.

❧ SEEING JESUS ❧

Since its release in 1979, *The Jesus Film* has been translated into over 1,800 languages and viewed more than seven billion times. The filmmakers wanted to create a historically accurate account of Jesus, and the dialogue comes directly from Scripture. Even the costumes used only the exact shades of dye of Jesus' day. The result was an unembellished portrayal of the life and ministry of Jesus.

Emotions run high when people see the film. The gospel becomes real. Afterward, many stay for discussion and prayer. When you read Peter's sermon in Acts 10, imagine Cornelius and his family hearing it! If you find yourself less than fully interested because you've heard it so many times already, then perhaps you need to, as the saying goes, "hear it again for the first time."   —D. G.

D. Jesus' Commission (vv. 42-43)

42. He commanded us to preach to the people and to testify that he is the one whom God appointed as judge of the living and the dead.

What we call the Great Commission, from Matthew 28:19-20, is worded this way:

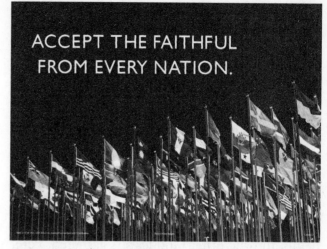

ACCEPT THE FAITHFUL FROM EVERY NATION.

Visual for Lesson 13. *Start a brainstorming session by asking learners for ways to make this imperative a reality.*

> Therefore go and make disciples of all nations, baptizing them in the name of the Father and of the Son and of the Holy Spirit, teaching them to obey everything I have commanded you.

The verse before us might be seen to specify additional elements of method and message of that commission. The methods so specified are *to preach* and *to testify;* the message is that Jesus was *appointed* by *God* to *judge . . . the living and the dead.*

When added to earlier references of Jesus' impartiality (Acts 10:34-35) and his title of "Lord of all" (10:36), the role of judge makes sense. The broad scope of Jesus' lordship is viable in his perfect impartiality as judge.

> *What Do You Think?*
> Which is God calling you to do: to *be* a cross-cultural missionary or to *support* one?
> *Digging Deeper*
> Is that question a false choice? Why, or why not?

43. All the prophets testify about him that everyone who believes in him receives forgiveness of sins through his name."

God fearers such as Cornelius likely had some knowledge of the witness of the Old Testament *prophets.* Thus it was appropriate for Peter to refer to them here, while in other contexts it may not have been (as in Acts 17:22-34).

No specific prophets are noted, but the Old Testament provides numerous examples of prophetic witness. Isaiah foresaw a day when people "will be forgiven" (Isaiah 33:24), through the one who "was pierced for our transgressions" (53:5), the "righteous servant" who would "justify many" (53:11).

In a similar vein, Jeremiah hoped for a day when the Lord would "forgive their wickedness" and "remember their sin no more" (Jeremiah 31:34). Daniel spoke of a time that would bring the "end to sin" and the Lord would "atone for wickedness" (Daniel 9:24). In speaking to Cornelius and the other God fearers gathered, Peter emphasized that the person who fulfilled such prophecies had arrived.

We note that Acts 10:36-43 may be a concise summary of a sermon that went on for hours. Perhaps there were many pauses to answer questions. Some students see in these eight verses a highly condensed version of the four Gospels.

> ### What Do You Think?
> How do you decide which of your witnessing opportunities should mention the Old Testament and which should not?
>
> *Digging Deeper*
> How do Acts 17:22-31 and 28:23 inform your response?

II. Two Outcomes
(ACTS 10:44-47)

A. Spirit Poured Out (vv. 44-46a)

44. While Peter was still speaking these words, the Holy Spirit came on all who heard the message.

On hearing Peter's message, these Gentiles might have had all types of questions. How could they be sure Jesus was the Messiah? They could have doubted the message like so many before. But before *Peter* could finish speaking, *the Holy Spirit came on all who heard the message.* If any further evidence was needed, that was it!

45. The circumcised believers who had come with Peter were astonished that the gift of the Holy Spirit had been poured out even on Gentiles.

The circumcised believers refers to those Christians present who were of Jewish descent; those *who had come with Peter* were six in number, according to Acts 11:12. To a man, they *were astonished* at God's giving *of the Holy Spirit* to the *Gentiles*.

As Peter would recount later, "As I began to speak, the Holy Spirit came on them as he had come on us at the beginning" (Acts 11:15). Those last nine words are a key to the importance and rarity of such an outpouring. It obviously had occurred only once before: on the day of Pentecost. This has caused some to refer to the outpouring of Acts 10:44-47 as "the Gentile Pentecost."

46a. For they heard them speaking in tongues and praising God.

The Spirit worked with this Gentile audience in a way similar to his work on the day of Pentecost, allowing them to speak *in tongues*. This is only the second instance in Acts where Luke describes speaking with tongues, which is the ability to speak in foreign languages that one has not studied (see Acts 2:6-12).

This was divine authentication of Gentile inclusion. For a Jewish audience who had experienced the outpouring of tongues at Pentecost, hearing of the same occurring among a Gentile audience would further stress that God is impartial.

❧ REFUGEES' RESPONSE ❧

When three refugees appeared at the gate of our compound in North Africa, we didn't know what God's Spirit was about to unleash. They knew my teammate was a Christian, and they wanted to learn more, even though their community did not allow Christianity.

They began reading and studying the Bible in Arabic. Meanwhile our mission team began to facilitate the work of translating the Bible into their local language. The reading group eagerly studied translated portions of Scripture as they became available. Other reading groups formed. Eventually, local leaders allowed Christianity to enter their community. Only God's Spirit could so quickly transform a community!

It all began with three refugees looking for someone to tell them about Jesus. What if my teammate had been busy or suspicious? What if Peter had been too proud or close-minded to meet with Cornelius? Will you make the effort to share Jesus and see what God's Spirit will do?

—D. G.

B. Baptism Enacted (vv. 46b-47)

46b-47. Then Peter said, "Surely no one can stand in the way of their being baptized with water. They have received the Holy Spirit just as we have."

For the first-century church, baptism followed as a response to the gospel message and faith in Christ (see Acts 2:38; 8:26-39; etc.). Consistent with this pattern, *Peter* asked rhetorically why *no one can stand in the way* of the new believers, *being baptized*.

Having seen the Holy Spirit at work in Cornelius and his household, Peter didn't have to ask whether or not they believed. The presence of God's *Spirit* made this clear! And so the first Gentiles entered the fellowship of God.

Conclusion

A. New Humanity

The scope of God's salvation is highlighted in today's pivotal text, when Gentiles received an outpouring of God's Spirit as Jews had earlier. Questions remained regarding what role former identity markers of God's people—markers such as circumcision, dietary laws, and observance of

HOW TO SAY IT

Caesarea Maritima	Sess-uh-*ree*-uh Mar-uh-*tee*-muh.
centurion	sen-*ture*-ee-un.
Cornelius	Cor-*neel*-yus.
Galilee	*Gal*-uh-lee.
Gentiles	*Jen*-tiles.
Joppa	*Jop*-uh.
Judea	Joo-*dee*-uh.
Mediterranean	*Med*-uh-tuh-*ray*-nee-un.
proselytes	*prahss*-uh-lights.
Pentecost	*Pen*-tih-**kost**.
Samaritans	Suh-*mare*-uh-tunz.

special days—would continue to play. Such questions were settled at the famous Jerusalem Council of Acts 15: these external markers were no longer essential to the people of God.

God's plan was to spread the news of salvation through his old-covenant people, the Jews (John 4:22). Jesus was Jewish, as were his closest disciples. All people who were not Jewish were lumped into a single category: Gentiles. (Samaritans could be a complicating additional category.)

To devout Jews, Gentiles were regarded as complete outsiders unless they adhered to the Law of Moses (Exodus 12:48-49; etc.). Today's passage overturned all this. We can do no better than allow the apostle Paul to summarize this change:

> Christ Jesus . . . [set] aside in his flesh the law with its commands and regulations. His purpose was to create in himself one new humanity. . . . For through him we both have access to the Father by one Spirit.
>
> —Ephesians 2:13-18

The good news of God's kingdom is now available to all who believe (see Romans 1:16). We should be on the lookout for people such as Cornelius—individuals who may be open to hearing the gospel, but who have never had it explained.

What Do You Think?
Which concept or imperative in today's lesson do you have the most trouble coming to grips with? Why?
Digging Deeper
How will you resolve this problem?

B. Prayer

Lord, it should not surprise us that you created for yourself a people from all humanity. Rid us of any tendency to set up walls within the body of Christ that your Spirit has already knocked down. In Jesus' name we pray. Amen.

C. Thought to Remember

God doesn't discriminate; salvation is for *all* people—period.

INVOLVEMENT LEARNING

Enhance your lesson with NIV® Bible Student (from your curriculum supplier) and the reproducible activity page (at www.standardlesson.com or in the back of the NIV® Standard Lesson Commentary Deluxe Edition).

Into the Lesson

Before class begins, rearrange the room so that the chairs/desks are difficult to access. As learners arrive, use this as a segue for a discussion on barriers. Write this on this board:

I am uncomfortable around people who are different from me in terms of _____.

Provide paper for learners to turn in answers anonymously; then you read aloud the responses. Discuss these differences and today's societal barriers. Ask what kinds of barriers, if any, should have a place in churches today and why.

Make a transition by pointing out that today's lesson speaks to the subject of barriers between Jews and Gentiles.

Into the Word

Have volunteers read aloud today's text, alternating with every verse. Use the Lesson Context to ensure that students grasp the pivotal nature of Peter's addressing a room of Gentiles.

Have ready slips of paper on which you've written names of celebrities, fictional characters, or Bible persons—one name per slip, one slip per student. Have the students line up with their backs to you; then tape a slip to each student's back. The students must then have conversations with one another and each try to figure out, from clues, what name is on his or her own back. Allow several minutes or until everyone has identified who they are.

Once the activity is complete, ask participants how they felt about their disadvantage—everyone else had access to a piece of critical information (the name) that they themselves weren't privy to.

Break the class into small groups and have them discuss what it was like for various segments of the Gentile world to be granted the same salvation opportunities as the Jews when the barrier of the Old Testament law came down.

Reconvene and allow the groups to share conclusions. After each is voiced, probe for evidence to separate fact from speculation. Then compare and contrast today's text with the account of the day of Pentecost in Acts 2. Draw a Venn diagram on the board to show things in common (where circles overlap) and things not in common (where circles do not overlap).

Option. Give each participant a US penny and challenge them to find on it the Latin phrase *E Pluribus Unum.* Have magnifying glasses available and/or an enlarged image from the internet. Ask who knows what it means. (*Expected response:* "out of many, one.") Say, "Leaving aside any discussion regarding its suitability as a motto for a country, of what usefulness is this slogan for the church?" Take the discussion deeper by asking what the foundation(s) of church unity should be. (*Option.* Explore the distinction between *unity* and *uniformity,* which you research in advance.)

Into Life

Have learners pair up for one-on-one role plays. Assign one person in each pair to be a Christian and the other to be a nonbeliever. The Christian's task is to share the message of today's lesson in a way appropriate to his or her conversation partner. After the determined amount of time, have each class member pair up with someone else and reverse roles to role-play the conversation again. If time allows, have a willing pair reenact its role play in front of the class. Discuss ways the conversation could be improved.

Option. Distribute copies of the "Broken Barriers" exercise from the activity page, which you can download. Announce a one-minute time limit to complete as indicated. Have participants discuss their entries and adjust their lists as desired.

Option. Distribute copies of the "Who Is My Gentile?" exercise from the activity page as a take-home. Promise to discuss results next week.

JUSTICE, LAW,
HISTORY

Special Features

Lessons
Unit 1: God Requires Justice

Unit 2: God: The Source of Justice

Unit 3: Justice and Adversity

QUARTERLY QUIZ

Use these questions as a pretest or as a review. The answers are on page iv of This Quarter in the Word.

Lesson 1

1. The Lord required Israel to serve him with all their heart and _____. *Deuteronomy 10:12*

2. The Israelites were not to use what kind of tools while building an altar? (iron, stone, bronze). *Deuteronomy 27:5*

Lesson 2

1. What gift did David grant to Mephibosheth? (land, money, clothing). *2 Samuel 9:7*

2. Ziba and his sons and servants were commanded to farm Mephibosheth's land. T/F. *2 Samuel 9:10*

Lesson 3

1. The promised child would be called Wonderful Counselor, Mighty God, Everlasting Father, and Prince of _____. *Isaiah 9:6*

2. This new ruler will reign from whose throne? (David's, Saul's, Isaiah's). *Isaiah 9:7*

Lesson 4

1. The Lord vents his wrath against his _____. *Nahum 1:2*

2. The Lord angers very quickly and easily. T/F. *Nahum 1:3*

Lesson 5

1. The Lord warned that Cain must rule over what? (sin, Abel, land). *Genesis 4:7*

2. The Lord gave Cain a mark to protect him from anyone taking his life. T/F. *Genesis 4:15*

Lesson 6

1. God promised that both Isaac and Ishmael would become great nations. T/F. *Genesis 21:13*

2. Ishmael "became an _____." *Genesis 21:20*

Lesson 7

1. God commanded the people not to spread _____ reports. *Exodus 23:1*

2. Only Israelites were to rest on the Sabbath. T/F. *Exodus 23:12*

Lesson 8

1. What positions were appointed by the people in Israel? (Pick two: judges, officials, kings, prophets, rulers). *Deuteronomy 16:18*

2. In difficult matters, Israel was to consult whom? (priests, Moses, idols). *Deuteronomy 17:9*

Lesson 9

1. "Remember that you were _____ in Egypt." *Deuteronomy 24:18*

2. The people were to leave the leftover olives and grapes from their trees for whom? (Pick two: fatherless, widows, priests, their children, God). *Deuteronomy 24:20-21*

Lesson 10

1. Who did David kill with the sword? (Uriah the Hittite, Nathan, ewe). *2 Samuel 12:9*

2. The Lord put David to death for his sin. T/F. *2 Samuel 12:13*

Lesson 11

1. The king denied Ezra all the requests he made. T/F. *Ezra 7:6*

2. Ezra appointed magistrates and _____. *Ezra 7:25*

Lesson 12

1. Bildad the Shuhite accused Job of talking like a blustering _____. *Job 8:1-2*

2. Bildad the Shuhite asserted, "Our days . . . are a _____." *Job 8:9*

Lesson 13

1. The things of the Lord are too _____ to understand. *Job 42:3*

2. God gave Job twice as many blessings as before. T/F. *Job 42:10*

QUARTER AT A GLANCE

by Jeff Gerke

Our holy God is perfectly just. He never finds himself confused or looking for legal precedent for his decisions. He does not turn a blind eye, even when he acts with mercy. Because justice is part of his character, God expects the people who follow him to also practice justice.

But when God's justice comes into contact with sinful humanity, things get messy. This quarter we look at Old Testament passages that reveal God's desire for justice to characterize human relationships. Just as his love extends to all people, from the street to the palace, so must just treatment reach all, regardless of status. Though justice easily is perverted by the powerful and the elite, God calls his people to a higher way: the way of justice.

God Requires Justice

God's law provides his people with a standard for justice. The first unit in this quarter illustrates how justice proceeds from God's own character and provides the basis for right human conduct and social order. Leaders of God's people must rely on God's law as they administer justice.

On earth, God's justice can and should be mirrored in human relationships. King David fulfilled his promise to Jonathan by extending provision to his deceased friend's son. Sometimes God brings justice personally through the exercise of his power and from the outpouring of his righteousness. The Messiah prophesied by Isaiah would bring perfect justice into his perfect reign. We humans can become angered when justice seems to be delayed. But Nahum's prophecies stand as a reminder that God sees the cruelty of the nations and judges them rightly.

God: The Source of Justice

The justice of God must be evident in the lives of his people. The second unit of this quarter's les-

sons examines the ramifications for justice as it plays out in human life. We find that uncontrolled anger leads to all kinds of negative consequences, from broken relationships to crime to war. The story of Cain and Abel illustrates well what happens when anger rules uncontested.

God expects his justice to be applied to all people, even those who oppose his purposes and his

> God calls his people to a higher way: the way of justice.

people. This includes the enemies of God and those who are oppressed and marginalized. Israel's own history of slavery in Egypt informs how they must live out justice, not favoring the powerful but showing equal concern for all people. We are reminded that God's justice is for our own well-being.

Justice and Adversity

God's justice is often perverted, miscarried, and ignored—to our own peril. When a king strays from the path of justice, who can rebuke him? When a whole nation has forgotten—or despised—the law of God, how can the people be saved? The third unit of the quarter explores how people who obey God can correct course when injustice has become the rule of the day.

God's representatives bear the responsibility of seeking God's justice in the face of all kinds of opposition. Sometimes, as with Job's friend Bildad, wrong doctrine about God sounds right and results in faulty condemnation of the innocent. The final lesson in the quarter illustrates the joy and life we find when we return to harmony with God's justice. Ultimately, though we work toward the reality of God's will enacted on earth as in Heaven, we are hopeful because justice does not depend on us alone. May this quarter's lessons remind us of what true justice looks like.

GET THE SETTING

by Mark S. Krause

ISSUES OF JUSTICE ARE rightly of grave importance to Christians. At the core of a biblical understanding of justice are Old Testament texts that speak to God's demand for justice among the people of Israel. This required doing the right thing from God's perspective, not for the enrichment, reputation, or benefit of the ruler or the elite. The just leader, judge, king, or prophet wisely taught and applied God's standards for human behavior.

What about justice, judgments, and the legal systems of other ancient societies? Did Israel display a marked difference in the area of justice compared to its neighbors?

Might Makes Right?

In the first book of Plato's *Republic* (published around 375 BC), Socrates (Plato's protagonist) poses the question of the nature of justice. Thrasymachus stated the popular view that justice is "the interest of the stronger" (*Republic* 4.16). Many people of his day understood justice as little more than the government ("the stronger") acting in its own best interests.

In a monarchy, this would mean that the king and his cohorts defined justice. Examples of self-proclaimed keepers of justice come from the notoriously cruel and unjust Assyrian Empire. Ancient written sources show that Sargon II styled himself as "king of righteousness" for acting to combat inequity in his chosen cities. Sennacherib was also lauded as a ruler who loved righteousness. As keepers of justice, these kings determined what was good and fair in their lands, often brutally putting down rebellions.

Although in practice the mighty define justice to their liking, Socrates understood justice to be a virtue that rose above situational factors like who had power. Greek and Roman laws generally reflected the idea that justice rendered to a person what was due. If a man committed a crime, punishment was his just deserts. If a woman was seeking to collect a debt, justice demanded she receive the money that was due to her.

Community Responsibility

This begs the question of what "rights" are due any person in a society. A community resolves this by its laws. A community devoid of laws faithfully carried out has no basis for determining justice beyond the whims of the strongest person or group. A crucial feature of the nation of Israel was the idea of "law" (Torah) given by the Lord, not the king. Although Moses was the "lawgiver" for the Torah, the people understood the Lord God himself as providing these laws through Moses. The just kept God's law, even the king.

Babylonian King Hammurabi predates Moses by several hundred years, but Hammurabi's insights into creating a system of justice have important parallels with the system of Israel. For example, Moses taught that a son who struck his father should be put to death (Exodus 21:15), whereas Hammurabi decreed that such a son should have a hand cut off (law 195). The Torah limits retaliation to "life for life, eye for eye, tooth for tooth" (Exodus 21:23-24), similar to Hammurabi's own decrees (laws 196, 197, 200). In these legal systems, the penalty for harmful actions is defined, and justice is its enforcement.

In Psalms and the Prophets, justice may be framed as the alleviation of oppression. Social justice advocates often turn to these passages, which identify the oppressed in standard categories: widows, orphans (the "fatherless"), and foreigners. In general, such people were the "poor and needy" and required the protection of the laws and rulers in the community if it were to be a community of justice (see Psalm 82:3-4). This ideal, although not always practiced in the nation of Israel, stood above other ancient nations' ideas of justice.

THIS QUARTER IN THE WORD

Mon, Nov. 29	The Law of Justice	Deuteronomy 5:6-21
Tue, Nov. 30	Follow the Path of God's Law	Deuteronomy 5:23-33
Wed, Dec. 1	Discern the Good	Romans 12:1-2, 9-21
Thu, Dec. 2	Written Law and Ark of Wood	Deuteronomy 10:1-11
Fri, Dec. 3	Jesus Fulfills the Law	Matthew 5:17-20
Sat, Dec. 4	Curses for Disobedience	Deuteronomy 27:14-26
Sun, Dec. 5	Obey the Statutes	Deuteronomy 5:1b-3; 10:12-13; 28:1-2
Mon, Dec. 6	Deaths of Saul and Jonathan Mourned	2 Samuel 1:1-12
Tue, Dec. 7	A Lament from a Just Heart	2 Samuel 1:17-27
Wed, Dec. 8	A Cry for Justice	Luke 18:1-8
Thu, Dec. 9	Mercy from the Son of David	Matthew 20:29-34
Fri, Dec. 10	David Made King over All Israel	2 Samuel 3:1-5; 5:1-5
Sat, Dec. 11	The King Rejoices in God	Psalm 21
Sun, Dec. 12	David Shows Kindness	2 Samuel 9:1-7, 9-12
Mon, Dec. 13	God's Holy People	Leviticus 19:1-2, 11-18
Tue, Dec. 14	Righteousness and Justice	Psalm 89:14-21
Wed, Dec. 15	Be Content; Pursue Righteousness	1 Timothy 6:6-12
Thu, Dec. 16	Do Justice, Love Kindness, Walk Humbly	Micah 6:1-8
Fri, Dec. 17	Seek God's Kingdom and Righteousness	Matthew 6:25-34
Sat, Dec. 18	God's King Will Judge with Righteousness	Isaiah 11:1-9
Sun, Dec. 19	God's Light Has Shined	Isaiah 9:1-7

Mon, Feb. 14	Job Suffers	Job 1:8-11, 13-22
Tue, Feb. 15	Habakkuk Struggles to See Justice	Habakkuk 1:12-17
Wed, Feb. 16	Suffering for Doing Right	1 Peter 2:20-25
Thu, Feb. 17	God Is in the Storm	Psalm 29
Fri, Feb. 18	Remove This Cup from Me	Mark 14:32-42
Sat, Feb. 19	God Speaks from the Whirlwind	Job 38:1-11
Sun, Feb. 20	God's Justice Is Unfathomable	Job 8:1-10, 20-22
Mon, Feb. 21	Abraham Pleads for Justice	Genesis 18:20-33
Tue, Feb. 22	Trust in God's Coming Justice	Psalm 37:1-11
Wed, Feb. 23	The Lord Loves Justice	Psalm 37:21-28, 34-40
Thu, Feb. 24	Righteousness, Peace, and Joy	Romans 14:13-23
Fri, Feb. 25	Jesus Demonstrates God's Justice	Matthew 12:1-13
Sat, Feb. 26	Job Cries Out for a Redeemer	Job 19:23-29
Sun, Feb. 27	Job's Fortunes Are Restored	Job 42:1-6, 10-17

Answers to the Quarterly Quiz on page 114

Lesson 1—1. soul. 2. iron. **Lesson 2**—1. land. 2. true. **Lesson 3**—1. 'Peace. 2. David's. **Lesson 4**—1. enemies. 2. false. **Lesson 5**—1. sin. 2. true. **Lesson 6**—1. true. 2. archer. **Lesson 7**—1. false. 2. false. **Lesson 8**—1. judges, officials. 2. priests. **Lesson 9**—1. slaves. 2. fatherless, widows. **Lesson 10**—1. Uriah the Hittite. 2. false. **Lesson 11**—1. false. 2. magistrates, judges. **Lesson 12**—1. blustering wind. 2. shadow. **Lesson 13**—1. wonderful. 2. true.

DESERVED PUNISHMENT
LESSONS 4, 5, 8, 9, 10, 11, 12

DUE PROCESS
LESSONS 7, 8, 9, 11

REQUIRED RESTITUTION
LESSONS 12, 13

ECONOMIC FAIRNESS
LESSON 9

A MORAL COMPASS REQUIRES ALL!

Lesson 1

Photo © Getty Images

Sheet 1 · Winter 2021–2022, *Adult Resources: Standard Lesson Quarterly®* Curriculum

TEACHING IS MORE THAN TALKING

Part 2: You Can Surprise Them   *Teacher Tips by Mark A. Taylor*

MOST TEACHERS REALIZE their students will learn more if they participate. But how can teachers help passive members become active learners? Plan surprises!

Engaging Readers

Write each point of your lesson outline on a different card and give these cards to class members. As you come to each section, ask these recruits to stand and read their point.

Ask class members to read Scriptures aloud instead of reading them yourself. Recruit volunteers you know will be willing to do this, even if it means asking them during the week before class.

Use the same approach if you've found quotes you want to use from literature or the news. Try taping these randomly to the bottoms of chairs and asking class members to read the quotes they find.

Engaging Observers

Give class members something to see besides you. Write the theme of the lesson (or a provocative question or quote) on poster board or your whiteboard. Write major points on the board and cover each one with paper and tape; uncover each point as you come to it. Draw or purchase maps for the wall or to project via a computer.

Show movie clips or videos of Christian speakers. In addition to Christian teaching videos, consider using a snippet from one of your minister's sermons. Funny and/or inspiring clips from video-sharing sites can also work.

Engaging Listeners

Play Christian or contemporary songs to introduce a lesson or to drive home the lesson application at the end of a session.

Engaging Writers

Ask class members to complete easy paper-and-pencil activities. Distribute an outline with blanks for class members to fill in as the class time progresses.

Distribute copies of a Scripture and ask members to mark it. Possible prompts: Circle the commands; underline the names for God; put a star beside the verse most meaningful to you; put a question mark beside the sections that seem unclear.

Distribute copies of a simple true/false pretest or posttest about the facts in that week's Scripture. After a few minutes, poll the class about each statement before explaining the right answer.

Use multiple-choice opinion questions in the first part of the lesson to introduce a theme; for example: "Do you feel more afraid of (a) wild animals, (b) being alone in the dark, or (c) getting lost in a strange neighborhood?" Poll students and ask volunteers to tell why they chose as they did.

Engaging Movers

Ask class members to raise their hands to show whether they agree or disagree with each statement in a list you read. Poll the class to see who has had any of several experiences. Divide the class into sections and ask members to raise their hands as the Scripture is read; for example, half raise hands when God commands; half raise hands when God is praised. Or imagine emotions in a Bible story. Instruct members to raise hands when they think Jesus is pleased, raise hands when they think the disciples are confused, and raise hands when you think the crowd is angry.

Write each item from a Bible story on a separate large sheet of paper and distribute these among volunteers. Ask them to come to the front and arrange themselves in the proper order; or ask the class to tell you the proper order.

Engaging All Learners!

Use a variety of ideas, and try something different in every session. Surprise students and you may also be surprised to see how well they respond!

JUSTICE AND OBEDIENCE

DEVOTIONAL READING: Deuteronomy 5:1-3; 10:12-13; 28:1-2
BACKGROUND SCRIPTURE: Deuteronomy 5; 10; 27; 28:1-2

DEUTERONOMY 5:1B-3

¹ Hear, Israel, the decrees and laws I declare in your hearing today. Learn them and be sure to follow them. ² The LORD our God made a covenant with us at Horeb. ³ It was not with our ancestors that the LORD made this covenant, but with us, with all of us who are alive here today.

DEUTERONOMY 10:12-13

¹² And now, Israel, what does the LORD your God ask of you but to fear the LORD your God, to walk in obedience to him, to love him, to serve the LORD your God with all your heart and with all your soul,¹³ and to observe the LORD's commands and decrees that I am giving you today for your own good?

DEUTERONOMY 27:1-10

¹ Moses and the elders of Israel commanded the people: "Keep all these commands that I give you today. ² When you have crossed the Jordan into the land the LORD your God is giving you, set up some large stones and coat them with plaster. ³ Write on them all the words of this law when you have crossed over to enter the land the LORD your God is giving you, a land flowing with milk and honey, just as the LORD, the God of your ancestors, promised you. ⁴ And when you have crossed the Jordan, set up these stones on Mount Ebal, as I command you today, and coat them with plaster. ⁵ Build there an altar to the LORD your God, an altar of stones. Do not use any iron tool on them. ⁶ Build the altar of the LORD your God with fieldstones and offer burnt offerings on it to the LORD your God. ⁷ Sacrifice fellowship offerings there, eating them and rejoicing in the presence of the LORD your God. ⁸ And you shall write very clearly all the words of this law on these stones you have set up."

⁹ Then Moses and the Levitical priests said to all Israel, "Be silent, Israel, and listen! You have now become the people of the LORD your God. ¹⁰ Obey the LORD your God and follow his commands and decrees that I give you today."

KEY TEXT

Now, Israel, what does the LORD your God ask of you but to fear the LORD your God, to walk in obedience to him, to love him, to serve the LORD your God with all your heart and with all your soul, and to observe the LORD's commands and decrees that I am giving you today for your own good? —Deuteronomy 10:12-13

Justice, Law, History

Unit 1: God Requires Justice

Lessons 1–4

Lesson Aims

After participating in this lesson, each learner will be able to:

1. Summarize God's requirements of the Old Testament covenant people.

2. Explain the connection between those requirements and the concept of justice.

3. Make a plan to be more consistent in one area of his or her Christian walk.

Lesson Outline

Introduction

A. Lessons from a Kite's Flight

A certain fable depicts the story of a kite and its owner. The kite enjoyed being taken outside and flying high above the ground. But the kite could go only as far and high as the length of its string. One day the kite began to complain about its lack of freedom: "It isn't fair for me to be held back by my owner's string. If only I could break loose from him, I could go wherever I wanted."

Soon after, the kite's wish came true when the string broke. For a few moments, the kite relished its newfound freedom. But a sudden strong gust of wind came along, and the kite soon found itself unable to control its flight. Before long, the wind swept the kite into a tangle of tree branches. The briefly free kite now hung captive. The freedom the kite longed for was its eventual ruin.

God's requirements are for our benefit. Any perceived restrictions on our freedoms are in our best interest. He intends that we accept his will as our own so that we might become a blessing for the world. This week's lesson highlights several times when the people of God are reminded of those edicts as they are called to create a just society in witness to the just God they served.

B. Lesson Context: Deuteronomy

This lesson's texts come from the Old Testament book of Deuteronomy. Its name means "second law." That is an appropriate title as Deuteronomy is the second instance of the giving of God's law to Israel—the first time being to the generation that followed the one of the exodus from Egypt.

Israel's long journey to the promised land of Canaan had come to its climax as the people had arrived east of the Jordan River (Deuteronomy 1:1). The previous generation of Israel, prevented from entering the promised land, had perished in the wilderness because of unbelief (1:35, 37). Deuteronomy details Moses' expounding on God's law to Israel (1:5) and his farewell address to a new generation on the verge of entering the promised land.

One way Deuteronomy can be studied is on the basis of Moses' four major addresses. The first reviews the ways God worked in and provided for Israel throughout the desert wanderings. The review culminated in a reminder that Israel was a people set apart, called to live in obedience to God (Deuteronomy 4:1-4).

The second address reviewed God's law for Israel and provided moral boundaries for living in the promised land (Deuteronomy 4:44–26:19).

Moses' third address explored the demands of covenant life and the dangers of disobedience. It culminated in a call for Israel to commit to following God and his laws (Deuteronomy 30:11-20).

In what became the final scene of Moses' life, his fourth address presented Joshua as the new leader for Israel (Deuteronomy 31:1-8). This address served as that man's commissioning as the people entered the promised land (32:48-52).

C. Lesson Context: Covenant

God desired that Israel be known as a people well acquainted with his righteous standards. He expressed that desire in terms of a covenant. The covenant served as the formal agreement between God and his people, describing how Israel was to live as a holy people and how God committed to making Israel his people.

Covenants were not unique to ancient Israel. Other ancient Near Eastern cultures used similar legal agreements, often made between a more powerful kingdom and a lesser kingdom. These agreements often included a historical narrative (detailing the history between the parties), stipulations for the submission of the lesser party, and curses or blessings for the disregard or obedience of the previously mentioned stipulations. For pagan cultures of antiquity, covenants provided legal precedent for how parties were to relate to one another, especially if a power differential was present.

Throughout Israel's history, God made several covenants with his people. Each detailed a different aspect of his commitment to and his expectations for the Israelites (see Genesis 9:8-17; 15:1-21; 2 Samuel 7:8-16; Jeremiah 31:31-34). This week's Scripture texts describe how Israel was to commemorate and commit to the covenant God made with them at Sinai (Exodus 19:3-8; 20:1-17; 24:3-8).

I. Binding Covenant
(DEUTERONOMY 5:1b-3)

This passage serves as the introduction to the heart of Israel's relationship with God: the Ten Commandments, also known as the Decalogue.

A. Its Principles (v. 1b)

1b. Hear, Israel, the decrees and laws I declare in your hearing today. Learn them and be sure to follow them.

Throughout Deuteronomy, the command to *hear* draws the attention and focus of *Israel* (see Deuteronomy 6:3-4; 9:1; 20:3). However, the command is more than a call to hear; it challenges the audience to live in obedience to that which is heard (compare James 1:22). God's *decrees and laws* are what Israel is called to hear and, therefore, obey.

Obedience begins by *hearing* and continues through proper action. To *learn* and *follow* God's laws communicates that Israel must accept God's commands, mediated through Moses, and make certain that those commands direct their behavior. Otherwise, true hearing had not occurred. The people needed to listen to Moses to learn what God had to say (Deuteronomy 34:10-12). The command to hear was especially important, given that the Lord made himself heard but not seen at Horeb (4:12, 15).

> *What Do You Think?*
> How can we ensure that our obedience to the Lord doesn't turn into legalism?
> *Digging Deeper*
> In addition to Luke 11:37-54, what passages help you most in this regard?

B. Its Parties (vv. 2-3)

2. The LORD our God made a covenant with us at Horeb.

Moses reminded Israel of where they had received God's law. Elsewhere, Scripture uses the names *Horeb* and Mount Sinai interchangeably as the designation of this location (see Exodus 19:18; Deuteronomy 1:6; 4:10; 1 Kings 8:9; 2 Chronicles 5:10; Psalm 106:19).

Now, a generation later, Moses recalled that moment when God *made a covenant with* Israel. This covenant reminded Israel of God's great acts of salvation and called Israel to live as God's people in light of that reality (see Lesson Context: Covenant).

What Do You Think?
How would you explain to someone the difference between the modern use of the word *covenant* (as in "community covenants") and how that word is used in the text?

Digging Deeper
Why is it important not to read the ancient word through the lens of the modern meaning?

3. It was not with our ancestors that the LORD made this covenant, but with us, with all of us who are alive here today.

This covenant was *not* merely an event for Israel's previous generations (see Exodus 20:1-21); its stipulations also applied to their current and future generations. A communal component to God's commands transcends generations. All Israel was bound by the covenant, even those not yet *alive* when it was given. Moses invited hearers to draw on collective memory and live as a people unified by the covenant.

II. Basic Duties

(DEUTERONOMY 10:12-13)

Preceding this passage, Moses again received the Ten Commandments and placed them in the ark of the covenant (Deuteronomy 10:1-5).

A. Crucial Question (v. 12a)

12a. And now, Israel, what does the LORD your God ask of you

Having confronted the people with their record of idolatry and rebellion (Deuteronomy 9:7-24), Moses set before them a rhetorical question that forced self-reflection to determine how best to live as people of God.

Centuries later, the prophet Micah would ask the same question of *Israel*. Both Micah and Moses were concerned with following God's law and ways. For Micah, following God's law meant "to act justly and to love mercy and to walk humbly with your God" (Micah 6:8). While Moses had a different focus (see commentary on Deuteronomy 10:12b-13, below), their respective answers were complementary, not contradictory. Following God's law implied a desire for justice and mercy.

B. Clear Answer (vv. 12b-13)

12b. but to fear the LORD your God,

The Lord's requirements of his people are remarkably simple. *To fear the Lord your God* meant to possess a reverential respect for him. Fearing God was at the heart of the covenant as God reminded Israel, "You shall have no other gods before me" (Deuteronomy 5:7; see also 5:29; 6:13, 24; 8:6; 13:4).

12c. to walk in obedience to him,

To walk in obedience translates the fear of the Lord into righteous conduct that honors his authority and his commands (Deuteronomy 5:33).

12d. to love him,

Previously, Moses had expressed the centrality of *love* for the Lord, challenging Israel to "love the Lord your God with all your heart and with all your soul and with all your strength" (Deuteronomy 6:5). One way for Israel to show this all-encompassing love was to abide by God's law (11:1).

12e. to serve the LORD your God with all your heart and with all your soul,

Love makes it a joy *to serve the Lord* with the totality of one's being. For ancient Israelites, the *heart* was regarded as the location of an individual's volition, while the *soul* implied the root of life. Serving God required the whole self and necessitated the total allegiance of God's people.

What Do You Think?
Which imperative of *fear, walk, love,* and *serve* will you focus on improving the most in the week ahead?

Digging Deeper
Who can be a mentor for you in this regard?

13. and to observe the LORD's commands and decrees that I am giving you today for your own good?

Moses concludes by stressing the importance of

obedience to the Lord. His *commands* and *decrees* did not exist to frustrate God's people. Instead, they were graciously given to his people for their *good*. God promised to bless his people as long as they obeyed his commands (Deuteronomy 11:27).

❧ *LEAN ON ME* ❧

In the mid-1960s, Bill Withers found himself working in a California manufacturing plant. Between shifts, Bill learned to play the guitar and began writing music. He found success as an artist and signed with a major record company. "Lean on Me," one of his well-known songs, reminds us of the need to recognize our interdependence.

Skeptics may accuse Christians of using God as a crutch. Yes, we are to lean on him, but we also get to walk with him, love him, and honor him with all our hearts, souls, minds, and strength.

How do you view the laws God gave to Israel? Do you see his instructions as loving commands, or harsh demands? Do you view his commands as a crutch, or an invitation to a deeper life? Perhaps another look at John 14:15 is in order.   —D. F.

III. Broader Instructions

(DEUTERONOMY 27:1-10)

Following the exposition of God's commands, Deuteronomy 27 describes instructions for a yet-to-occur covenant renewal ceremony.

A. Recording the Law (vv. 1-4)

1. Moses and the elders of Israel commanded the people: "Keep all these commands that I give you today.

Moses would not be alive when the people of Israel entered the promised land (Deuteronomy 31:2; 34:1-5). Therefore, this address sets the stage for him to transfer his leadership responsibilities. Israel would soon enter the promised land under Joshua's direction (31:23; 34:9; Joshua 1:1-2).

Moses reminded the people of the necessity of keeping God's *commands* (see commentary on Deuteronomy 27:9-10, below). The commands were binding not only in the immediate moment but also as Israel possessed the land.

2-3. When you have crossed the Jordan into

the land the LORD your God is giving you, set up some large stones and coat them with plaster. Write on them all the words of this law when you have crossed over to enter the land the LORD your God is giving you, a land flowing with milk and honey, just as the LORD, the God of your ancestors, promised you.**

Moses described a yet-to-occur ceremony in which Israel would commemorate its covenant with God. After Israel *crossed the Jordan into the land*, they were to remember God's covenant and renew their obligation to obey his commands. While it's possible the ceremony happened on the exact day they crossed the river (see Joshua 4), more likely Moses was referring to a general time afterward.

The practice of whitewashing *stones* and painting the law on them was a practice popularized by ancient Egyptians. Whereas other cultures would carve the words of the law into wood or stone, ancient Egyptians would paint the words of the law onto whitewashed stones.

To write every line of the law would constitute a project too large to be of any practical value. One possibility is that the Ten Commandments, which provided a kind of "constitution" for Israel, were written on the stones. Others note that perhaps the law's blessings and curses were written, reminding Israel of the consequences of obedience and disobedience (Deuteronomy 27:15–28:68).

Previously, *the Lord . . . God* had promised to Moses that he would "bring [Israel] . . . into a good and spacious land, *a land flowing with milk and honey*" (Exodus 3:8). Now Israel would see the fulfillment of this promise.

HOW TO SAY IT

Canaan	*Kay*-nun.
Decalogue	*Dek*-uh-log.
Ebal	*Ee*-bull.
Gerizim	*Gair*-ih-zeem or
	Guh-*rye*-zim.
Horeb	*Ho*-reb.
Jordan	*Jor*-dun.
Sinai	*Sigh*-nye or
	Sigh-nay-eye.

Visual for Lesson 1. *Begin the lesson by asking the class how each of these directions is necessary for justice to be practiced.*

4. And when you have crossed the Jordan, set up these stones on Mount Ebal, as I command you today, and coat them with plaster.

With one exception, this verse repeats much of the information found previously. That exception is the inclusion of the location where this ceremony is to occur, *Mount Ebal*. This mountain, located west of the Jordan River and north of Jerusalem, is mentioned in tandem with another nearby mountain, Mount Gerizim (Deuteronomy 11:29; 27:12-13; Joshua 8:33).

Later, Moses instructed that 6 of the 12 tribes of Israel were to stand on Mount Gerizim and proclaim the covenant blessings (Deuteronomy 27:12), while the remaining 6 tribes were to stand on Mount Ebal and announce the curses of covenant disobedience (27:13). The valley between these two mountains provided a natural amphitheater to highlight the voices. The ceremony took place under the direction of Joshua (Joshua 8:30-33).

B. Raising the Altar (vv. 5-8)

5. Build there an altar to the Lord your God, an altar of stones. Do not use any iron tool on them.

Israel was to *build there an altar* made of *stones* for the worship of *God*. Previously, God told Israel that any tool used on an altar would cause the altar to be defiled (Exodus 20:25). The prohibition of using an *iron tool* may be linked to the pagan religious practices of neighboring peoples, such as the Canaanites. Israel's altar was to be wholly different from altars to false gods.

6. Build the altar of the Lord your God with fieldstones and offer burnt offerings on it to the Lord your God.

As no iron tool could be used on *the altar*, these *fieldstones* were whole and uncut (see Joshua 8:31). Upon the altar Israel presented their *burnt offerings*. During these offerings, an entire animal was burned on the altar, symbolizing the worshipper's complete surrender to God (Leviticus 1:1-17).

7. Sacrifice fellowship offerings there, eating them and rejoicing in the presence of the Lord your God.

Following burnt offerings, *fellowship offerings* burned only a portion of the sacrificial animal; remaining portions were to be used by the worshippers in what amounted to a fellowship-with-God meal (Leviticus 3:1-17).

This would provide a time for Israel to rejoice *in the presence of the Lord* as the meal reminded them of God's presence and faithfulness (see Exodus 20:24). These acts of worship were to be acts of celebration!

> *What Do You Think?*
> What greater personal attention do you need to give to the idea of rejoicing in God?
> *Digging Deeper*
> What are various ways to do so? Give biblical examples of such variety.

8. And you shall write very clearly all the words of this law on these stones you have set up."

The previous instructions are repeated, thereby stressing the importance of *the words of this law* (see commentary on Deuteronomy 27:3).

The Hebrew phrase translated *very clearly* describes the act of engraving words on a stone (see Habakkuk 2:2). This act was to be completed with intentionality and purpose, not haphazardly.

❧ *Knowing Before Doing* ❧

Have you ever heard the saying "Pale ink is better than the most retentive memory"? Every Friday

I examine my calendar, look at the coming week, and create a to-do list. Additional tasks may arise, but my to-do list keeps me on task. The ink of my to-do list focuses my memory.

God instructed kings, prophets, disciples, and apostles to put his truth into writing. The Law of Moses, David's psalms, John's eyewitness testimony, and Paul's letters detail God's revelation for our lives. As people of God, we are called to live in accordance with his instruction. But we can't *live* those instructions until we *know* them. Here's a one-question test in that regard: Considering Jesus' statement "If you love me, keep my commands" (John 14:15), how do you honor the two he called most important (see Matthew 22:37-40)?   —D. F.

C. Reminding the People (vv. 9-10)

9. Then Moses and the Levitical priests said to all Israel, "Be silent, Israel, and listen! You have now become the people of the LORD your God.

Moses' exhortations focused the attention of the audience and drew them into a position of *silent* worship before God (compare Nehemiah 8:11; Zephaniah 1:7; Zechariah 2:13).

Those gathered before *Moses* were a generation removed from those who had experienced personally the establishment of God's covenant. As such, this new generation needed to affirm their commitment to be God's covenant *people*.

What Do You Think?
What can you do to overcome a tendency to talk too much and listen too little?
Digging Deeper
What biblical examples can you give of this kind of tendency?

10. Obey the LORD your God and follow his commands and decrees that I give you today."

As a covenant people, Israel was held to certain standards of obedience: God's *commands and decrees*. The Israelites' obedience did not cause them to be the people of God. Instead, their obedience was to be grounded in the fact that they were in covenant with God (Deuteronomy 8:1-6).

Conclusion
A. That One Thing

Few are considered experts in the realm of corn cultivation. However, this is exactly the one thing for which Orville Redenbacher (1907–1995) was known. By the mid–twentieth century, he had perfected techniques that paved the way for mass consumption of popcorn. His name and likeness were associated with accessible popcorn snacks. A 1987 commercial for his brand described the focus of his work: "Do one thing, and do it better than anyone."

The "one thing" for Israel was to be their *obedience* to God and his law. This was how they were to live according to the covenant. Moses recognized this requirement, and it's the main reason imperatives like *obey*, *keep*, *serve*, and *do* are found throughout this week's Scripture text. A people obedient to the commands of God would have a proper understanding of justice and just living (see Leviticus 19:15-16; Deuteronomy 16:20; Isaiah 1:17; Zechariah 7:9).

It was one thing for Israel to write God's laws on stones; it was quite another thing to practice faithful obedience to those laws. May we write God's laws on our hearts and practice faithful obedience in all areas of our lives (2 Corinthians 3:3).

B. Prayer

Father, may we recognize that the challenge placed before the ancient Israelites is the challenge placed before us today. May we be more than hearers of your Word; may we resolve to be doers as well. In Jesus' name we pray. Amen.

C. Thought to Remember
Obedience to God must remain
our top priority.

VISUALS FOR THESE LESSONS

The visual pictured in each lesson (example: page 126) is a small reproduction of a large, full-color poster included in the *Adult Resources* packet for the Winter '21-'22 Quarter. That packet also contains the very useful *Presentation Tools* CD for teacher use. Order No. 2629122 from your supplier.

INVOLVEMENT LEARNING

Enhance your lesson with NIV® Bible Student (from your curriculum supplier) and the reproducible activity page (at www.standardlesson.com or in the back of the NIV® Standard Lesson Commentary Deluxe Edition).

Into the Lesson

Distribute the following open-end sentences on slips of paper (one slip per learner; repeat sentences as necessary).

Children need to learn obedience because . . .

The biggest problem caused by disobedience is . . .

Here's what happened when I disobeyed . . .

Discuss completions in one of two ways: either (1) form discussion pairs or triads of learners who have the same sentence, or (2) form discussion pairs or triads of learners who have the same sentences.

After three or four minutes, allow volunteers to share responses with the whole class. Make sure to hear at least one response for each sentence.

Lead into Bible study by saying, "Obviously, obedience is a big deal for people today. This was a challenge for God's people in ancient times too."

Into the Word

Prepare a brief lecture to remind class members of the setting and history of today's texts. Use material from the Lesson Context above.

Divide the class into pairs or triads (consider using the same groupings as for the introductory activity). Ask students to survey today's texts to list every verse that contains a command to obey. Beside each verse, they can explain or paraphrase the admonition.

After several minutes, call the class together to share answers. Discuss, "Why did Moses make each of the exhortations we find here?"

Option. Distribute copies of the "Hear Here" exercise from the activity page, which you can download. Ask all class members to complete this activity after finishing the above.

Next distribute copies of a chart (you prepare) that feature these three headings:

Activity / Purpose / Today

In the pairs or triads formed above, have class members list in the first column elements of the ceremony/worship described in Deuteronomy 27:1-10. Under the second heading, have them list the purpose for each element. Allow about five minutes to complete these two columns. After you call time, ask volunteers to share responses with the whole class.

Into Life

Send class members back to their groups to make a list under the *Today* heading. For each item in the worship ceremony described in Deuteronomy, class members should list a comparable aspect or principle of worship today. After calling time, reconvene for whole-class sharing and discussion. Use the following discussion prompts as needed:

1–How prominent should God's Word be in our services?
2–How meaningful is the use of Scripture in our services?
3–Why is it important for us to know and reflect on Scripture?
4–How can we make the teaching of Scripture more central to daily living?

Remind students that the theme of this lesson introduces the theme of the whole quarter: justice. Send class members back to their groups one more time and challenge them to look again at the five admonitions in Deuteronomy 10:12-13. For each one, they should think of ways that heeding it contributes to justice in the world. After several minutes, discuss as a class.

Option. Distribute copies of the "Doing What God Wants" exercise from the activity page as a take-home devotional work. Close with five prayers that ask God's help in heeding the five admonitions listed in the take-home activity, one request per prayer.

JUSTICE AND KINDNESS

DEVOTIONAL READING: 2 Samuel 9:1-7, 9-12
BACKGROUND SCRIPTURE: 2 Samuel 9

2 SAMUEL 9:1-7, 9-12

¹ David asked, "Is there anyone still left of the house of Saul to whom I can show kindness for Jonathan's sake?"

² Now there was a servant of Saul's household named Ziba. They summoned him to appear before David, and the king said to him, "Are you Ziba?"

"At your service," he replied.

³ The king asked, "Is there no one still alive from the house of Saul to whom I can show God's kindness?"

Ziba answered the king, "There is still a son of Jonathan; he is lame in both feet."

⁴ "Where is he?" the king asked.

Ziba answered, "He is at the house of Makir son of Ammiel in Lo Debar."

⁵ So King David had him brought from Lo Debar, from the house of Makir son of Ammiel.

⁶ When Mephibosheth son of Jonathan, the son of Saul, came to David, he bowed down to pay him honor.

David said, "Mephibosheth!"

"At your service," he replied.

⁷ "Don't be afraid," David said to him, "for I will surely show you kindness for the sake of your father Jonathan. I will restore to you all the land that belonged to your grandfather Saul, and you will always eat at my table."

. . . .

⁹ Then the king summoned Ziba, Saul's steward, and said to him, "I have given your master's grandson everything that belonged to Saul and his family. ¹⁰ You and your sons and your servants are to farm the land for him and bring in the crops, so that your master's grandson may be provided for. And Mephibosheth, grandson of your master, will always eat at my table." (Now Ziba had fifteen sons and twenty servants.)

¹¹ Then Ziba said to the king, "Your servant will do whatever my lord the king commands his servant to do." So Mephibosheth ate at David's table like one of the king's sons.

¹² Mephibosheth had a young son named Mika, and all the members of Ziba's household were servants of Mephibosheth.

KEY TEXT

David asked, "Is there anyone still left of the house of Saul to whom I can show kindness for Jonathan's sake?" —**2 Samuel 9:1**

Justice, Law, History

Unit 1: God Requires Justice

Lessons 1–4

Lesson Aims

After participating in this lesson, each learner will be able to:

1. Summarize the history behind David's kindness to Mephibosheth.

2. Evaluate David's motives in doing so.

3. Make a commitment to show kindness to a marginalized person in the week ahead.

Lesson Outline

Introduction

A. Kindness from Memory

Khaled Hosseini's 2004 novel *The Kite Runner* is a gripping story of childhood friendship, betrayal, and the search for redemption. Set in Afghanistan, the story traces the life story of Amir, the young son of a wealthy family, who befriends Hassan, the underprivileged son of his father's servant. The boys become friends, but the difference in status between them leads to a grueling separation that haunts Amir for many years. Some decades later, following Hassan's death, Amir searches for Hassan's son in order to rescue him from abuse and show him kindness for his father's sake.

Similar themes of friendship, redemption, and rescue arise in the books of 1 and 2 Samuel through the story of David and Jonathan. Long after he could no longer enjoy a friendship with Jonathan, David remembered his promises and looked for the chance to show kindness to his friend's son.

B. Lesson Context

In the Christian arrangement of the Old Testament, 1 and 2 Samuel are part of the historical books (Joshua–Esther). They record the transition from being governed by the Lord (theocracy) to an earthly king (monarchy, beginning around 1050 BC). The man Samuel, after whom the books were named, was a pivotal figure: the last of the judges and the first of the prophets (see Acts 3:24; 13:20).

While Samuel was well respected throughout the land, his sons did not enjoy the same esteem (1 Samuel 8:1-3). The Israelites, tired of the abuses of Samuel's sons, demanded that Samuel give them an earthly king "like all the nations" (8:5). This flew in the face of God's desire for Israel to be a priestly, holy nation under his rule (Exodus 19:6; 1 Samuel 12:12-16). But the Lord did as they desired, choosing Saul to be king. But Saul did not faithfully carry out the Lord's commands (13:7-14; 15:1-35). The Lord rejected Saul and had Samuel anoint David to be Saul's successor (13:14; 16:1).

Though Saul was initially fond of David and took him into his court (1 Samuel 16:21-22), the king knew that David was chosen to succeed him

(20:30-31). He grew fearful and even murderous when David's renown started to surpass his own (18:6-16, 25, 29; 19:9-10; 23:7-8; 26:1-2).

Yet for all of Saul's paranoid attacks on him, David consistently refused to harm or retaliate against Saul (1 Samuel 24:6; 26:11; 2 Samuel 1:16). In spite of his complicated interactions with Saul, David's most loyal and trusted friend was none other than Saul's oldest son, Jonathan (1 Samuel 18:1-4). Their friendship resulted in a covenant that obligated both parties. Jonathan would protect and support David, while David pledged to show kindness to Jonathan's family (20:12-17).

Material in 1 and 2 Samuel is sometimes arranged thematically rather than chronologically. So the relationship between events in David's life can be hard to determine. This is especially true of David's ordering the deaths of several of Saul's sons (2 Samuel 21:1-9). It seems at first glance that the incident in 2 Samuel 21 must have occurred after our story (see 9:1a, below). But it also could have been included in the latter chapters of 2 Samuel to fit with other stories about David's fallibility (example: 24:1-17).

Clues from the surrounding material place today's text some 15 to 20 years after David began his reign in 1010 BC. David had spent much of his time solidifying his control as king over all Israel by defeating enemies both within and without (examples: 2 Samuel 2:8-32; 5:6-25). Saul and Jonathan had been dead for some time (1 Samuel 31). Another of Saul's sons, Ish-Bosheth, ruled in the northern tribes until his own death, at which time David began his rule over all of Israel (2 Samuel 5:1-5). But the tribes had shown their preference for a descendant of Saul on the throne (2:8-9). In situations such as this one, it was often top priority for a king from a new ruling family to kill off all members of the previous king's household, thereby eliminating any rivals (examples: 1 Kings 15:29; 16:11).

I. A Promise Remembered
(2 SAMUEL 9:1-4)
A. David's Search (vv. 1-3a)

1a. David asked, "Is there anyone still left of the house of Saul

David had vowed against destroying Saul's house, both to *Saul* and to Jonathan (1 Samuel 24:20-22; the circumstances of 2 Samuel 21:1-9 did not constitute unfaithfulness to his oath). In spite of potential threats to his rule, David determined to keep his promises and spare the lineage of his friend and his former king.

How could David not know whether anyone of Saul's household still lived? For one thing, he had been busy with wars, establishing Jerusalem as his capital, and trying to move the ark. How was he meant to keep track of who died in those years? But the answer may be even simpler than that: Saul's family was hiding. Knowing that David had been crowned king first in Judah and then over all Israel, any remaining sons of Saul would have to fear that they would be executed to prevent their trying to regain the throne.

1b. "to whom I can show kindness for Jonathan's sake?"

Some have said that David's motives here may have involved keeping his enemies close, so as to make sure they did not plot his overthrow (compare 1 Kings 2:36-38). Or similarly, he may have thought that being kind to Saul's family might score him political points with any remaining supporters of Saul's dynasty. Knowing that people rarely have pure motivations, it is possible that David valued both keeping potential usurpers close *and* scoring points with Saul's supporters. But his main motivation was neither of these things.

David's pledge to Jonathan went so far as to ensure continual *kindness* to the same, even after "the Lord has cut off every one of David's enemies from the face of the earth" (1 Samuel 20:15).

HOW TO SAY IT

Ammiel	*Ah*-mih-el.
Ish-Bosheth	Ish-*Bo*-sheth.
Lo Debar	Low *Dee*-bar.
Makir	*May*-ker.
Mephibosheth	Meh-*fib*-o-sheth.
Mika	*My*-ka.
theocracy	thee-*ok*-ruh-see (*th* as in *thin*).
Ziba	*Zih*-bah.

Second Samuel 8 details David's military defeat of all Israel's surrounding enemies (2 Samuel 8:1-14). It is fitting that after we hear of David's enemies being cut off from the face of the earth, we hear of his determination to find someone to care for *for Jonathan's sake.*

This kindness often describes acts of loyalty or trustworthiness within the context of a promise (example: Joshua 2:12). The same Hebrew word is frequently translated "love" when referring to God's actions within the covenant (Exodus 20:6; Deuteronomy 7:12; etc.). Kindness like this is built into the character of God (see Exodus 34:6; Numbers 14:19).

Covenants were struck in situations where a power imbalance existed. At the time that David and Jonathan committed to their own covenant, Jonathan was the heir to Saul's throne and David was a soldier, albeit a very popular one. By the time David was looking for an opportunity to act on this covenant, Jonathan was dead and David himself was king instead. David's adherence to the covenant years later depended solely on his faithfulness toward Jonathan, not to any possible falling out of their friendship.

> *What Do You Think?*
> Under what circumstances should you promote memorializing a fellow servant of God?
> *Digging Deeper*
> What guardrails would you suggest for helping keep that memorialization focused ultimately on Jesus?

2. Now there was a servant of Saul's household named Ziba. They summoned him to appear before David, and the king said to him, "Are you Ziba?" "At your service," he replied.

Ziba held high position among the servants in Saul's *household* even after Saul's death, demonstrated here by his being the one called into David's presence. He was the manager of Saul's estate at this point and had become wealthy as a result (see 2 Samuel 9:10, below). Other episodes affirm Ziba's continued status (16:1-4; 19:15-30). Ziba would be sure to know all about Saul's remaining descendants.

Referring to himself as being *at* [David's] *service* identified Ziba as being loyal to David. This was important to establish if Ziba worried that David might take revenge on the house of Saul, despite the king's claim to want to be kind to someone in the family. However, David had shown time and again that he did not desire to wipe out Saul's family or his soldiers (examples: 2 Samuel 3:6–4:12).

3a. The king asked, "Is there no one still alive from the house of Saul to whom I can show God's kindness?"

David restated his question (see 2 Samuel 9:1, above), now to a man who should have known the answer. Although the question would not be redundant to Ziba, who was hearing it for the first time, the repetition emphasizes for the reader David's urgent desire. The slight difference of showing *God's kindness* (rather than "for Jonathan's sake" in verse 1b) recalls God's favor expressed through and as a result of his covenant with Israel (examples: Exodus 15:13; "love" in Deuteronomy 7:7-9).

> *What Do You Think?*
> What are some ways to ensure that God gets the credit in your acts of kindness?
> *Digging Deeper*
> What texts in addition to Mark 9:41 and Luke 17:10 inform your answer?

B. Ziba's Knowledge (vv. 3b-4)

3b. Ziba answered the king, "There is still a son of Jonathan; he is lame in both feet."

The first mention of this *son* comes in a passing note in 2 Samuel 4:4. He was five years old when Saul and *Jonathan* died in battle. At that time, his nurse fled with the boy, likely thinking that David would come to eliminate him (compare the similar story of Joash in 2 Kings 11:1-3). Unfortunately, though, the boy fell during the flight and suffered permanently crippling injuries. As *Ziba* spoke, that child would probably be in his early to mid 20s.

Ziba did not mention the child's name in his reply to David, but seems quick to have mentioned his disability. Maybe he knew David would immediately know which son Ziba was referring to. Perhaps he sought to reassure David that Jonathan's son was no threat, so that David would not seek to kill him. Or perhaps he hoped that David would do exactly that, relieving Ziba of any obligation to provide for him (see 2 Samuel 9:7, below).

> **What Do You Think?**
> How should a person's disabilities affect your responses to the previous two questions, if at all? Why?
>
> *Digging Deeper*
> Considering 2 Samuel 16:1-4; 19:24-30, how should you deal with third-party reports that bring up questions of worthiness?

4. "Where is he?" the king asked. Ziba answered, "He is at the house of Makir son of Ammiel in Lo Debar."

Lo Debar was a village east of the Jordan River, in Gilead and associated with the tribe of Gad (Joshua 13:24-28). It was located much closer to Ish-Bosheth's political center, Mahanaim (Joshua 21:38; 2 Samuel 2:8), than to David's capital, Jerusalem (5:5). Although *Makir* had probably been a supporter of Saul originally, we later learn that he supported David and his men during Absalom's revolt (17:24-29). The outcome of David's inquiry here may have changed the man's loyalties (see 9:9, below).

Nothing more is known about Makir's father, *Ammiel*.

❧ *Enabled to Aid* ❧

I often saw her, bent nearly in half, making her way down the street in the Ukrainian city where I lived. One day we started talking. She told me about surviving the Holodomor, a horrifying famine in Ukraine in the 1930s. In an effort to stifle Ukrainian resistance to Soviet rule, Stalin enacted policies that resulted in widespread starvation; at least 3.9 million Ukrainians died as a result. My new friend was left with debilitating disabilities caused by severe malnourishment in her childhood.

Over the next few weeks, I learned she had few family members to care for her. But one day when I knocked on her door, a stranger opened it. My friend had found some boarders to share her small apartment and care for her. They provided comfort and much-needed financial help to this woman who had seen so much tragedy.

Though my Ukrainian friend sought out help, there are many others who need us to ask after their well-being and take initiative to help. What step can you take today to give aid and comfort?

–L. M.-W.

II. A Promise Fulfilled
(2 Samuel 9:5-7, 9-12)
A. Mephibosheth's Arrival (vv. 5-6)

5-6. So King David had him brought from Lo Debar, from the house of Makir son of Ammiel. When Mephibosheth son of Jonathan, the son of Saul, came to David, he bowed down to pay him honor.

Mephibosheth immediately honored *David* and addressed him with the deferential language appropriate when speaking to a king, echoing Ziba's words (see 2 Samuel 9:2, above). As a potential rival to the throne—being *son of Jonathan,* who was the firstborn *son of* the dead King *Saul*—Mephibosheth must have felt the tension in this moment. Accordingly, his first aim was to assure David that he was not a threat to his throne.

B. David's Declaration (vv. 7, 9-10)

7. "Don't be afraid," David said to him, "for I will surely show you kindness for the sake of your father Jonathan. I will restore to you all the land that belonged to your grandfather Saul, and you will always eat at my table."

Given the practice of familial annihilation discussed above, Mephibosheth may have expected to receive anything but kindness from David (compare 2 Samuel 19:28). But *David* immediately offered reassurance to Mephibosheth that he need not *be afraid*. David's summons was not, as it turns out, a ruse to flush Mephibosheth out of hiding. Instead, David wanted to show him *kindness for the sake of [his] father* in order to keep his covenant with *Jonathan*. Mephibosheth would eat at the king's *table,* just as David had once eaten at Saul's table (1 Samuel 20:24-27).

David's desire to *restore* to Mephibosheth the estate of his father suggests that David had gathered additional information beyond what is stated in these verses. Mephibosheth's living in Lo Debar in Makir's house makes clear that he wasn't living on any of Saul's lands, whether or not he was seeing any other benefit from the properties. Having *the land* restored cemented that Mephibosheth would receive whatever wealth was to be made from his grandfather's holdings.

> **What Do You Think?**
> What criteria will you use to decide which of your acts of kindness will be done anonymously and which will be a public witness?
> *Digging Deeper*
> What texts in addition to Matthew 5:14-16 and 6:1-4 help you resolve this tension?

Mephibosheth seemed sincerely and humbly grateful for David's kindness to him (compare 2 Samuel 9:8, not in our printed text). Mephibosheth no doubt knew of his father's friendship with David and probably heard stories of Jonathan's aid to David.

9. Then the king summoned Ziba, Saul's steward, and said to him, "I have given your master's grandson everything that belonged to Saul and his family.

David had come to possess Saul's land (see 2 Samuel 12:8; also lesson 10), whether because of his marriage to Michal (compare Numbers 27:8) or as forfeiture to his throne after the failure of Ish-Bosheth's brief reign. By returning Saul's property to Jonathan's son, David executed not only kindness but also restorative justice (Leviticus 25:23-28). Perhaps Ziba had taken advantage of Mephibosheth's disabled condition and commandeered Saul's estate for himself. His motives are not analyzed here, but later events suggest this would be in character for the *steward* (see 2 Samuel 9:10-11a, below).

10a. "You and your sons and your servants are to farm the land for him and bring in the crops, so that your master's grandson may be

provided for. And Mephibosheth, grandson of your master, will always eat at my table."**

Although *Mephibosheth* would *eat* in David's house, *the land* would provide for the rest of Mephibosheth's family (see 2 Samuel 9:12, below) and for the servants supported through their own work.

10b. (Now Ziba had fifteen sons and twenty servants.)

Ziba had apparently grown wealthy as a result of his control over Saul's estate, having *twenty servants* of his own, as well as *fifteen sons*. His work on the land would continue to support his own household as well as Mephibosheth's.

C. The New Normal (vv. 11-12)

11a. Then Ziba said to the king, "Your servant will do whatever my lord the king commands his servant to do."

Once again *Ziba* emphasized his loyalty to David, calling himself his *servant* twice. Though he did not protest David's decree, he nonetheless looked for an opportunity to have it annulled. His chance came years later when David fled the palace during Absalom's rebellion (see 2 Samuel 15:37–16:4; contrast 19:24-30).

11b. So Mephibosheth ate at David's table like one of the king's sons.

Whereas Jonathan had "loved [David] as himself" (1 Samuel 18:1), now David would care for Jonathan's son as his own son. David's care for *Mephibosheth* yields a more satisfying conclusion to the story of David and Jonathan, which otherwise would have had a disheartening end.

❧ *HEALING THROUGH HELPING* ❧

Rick and Samantha's son was 19 when he died. Just as he was growing into a man, he was stricken with a rare disease that killed him quickly. His parents spent months in shock, mulling over what had happened—wondering if they could have seen the signs earlier, gotten him treatment earlier, somehow prevented his dying.

Then Rick and Samantha began to think about how to help others. In their grief, they met other families with children suffering from the same disease their son had. They began raising money for research, sponsoring fund-raising events and banquets. Their network of friends expanded as they supported others in similar situations. In the process of helping other families heal, Rick and Samantha have found healing themselves.

Similarly, David no doubt found healing from the loss of his friend Jonathan by reaching out to Jonathan's son. Think of your own vulnerabilities and emotional pain. How can you move toward healing by helping another?   –L. M.-W.

12. Mephibosheth had a young son named Mika, and all the members of Ziba's household were servants of Mephibosheth.

Jonathan's grandson *Mika* would carry on the family (see 1 Chronicles 8:34-35, where Mephibosheth is called Merib-Baal).

Though one might expect David's sons to have some feelings about Mephibosheth's new role in their family, no hostilities between them are noted here or elsewhere.

Conclusion

A. Kindness from Experience

When I was a poor college student, times were tight financially and I received many kindnesses from God's people who helped me through. Small gifts paid for meals, books, and gas and always seemed to come when I needed them most. Now that I'm older, employed full-time, and the tables have turned, I try to remember those days and give some help to poor college students when the opportunity arises.

For David, the idea that he would help others based on his own remembrances and experiences is a running theme throughout today's text. He showed kindness and justice to Mephibosheth, partly because David had pledged to do so but also because he had received the same from Jonathan. And David remembered the ordeals he suffered at the hands of an unpredictable Saul and sought to rectify the misdeeds of that predecessor. But most of all, as a man after God's own heart (1 Samuel 13:14; Acts 13:22), David sought to display in his kingship the characteristics of divine justice that were required of Israel as a whole. He

DO YOUR FRIENDSHIPS NURTURE KINDNESS?

Visual for Lesson 2. *Point to this visual while discussing verse 1, and ask volunteers to give examples from their own friendships.*

knew that he must fear, serve, and love God with all his heart and soul (see Deuteronomy 10:12; also lesson 1).

The same is true today. We are called to remember the kindness that God has shown us—especially through Jesus' life, death, and resurrection—and show that kindness to others. This may mean providing for the needs of others in our community; it could mean making restitution for wrongs that we did not commit. Justice and kindness call us to go beyond loving our friends to loving even those people who may be enemies (Matthew 5:43-48). In this way, we demonstrate the covenant kindness of our God.

What Do You Think?
  Which principle in today's text will you have the most problem integrating into your life?
Digging Deeper
  What action will you take this week to resolve this problem?

B. Prayer

Father, you have shown us many kindnesses and given us examples to follow in your Word. May we show your love, kindness, and justice to others in return. In Jesus' name we pray. Amen.

C. Thought to Remember

Show God's kindness—keep your promises.

INVOLVEMENT LEARNING

Enhance your lesson with NIV® Bible Student (from your curriculum supplier) and the reproducible activity page (at www.standardlesson.com or in the back of the NIV® Standard Lesson Commentary Deluxe Edition).

Into the Lesson

Before class begins, write on the board several of the following sentences with words scrambled.

Justice leads to kindness.
True justice is sometimes surprising.
Not everyone wants justice.
It's never too late to be kind.
It's possible to ignore justice.

Allow a few minutes for learners to unscramble the sentences. Ask for them to be read aloud. Ask volunteers to tell whether they agree or disagree with a given sentence and to share an example of why they believe it's true or not.

Alternative 1. Create a handout to distribute for small-group work.

Alternative 2. Before class, place at each chair a copy of the "Why Be Kind?" exercise from the activity page, which you can download. Students can begin work on as they arrive.

Make a transition by saying, "How are kindness and justice connected? David's actions today give us some insight into this question."

Into the Word

Recruit three volunteers to explain the background material for this week's lesson by preparing a 90-second story beginning with one of these phrases:

Let me tell you about Saul
Let me tell you about Jonathan
Let me tell you about Mephibosheth.

After their presentations, have the text read aloud, then distribute handouts (you create) with the following nine sentences on all handouts. Form groups of three or four to put the sentences in the correct biblical order.

1–David promised to restore to Mephibosheth all the land that had belonged to his grandfather Saul.

2–David promised that Mephibosheth would always eat at his table.

3–Ziba, a servant of Saul's household, appeared before the king.

4–David summoned Jonathan's son Mephibosheth to appear before him.

5–Mephibosheth had Ziba and all his sons as his servants.

6–Ziba promised to follow David's orders.

7–David asked whether anyone from Jonathan's family line was still living.

8–David told Ziba that Mephibosheth would receive everything that had belonged to Saul and his family.

9–Ziba told David that Jonathan's son was still alive.

After several minutes, ask the groups to report (*expected order: 7, 3, 9, 4, 1, 8, 2, 6, 5*). Discuss by asking how the five sentences that opened the class apply to today's story.

Option. Distribute copies of the "www.Ziba&Mephibosheth.edu?" exercise from the activity page. Allow study pairs several minutes to complete the activity before whole-class sharing.

Into Life

Brainstorming. Write this header on the board

Victims of Injustice

Give class members 90 seconds to call out responses; list them under the heading.

Then write a second heading beside the first:

How Kindness Could Help

Discuss how each example listed could be remedied by acts of kindness. As learners share, make a list under this second heading. Ask the class how they as individuals or as a group could begin to show kindness in one of the examples. Close with prayer for participants to commit to pursuing at least one idea from the second list.

JUSTICE AND RIGHTEOUSNESS

DEVOTIONAL READING: Isaiah 9:1-7
BACKGROUND SCRIPTURE: Isaiah 9:1-7

ISAIAH 9:2-7

² The people walking in darkness
 have seen a great light;
on those living in the land of deep
  darkness
 a light has dawned.
³ You have enlarged the nation
 and increased their joy;
they rejoice before you
 as people rejoice at the harvest,
as warriors rejoice
 when dividing the plunder.
⁴ For as in the day of Midian's defeat,
 you have shattered
the yoke that burdens them,
 the bar across their shoulders,
 the rod of their oppressor.
⁵ Every warrior's boot used in battle
 and every garment rolled in blood
will be destined for burning,
 will be fuel for the fire.
⁶ For to us a child is born,
 to us a son is given,
 and the government will be on his
  shoulders.

And he will be called
 Wonderful Counselor, Mighty God,
 Everlasting Father, Prince of Peace.
⁷ Of the greatness of his government and
  peace
 there will be no end.
He will reign on David's throne
 and over his kingdom,
establishing and upholding it
 with justice and righteousness
 from that time on and forever.
The zeal of the LORD Almighty
 will accomplish this.

KEY TEXT

Of the greatness of his government and peace there will be no end. He will reign on David's throne and over his kingdom, establishing and upholding it with justice and righteousness from that time on and forever. The zeal of the LORD Almighty will accomplish this. —**Isaiah 9:7**

Photo © Getty Images

JUSTICE, LAW, HISTORY

Unit 1: God Requires Justice

LESSONS 1–4

LESSON AIMS

After participating in this lesson, each learner will be able to:

1. Describe the historical background to Isaiah's prophetic ministry.

2. Explain the importance of Isaiah 9 in the New Testament.

3. Write a reminder of how anticipating Jesus' coming should contribute to his or her joy daily.

LESSON OUTLINE

Introduction
  A. Utter Darkness
  B. Lesson Context
I. The Great Reversal (Isaiah 9:2-5)
  A. Light to Shine (v. 2)
  B. Joy to Erupt (v. 3)
    Gathered at the Table
  C. Historical Analogy (vv. 4-5)
II. The Promised Child (Isaiah 9:6-7)
  A. His Names (v. 6)
    What's in a Name?
  B. His Government (v. 7)
Conclusion
  A. A Dark State
  B. Prayer
  C. Thought to Remember

Introduction

A. Utter Darkness

For a year I taught at a Christian high school in Oklahoma where there were rocky hills with caves. One Sunday afternoon one of my fellow teachers took me and some students to go spelunking. We entered the four-foot-tall opening. Within a few yards we reached a rock outcropping with a key-shaped opening, requiring us to scoot along on our bellies. Only a narrow slit in the rock allowed the right leg to reach the ground to power forward, while the left leg trailed behind. After a few feet the cave opened up some, and we walked hunched over for what seemed quite a distance. We eventually reached a larger chamber in which we could all stand. Then my friend had everyone turn off their flashlights. We were far enough into the cave that there was absolutely no light coming in from the outside. That was the darkest physical darkness I have ever been in! Had I been lost in that cave with no light, I am sure panic would soon set in.

In the beginning God created physical light (Genesis 1:3-5). And then, at just the right time, Jesus arrived in the world as our spiritual light (John 1:1-5). Isaiah prophesied his coming centuries in advance, offering hope to all who would believe.

B. Lesson Context

Isaiah lived and prophesied in the eighth century BC, with access to the royal court in Judah (see 2 Kings 19:1–20:19; Isaiah 37–39). Some students suggest that the book of Isaiah includes part of the official court records during his service to various kings (see 2 Chronicles 26:22; 32:32). His ministry spanned the reigns of four kings (see Isaiah 1:1; this indicates a date range of approximately 740–680 BC). Isaiah was perhaps martyred in the early years of a fifth king, the wicked Manasseh (compare Hebrews 11:37).

Isaiah 9:2-7, today's text, must be understood in the larger context of Isaiah 7–12. This section is often called The Book of Immanuel because of its focus on the promised blessing of God's presence; "God with us" is the meaning of the word

Immanuel (Isaiah 7:14; 8:8-10; Matthew 1:23). The immediate need for that divine presence was a war that saw Syria and the northern kingdom of Israel in an alliance against Judah, the southern kingdom of divided Israel (Isaiah 7:1).

In reaction, the prophet Isaiah brought a message of hope to Judah's ungodly King Ahaz. The young and inexperienced king (2 Kings 16:2) was frightened, along with all of Judah, by the political winds (Isaiah 7:2). The prophet encouraged Ahaz to trust the Lord in this matter. Isaiah even offered Ahaz a sign from the Lord (7:11).

For some reason, Ahaz refused to ask for a sign (Isaiah 7:12). Perhaps he already had in mind an alliance with the Assyrians (2 Kings 16:7). But the Lord gave the "house of David" (represented by Ahaz) a sign anyway: a child to be known as Immanuel (Isaiah 7:13-14). Before this child could reach an age of accountability, the two threats in the north would be destroyed (7:7-9, 15). Since Ahaz had refused to ask for a sign, the sign that was nevertheless provided therefore remained a "distant" prophecy for a remnant of God's people, not to be fulfilled until Immanuel truly would come in ultimate victory.

The importance of the prophet Isaiah is seen in the fact that he is mentioned by name over 20 times in the New Testament—more than all other prophets combined.

I. The Great Reversal
(Isaiah 9:2-5)
A. Light to Shine (v. 2)

2. The people walking in darkness have seen a great light; on those living in the land of deep darkness a light has dawned.

The prophetic word was so certain that Isaiah spoke of the prophecy as having already been fulfilled. *The people* had continued to walk (that is, live) as if in the darkest part of the night (compare Isaiah 5:30; 8:22). These were the Lord's own people, whose ways the Lord had instructed Isaiah not to adopt (8:11). They apparently had no desire to walk in the light (compare John 3:19-20). They preferred *the land of deep darkness* of mind and spirit, bereft of God's presence (compare Psalm 23:4).

Yet it is on people who seem to prefer darkness that *a great light* comes. They *have seen* (personal experience) this light and *on those . . . a light has dawned* (objective fact). Light is a figure of speech for God himself or for his divine presence (see Isaiah 60:1-3; 2 Corinthians 4:6; 1 John 1:5; Revelation 21:23; 22:5).

Matthew quoted Isaiah 9:2 to refer to Jesus (Matthew 4:16). Jesus' ministry was like a great light bursting on an unworthy people. Yet in spite of Jesus' great miracles and authoritative teachings, most chose not to walk in the light. As a result, Jesus condemned them (see Matthew 11:21-24). In other words, they should have known better.

What Do You Think?
What personal experiences of spiritual darkness would be most valuable to pass along to others as warnings?
Digging Deeper
How and when will you do so?

B. Joy to Erupt (v. 3)
3a. You have enlarged the nation

The nation of Israel would be *enlarged* many times over in terms of both population and boundaries (see Isaiah 26:15; 54:1-3). Following Jesus' ministry, this expansion was caused by the great influx of Gentiles into the kingdom of God, not of David, in fulfillment of the first promise of God to Abraham (Genesis 12:3).

And it did not happen overnight. The fulfillment of this verse was neither in national Judah nor in the northern kingdom of divided Israel. Judah was weak compared to the world powers and was never a powerful nation after Assyria consolidated control over the region. Even after the return from Babylonian exile in the sixth century BC, times were very difficult. The multiplying of the nation must refer to a spiritual reality.

3b. and increased their joy;

This verse contains an uncertainty in the Hebrew, and not all translations are alike. The problem is that the Hebrew word for *to it* or *to them*, which here is translated *their*, sounds exactly like the Hebrew word for *not* (a homonym). It would be easy for a copyist of Hebrew to write *not* when another person actually is saying *to it/them* (or vice versa) during verbal dictation. This uncertainty between *not* and *to it/them* occurs over a dozen times in the Hebrew Old Testament. If *to it* was the original intent, then the idea is what we see here in the translation of the *New International Version*. Thus the enlarging of the nation is cause for the increase in *joy*.

The *King James Version*, by contrast, has "and not increased the joy" in the first line. The result is a rapid shift from the positive "you have enlarged the nation" of verse 3a to the negative "not increased the joy." One explanation of this shift proposes that the prophet at first is foreseeing the people dwelling in darkness; then the light dawns (Isaiah 9:2), and nation is multiplied (9:3a). But that is followed by a time of difficulty (lack of joy).

3c. they rejoice before you as people rejoice at the harvest, as warriors rejoice when dividing the plunder.

To the situation just noted, Isaiah compared the future joy from the light to two of the greatest occasions for joy in the ancient world: *harvest* time (Exodus 23:16; Deuteronomy 16:13-15) and the victorious end of war, indicated by *dividing the plunder* thereof (Numbers 31:25-47; 1 Samuel 30:16; etc.). Both events are considered gifts from God (see Deuteronomy 28:2-8). The outcomes of harvest and war were matters of life and death. No wonder Isaiah used these as comparisons for the forthcoming joy when the light would arrive!

> *What Do You Think?*
> How will you ensure that what most causes joy for God is also what most causes joy for you?
> *Digging Deeper*
> What Scripture text most challenges you to do so? Why?

❧ GATHERED AT THE TABLE ❧

On college game days, my team was ready. We had analyzed the previous Saturday's game, gone over scouting reports, and practiced daily. We knew our game plan, and we were mentally and physically ready to execute it.

Saturday mornings were spent together in the equipment locker room. We saw ourselves as a great army preparing for battle as we strapped on our gear, donned our colors, and applied war paint to our faces. On game days the earth shook with the energy of our hard work.

The victorious outcome outweighed the fact that afterward we could barely walk for the bruises and cuts that tattooed our bodies. Even so, we sat around a banquet table, cheering and laughing and loving one another. We rejoiced in the "harvest" as we emotionally shared the "spoils."

God's promise is of a joy infinitely greater. The joy Israel would experience is like a victorious team gathered around a banquet table. What hard work are you doing now in anticipation of the joy God will lay out before his people? For a hint along these lines, see 1 Corinthians 3:8-15.
—W. L.

C. Historical Analogy (vv. 4-5)

4. For as in the day of Midian's defeat, you have shattered the yoke that burdens them, the bar across their shoulders, the rod of their oppressor.

The analogy in view is freedom from foreign domination. *The day of Midian's defeat* refers to Gideon's defeat of the Midianites, over 400 years in the past at this point (Judges 6–8). Gideon's actions triggered knowledge that his victory could only have been an act of God (7:2-14). No one expected victory in Gideon's day, and no one would expect it in Jesus' day. Skeptics said things like "How can the Messiah come from Galilee?" (John 7:41) and "Look into it, and you will find that a prophet does not come out of Galilee" (7:52). The people who made this statement were wrong: Jonah was from Galilee (2 Kings 14:25).

Some students see echoes of the exodus from Egypt in the use of such words as *yoke* and *bar* (Leviticus 26:13), *shoulders* (Psalm 81:6), and *oppressor* ("slave drivers" in Exodus 5:6, 10, 14). The exodus events were of divine origin, as will be the birth of a special child (Isaiah 9:6, below).

The imagery is of a disenfranchised, subjugated people. This would be the status of the Jews under Roman rule in the time of Jesus. Regarding *burdens* and the nature of oppression, see also Isaiah 10:27; 14:25; 49:26; 60:14. But Jesus came to grant deliverance from bondage to a different, more oppressive master: sin (Galatians 5:1; etc.).

> **What Do You Think?**
> What modern metaphor could you use to compare and contrast the yoke of Galatians 5:1 with the yoke of Matthew 11:29-30?
> *Digging Deeper*
> How might your choice of metaphor change, based on various contexts? Give examples.

5a. Every warrior's boot used in battle and every garment rolled in blood

Every warrior's boot [and] garment rolled in blood represents the dead and wounded. Imagine thousands of soldiers engaged in hand-to-hand combat with weapons such as spears, swords, and cudgels. The suffering and gore would be immense.

5b. will be destined for burning, will be fuel for the fire.

The end of warfare is another reason for great rejoicing. Once the people are liberated (Isaiah 9:4, above), a spreading peace will allow the *burning* of the blood-stained garments of the previous statement. There will be no more need for these. This outcome matches what the prophet foresees in Isaiah 2:4 (compare Psalm 46:9; Zechariah 9:10).

II. The Promised Child
(ISAIAH 9:6-7)
A. His Names (v. 6)

6a. For to us a child is born, to us a son is given, and the government will be on his shoulders.

The ultimate reason for joy is the birth of an extraordinary *child*. He is *given* to us by God. This is not said of other births, although this child was to have been a sign to Ahaz—a sign he refused (see Lesson Context)!

Some identify the child as Hezekiah, the son of Ahaz. But this does not match the chronology of Hezekiah's birth. And, more importantly, no mere human king is in view, but rather an end-times figure, the Messiah. Furthermore, neither Heze-

kiah nor anyone else from Isaiah's time accomplished what is in this passage.

Isaiah 7:14 requires us to conclude that this child is to be the coming Immanuel ("God with us"). The role of this *son* is to administer *the government*. The greatest promise of God is not merely the end of a short-term crisis. Rather, God promises to send a King who will surpass what his people have seen in their rulers. As with Psalm 89, the language here about the birth of a son reminds us of the promises to the patriarchs and to David of sons through whom God would bring promised blessings (example: 2 Samuel 7:11-16). The Son will bear the burden of responsibility for the rule and dominion over the Lord's people (see Matthew 28:18). When his shoulder bears the rule of government, it frees the people from the violence they had endured (Isaiah 9:4, above).

6b. And he will be called Wonderful Counselor,

Names are significant throughout Isaiah's ministry and in his confrontation with kings, especially Ahaz (Isaiah 7:3; 8:1-3; etc.). The set of names we see starting here reminds us of "throne names" used for newly crowned kings. These names give the nature and character of this child and his perfect rule. Egyptian coronation liturgies exhibited such names to encourage qualities desired in the newly crowned monarch (compare and contrast 2 Kings 24:17).

Four paired descriptions mark him as extraordinary. First is *Wonderful Counselor*. We have weakened the meaning of *wonderful* in the English language. Today this word means something like "really, really good." When one experiences the wonderful in this sense, one knows that this is a miraculous work of God Almighty (example: Isaiah 29:14).

To combine this with the function of counselor means that Isaiah foresaw someone who knows

HOW TO SAY IT

Ahaz	*Ay*-haz.
Hezekiah	Hez-ih-*kye*-uh.
Manasseh	Muh-*nass*-uh.
shalom *(Hebrew)*	shah-*lome*.

all the questions and has all the answers. This can be only God himself (compare Isaiah 25:1). Solomon, David's son, also was given great wisdom that could be explained only supernaturally (see 1 Kings 3). This child perhaps is presented as the "new Solomon," who gives supernatural counsel to his subjects (see Isaiah 11:2). Even so, the child is to be greater than Solomon (Luke 11:31). The child's wise, supernatural counsel will be the exact opposite of that of the supposedly wise counselors of Isaiah 19:11.

6c. Mighty God,

The next prophetic designation amplifies the previous. The descriptive word *Mighty* is drawn from the world of war heroes (compare Genesis 10:8). We might liken this to our term *invincible,* the one who cannot be defeated. The coming child will not be bested by any army, human or otherwise, in the reign of his universal government (see Isaiah 42:13). *Mighty God* is used also in Isaiah 10:21 to refer to the Lord. Here the name ascribes deity to the child (see John 1:1). Revelation 1:8 refers to Jesus as "the Almighty" and may be drawing on this name.

6d. Everlasting Father,

This exact title is found only here in the Old Testament. Indeed, the Old Testament rarely uses the term *Father* to refer to God (examples: Psalm 68:5; 89:26; Malachi 2:10). It remains for Jesus to teach humans that God is our Father in a universal, loving, and holy way. This title emphasizes the Father's eternal nature and/or his control over eternity and time itself. The concept of eternity was difficult to grasp in Isaiah's day and remains so for us. The eternality of God, however, is a characteristic that sets him apart in a decisive way (see Isaiah 57:15). This too seems to ascribe divinity to the child: born into time, he transcends time. The child will bring about conditions in the new government that will fulfill the role of the divine fatherhood of God (see Psalm 103:13; Isaiah 63:16).

6e. Prince of Peace.

War characterizes earthly kingdoms. The only son of David we know of who did not go to war was Solomon, yet Solomon established his reign with bloodshed (1 Kings 2:25, 46). Solomon's name means "peace," but the promised child will be the ultimate *Prince of Peace.* This is not *prince* in the sense of a king-in-waiting. Rather, it is *prince* in the sense of ruler of a people, a virtual synonym with "king" or "monarch." He brings peace between God and humanity by way of reconciliation and redemption (see John 14:27; Romans 5:1-11).

> **What Do You Think?**
> Which description in this verse will most motivate your service to Christ this week? Why?
> *Digging Deeper*
> Which description most motivates you to further study of its significance?

❧ WHAT'S IN A NAME? ❧

My parents spent a lot of time reading baby-naming books, trying to find my name. The book they chose gave characteristics of names instead of definitions. *When you hear this name, who do you see, and what are they like?* Each name had character and a legacy.

They settled on Wyatt, after Wyatt Earp, one of the most famous gunslinging lawmen of the Old West. And he was a cowboy through and through. The name evokes a tough, adventurous man who sat a horse well, rode next to herds of thundering buffalo, and slept with a saddle for a pillow beneath a quilt of starlight. I've carried in my name the hope to grow into a man who earns it. I want people to hear my name and glimpse something true about me.

The names God gave his Messiah are like this. He *is* what his names suggest. How will you celebrate the man behind the names?   —W. L.

B. His Government (v. 7)

7. Of the greatness of his government and peace there will be no end. He will reign on David's throne and over his kingdom, establishing and upholding it with justice and righteousness from that time on and forever. The zeal of the LORD Almighty will accomplish this.

The promise to Abraham in Genesis 12:3

became, at Sinai, the purpose of Israel's existence (Exodus 19:5-6). The broader redemptive work through David is found in a promise that his dynasty will never *end* (compare 2 Samuel 7:16). But the coming child would be in a different category from any earthly monarch. His reign is characterized in five ways that no normal human ruler can ever measure up to.

First, his reign is to be endlessly increasing, as opposed to the rise and fall of empires throughout history. Second, it is to be endlessly peaceful, never at war or preparing for war. It advances because of its *peace*, not in spite of it. Third, it is to be tied to the most beloved ruler of Israel, King David. Fourth, it is to be established on true *justice and righteousness*, not on brute strength and aggression. Fifth, its existence and increase are guaranteed by *the zeal of the Lord*. This is to be a primary matter for the all-powerful God of Israel. Such zeal cannot be thwarted by anyone or anything.

Jesus' dominion will be characterized by peace, not war. His agenda will be reconciliation and *shalom*. His *kingdom* is established not just as an end to war, but as positive harmony and goodwill—the kind of peace that Israel had not known. His *government* and peace expand forever because people from all nations will be at peace with God (Zechariah 14:9, 16-17; Romans 11:25-32; Ephesians 2:11-17). The angel Gabriel quoted from this passage when he announced to Mary that she would bear a son, Jesus (Luke 1:32-33).

> ### What Do You Think?
> What is the single most important action you can take this week to bring your priorities and zeal in line with God's?
>
> *Digging Deeper*
> How might Satan distract you from this task?

Conclusion

A. A Dark State

There's hide-and-seek, and then there's Hide-and-Seek: Dark Edition. Imagine a warm house on a cold winter night, all the lights off. Two parents go searching for their whispering and

WONDERFUL, COUNSELOR, THE MIGHTY GOD, THE EVERLASTING FATHER, THE PRINCE OF PEACE

Visual for Lesson 3. *Allow one minute for silent reflection on Jesus' titles and fulfillment of their meanings before concluding the class with prayer.*

shushing children. Their hiding places would be laughable in daylight, but in the dark they are effectively invisible behind a pillow or wrapped in a curtain. Perhaps the mother can sense her child's presence, but it's not until he jumps out or giggles that she can place him. Darkness certainly adds drama to hide-and-seek.

The people living before Jesus lived in a state of darkness. Spiritually, they walked around with hands outstretched, hoping not to run into something dangerous. Fear and anxiety lurked in that state of unpredictability and loss in a deadly game of hiding from God, trying to keep sins in darkness.

We no longer live in the darkness, hands outstretched, hoping to avoid danger. We live in the light of Jesus' sacrifice, which has illuminated our paths! What then will you do? Will you continue to live as though you have not seen the light? Will you leave little children in the dark, never trying to find them? The game only ends in victory when the light comes on and everyone is safe in God's home.

B. Prayer

Father, we thank you for your care for all the world. May we be worthy ambassadors of the kingdom of the Messiah. In Jesus' name we pray. Amen.

C. Thought to Remember

Jesus the King is like no other!

INVOLVEMENT LEARNING

Enhance your lesson with NIV® Bible Student (from your curriculum supplier) and the reproducible activity page (at www.standardlesson.com or in the back of the NIV® Standard Lesson Commentary Deluxe Edition).

Into the Lesson

Form pairs of students and ask them to share with each other the deepest physical darkness they ever experienced. Allow one minute of sharing before announcing time to switch so the second partner has time to share. After two minutes of conversation, ask a few volunteers to share their *partner's* experience, and then discuss briefly: "Why is complete darkness something we fear?"

Ask the pairs next to consider silently their darkest spiritual experience. (Be sensitive to what you know of your class members when considering whether this is an appropriate question for their particular experiences.) Do not allow this activity to last longer than one minute. After that minute, tell students that today's text points to the greatest darkness of all.

Into the Word

Using today's Lesson Context, briefly explain the historical context for today's passage from Isaiah. Follow with a reading of the lesson text aloud.

Form the class into three groups: **Signs of Victory Group**, **Literal Meaning Group**, and **Spiritual Implication Group**. Point the groups to Isaiah 9:2-7 and ask them to list what belongs under their group name. Expect that there will be some overlap in answers. Allow time for discussion; be prepared to resolve disagreements.

Option. Play a recording of "Unto Us" from *The Messiah*, which you can find online. While students listen, have them mark the phrases from Isaiah 9:2-7 that are lyrics in the song. This can be accomplished in their Bibles or on copies of today's printed text (you provide). Ask volunteers to tell what they've highlighted.

Discuss what parts of Isaiah's prophecy would be most difficult to understand *if* the class did not have knowledge of Jesus. What parts would be most encouraging in that case?

Ask class members to form new groups as follows: **Wonderful Counselor Group; Mighty God Group; Everlasting Father Group; Prince of Peace Group.** Each group is to write a job description for Jesus to show him fulfilling their assigned group's title: After five minutes, call for conclusions in whole-class discussion.

Option. For deeper discussion, follow the above by distributing copies of the "Looking at the Light" exercise from the activity page, which you can download, to be completed as indicated.

Into Life

Put class members back into their groups above to discuss how Jesus offers light that our culture needs today through the specific attribute assigned to that group. If your learners need examples, these are possibilities:

- **Wonderful Counselor Group**: guidance for how we plan our lives.
- **Mighty God Group**: for recognizing that we're not in control.
- **Everlasting Father Group**: for realizing that this world is not the end.
- **Prince of Peace Group**: for encouragement to live with contentment in an age of discontent.

After five minutes, ask class members to share from their ideas. Then ask which title for Jesus brings the most hope personally and why.

Option. Distribute copies of the "No Santa" exercise from the activity page. Have students work individually for one minute before comparing their cards with others in ensuing whole-class discussion. For each sentiment, ask the class, "Why is this message so important for our world today?"

Close with a prayer of thanks for Jesus, whose rule is a reason to celebrate not only at Christmas but always for those who have submitted to him as Lord.

JUSTICE AND DELIVERANCE

DEVOTIONAL READING: Nahum 1:1-3, 6-8, 12-13, 15
BACKGROUND SCRIPTURE: Nahum 1

NAHUM 1:1-3, 6-8, 12-13, 15

¹ A prophecy concerning Nineveh. The book of the vision of Nahum the Elkoshite.

² The LORD is a jealous and avenging God;
    the LORD takes vengeance and is filled
      with wrath.
The LORD takes vengeance on his foes
    and vents his wrath against his enemies.
³ The LORD is slow to anger but great in
      power;
    the LORD will not leave the guilty
      unpunished.
His way is in the whirlwind and the storm,
    and clouds are the dust of his feet.

⁶ Who can withstand his indignation?
    Who can endure his fierce anger?
His wrath is poured out like fire;
    the rocks are shattered before him.
⁷ The LORD is good,
    a refuge in times of trouble.
He cares for those who trust in him,
⁸   but with an overwhelming flood
he will make an end of Nineveh;
    he will pursue his foes into the realm of
      darkness.

¹² This is what the LORD says:

"Although they have allies and are
      numerous,
    they will be destroyed and pass away.
Although I have afflicted you, Judah,
    I will afflict you no more.
¹³ Now I will break their yoke from your
      neck
    and tear your shackles away."

¹⁵ Look, there on the mountains,
    the feet of one who brings good news,
    who proclaims peace!
Celebrate your festivals, Judah,
    and fulfill your vows.
No more will the wicked invade you;
    they will be completely destroyed.

KEY TEXT

The LORD is a jealous and avenging God; the LORD takes vengeance and is filled with wrath. The LORD takes vengeance on his foes and vents his wrath against his enemies. —**Nahum 1:2**

Photo © Getty Images

Justice, Law, History

Unit 1: God Requires Justice
LESSONS 1–4

LESSON AIMS

After participating in this lesson, each learner will be able to:

1. Summarize the historical context of Nahum's prophecy.

2. Explain why God's justice is necessary to the spread of good news.

3. Explain how to present the gospel both in terms of God's wrath and salvation available through Christ.

LESSON OUTLINE

Introduction

A. Ready to Receive

Who was the last person to deliver really good news to you? Maybe a doctor or nurse told you that mother and child are safe following a difficult labor, or the treatments worked and your spouse's cancer is in remission. Perhaps a teenager you love decided to dedicate his life to following Jesus. A weatherman declared that the hurricane would not land, or a sales associate told you the appliance you needed was available at a deep discount. The car repair you were worried about was simple. All kinds of people deliver good news.

This time of year, we might think of the shepherds in the field (Luke 2:8-20) or the Magi from the east (Matthew 2:1-12) who received the good news of Jesus' birth. All these carried with them the good news that Jesus was born. Long before this, however, the day of peace was anticipated in the days of a ruthless world power, whose end was indeed good news for Judah. And that good news prepared the people to receive the Messiah, who would fulfill these prophecies in ways no one had imagined.

B. Lesson Context

The historical setting of the book of Nahum is of utmost importance to understanding its message of hope for Judah. Even so, only one historical event is cited in the book's three chapters —the destruction of Thebes (Nahum 3:8-10; compare Jeremiah 46:25). Ashurbanipal of Assyria (reigned 669–633 BC) sacked that Egyptian city in 663 BC. This indicates that the book of Nahum was written sometime after the fall of Thebes but before the predicted fall of Nineveh, a major city of the Assyrian Empire. That fall became reality in 612 BC (see below). Therefore, a date during the reign of righteous King Josiah of Judah (641–609 BC) makes the most sense. This can be further narrowed to between 625 and 612 BC as most likely, since judgment is predicted for Judah's enemies, not for Judah itself.

The Assyrians certainly played a role in God's disciplining of Judah. The Lord allowed its evil King Manasseh (reigned 697–643 BC; see

2 Chronicles 33:1-9) to be exiled by the Assyrians. The Assyrians were renowned for their cruelty. They had a practice of torturing the leaders of captive cities or nations as a warning not to rebel. In Manasseh's case, the Assyrians put a hook in his nose, bound him with chains, and led him away. While in prison Manasseh turned to God (33:10-13). When he returned to Jerusalem, he led in a spiritual revival (33:14-16).

Such a revival had not occurred in the northern kingdom of Israel. Neither kings nor people there repented of their evil, so the Lord used the Assyrians' violence as a tool of punishment. Whereas Judah suffered threats of violence and periodic incursions, Samaria, northern Israel's capital city, was captured after a three-year siege, in 722 BC (2 Kings 17:5-6; 18:9-12). Sargon II's boast that he led captive over 27,000 people was preserved in Assyrian cuneiform text. This is when Israel as a nation disappeared from the world stage.

Nineveh hit its peak in power as Ashurbanipal's capital in the mid-seventh century BC, just before its destruction. Following Ashurbanipal's death, kingdoms that had come under Assyrian control rebelled. Among these were the Babylonians and the Medes. Their armies came together to sack Nineveh in 612 BC. Following this, Babylon displaced Assyria as the major power in the region.

I. Prophecy
(Nahum 1:1)
A. Place Indicted (v. 1a)

1a. A prophecy concerning Nineveh.

Prophets often began their prophecies using a word that can be translated "burden" (examples: Isaiah 13:1 and Zechariah 9:1 in the *KJV*). The same word is also translated "inspired utterance" in Proverbs 30:1; 31:1. The *prophecy* that follows is often one of judgment, and that is the case here. This is a weighty call, not a trivial or light matter.

The city of *Nineveh* was located on the Tigris River, site of present-day Mosul, Iraq (see Lesson Context). Nineveh was first mentioned in the Bible when a descendant of Noah's son Ham built it (Genesis 10:11).

B. Prophet Identified (v. 1b)

1b. The book of the vision of Nahum the Elkoshite.

The vision is another way to refer to the prophecy being revealed in this *book* (compare Isaiah 1:1). The same Hebrew word can also be translated "revelation" (Proverbs 29:18; Habakkuk 2:2-3), which emphasizes that God provided both the experience and the wisdom to understand its significance.

Nahum means "repentings" or "compassion" (compare Hosea 11:8). He is the only person in the Old Testament with that name and is not the Nahum named in Jesus' genealogy (Luke 3:25). Nahum did not provide the names of his ancestors, only that he was from a town called Elkosh. At least four places have been suggested for its location: one north of Nineveh, site of modern Alkush, about two miles north of modern Mosul, Iraq (see Lesson Context); two in Galilee (including Capernaum, which means "town, or village, of Nahum"); and one near Jerusalem in Judah. The latter is preferred by most scholars.

Jonah and Nahum are the two Old Testament prophets whose prophecies focused on a coming judgment on Nineveh. Nahum's prophecy differs from Jonah's in two key ways: (1) Nahum was told to preach in Judah *about* Nineveh, not *in* Nineveh itself; and (2) Nahum's prophecy was fulfilled. Jonah's was unfulfilled because God chose mercy over judgment when the people repented (see Jonah 3:6-10; Matthew 12:41). Zephaniah, a contemporary of Nahum, also named Nineveh in the context of judgment coming to all of Assyria (Zephaniah 2:13).

II. Portrayals
(Nahum 1:2-3, 6-8, 12a)
A. Punishment for Foes (v. 2)

2. The Lord is a jealous and avenging God; the Lord takes vengeance and is filled with wrath. The Lord takes vengeance on his foes and vents his wrath against his enemies.

We should take care to understand what it means for *the Lord* to be *jealous*. God's jealousy is not like that of a boy who has a fit if he sees his girlfriend flirting with someone else. The biblical concept of jealousy when applied to *God* indicates a profound sense of caring and commitment. This is even more apparent where a word in the original language is translated "jealousy" in one passage but "zeal" in another.

For example, the Hebrew noun translated "jealousy" in Ezekiel 8:3, 5 and Zechariah 8:2 is rendered "zeal" in Isaiah 9:7; 37:32; 59:17; 63:15. In the New Testament, the Greek noun translated "jealousy" in 2 Corinthians 11:2 is the same one translated "zeal" in Philippians 3:6. Overlap in meaning is affirmed in English by a dictionary entry that offers one meaning of jealousy as "zealous vigilance." The common idea is one of fervency.

In this verse, God's jealousy is more closely linked to his protecting his people from violence and oppression that often results when hostile nations worship violent and oppressive false gods. Sennacherib (reigned 704–681 BC), an Assyrian king during the time of Hezekiah's reign (about 716–687 BC), learned this lesson the hard way in 701 BC. Sennacherib had captured many cities in Judah, so the Lord—protecting both his name and his people—struck the Assyrian army, and 185,000 soldiers died in one night (2 Kings 18:13-37; 19:34-36; Isaiah 36–37).

Repetition in Hebrew prophecy, which was often written as poetry, serves to emphasize the point being made. In this verse, God's *vengeance* and *wrath* become more frightening and immediate through Nahum's insistence that God will act out of his righteous rage (compare Nahum 2:13; 3:5-7). As Hebrews 10:31 says, "It is a dreadful thing to fall into the hands of the living God."

❧ *Our Zealous, Jealous God* ❧

Ever been attacked by a Canada goose? Each spring a pair of long-necked Canada geese build a nest in the tall grass next to a pond near the trail where my wife and I take our daily walks. We have learned to beware of the geese. When the female lays her eggs, the male becomes quite protective. Step anywhere near the nest, and he will sound a warning honk. Get too close and he will run toward you aggressively. Even in a common goose, there's a God-given instinct to protect.

Have you ever wondered why the Bible describes the Lord as a jealous God? He is protective and passionate. He doesn't sit passively on his throne. Sin rouses God's righteous indignation, but not because he hates us. On the contrary: he loves us too much to sit by idly when out-of-control wickedness threatens our relationship with him. Aren't you glad our heavenly Father isn't apathetic, indifferent, and unemotional about us? Can the same be said about your attitude toward him?

—D. F.

B. Power to Accomplish (vv. 3, 6)

3. The LORD is slow to anger but great in power; the LORD will not leave the guilty unpunished. His way is in the whirlwind and the storm, and clouds are the dust of his feet.

If the nation of Assyria deserved to be punished, why had God not done something earlier? God waits patiently because he wants everyone to repent; he does not wish for anyone to perish (2 Peter 3:9). God does not react in haste (see Jonah 3).

But God's patience does have its limits. And when his patience ends, he still has the *power* to hold *the guilty* accountable. The people of Noah's day had gone too far from God and acted wickedly, so God sent the flood (Genesis 6–8). Having promised never to destroy the whole world with water again (9:8-11), God still reserved the right to act in judgment (examples: chapter 19; 2 Peter 3:10-12; Revelation 6:12-17).

Although God acts as a judge, this verse describes him as more of a righteous warrior (compare Revelation 19:11-16). Unlike human fighters, he has all of nature at his command as his weapons. *The whirlwind* forms in the sky and reaches to earth; *the storm* can yield thunder and lightning, hail, destructive rains, and more (compare Job 38:22-23). *Clouds* parallel these terms and encompass weather more generally. Not only does God command these (examples: 2 Kings 2:1; Mark 4:39-41), but they are as distressing to him as *the dust* that kicks up as he walks in his heavens—that is to say, not at all.

Yet even dust can serve his purposes, as seen in the plague of boils that resulted from Moses' obeying God's command (Exodus 9:8-9). Nahum 1:4-5 (not in our printed text) continues to describe God's power in terms of his authority over the forces and features of our world.

> **What Do You Think?**
> What are some indications that your expressions of anger are not modeled after God's?
>
> *Digging Deeper*
> What plan can you enact to be more accountable in improving in this area?

❧ STUCK IN THE MUD ❧

Not heeding the counsel of one's spouse can be dangerous—but so can heeding it! We were driving to our friends' new home for dinner when I accidentally made a wrong turn into someone else's narrow driveway. My wife advised, "Just pull into the grass and turn around."

Despite my voiced reservations about getting stuck, I did as she said. As soon as the car was off the paved driveway, the front tires sank into the soft soil. Tempers flared as tires spun. We ended up paying a tow-truck driver $50, arriving 90 minutes late, and exchanging glares the rest of the evening.

That night we both flared uncharacteristically into frustrated anger. But unlike the two of us in a marital spat, God's wrath is righteous indignation, not impulsive temper tantrums. He doesn't explode with unrestrained rage, nor does he hold grudges (Psalm 103:8-9). What needs to happen for your anger to be more like his?   —D. F.

6. Who can withstand his indignation? Who can endure his fierce anger? His wrath is poured out like fire; the rocks are shattered before him.

The recognition of the Lord's power caused Nahum to ask two rhetorical questions. These ask the same thing and in doing so emphasize the impossibility of the answer. No one can withstand God's *indignation* and *his fierce anger*—no person, no nation, no power. Not even the

strongest or the strongest-willed has the ability to resist God.

God's *wrath* is like a volcano; lava *like fire* is *poured out*. The eruption sends *rocks* into the air. Nothing in the path of a volcano—or the Lord in his righteous anger—can survive. Any resistance is futile.

> **What Do You Think?**
> What problems can we avoid by making sure we acknowledge the wrath of God as the Bible intends?
>
> *Digging Deeper*
> What Scripture passages do you find most helpful in framing your response?

C. Protection for His People (v. 7)

7. The LORD is good, a refuge in times of trouble. He cares for those who trust in him,

All of God's many attributes are tempered by the fact that he *is good* (Matthew 19:16-17). He creates good things (examples: Genesis 1:4, 10, 12, 18, 21, 25, 31). He gives good gifts (Exodus 3:8; James 1:17). Those who *trust in him* experience his goodness in protection from harm. The phrase *he cares for those* anticipates Jesus' self-disclosure that he is the good shepherd who knows his sheep and cares for them (John 10:14-15). On the Lord as *a refuge*, compare Psalm 31:2; contrast 52:7.

D. Pursuit of His Enemies (vv. 8, 12a)

8. but with an overwhelming flood he will make an end of Nineveh; he will pursue his foes into the realm of darkness.

Nahum often used poetic imagery to describe Nineveh's destruction, but two factors here were literally fulfilled. The Tigris River ran along the western side of Nineveh, and a tributary from the east joined it there. A severe flooding in both rivers at once would be too much for the foundations of the mighty city. During the Babylonian siege on Nineveh, *an overwhelming flood* occurred that damaged the walls of the city and that helped to bring about the *end* of that great city (compare Nahum 2:6, 8). After that, the figurative flood of Babylonians and Medes took the city (see Lesson Context).

Many ancient cities suffered capture and destruction, and new cities were built on top of the ruins. But Nineveh was never rebuilt. Figuratively, *darkness* also overwhelmed Nineveh. There is no indication that God used the same darkness in Nineveh as he chose in Egypt (Exodus 10:21-23). Rather, the fate of the city was similar to what was believed of a dead person—existing in some dark place, never to be offered opportunity to enter God's presence (contrast Jonah 2). Still, darkness playing a part in releasing God's people from oppression is poignant.

Nahum 1:9-11 (not in our printed text) again taunts Nineveh with the futility of opposing the Lord.

12a. This is what the LORD says: "Although they have allies and are numerous, they will be destroyed and pass away.

This is what the Lord says is a phrase used hundreds of times in the Old Testament (with some variation) to introduce a prophecy given by God (compare Isaiah 1:2; Hosea 1:1; etc.). What he revealed about Nineveh would happen as surely as if it had already happened; the prophecy was entirely trustworthy.

The people of Nineveh would foolishly behave as though they were secure as a result of their political alliances and national strength. In this case the Ninevites' might combined with their numerical superiority to create a false sense of security.

God's anger:
Slow but powerful.

Visual for Lesson 4. *Discuss with the class how God's anger being like lava (instead of the more typical fire) changes the metaphor.*

III. Promises
(NAHUM 1:12b-13, 15)
A. An End of Affliction (v. 12b)
12b. "Although I have afflicted you, Judah, I will afflict you no more.

The subject of God's address changes here from Assyria (represented by Nineveh) to *Judah*. Assyria, the instrument of God's anger, had gone too far and would be stopped (Isaiah 10:5-7). The Assyrians' violence and oppression would not *afflict* God's people forever.

B. Peace for His People (vv. 13, 15)
13. "Now I will break their yoke from your neck and tear your shackles away."

A wooden yoke was placed on the necks of animals for pulling heavy loads or plowing. While it was a mere tool on a beast of burden, people were never meant to bear the kind of *yoke* in view here. The yoke therefore became a symbol of oppression (contrast Matthew 11:29-30). Assyrian bondage of Judah would end.

The Lord spoke once again to Nineveh in Nahum 1:14 (not in our printed text). His declaration left no doubt as to the fate of the city and its false gods.

What Do You Think?
What line of reasoning would you use to convince a new believer that attempting to live a yoke-free life will result in the heaviest yoke of all?
Digging Deeper
Considering the importance of good timing, when should you point out Galatians 5:1?

15a. Look, there on the mountains, the feet of one who brings good news,

The opening words of this verse are similar to those of Isaiah 52:7, which itself is quoted in Romans 10:15. In Isaiah's context, the *good news* was that Babylonian exile would end and the people of Judah would be restored to their land. For the apostle Paul, the words in Romans find their ultimate meaning in the march of the news regarding Jesus Christ. For Nahum and pre-

Babylonian Judah, the good news was that Assyria would fall.

15b. who proclaims peace!

Peace had been a blessing available to the people in the promised land if they remained faithful to the Lord (Leviticus 26:1-6). This peace was to include cooperation from the land in agriculture, victory over foes, and most importantly, God's presence; in short, reversals of the curses found in Genesis 3. This too is ultimately fulfilled in Jesus (see John 14:27; 16:33; Acts 10:36).

> **What Do You Think?**
> In working to promote a just peace, what are some ways to stay on guard against unbiblical concepts of "peace"?
>
> *Digging Deeper*
> In addition to Jeremiah 6:14 and Ezekiel 13:10, what texts help most in framing your answer?

15c. Celebrate your festivals, Judah, and fulfill your vows. No more will the wicked invade you; they will be completely destroyed.

As a result, Nahum challenged *Judah* to *celebrate* the various *festivals* prescribed in the Law of Moses. The implication is that some type of restriction had hindered the free exercise of worship for the people of God. Or, more troublingly, the people hadn't been very dedicated to their celebrations to begin with and had used foreign interference as an excuse not to *fulfill* their *vows* (compare Psalm 61:8; contrast Jeremiah 44:25). With the destruction of *the wicked*, however, the people would be free once again to choose devotion to God and enjoy the blessings that came with it.

Conclusion

A. Good News!

The destruction of Nineveh fulfilled Nahum's prophecy. The city's destruction was complete, and so too was the end of Assyria's dominance. The pending doom of Nineveh was the greatest part of Nahum's prophecy, but closely related was the word of deliverance for Judah. This comforted a people who had been oppressed by Assyria for decades.

Injustice still exists, and God still intends to act to bring justice and deliver his people. But he sees the global picture, so his timetable differs from what we might desire. In his treatment of Assyria, he did not act in haste. At the right time in God's plan, the nation of Assyria came to an end. It had fulfilled its purpose. God's justice prevailed. God's timing is always perfect (example: Galatians 4:4-5).

For this reason, we share the love of Jesus, not only at Christmastime but also year-round. The gospel truth about Jesus is the reason we have hope of eternal life. And what better news could there be than a future with the Lord in his Heaven?

> **What Do You Think?**
> Which concept or description in today's text most conflicts with your ideas regarding how God "should" be or act?
>
> *Digging Deeper*
> What action will you take to resolve this?

B. Prayer

God in Heaven, help us to shape our lives to show that we truly believe that you are holy, just, and loving. Today we especially thank you for giving us your Son. In his name we pray. Amen.

C. Thought to Remember

Use your feet to spread the gospel!

HOW TO SAY IT

Ashurbanipal	*As*-shure-**bah**-nee-pahl.
Capernaum	Kuh-*per*-nay-um.
cuneiform	*koo*-nee-eh-**form**.
Elkoshite	*El*-kuh-shite.
Manasseh	Muh-*nass*-uh.
Medes	Meeds.
Nahum	*Nay*-hum.
Nineveh	*Nin*-uh-vuh.
Sennacherib	Sen-*nack*-er-ib.
Thebes	*Theebz* (*th* as in *thin*).
Tigris	*Tie*-griss.
Zephaniah	Zef-uh-*nye*-uh.

INVOLVEMENT LEARNING

Enhance your lesson with NIV® *Bible Student (from your curriculum supplier) and the reproducible activity page (at www.standardlesson.com or in the back of the* NIV® *Standard Lesson Commentary Deluxe Edition).*

Into the Lesson

Divide your class in half and ask those in each half to form triads. Triads in the first half are to think of at least one example for this prompt: "He got what he deserved when . . ." Triads of the other half are to discuss examples for "She didn't get the punishment she had coming to her when . . ." (Caution not to use names of politicians or people personally known in your church.)

After five minutes, ask how people react when someone's punishment is evidently just. After a few minutes, ask about the opposite.

Lead to Bible study by saying, "Today's text will lead to fresh thoughts about how and why God ensures justice."

Into the Word

Discuss the historical background for today's prophecy based on material from the Lesson Context. After having the text read aloud, distribute handouts (you create) with the following tasks and questions. (*Option.* You can put only one of the six per handout or all six on every handout, depending on time available and the nature of your class.)

1–List all the words in today's text that describe God. Which is the newest picture to you? Which makes you most uncomfortable? Which is most encouraging?

2–How should those who actively opposed God have been warned, based on the prophecies in this passage? List specific examples.

3–What images in these verses indicate how God will overwhelm all those who oppose him?

4–Name a key factor or two that will ensure God's favor.

5–How were the citizens of Judah to respond to this prophecy from Nahum?

6–List appropriate responses of Christians today to this ancient prophecy.

Have students work in their same groups formed for Into the Lesson. After no more than

10 minutes, reconvene for whole-class discussion of results. Use task number 6 as a transition to the Into Life segment.

Alternative. For a more general, open-ended approach, distribute instead copies of the "Our Just God" exercise from the activity page, which you can download. Have students complete the exercise in their groups. Discuss results. The "Good News" exercise from the activity page can be used after either alternative for expanded consideration.

Into Life

Continue the discussion by asking how our understanding of God-as-just would be changed if He had not carried through with his judgment on Assyria as prophesied by Nahum. Challenge learners, again in their groups, to prepare an "elevator speech"—an explanation that can be offered in the time it takes an elevator to close its doors and open them again—explaining the gospel both in terms of God's wrath to be avoided and salvation through Christ to be embraced. After no more than 10 minutes, reconvene for whole-class discussion.

Option. Ask students to use the blank side of one of the handouts to write a commitment prayer about living for God in the new year. Direct them to consider words, phrases, and ideas from today's text. State that you will offer opportunities for sharing results with the class as a whole, but you will not put any on the spot to do so. Offer that opportunity after no more than one minute to jot down thoughts for their individual prayers.

Close the class with sentence prayers, led by volunteers (possibly recruited in advance) to voice specific individuals (named or unnamed) who need to hear the message of justice (wrath to come) alongside the message of restoration offered through Christ (forgiveness). You as teacher can offer the last of the prayers to wrap up.

JUSTICE, VENGEANCE, AND MERCY

DEVOTIONAL READING: Genesis 4:1-13
BACKGROUND SCRIPTURE: Genesis 4

GENESIS 4:1-15

¹ Adam made love to his wife Eve, and she became pregnant and gave birth to Cain. She said, "With the help of the LORD I have brought forth a man." ² Later she gave birth to his brother Abel.

Now Abel kept flocks, and Cain worked the soil. ³ In the course of time Cain brought some of the fruits of the soil as an offering to the LORD. ⁴ And Abel also brought an offering— fat portions from some of the firstborn of his flock. The LORD looked with favor on Abel and his offering, ⁵ but on Cain and his offering he did not look with favor. So Cain was very angry, and his face was downcast.

⁶ Then the LORD said to Cain, "Why are you angry? Why is your face downcast? ⁷ If you do what is right, will you not be accepted? But if you do not do what is right, sin is crouching at your door; it desires to have you, but you must rule over it."

⁸ Now Cain said to his brother Abel, "Let's go out to the field." While they were in the field, Cain attacked his brother Abel and killed him.

⁹ Then the LORD said to Cain, "Where is your brother Abel?"

"I don't know," he replied. "Am I my brother's keeper?"

¹⁰ The LORD said, "What have you done? Listen! Your brother's blood cries out to me from the ground. ¹¹ Now you are under a curse and driven from the ground, which opened its mouth to receive your brother's blood from your hand. ¹² When you work the ground, it will no longer yield its crops for you. You will be a restless wanderer on the earth."

¹³ Cain said to the LORD, "My punishment is more than I can bear. ¹⁴ Today you are driving me from the land, and I will be hidden from your presence; I will be a restless wanderer on the earth, and whoever finds me will kill me."

¹⁵ But the LORD said to him, "Not so; anyone who kills Cain will suffer vengeance seven times over." Then the LORD put a mark on Cain so that no one who found him would kill him.

KEY TEXT

The LORD said, "What have you done? Listen! Your brother's blood cries out to me from the ground."

—Genesis 4:10

Justice, Law, History

Unit 2: God: The Source of Justice
Lessons 5–9

Lesson Aims

After participating in this lesson, each learner will be able to:

1. Describe Cain's troubled relationships.

2. Explain the implications of Cain's action in light of Hebrews 11:4 and 1 John 3:12.

3. Commit to true repentance of his or her sins.

Lesson Outline

Introduction

A. Acing Sisterhood

The Williams sisters *know* tennis. Together Serena and Venus have dominated the women's field, winning 14 Grand Slam doubles titles. They both excel in singles competition as well, although the younger sister has been the brighter star. As of this writing, Serena has won a staggering 73 singles titles while Venus has 49 of her own.

Serena's relatively greater successes could have made Venus bitter. The 19–12 record of Serena's wins against Venus in head to head matches could have soured their relationship. Instead, the competition seems to fuel their continued excellence. Both sisters understand the struggles of performing at the highest level of their sport. Instead of giving in to jealousy over their relative successes, the sisters demonstrate their love by cheering each other on, always hoping for the other's success.

What an example of sibling love! But we know that many siblings do not take joy in the other's accomplishments. Our text today does not explore a relationship like Serena and Venus have; it sadly shows us what happens when evil takes root in a brother's heart.

B. Lesson Context

The first part of the book of Genesis is general history (also called primeval history). As Moses introduced new people or nations throughout this section, the emphasis very quickly moved to the person or entity that he intended to feature at that point. For example, the accounts of the first sin and the first murder are set forth in Genesis 3 and 4 (see below), but the goal is to get to another son of Adam and Eve—namely, Seth. Notice the focus on him in Genesis 5:1-4. In Genesis 5:6-26, we see repeatedly that a certain descendant "had . . . sons and daughters," but the only one mentioned by name in each case is the one leading to Noah and the flood. This trend continues until the account finally reaches Abram and stays focused on his family (see lesson 6).

Today's passage comes early in the general history as it focuses on the first human family. The account begins immediately after the fall (Genesis 3).

It is worth naming four consequences of sin already in the world at this stage. Two are listed in Genesis 3:16: (1) the woman will experience pain in childbirth, and (2) her desire will be for her husband and he will rule over her. Most scholars agree that the woman's anticipated "desire" for her husband and his expected "rule" over her are not ideal, but are fallen in nature. This interpretation is grounded in part on the observation that the same words for "desire" and "rule" occur in Genesis 4:7 to describe Cain's conflicted relationship with sin (see below).

Relevant consequence (3) is that God had cursed the ground on account of sin (Genesis 3:17). This means that humans have to work the ground with hard labor. Food was no longer easy to come by. Noteworthy consequence (4) is that God barred Adam and Eve from the Garden of Eden so they could no longer partake of the tree of life (3:23-24). Without such access, they eventually died.

I. Sibling Rivalry
(Genesis 4:1-7)
A. Eve's Sons (vv. 1-2)

1a. Adam made love to his wife Eve, and she became pregnant and gave birth to Cain.

The conception and birth of the first human offspring follow what people through the generations have known as the ordinary course of events. Unlike *Adam* and *Eve*, *Cain* was a child born through ordinary human sexual reproduction.

1b. She said, "With the help of the Lord I have brought forth a man."

Cain's name is a play on words. First, it has some of the same Hebrew consonants as the word Eve used to describe how she had *brought forth a man*. Second, Eve specified that *the Lord* helped her beget her first son. She did not mention Adam. Alone, this observation has ambiguous meaning, but combined with the third and most remarkable insight, we get a clearer picture of her meaning.

Referring to a newborn baby as *a man* is unique to Eve's experience with Cain. The same Hebrew word is translated "husband" and was used when God told Eve that she would desire Adam and he

would rule over her (Genesis 3:16). In the ancient world, naming infers the authority of the name giver. Adam's rule over her was demonstrated immediately when he named her Eve (3:20; compare 2:19; 17:5, 15; 41:45; Daniel 1:7).

But God also acknowledged that the woman would have desire for her man. This likely means in part that she would want the power she experienced her husband exercising over her. Thus in taking the initiative to name their son, in stating that she has named a "man," and in emphasizing her direct relationship to God in this process, Eve may be asserting her own authority in response to the authority that Adam exercised when he named her.

2a. Later she gave birth to his brother Abel.

There is no fanfare in learning Abel's name. Nor is its meaning very grand, given that the Hebrew word can refer to something that is vain (examples: Job 9:29; Psalm 39:6), something of little substance that disperses quickly into the air (see Hosea 6:4; 13:3; compare James 4:14). The name *Abel* proves to be tragically apt for Eve's second son (see Genesis 4:8, below).

2b. Now Abel kept flocks, and Cain worked the soil.

We should not draw too fine a distinction between *Abel* and *Cain* in their work. Though the former specialized in keeping *flocks* of sheep and the latter on working *the soil*, modern subsistence-level farming (and agriculture throughout the ages) suggests that they were working together to keep the ground productive and the animals healthy. It should be noted that God had cursed the ground because of sin (see Lesson Context).

Even so, a distinction certainly was made between shepherds and farmers in the ancient Near East. For instance, the Egyptians looked down on the Hebrews for being shepherds, a profession they disdained (Genesis 46:34). But that was several centuries later; it's hard to tell for sure what distinction was really made between Cain's and Abel's work.

B. The Sons' Offerings (vv. 3-5a)

3-4a. In the course of time Cain brought some of the fruits of the soil as an offering to

the LORD. And Abel also brought an offering—fat portions from some of the firstborn of his flock.

Perhaps Adam taught *Cain* to offer a portion *of the fruits of the soil* to *the Lord*. Nowhere are we told that God explicitly asked this of the first family. But even before being codified into Israel's laws (example: Leviticus 2), righteous men offered gifts to God (example: Genesis 8:20-21). *Abel* apparently followed either his father's or his older brother's lead.

4b-5a. The LORD looked with favor on Abel and his offering, but on Cain and his offering he did not look with favor.

God's accepting Abel's *offering* and not Cain's has led to all sorts of speculation. Most propose that Cain didn't actually do anything wrong. Some have theorized that God preferred shepherds to farmers, in contrast to the Egyptians who despised shepherds (see Genesis 46:34). A related explanation is that God had less regard for Cain's offering because it reminded him of the cursed soil. *Cain* had to wrestle with the cursed soil to get it to produce food, whereas a shepherd like *Abel* had to care for his flock. In short, the theory is that God preferred the offering of Abel because of what it signified in that time and place.

Instead, we understand that Abel brought the best of his flock as later required in Israel's laws (the firstborn and fat portions; see Leviticus 3; Deuteronomy 12:5-7), and Cain did not (Hebrews 11:4). This is an early introduction to a series of events in which God preferred a younger son to the firstborn in the face of cultural convention (example: Genesis 21:12; see lesson 6). While God had reason other than Abel's birth order to prefer the man's sacrifice, this account does pave the way for this theme to be pursued throughout the book.

C. God's Warning (vv. 5b-7)

5b-6. So Cain was very angry, and his face was downcast. Then the LORD said to Cain, "Why are you angry? Why is your face downcast?

It is little wonder *Cain* felt snubbed. God rec-ognized this and initiated a conversation with him by asking questions. This echoes his approach to Adam and Eve after they sinned (Genesis 3:9, 11, 13). God was not ignorant of their deeds and thoughts. Like a good teacher, he drew them out of their negative inner monologue.

What Do You Think?
How can you learn to identify the first seedlings of sin during painful times?
Digging Deeper
Will your answer depend on whether the pain is your own fault? Why, or why not?

This tactful approach from the powerful Creator emphasizes God's loving desire for relationship. Though he was not pleased with Cain's sacrifice, God still actively sought out a relationship with the man. From the very beginning, then, we see *the Lord* seeking to save the lost (see Luke 19:10).

What Do You Think?
In what ways can you be more alert for the voice of God?
Digging Deeper
What might you gain in doing so? What traps are there to avoid?

❧ CAIN IS CRYING ❧

A brief internet search of "why my kid is crying" can reveal all sorts of hilarious causes for a meltdown. Sometimes a toddler's favorite cup is in the dishwasher, unavailable *right now* for a drink. Or Dad's shoes don't fit her. Or he can't achieve the physical impossibility of picking up a book he is sitting on or riding a bus that is on a television show. The reasons are as varied as the children themselves.

And while children can cry about all sorts of silly things, sometimes they are in a tizzy because their parents won't let them do something dangerous. His mom won't let him eat garbage or drink out of a bottle he found on the road. Her mom won't let her run into the road.

In a childlike tantrum, Cain was too self-centered to see God's intervention as mercy. When God reaches out to correct you, what do you have in common with Cain . . . and the children? —J. K.

7. "If you do what is right, will you not be accepted? But if you do not do what is right, sin is crouching at your door; it desires to have you, but you must rule over it."

God's question here implies what the writer of Hebrews asserted: that Cain was not accepted because he did not do well (11:4; see Genesis 4b-5a, above). Failure to do what one knows to be right opens the door to *sin*. God's warning contains a heartbreaking echo of the antagonistic relationship between Adam and Eve that was a consequence of their disobedience (3:16; see Lesson Context and 4:1b, above).

This is God's first instruction about sin, and it rings as true for us today. Ruling over sin isn't a matter of obsessing about it; it is about busying ourselves with doing the right thing. The first step to inviting sin into our lives is to neglect doing what we ought to be doing. It is the vacuum created by inactivity in righteousness that sucks wickedness into our lives.

> *What Do You Think?*
> What are some ways to resist Satan's pull against the Lord's correction?
> *Digging Deeper*
> What texts of Scripture can help you most in that regard? Why?

II. Divine Mercy
(GENESIS 4:8-15)
A. Fratricide (v. 8)

8. Now Cain said to his brother Abel, "Let's go out to the field." While they were in the field, Cain attacked his brother Abel and killed him.

Rather than heed God's warning, *Cain* committed the first murder, probably even the first premeditated murder. Cain did not slay *Abel* at home, but instead led him into *the field*. It's unclear why this place was better to kill his brother than another. Maybe this was where Abel raised his sheep, or where Cain raised his own crops. Or maybe he meant to hide the evidence of his sin against his brother, burying him where he was struck or making the murder look like a workplace accident.

Cain is an example of the extreme opposite of what a Christian ought to be. His problem was that he "belonged to the evil one," the devil (1 John 3:12). As a result, he did wrong instead of right. But instead of repenting, Cain went wild with jealousy.

So I am warned. If I feel inclined to hate a fellow Christian, is it possibly because he or she is more *righteous* than I am? Should I be cleaning up my own way of living instead of envying someone whose godly living wins for him or her some honor that is denied to me?

B. Consequences (vv. 9-12)

9a. Then the LORD said to Cain, "Where is your brother Abel?" "I don't know," he replied.

The Lord again confronted *Cain* with a question (see Genesis 4:5b-6, above). Cain's lie indicated that he thought he could play dumb and God would be none the wiser. This lack of both respect and holy fear was reflected in Cain's inferior sacrifice (see 4:4b-5a, above).

9b. "Am I my brother's keeper?"

Here is another play on words. Abel was earlier introduced as a keeper of flocks (Genesis 4:2, above). In essence Cain asked God, "Am I the *keeper* of the keeper?"

> *What Do You Think?*
> Where will you draw the line between being your "brother's keeper" and not?
> *Digging Deeper*
> How do Acts 18:5-6 and James 5:20 help you answer that question?

❧ WAY TO GROW! ❧

"Straighten up!" Mom would often snap, but only on New Year's Day would we obey. That's when Mom would open the door to the utility room and back us up against it. With our heels

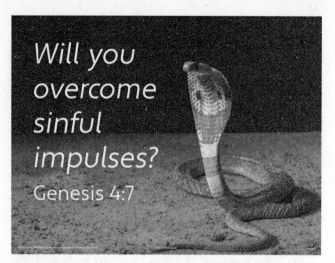

Will you overcome sinful impulses?

Genesis 4:7

Visual for Lesson 5. *Pose this question as an introduction to the discussion questions associated with verse 7.*

against the door and our chins up, we would each stretch to optimum height. A line was drawn that indicated our growth for the past year, marked with our initials and the date. Then Mom would say, "My! How you have grown!"

God offered Cain two paths to spiritual growth: a warning to heed and a chance at truthful repentance. But Cain remained defiant. As we enter 2022, "How's it growing?" might not be a slip of the tongue. Ask yourself: *Have I accepted the discipline of the Lord? Am I growing in knowledge of my God?* If the answer to these questions is yes, it wouldn't be a slip of the tongue to exclaim, "Way to grow!"   —C. T.

10. The LORD said, "What have you done? Listen! Your brother's blood cries out to me from the ground.

This time the Lord's question is rhetorical. There's no need for Cain to say anything, because Abel's *blood* was crying out loudly. God will later declare the shedding of innocent blood to be a pollution on the land (Numbers 35:33).

11. "Now you are under a curse and driven from the ground, which opened its mouth to receive your brother's blood from your hand.

Genesis 3–9 emphasizes that the estrangement between humans and God resulted not only in consequences for people but also for nonhuman creation (examples: Genesis 3:14-15, 17-19; 6:11-21). This being the case, we ought to be care-

ful not to reduce God's concern just to people. Though we are made in his image and occupy a special position in his creation (1:27-28), God is not *solely* concerned with the consequences of sin on humans. He still cares for his creation (examples: Jonah 4:11; Matthew 10:29). For this reason, salvation is an all-out, multidimensional solution to the global sin catastrophe (see Romans 8:18-23).

12. "When you work the ground, it will no longer yield its crops for you. You will be a restless wanderer on the earth."

If Cain could not be trusted with his brother's life, he could not be trusted with God's land. The land itself would resist all of Cain's efforts to wrest sustenance from it (compare Deuteronomy 28:15-24). And Cain could not simply run away from this problem. He could not find greener pastures elsewhere and resume his farming profession. No piece of land anywhere would cooperate with the first person who defiled the soil with human blood. He was therefore consigned to a life of roaming without a homeland.

C. Limiting Consequences (vv. 13-15)

13. Cain said to the LORD, "My punishment is more than I can bear.

The word translated *punishment* here has three senses, any one of which could be appropriate in this context: (1) It can refer to the wicked deed Cain committed. While in English we would think of punishment as a consequence of a misdeed, this sense implies that the action has natural consequences of its own that will now play out. (2) The word could refer to the guilt Cain bore or felt because of what he did. And finally, (3) it could refer to the sentence that he has received, the most natural English understanding. This final sense is preferable because Cain did not ask for forgiveness or mercy.

14a. "Today you are driving me from the land, and I will be hidden from your presence;

When Cain's parents were forced out of the garden, God's presence remained with them, even though they might have believed that God would abandon them. His faithfulness to them was evident in providing clothing (Genesis 3:21), helping

Eve in childbirth, and continuing conversations with Cain.

But Cain connected his wandering status with separation from God's presence. Did he understand that sin creates a rift between people and God (Romans 3:23; Ephesians 4:18)? Or did he believe that God's geographic reach was limited to his parents' home? Perhaps Cain viewed his connection with the soil as his primary contact point with God. He would meet God each day as he worked in God's good creation.

In any case, the murderer believed he was being sent outside of God's care. The Lord would not be his keeper (see Genesis 4:9b, above; contrast Psalm 23).

14b. "I will be a restless wanderer on the earth, and whoever finds me will kill me."

Cain's concern regarded his own family's desire for vengeance for Abel. He was convinced that his guilt would be known in any case and that, while God did not kill him outright now, he was effectively sentencing Cain to death.

15. But the LORD said to him, "Not so; anyone who kills Cain will suffer vengeance seven times over." Then the LORD put a mark on Cain so that no one who found him would kill him.

Quite in character, God responded with mercy. He recognized the truth in Cain's concern. People are inclined toward evil from birth (Genesis 8:21), and the desire for revenge is often a powerful motivator to act with evil, violent intent. Vengeful people do not trust God or leave vengeance to him; they take it upon themselves to repay evil. They organize mob actions against the Cains of this world. They authorize and deputize someone who is willing to do whatever necessary to rid the world of any and all threats to their community.

Cain would have to live with the consequences of his sin, but he would live nonetheless. We often experience the same. While our sins come with consequences, we know that through Christ we are spared death that is the natural consequence of sin (Romans 6:23).

The text provides no clue as to what Cain's *mark* might have been. Perhaps it was a unique physical feature that served as a deterrent. Or per-

haps it was a visible sign of a sevenfold level of *vengeance*, should anyone lay a hand on him.

Conclusion

A. Mercy on Mercy

Cain was not the first to benefit from God's mercy. It permeates the early chapters of Genesis. He cares for the innocent and the wicked alike in ways that we are typically slow to understand (Matthew 5:45). God does not delight in the death of the wicked but longs for them to repent and live (Ezekiel 18:23). And though we were all enemies of God, Christ died for us (Romans 5:10).

So may we all learn *what* it means that vengeance belongs to God and *how* to bless those who persecute us—and so overcome evil with good (Romans 12:14-21). May we, like Abel, offer pleasing sacrifices to our Lord. May we, unlike Cain, ask for the Lord's mercy and so experience the peace of reconciliation.

> *What Do You Think?*
> What principle from today's text will you have the most problem integrating into your life?
> *Digging Deeper*
> What plan can you enact to resolve this difficulty?

B. Prayer

Merciful and just God, teach us to trust in your justice and in your timing. Give us the faith to extend your mercy, which you have lavishly poured on us, to a wicked world that needs it neither more nor less than we do. In Jesus' name we pray. Amen.

C. Thought to Remember

God calls all people to turn to him and live.

HOW TO SAY IT

Leviticus	Leh-*vit*-ih-kus.
Moses	*Mo*-zes or *Mo*-zez.
primeval	pry-*mee*-vuhl.
Terah	*Tair*-uh.

INVOLVEMENT LEARNING

Enhance your lesson with NIV® Bible Student (from your curriculum supplier) and the reproducible activity page (at www.standardlesson.com or in the back of the NIV® Standard Lesson Commentary Deluxe Edition).

Into the Lesson

Present two closed boxes of different sizes. Have hidden in each box a "prize," one pleasant (example: candy) and one worthless (example: empty candy wrapper).

Ask a volunteer to choose one box without looking inside. Before choosing, the volunteer is allowed to ask one question about the boxes' contents (except "What's in the boxes?" or similar). Allow the class as a whole to coach him or her regarding choice of the question and box.

After the volunteer poses the question and makes the choice, ask, how the question helped make the decision. Then allow the student to look into the chosen box as you reveal what was in the other one. Discuss how advance thinking influences one's decision-making process.

Alternative. Divide participants into two teams and give each team a set of double-six dominoes. Have teams take no more than five minutes to set up a row or rows that will fall when the first domino is pushed. When time is up, knock down the first domino in one team's row and watch them fall. Before knocking down the other team's row, ask, "What could we do to this lineup to ensure that they *won't* fall?" Do whatever is suggested to demonstrate.

After either activity, say, "Every decision and action has consequences—sometimes these are very predictable and sometimes they aren't. Today we will explore which should have been which as we consider one man's actions and God's reactions."

Into the Word

Ask a volunteer to read aloud Genesis 4:1-8. Then divide the class in half, designating one half to be the **Offering Group** and the other to be the **Attitude Group**. Each group is to consider how things might have turned out differently if Cain's heart had been different, with the **Offering Group**

considering verses 1-5 and the **Attitude Group** considering verses 6-8.

After groups have reached their conclusions, have volunteers from each group role-play the story to show the implications of each of these crossroads for Cain.

Alternative. Distribute copies of the "Crossroads" exercise from the activity page, which you can download. Have students work in groups of two or three to complete as directed. After a few minutes, reconvene for whole-class discussion of conclusions.

Ask a volunteer to read Genesis 4:9-15. Divide the class into three groups to compare and contrast that passage with 3:9-24. **Confrontation Group:** compare/contrast 3:9-13 with 4:9-10; **Cursed Earth Group:** 3:14-19 with 4:11-12; **Mercy Group:** 3:20-24 and 4:13-15. Put those assignments on handouts along with these two questions:

1–In what ways are these accounts similar and in what ways are they different?
2–How do these passages portray the justice, vengeance, and mercy of God?

Share findings in whole-class discussion.

Into Life

Invite participants to share ways they use memory devices (mnemonics) to remember important things. Then challenge small groups to develop a way to help them remember how to respond to their own sinful expressions of anger (based on God's counsel to Cain in Genesis 4:6-7). After a few minutes, ask the groups to share and compare their tactics to prioritize repentance with the whole class.

Alternative. Distribute copies of the "Anger Two Ways" exercise from the activity page as a take-home. Suggest that some volunteers come to the next class prepared to share what they learned through this activity.

INJUSTICE AND HOPE

DEVOTIONAL READING: Genesis 21:8-21
BACKGROUND SCRIPTURE: Genesis 21:8-21

GENESIS 21:8-20

⁸ The child grew and was weaned, and on the day Isaac was weaned Abraham held a great feast. ⁹ But Sarah saw that the son whom Hagar the Egyptian had borne to Abraham was mocking, ¹⁰ and she said to Abraham, "Get rid of that slave woman and her son, for that woman's son will never share in the inheritance with my son Isaac."

¹¹ The matter distressed Abraham greatly because it concerned his son. ¹² But God said to him, "Do not be so distressed about the boy and your slave woman. Listen to whatever Sarah tells you, because it is through Isaac that your offspring will be reckoned. ¹³ I will make the son of the slave into a nation also, because he is your offspring."

¹⁴ Early the next morning Abraham took some food and a skin of water and gave them to Hagar. He set them on her shoulders and then sent her off with the boy. She went on her way and wandered in the Desert of Beersheba.

¹⁵ When the water in the skin was gone, she put the boy under one of the bushes. ¹⁶ Then she went off and sat down about a bowshot away, for she thought, "I cannot watch the boy die." And as she sat there, she began to sob.

¹⁷ God heard the boy crying, and the angel of God called to Hagar from heaven and said to her, "What is the matter, Hagar? Do not be afraid; God has heard the boy crying as he lies there. ¹⁸ Lift the boy up and take him by the hand, for I will make him into a great nation."

¹⁹ Then God opened her eyes and she saw a well of water. So she went and filled the skin with water and gave the boy a drink.

²⁰ God was with the boy as he grew up. He lived in the desert and became an archer.

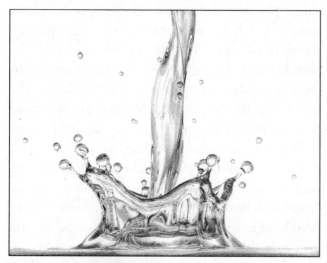

KEY TEXT

God heard the boy crying, and the angel of God called to Hagar from heaven and said to her, "What is the matter, Hagar? Do not be afraid; God has heard the boy crying as he lies there. Lift the boy up and take him by the hand, for I will make him into a great nation." —**Genesis 21:17-18**

Photo © Getty Images

JUSTICE, LAW, HISTORY

Unit 2: God: The Source of Justice
LESSONS 5–9

LESSON AIMS

After participating in this lesson, each learner will be able to:

1. List key features of the relationships among the six individuals (including God).

2. Compare and contrast Abraham's distress with that of Sarah and Hagar.

3. Write a prayer of praise for God's presence during a difficult time of life.

LESSON OUTLINE

Introduction
A. Deaf "Gods"

Isaiah 44:10-20 provides an incisive "mocku-mentary" of ancient Near East idolatry. Someone plants a tree and the rain waters it. Then someone cuts down that tree and uses half of it for firewood. Then a craftsman carves the other half into an image, claims it is a god, and asks it to save him. How, Isaiah wondered, could anyone in his or her right mind do such a thing? A block of wood does not have understanding. It neither sees nor hears, let alone acts in history to save.

Idolatry hasn't changed much over the centuries. And beyond that type of idol, people who have achieved fame are often idolized. Yet these people were once babies—utterly dependent on their parents for everything. But because a person is a household name, some hang on their every word, expecting inspiration that will put life on the right path. But these idols cannot save either.

The truth is, only God can hear, speak, and act to save. He hears the cries of his people and heeds the pleas of the oppressed. In today's passage, we see the God of Abraham listening attentively and offering a word of true hope.

B. Lesson Context

The second part of the book of Genesis could be called personal history (see Lesson Context from lesson 5). It is about people who have purpose in the plan of God to bring the Messiah into the world at just the right time (Galatians 4:4). This section of Genesis begins with Genesis 11:27. The focus is on the descendants of Abraham who continue through Isaac, Jacob, and the latter's 12 sons.

When God called Abraham and Sarah (then Abram and Sarai) to leave Ur, he promised to bring them to the land he would give them and to make Abraham's family a great nation (Genesis 12:1-3). Abraham entered Canaan at age 75, and he was told that this was the land that God planned to give to Abraham's descendants (12:7). After Abraham and his nephew Lot went their separate ways, Abraham was again told that all the land he could see would be given to his descendants (13:15). Yet Sarah was unable to conceive a child

(Genesis 11:30). She sought to overcome her barrenness by asking Abraham to impregnate one of her slaves (16:2-3). Sarah's logic in this seems strange to us. Why would a wife willingly allow her husband to have an intimate relationship with another woman? This seems to be a recipe for disaster! But the logic of this practice, common at the time, went something like this: "If my slave produces a child, that child will be mine, just like his mother is my property." Sarah thought she could have a son in this secondary way and thus please her husband.

One of their slaves was an Egyptian named Hagar (Genesis 16:3). She presumably came into their household when the family sojourned in Egypt (12:16). Hagar was Sarah's personal attendant. When Abraham and Sarah's attempts to produce a child were unsuccessful, Sarah offered Hagar to Abraham (never asking the slave's consent), hoping this union would yield a child. This attempt to run ahead of God turned out to be a bad idea, as Genesis 16:4b-6 shows.

When Hagar conceived, it created a rift between the two women. Hagar looked down on Sarah (Genesis 16:4), and Sarah retaliated with harsh treatment. When Hagar fled, God comforted her and encouraged her to return to Abraham and Sarah, with the promise that God would bless her offspring (16:9-12). The baby born to Abraham and Hagar was named Ishmael (see 21:17b, below).

Eventually God made it clear to Abraham that Sarah would bear him a son (Genesis 18:1-15). Isaac, the child of this miraculous conception, would become the heir to God's promise to Abraham. Yet with Ishmael still in the mix as Abraham's firstborn son, the situation was ripe for more conflict—which brings us to today's passage.

I. The Last Laugh
(GENESIS 21:8-13)
A. What Sarah Saw (vv. 8-9)

8. The child grew and was weaned, and on the day Isaac was weaned Abraham held a great feast.

We are not told when exactly a baby was expected to be *weaned*. Much later in Israel, Han-

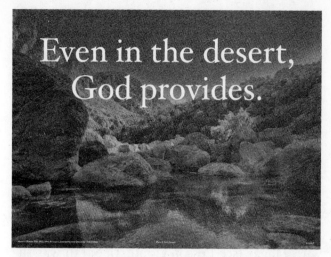

Visual for Lesson 6. *Allow one minute for silent personal reflection on this truth before discussing the questions associated with verse 19.*

nah (another barren woman whom God enabled to conceive) entrusted her son Samuel into the care of Eli to be raised as a priest after he was weaned (1 Samuel 1:22-24). This likely did not occur before Samuel was 3 years old, perhaps closer to 4.

Isaac's weaning was an event to be celebrated. He no longer depended on his mother's breastmilk for sustenance, which allowed him to spend more time with his father and the other men. This important rite of passage for any young boy was especially important for the child of promise, born in miraculous circumstances.

9. But Sarah saw that the son whom Hagar the Egyptian had borne to Abraham was mocking,

Referring to Ishmael as *the son [of] Hagar the Egyptian* emphasizes his relationship to his slave mother rather than to his father. Ishmael was 14 years older than his half brother Isaac (compare Genesis 16:16; 17:25 with 21:5), making Ishmael about age 17 when this event took place (see 21:8, above).

We are never told exactly what Ishmael said and/or did to draw the accusation of *mocking*. The Hebrew word is the same behind the name Isaac, which means "laughter." The word can imply simple amusement, but other contexts reveal darker possibilities. The same word was used when Lot's sons-in-law thought he was kidding around about the imminent destruction of Sodom (Genesis

19:14). The word also described the frivolity of the idolatrous Israelites with their golden calf (Exodus 32:6). The term further characterized how a husband and wife enjoyed romantic time together (Genesis 26:8), appropriate within a marriage but sinful in other contexts. The final possibility of inappropriate touch is most disturbing.

Sarah's sensitivity to anything to do with Hagar or Ishmael may lead us to assume that she over-reacted to a teasing insult to Isaac rather than molestation or abuse. Whatever was happening, it provoked Sarah to act decisively. Given her history with Hagar (see Lesson Context), Sarah was the worst person to witness Ishmael's misbehaving.

B. What Sarah Said (vv. 10-11)

10a. and she said to Abraham, "Get rid of that slave woman and her son,

As God cast the first couple out of Eden (Genesis 3:24) and later drove Cain from the soil (4:14; see lesson 5), so Sarah called *Abraham* to expel Hagar and Ishmael from their camp. We should hesitate to evaluate this action in a moral sense, given the fact of God's approval (21:12, below). With our knowledge that God worked through Isaac, we might be tempted to excuse Sarah's request as a pragmatic change-of-address request.

We might ask ourselves, *Do the ends justify the means?* It was cruel to cast out the *slave woman and her son*—a son born because Sarah herself had willed Abraham to impregnate Hagar. Referring to Hagar and Ishmael in the third person rather than by name may have been Sarah's way of depersonalizing them and distancing them as legitimate recipients of Abraham's concern. Subjecting Hagar and Ishmael to starvation, exposure, and violence then seemed tolerable to Sarah in some sense.

> *What Do You Think?*
> How do you as an adult believer discern when to allow children to work out their own conflicts and when to step in to protect one child against another?
> *Digging Deeper*
> In the case of intercession, how do you demonstrate God's love to the offending child?

10b. "for that woman's son will never share in the inheritance with my son Isaac."

When the law is later given at Sinai, it will be mandatory for the firstborn son to inherit a double portion of his father's estate at the father's death (see Deuteronomy 21:15-17). But Sarah was unwilling to see Ishmael even as an heir equal to her own *son.*

❧ *THE WICKED STEPMOTHER* ❧

Fairy tales exploit negative stereotypes about stepmothers. These stereotyped individuals in story lines serve as foils for conflict and the ultimate triumph of children. Cinderella's stepmother forced her to live as a servant in her father's house. Hansel and Gretel's stepmother sent them out of the house when food became scarce. While we might like to think that such characterizations are entirely imagined—that no adult, no matter her position, would mistreat children—we must admit that there is some truth here.

Disappointingly, Sarah sounds like the wicked stepmother here. Jealousy, pride, fear—all played a part in Sarah's disregard for Ishmael. And yet God worked through Sarah, Abraham, Isaac, Hagar, and Ishmael for his purposes. Be alert for how our Father, who watches the women and children this world rejects, may work.   —J. K.

11. The matter distressed Abraham greatly because it concerned his son.

Abraham rightly loved *his son* Ishmael. The father was not naïve about the dangers that the boy and his mother would face if sent away. Perhaps Abraham thought both sons would share his inheritance; after all, when God specified that Abraham's heir would be his own flesh and blood, Sarah was not mentioned (Genesis 15:4). And if Abraham understood that God intended for

HOW TO SAY IT

Beersheba	Beer-*she*-buh.
Gerar	*Gear*-rar (*G* as in *get*).
Hagar	*Hay*-gar.
Ishmael	*Ish*-may-el.
Keturah	Keh-*too*-ruh.
Paran	*Pair*-un.

only *one* nation to descend from Abraham, then that man could be excused for thinking that his two sons would both contribute to that one people. Ishmael's banishment would throw all these assumptions into disarray.

> **What Do You Think?**
> In conflicts between others, under what circumstances would you be a peacemaker? a problem solver? a silent bystander?
>
> *Digging Deeper*
> How do Proverbs 26:17 and Matthew 5:9 help inform your answer?

C. What God Said (vv. 12-13)

12. But God said to him, "Do not be so distressed about the boy and your slave woman. Listen to whatever Sarah tells you, because it is through Isaac that your offspring will be reckoned.

We might conclude quickly that it's God's will for Hagar and Ishmael to move away. But recognizing three ways to speak of "God's will" is important. The first is that of God's *purposive will* (referring to God's desire and decision; examples: Genesis 1:1; Acts 2:23). The second is that of his *prescriptive will* (referring to God's desire and human decision; examples: Hosea 6:6; Matthew 23:37). The third is that of his *permissive will* (referring to human desire and God's permission; examples: Acts 14:16; James 4:13).

The third of these three is in view here. In other words, God was willing to work within Sarah's desire as he moved his own plan forward. He would act in genuine partnership with Abraham and *Sarah*. Sometimes humans take initiative, and then God responds to their actions. This had been so in Abraham's case at least since Sarah decided to have a child by Hagar.

It is one thing to say that God wanted Sarah to cast away her servant and Abraham's son; it is another thing to say that God allowed it and saw it as a way to carry out his larger promises for his people. Those larger promises revolved around *Isaac*—not Ishmael. So God told Abraham to accept the will of his wife.

13. "I will make the son of the slave into a nation also, because he is your offspring."

In working with Sarah's decision, God did not ignore Hagar or become indifferent to Ishmael. Although God was always going to fulfill his promises through Sarah's child, he chose to also *make* Ishmael *a nation* because he too was Abraham's son (see Genesis 21:18, below). Even so, Abraham left his entire estate to Isaac (25:5).

After Sarah died, Abraham had additional sons with Keturah (Genesis 25:1-4). These sons do not appear to receive the same blessing as Ishmael, but Abraham sent them away from Isaac's family with gifts before he died (25:6).

II. A Lasting Promise
(GENESIS 21:14-20)

A. Hagar's Wandering (vv. 14-16)

14a. Early the next morning Abraham took some food and a skin of water and gave them to Hagar. He set them on her shoulders and then sent her off with the boy.

In this instance, as in the story of Isaac's near sacrifice, Abraham's obedience to the Lord was seen in his immediate action *early the next morning* (Genesis 22:3). The only record we have of *Abraham* and Ishmael together after this is when Ishmael returned to help Isaac bury their father (25:9); whether Ishmael spent time with his dying father is unknown. There is no record of Hagar ever returning to see Abraham.

14b. She went on her way and wandered in the Desert of Beersheba.

Beersheba was in southern Canaan, west of Gerar, where Abraham had settled (Genesis 20:1). Later, the entire promised land could be measured from Dan in the north to Beersheba. Indeed, the phrase "from Dan to Beersheba" became a catchphrase in that regard (Judges 20:1; 1 Samuel 3:20; 2 Samuel 3:10; 17:11; 24:2, 15; 1 Kings 4:25). Hagar likely intended to return to Egypt and eventually did so (Genesis 21:21). Her wandering in the desert foreshadowed Israel's own experience on their journey out of Egypt (Deuteronomy 2:1). Later Abraham would designate a well in the area by the name Beersheba (Genesis 21:31). Isaac and

Jacob both had significant spiritual experiences in the area (26:23-25; 46:1-4).

15. When the water in the skin was gone, she put the boy under one of the bushes.

We are not told how long Hagar wandered in the desert before running out of provisions, though we would expect that Abraham had sent her and *the boy* away with as much as they could carry. *Put* in this verse is the same term used when Joseph was thrown into a well and left for dead (Genesis 37:22, 24; see also Exodus 1:22). We can assume that for Hagar to be able to leave her teenage son *under one of the bushes*, he had no strength to change his circumstance.

16a. Then she went off and sat down about a bowshot away,

Here a play on words measures this distance in terms of *a bowshot*, foreshadowing Hagar and Ishmael's own near future (see Genesis 21:20, below).

16b. for she thought, "I cannot watch the boy die." And as she sat there, she began to sob.

The last time Hagar ran away, pregnant with Ishmael, God met her by a spring of water and promised that Ishmael would grow into manhood (Genesis 16:7-12). At that time, she called the Lord "the One who sees me" (16:13). It must have seemed to her that God was breaking this promise and refusing to see their current plight. Not giving a thought to her own likely death, she sobbed for her *boy*.

> **What Do You Think?**
> Without giving directive advice, how would you counsel someone who feels hopeless?
>
> *Digging Deeper*
> Under what circumstances would sharing Romans 8:28 and/or 2 Corinthians 4:7-9 *not* be a good idea?

B. God's Hearing (vv. 17-18)

17a. God heard the boy crying, and the angel of God called to Hagar from heaven and said to her, "What is the matter, Hagar? Do not be afraid;

The angel of God opened a conversation with *Hagar* as "the angel of the Lord" had done previously: with a question about her status (Genesis 16:7-8). But this time the angel didn't wait for an answer. Instead, the unanswered question is immediately followed by the command *not [to] be afraid*. Throughout the Bible, this command shows up dozens of times, often when humans encounter God or angelic beings (see Joshua 8:1; Matthew 28:5; Luke 1:13, 30).

Hagar would not have the language of God's love driving out fear, but surely her experience confirms the apostle John's words in 1 John 4:16-18. Because God loved both Hagar and Ishmael, the mother had no reason to fear for her child. When God calls his people to fear not, he calls them to love him and trust in his plans for them.

17b. "God has heard the boy crying as he lies there.

We may wonder why the angel told Hagar that God *heard the boy*, even though Hagar was the one weeping audibly in the previous verse. Nowhere in Genesis 21 is Ishmael referred to by name, which is a combination of the Hebrew words that mean "God hears" (Genesis 16:11). By emphasizing that he heard the teenager, God showed Hagar that he was looking after her son personally. He proved her son's name to be reassuringly true, even when it seemed that not even the boy's mother had the capacity to listen to him any longer.

18. "Lift the boy up and take him by the hand, for I will make him into a great nation."

God already had promised that Ishmael would become *a great nation* (Genesis 17:20), and God planned to keep his promise. The only other person to whom God made such a promise was Abraham (12:1-2). Ishmael would have 12 sons (25:12-18) as would Isaac's son Jacob (49:1-28). These Ishmaelites show up in Joseph's story (see 37:25-28). They were nomadic people, generally living in northern Arabia.

C. God's Help (vv. 19-20)

19. Then God opened her eyes and she saw a well of water. So she went and filled the skin with water and gave the boy a drink.

Why Hagar could not see the *well* before is not clear. Perhaps her exhaustion and dehydration prevented her from seeing what was right before her eyes. This *water* was enough to revive Ishmael and keep her hope alive. The God whom she previously declared to be the God who "sees me" (Genesis 16:13) had opened her own eyes.

What Do You Think?
What has to happen for you to "open your eyes" (physically or spiritually) more fully to God's blessings?
Digging Deeper
Are the eye-opening actions of Psalm 119:18 and Ephesians 1:18 your responsibility or God's?

❧ *I Hit My Knees, Hard!* ❧

On Saturday, January 13, 2018, the Hawaii Emergency Management Agency sent an alert to tens of thousands of Hawaii cell phones that warned of an inbound ballistic missile. The alert caused immediate panic in many who saw it. Only minutes later, relief came in a second message confirming that the first was a false alarm.

My friend Diana had been in Hawaii at the time. She told me she immediately fell to her knees when she read the text. "And when I got up, I asked the Lord for two things: help me be brave, and if I die today, please make it quick. Other than that, I knew that I was ready to go."

Her testimony was short, but powerful. Hagar might tell a similar story. In her crying, the Spirit of God heard her and cared for her and her son. No matter how dire the situation, God hears and God loves.
—C. T.

20a. God was with the boy as he grew up.

God kept his promise to Hagar. His presence *with the boy* serves as a reminder that, though God looks after his chosen people in a special way, he also cares for people beyond that group (compare Matthew 5:45). Indeed, God set apart Abraham's family through Isaac precisely to bless all nations (Genesis 12:3). How great to serve a God who has always loved the whole world and chose to demonstrate it through his Son (John 3:16-18)!

20b. He lived in the desert and became an archer.

Ishmael's becoming *an archer* completes the play on words from verse 16. More importantly, it also fills out some of God's original declaration about the boy's future. The last time God spoke with Hagar, he told her that Ishmael would become a wild man at odds with others (Genesis 16:12), a characteristic one might expect from a boy growing to maturity *in the desert* without a father to guide him or a community to mold him. Bows were the weapon of choice in Ishmael's time—for hunting (27:3) and waging war (1 Samuel 31:3). These skills undoubtedly contributed much to his survival and eventual prosperity.

Conclusion
A. God Who Hears

Hagar had a difficult life. But as Ishmael's name reminds us, God hears! Abraham's God, who loved both Isaac and Ishmael, is the Lord of all creation. He cares for all people, and he keeps his promises. He hears all cries of injustice, and he responds with a message of hope. That message must be preached, taught, and lived by his people before the watching world, which is desperate for a better story than the divisions that so often define our lives. When *we* hear, the world might begin to believe that God also hears.

What Do You Think?
How will you resolve the principle or precedent in today's text that you have the most trouble with?
Digging Deeper
When will you start that process?

B. Prayer

God who hears, we raise our voices to you. Strengthen our hope so the world may have hope in you through our faithful witness. In Jesus' name we pray. Amen.

C. Thought to Remember

Call out to the God
who hears.

INVOLVEMENT LEARNING

Enhance your lesson with NIV® Bible Student (from your curriculum supplier) and the reproducible activity page (at www.standardlesson.com or in the back of the NIV® Standard Lesson Commentary Deluxe Edition).

Into the Lesson

Give each participant several self-stick notes on which to write different *kinds* of relationships, one per note. As they take no more than a minute to do so, draw a spectrum line across the board; write "adversity/tension" on one end and "peace/trust" on the other end.

Have volunteers stick their notes along the line, to indicate the general quality of their own relationships. When all those willing to post notes have done so, review them for trends. Follow this by asking participants to share why some types of relationships tend to be more tense or more peaceful.

Alternative. Invite participants to mention characters from books or movies who were underdogs. After each example, pose the following questions to the whole group: 1–What made the underdog's goal seem unattainable? 2–What made the difference and turned the story around?

After either activity, say, "Challenging relationships or situations can make us fearful and without hope. But today's lesson has the cure."

Into the Word

Ask a volunteer to read Genesis 21:8-13. Then have three volunteers play the roles of Abraham, Sarah, and Hagar, each one taking turns telling this part of the story in "their own words" (it's best to recruit these actors in advance). Allow opportunities for reactions and feedback. For whole-class discussion, ask how perspective and personal emotions affected the ways the characters saw and responded to this complicated situation.

Have a volunteer read Genesis 21:14-20. Challenge participants to think of as many other examples as possible of God or an angel telling someone to "fear not." As participants name these instances, list them on the left side of the board under a column titled *Example.* Then divide the class into small groups and assign one or two examples to each. Challenge them to find the book, chapter, and verse of the instance and read it in context. While groups work, add columns on the board headed *Reference* and *Reason Not to Fear.* Have each group choose a volunteer to come to the board to make appropriate entries under the headers. Do your own research in advance so you can mention instances that class members miss.

Option 1. Have participants choose a partner as you distribute copies of the "Relationship Dynamics" exercise from the activity page, which you can download. After pairs complete the exercise, reconvene for whole-class discussion.

Option 2. For deeper study and possible input for *Option 1,* distribute copies of the "Hagar and God" exercise from the activity page to complete together. Allow time for whole-group discussion and insights.

Into Life

Write this phrase across the top of the board:

Praise be to the God who . . .

Invite participants to think of a way to complete the phrase to describe their experiences with God. Have volunteers come forward and write their responses on the board.

Follow by asking why the meaning of the name *Ishmael* ("God hears") is significant. Encourage participants to recall a difficult time they were able to endure, when all hope seemed lost. Challenge them to recall the presence of God during that time and how He restored hope.

Alternative. Instruct participants to think about a difficult and seemingly helpless season of life and connect it with a hymn, Bible verse, etc., that strengthened them to walk through that time. Invite individuals to quote, read, or even sing the words that helped them as a testimony and act of praise to God for His faithfulness. Come prepared to do so yourself.

JUSTICE AND FAIRNESS

DEVOTIONAL READING: Exodus 23:1-12
BACKGROUND SCRIPTURE: Exodus 23

EXODUS 23:1-12

¹ "Do not spread false reports. Do not help a guilty person by being a malicious witness.

² "Do not follow the crowd in doing wrong. When you give testimony in a lawsuit, do not pervert justice by siding with the crowd, ³ and do not show favoritism to a poor person in a lawsuit.

⁴ "If you come across your enemy's ox or donkey wandering off, be sure to return it. ⁵ If you see the donkey of someone who hates you fallen down under its load, do not leave it there; be sure you help them with it.

⁶ "Do not deny justice to your poor people in their lawsuits. ⁷ Have nothing to do with a false charge and do not put an innocent or honest person to death, for I will not acquit the guilty.

⁸ "Do not accept a bribe, for a bribe blinds those who see and twists the words of the innocent.

⁹ "Do not oppress a foreigner; you yourselves know how it feels to be foreigners, because you were foreigners in Egypt.

¹⁰ "For six years you are to sow your fields and harvest the crops, ¹¹ but during the seventh year let the land lie unplowed and unused. Then the poor among your people may get food from it, and the wild animals may eat what is left. Do the same with your vineyard and your olive grove.

¹² "Six days do your work, but on the seventh day do not work, so that your ox and your donkey may rest, and so that the slave born in your household and the foreigner living among you may be refreshed."

KEY TEXT

Do not follow the crowd in doing wrong. When you give testimony in a lawsuit, do not pervert justice by siding with the crowd, and do not show favoritism to a poor person in a lawsuit. —**Exodus 23:2-3**

Photo © Getty Images

JUSTICE, LAW, HISTORY

Unit 2: God: The Source of Justice
LESSONS 5–9

LESSON AIMS

After participating in this lesson, each learner will be able to:

1. Identify the ratio of positive commands ("do") to negative ones ("do not").

2. Suggest a reason for that ratio.

3. Express one or more ways to avoid following sinful cultural trends.

LESSON OUTLINE

Introduction

A. Law from a Loving God

"Meet your new family," said the judge to Bill and Rosa. For the previous year or so, the couple had welcomed into their home three siblings under age 5. Finally the adoption process was complete. As the courtroom erupted in applause by members of their church family, Bill and Rosa took their three little children in their arms. The smiles on every face and tears in every eye signaled the power of justice and love. Law and family worked together for the improvement of lives.

All nations and cultures have vulnerable people, often those who are very young or very old. All cultures develop ways of caring for such people. The Bible has much to say in this regard as it directs our actions—individually and corporately—toward the benefit of everyone we encounter.

B. Lesson Context

To understand the laws under consideration in today's text, we must pay attention to their contexts (plural). On a larger scale, Exodus 21–23 is often called the Covenant Code because it gives foundational rules for ancient Israel's corporate life. In other words, the laws reflect how people were to conduct themselves in typical, everyday situations. This collection of laws is the basis of longer discussions in Leviticus 17–27 and Deuteronomy 12–26.

Within Exodus, the Covenant Code comes immediately after the Ten Commandments. While that shorter list includes 10 distinct laws, expressed for easy memorization, the longer list of the Covenant Code repeats itself and arranges topics more by association ("speaking of X, consider also Y"). That sort of organization appears in today's lesson.

The sequence of the laws influences meaning. Readers should not think of them as sound bites but as a web of required behaviors that collectively reflected the character of those practicing them.

On a smaller scale, today's text of Exodus 23:1-12 concentrates on issues of justice. Verses 1-9 fit closely with the end of chapter 22, while verses 10-12 open up a discussion of the proper use of time for worship and rest. The two major sections of the text at hand use the same sort of lock-and-key organizational technique common in Israelite legal texts and in the book of Proverbs. That is, several statements on obviously related themes follow each other. Then the topic seems to change, and then it returns to the original subject.

This pattern challenges the reader to see previously unconsidered dimensions of both the main idea on the ends of the list and a seemingly different idea wedged into the middle. In this case, Exodus 23:4-5 seems to change the subject covered in verses 1-3 and 6-8, all of which feature a courtroom setting. Verses 4-5 envision encounters out in the field or on the road. The apparent change of topics reminds the reader that lying in court does not occur in the abstract but at the expense of real people and relationships. Conversely, the text's connection between judicial proceedings and ordinary helpfulness toward enemies reminds the reader that even the most mundane incidents of life have wider societal implications.

These laws apply concretely the more general command to "love your neighbor as yourself" (Leviticus 19:18). Since people tend to extend greatest love to friends and family members while treating others less favorably, the Law of Moses identifies classes of people who deserved respect in the Israelites' interactions with them. The law does not allow for rationalizing, self-indulgence, or sanctimonious self-justification. Rather, it demanded that the Israelites take seriously their status as peers with all other human beings and as fellow subjects of their Creator. This fact is reflected in the apostle Paul's statement that "whoever loves others has fulfilled the law" (Romans 13:8).

These laws also assumed that the Israelites *wanted* to be people of integrity. The Israelites should have wanted to act justly, even when pushed to do otherwise or when conflict made them want to take personal revenge. They were to have recognized their own faults and temptations to misbehavior and take steps to correct them.

HOW TO SAY IT

Français *(French)*	Fraun-*say*.
parlez-vous *(French)*	par-lay-*voo*.
Septuagint	Sep-*too*-ih-jent.

I. Justice in Court and Home
(Exodus 23:1-8)
A. Rules of Due Process, Part 1 (vv. 1-3)

1. "Do not spread false reports. Do not help a guilty person by being a malicious witness.

The first law in the chain prohibits giving *false reports* (also known as perjury) in court. The two halves of the verse do not merely say the same thing, however. The first clause offers a general command against lying such as would harm another person (compare Exodus 20:16; Deuteronomy 5:20), while the second clause addresses a subset of the first clause in forbidding conspiracy to commit perjury. Cooperating with others to harm a third party undermines any justice system and leads to societal conflict and violence. When a legal system is corrupt, everyone eventually suffers (compare 1 Kings 21:8-14 and Matthew 26:59-60).

> *What Do You Think?*
> What are some ways to guard your mind and tongue against dishonesty?
> *Digging Deeper*
> What principles in Ephesians 4:25; Colossians 3:9; and Titus 1:2 help you most in this regard?

2. "Do not follow the crowd in doing wrong. When you give testimony in a lawsuit, do not pervert justice by siding with the crowd,

The first clause states a general requirement: an ancient Israelite was not to determine correct behavior by what everyone else was doing. The specific reference may be to mob action (compare Acts 7:57-58; 17:5); at the least it refers to a crowd mentality that perpetuated common prejudices that denied the divinely determined rights of others.

The meaning of the second clause is more obscure. The Hebrew verb translated *pervert* occurs a second time, translated *siding with*, to create a memorable play on words that is difficult for translators. The verb used by the ancient Greek translation called the Septuagint occurs in the New Testament three times: in Romans 3:12; 16:17; and 1 Peter 3:11—all implying a departure or turning of some sort. The verse at hand seems to say the same thing twice, though the second clause narrows possible interpretations of the first clause to fit in the ongoing discussion of these verses.

> **What Do You Think?**
> What can you do better to resist temptation to go along with the crowd?
> *Digging Deeper*
> What have you learned from your past failures in this regard?

3. "and do not show favoritism to a poor person in a lawsuit.

The law forbids bending the legal system, even when it seems to level the playing field. Judges must decide cases solely on the evidence. Leviticus 19:15 repeats the verb translated *show favoritism* in affirming the flip side of the coin: that judges were not to "show . . . favoritism to the great" in legal proceedings. See Exodus 23:6, below.

B. Helping an Enemy (vv. 4-5)

4. "If you come across your enemy's ox or donkey wandering off, be sure to return it.

This verse and the next assume that people have enemies. In envisioning ideals, the law is also practical. Even when a person is hated, Israelites were not to hate and be vindictive in return. Jesus' call to pray for enemies and resist repaying evil for evil (Matthew 5:43-48) makes a general statement about a principle that was already in the law.

In agricultural societies like that of ancient Israel, beasts of burden provided labor for plowing and threshing, dung for fuel, transportation for family members, etc. For a poor farming family, the loss of one such animal would create a major financial hardship. On the other hand, rustling allowed poor people to add to their assets at the expense of others. In a time when 98 percent of people farmed, the residents of farming villages had to help each other survive and flourish as they exhibited the love and holiness of God to one another.

❧ LOVING THE FORMER FRIEND ❧

Alex's affair had carried on with one of Emma's friends. And soon enough, Emma became the ex-wife while Alex wed the now-former friend, Zoe. The children of the families found the new role of step-siblings thrust upon them. Emma was devastated.

One day Emma found herself running late in picking up her children from school. When she arrived, there were her three kids . . . and Zoe's two children. The on-duty teacher told her that her ex-friend's car had broken down and the woman would be *very* late picking up the kids, who wilted in the soaring heat. Emma decided to take pity on the children and bring them home with her to wait for their mother.

God commands us to care for our enemies. How easy it would have been for Emma merely to take her own children and leave! But she knew what was right. How will you love an enemy this week?

—P. L. M.

5. "If you see the donkey of someone who hates you fallen down under its load, do not leave it there; be sure you help them with it.

The law depicted four phases of a decision-making process: (1) spotting an animal in difficulty, (2) realizing that it belonged to an enemy, (3) checking one's own motives, and (4) deciding to help despite the underlying personal relationship. The law did not state how the animal's owner might be identified as such. Was the owner present? Or did living in close quarters in the village make the identification possible? The law exhibited no concern for that detail; the law made an absolute demand on the Israelites. No matter how sorely tempted one was to avoid helping an enemy, concerns for the animal's welfare, societal harmony, and honoring God dictated giving assistance.

The last part of the verse can be interpreted in several ways. One interpretation might be "you shall *surely* leave [it] with him." More broadly, the line implies that the person obedient to the law was not to take advantage of the animal's (and the enemy's) distress.

Jesus later built on this and similar laws in his disputes about doing good on the Sabbath. If Jesus' opponents would rescue a trapped animal on the Sabbath, how much more should they help a fellow human being (Matthew 12:9-14; see also Luke 14:1-6; John 5:1-18)!

C. Rules of Due Process, Part 2 (vv. 6-8)

6. "Do not deny justice to your poor people in their lawsuits.

While Exodus 23:3 banned the Israelites' favoring a *poor* person in legal proceedings merely because of his or her poverty, the verse before us forbids the opposite. Considered alongside Leviticus 19:15, God's rule is clear: that anyone involved in a dispute, especially a witness or a judge, must decide fairly without regard to external factors such as the socioeconomic status of the persons involved.

7a. "Have nothing to do with a false charge

People are often inclined to get as close as possible to the line separating truth telling from lying without actually crossing that line. Think of how often we have heard (and voiced) half-truths, or quotes of others out of context. And what about a lack of being forthcoming when questioned! But the command here broadly required an Israelite to stay far away from deception.

> **What Do You Think?**
> As you keep your distance from dishonesty, in what kinds of cases should you confront it according to Ephesians 5:11?
> **Digging Deeper**
> What dangers should you anticipate in doing so?

7b. "and do not put an innocent or honest person to death,

This part of the verse moves from deceptive speaking to murder of those undeserving of death. By setting the two forbidden actions side by side, the verse reminds readers of the potential for abusive situations to escalate.

7c. "for I will not acquit the guilty.

This declaration offers a reason to keep God's laws. He had extended mercy to Israel by delivering them from heartless Egyptian slavery. Thus the Israelites dare not become a heartless society themselves (compare Matthew 18:23-35). God will not cheapen his gift of redemption by turning a blind eye on wickedness.

8. "Do not accept a bribe, for a bribe blinds

those who see and twists the words of the innocent.

Like intimidating witnesses or lying in open court, bribery can negatively affect the outcome of any dispute. The word translated *bribe* appears 26 times across 24 verses in the Old Testament that results in injustice against an innocent party (example: 1 Samuel 8:3). Centuries later, prophets would complain often and loudly about judicial corruption traceable to bribery (Isaiah 1:23; Amos 5:12; Micah 3:11; etc.). Bribery can be thought of as purchasing a certain outcome in court. Such a "purchase" may go as far as ensuring the slaying of an innocent person. (Deuteronomy 27:25 explicitly connects the two.) Thus these bribery texts imply the threat that this corrupt practice posed to the entire social structure of ancient Israel (compare Proverbs 15:27). And sometimes the bribery texts emphasize God's dismay at such behavior, since God has called on Israel to imitate the divine justice extended to all of them (see Ezekiel 22:12).

The verse before us is unusual, however, in its reason for avoiding bribery: such an action corrupts the very character of the ones involved. A judge receiving a bribe abandons the very qualification for being a judge: wisdom. A temporary advantage, gained to the detriment of others, can corrode the very soul of the person gaining that advantage, as well as harming many others. And a system that tolerates such behavior sooner or later decays into conflict as distrust builds.

II. Justice in Economic Matters
(Exodus 23:9-12)

A. Care for Migrants (v. 9)

9a. "Do not oppress a foreigner;

A foreigner living away from his or her homeland is often without the support system of family and friends. In ancient Israel, as in most nations before modern times, the extended family or clan was the basic unit of social organization. Family units provided financial, physical, and emotional support for their members. The migrant might have no support system. Therefore laws were needed to protect that person.

9b. "you yourselves know how it feels to

be foreigners, because you were foreigners in Egypt.

For this analogy to make sense, the hypothetical *foreigners* in the first clause must be non-Israelites. Many migrants must have been refugees, given the many wars in the history of the Middle East. Because Israel's collective memory centered around its experiences in Egyptian bondage, the core story of the Israelites—individually and collectively—had to show empathy toward similarly vulnerable people, honoring their divinely given rights (compare Exodus 23:8, above).

Laws protecting foreigners appear several times in Exodus. The Ten Commandments protected them during the observance of the Sabbath, when they also may rest (Exodus 20:10; compare Deuteronomy 5:14). Exodus 22:21-24 links them with widows and orphans as vulnerable people lacking family ties and, therefore, social protection. A legal case between a foreigner and an Israelite was to be judged just as if the case was between two Israelites (Deuteronomy 1:16). The law forbade mistreating them, threatening divine punishment of those who did so.

> *What Do You Think?*
> How do 1 Peter 1:1 and 2:11 help you apply this text in a spiritual sense?
> *Digging Deeper*
> What are examples of cases in which doing nothing was actually a form of oppression?

❧ *PARLEZ-VOUS FRANÇAIS?* ❧

The facility where I worked employed many Certified Nursing Assistants (CNAs) from West Africa. Some were not fluent in English, which could make the hiring process difficult. One CNA was offered a position but missed deadlines to enroll in onboarding classes because of the language barrier. Hearing this, her face fell, anxiety and uncertainty etched on it.

But she made it the next time around. During my presentation, I let it be known that I speak French. When I spoke directly to our new West African team member, her eyes lit up, and the smile on her face was such a beautiful contrast to her previous downcast countenance. My heart leaped for joy to be able to give a little comfort to someone in a foreign land.

The Israelites knew what it was like to be strangers in a strange land. Even more than Israel, Christians are strangers even in our home countries (see Philippians 3:20; 1 Peter 2:11). So what will you do when you have the opportunity to comfort a stranger? —P. L. M.

B. The Sabbatical Year (vv. 10-11)

10-11. "For six years you are to sow your fields and harvest the crops, but during the seventh year let the land lie unplowed and unused. Then the poor among your people may get food from it, and the wild animals may eat what is left. Do the same with your vineyard and your olive grove.

It is unclear whether this law required all land to lie fallow in *the seventh year,* or if a rotation of crops should occur. Nor is it clear whether allowing the land to remain *unplowed* means not harvesting the field in addition to not even planting it. Ambiguities here receive greater clarity in Leviticus 25:1-7, which is a sort of commentary on this earlier text. Leviticus expressly forbade sowing any seed during the seventh year.

The owners of the *land* should have stored a year's worth of food for their families, allowing any surpluses to go to *poor,* landless *people.* The last part of verse 11 closes a possible loophole, so that not only fields but also vineyards and olive groves must not be harvested. These three major food sources (for bread, wine, and olive oil), constituted the core of the Israelite diet, and so the law aimed at comprehensiveness. Relying on God's generosity for large parts of the food supply would allow those keeping the law to live in solidarity with each other regardless of income. They all must trust in God's care for them.

C. The Sabbath Day (v. 12)

12. "Six days do your work, but on the seventh day do not work, so that your ox and your donkey may rest, and so that the slave born in your household and the foreigner living among you may be refreshed."

Six days here echoes the six years of verse 10. The law of the Sabbath Day (*the seventh day*) here returns to the theme of helping domesticated animals, as seen in verses 4-5. In this instance, the help is *rest* rather than some other active intervention.

This text differs from the Sabbath laws in the Ten Commandments (Exodus 20:8-11; Deuteronomy 5:12-15) in two ways. First, the verse before us does not give a warrant for the law (elsewhere justified by referring to the creation of the world or to God's deliverance of Israel in the exodus). And second, it does not command the recipient's family to rest. That latter point went without saying, while the former points to the fact that the Ten Commandments, despite their brevity, richly develop important details.

This version of the Sabbath law does name those members of the household most vulnerable to self-centered action on the part of the family head. So, *the slave born in your household* as well as *the foreigner* living with the family had the right to rest just as much as did the citizens of Israel.

Visual for Lessons 7 & 8. *While discussing verse 8, ask the class what role Christians should or do play in making sure that justice remains unbiased.*

> **What Do You Think?**
> What steps can you take to achieve a better balance between work and rest?
> *Digging Deeper*
> What relationship do you see between such a balance and spiritual health (or lack thereof)?

Conclusion

A. Seeking Justice

One of the most powerful treatments of the nature of God appears in Exodus. It contains a richly layered set of stories exploring the question "What sort of God do we have in our midst?" This story lies behind all of Israel's laws. Rather than creating a long philosophical discussion on God, the scroll of Exodus weaves together stories about divine actions and conversations around them. As it reveals a God who practices a radical commitment to mercy, Exodus does not avoid the challenges that belief in a redeemer God poses.

The 600-plus laws in the Old Testament do not address every imaginable circumstance. Even so, they lay out enough specific examples to allow thinking people to figure out how to act in situations not explicitly named. The Law of Moses invites reflection. Those following it ask questions that will shape commitments and attitudes for a lifetime.

A remarkable feature of today's church in much of the Western world is its distance from the poorest among us. American Christians, in particular, often seem to live in a bubble. Wealth is taken as proof of God's blessing, which can lead us to blame others for their alleged failures if they do not obtain it. We are slow to acknowledge how decisions of past generations still affect people's lives. And those most vulnerable pay the price for that self-deception.

The Law of Moses, while aimed at the people of Israel, offers guiding principles for the church as well. Life together requires practical actions that show love for difficult people. In this way, we can fulfill the law: to love our God, and to love both neighbors and enemies, wherever they are found.

B. Prayer

Father, continue to teach us to be generous to our enemies, loyal to our friends, honest in all our dealings, and compassionate toward all in need. Make us people who always treat the poor with respect and care. In Jesus' name we pray. Amen.

C. Thought to Remember

Drawing near to God requires caring for others.

INVOLVEMENT LEARNING

Enhance your lesson with NIV® Bible Student (from your curriculum supplier) and the reproducible activity page (at www.standardlesson.com or in the back of the NIV® Standard Lesson Commentary Deluxe Edition).

Into the Lesson

Have the class brainstorm ways that people justify their actions by saying, "Everybody does it!" List responses on the board. After you have about six, have the group rank-order them from least to most harmful and give reasons.

Make a transition by saying, "As we consider the challenge to be countercultural in honoring God, let's stay alert to how that challenge may be broken down into issues of *who, what, where, when, why,* and *how.*"

Into the Word

Ask a volunteer to read Exodus 23:1-12. Then divide the class into five groups. Give each group a large index card on which you have printed a group name and a Scripture reference as follows: **Sabbath Group**–Exodus 20:8; **Murder Group**–Exodus 20:13; **Theft Group**–Exodus 20:15; **Witness Group**–Exodus 20:16; **Love Group**–Leviticus 19:18. Have these identical instructions printed on all five cards:

1–Look up the reference and write the full verse on the front of the card.

2–On the back of the card, write the commands in Exodus 23:1-12 that relate to the text on the front of the card.

3–Provide scriptural examples of the law being obeyed or disregarded and what resulted from those attitudes and actions.

Work through Exodus 23:1-9 and allow groups to present discoveries, saving the **Sabbath Group** for last.

Option. Instead of step 3 above, instruct each group to plan a short skit, creating a modern-day scenario to demonstrate their card subject in two parts: (1) the wrong thing to do and (2) how to correct that behavior based on the given law(s). Have each group perform their skit for the whole group, saving the **Sabbath Group** for last.

Alternative. Divide the whole group into small groups of two or three. Distribute copies of the "To Do or Not to Do" exercise from the activity page, which you can download. Have all groups complete the entire activity and then compare results. (*Alternative.* Assign each group a section of the activity to complete.) Share results in the ensuing whole-class discussion.

As the **Sabbath Group** presents last, ask who and/or what benefits from the command to rest. (*Expected response*: both animals and people.) Divide the class into two groups, one group to focus on animals and the other group to focus on people. Each should find additional scriptural evidence of God's concern for animals and people. Have the groups discuss these issues as well (distribute on handouts you create):

1–Is the issue of sabbath rest still valid in the new covenant era? Why, or why not?

2–If still valid, what forms would be appropriate for honoring it?

3–Would two half-days of rest be the same as one full day? Why, or why not?

Have volunteers groups present their conclusions; brace for lively discussion!

Into Life

Ask participants which sins listed in today's passage seem to trouble Christians the most. As opinions are forthcoming, say, "Rather than just *not* doing the wrong thing, what is a pro-active *right* thing we can do instead?" Write the group's ideas on the board; encourage participants to put these into action this week.

Option. Distribute copies of the "Who Is My Neighbor?" exercise from the activity page. Spend a few minutes in group discussion clarifying the categories. Challenge participants to take the page home to reflect on and respond to during the week. State that participants should be prepared to discuss the results of this activity during the next class session.

JUSTICE, JUDGES, AND PRIESTS

DEVOTIONAL READING: Deuteronomy 16:18-21; 17:8-13
BACKGROUND SCRIPTURE: Deuteronomy 16:18-20; 17:8-13; 19:15-21

DEUTERONOMY 16:18-20

18 Appoint judges and officials for each of your tribes in every town the LORD your God is giving you, and they shall judge the people fairly. 19 Do not pervert justice or show partiality. Do not accept a bribe, for a bribe blinds the eyes of the wise and twists the words of the innocent. 20 Follow justice and justice alone, so that you may live and possess the land the LORD your God is giving you.

DEUTERONOMY 17:8-13

8 If cases come before your courts that are too difficult for you to judge—whether bloodshed, lawsuits or assaults—take them to the place the LORD your God will choose. 9 Go to the Levitical priests and to the judge who is in office at that time. Inquire of them and they will give you the verdict. 10 You must act according to the decisions they give you at the place the LORD will choose. Be careful to do everything they instruct you to do. 11 Act according to whatever they teach you and the decisions they give you. Do not turn aside from what they tell you, to the right or to the left. 12 Anyone who shows contempt for the judge or for the priest who stands ministering there to the LORD your God is to be put to death. You must purge the evil from Israel. 13 All the people will hear and be afraid, and will not be contemptuous again.

KEY TEXT

Appoint judges and officials for each of your tribes in every town the LORD your God is giving you, and they shall judge the people fairly. —**Deuteronomy 16:18**

Photo © Getty Images

• 177

Justice, Law, History

Unit 2: God: The Source of Justice
Lessons 5–9

Lesson Aims

After participating in this lesson, each learner will be able to:

1. Identify the type or types of justice at hand.

2. Contrast characteristics of just judges and their rulings with those of unjust judges.

3. Create a list of go-to advisers for challenging situations.

Lesson Outline

Introduction

A. The Journey to Judgeship

Becoming a judge is a rigorous and demanding (not to mention expensive!) process. The process includes specialized, post-graduate education at a law school to earn a JD (juris doctor) degree, passing the bar exam, completing a judicial clerkship, and practicing law by prosecuting and/or defending cases in court. Only at that point does one stand a chance of being elected or appointed to the bench.

The entire process often takes decades. The education, training, and experience a potential judge receives during years of preparation provide the necessary foundation needed to render right judgments based in law.

Becoming a judge in Old Testament Israel was radically different from the process required nowadays. But a necessary element for *continuing* as a judge remains the same as it did some 34 centuries ago—a key issue in this week's lesson.

B. Lesson Context

Moses himself appointed the first judges (Exodus 18:24-26), but no formalized program existed for training to become a judge in the Israel of Moses' day (about 1447 BC). There was a certain kind of "bar exam" that an individual had to pass before being appointed to judge. The first stated criteria for passing were four in number: (1) capability, (2) fear of God, (3) trustworthiness, and (4) hatred of dishonest gain (18:21). Moses received these criteria from his father-in-law, Jethro, shortly after leading the Israelites out of Egypt but before reaching Mount Sinai (19:1, 20). The individuals who met these criteria assisted Moses as judges, providing rulings on the legal cases of the people brought before them (18:26). During Israel's sojourn to the promised land, they received many more instructions that distinguished just from unjust behavior. Some are recorded in Exodus 23:1-12, the text of last week's lesson.

The focus of the book of Exodus is on the first generation of the new nation of Israel. But as the book of Deuteronomy opens, 40 years had passed, and a new generation of Israelites needed to hear the law expounded (Deuteronomy 1:1-5). This included reiterating the characteristics of a proper judicial system in general and the requirements of judges in particular (1:16-18).

The exact steps of appointment processes for judges isn't clear. Hundreds of years after Moses, Absalom used subversion to get himself appointed as judge by popular acclamation (2 Samuel 15:1-6). Later, King Jehoshaphat (reigned 872–848 BC) appointed judges personally (2 Chronicles 19:4-7). In 458 BC, Ezra was charged with appointing judges in his capacity as a priest and an expert in the law (Ezra 7:25). Stricter, more specific requirements for serving as a judge are found in Ezekiel 44:15-27.

This lesson considers how the leaders of Israel, namely judges and priests, were to advocate for and implement justice among the people of Israel. This week's lesson comes from the portion of Deuteronomy where Moses spoke on various leadership positions and how they were to function. Judges (Deuteronomy 16:18–17:13), kings (17:14-20), priests (18:1-8), and prophets (18:14-22) are among those groups described by Moses. Today's lesson will illustrate how the Lord demands just judgment and desires his covenant people to be led by individuals who exhibit the ability to practice just judgment among them.

I. General Goals
(Deuteronomy 16:18-20)

A. Responsible People (v. 18)

18. Appoint judges and officials for each of your tribes in every town the LORD your God is giving you, and they shall judge the people fairly.

Moses prescribed two groups of leaders for the community. The *judges* were those leaders tasked with exacting decisions of justice for the people. These individuals were considered leaders of the community and, as such, were often mentioned alongside the priests (Deuteronomy 19:17) and the elders (21:2).

Officials served the people of Israel in a different fashion than judges. These individuals assisted the judges in providing leadership and just deci-

sion making for the people of God as they presented themselves before God (Deuteronomy 31:28; Joshua 8:33; 24:1).

The Hebrew word rendered *fairly* can also mean "righteous," or the idea of pursuing a right relationship with God as well as right and fair relationships with other humans (see lesson 9 commentary on Deuteronomy 24:12-13; see also Leviticus 19:15, 36; Deuteronomy 1:16; 25:15; Job 8:3; Isaiah 51:5). For Israel, fair and righteous action was not a hypothetical to be wished for but tangible acts of following the just laws that God had set forth.

Legal proceedings often took place at the gates of *every town*. These gates served as the center of the town's public life and constituted the location where significant administrative and legal decisions were made (see Genesis 19:1; Deuteronomy 22:15; Ruth 4:1, 11; 1 Kings 22:10). In essence, the gates were a public forum in which accountability to God's law was acknowledged by all.

❧ *THE FAIR JUDGE* ❧

My brother and I are as different as brothers could be. He has a gentle demeanor and a laid-back attitude. I, on the other hand, have a tightly wound disposition and intense inclination. When we were younger, he always reminded me that he was bigger and older. These reminders spurred me to prove myself, often leading to backyard brawls between us. During one such brawl he hung me by my shirt collar on a coat rack.

Our fights rarely resolved anything, leading us to seek an authority figure to adjudicate who was in the right and who was in the wrong. In most cases, this authority figure was our father. We agreed to his decisions because he was a good and trustworthy judge, bound to impartiality by his love for both his sons.

HOW TO SAY IT

Absalom	*Ab*-suh-lum.
Ahab	*Ay*-hab.
Jehoshaphat	Jeh-*hosh*-uh-fat.
Jezebel	*Jez*-uh-bel.
Levitical	Leh-*vit*-ih-kul.
Naboth	*Nay*-bawth.

For the nation of Israel, in matters too difficult to settle, the involved parties appeared before the priests and the judge. These leaders provided fair and just rulings. They gave voice to God's people of God's desire for just and fair treatment. Undoubtedly you have experienced conflicts too difficult or too heated for fair judgment. When these conflicts arise, how do you resolve them? Do you appeal to wise and loving individuals to provide insight?

—W. L.

B. Reliable Principles (vv. 19-20)

19a. Do not pervert justice

To *pervert* refers to the act of twisting, skewing, withholding, or distorting. In this case, it affects one's ability to practice right and fair *justice*. Later texts describe individuals who withhold justice as being "cursed" (Deuteronomy 27:19).

The act of perverting justice was quite concerning for the needy individuals in the land, especially the stranger, the fatherless, and the widow (Deuteronomy 24:17; see lesson 9).

19b. or show partiality.

Administrators of justice were not to *show* undue *partiality* based on the social standing of other individuals. Scripture declares that all people are equal before God and, therefore, he does not show partiality, or favoritism (Deuteronomy 10:17; Acts 10:34; Romans 2:11). Therefore, the people of God are to demonstrate a life committed to showing impartial justice (Leviticus 19:15; 2 Chronicles 19:7).

19c. Do not accept a bribe, for a bribe blinds the eyes of the wise and twists the words of the innocent.

Finally, administrators of justice must be wary of accepting a *bribe*, or a gift, lest their judgment become clouded. This is not the only instance where the people of God are called to avoid bribes. Moses warned Israel that "a bribe *blinds* those who see and *twists the words of the innocent*" (Exodus 23:8). Bribes and influencing gifts distorted the leader's ability to judge rightly in the manner God required. When this occurred, justice became a commodity that could be bought and sold. Such individuals were called "wicked" as they "pervert the course of justice" (Proverbs 17:23).

Years later, the sons of Samuel would be appointed as Israel's leaders (1 Samuel 8:1). However, the sons were more interested in receiving personal gain from the position they were in than the process of exacting justice among the people (8:3).

20. Follow justice and justice alone, so that you may live and possess the land the Lord your God is giving you.

Just as reflected in the English translation, the Hebrew words behind the phrase *justice and justice alone* read as the repetition of the Hebrew word for "just" (see commentary on Deuteronomy 16:18, above). Repetition of a single word in this manner signifies the word's magnitude and its importance for the reader or hearer. As a result, complete and absolute justice with no compromise must be the passion for all God's people.

As Israel and its leaders made efforts to *follow* the just living that God required, a positive consequence would be their continued residence in *the land* given to them by God. Their ability to *live* in and *possess* the promised land had nothing to do with their own virtue; it was a matter of making the Lord's priorities *their* priorities. As Israel made justice a priority, God's priorities for justice became Israel's top priority.

> **What Do You Think?**
> How do you show respect for your congregational leaders when you find yourselves in a disagreement of consequence?
> *Digging Deeper*
> How do you show respect for leaders outside of your congregation with whom you rarely (if ever) agree?

II. Specific Challenges
(Deuteronomy 17:8-13)
A. Difficult Instances (vv. 8-11)

8. If cases come before your courts that are too difficult for you to judge—whether bloodshed, lawsuits or assaults—take them to the place the Lord your God will choose.

In especially challenging instances, Moses prescribed the steps and actions for those making judgment in legal *cases*. The use of *your* refers to local judges or courts who were unable to resolve a particularly controversial or challenging legal case.

Such cases often involved an intent to kill (*bloodshed*), legal claims (*lawsuits*), or physical injury (*assaults*).

In these situations, the involved parties were to *take them* to the location chosen by *God*. The exact identity of the involved parties is unclear and could include either the tribunal of judges or the parties of the dispute. Previous precedent suggests that it was the duty of the local judges to take this step and confer at the indicated location (compare Exodus 18:13-20).

This *place* was mentioned previously in more detail as a place of sacredness—a place where the Lord would "put his Name" (Deuteronomy 12:5, 21). In that place, in what became a central sanctuary, the Israelites offered their sacrifices, tithes, special gifts, and vows (12:11). This location served Israel not only for its legal needs but also for its sacred and ceremonial needs.

> ### What Do You Think?
> What current familial or other conflicts could benefit from the wise counsel of spiritual leaders?
>
> ### Digging Deeper
> What obstacles do you need to overcome in order to benefit from that counsel?

9. Go to the Levitical priests and to the judge who is in office at that time. Inquire of them and they will give you the verdict.

For these challenging cases, the *Levitical priests* and the *judge* provided the final ruling (see Deuteronomy 19:17). The exact identity of the judge is unknown. The person's position likely came from a precedent made by Moses years before (see Lesson Context; Exodus 18:13-20).

Priests were Levites, members of the tribe of Levi. These individuals guided the religious practice of Israel by officiating times of worship (Numbers 18:5-7), teaching the stipulations of the Law of Moses (Leviticus 10:8-11), and guiding the proper actions of life—even as related to health—within the community of God's people (Deuter-

Visual for Lessons 7 & 8. *While discussing verse 19, ask the class what role Christians should or do play in making sure that justice remains unbiased.*

onomy 24:8). Unlike other tribes of Israel, Levites owned no land, but lived on properties donated by the Israelites (Numbers 18:20; Joshua 21:1-42).

The involvement of religious leaders with seemingly "nonreligious" judicial cases might seem inappropriate from a modern perspective. However, Old Testament Israel had the singular responsibility to follow God's laws in every realm of life. Because of the all-encompassing nature of their covenant relationship with God (Deuteronomy 5:1b-3), there was no distinction between sacred and secular.

The Levitical priests and the judge made their *verdict* based on their understanding of civil and criminal law, thereby acting as leaders of God's covenant people.

King Jehoshaphat of Judah (reigned 872–848 BC) served as an example of this text's prescriptions. Jehoshaphat appointed judges and priests in Jerusalem for the administration of justice (2 Chronicles 19:5, 8). In following the words of Moses, the king warned the counsel to "judge carefully, for with the Lord our God there is no injustice or partiality or bribery" (19:7; see commentary on Deuteronomy 16:19, above).

10. You must act according to the decisions they give you at the place the LORD will choose. Be careful to do everything they instruct you to do.

Whatever sentences the judges and Levites render, the involved parties must abide by those decisions. Their decision was final! The reminder that their verdict occurred in *the place the Lord will choose* reinforces the sacredness of that location and, therefore, the decisions made there.

11. Act according to whatever they teach you and the decisions they give you. Do not turn aside from what they tell you, to the right or to the left.

Moses emphasized strict obedience to what the Levites and the judge *teach* and *the decisions they give*. All parties involved were not to deviate from the decision rendered.

Elsewhere, Moses described obedience to God's law in similar terms, exhorting Israel to "be careful to do what the Lord your God has commanded you; do not turn aside *to the right or to the left*" (Deuteronomy 5:32). The pointed counsel prepared hearers for a solemn warning if they failed to adhere to Moses' guidelines.

> **What Do You Think?**
> How does Deuteronomy 17:11 help you practically follow Jesus' admonition in Matthew 7:13-14, if at all?
> *Digging Deeper*
> Are you in a position to judge wisely and help others remain on the straight path? Why or why not?

B. Defiant Individuals (vv. 12-13)

12. Anyone who shows contempt for the judge or for the priest who stands ministering there to the LORD your God is to be put to death. You must purge the evil from Israel.

The individual who defied the ruling of *the judge* or *the priest* was described as acting out of *contempt*. The Hebrew word behind this term describes an individual acting out of pride or haughtiness of heart (compare Deuteronomy 17:12; Proverbs 11:2; Jeremiah 49:16). These defiant individuals acted pridefully as they disregarded the given judgment of the ordained leadership who *stands ministering there to the Lord your God.*

Such defiance and contempt also brought harm to the community of Israel. Upon an initial inspection, that the defiant individual shall *be put to death* seems harsh or disproportionate to the

initial act that brought them to this place. However, the following line indicates the measures the community was required to take to protect *Israel* from *evil*.

Israel's law described other instances that necessitated capital punishment (among others), such as a rebellion against God (Deuteronomy 13:5), a false prophet (18:20-22), or an insubordinate family member (21:18-21). In these instances, the primary concern was that the people of God maintained holiness in their covenant relationship and that evil no longer polluted the covenanted people.

> **What Do You Think?**
> What about your witness of God's holiness might cause others to act with greater respect toward him?
> *Digging Deeper*
> How will greater obedience strengthen your witness?

❧ DISCIPLINE AND TRUE FREEDOM ❧

My college football team was poised to play for a national championship. As we prepared for the occasion, three teammates violated team rules and skipped team workouts. Because of their contempt for the team rules, these teammates were kicked off the team, purged from our locker room.

Such a harsh act was necessary. As a team, we were committed to one another, united in our goals, and dedicated to the values of the football program. We could not tolerate individuals showing disregard for these values. Only when we adhered, in love, to our values were we free to become the best version of our team.

God's people of all ages are called to live disciplined lives, following God's expectations and mandates. In what aspects of your life do you need discipline in order to follow God's expectations? What distractions do you need to purge from your life so that you might become a more disciplined follower of God?   —W. L.

13. All the people will hear and be afraid, and will not be contemptuous again.

The harsh actions of the previous verse were revealed to have another, more communal function: as a deterrent to any further *contemptuous* behavior.

That Israel *will hear and be afraid* of such punishment served as a powerful motivation for avoiding the conduct resulting in that degree of disciplinary action (see Deuteronomy 13:11; 17:13; 19:20). God required that his people live justly. He had strong consequences for those who refused to live in that manner or who distracted others from that same quest for justice.

The Old Testament *does* record numerous examples of how justice became disregarded by those in power, a problem that the Lord's prophets called attention to when they saw it happening. The prophet Amos indicted the people in his day were guilty of that disregard; Amos described them as those who "turn judgment into bitterness and cast righteousness to the ground" (Amos 5:7).

At times the innocent were punished and the guilty went free, as in the case of Naboth's vineyard (see 1 Kings 21). When such conditions as these exist within a society, it is not long before people become accustomed to calling "evil good and good evil" (Isaiah 5:20). Justice according to God's standard becomes harder and harder to find in such a morally corrupt environment.

Conclusion

A. Operation Greylord Revisited

The 14-year period 1980–1994 was bittersweet for the American judicial system as Operation Greylord began and ended. Greylord was the name of an undercover FBI investigation into alleged corruption in the judicial system in Cook County, Illinois. The "bitter" part was that the allegations proved to be true. In the end, 15 judges were convicted on various counts of bribery, mail fraud, racketeering, income-tax violations, etc. The depth of the systemic corruption was underlined as dozens of others—including lawyers, deputy sheriffs, policemen, and court officials—were also convicted.

The "sweet" part was that an accountability system existed to expose and correct such corruption. Despite that, we will never know how far and to whom the ripple effects of the corruption extended.

Work toward a just system begins by acknowledging the need for four distinct kinds of justice: (1) *distributive justice* to ensure economic fairness (see Deuteronomy 24:14-15; 2 Thessalonians 3:10; James 5:4), (2) *restorative justice* to require restitution by an offender (see Exodus 22:1-15; Luke 12:58-59; 18:3-5; 19:8), (3) *retributive justice* to punish offenders because they deserve it (Deuteronomy 25:2; Romans 13:4-5), and (4) *procedural justice* for ensuring fairness in application of rules by due process (see Exodus 23:3 [lesson 7]; James 2:1-9). The fourth of these is the starting point, the one the other three depend on as a prerequisite. Humans have a duty to work for all four, but our work begins with the fourth. This obligation has been unchanged since today's lesson text was penned. Our efforts here form part of the salt and light that Jesus commanded us to be (see Matthew 5:13-16). We do so as citizens of the kingdom that is "not of this world" (John 18:36), as we honor the ruler of that heavenly kingdom.

Whereas previous lessons on justice have examined justice alongside various qualities such as kindness and righteousness, today's lesson considers justice alongside some of those officials who were supposed to administer it in Old Testament Israel, namely, judges and priests.

> *What Do You Think?*
> What action have you been putting off that this lesson has given new urgency to?
> *Digging Deeper*
> What first steps will you take toward that task?

B. Prayer

God of justice, our world often voices its desire for justice; yet how we need to return to your Word for a true understanding of this principle! Show us your justice in the world. In Jesus' name we pray. Amen.

C. Thought to Remember

No one is exempt from
practicing justice!

INVOLVEMENT LEARNING

Enhance your lesson with NIV® Bible Student (from your curriculum supplier) and the reproducible activity page (at www.standardlesson.com or in the back of the NIV® Standard Lesson Commentary Deluxe Edition).

Into the Lesson

Begin class by asking about television shows or movies that feature a judge as a central figure. Focus on one who is well known. Ask for descriptions of that judge and jot responses on the board. Then ask whether this judge exhibits the kind of character the class thinks is appropriate for a judge. Ask how that character is revealed in the judge's treatment of people and in decisions rendered. (*Option.* For large classes, divide into smaller groups to discuss; create handouts as appropriate. Allow time for the groups to share.)

Alternative. Distribute index cards that each have a simple action command written on them (examples: stand on one leg; whistle three notes). When everyone has a card, each person will read the command aloud and then do what it says. Then let the group express their likes and dislikes of the commands, and why.

After either activity, say, "When do we submit to the requests or commands of others, and when do we resist? Let's find out!"

Into the Word

Ask a volunteer to read aloud Deuteronomy 16:18-20 and 17:8-13. As a class, discuss the characteristics of an ideal judge based on these verses. Jot key ideas on the board.

Divide the class into small groups of three to four. Using the main points on the board and any additional ideas of your own, have each group create a campaign slogan and platform for electing a hypothetical judge to office. Provide paper and markers for each group to creatively display their information as a flyer.

When groups are finished, ask a volunteer from each group to represent a spokesperson for the campaign, showing their flyer and sharing their information with the whole group. Highlight commonalities and differences between the flyers. Make notes on the board as appropriate.

Identify common threads and points of departure as you compare and contrast the flyers with the Scripture text. (*Option.* To introduce a surprise element, do not have the text read aloud until *after* the groups finish their work and discussion has ensued.)

Alternative. Distribute copies of the "Job Description" exercise from the activity page, which you can download. Allow groups of three to four to work through the activity as directed. After 10 minutes or so, have groups compare and contrast their documents in the ensuing whole-class discussion.

Into Life

Continuing in the same small groups, distribute handouts (you prepare) on which are printed the following questions:

1–What positions in the church are most like that of the judges of ancient Israel (as described in the lesson text, not as in the book of Judges)?

2–What similarities cause you to reach that conclusion?

3–How are the positions different and what accounts for those differences?

Instruct groups to add or update information to their campaign flyers or job description to better fit the church position discussed. Have groups defend their revisions in whole-class discussion.

Have participants work alone for no more than one minute to make a list of up to five friends and/or acquaintances who possess qualities noted in the text. Encourage participants to make this their list of go-to advisers when they face situations that are too difficult to resolve on their own.

Option. If you used the "Job Description" exercise above, distribute copies of the "Personal Statement" exercise from the activity page as a take-home. To encourage its completion, state that you will call for results at the beginning of the next class session.

JUSTICE AND THE MARGINALIZED

DEVOTIONAL READING: Deuteronomy 24:10-21
BACKGROUND SCRIPTURE: Deuteronomy 24:10-21

DEUTERONOMY 24:10-21

10 When you make a loan of any kind to your neighbor, do not go into their house to get what is offered to you as a pledge. 11 Stay outside and let the neighbor to whom you are making the loan bring the pledge out to you. 12 If the neighbor is poor, do not go to sleep with their pledge in your possession. 13 Return their cloak by sunset so that your neighbor may sleep in it. Then they will thank you, and it will be regarded as a righteous act in the sight of the LORD your God.

14 Do not take advantage of a hired worker who is poor and needy, whether that worker is a fellow Israelite or a foreigner residing in one of your towns. 15 Pay them their wages each day before sunset, because they are poor and are counting on it. Otherwise they may cry to the LORD against you, and you will be guilty of sin.

16 Parents are not to be put to death for their children, nor children put to death for their parents; each will die for their own sin.

17 Do not deprive the foreigner or the fatherless of justice, or take the cloak of the widow as a pledge. 18 Remember that you were slaves in Egypt and the LORD your God redeemed you

from there. That is why I command you to do this.

19 When you are harvesting in your field and you overlook a sheaf, do not go back to get it. Leave it for the foreigner, the fatherless and the widow, so that the LORD your God may bless you in all the work of your hands. 20 When you beat the olives from your trees, do not go over the branches a second time. Leave what remains for the foreigner, the fatherless and the widow. 21 When you harvest the grapes in your vineyard, do not go over the vines again. Leave what remains for the foreigner, the fatherless and the widow.

KEY TEXT

Remember that you were slaves in Egypt and the LORD your God redeemed you from there. That is why I command you to do this. —**Deuteronomy 24:18**

Photo © Getty Images

JUSTICE, LAW, HISTORY

Unit 2: God: The Source of Justice

LESSONS 5–9

LESSON AIMS

After participating in this lesson, each learner will be able to:

1. Describe ways Israel showed justice toward the marginalized.

2. Explain the importance of Israel's remembrance of God's redemption.

3. Suggest one practical way he or she can help a marginalized individual or family.

LESSON OUTLINE

Introduction

A. Ignorance and Want

In Charles Dickens's *A Christmas Carol*, the Ghost of Christmas Present guides Ebenezer Scrooge on a tour of various scenes around London. Some scenes highlight holiday celebrations, while others show poverty-stricken individuals, including Scrooge's own employee, Bob Cratchit.

Toward the end of the tour, the ghost reveals two destitute children beneath the folds of his robe, a boy named Ignorance and a girl named Want. The ghost warns Scrooge, "Beware them both . . . but most of all beware this boy."

Through these characters, Dickens drew his readers' attention to issues of ignorance and want regarding the economic challenges of his day, which was mid-nineteenth-century England. Many people of that time and place experienced want and neglect and were otherwise marginalized. Those who were better off often adopted a stance of willful ignorance toward the situation. Scrooge's next words aptly describe that attitude: "Cover [the children Ignorance and Want]; I do not wish to see them." Unfortunately, many still react this way, avoiding issues of economic justice by looking the other way. Deuteronomy 24:10-21 has important things to say in this regard.

B. Lesson Context

Previous lessons from this quarter focused on other aspects of God's law: his covenant with Israel (lesson 1), which served as the foundation for the law, and those individuals tasked with ruling on God's law (lesson 8). This lesson turns to the details of God's law for Israel. These laws make up the bulk of Deuteronomy's content and are a central theme of the Torah, the first five books of the Old Testament.

The Hebrew word *torah* can mean "teaching" or "law," specifically God's laws for ancient Israel. These laws depicted how the Israelites were to live rightly with each other, with their neighboring peoples, and with their God.

Today's Scripture text comes from Moses' second address in Deuteronomy to the people of Israel, with the detailed covenant stipulations that God required for his people (Deuteronomy 12:1–26:19). Moses' address began with a detailed description of proper worship of God (12:1–16:17) and continued with descriptions of proper justice in law (16:18-20; 17:8-13), regulations regarding the handling of violent acts (19:1–21:23), and issues of marriage (22:13-30), among other things, as God provided an ordered description of a new society.

For Israel, part of being God's covenant people was the just and proper treatment of poor and otherwise marginalized individuals. Previously, Moses had reminded the Israelites that poor people would always be part of the population (Deuteronomy 15:11; compare John 12:18). As a result, Moses commanded an openhanded policy toward these individuals, requiring generous giving without resentment (Deuteronomy 15:10). Today's Scripture expands on this theme.

I. Just Lending
(DEUTERONOMY 24:10-13)

A. Respecting the Person (vv. 10-11)

10-11. When you make a loan of any kind to your neighbor, do not go into their house to get what is offered to you as a pledge. Stay outside and let the neighbor to whom you are making the loan bring the pledge out to you.

Moses described a situation in which a *neighbor*—a fellow Israelite—needed a loan. Elsewhere, the law forbade Israelites from charging interest on loans made to other Israelites (Exodus 22:25; Deuteronomy 23:19-20).

However, lenders were allowed to receive collateral, or a *pledge*, as security for a loan. Even then, certain restrictions remained for what lenders could take as a pledge; taking as a pledge a person's method of livelihood was forbidden (Deuteronomy 24:6; compare Job 24:3), as was taking a widow's clothing (Deuteronomy 24:17; see commentary below).

To maintain the borrower's dignity, the lender was not permitted to enter the borrower's *house*. Instead, the lender was required to *stay outside* the borrower's dwelling, allowing the borrower to *bring the pledge out*. In this situation, the bor-

rower controlled what was offered as pledge, with dignity and respect maintained.

As Old Testament history unfolded, the dangers of putting up security, or collateral, came to be recognized, but the practice was not outright banned for Israel (see Proverbs 17:18; 20:16; 22:26; 27:13).

B. Respecting the Pledge (vv. 12-13)

12. If the neighbor is poor, do not go to sleep with their pledge in your possession.

The law added extra clarification for loans made to *poor* individuals. Such lending stipulations were required because of the extra vulnerability poor individuals may have faced. Furthermore, the law specifically prohibited lenders from charging interest on loans in these situations (Exodus 22:25; Leviticus 25:35-37).

13. Return their cloak by sunset so that your neighbor may sleep in it. Then they will thank you, and it will be regarded as a righteous act in the sight of the LORD your God.

Additionally, lenders were limited on what could be done with a pledge of a borrower's *cloak*. If that was all a poor individual could provide as a pledge, then the lender was prohibited from keeping it overnight (compare Leviticus 19:13); the clothing had to be returned by *sunset*. This limitation protected the borrower's health during the night (Exodus 22:26). Lenders were to be compassionate in their lending practices because God is compassionate (22:27; Psalm 116:5).

The lender's act resulted in two outcomes. First, the borrower would *thank* the lender. One can picture the borrower, preparing for a good night's sleep, offering a prayer of thanksgiving to God for the lender's kindness.

HOW TO SAY IT

Babylonian	Bab-ih-*low*-nee-un.
Boaz	*Bo*-az.
Hammurabi	Ham-muh-**rah**-bee.
Malachi	*Mal*-uh-kye.
Mediterranean	Med-uh-tuh-**ray**-nee-un.
Torah (*Hebrew*)	*Tor*-uh.
Zechariah	Zek-uh-**rye**-uh.

Second, the lender's gesture would be judged by the *Lord* and deemed as *a righteous act*. Such acts were considered right standing in God's eyes and conformed to the demands of God's law and covenant (see Genesis 15:6; Deuteronomy 6:25; Isaiah 56:1; compare Luke 1:6). God desired his people to live in this manner because his own nature is one of righteousness and justice (see Psalms 9:8; 11:7; 33:5; 36:6; 103:6; Isaiah 33:15; Jeremiah 9:24; compare 1 John 3:7). Lending practices as prescribed by the law served as an example of the just and equitable actions the Lord wants his people to pursue, especially toward the marginalized.

> ### What Do You Think?
> Is the respect you offer to people poorer than you different from what you offer to those who are wealthier? If so, how?
>
> ### Digging Deeper
> Consider Matthew 25:40, 45. Does this add importance to how you treat the poor? Why or why not?

II. Just Labor
(Deuteronomy 24:14-15)
A. Oppression Forbidden (v. 14)

14a. Do not take advantage of a hired worker who is poor and needy,

The concern for justice among the *poor and needy* extended to hired hands. After their experience of slavery in Egypt, Israelites were not permitted to be sold as slaves (Leviticus 25:42). However, an Israelite who experienced economic difficulty to the point of losing everything might serve other Israelites as *a hired worker,* or "stranger" (25:35). Such individuals had the expectation of eventually receiving freedom (25:40; see also Exodus 21:2; Deuteronomy 15:12). The status of such a person is sometimes known as indentured servant.

14b. whether that worker is a fellow Israelite or a foreigner residing in one of your towns.

Prescriptions to protect hired hands were enacted to maintain the economic livelihood, dignity, and ability of impoverished individuals, *Isra-*

elite or not, to continue to live among the people of God (Leviticus 25:35-36).

Most requirements also extended to *a foreigner residing in* the *towns* of Israel. Qualifying this with "most" admits the exception found in Leviticus 25:44-46a. Without just treatment, these workers could become further marginalized.

God's people, however, were not to mistreat these individuals. Even in (or especially in) hiring and working practices, God's people were to practice justice. The most obvious way to do so was through the timely deliverance of wages (next verse).

B. Opportune Wages (v. 15)

15a. Pay them their wages each day before sunset, because they are poor and are counting on it.

Workers were paid for their labors at the end of an agreed time of work. However, the hired worker who was *poor* was to receive their agreed upon wages at the end of each day, before *sunset*. This worker, perhaps living a hand-to-mouth existence, depended on such timely pay to provide for daily necessities (see Leviticus 19:13; Matthew 20:8).

> ### What Do You Think?
> What aid does your congregation offer the poor, which would be missed if that support vanished?
>
> ### Digging Deeper
> How do you contribute to that ministry?

15b. Otherwise they may cry to the Lord against you, and you will be guilty of sin.

If workers were treated unjustly, it would be within their power to *cry* out *to the Lord* for help and justice (Exodus 22:22-23; James 5:4). As failing to return a poor person's pledge at the end of the day would be considered unrighteous (see commentary on Deuteronomy 24:13, above), withholding pay from a poor person at the end of the day would be considered a *sin*.

Centuries later, the prophet Malachi warned Israel that God would "come to put you on trial . . . against those who defraud laborers of their wages" (Malachi 3:5). God would deal decisively and swiftly with those who did not show justice to their workers.

❧ BEWARE OF OPPORTUNISM! ❧

During the coronavirus pandemic of 2020, an enterprising but unscrupulous couple used the demand for hand sanitizer for their own profit. They traveled to nearby towns and purchased all the hand sanitizer they could find, storing up cases of the in-demand product. They advertised their newly acquired product at vastly inflated prices. While hand sanitizer shortages were prevalent, the couple charged several times the suggested retail! People readily purchased the hand sanitizer at the grossly inflated price. Eventually, the government intervened and redistributed the product to those in need.

During a crisis that necessitated a compassionate response, this couple exploited others for profit and caused an inequitable situation. God requires his people to not take advantage of others. While many people see crises as an opportunity for personal gain, God requires fairness. What can you do to ensure that you are part of the solution rather than part of the problem?   —C. R. B.

III. Just Community
(DEUTERONOMY 24:16-18)
A. Commanding Punishment (v. 16)

16. Parents are not to be put to death for their children, nor children put to death for their parents; each will die for their own sin.

The principle described here stands in contrast to other law codes of the ancient world. The Babylonian law code of Hammurabi prescribed that if a builder built a house that collapsed, causing the death of the homeowner's son, the builder's son was to be put to death.

In contrast, Hebrew law required certain parameters to allow for just treatment of innocent family members who were vulnerable to harm because of the actions of a relative. The given stipulation would prevent a potentially endless chain of revenge.

However, this principle does not contradict what is found elsewhere regarding God's "punishing the *children* for the sin of the *parents* to the third and fourth generation of those who hate me" (Deuteronomy 5:9). While each person will surely experience the consequences of their *sin*, the repercussions of those sins are often experienced by others. We may think of a parent today who is justly sent to prison for a crime, with side effects of their family suffering destabilization in their relationships and finances.

> **What Do You Think?**
> What encouragement can you offer to Christian parents, based on this verse?
> *Digging Deeper*
> How would your encouragement change when offered to children of unbelieving parents?

B. Caring for the Needy (v. 17)

17. Do not deprive the foreigner or the fatherless of justice, or take the cloak of the widow as a pledge.

All Israelites were tasked with looking out for the marginalized and the defenseless among them. The Hebrew words translated *foreigner, fatherless,* and *widow* occur together in triads in 11 verses in the book of Deuteronomy, emphasizing God's concern for these vulnerable people (see also Psalms 94:6; 146:9; Jeremiah 7:6; 22:3; Ezekiel 22:7; Zechariah 7:10; Malachi 3:5).

To *take the cloak of the widow as a pledge* is in the same category as taking the garment of a poor man—forbidden (Deuteronomy 24:12-13, above). Furthermore, lenders who had wrongly taken such garments in pledge sometimes worsened the offense by taking those items to pagan worship (see Amos 2:8).

The law provided numerous reminders to God's people to uphold justice for those who needed it most (Exodus 23:6, 9; Leviticus 19:33-34; Proverbs 22:22). Concern for these three groups extends into the New Testament as well (see Matthew 25:35-36; Acts 6:1-5; 1 Timothy 5:3, 16; Hebrews 13:2; James 1:27).

God desires justice for needy individuals and his people are to desire the same. Following God's

GOD'S JUSTICE KNOWS NO BOUNDARIES.

Visual for Lesson 9. *Discuss what role Christians play in seeking justice on a global scale. How has that role changed over the past 50 years?*

commands for just living requires extra attention to vulnerable people.

C. Corporate Memory (v. 18)

18. Remember that you were slaves in Egypt and the LORD your God redeemed you from there. That is why I command you to do this.

Moses reminded the second generation of Israelites of their history as slaves in the land of *Egypt*. That along with God's redemptive act served as the foundation for Israel's identity (see Deuteronomy 5:15; 7:8; 9:26; 13:5; 15:15; 16:12; 24:22).

The corporate memory of that bondage and their following redemption was to motivate the Israelites to compassionate treatment of the marginalized. That would happen as the Israelites remembered their own suffering and marginalization as slaves in Egypt. To treat others as they had been treated by God was the watchword for Israel (compare Matthew 18:23-35). They were to remember that *God redeemed* them from that situation and provided justice where injustice reigned.

⅔ THE POWER OF MEMORY ⅔

A young family, expecting their first child, recently moved in next door. One day the young husband caught my attention and hesitantly asked, "Do you have a battery charger I could borrow?" I said, "Of course," retrieving the charger from my garage. I told him to keep it as long as needed.

A week later, he brought back the charger and asked why I didn't hesitate lending it to him. I answered him with a story: "When my wife and I were newly married and had our first son, we were living paycheck to paycheck. My car battery was dying, and I was desperate to get back and forth to work. I asked my neighbor, Harvey, if I could borrow his battery charger. He did not hesitate. I used the charger every night. I wanted to treat you the same way Harvey treated me. That's why I didn't hesitate."

On hearing the story, the young man replied, "That was exactly my situation! Maybe I can help my neighbor someday. Thanks!"

One's memory serves as a powerful tool for inviting action. For the people of Israel, memory of God's redemptive acts—especially from bondage in Egypt—served to remind them of how to treat others. How do memories of God's work in your life shape your behavior?   —C. R. B.

> **What Do You Think?**
> What do you remember that helps you keep the Lord's commands?
> *Digging Deeper*
> What can you do to strengthen your memory in preparation for particularly trying times?

IV. Just Harvest
(DEUTERONOMY 24:19-21)
A. Regarding Grain (v. 19)

19a. When you are harvesting in your field and you overlook a sheaf, do not go back to get it. Leave it for the foreigner, the fatherless and the widow,

In addition to justice in lending practices, justice to the vulnerable was also to be seen in agrarian practices at harvest times. Often the poorer Israelites would work in the fields during the annual harvest time (compare 2 Kings 25:12). The work of *harvesting* was completed with a hand sickle, cutting bundles of grain and binding each into a *sheaf.* Written in terms of what the landowner did *overlook* should have encouraged the underprivileged to boldness in retrieving the grain accidentally left behind. There should have been no worry that the landowner would later demand it back.

Furthermore, the law made clear that the edges of the fields be left unharvested and only a single harvest occur so that "the poor and *foreigner*" might harvest from the fields for their own sustenance (Leviticus 19:9-10; 23:22). This legislation is seen enacted in the narrative of Ruth, a foreign widow who gleaned the leftover grain from the fields of her Hebrew relative, Boaz (Ruth 1:22–2:3).

19b. so that the LORD your God may bless you in all the work of your hands.

The phrase *that the Lord your God may bless you* occurs three times in the book of Deuteronomy: here and in 14:29 and 23:20. In all three cases, God's blessing is contingent on meeting the needs of others. The Lord will bless those who honor his laws and treat the marginalized with respect and compassion (see Proverbs 19:17).

B. Regarding Produce (vv. 20-21)

20-21. When you beat the olives from your trees, do not go over the branches a second time. Leave what remains for the foreigner, the fatherless and the widow. When you harvest the grapes in your vineyard, do not go over the vines again. Leave what remains for the foreigner, the fatherless and the widow.

Grape and olive crops were often planted together using a method called polyculture, the practice of growing several crops side by side, which was made popular in the Mediterranean region. Each crop contributed to the health and well-being of the other.

Harvesting olives required that a harvester beat the *branches* of the olive *trees* with a long stick. Most ripe olives would fall to the ground; and any olives remaining on the branches were to be left for the *foreigner*, the *fatherless*, and the *widow*. The same generous harvesting principle was applied to the gathering of *grapes*. What remained following the first harvest was to be left for the needy. The people of God should cultivate not only their crops but also the same kind of generous spirit that the Lord had shown to them.

What Do You Think?
What characteristics of offering your "leftovers" to others make it a respectful act?
Digging Deeper
What should you avoid so that such offerings do not become demeaning?

Conclusion

A. Ignorance and Want, Today

The physical needs of others confront us daily. Applying God's principles for an ancient culture, where 98 percent of people lived on farms, to our modern culture, where only 2 percent do, is a challenge. But a common-ground starting point is that people of God in all times should live in such a way as to respect the dignity of those in need. Granted, it may take some challenging conversations and creative thinking on our part to apply these principles in specific and helpful ways. This lesson's Scripture text provides principles of justice that each and every follower of God should model and help enact.

Ignorance and want continue to manifest themselves today. Unlike Scrooge, we should not desire that injustice be hidden from our eyes. Our heavenly Father has made it clear that his heart and his compassion are with those in need. Are ours?

What Do You Think?
What practical help can your congregation offer vulnerable people in your community?
Digging Deeper
What role can you play in either starting or continuing such efforts?

B. Prayer

Father, we pray that you will help us always to see our neighbors as you see them, especially those who are often ignored or treated with contempt. Help us to treat them justly, with the mercy that you have shown us. In Jesus' name. Amen.

C. Thought to Remember

Remembering how God has treated us should always govern how we treat others.

INVOLVEMENT LEARNING

Enhance your lesson with NIV® Bible Student (from your curriculum supplier) and the reproducible activity page (at www.standardlesson.com or in the back of the NIV® Standard Lesson Commentary Deluxe Edition).

Into the Lesson

Before class, obtain a deck of playing cards and remove all cards numbered from 5 to 10, leaving only the 28 cards of ace through 4 and Jack through King across 4 suites. Shuffle the 28 cards thoroughly.

As class begins, give each attendee one card and say that no one is to look at his or here card. Review the card values: 2 is the lowest value; ace is the highest value. Explain that each person's card value determines his or her social value for this activity.

Learners should then hold their cards against their foreheads so others can see them but the person with the card cannot. The object is to form community associations with people of "value." Participants must try to discern their relative "value" based on the way others treat them as they mingle; card values are not to be discussed directly. Allow a few minutes to interact; give a one-minute notice for learners to form two groups, according to their similar "values." Then let participants look at their own cards and discuss the experience.

To transition, say, "Society tends to define people's value by outward appearances and status symbols. But let's see if that lines up with how God calls us to treat one another."

Into the Word

Ask three volunteers to read the three segments Deuteronomy 24:10-13, 14-15, and 19-21 aloud. Divide the class into three groups: the **Lending Group** to consider Deuteronomy 24:10-13), the **Oppressing Group** for 24:14-15), and the **Harvesting Group** for 24:19-21. Give each group a card (you prepare) on which are printed the following questions:

1–What are the examples of exploitation and of honoring others in this Scripture?

2–What are modern-day examples of exploitation?

3–What are modern-day examples of honoring one another?

After small-group discussion, ask a volunteer from each group to report the group's response to the class. Then ask a volunteer to read Deuteronomy 24:17-18 aloud. Reshuffle the groups to be the **Stranger Group**, the **Fatherless Group**, and the **Widow Group**. Write this question on the board for to all groups to answer:

How has the vulnerability of your group's namesake changed since Old Testament times, if at all?

Have one member of each group share their conclusions with the class.

Ask a volunteer to read Deuteronomy 24:16 aloud. As a class, discuss how this prohibition relates to the other commands before and after it. Focus last on its relationship to Deuteronomy 24:17-18. Consult the commentary as necessary to clear up misconceptions.

Into Life

Have the three groups plan a workday to meet some basic needs of the population named in their groups. They should brainstorm local organizations that can provide guidance and opportunities for appropriate service, then gather information in order to make contact throughout the week. Tell the class that next week the groups will set dates to serve together.

Option 1. Distribute copies of the "Color Coding" exercise from the activity page, which you can download, as a take-home activity. To encourage completion, promise to discuss results and insights gained at the beginning of next week's class.

Option 2. Distribute copies of the "Examples to Follow" exercise as a take-home activity. To encourage completion, say that you will ask for volunteers next week to share how this exercise challenged or inspired them. Promise also to discuss how the class as a whole can respond in a practical way.

NATHAN CONDEMNS DAVID

DEVOTIONAL READING: 2 Samuel 12:1-9, 13-15
BACKGROUND SCRIPTURE: 2 Samuel 12

2 SAMUEL 12:1-9, 13-15

1 The LORD sent Nathan to David. When he came to him, he said, "There were two men in a certain town, one rich and the other poor. 2 The rich man had a very large number of sheep and cattle, 3 but the poor man had nothing except one little ewe lamb he had bought. He raised it, and it grew up with him and his children. It shared his food, drank from his cup and even slept in his arms. It was like a daughter to him.

4 "Now a traveler came to the rich man, but the rich man refrained from taking one of his own sheep or cattle to prepare a meal for the traveler who had come to him. Instead, he took the ewe lamb that belonged to the poor man and prepared it for the one who had come to him."

5 David burned with anger against the man and said to Nathan, "As surely as the LORD lives, the man who did this must die! 6 He must pay for that lamb four times over, because he did such a thing and had no pity."

7 Then Nathan said to David, "You are the man! This is what the LORD, the God of Israel, says: 'I anointed you king over Israel, and I delivered you from the hand of Saul. 8 I gave your master's house to you, and your master's wives into your arms. I gave you all Israel and Judah. And if all this had been too little, I would have given you even more. 9 Why did you despise the word of the LORD by doing what is evil in his eyes? You struck down Uriah the Hittite with the sword and took his wife to be your own. You killed him with the sword of the Ammonites.'"

. . . .

13 Then David said to Nathan, "I have sinned against the LORD."

Nathan replied, "The LORD has taken away your sin. You are not going to die. 14 But because by doing this you have shown utter contempt for the LORD, the son born to you will die."

15 After Nathan had gone home, the LORD struck the child that Uriah's wife had borne to David, and he became ill.

KEY TEXT

Nathan said to David, "You are the man!" —**2 Samuel 12:7a**

Photo © Getty Images

JUSTICE, LAW, HISTORY

Unit 3: Justice and Adversity
LESSONS 10–13

LESSON AIMS

After participating in this lesson, each learner will be able to:

1. List the positions held by David, Nathan, Uriah, and Bathsheba.

2. Compare and contrast the reaction of David with that of Saul when confronted with personal sin.

3. Commit to reading Psalm 51 daily in the week and make it a personal prayer of confession, repentance, and restoration.

LESSON OUTLINE

Introduction

A. Confrontations

Confrontations are hard for me. In my years as a professor, I have unfortunately had to confront many students for cheating. I get varied reactions: from outright denial, to hedging and excuse making, to full and immediate confession. Though I hope for an admission of guilt at some point, I never know how things are going to go. But things are easier and the consequences are lighter when a confession comes forth.

Scripture tells us about many such confrontations. It is clear that God holds humans accountable (examples: Genesis 3:9-19; 4:6-15 [see lesson 5]; 1 Kings 18; Jeremiah 21). Sin must be confronted, especially when committed by those in powerful positions. What happens *after* confrontation reveals the character of the accused—and of God.

B. Lesson Context

At the time of today's lesson, the Israelite army was fighting the Ammonites (Genesis 19:38; Deuteronomy 2:19). The date was about 990 BC. The particular backdrop for us is a siege of the Ammonite capital, Rabbah. This was located at the site of the modern city of Amman, Jordan. Situated at the sources of the Jabbok River, the city was about 40 miles east of Jerusalem.

With a good general directing his army, a king could stay home to take care of administrative concerns or personal matters. King David had such a man in Joab (2 Samuel 8:16). Although not without ethical problems of his own (see 3:30), Joab was a fierce and unrelenting warrior, at that time very loyal to David. One day while home, David seemed to have been enjoying a nap on the roof (compare 1 Samuel 9:25). After waking, he began to walk around the roof (2 Samuel 11:2).

The highest point in Jerusalem was Mount Zion. Next to the mount on the south side was David's palace, making his rooftop the second highest position in the small city (probable size: about 2,000 people within 12 acres). This is how David could have observed activity on a nearby rooftop (2 Samuel 11:2b).

What David saw was the woman Bathsheba performing a ritual bath for purification (see 2 Samuel 11:4; compare Leviticus 15:19-24). David may have known Bathsheba's family, for her father was Eliam, thought to be the son of one of David's counselors Ahithophel (see 2 Samuel 11:3; 15:12; 16:23).

King David's notice of Bathsheba quickly turned to lust. He ended up sleeping with her, which resulted in a pregnancy (2 Samuel 11:5). David tried to influence her husband, Uriah, to go to his own house before returning to battle. That way everyone (except David and Bathsheba) would think that the baby was Uriah's. But Uriah's sense of honor kept him from spending time with his wife (11:6-13). Little did Uriah know that his sense of honor sealed his fate (11:14-17), as he carried his own death warrant back to Joab. After Uriah's death, David took Bathsheba as his own wife.

Nine months later, it looked as though David had gotten away with these crimes.

I. Tale of Two Men
(2 SAMUEL 12:1-6)
A. Contrasting Fortunes (vv. 1-3)
1a. The LORD sent Nathan to David.

Biblical narratives often present people's actions without offering God's evaluation of their deeds. But the writer of 2 Samuel could not resist the arresting understatement, "The thing that David had done displeased the Lord" (11:27).

Nothing is known of the prophet *Nathan* other than what is recorded in conjunction with David's reign (2 Samuel 7; 1 Kings 1; 1 Chronicles 29:29). Prophets existed in Israel's history before the monarchy, but their number and role seem to have increased after a human king was enthroned. True prophets were called directly by *the Lord* (example: Jeremiah 7:1-8). Among their important roles was to hold Israel's civil authorities in check (examples: 1 Samuel 13:11-14; 1 Kings 21:17-29). All in all, the prophet Nathan demonstrated respect for the Lord's anointed and fear of the Lord that led him to take on a potentially suicidal mission before *David*.

1b. When he came to him, he said, "There

were two men in a certain town, one rich and the other poor.

Nathan could have chosen a more direct approach to confronting David, but he chose to start with a parable. Old Testament prophets often used metaphors and symbolism to speak against evil in their nation (examples: Isaiah 5:1-7; Jeremiah 2:20-30) or even to entrap the king with his own ruling (2 Samuel 14:1-20; 1 Kings 20:35-43).

The description of *two men in a certain town* primed David for a story of conflict. The fact that *one [was] rich and the other poor* further heightened the likelihood of conflict, especially of injustice based on disparity of power.

> *What Do You Think?*
> How can a story help prepare a person to face a confrontation?
> *Digging Deeper*
> In what situations is this technique appropriate?

2-3a. "The rich man had a very large number of sheep and cattle, but the poor man had nothing

Since farm animals were an indication of wealth (example: 1 Samuel 25:2), the difference in power and status between the two men was made more apparent from the description of what both men possessed. Nathan's choice of *sheep and cattle* as the principal indicator of wealth likely resonated with David, who grew up working as a shepherd for his family (16:11; 2 Samuel 7:8). It also set up the potential conflict between the two as more emotional than if only gold was at stake.

3b. "except one little ewe lamb he had bought. He raised it, and it grew up with him and his children. It shared his food, drank from his cup and even slept in his arms. It was like a daughter to him.

With expert rhetorical flair, Nathan piled on more detail about the nearness and dearness of the *one little ewe lamb* to the poor man. David had protected his father's sheep fiercely (1 Samuel 17:34-35). Nathan's story would have stirred David's sympathies even before the crime was revealed.

Nathan's story also contains hints at its

meaning. That the sheep *slept in* the man's *arms* alludes to David's holding Bathsheba (2 Samuel 11:4). That the sheep *was like a daughter to him* also hints at Bathsheba, whose name means something like "daughter of abundance." For those in the know, it's obvious what Nathan is getting at—but still not to David (see 12:5-6, below).

B. Blatant Injustice (v. 4)

4. "Now a traveler came to the rich man, but the rich man refrained from taking one of his own sheep or cattle to prepare a meal for the traveler who had come to him. Instead, he took the ewe lamb that belonged to the poor man and prepared it for the one who had come to him."

In the days before hotels and restaurants, it was unremarkable for a *traveler* to seek room and board from a private citizen. Any virtuous person, wealthy or not, in the ancient world practiced hospitality to prevent a stranger from becoming the victim of violence (examples: Genesis 19:1-11; Judges 19:16-28).

The rich man followed convention by preparing a meal for the visitor (compare Genesis 19:3; Judges 19:20-21). But such hospitality, he may have reasoned (falsely), was the responsibility of the whole town, and not just himself. He therefore confiscated the poor man's *ewe lamb* for the occasion. No one hearing the story would believe that the man was justified in this, especially given the wealth disparity between the two citizens.

> *What Do You Think?*
>   What prevents you from taking advantage of
>   others based on your relative privilege?
> *Digging Deeper*
>   Instead of simply not taking advantage, what
>   verses guide you in actively blessing others?

C. Angry Verdict (vv. 5-6)

5. David burned with anger against the man and said to Nathan, "As surely as the LORD lives, the man who did this must die!

The differences in status and resources between the two men, combined with the rich man's heart-less action, made the guilt of the rich man appallingly clear. David's initial instinct as judge was to pass the death sentence on the man for his egregious behavior, which ironically would be appropriate for both adultery and murder (Exodus 21:12; Leviticus 20:10), but not theft (Exodus 22:1-15; exceptions: 21:16; 22:2).

6. "He must pay for that lamb four times over, because he did such a thing and had no pity."

Perhaps realizing that death was not a prescribed punishment for the theft of a *lamb*, no matter how precious, David gave a more realistic verdict. Fourfold recompense is the stipulated penalty in Exodus 22:1 for stealing a sheep.

David did not realize that he had stepped on a land mine that Nathan had planted. The psychological concept of projection can give some insight into David's words here. Though he was not consciously thinking of his own sin, he could harshly rebuke someone else exhibiting the same kind of behavior. This suggests that David subconsciously was quite aware of his guilt and felt the shame of his actions but had not yet confessed it to himself or the Lord (see 2 Samuel 12:13a, below).

> *What Do You Think?*
>   Why might you be inclined to judge someone
>   more harshly for sins that you also struggle
>   against?
> *Digging Deeper*
>   How can you remove the "plank" from your eye
>   in order to help with the "speck" in another's
>   (Matthew 7:3)?

II. Tale of the King
(2 SAMUEL 12:7-9)
A. The Guilty One (v. 7a)

7a. Then Nathan said to David, "You are the man!

Clues in the surrounding text indicate that this conversation between *Nathan* and *David* took place months after the offenses occurred (see Lesson Context), on the occasion of the child's birth (see 2 Samuel 12:14-15, below). By then David had had time to rationalize his sins away and bury them in his mind. But try as he might, he could not forget what he had done, and he now stood exposed before an all-knowing, all-seeing God (Psalms 11:4-7; 139:7-12). David himself was the rich *man*.

❧ *AM I GUILTY?* ❧

"Remember, we frequently have children on campus, so we all need to slow down in our driveway and parking lot." I nodded in agreement as I read the email from the facilities manager. I had seen coworkers driving too fast around the road that curved to our office. I tried to suppress my irritation. *Why can't they just slow down?*

A few days later I pulled into the parking lot in a rainstorm. I saw headlights in my rearview mirror as I parked. The facilities manager was leaning his head out of the window as I stood in the rain.

"David, you need to slow down," he said.

Flabbergasted, I mumbled an apology and retreated inside. It had never once entered my mind that the warning email might apply to *me*. But I was guilty.

Why is it so hard to judge ourselves? The next time you encounter a call for changed behavior, put yourself in the hot seat. Are you guilty?

—D. G.

B. The Blessed One (vv. 7b-8)

7b. "This is what the LORD, the God of Israel, says: 'I anointed you king over Israel, and I delivered you from the hand of Saul.

Nathan reminded David of the favor that the Lord had shown him (see Lesson Context, above; see also lesson 2). Very clearly he must have remembered the day he was summoned from the pasture to be *anointed* as *king* (1 Samuel 16:1-13). He also could not forget his years of fleeing from *Saul* (21:10; 23:7-8; etc.).

8. "'I gave your master's house to you, and your master's wives into your arms. I gave you all Israel and Judah. And if all this had been too little, I would have given you even more.

For a new king to assume possession of the former king's *wives* as well as his *house* was the apparent custom of the day. This does not mean that David married the women but, instead, that they were part of the package deal now under his control of *Israel* and *Judah* as Saul's successor (2 Samuel 5:1-5). David's acquisition of Saul's harem was thus a blessing representing God's giving him the kingship.

And the list of blessings does not stop there! God gave David the promise of an ongoing dynasty and a name like the greatest men on earth (2 Samuel 7:9). How much more could David possibly want? And *if all this had been too little*, the Lord had more to give!

C. The Ungrateful One (v. 9)

9a. "'Why did you despise the word of the LORD by doing what is evil in his eyes?

Disobeying *the Lord* in the face of such extravagant evidence of favor was a wicked, sinful betrayal. In the course of events, David had violated the foundational commandments against coveting, adultery, and murder (Exodus 20:13-14, 17).

9b. "'You struck down Uriah the Hittite with the sword and took his wife to be your own. You killed him with the sword of the Ammonites.'"

For the first time, Nathan named *Uriah the Hittite*. He called Bathsheba only Uriah's *wife*, not by her own name, emphasizing that David *took* a *wife* who was not his to take (see 2 Samuel 12:15, below; compare Matthew 1:6).

The consequences listed in 2 Samuel 12:10-11 (not in today's printed text) fit the crime (see also 2 Samuel 12:14, below). Because David had Uriah murdered by *the sword of the Ammonites*, the sword—representing military violence—would torment his own household (see fulfillment in 13:29; 18:14; 1 Kings 2:24-25). Since he took the wife of another man to be his own, someone close to him would now take his wives (see fulfillment in 2 Samuel 16:21-22).

HOW TO SAY IT

Eliam	Ih-*lye*-am.
Joab	*Jo*-ab.
Uriah	Yu-*rye*-uh.

III. Moving Beyond the Tales
(2 SAMUEL 12:13-15)
A. Confession (v. 13a)

13a. Then David said to Nathan, "I have sinned against the LORD."

Prophets often spoke truth to power only to find that power was not willing to listen (examples: 1 Kings 18:16-18; Jeremiah 36:1-26) or made excuses (example: 1 Samuel 15:13-21). But unlike Saul before him, *David* offered no excuses. Nor did he lash out at *Nathan* for denouncing him. Instead, he confessed the awful truth in the plainest language. Had he not *sinned* first *against the Lord*, the rest—Uriah, Bathsheba, and the countless others who would be affected by the consequences of his actions—would not have become his victims.

David was anointed king because he was a man after God's own heart (compare Acts 13:22). His confession here is surely one indication of why. Contrasting David with a later king, the Lord said that David had "followed me with all his heart, doing only what was right in my eyes" (1 Kings 14:8). Similar statements about David's wholehearted devotion to the Lord come in other comparisons (9:4; 11:6; 2 Kings 14:3; 18:3; 22:2). Only once later did the Lord add the qualifier, "except in the case of Uriah the Hittite" (1 Kings 15:5).

This should hearten the believer who continues

Sin always yields consequences.

Visual for Lesson 10. *Allow one minute of self-examination for any unconfessed sins for which participants need to repent.*

to struggle against sin; confession allows the heart to once again be fully devoted to the Lord. With this admission of sin, David would at last begin to unburden himself. He had felt the weight of his sin in his bones (Psalm 32:3-4). David went on to write a penitential prayer for cleansing and restoration (Psalm 51). Confession was the first step on the path to forgiveness for David, and is for us (1 John 1:9).

B. Mercy (v. 13b)

13b. Nathan replied, "The LORD has taken away your sin. You are not going to die.

David deserved to die for his crimes (see 2 Samuel 12:5, above). But *the Lord* once again showed himself to be compassionate, gracious, and forgiving of transgression and sin (compare Exodus 34:6-7). Even so, David would experience both punishment and consequence.

❧ *REMORSE* ❧

For my young daughter, stay-at-home orders represented her best defense against contracting COVID-19. She has chronic lung disease, so the virus could easily prove lethal for her. Even a simple cold could put her in the hospital, where she would be more at risk for exposure.

Her home-health nurses still reported for their usual 12-hour shifts. But when one nurse mentioned that her own child had a fever, my wife and I were alarmed. We asked the nurse to return home until everyone in her household had been symptom-free for two weeks.

It's possible that we would have kept her on if we were comfortable that she understood our concerns. But instead we parted ways with the nurse. King David modeled the humility we were looking for when he acknowledged his wrongdoing. This opened the door for forgiveness and renewal of his relationship with God. Can you follow David's example, or will you instead seek to justify yourself?
—D. G.

C. Consequences (vv. 14-15)

14. "But because by doing this you have shown utter contempt for the LORD, the son born to you will die."

As king in Israel, David brought dishonor not only to himself but also to God. Not only had David's sin of adultery snowballed into murder; it would cause enemies who already displayed *utter contempt for the Lord* (and possibly even people within Israel) to blaspheme God all the more (compare Matthew 18:6-7)! Far from shepherding the people in greater faithfulness to their God, David had demonstrated blatant disregard for God's standards.

The death of this innocent *son* is stunning as a punishment for David's sin. But while it may seem to go against God's own declaration that he does not punish the child for the parent's sin (Deuteronomy 24:16; Ezekiel 18:20), we need not assume that the child's death was a form of punishment for the baby. His death along with the record of Nathan's prophecy would be concrete evidence to the nation that the Lord saw David's sin and took it seriously. This example would, ideally, cause them to take their own sins seriously, knowing that God did not spare even his chosen king from discipline.

> *What Do You Think?*
> How do open secrets concerning a person's sins harm communities in which that person participates?
> *Digging Deeper*
> How can bringing those secrets to light help heal the damage?

15. After Nathan had gone home, the LORD struck the child that Uriah's wife had borne to David, and he became ill.

Bathsheba is again referred to as *Uriah's wife* to highlight the depravity of David's acts (see 2 Samuel 12:9b, above). For the next seven days, David would watch and pray as *the child* sickened and eventually died (12:16-20).

A sense of God's mercy and forgiveness would come with Solomon's birth (2 Samuel 12:24-25). He continued the royal line that led to Jesus (Matthew 1:6-7). Through the prophet Nathan, the Lord confronted David. But the Lord did not give up on David or his enduring dynasty (1 Kings 11:38; Jeremiah 23:5-6; Acts 2:29-31).

> *What Do You Think?*
> How do you guard against reading every negative consequence of your actions as a punishment from God?
> *Digging Deeper*
> How can you minister to others who fear that God is most often angry with them?

Conclusion
A. Accountability

There is always a temptation when reading a story to put oneself in the shoes of the hero. *I* would run into a burning building to save a child. *I* would step in if I saw blatant discrimination in front of me. Of course I would be Nathan, confronting the sins of the powerful.

But there is much to be gained by resisting the urge to identify with the hero. And if we're being honest, we are frequently more like David than a hero. We think our sins have passed by without consequence, that maybe even God didn't notice. We squash any gnawing guilt. If no consequences manifest themselves, we must have been forgiven!

Let David's story warn us against such attitudes. Our sins have consequences in others' lives. And sins we ignore instead of confess harden our hearts to other sins, making us complicit in the wickedness of others.

The tendency to abuse our own influence must constantly be held in check. We must be willing not only to hold others to account but also to listen when Christian brothers and sisters do the same for us. By doing so we will fulfill the words of Christ: "First take the plank out of your own eye, and then you will see clearly to remove the speck from your brother's eye" (Matthew 7:5).

B. Prayer

Father, give us the boldness to speak truth to power and the humility to recognize our need for accountability. In Jesus' name we pray. Amen.

C. Thought to Remember

Confess your sins and turn
to the Lord.

INVOLVEMENT LEARNING

Enhance your lesson with NIV® Bible Student (from your curriculum supplier) and the reproducible activity page (at www.standardlesson.com or in the back of the NIV® Standard Lesson Commentary Deluxe Edition).

Into the Lesson

Mention a public figure who was caught in a crime or scandal (example: Jeffrey Epstein's sex trafficking). Invite the whole group to outline the main details of the case. Ask for reactions when class member heard of this person's arrest. Ask if the outcome seemed satisfactory or not to most. As a transition, note that today's text leads us to consider a bigger, behind-the-scenes picture of scandals and crimes.

Into the Word

Ask a volunteer to read aloud 2 Samuel 12:1-6. Divide into small groups to "modernize" the story that Nathan told in order to set David up (example: instead of a sheep, perhaps it could be a family's dog or cat that is taken). Have groups read their modifications in the ensuing whole-class discussion. Give a token prize to the most creative recasting of the story. Then pose this question for discussion: "What response to Nathan's description of David's misdeed would you consider just in our time?"

Ask a volunteer to read aloud 2 Samuel 12:7-9, 13-15. Distribute handouts (you prepare) to groups you designate as **David's Deeds** (for considering 12:7-9) and **King's Confession** (for considering 12:3-15). Have groups "grade" Nathan or David from A+ to F– regarding the thoroughness of each man's declaration. (*Option.* If you wish, you can also include a third group to do the same with 7:10-12, not in today's printed text.)

Allow groups time to discuss and formulate their grades. As each group presents and defends its grading in the ensuing whole-class discussion, encourage the other group(s) to be contrarian and challenge the grading. Invite participants to summarize the characters of Nathan and David, as reflected in the text.

Option. Distribute to study pairs copies of the "Saul vis-à-vis David" exercise from the activity page, which you can download. Instruct learners to compare and contrast the two accounts as they complete the exercise as indicated.

Into Life

Invite participants to cross-reference today's passage with Psalm 51, the song David wrote in association with his repentance. Ask three volunteers to read it aloud in sections: Psalm 51:1-6, 7-13, and 14-19. Play, sing, or read the lyrics of the hymn "Whiter than Snow" or praise song that is similar to this psalm. Encourage participants to read Psalm 51 throughout the week ahead and make it a personal prayer of confession, repentance, and restoration. (*Option.* To enhance this proposal, distribute copies of the "Psalm 51" exercise from the activity page, which you can download, to be completed as a take-home.)

Form pairs or triads of learners to think of a modern scenario that would call for the kind of confrontation that Nathan used and prepare a role play for the class in that regard. Be prepared to give some hints to groups that are struggling with the assignment.

After all pairs or triads have performed their brief role plays, pose the following questions (write them on the board) for whole-class discussion:

What kinds of situations call for Nathan's type of confrontation?

In what kinds of situations would Nathan's technique be ineffective?

In what kinds of situations would Nathan's technique be seen as downright manipulative?

Tip: Do not write all three questions on the board at once. Write the second question only after the discussion has run its course on the first; similarly, write the third question only after the discussion has run its course on the second. Allow periods of silence to run 15 seconds—don't jump in to fill silence too quickly!

EZRA AND THE LAW

DEVOTIONAL READING: Ezra 7:1-10, 23-26
BACKGROUND SCRIPTURE: Ezra 7:1-26

EZRA 7:1-10, 23-26

¹ After these things, during the reign of Artaxerxes king of Persia, Ezra son of Seraiah, the son of Azariah, the son of Hilkiah, ² the son of Shallum, the son of Zadok, the son of Ahitub, ³ the son of Amariah, the son of Azariah, the son of Meraioth, ⁴ the son of Zerahiah, the son of Uzzi, the son of Bukki, ⁵ the son of Abishua, the son of Phinehas, the son of Eleazar, the son of Aaron the chief priest— ⁶ this Ezra came up from Babylon. He was a teacher well versed in the Law of Moses, which the Lord, the God of Israel, had given. The king had granted him everything he asked, for the hand of the LORD his God was on him. ⁷ Some of the Israelites, including priests, Levites, musicians, gatekeepers and temple servants, also came up to Jerusalem in the seventh year of King Artaxerxes.

⁸ Ezra arrived in Jerusalem in the fifth month of the seventh year of the king. ⁹ He had begun his journey from Babylon on the first day of the first month, and he arrived in Jerusalem on the first day of the fifth month, for the gracious hand of his God was on him.

¹⁰ For Ezra had devoted himself to the study and observance of the Law of the LORD, and to teaching its decrees and laws in Israel.

. . . .

²³ Whatever the God of heaven has prescribed, let it be done with diligence for the temple of the God of heaven. Why should his wrath fall on the realm of the king and of his sons? ²⁴ You are also to know that you have no authority to impose taxes, tribute or duty on any of the priests, Levites, musicians, gatekeepers, temple servants or other workers at this house of God.

²⁵ And you, Ezra, in accordance with the wisdom of your God, which you possess, appoint magistrates and judges to administer justice to all the people of Trans-Euphrates—all who know the laws of your God. And you are to teach any who do not know them. ²⁶ Whoever does not obey the law of your God and the law of the king must surely be punished by death, banishment, confiscation of property, or imprisonment.

KEY TEXT

Ezra had devoted himself to the study and observance of the Law of the LORD, and to teaching its decrees and laws in Israel. —**Ezra 7:10**

Justice, Law, History

Unit 3: Justice and Adversity
LESSONS 10–13

LESSON AIMS

After participating in this lesson, each learner will be able to:

1. Summarize Ezra's role in the exiles' return to Jerusalem.

2. Explain why Ezra was the right leader for that journey.

3. Make a plan to study the ways his or her spiritual heritage has affected personal beliefs and practices.

LESSON OUTLINE

Introduction

A. Researching Roots

By the year 2016, personal genetic testing became broadly accessible and popular. Various companies promised to provide extensive insight into a person's health and ancestry, all based on a person's genetic profile.

Some tests compare a person's results with the results from other participants to reveal familial relationships. These results sometimes provide intriguing insights—and the potential for making connections with previously unknown family members or discovering of famous (or infamous!) relatives. Through these programs, our ability to connect with and learn from past generations has been greatly enhanced. Law enforcement has also benefited as DNA from crime scenes is compared against genetic databases.

Ancestral background plays a crucial role in today's lesson. Because of Ezra's ancestry and his skilled knowledge of God's law, he was the right individual to lead his people back to their ancestral homeland.

B. Lesson Context

After the death of King Solomon in about 930 BC, the nation of Israel experienced political and religious upheaval. The 12 tribes of Israel were divided into 10 northern tribes (designated the kingdom of Israel) and 2 southern tribes (designated the kingdom of Judah; see 1 Kings 12:1-24; 2 Chronicles 10:1–11:4).

Following this division, the king of the kingdom of Israel established two places of worship —at Bethel, just 10 miles north of Jerusalem, and at Dan, farther to the north. At each location a golden calf was placed (1 Kings 12:28-29; 2 Kings 10:29). This act was a blatant disregard for what the Lord had prescribed regarding the place and manner of worship (Deuteronomy 12:5, 11). Idolatry such as this eventually led to the destruction and captivity of the kingdom of Israel by the Assyrians around 722 BC (see 2 Kings 17:5-6; 1 Chronicles 5:26).

The southern kingdom of Judah experienced a similar fate. After decades of immoral worship, in contradiction to the words of God's prophets, Jerusalem (the capital of Judah) was destroyed by the Babylonians in 586 BC (2 Chronicles 36:14-20). During this conquest, Solomon's temple was destroyed and the people of Judah were exiled. The land of Judah was desolate—without its people, its king, its capital, and its temple.

Within this context, the book of Ezra described two waves of Jewish captives returning to their homeland. It is extremely important for understanding the book of Ezra to distinguish between the two waves. The first took place in about 538 BC after Cyrus, king of Persia and conqueror of Babylon, decreed that captives could return to Jerusalem to build a temple (Ezra 1:2; compare 2 Chronicles 36:22-23). These returnees first rebuilt the altar in 537 BC (Ezra 3:1-6), then began work on rebuilding the temple (3:7-13). After opposition (4:1-5) and a brief delay (4:24), the temple was completed in 516 BC (6:15).

Today's lesson focuses on those who returned to Judah in 458 BC, 80 years after the first return. This return was led by Ezra, an expert in God's law, whose life focused on proper worship of God.

Over a century had passed since the Babylo-

HOW TO SAY IT

Ahitub	A-*high*-tub.
Amariah	Am-uh-**rye**-uh.
Aramaic	Air-uh-**may**-ik.
Artaxerxes	Are-tuh-*zerk*-seez.
Azariah	Az-uh-*rye*-uh.
Baal	*Bay*-ul.
Bethel	*Beth*-ul.
Eleazar	El-ih-*a*-zar or E-lih-*a*-zar.
Euphrates	You-*fray*-teez.
Ezra	*Ez*-ruh.
Hilkiah	Hill-*kye*-uh.
Josiah	Jo-*sigh*-uh.
Judah	*Joo*-duh.
Nebuchadnezzar	*Neb*-yuh-kud-**nez**-er.
Nisan	*Nye*-san.
Phinehas	*Fin*-ee-us.
Seraiah	Se-*ray*-yuh or Se-*rye*-uh.
Shallum	*Shall*-um.
Zadok	*Zay*-dok.

nians had taken Ezra's ancestors captive. In the midst of their captivity, the foundation that undergirded the actions of Ezra and his people was their faith in God and hope to return to their homeland. Only in Jerusalem could Ezra and his people worship properly, at the rebuilt temple.

I. Ezra's Qualifications
(EZRA 7:1-6)
A. Physical Lineage (vv. 1-5)
1a. After these things,

This phrase refers to the events of Ezra 6: the completion and dedication of the rebuilt temple (Ezra 6:13-18). Most scholars put approximately 57 years between the events of Ezra 6 and the events of today's text.

1b. during the reign of Artaxerxes king of Persia,

In antiquity there were three Persian rulers with the name *Artaxerxes*. This one is Artaxerxes I, who reigned 465–424 BC. Since the other two reigned much later (404–359 BC and 359–338 BC), there was no need for Ezra to distinguish among them. Artaxerxes I is the same individual who would later send Nehemiah to Jerusalem (Nehemiah 2:1).

1c. Ezra son of Seraiah, the son of Azariah, the son of Hilkiah,

The following genealogy traced the ancestry of *Ezra* back to Aaron, the first high priest (see Exodus 28:1), and validated Ezra's role as priest (see Ezra 7:11, not in today's text).

The genealogy relates Ezra to several prominent priests with the expression *son of*, an idiom meaning "descendant." This idiom does not necessarily indicate a direct father-son relationship.

In the Old Testament, at least 11 individuals were named *Seraiah* (see 2 Samuel 8:17; 1 Chronicles 4:13, 35; Ezra 2:2; Nehemiah 10:2; 11:11; 12:1; Jeremiah 36:26; 40:8; 51:59). The individual mentioned here was likely the high priest when Nebuchadnezzar's forces captured and destroyed Jerusalem in 586 BC (see 2 Kings 25:8, 18).

The Old Testament mentions more than 20 individuals with the name *Azariah*, including a second individual in Ezra's genealogy (see commentary on Ezra 7:3, below; see 1 Kings 4:5;

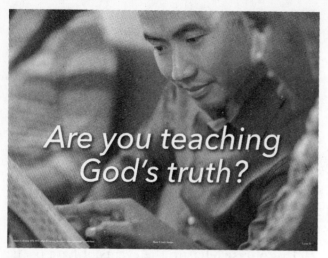

Are you teaching God's truth?

Visual for Lesson 11. *Allow one minute for silent personal reflection on this question, following the lesson's conclusion.*

2 Kings 14:21; 1 Chronicles 2:8, 38; 6:9; etc.). This name likely refers to a priest and official in the service of King Solomon (see 1 Kings 4:2).

In 622 BC, during the reign of King Josiah, the high priest *Hilkiah* found the Book of the Law neglected in the temple (see 2 Kings 22:3, 8).

2. the son of Shallum, the son of Zadok, the son of Ahitub,

Some 14 individuals in the Old Testament share the name *Shallum* (see 2 Kings 15:10-15; 22:14; 1 Chronicles 2:41; 3:15; 4:25; 2 Chronicles 28:12; etc.). In Ezra's day, temple gatekeepers were one of the first exiles to return to Judah (Ezra 2:42; see 1 Chronicles 9:17). Their role was critical as they protected the entrance to the temple and the sacred items located in the temple (9:23; 15:23)

3-4. the son of Amariah, the son of Azariah, the son of Meraioth, the son of Zerahiah, the son of Uzzi, the son of Bukki,

For further detail about the ancestral background of the tribe of Levi, one might turn to 1 Chronicles 6:1-81, where a detailed genealogy lists the relatives of Levi and Aaron. Some names from Ezra 7 are omitted in the genealogy of 1 Chronicles 6. However, their lack of inclusion is not an issue as it was uncommon to list every member of every generation.

5. the son of Abishua, the son of Phinehas, the son of Eleazar, the son of Aaron the chief priest—

Beyond his service as high priest from the tribe of Levi, very little is known about *Abishua* (1 Chronicles 5:30-31; 6:50).

Upon seeing Israel's sin with Baal, *Phinehas* is recorded to have killed an Israelite man and a Midianite woman (see Numbers 25:3-8). His act of violence was seen as an act of righteousness, turning away the wrath of the Lord and establishing a "covenant of peace" (25:11-12; see Psalm 106:28-31).

Eleazar followed in his father's priestly duties upon Aaron's death (Numbers 20:25-29). Additionally, Eleazar assisted Joshua in distributing land to the tribes of Israel (Joshua 14:1).

One might consider biblical genealogies boring and useless, but they stand as historical record and are essential to show the validity of certain roles. For Ezra, these genealogies validated his role as leader and priest of his people. The importance of this is seen in the identical wording (in both Hebrew and English) of Ezra 2:62 and Nehemiah 7:64.

> *What Do You Think?*
> What role, if any, should physical or spiritual genealogy play in your life? Why?
> *Digging Deeper*
> What boundaries do 1 Timothy 1:4 and Titus 3:9 establish in this regard?

❧ *AN ENDURING LEGACY* ❧

Amanda experienced a difficult childhood. By her 10th birthday, her parents had divorced. One parent dealt with a prescription drug addiction, and the other parent died by the time Amanda was in middle school. Because of these challenges, Amanda was forced to care for her younger brother.

Eventually, Amanda's grandmother became the primary legal caregiver for Amanda and her brother. Their grandmother cared in ways they had never previously experienced. She attended parent-teacher conferences, provided school supplies for the children, and cooked nourishing meals daily. She was present for all the ups and downs Amanda experienced during high school. Says Amanda, "Without my grandma's example for me, I don't know where I'd be today."

The legacy of Amanda's grandmother will be long-lasting as it extends to Amanda's children and grandchildren. When a family member's care and support counteract the challenges of life and affect future generations in the process, a legacy is established. How will your legacy encourage leadership and healing for future generations? What kind of legacy will you leave?   —L. M.-W.

B. Spiritual Preparation (v. 6)

6a. this Ezra came up from Babylon.

With Ezra's role validated by his genealogy, the narrative turns to Ezra's specific task: leading a journey *from Babylon* to Jerusalem. The distance between the two cities was approximately 880 miles and would take extensive planning.

6b. He was a teacher well versed in the Law of Moses, which the LORD, the God of Israel, had given.

Ezra was more than merely a priest. He is described as a *teacher,* or scholar, of *the Law of Moses.* As the legal scholars of the day, teachers of the Law (also called scribes) were highly regarded as they studied the ancient law given to Moses, provided accurate interpretation, and taught it to others (compare Nehemiah 8).

The ease at which Ezra understood the complex nuances of law is indicated by his description as *well versed.* This implies his skilled comprehension.

Ezra's focus on the law did not lie with its editorial foundations; he was not concerned with whether there were multiple authors of the law over several centuries. Instead, his focus lay with the reality that it was *the Lord, the God of Israel* who *had given* the law.

6c. The king had granted him everything he asked, for the hand of the LORD his God was on him.

As *the king had granted* Ezra's requests and needs for the upcoming journey, it seems that Artaxerxes's attitude had changed. Elsewhere, the king ordered that work on rebuilding the city of Jerusalem stop until he issued a new decree (Ezra 4:21). However, the king changed his opinion and supported Ezra's journey. Artaxerxes even contributed great quantities of silver and gold for the work in Jerusalem (8:25-27). Ezra prepared

for this moment, knew the needs of the journey, requisitioned necessary resources, and secured the complete confidence of the king.

The hand of the Lord is referred to throughout the latter half of Ezra and acknowledges the source of the blessings bestowed on this journey and the following rebuilding projects in Jerusalem (see Ezra 7:6, 9, 28; 8:18, 22, 31). This journey would be successful because it was blessed by the Lord.

> **What Do You Think?**
> What does Ezra's favor with the king suggest regarding how you should view and interact with governing authorities?
> *Digging Deeper*
> How do Acts 5:29; Romans 13:1-7; Titus 3:1; Hebrews 11:23; and 1 Peter 2:13-17 help frame your response?

II. Ezra's Journey
(EZRA 7:7-10)
A. Travel Companions (v. 7)

7. Some of the Israelites, including priests, Levites, musicians, gatekeepers and temple servants, also came up to Jerusalem in the seventh year of King Artaxerxes.

The total number of those who traveled *to Jerusalem* numbered fewer than 2,000 (Ezra 8:1-14). This group included the *priests* and the *Levites,* individuals necessary for proper worship in the newly built temple; *musicians* and *gatekeepers,* necessary for rightly ordered worship; and other *Israelites.*

The *temple servants* were individuals who had given their lives to work and minister in the temple in a non-priestly manner (see 1 Chronicles 9:2; Ezra 8:20).

B. Journey's Length (vv. 8-9a)

8. Ezra arrived in Jerusalem in the fifth month of the seventh year of the king.

As a careful scribe, Ezra gives additional information about the chronology of the trip. The entire journey took place *in the seventh year of the king,* Artaxerxes, corresponding to 458 BC.

9a. He had begun his journey from Babylon on the first day of the first month, and he arrived in Jerusalem on the first day of the fifth month,

The journey *from Babylon* began on *the first day of the first month*, the Jewish month of Nisan (late March to early April). Ezra arrived *in Jerusalem* on *the first day of the fifth month*, the Jewish month of Ab. This date would be to August 4, 458 BC.

As the Jewish calendar is based on lunar months, each month is approximately 29.5 days. Therefore, the travel time was approximately 118 days, including Sabbath Days for rest. Because this group likely included animals, children (Ezra 8:21), and cargo (8:24-30), those would have necessitated a slower rate of travel: approximately nine miles a day.

> *What Do You Think?*
> What steps can you take to avoid the danger of enslavement in the "spiritual Babylon" culture that surrounds us?
> *Digging Deeper*
> How do texts such as 2 Corinthians 5:16; 10:4; 11:18-20; Galatians 4:8-9; and 1 Peter 5:13 speak to this issue?

C. God's Blessing (vv. 9b-10)

9b. for the gracious hand of his God was on him.

The arrival of the travelers to Jerusalem gave evidence that the providence and blessing of *the gracious hand of his God* was upon Ezra (see commentary on Ezra 7:6, above).

10. For Ezra had devoted himself to the study and observance of the Law of the LORD, and to teaching its decrees and laws in Israel.

Ezra's role as a scribe and teacher is seen by the ways *the Law of the Lord* affected his life and the lives of others. It was not enough that he wanted to *study* teach God's law. The desire to practice *observance* of God's law implied a full understanding of the law's life-changing affect. Ezra's dedication to his calling undoubtedly changed Israel for the better and encouraged proper worship as the travelers returned to their homeland (compare Nehemiah 8).

> *What Do You Think?*
> What disciplines do you find helpful in motivating you to seek, do, and teach God's will?
> *Digging Deeper*
> What activities have you noticed that work against this ideal?

III. Ezra's Obligations
(EZRA 7:23-26)

The intervening verses consist of the words of King Artaxerxes in a letter to Ezra. The text of this letter was written in Aramaic, the official language of the Persians. This letter granted Ezra authority to determine the proper location to observe God's law (Ezra 7:14).

A. What to Do, Part 1 (v. 23)

23. Whatever the God of heaven has prescribed, let it be done with diligence for the temple of the God of heaven. Why should his wrath fall on the realm of the king and of his sons?

Whether Artaxerxes regarded Israel's *God* as the one, true God is undetermined. However, at the very least, he held a high regard for the Israelites' God. The king ordered obedience to the commands of God as they related to *the temple* of God. The expression *the God of heaven* admits that Ezra's God is not just the God of Israel; this God is much greater, and Artaxerxes recognizes the scope of God's domain.

However, it is also possible that Artaxerxes acted pragmatically, not wanting to incur divine *wrath* and desiring to maintain order among those in his kingdom (see Ezra 1:2-4, 6:10).

❧ *RECOGNIZING A NEED* ❧

Our church began collecting backpacks filled with school supplies to distribute to students at our local school. After an initial hesitation, the school's principal accepted our help and showed us further needs of the students. Our church collected and distributed meals for children home alone during the day on Christmas break. Later, our church organized a program to provide tutoring assistance.

Ezra recognized the needs of his people,

organized King Artaxerxes's donations, and envisioned ways to meet the needs of the people (Ezra 7:15-22). My church saw the needs of our community, organized the resources and abilities of our church community, and provided ways to meet the needs of our neighbors. As a person of faith, how can you reach out to your neighbors in need, even by sharing your own resources? —L. M.-W.

B. What Not to Do (v. 24)

24. You are also to know that you have no authority to impose taxes, tribute or duty on any of the priests, Levites, musicians, gatekeepers, temple servants or other workers at this house of God.

It was customary for the Persians not to levy taxes on priests of any kind of religious order. Decades before Ezra, Persian King Darius the Great exempted servants of the cult of Apollo from paying *taxes* and *tribute* to the state. Artaxerxes continued that precedent to include all who served at the *house of God* in Jerusalem.

C. What to Do, Part 2 (v. 25)

25. And you, Ezra, in accordance with the wisdom of your God, which you possess, appoint magistrates and judges to administer justice to all the people of Trans-Euphrates—all who know the laws of your God. And you are to teach any who do not know them.

Artaxerxes had developed a very high regard for *Ezra* and empowered Ezra to establish just and consistent guidance on the *laws of . . . God.* Undoubtedly, Ezra's identity as an expert on God's laws allowed him to accurately *know* and *teach* others in the same regard.

The region known as the *Trans-Euphrates* refers to the area across the Euphrates River to the west. This highlights the geographic extent of the Persian Empire (see Ezra 4:10; Nehemiah 2:7, 9; 3:7), which stretched from the Euphrates to the eastern end of the Mediterranean Sea, and from northern Syria to the border of Egypt.

D. Penalty for Disobedience (v. 26)

26. Whoever does not obey the law of your God and the law of the king must surely be punished by death, banishment, confiscation of property, or imprisonment.

In a surprising move, Artaxerxes required people to obey both *the law of the king* and *the law of . . . God.* Years before, Darius the Great made a similar demand, requiring obedience to "the God of heaven" and the word of the king (Ezra 6:9-12).

> *What Do You Think?*
> Which motivates you more as a Christian: expectation of eternal reward or fear of judgment? Why?
> *Digging Deeper*
> How is this evident in your life?

Conclusion

A. Be an Ezra!

Leaders must cast vision and invite others to see that vision similarly. Leaders must address immediate decisions, favors, or requests made to them by their followers. By reading widely, listening to the advice of experts, and preparing for all possible scenarios, thoughtful and successful leaders are able to face a variety of challenges.

Ezra flourished as a leader because he focused on what really mattered: the wisdom of God and law of God. He studied God's Word and law in order that he might teach and lead Israel well. Because of his determination in study, combined with his priestly background, Ezra showed to be the most capable leader for Israel's return to Jerusalem. He became an example to following generations of a God-focused leader. The primary goals of his life were to study, to do, and to teach God's Word! Is Ezra a model for you?

B. Prayer

Almighty God, we are thankful for the example of Ezra. May we too be good examples as we take on our daily tasks, and may others see that your Word guides our lives. In the name of Jesus. Amen.

C. Thought to Remember

Follow Ezra's example!

INVOLVEMENT LEARNING

Enhance your lesson with NIV® Bible Student (from your curriculum supplier) and the reproducible activity page (at www.standardlesson.com or in the back of the NIV® Standard Lesson Commentary Deluxe Edition).

Into the Lesson

Create three columns across the board with these three headers:

Physical Trait / Character Quality / Family Heirloom

Leave room for a fourth column to be added during the Into Life segment.

Ask participants what has been passed down through the generations of their families in these areas. Write participants' responses in the appropriate column. (Possible answers might include things such as baldness, freckles, sense of humor, silver candlesticks, etc.) Challenge responders to trace their mentioned traits, qualities, or heirlooms as far back as possible and to consider how these may have shaped their identities. (Caution: don't let this drag out too long.)

Make a transition by saying, "Inheriting traits, troubles, and trinkets from our ancestors is nothing new. But there's something valuable to learn in this regard from today's text."

Into the Word

After having Ezra 7:1-5 read aloud, put participants in small groups of three or four. Provide each group with a poster board and markers. Challenge groups to create a visual depiction of the lineage of Ezra, as it is recorded in Ezra 7:1-5. This depiction can take the form of a time line, a family tree, stick figures, etc.

After groups finish and compare results, ask what the people in the lineage had in common (*expected answer:* Ezra was from a long line of Levitical priests). Discuss why such roots were important to the returned exiles (*answer:* see Ezra 2:62; Nehemiah 7:64).

Ask a volunteer to read Ezra 7:6-10 aloud. Discuss the significance of God's hand in these verses as they relate to the king's granting Ezra's requests and Ezra's safe arrival in Jerusalem. Contrast these with the admission in Ezra 8:22.

Option. To dig deeper into the issue of God's guiding hand, keep the participants in the same groups and give each a handout (you prepare) featuring a two-column table titled "The Influence of God's Hand." Head the first column *References* and the second column *Preexilic vs. Postexilic.* List the following texts under the *References* header: Exodus 14:31; Joshua 4:23-24; Judges 2:15; 1 Samuel 7:13; 2 Chronicles 30:12; Ezra 7:6, 9, 28; 8:18, 22, 31; 9:7; Nehemiah 2:8, 18.

Include instructions to compare and contrast the postexilic texts (that is, texts from Ezra and Nehemiah) with the preexilic texts (all the texts other than Ezra and Nehemiah). Determine how God changed his approach in moving from times before the exile of 586 BC to times after the exile of 538 BC and following, if at all.

Then have Ezra 7:23-26 read aloud. Ask each group to choose a scribe. Ask groups to write a job description, in modern-day format, based on what Ezra was given authority to do and what he did not have authority to do. (*Option.* You can use the "Job Description" handout from the activity page of lesson 8 if you desire.) Ask what challenges and rewards Ezra might have experienced.

Into Life

Add a fourth column headed *Spiritual Heritage* to the other three columns on the board. Ask, "What spiritual beliefs and practices have been passed down to you from spiritual or physical ancestors?" Write responses under the new header. Challenge learners to take no more than one minute individually to create a first draft of a plan and commitment to study how their spiritual heritage has affected their beliefs and practices.

Options. Read aloud Nehemiah 8:1-6 to show the response to Ezra's teaching. Distribute copies of "The Effects of God's Word" and/or "Looking Forward" exercises from the activity page, which you can download, as take-homes.

BILDAD MISSPEAKS GOD'S JUSTICE

DEVOTIONAL READING: Job 8:1-10, 20-22
BACKGROUND SCRIPTURE: Job 8

JOB 8:1-10, 20-22

1 Then Bildad the Shuhite replied:

2 "How long will you say such things?
 Your words are a blustering wind.

3 Does God pervert justice?
 Does the Almighty pervert what is
 right?

4 When your children sinned against him,
 he gave them over to the penalty of
 their sin.

5 But if you will seek God earnestly
 and plead with the Almighty,

6 if you are pure and upright,
 even now he will rouse himself on your
 behalf
 and restore you to your prosperous state.

7 Your beginnings will seem humble,
 so prosperous will your future be.

8 "Ask the former generation
 and find out what their ancestors
 learned,

9 for we were born only yesterday and know
 nothing,
 and our days on earth are but a shadow.

10 Will they not instruct you and tell you?
 Will they not bring forth words from
 their understanding?"

. . . .

20 "Surely God does not reject one who is
 blameless
 or strengthen the hands of evildoers.

21 He will yet fill your mouth with laughter
 and your lips with shouts of joy.

22 Your enemies will be clothed in shame,
 and the tents of the wicked will be no
 more."

KEY TEXT

Bildad the Shuhite replied: "How long will you say such things? Your words are a blustering wind."
—Job 8:1-2

Photo © Getty Images

JUSTICE, LAW, HISTORY

Unit 3: Justice and Adversity

LESSONS 10–13

LESSON AIMS

After participating in this lesson, each learner will be able to:

1. Summarize Bildad's explanation for Job's suffering.

2. Explain the error of Bildad's conclusion.

3. Be "Bildad" in a role-play of improved counseling of friends in distress.

LESSON OUTLINE

Introduction

A. Premises and Conclusions

Aristotle, a Greek philosopher who lived 300 years before Christ, influenced modern understandings of philosophy and rhetoric. Other aspects of his work focused on syllogisms, which are logic arguments where a conclusion is required by two premises.

One of Aristotle's famed syllogisms goes as follows: *All men are mortal. Socrates is a man. Therefore, Socrates is mortal.* The first phrase is called the major premise, while the second phrase is called the specific premise. If the two premises are properly stated, then the resulting conclusion will be valid.

In the midst of Job's suffering, his friends—who lived hundreds of years before Aristotle—attempted to explain Job's suffering through an implied syllogism. Their syllogism, espoused by Bildad in this lesson's text, went as follows: *Only wicked people suffer. Job suffers. Therefore, Job is wicked.* In the perspective of Job's friends, the premises were true, so it would seem the conclusion was validated!

B. Lesson Context

The book of Job is among the oldest biblical texts, and it deals with one of humanity's oldest challenges: maintaining hope in the face of suffering. The text also addresses another shared experience: the desire for justice in the midst of suffering.

Job's suffering was the catalyst for his friends' arrival. At the onset of the book, Job was described as "blameless and upright," one who actively "feared God and shunned evil" (Job 1:1). However, Job experienced undue tragedy. His flocks and servants were taken or killed (1:13-17), his 10 children died (1:2, 18-19), and he was afflicted with intense physical suffering (2:7). Without an explanation for the tragedies, Job remained faithful to God and "did not sin in what he said" (2:10).

Job's friends—Bildad, Eliphaz and Zophar—are introduced when, on hearing of Job's suffering, they "met together . . . to go and sympathize with him and comfort him" (Job 2:11). When they reached Job, they were shocked at his appearance and were unable to recognize him. They raised their voices, wept, and took a posture of mourning, remaining silent "for seven days and seven nights" (2:12-13).

Finally Job spoke, pouring out his anguish in great torrents of despair. His suffering overwhelmed him to the point of his cursing his own birth (Job 3:3). Job cried out that the thing he dreaded in life had happened: he experienced no consolation and no peace (3:25-26).

In response to Job's lament, his friends spoke in cycles of back-and-forth discussions. Eliphaz and Bildad each addressed him three times, while Zophar addressed him twice. Each argument was countered by Job. This lesson's Scripture text highlights Bildad's first response to Job's lament. It is reasonable to conclude that Job's friends were sincere in wanting to care for Job, even though their counsel was incompetent (see Job 6:21; 16:2).

I. Condemnation
(Job 8:1-4)
A. Blowing Winds (vv. 1-2)
1. Then Bildad the Shuhite replied:

This is the first instance where *Bildad* speaks. His origins are mysterious, and there is little information to gather from the biblical text. Bildad's designation as *the Shuhite* was possibly a tribal name from an ancient ancestor. His ancestry may have been traced to Shuah, a child of Abraham and Keturah (see Genesis 25:2; 1 Chronicles 1:32).

2. "How long will you say such things? Your words are a blustering wind.

Bildad's speech follows a lengthy lament spoken

HOW TO SAY IT

Bildad	*Bill*-dad.
Eliphaz	*El*-ih-faz.
Shuah	*Shoe*-uh.
Shuhite	*Shoe*-hite.
Socrates	*Sock*-ruh-teez.
Zophar	*Zo*-far.

by Job (Job 6–7). *Such things* spoken by Job consisted of his bemoaning the unjust nature of his suffering. Job did not question God's sovereignty but questioned the wisdom of his friends (6:11-30). Job's speech culminates in a pointed protest against God (7:11-21).

Bildad did not waste time expressing his disapproval of Job's lament. By describing Job's words as *a blustering wind*, Bildad used Job's own word against him (see Job 6:26). To Bildad, Job's words, while desperate, were meaningless and empty. That Job reeled over his multitude of losses (most significantly the death of his children), should give us a sense of how hurtful Bildad's reply must have felt to Job. Bildad was, after all, one of Job's closest friends.

> *What Do You Think?*
> What role should the correcting of doctrine play when comforting a friend in mourning?
> *Digging Deeper*
> What factors might cause you to reconsider your general response?

B. Blasphemous Claims (v. 3)
3. "Does God pervert justice? Does the Almighty pervert what is right?

The structure of this verse is such that the two questions are, essentially, the same. Such is an example of literary parallelism, common in Old Testament wisdom literature. This form of parallelism exists when two phrases carry the same meaning but with slightly altered and/or synonymous language. A similar example is stated by the prophet Isaiah: "Justice is driven back and righteousness stands at a distance" (Isaiah 59:14).

The Hebrew verb translated *pervert* means to bend, falsify, or make crooked (compare Ecclesiastes 1:15; 7:13; Amos 8:5). The primary thrust of Bildad's argument was rooted in his observation of the nature and character of *God* the *Almighty*. God does not bend or falsify *justice*. Elihu, another friend of Job, later echoed Bildad's sentiments, affirming, "It is unthinkable that God would do wrong, that the Almighty would pervert justice" (Job 34:12).

Visual for Lesson 12. *Allow one minute for silent personal reflection on this truth before discussing the questions associated with verse 6.*

Bildad's assertion is true. God himself is the standard of justice and righteousness, and he cannot violate his own character. He *is* just, and Job did not argue that point.

C. Blistering Accusation (v. 4)

4. "When your children sinned against him, he gave them over to the penalty of their sin.

Bildad used Job's deceased *children* to illustrate his assumptions about the manner of God's justice. Previously, the actions of his children greatly concerned Job. Job "would make arrangements for them to be purified" because they may "have *sinned,* and cursed God in their hearts" (Job 1:5). What Bildad proposed provides an example of retributive justice.

Retributive justice argues that God blesses the righteous and, conversely, curses the wicked. Bildad supposed that Job's children sinned and so their deaths were the result of their wickedness. This concept finds similarities in the Law of Moses. The promise of blessings came with obedience to God's law (Deuteronomy 28:1-14), while the promise of curses accompanied disobedience to God's law (28:15-68). Bildad's assumptions appear accurate; God blesses obedience and punishes disobedience (compare 11:26-28; 1 Samuel 15:22-23).

However, God sometimes works differently. Perhaps he chastens the righteous in order for their further refinement (see John 15:2-3) or allows the wicked to experience prosperity during their earthly lives (see Psalm 73:3; compare 103:10).

Bildad erred by assuming that Job's hardships were the inevitable outcome of *sin.* Bildad's strong desire to speak on behalf of God led him to make sweeping assertions. Such assertions carry little value, as the author of Ecclesiastes describes: "The righteous and the wise and what they do are in God's hands, but no one knows whether love or hate awaits them" (Ecclesiastes 9:1).

The existence (or nonexistence) of physical and material blessings does not correlate to a person's spiritual vitality. A righteous individual may inexplicably experience hardship and suffering. This does not imply God's absence or the wickedness of the individual.

Ultimately, it was not up to Job or Bildad to explain Job's hardship and suffering. Instead, their interaction highlights that a silent presence often can provide the best comfort to those who are suffering. Bildad could have better served his friend through the comfort of silence and presence—as he started out doing in Job 2:13.

> *What Do You Think?*
> What danger exists in assuming God's motives behind earthly events?
> *Digging Deeper*
> How can you guard against thinking or speaking in ways that assume you know why God has allowed something to happen?

II. Exhortation
(JOB 8:5-7)
A. Urgent Response (v. 5)

5. "But if you will seek God earnestly and plead with the Almighty,

Bildad transitioned from condemnation to exhortation. Bildad concluded that Job was less sinful than others because the Lord spared Job's life, at least for the time being. In this perspective, unless Job did *plead* to the mercy of *the Almighty,* there was no guarantee that his life would be spared.

The time for Job's lament had passed, and

Bildad challenged him to *seek God earnestly* and make request of *God* in a rapid and timely manner.

B. Favorable Reply (vv. 6-7)

6. "if you are pure and upright, even now he will rouse himself on your behalf and restore you to your prosperous state.

The theme of God's awakening occurs in the psalms, where the psalmist pleaded for God to "awake" and "rise" in order to defend the psalmist (Psalm 35:23). Similarly, the prophet Isaiah called for God to "awake" for the sake of restoring Israel (Isaiah 51:9). In these occurrences, God is called to action for the sake of his people.

In a similar way, Bildad promised that God *will rouse himself* to *restore* a truly righteous Job. God's awakening does not imply that God is unaware or unavailable; the psalmist provides a reminder of the ever-present nature of God as one who "will neither slumber nor sleep" (Psalm 121:3-4).

Bildad proposed that the most notable way God would act for Job is through the restoration of Job's *state*. The Hebrew word is here referring to Job's overall circumstances (compare Job 5:24) but can also describe a pasture for rest, be it for a flock of sheep (see 2 Samuel 7:8) or a group people (see Isaiah 32:18).

The Hebrew word behind *prosperous* implies peace, safety, restoration, and a return to wholeness. Bildad exhorts Job with hopes that Job can lead a restored existence, reflective of a righteous life.

> *What Do You Think?*
> How do you contradict doctrine that sounds right but is actually fundamentally flawed?
> *Digging Deeper*
> How does your approach differ if you are speaking to an unbeliever?

7. "Your beginnings will seem humble, so prosperous will your future be.

At the onset of Job's story, he is said to be "the greatest man among all the people of the East" (Job 1:3). Bildad argued that if Job sought God and returned to righteousness, then he would experience an increase in prosperity and his previous life would *seem humble* in comparison.

This verse reveals one of the great ironies in the book of Job—and perhaps all the Bible. Bildad's words were unknowingly prophetic in describing Job's future. Eventually, Job was granted more children and more wealth, but not because of Bildad's advice (see Job 42:12-14).

> *What Do You Think?*
> In what ways do you link material wealth with God's blessing?
> *Digging Deeper*
> What Scriptures contradict doctrines that suggest God always gives wealth to those he favors?

III. Reflection
(Job 8:8-10)
A. Search the Past (v. 8)

8. "Ask the former generation and find out what their ancestors learned,

Recognizing the limitations of his experience, Bildad appealed to the tradition of *the former generation*. Perhaps Bildad anticipated that a search of *what their ancestors learned* would confirm his view of God's justice, thus making clear Job's next steps.

Bildad's error, though, came in assuming that the tradition they have inherited was normative. It is one thing to accept tradition with a critical eye; it is something else altogether to use it to draw uncritical, sweeping generalizations. The latter is what Bildad seemed to do to bolster his claims about the nature of God's justice.

B. Learn from the Past (vv. 9-10)

9-10. "for we were born only yesterday and know nothing, and our days on earth are but a shadow. Will they not instruct you and tell you? Will they not bring forth words from their understanding?"

The appeal to the past is rooted in life's tenuous nature, as *our days* are but *a shadow* (see Psalms 102:11; 144:4; Ecclesiastes 8:13). Previously, Job cried out, "Teach me . . . show me where I have been wrong" (Job 6:24). In response, Bildad pointed to the teachings of the ancestors and the *words from their understanding.*

Like Bildad, when faced with a crisis, we might be tempted to provide comfort by appealing to past experiences, whether personal or anecdotal. The impulse to do so might arise from our feelings of discomfort and inadequacy during the crisis, especially if we struggle with what to do or say. In moments when we feel a sense of discomfort, we can remember Bildad's approach and behave differently, choosing to be present and quiet, if necessary.

> *What Do You Think?*
> What safeguards are necessary when studying with fellow believers about the Lord's ways?
> *Digging Deeper*
> Do these safeguards differ from generation to generation? Why or why not?

❧ THE WISDOM OF A MENTOR ❧

As a new mother, the pressures of parenting weighed heavily on me. I lived far from my extended family and did not have the support of other mothers. I wanted to learn from the wisdom of other mothers who could guide me and offer encouragement.

In an effort to find that support, I asked the minister of my church if church leadership had ever considered starting a mentoring program for new mothers. My minister responded that they had tried to start such a program, but it did not take root. The minister elaborated that "a lot of [the mothers] feel they made too many mistakes with their own children to be of use to another person."

I felt deflated; I longed to learn from former generations and apply their wisdom to my own parenting practices.

Bildad challenged Job to seek wisdom from previous generations. For Job's situation, that challenge was not helpful. On the other hand, godly individuals can provide helpful insight and wisdom that coincides with the wisdom of Scripture. What traits do you look for in a mentor? How are you fostering traits of godliness in your life?

Can you live up to the words of the apostle Paul, "Follow my example, as I follow the example of Christ" (1 Corinthians 11:1)?   —L. M.-W

IV. Projection
(JOB 8:20-22)
A. Double Retribution (v. 20)

20. **"Surely God does not reject one who is blameless or strengthen the hands of evildoers.**

Bildad continued to project assumptions of God's justice. The Hebrew word translated *blameless* here is also translated that way in Job 1:1, which establishes that Job was indeed "blameless and upright" (Job 1:1). But Bildad seems to have been looking at Job's tragedies to conclude the opposite. Thus Bildad has constructed a syllogism as follows:

Major Premise:	God does not cast away those who are perfect.
Specific Premise:	God has cast Job away (as evidenced by Job's troubles).
Conclusion:	Job is not perfect and, therefore, needs to repent.

The problem lies in the specific premise, which everyone assumed to be true. But the narrative of the first two chapters of this book—unknown to Job and his friends—informs us otherwise.

The flip side of the idea is found in the tradition of biblical wisdom literature that describes the righteous experiencing God's blessings. These individuals are like a "well-watered plant" (Job 8:16; compare Psalm 1:3).

Eliphaz made similar claims (Job 4:7-9), which Job would later refute (see Job 12:6). Various Old Testament voices reflect Job's sentiment, lamenting the ways the wicked seem to flourish, even as they speak against God (see Jeremiah 12:1; Malachi 3:15). Jesus' teaching reminds us that the righteous and unrighteous alike receive rain and sunshine (see Matthew 5:45). When compared to Bildad's assumptions, a fuller understanding of Scripture creates a big problem for those determined to maintain a rigid understanding of how God works.

B. Double Vindication (vv. 21-22)

21. "He will yet fill your mouth with laughter and your lips with shouts of joy.

What greater satisfaction could Job experience than for God to *fill his mouth with laughter* and his *lips with shouts of joy* after recovering from such prolonged lament, personal loss, and intense pain? But Bildad's implied solution—that Job needs to repent—follows from defective reasoning.

❧ VICTORY FROM AFFLICTIONS ❧

For several years, I lived in Eastern Europe and experienced the celebrations of May 8. Every year on this day, people flood parks and downtown areas to celebrate Victory in Europe day (VE-day). It was on that day in 1945 that Allied forces formally accepted the surrender of Nazi Germany, thus ending World War II in Europe. After VE-day, people felt free to rebuild from the rubble of war.

Some celebrants lived through the war and remembered the fear and deprivation they endured during that time. They remembered losing loved ones, being displaced from their homes, and scavenging for food and shelter. For these individuals, VE-day celebrations serve as a reminder of previous afflictions and eventual freedoms.

Though not as Bildad envisioned, Job did find freedom from his afflictions and again experienced joy. How has God freed you from afflictions and filled your heart with joy? May the words of the psalmist become your worship: "The Lord has done great things for us, and we are filled with joy" (Psalm 126:3).　　　—L. M.-W

22. "Your enemies will be clothed in shame, and the tents of the wicked will be no more."

The false logic continued as Bildad again unknowingly spoke prophetic words (see commentary on Job 8:7, above). Yet this time Bildad's words addressed his own future situation before God—Bildad, Eliphaz, and Zophar are the ones *clothed in shame* (see 42:7-9).

God's ultimate and lengthy response was to affirm his own sovereignty (Job 38–41). In a general sense, this corrected Bildad's faulty assumptions.

> *What Do You Think?*
> What Scriptures suggest that Bildad's statement in Job 8:22 is true?
> *Digging Deeper*
> When have you needed to hear this promise?

Conclusion

A. The Greatest Ministry

Being present to someone in the midst of a tragedy presents unique challenges. In an effort to explain the suffering, we may put too much pressure on ourselves to comfort in a wrong way. Platitudes will likely overstep the bounds of what is helpful. At best, our words might be little more than hollow clichés; at worst, they might cause further harm.

Bildad's counterproductive interaction with Job reminds us of the best ministry we might offer: the ministry of presence in the midst of difficult seasons. At first, Job's friends approached him in this manner (Job 2:13). But their silent presence changed to unhelpful arguments. They were quick to suppose that wickedness was the primary reason for Job's suffering. However, Bildad's logic did not account for the entire story of how God works. In reality, wicked individuals might experience blessing, while righteous individuals might experience suffering. Unbeknownst to everyone present, Job's suffering was an example of the latter.

When others experience suffering, our natural response is to *be with* them. To draw near, cry, and share in grief is an appropriate course of action to comfort the sufferer. Conjecture on God's behalf is unwise and unnecessary. Sitting silently with a grieving person often provides the best support.

B. Prayer

God of all comfort, grant us the patience to be silent for as long as it is needed in difficult moments. Help us say only what will be received as grace and comfort. In Jesus' name. Amen.

C. Thought to Remember

Our loving presence is the greatest ministry we have to offer those who are suffering.

INVOLVEMENT LEARNING

Enhance your lesson with NIV® Bible Student (from your curriculum supplier) and the reproducible activity page (at www.standardlesson.com or in the back of the NIV® Standard Lesson Commentary Deluxe Edition).

Into the Lesson

Lead the group in playing "Two Truths and a Lie." Have three volunteers each think of two little-known facts about themselves along with one plausible non-fact. Have each volunteer come to the board in turn and write on it their three statements. Then invite the class as a whole to vote on which of the three statements is the lie. Have the volunteers identify the truths and lies. (*Option.* Allow a certain number of yes/no questions to be asked of each volunteer.)

Pose the following questions for whole-group discussion, which can serve as a transition to Bible study:

1–How did you determine which statement was false?

2–Why is it sometimes challenging to discern lies from the truth?

Into the Word

Divide the class into four small groups to study today's passage. Designate them **Pervert Justice Group, Seek God Group, Ancestors Group,** and **Rejoice Group.** Assign the four groups the four text segments of Job 8:1-4, 5-7, 8-10, and 20-22, respectively. Distribute handouts (you create) with these identical instructions:

1–Identify elements of truth, if any, in Bildad's words.

2–Identify incorrect information or false presuppositions.

3–Create a short phrase that sums up what Bildad is saying in the group's text segment.

After each section is considered in small groups, compare conclusions in ensuing whole-class discussion. Be alert for conclusions of one group that don't match conclusions of another group. Refer to the commentary as necessary to resolve issues.

Following the discussion, ask each group to think of at least two examples from the Bible (specific verses or broader stories) that refute Bildad's

position. Challenge groups to use their examples as a basis to create a new short phrase to counter Bildad's words.

Option. Form learners into study pairs and announce a closed-Bible pop quiz. Distribute copies of the "Fact-Check the Speech" exercise from the activity page, which you can download. Allow a few minutes for the pairs to complete as directed. When pairs are finished, have them score their own work.

Option. For a deeper study of defective beliefs that Christians sometimes embrace, distribute copies of the "Say What?" exercise from the activity page. Form learners into study pairs or triads to complete it as indicated. After subsequent whole-class discussion, ask if participants have more entries for the list.

Into Life

Have participants pair off to role-play this situation: one person will represent a person experiencing great loss and the other a trusted friend who is doing his or her best to provide comfort.

Ask participants first to imitate Bildad's approach in the texts and then to alter it. Allow time for each member of pairs to act in both roles. Note: this happens only between members of pairs, not before the whole class.

Reconvene and ask for after-action reports. Some questions that you, the teacher, can ask of role-play pairs for the benefit of the class are:

1–What did you find most useful in this exercise?

2–What did you find to be the most intimidating?

3–What "God-talk" errors did you make that were similar to that of Bildad, if any?

4–Did anyone quote Romans 8:28 or other passages? If so, was that a useful thing to do?

5–What role did silence play, if any? (See Job 2:13.)

Draw the discussion to a close with a consideration of Job 16:1-5 and 42:7.

JOB AND THE JUST GOD

DEVOTIONAL READING: Job 42:1-11
BACKGROUND SCRIPTURE: Job 42

JOB 42:1-6, 10-17

¹ Then Job replied to the LORD:

² "I know that you can do all things;
   no purpose of yours can be thwarted.
³ You asked, 'Who is this that obscures my
      plans without knowledge?'
   Surely I spoke of things I did not
      understand,
   things too wonderful for me to know.

⁴ "You said, 'Listen now, and I will speak;
   I will question you,
      and you shall answer me.'
⁵ My ears had heard of you
   but now my eyes have seen you.
⁶ Therefore I despise myself
   and repent in dust and ashes."

· ·

¹⁰ After Job had prayed for his friends, the LORD restored his fortunes and gave him twice as much as he had before. ¹¹ All his brothers and sisters and everyone who had known him before came and ate with him in his house. They comforted and consoled him over all the trouble the LORD had brought on him, and each one gave him a piece of silver and a gold ring.

¹² The LORD blessed the latter part of Job's life more than the former part. He had fourteen thousand sheep, six thousand camels, a thousand yoke of oxen and a thousand donkeys. ¹³ And he also had seven sons and three daughters. ¹⁴ The first daughter he named Jemimah, the second Keziah and the third Keren-Happuch. ¹⁵ Nowhere in all the land were there found women as beautiful as Job's daughters, and their father granted them an inheritance along with their brothers.

¹⁶ After this, Job lived a hundred and forty years; he saw his children and their children to the fourth generation. ¹⁷ And so Job died, an old man and full of years.

KEY TEXT

Surely I spoke of things I did not understand, things too wonderful for me to know. —**Job 42:3b-c**

Justice, Law, History

Unit 3: Justice and Adversity
Lessons 10–13

Lesson Aims

After participating in this lesson, each learner will be able to:

1. Summarize Job's response to the Lord.
2. Identify changes in Job's view of God.
3. Write a respectful letter to God regarding a perceived injustice.

Lesson Outline

Introduction

A. The Courage to Hope

A diving accident at the age of 17 left Joni Eareckson Tada paralyzed. Bound to a wheelchair and unable to use her hands, she spent two years in rehabilitation learning how to deal with her new reality. Over the years her ministry has expanded to include a successful writing, speaking, and painting career. Additionally, she launched a ministry centered on helping people impacted by disability.

However, her life has been filled with many trials. She has lived with bouts of intense pain, pneumonia, and breast cancer. As she wrote about the suffering she experienced, she recalled God's promises to Joshua, promises to never leave or forsake (see Deuteronomy 31:6). God's promises of his presence gave Joni the courage to hope in the midst of dark nights.

Joni's story of suffering, lament, and hope parallels that of Job's life in some ways. In the midst of a dark time of lament and suffering, Job realized he had to cling to the hope that only a just God could provide.

B. Lesson Context

Job's response, described in this week's lesson, follows a lengthy and pointed reprimand from God. Out of a storm (Job 38:1; 40:6), God appeared to Job and warned him to "brace yourself like a man; I will question you, and you shall answer me" (38:3). Elsewhere in Scripture, God spoke to humanity through what could only be described as a storm (compare Exodus 19:16; Ezekiel 1:4; contrast 1 Kings 19:11-12). Out of the midst of this storm came the voice of God, demanding full attention as he presented his glory.

From that point, God proceeded to ask questions concerning Job's knowledge and understanding of the world, beginning with, "Where were you when I laid the earth's foundations? Tell me, if you understand" (Job 38:4).

After asking about Job's understanding of the observed world (Job 38:5–39:30), God invited Job to provide an answer (40:2). In a response that mirrored his later reply (see commentary on 42:3b, below), Job expressed that he could not provide answers to God's line of questioning and was in no place to accuse God further (40:4-5). God's response became even more pointed as he asked Job if he would "discredit my justice" and "condemn me to justify yourself" (40:8). God made it clear that Job, as a mere creature, was in no position to question the justice and judgment of the eternal Creator.

God's response was not an attempt to belittle Job or to provide answers for Job's suffering and lament. Rather, God's intent was to show Job the limit of his understanding of God's purposes and plans. God's just nature will not be thwarted, brought into question, or limited by humanity.

I. God's Plans
(JOB 42:1-2)

1-2. Then Job replied to the LORD: "I know that you can do all things; no purpose of yours can be thwarted.

After hearing God's blistering reply, *Job* responded. By saying *I know*, Job's answer mirrored God's previous line of questioning Job's knowledge and understanding (see Job 38:5, 18, 21, 33; 39:1, 2). Elsewhere, Job used the same sentiment to speak of his confidence in God's redemption: "I know that my redeemer lives" (19:25).

The object of Job's knowledge is the expanse of God's sovereign power and work. Job notes that *no purpose* takes place outside of the purview of God's divine wisdom. Throughout Scripture, other individuals have reflected on the extent of God's wisdom, power, and work in the world (see 2 Chronicles 20:6; Isaiah 14:27; Acts 4:30; 6:8).

HOW TO SAY IT

Abihu	Uh-*bye*-hew.
Behemoth	*Bee*-heh-moth or Beh-*hee*-moth.
Elihu	Ih-*lye*-hew.
Jehoiada	Jee-*hoy*-uh-duh.
Leviathan	Luh-*vye*-uh-thun.
Nadab	*Nay*-dab.
Sinai	*Sigh*-nye or *Sigh*-nay-eye.
theophany	the-*ah*-fuh-nee.

As a finite human, Job realized that nothing takes place beyond God's wisdom and knowledge, even the events that caused Job to experience suffering (see Job 1:13-22; 2:7-10).

II. God's Words
(JOB 42:3-4)
A. Question Restated (v. 3)

3a. "You asked, 'Who is this that obscures my plans without knowledge?'

Job restates God's accusation (see Job 38:2) and, therefore, introduces his own self-judgment (see commentary on 42:3b, below). God's original question served as an indictment against Job for speaking of things he did not understand.

Job's friend Elihu also recognized the folly of Job's words, saying, "Job speaks without knowledge; his words lack insight" (34:35) and "Job opens his mouth with empty talk; *without knowledge* he multiplies words" (35:16).

Because of God's indictment and Elihu's sharp rebuke, Job realized that the *plans* and purpose of God would not be thwarted (see Proverbs 19:21).

3b. "Surely I spoke of things I did not understand, things too wonderful for me to know.

Job admitted he spoke in ignorance. Previously, Job showed remorse for his words toward God (see Job 40:3-5). Now, after the Lord's further challenge (see 40:6–41:34), Job woefully expressed that he misspoke of *things too wonderful . . . to know.*

God had shown Job the extent of his power over creation (38:4–39:30), including the creatures Behemoth (40:15-24) and Leviathan (41:1-34). God's ways, including his justice, would not be called into question (40:8). Job now realized that God's justice and providence were too wonderful!

> *What Do You Think?*
> What are some situations in which we can do no better than to say exactly what Job says here?
> *Digging Deeper*
> What consequences could be in store for failure to do so?

The Lord surpasses
understanding.
-John 3:8

Visual for Lesson 13. *Point to this visual as an introduction to the discussion questions associated with verse 3.*

B. Request Replayed (v. 4)

4. "You said, 'Listen now, and I will speak; I will question you, and you shall answer me.'

God's previous imperatives to Job are repeated (see Job 38:3; 40:7). Job was to *listen* as God would *speak* to and demand an *answer* of Job. Initially, Job declined to respond to the demands of God. However, Job's repetition of these imperatives signals Job's coming confession, repentance, and new perspective.

III. God's Presence
(JOB 42:5-6)
A. Vision of God (v. 5)

5. "My ears had heard of you but now my eyes have seen you.

One's faith in God grows by encountering him, often in peculiar ways. Whether in times of hardship or celebration, hearing the message and seeing the work of God can bolster our faith (see Acts 4:13-20; Romans 10:17).

Job's description of his experience with God can be understood as a theophany, a specific appearance or manifestation of God to humanity. Such instances are temporary and often accompanied by great physical indication, such as a fire, cloud, or earthquake.

When Moses asked to see the glory of the Lord, God replied, "You cannot see my face, for no one may see me and live" (Exodus 33:20; com-

pare 19:20-21; Judges 6:22-23; 13:20-22). However, others testified to seeing what seemed to be a direct appearance of God in human form. Jacob stated that he "saw God face to face" (Genesis 32:30). Moses, Aaron, Nadab, Abihu, and the elders of Israel "saw the God of Israel" (Exodus 24:10). Additionally, Moses conversed directly with God: "The Lord would speak to Moses face to face, as one speaks to a friend" (33:11).

Scripture describes other instances of God's disclosure to humanity. The Lord appeared to Abraham to confirm the promise of offspring (Genesis 12:7). Moses experienced the direct voice of God in the desert in the form of a fire in the midst of a bush (Exodus 3:2-4) and on Mt. Sinai in the midst of thunder, lightning, and smoke (19:18; 24:15-18). God appeared to King Solomon in a dream (1 Kings 3:5). The prophet Elijah heard the voice of God after intense winds, an earthquake, and fire (19:11-13). These disclosures of God provided confidence of God's work in the lives of his people.

How might Job have *heard* and *seen* the Lord and his deeds? As a "blameless and upright" man who "feared God and "shunned evil" (Job 1:1), Job might have attended religious ceremonies or heard the teachings of God from elders. In his holiness, Job longed to see God with his own eyes (19:26-27). Now Job's longing came to fruition as he heard directly from the voice of God.

❧ CONVERSATION IS A TWO-WAY STREET ❧

I'm not sure how your conversations with God sound, but mine tend to be one-sided. Either I'm rambling about something menial or I'm venting about some perceived injustice. Sometimes my frustration grows when it seems like I'm not "hearing" from him.

Recently, I committed time to be silent and listen to God. There would be no distractions or no ramblings; I would sit in silence. During this time, I heard God's voice! He spoke to me, quietly and lovingly. In my excitement, I asked why it had taken so long to hear from him. He asked why it had taken so long for me to listen. Of course, this experience did not overrule Scripture itself as the primary voice from God. Rather, I used Scripture as the means of measuring and interpreting this experience.

In our conversations with God, we sometimes get in our own way. We miss hearing his voice because we're not giving space to listen. It's called a conversation because it involves two speakers; otherwise, it's just a monologue. When God convicted me of this, I committed to listening better to him.

If you think God isn't speaking, are you really listening? What distractions do you need to quiet so you can hear? Sometimes all it takes to hear is to look up (see Psalm 19:1-4). —K. D.

B. Vision of Self (v. 6)

6a. "Therefore I despise myself

Job's vision of God was both overwhelming and humbling. The Hebrew word translated *despise* is used elsewhere to speak of God's judgment (Jeremiah 6:30) and an individual's rejection of the word of the Lord (1 Samuel 15:23). Though a sense of rejection is implied in this word, the underlying Hebrew text is unclear as to what Job rejects.

As the personal pronoun *myself* is not explicit in the Hebrew text, an assumption must made as to the object of Job's despisement. The first possibility is that Job despises his improper and accusatory words directed to God. These were words that he "spoke" but "did not understand" (Job 42:3b, see commentary above).

The second possibility proposes a verbal construction with the verb "repent" (see Job 42:6b, next). In this construction, both verbs refer to the same object: himself. Both possibilities are consistent with the text and the nature of Job. Upon hearing the pointed words of God, Job rejected his previous thoughts, actions, and words.

6b. "and repent

Both modern and Hebrew usage of the word *repent* indicates the notion of feeling remorse and contrition (see Jeremiah 31:19). It is important to note that Job is not repenting as his friends had prescribed (see Job 34:33); he was not repenting for any unknown wrongdoing that was supposed to have prompted his suffering and misfortune. Instead, Job repented of and grieved over the ways he had misconstrued and misrepresented the just and all-powerful God.

6c. "in dust and ashes."

There is a play on words to describe the location of Job's act of remorse and contrition. Sitting in or covering one's self with *ashes* was a common occurrence for situations of lament and sorrow (see 2 Samuel 13:19; Esther 4:1, 3; Job 2:8; Jeremiah 6:26).

Additionally, the mention of *dust* alludes to the creation of humans and the tenuous nature of life (see Genesis 2:7; 3:14; Job 10:9). Job may very well have been lamenting *in* dust and ashes. However, he may also have been describing his human status before God as, eventually, he would return to dust and ashes (compare Job 30:19).

Abraham echoed a similar sentiment. Upon hearing of the Lord's impending destruction of the city of Sodom, Abraham advocated to the Lord for the city on behalf of the righteous (Genesis 18:23-25). In doing so, Abraham acknowledged his human finitude, saying that he was "nothing but dust and ashes" (18:27). When confronted with the plans of the all-powerful God of the universe, Abraham and Job recognized their finitude.

> **What Do You Think?**
> Instead of using dust and ashes, what physical acts or substances best accompany repentance today? Why?
>
> *Digging Deeper*
> What Scripture texts guide your response?

IV. God's Blessings
(Job 42:10-17)
A. Job Restored (v. 10)

10. After Job had prayed for his friends, the LORD restored his fortunes and gave him twice as much as he had before.

Before God restored *Job*, he addressed Job's *friends* (see lesson 12) and ordered them to sacrifice burnt offerings (see Job 42:7-9, not in today's text). Job's friends followed God's directives, after which Job *prayed for* them. The Lord then began the process of restoring Job.

Older English translations of this passage state that the *Lord* "turned the captivity" of Job. This idea alludes to Scripture texts where a captive people returned to their homeland and experienced a new, restored life (see Jeremiah 30:3, 18). In a similar manner, in his time of suffering, Job experienced a form of captivity. However, God freed Job from this captivity and blessed him with *twice as much as he had before.*

❧ SOMETHING BETTER ❧

Pam had a job she completely loved. She found the work fulfilling and enjoyed working with supportive and trustworthy people. The job presented challenges but was better than any other job she held. However, that bliss was short-lived; the day after her work anniversary, Pam was abruptly fired.

She felt utterly blindsided! She called me in tears, questioning how this could have happened. She couldn't make sense of why God would take away this job. I was unable to provide an answer, but I reminded her that God was still in control.

Over time, Pam learned to release her anger and confusion. She learned to find joy and fulfillment outside her job. Eventually, a new employment opportunity arrived with another company. Soon Pam came to love her new workplace just as much as the previous one.

Pam's abrupt firing still doesn't make sense, but I know God is in control during confusing and maddening situations. When these situations occur, you can believe that he will continue to work in your life. Will you let him?   —K. D.

B. Job Rewarded (vv. 11-17)

11a. All his brothers and sisters and everyone who had known him before came and ate with him in his house. They comforted and consoled him over all the trouble the LORD had brought on him,

The Lord's blessing (Job 42:10) is given further detail, this time through the renewed and restored relationships of Job. Previously, Job lamented that *his brothers and sisters* had been "alienated" from him, and *everyone who had known him before* was "estranged" (19:13; compare 19:19). Those closest to Job had turned against him, believing that Job had sinned greatly against God. But in light of Job's vindication and reward, they returned

and *ate with him in his house* to signify a renewed fellowship.

11b. and each one gave him a piece of silver and a gold ring.

Their gifts of *silver* and *gold* could have been seen as an act of honor and respect toward a restored Job. Additionally, these gifts could have been the means through which God chose to restore Job's economic fortunes.

> *What Do You Think?*
> What guardrails can you erect to keep yourself from being a fair-weather friend?
> *Digging Deeper*
> Which of the following passages speak to you most directly in this regard: Proverbs 14:20; 17:17; 18:24; 19:4, 6; 25:20? Why?

12. The LORD blessed the latter part of Job's life more than the former part. He had fourteen thousand sheep, six thousand camels, a thousand yoke of oxen and a thousand donkeys.

The Lord doubled the amount of livestock owned by Job (see Job 1:3). God's act highlights the generous nature of his grace and blessing (see Genesis 12:3; Exodus 34:6-7; Titus 2:11; 2 Peter 1:3).

13. And he also had seven sons and three daughters.

Notably, the number of Job's children remains the same (compare Job 1:2). One cannot help but wonder why Job's estate doubled in size but not the number of his children. It would seem that a natural explanation is best; it would be reasonable to assume that Job and his wife needed time to have 10 more children.

One temptation in reading this part of the story might be to inadvertently think that Job's *seven sons and three daughters* replaced Job's killed children (Job 1:18-19). Certainly Job and his wife continued to live with the scars of their tremendous loss. The addition of a child can never replace the loss of another.

14-15. The first daughter he named Jemimah, the second Keziah and the third Keren-Happuch. Nowhere in all the land were there found women as beautiful as Job's daughters,

and their father granted them an inheritance along with their brothers.

Much has been made over the fact that the names of *Job's daughters* are explicitly given. It is not uncommon in ancient epics, however, for heroic or successful women to be named and granted a place of prominence.

That the daughters and *their brothers* received an *inheritance* might provide evidence for why the text of Job is thought to be one of the oldest in the Old Testament. Old Testament law stipulated that daughters only received an inheritance if their father had no son (see Numbers 27:5-8).

One might conjecture that Job's generous act of providing an inheritance for both his daughters and sons makes sense in a historical context apart from Israel's law. Perhaps Job's life predated the priestly law, thus placing his narrative within the time of the patriarchs—Abraham, Isaac, and Jacob. However, that conjecture may not be accurate, and Job's generosity toward his daughters could simply be a demonstration of gratitude toward God for his act of blessing.

> *What Do You Think?*
> What is one countercultural thing you can do this week that honors the Lord?
> *Digging Deeper*
> What countercultural things have you seen Christians do that dishonored the Lord?

16-17. After this, Job lived a hundred and forty years; he saw his children and their children to the fourth generation. And so Job died, an old man and full of years.

Some debate exists as to whether *Job* died at the age of one *hundred and forty years* or lived for another 140 years. Regardless, his long life further illustrates his commitment to righteousness (compare Psalm 91:16). Job's epitaph parallels Abraham's (Genesis 25:8), Isaac's (35:28-29), David's (1 Chronicles 29:28), and Jehoiada's (2 Chronicles 24:15-16). As Job's narrative ends, the words of Moses resonate as an appropriate description of Job's life: "Walk in obedience to all that the Lord your God has commanded you, so that you may live and prosper and prolong your days in the land

that you will possess" (Deuteronomy 5:33). Job lived in righteous obedience to God's commands, and God blessed him as he lived in the land.

Conclusion

A. Give Us an Explanation!

It's highly unlikely that any of us have had 10 children die and have lost all possessions, etc., as Job did. Even so, our reactions during challenging circumstances often mirror Job's. He lamented in unknowing, and allowed the intensity of his emotions to govern his speech toward God. After Job experienced God's presence and pointed line of questioning, Job realized his insignificance and the baseless nature of his questioning of God. Job had questioned his just God, only to realize he spoke out of turn. Job learned firsthand that God's purpose or plan may not be evident to human eyes, but God remains just in the midst of it all.

Often, when faced with unexplainable and challenging circumstances, we want answers and explanations for the reason for our suffering. So we ask *why* relentlessly, implying that answers will satisfy the longing of our souls as they explain the unexplainable. But a greater salve for our wounded souls is an overwhelming vision of God, in which his eternal presence and wise counsel become the anchor for our lives and guide us to whatever he might have next for us.

> *What Do You Think?*
> What aspect of today's text do you see most difficult as addressing modern problems or applying to life today?
> *Digging Deeper*
> How will you go about resolving this difficulty?

B. Prayer

God of infinite wisdom, remind us that we do not see as you see. Give us confidence to trust that you are just and worthy of full obedience. In Jesus' name. Amen.

C. Thought to Remember

Instead of asking *why*, ask, "What's next?"

INVOLVEMENT LEARNING

Enhance your lesson with NIV® Bible Student (from your curriculum supplier) and the reproducible activity page (at www.standardlesson.com or in the back of the NIV® Standard Lesson Commentary Deluxe Edition).

Into the Lesson

Give each participant a blank index card on which to write the name of a favorite novel or movie. Collect and redistribute the anonymous cards, making sure no one receives his or her own card back. Have each participant guess the writer of the card held. The writer should then tell why he or she liked the ending of the book or movie chosen.

Alternative. Distribute copies of Image 1 of the "New Perspective" exercise on the activity page, which you can download. Have participants guess what it depicts (*answer*: grain of sand). Then distribute copies of Image 2 and let participants know that the subject matter is the same thing. Finally, distribute copies of Image 3 and pose the following two questions to the whole group. (Do not state both questions together; allow responses to the first question before posing the second.)

1–Why did the grain of sand seem so big and important in Image 1?
2–When did it become clear that you were looking at mere sand?

Invite participants to give other examples of things (or experiences) that become clearer as one "zooms out" or see the bigger picture.

After either alternative, say, "Today's lesson describes one man's experience of gaining greater perspective about God's work in his life. Let's take a look."

Into the Word

Ask a volunteer to read Job 42:1-6. Then play some randomly recorded sounds, each one just a few seconds long. (Some possibilities are popcorn popping, children laughing, water running, and/or birds chirping.) Invite participants to guess what the sounds are. After correct responses, press for more details, particularly details that cannot be known by sound alone. (For instance, you could ask for the ages and number of children

laughing, since these cannot be determined accurately by sound alone.) As participants make their guesses, display pictures (you provide) that correlate with each sound as you play them again.

Then ask the group to distinguish between the values gained by hearing vs. seeing. Jot responses on the board as you guide participants in connecting the discussion with Job 42:5. (*Option.* For deeper study on hearing and seeing, compare and contrast Job 42:5 with Job 13:1; Matthew 13:13-17; John 20:29; 1 John 1:1-3.)

After a volunteer reads Job 42:10-17, have participants compare the new riches Job received with what he lost in Job 1:3. Challenge participants to consider other ways Job was blessed, beyond what is specifically listed. (*Possible responses:* restored relationships with neighbors, wife, and friends; stronger faith and love for the Lord.) List all on the board as mentioned. Make a transition to the Into Life segment by asking participants to review the list on the board and choose one blessing that stands out as something especially valuable. Offer the chance to share why as time allows.

Into Life

Share a personal story about going through a difficult trial and learning to trust God in the midst of it. Then ask for volunteers to share with the class a personal experience they had that was difficult, and how they have seen God's mercy and redemption through it.

Alternative: Distribute the "A Sincere Prayer" exercise from the activity page for learners to complete in study pairs.

Distribute handouts (you prepare) headed "A Letter to God." Invite leaners to write a letter to God in the week ahead regarding a perceived injustice. Caution them not to question God's justice, but rather to seek guidance to help correct the injustice. Encourage them to be prepared to share a brief reflection of this experience next time.

GOD FREES AND
REDEEMS

Special Features

Lessons
Unit 1: Liberating Passover

Unit 2: Liberating Gospels

Unit 3: Liberating Letters

QUARTERLY QUIZ

Use these questions as a pretest or as a review. The answers are on page iv of This Quarter in the Word.

Lesson 1

1. The Lord "moved the heart" of Cyrus, king of _____. *Ezra 1:1*

2. To rebuild the "house of the Lord," Cyrus permitted some Jews to return to what city? (Bethlehem, Hebron, Jerusalem?) *Ezra 1:5*

Lesson 2

1. The temple's gold and silver vessels were stolen and brought to Babylon by whom? (Darius, Nebuchadnezzar, Xerxes?) *Ezra 6:5*

2. Israel's priests were to offer prayers for the king and his sons. T/F. *Ezra 6:9-10*

Lesson 3

1. The exiles rebuilt following the decrees of Kings Cyrus, Darius, and _____. *Ezra 6:14*

2. After exile, the elders of the Jews slaughtered the Passover lamb. T/F. *Ezra 6:20*

Lesson 4

1. How many years in the wilderness did God lead his people? (4, 14, 40?) *Deuteronomy 8:2*

2. The fathers of the Israelites previously knew of manna. T/F. *Deuteronomy 8:3*

Lesson 5

1. The crowd that went before Jesus shouted, "Hosanna to the Son of _____." *Matthew 21:9*

2. Crowds called Jesus a "teacher" from Nazareth. T/F. *Matthew 21:11*

Lesson 6

1. During the meal, Jesus said one of the Twelve would _____ him. *Matthew 26:21*

2. Before going to the Mount of Olives, Jesus and the disciples sang a hymn. T/F. *Matthew 26:30*

Lesson 7

1. Who rolled away the stone that sealed Jesus' tomb? (a disciple, an angel, a guard?) *Matthew 28:2*

2. The women at the empty tomb experienced fear and _____. *Matthew 28:8*

Lesson 8

1. Jesus taught that knowing (truth, justice, peace?) would set people free. *John 8:32*

2. Jesus' audience claimed they had never been in bondage to anyone. T/F. *John 8:33*

Lesson 9

1. Baptism into Christ Jesus is baptism into his death. T/F. *Romans 6:3*

2. Followers of Jesus are to offer themselves to God as instruments of _____. *Romans 6:13*

Lesson 10

1. Present sufferings are not worth comparing to the glory to "be _____ in us." *Romans 8:18*

2. God's predestination leads to being conformed to the image of his Son. T/F. *Romans 8:29*

Lesson 11

1. Why did Paul say the law was added? (transgressions, punishments, services?) *Galatians 3:19*

2. Paul compared the law to a guardian. T/F. *Galatians 3:25*

Lesson 12

1. Paul taught that people who tried to be "justified by the law" have fallen away from grace. T/F. *Galatians 5:4*

2. The law is _____ by showing love to one's neighbor. *Galatians 5:14*

Lesson 13

1. People under the Spirit's leading are not "under the _____." (flesh/Spirit/law?) *Galatians 5:18*

2. Love, joy, and peace are considered among what? (fruit of the Spirit, works of merit, fruit of the flesh?) *Galatians 5:22*

QUARTER AT A GLANCE

by Mark Hamilton

How can humans live freely? The concept of freedom can have different meanings for different people. For some people, freedom means unchecked following of a person's impulses and desires. In this regard, there is no concern for how so-called freedom affects others. Undisciplined living destroys freedom rather than enhancing it. This quarter's Scriptures address three themes of true freedom in God: the power of memory, the significance of right belief, and the role of responsibility.

Memory and Freedom

As ancient Israel remembered their liberation from Egypt, the memory reinforced the nature of their relationship with God. Centuries after they left captivity, they remembered God's act of liberation. Three lessons from the Old Testament book of Ezra describe how they rebuilt the temple and experienced liberation. As a result of their freedom, they were filled with joy and celebration, an acknowledgment of God's faithfulness to his people.

However, in the midst of their freedom, Israel was called to submit. The Law of Moses reminded them of the great blessings they would receive if they obeyed God's call on their lives (Deuteronomy 8:1-11). This obedience was rooted in their memory of God's liberation in their history. As they remembered and followed God's commands, they would experience true freedom. All God's people must remember their story as a people called out of bondage and into a new life.

Right Belief and Freedom

Christian freedom requires right belief and faithful action. When either is lacking, freedom is defined by made-up rules or self-indulgent expressions. This quarter's lessons from Jesus' triumphal entry into Jerusalem (Matthew 21:1-11) and his Passover feast with his disciples (26:17-30) show how the world had certain expectations of freedom. However, as Jesus followed his Father's direction, he brought a new kind of freedom, one established in his resurrection (28:1-10).

Jesus triumphed over the bondage of death and sin. As a result, his Father frees all who follow him. His disciples knew this, as Jesus had already called them to "know the truth" (John 8:32). As disciples follow Jesus, they can be "free indeed" (8:36). Those who follow Jesus' life, death, and resurrection gain freedom. True freedom comes through right belief in the work of Jesus Christ.

Responsible Freedom

Finally, true freedom is not null of responsibility. Instead, because of Christ's resurrection, Christians are to live freely and responsibly through submission. This comes as we imitate his life and are "clothed . . . with Christ" (Galatians 3:27). Through baptism, Christians join him in death so that they may join him in a new life, freed from the power of sin (Romans 6:3-4).

> *Proper expression of freedom is rooted in ethical concern for others.*

As a result, Christians are called to use their freedom in Christ to show love toward their neighbors (Galatians 5:14). Proper expression of freedom is rooted in ethical concern for others. To empower this, God gave the Holy Spirit to his followers. Through the Spirit, Christians live free and responsible lives, expressing the fullness of the Spirit in their actions (5:16-25).

This quarter's lessons will show that true freedom comes through the sustained acceptance of God's leading in our lives. When the people of God remember his work, they experience true freedom. Through this quarter, may we be reminded that God invites us to live freely and responsibly for him and for our community.

· 227 ·

GET THE SETTING

by Mark S. Krause

OPPRESSION FOLLOWED BY freedom followed by oppression. The history of Israel stretched for two millennia and followed a similar cycle, with seasons of oppression and freedom. Through this context, the nation of Israel understood God's liberation.

Oppression in the Old Testament Era

God's call sent Abraham and his family of nomadic herdspeople from Mesopotamia, located in modern-day Iraq, to the land of Canaan, located in modern-day Palestine. Famine eventually led Abraham's descendants to relocate to Egypt. After the famine, Abraham's descendants stayed in Egypt but retained a separate identity. Egypt's pharaohs exploited their separatism and subjugated the people. The cycle of oppression began, and the people experienced brutal slavery as they were exploited for royal construction projects.

Through Moses' leadership, God delivered the people from bondage. This act serves as the grand narrative of the Old Testament. However, oppression continued. Against the guidance of God (see 1 Samuel 8:11-18), the emergence of a Jewish king provided some freedom. King David dealt with localized threats and brought peace to the people. However, the peace Israel desired was short-lived. Invasions from the Assyrians (734–721 BC) and from the Babylonians (586–539 BC) brought oppression to Israel again.

Oppression in the Intertestamental Era

The intertestamental era consists of the roughly 400 years between the events of the Old and New Testaments. During that time, Israel continued to experience oppression and limited freedom. In 331 BC, the Greek King Alexander the Great (reigned 336–323 BC) took control of the Jewish land and people. However, his rule tolerated expressions of relative autonomy among the Jewish people.

At Alexander's death, his kingdom was divided into smaller kingdoms. Israel's central geographic location was advantageous for the kingdoms. As a result, Israel experienced turmoil and strife as rival kingdoms sought to control the area. Eventually, the Seleucids came to power. The tensions between the Seleucids and Jews came to a head when Seleucid ruler Antiochus IV (reigned 175–164 BC) looted Jerusalem, desecrated the temple, and killed thousands of Jews.

As a result, the Jews responded in what is known today as the Maccabean Revolt. The Jews took control of the Jerusalem temple area in 164 BC. The revolt eventually freed Jews from oppression. After a series of smaller conflicts, Seleucid rule was removed from Israel in 142 BC. Israel was free and a period of peace was established. For 79 years they lived free from oppression. However, that changed in 63 BC when the Roman general Pompey invaded Jerusalem, entered the temple, and ended nearly a century of Jewish independence. The cycle of oppression continued.

Oppression in the New Testament Era

Roman oppression was a defining reality for the writers and the audiences of the New Testament. As Jerusalem was located far from Rome, the Romans established local rulers—"client kings"—to oversee the will of the empire among Jews. Through Herod the Great (ruled 37–34 BC) and his successors, Roman rule was expressed to the Jews.

Tensions between Jews and Romans simmered for a time, but came to a head in a series of conflicts between the Jews and the Romans that spanned 70 years (AD 66–136). The conflict culminated in the annihilation of Jewish influence in the region. Oppression had led to eviction, and by the second century, Jews were banished from Jerusalem.

The story of Israel is one of a constant cycle of oppression and freedom. Against this context, Scripture declares God's freedom and liberation.

THIS QUARTER IN THE WORD

Mon, Feb. 28	Prepare the Way of the Lord	Isaiah 40:1-11
Tue, Mar. 1	Being God's Instrument	Isaiah 45:1-10
Wed, Mar. 2	God Will Provide for Every Need	Philippians 4:10-19
Thu, Mar. 3	Lift Up Your Eyes to God	Isaiah 40:12-15, 21-31
Fri, Mar. 4	Live Freely but Responsibly	1 Peter 2:13-17
Sat, Mar. 5	Light Dawns for the Righteous	Psalm 97
Sun, Mar. 6	Cyrus Permits Jews to Return Home	Ezra 1:1-8, 11; 2:64-70
Mon, Mar. 7	Rebuilding the Temple and Praising God	Ezra 3:8-13
Tue, Mar. 8	Jews Discouraged from Rebuilding	Ezra 4:1-5
Wed, Mar. 9	Worship at the Heavenly Throne	Revelation 5
Thu, Mar. 10	Bowing in Praise	Psalm 138
Fri, Mar. 11	The Time to Rebuild Has Come	Haggai 1
Sat, Mar. 12	The Temple's Foundation Laid	Haggai 2:1-9, 15-19
Sun, Mar. 13	God Provides Through King Darius	Ezra 6:1-12
Mon, Mar. 14	Keep Holy Convocations	Leviticus 23:4-8
Tue, Mar. 15	God Institutes the Passover	Exodus 12:1-14
Wed, Mar. 16	Instructions for the Passover	Exodus 12:21-28, 50-51
Thu, Mar. 17	Praise the Name of the Lord	Psalm 113
Fri, Mar. 18	Christ Our Passover	1 Corinthians 5:7-8; 10:1-4
Sat, Mar. 19	Praise for God's Liberation	Psalm 114
Sun, Mar. 20	Returned Exiles Keep the Passover	Ezra 6:13-22

Mon, May 16	Children and Heirs Through God	Galatians 4:1-7
Tue, May 17	Losing All for Christ	Philippians 3:1-8a (end with "my Lord")
Wed, May 18	Press Toward the Goal	Philippians 3:8b-14 (begin with "For whose sake")
Thu, May 19	Let Us Love One Another	1 John 4:7-13
Fri, May 20	Love and Pray for Your Enemies	Matthew 5:43-48
Sat, May 21	Avoid Strife; Love Always	Proverbs 17:13-17
Sun, May 22	Faith Working Through Love	Galatians 5:1-15
Mon, May 23	The Righteous Yield Fruit	Psalm 1
Tue, May 24	Abide in Christ and Bear Fruit	John 15:1-8
Wed, May 25	Wisdom's Harvest of Righteousness	James 3:13-18
Thu, May 26	The Spirit Produces a Fruitful Field	Isaiah 32:9-20
Fri, May 27	Known by Their Fruits	Matthew 7:15-20
Sat, May 28	God's Presence Brings Fruitfulness	Ezekiel 47:1-7, 12
Sun, May 29	Live by the Spirit	Galatians 5:16-26

Answers to the Quarterly Quiz on page 226

Lesson 1—1. Persia. 2. Jerusalem. **Lesson 2**—1. Nebuchadnezzar. 2. true. **Lesson 3**—1. Artaxerxes. 2. false. **Lesson 4**—1. 40. 2. false. **Lesson 5**—1. David. 2. false. **Lesson 6**—1. betray. 2. true. **Lesson 7**—1. an angel. 2. joy. **Lesson 8**—1. truth. 2. true. **Lesson 9**—1. true. 2. righteousness. **Lesson 10**—1. revealed. 2. true. **Lesson 11**—1. transgressions. 2. true. **Lesson 12**—1. true. 2. fulfilled. **Lesson 13**—1. law. 2. fruit of the Spirit.

ii

Mon, Mar. 21	Remember God's Blessings	Deuteronomy 8:12-20
Tue, Mar. 22	Hear and Act	James 1:19-27
Wed, Mar. 23	Show Humility and Resist the Adversary	1 Peter 5:5-9
Thu, Mar. 24	Bless the Lord, O My Soul	Psalm 103:1-10
Fri, Mar. 25	God's Love Is Everlasting	Psalm 103:11-22
Sat, Mar. 26	Remember Christ and Endure	2 Timothy 2:8-13
Sun, Mar. 27	Keep the Lord's Commandments	Deuteronomy 8:1-11
Mon, Mar. 28	Help Comes from the Lord	Psalm 121
Tue, Mar. 29	The First Will Be Last	Matthew 20:1-16
Wed, Mar. 30	The Greatest Must Be a Servant	Matthew 20:17-28
Thu, Mar. 31	Faithful Appear Before God	Exodus 34:23-27
Fri, Apr. 1	Jesus Weeps over Jerusalem	Luke 19:41-44
Sat, Apr. 2	Trust in the Lord	Psalm 125
Sun, Apr. 3	Hosanna to the Son of David!	Matthew 21:1-11
Mon, Apr. 4	God Is Gracious and Righteous	Psalm 116:1-15
Tue, Apr. 5	Celebrate Where God Chooses	Deuteronomy 16:1-8, 15-17
Wed, Apr. 6	Jesus Anointed	Matthew 26:1-2, 6-16
Thu, Apr. 7	Do This in Remembrance	1 Corinthians 11:23-26
Fri, Apr. 8	Disciples Love One Another	John 13:31-35
Sat, Apr. 9	God's Care Endures Forever	Psalm 118:1-9
Sun, Apr. 10	Jesus Shares Passover	Matthew 26:17-30
Mon, Apr. 11	John Proclaims the Lamb of God	John 1:29-36
Tue, Apr. 12	Jesus Prays in Gethsemane	Matthew 26:36-46
Wed, Apr. 13	Jesus Is Arrested	Matthew 26:47-56
Thu, Apr. 14	Jesus Is Crucified	Matthew 27:35-43, 45-50
Fri, Apr. 15	Why Have You Forsaken Me?	Psalm 22:1-9, 14-19
Sat, Apr. 16	God Is My Salvation	Psalm 118:14-17, 19-29
Sun, Apr. 17	Jesus Is Risen!	Matthew 28:1-10

iii

Mon, Apr. 18	Remember You Were Slaves	Deuteronomy 15:12-15
Tue, Apr. 19	Children of the Promise	Galatians 4:21-31
Wed, Apr. 20	Anointed to Proclaim Good News	Isaiah 61:1-3
Thu, Apr. 21	The Light of the World	John 8:12-20
Fri, Apr. 22	Jesus Is from Above	John 8:21-30
Sat, Apr. 23	I Delight in Your Commands	Psalm 119:41-56
Sun, Apr. 24	Jesus Brings True Freedom	John 8:31-38
Mon, Apr. 25	Out of the Depths I Cry	Psalm 130
Tue, Apr. 26	Go and Sin No More	John 7:53–8:11
Wed, Apr. 27	Righteousness Disclosed in Christ	Romans 3:19-31
Thu, Apr. 28	The Justified Have Peace with God	Romans 5:1-11
Fri, Apr. 29	God's Free Gift Brings Life	Romans 5:12-21
Sat, Apr. 30	Seek the Lord and Find Joy	Isaiah 55:6-13
Sun, May 1	Baptized into Christ's Death	Romans 6:1-14
Mon, May 2	No Longer Slaves of Sin	Romans 6:15-23
Tue, May 3	God Bestows the Spirit	Ezekiel 36:25-30
Wed, May 4	We Have Died to the Law	Romans 7:1-13
Thu, May 5	A Struggle to Obey	Romans 7:14-25
Fri, May 6	No Condemnation for Heirs	Romans 8:1-4, 10-17
Sat, May 7	Receive the Holy Spirit	John 20:19-23
Sun, May 8	All Things Work Together for Good	Romans 8:18-30
Mon, May 9	Receiving the Spirit Through Faith	Galatians 3:1-5
Tue, May 10	The Blessing Comes Through Christ	Galatians 3:6-17
Wed, May 11	God's Power Grants Life and Godliness	2 Peter 1:2-4
Thu, May 12	Betrothed in Faithfulness	Hosea 2:16-23
Fri, May 13	A Wise and Faithful Builder	Luke 6:45-49
Sat, May 14	Walk Blameless Before God	Genesis 17:1-8
Sun, May 15	No Longer Subject to the Law	Galatians 3:18-29

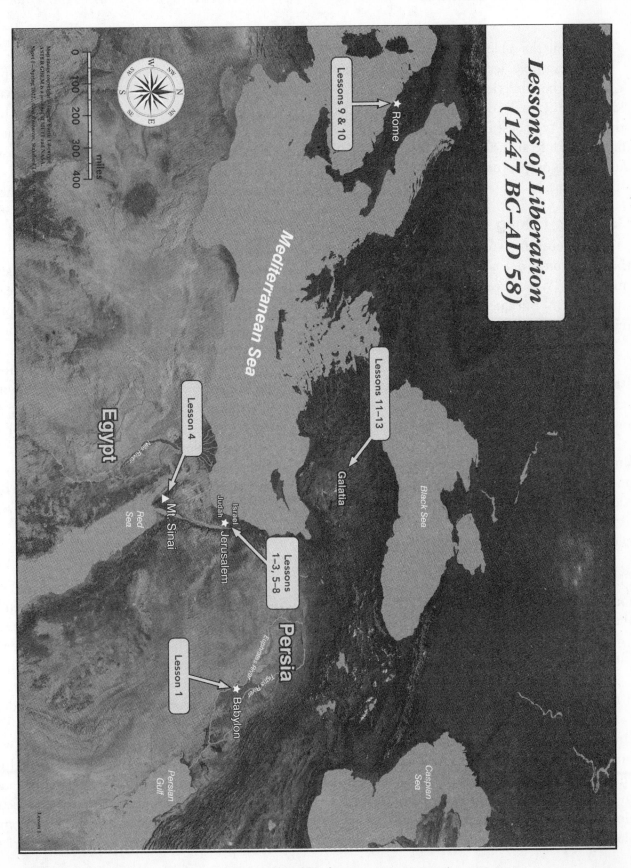

Lessons of Liberation
(1447 BC–AD 58)

Lessons 9 & 10 → ★ Rome

Lessons 11–13 → Galatia

Lesson 4 → ▲ Mt. Sinai

Egypt

Mediterranean Sea

Israel
Judah
★ Jerusalem ← Lessons 1–3, 5–8

Red Sea

Nile River

Persia

Euphrates River
Tigris River

Lesson 1 → ★ Babylon

Black Sea

Caspian Sea

Persian Gulf

N NE NW W E S SE SW

0 100 200 300 400
miles

TEACHING IS MORE THAN TALKING

Part 3: Let Them Talk Too   *Teacher Tips by Mark A. Taylor*

Studying the Bible is more than learning facts. For example, learners may need to wrestle with the subtleties of the biblical text to consider how they will respond to its demands. For adults, this type of learning can happen through dialogue. Here are a few ways to encourage discussion and deepen understanding in your Bible study groups.

Get Them Talking

There's nothing wrong with asking questions that have only one answer. For example, you might ask, "What three points does Paul make in this chapter?" But questions like this do not promote discussion—they may stifle it!

A better practice is to ask open-ended questions. For example, you might ask, "Which of Paul's points has the most relevance for today's readers?" By asking open-ended questions, you invite deeper reflection of your learners.

Ask an open-ended question and set a time limit of two minutes. Ask the class to shout out answers as you write their answers on the board. Don't rephrase or correct the answers; write them as they are stated. After the time limit, ask the class to choose the best answers.

Divide the whole class into three small groups. Have the groups discuss questions before you ask for their answers. This will get all learners, not just the most vocal ones, thinking and talking.

Give Them Time

Ask a question and be willing to say nothing afterwards. Some learners are internal processors and won't answer until they've had adequate time to think. If no one answers after 60 seconds, restate the question using different words. In some cases, silence can provoke a quiet learner to answer. However, never answer your own question. If you're willing to answer your own questions, the class will let you!

Keep It Going

When learners ask a question, do not answer it—at least not at first. Other learners may be willing to answer and discuss the question. Imagine class discussion as learners tossing a ball between themselves. The most fruitful discussions occur when learners toss the ball back and forth between each other, rather than catching the ball—answering a question—that comes from you.

Keep Control

If a learner says something that doesn't seem to relate to the conversation at hand, ask the learner to explain the statement further. Their explanation may help you and the group make a connection between their comment and the conversation.

If a learner asks a question that's off subject, compliment them for their contribution, then say, "This isn't really what we're talking about now, but it's important." If the whole discussion gets off track, apologize, don't criticize, and politely return conversation to the main topic. If conversation seems out of control, say, "Let's take a break for five minutes. When we return, we'll move forward with the lesson."

Show the Progress.

As the study proceeds, remind learners of what the class has discussed up to that point, then lead the class to the next topic. The goals of Bible study are twofold: First, learners should conclude what the Scripture text meant for original audiences and what it means for modern audiences. Second, in light of that knowledge, learners should decide how they will act in response.

As the teacher, before class begins, know where you want to take learners. To be successful in this regard requires thorough preparation, sometimes more than what is required to plan a lecture. Invest in your class, and your learners will come to love and know God better through the experience.

FREED FROM CAPTIVITY

DEVOTIONAL READING: Ezra 1:1-18, 11; 2:64-70
BACKGROUND SCRIPTURE: Ezra 1; 2:64-70

EZRA 1:1-8, 11

¹ In the first year of Cyrus king of Persia, in order to fulfill the word of the LORD spoken by Jeremiah, the LORD moved the heart of Cyrus king of Persia to make a proclamation throughout his realm and also to put it in writing:

² "This is what Cyrus king of Persia says:
"'The LORD, the God of heaven, has given me all the kingdoms of the earth and he has appointed me to build a temple for him at Jerusalem in Judah. ³ Any of his people among you may go up to Jerusalem in Judah and build the temple of the LORD, the God of Israel, the God who is in Jerusalem, and may their God be with them. ⁴ And in any locality where survivors may now be living, the people are to provide them with silver and gold, with goods and livestock, and with freewill offerings for the temple of God in Jerusalem.'"

⁵ Then the family heads of Judah and Benjamin, and the priests and Levites—everyone whose heart God had moved—prepared to go up and build the house of the LORD in Jerusalem. ⁶ All their neighbors assisted them with articles of silver and gold, with goods and livestock, and with valuable gifts, in addition to all the freewill offerings.

⁷ Moreover, King Cyrus brought out the articles belonging to the temple of the LORD, which Nebuchadnezzar had carried away from Jerusalem and had placed in the temple of his god. ⁸ Cyrus king of Persia had them brought by Mithredath the treasurer, who counted them out to Sheshbazzar the prince of Judah.

. . . .

¹¹ In all, there were 5,400 articles of gold and of silver. Sheshbazzar brought all these along with the exiles when they came up from Babylon to Jerusalem.

EZRA 2:64-70

⁶⁴ The whole company numbered 42,360, ⁶⁵ besides their 7,337 male and female slaves; and they also had 200 male and female singers. ⁶⁶ They had 736 horses, 245 mules, ⁶⁷ 435 camels and 6,720 donkeys.

⁶⁸ When they arrived at the house of the LORD in Jerusalem, some of the heads of the families gave freewill offerings toward the rebuilding of the house of God on its site. ⁶⁹ According to their ability they gave to the treasury for this work 61,000 darics of gold, 5,000 minas of silver and 100 priestly garments.

⁷⁰ The priests, the Levites, the musicians, the gatekeepers and the temple servants settled in their own towns, along with some of the other people, and the rest of the Israelites settled in their towns.

KEY TEXT

When they arrived at the house of the Lord in Jerusalem, some of the heads of the families gave freewill offerings toward the rebuilding of the house of God on its site. —**Ezra 2:68**

GOD FREES AND REDEEMS

Unit 1: Liberating Passover

LESSONS 1–4

LESSON AIMS

After participating in this lesson, each learner will be able to:

1. Recount the who, what, when, where, why, and how of Cyrus's proclamation and its result.

2. Explain the significance of King Cyrus's proclamation.

3. Write a prayer of thanks for release from a personal "captivity."

LESSON OUTLINE

Introduction

A. Rebuilding a Home

Tornadoes ripping through rural Oklahoma communities. Fires engulfing whole buildings and homes in the Pacific Northwest. Storm surges flooding homes in the gulf coast of Louisiana. Behind these tragic events are the stories of whole communities that lost everything. When losses include family photos, treasured heirlooms, or even favorite toys, these disasters can hurt deeply and such losses might be irreplaceable! However, out of the ruins, memories remain and can provide a foundation for beginning the rebuilding.

The first chapters of Ezra tell the story of a grand reconstruction project for Israel. Older Israelites had vivid memories of their preexilic life (Ezra 3:12); however, memories alone would not complete the reconstruction project. Israel needed help from an unlikely source. Their memories, combined with unlikely assistance, set Israel on the path of following God's requirement as they resettled their homeland.

B. Lesson Context

The text of Ezra tells the story of the Jewish people during the sixth and fifth centuries BC. In 586 BC, the Babylonian Empire, led by King Nebuchadnezzar, laid siege to Judah and destroyed Jerusalem (2 Kings 24:10-14; 25:1-10; 2 Chronicles 36:17; Jeremiah 52:4-5, 12-16). The siege's culmination was the destruction of the Jewish temple and the removal of its treasures (2 Kings 24:13; 2 Chronicles 36:18-19; Jeremiah 52:13). The removal of the treasures and the people of Judah was prophesied by Isaiah (2 Kings 20:16-17). The Babylonians carried the people of Judah —with the exception of the poorest individuals— into captivity (24:14; 2 Chronicles 36:20; compare Deuteronomy 28:36).

However, Babylon's rule was short-lived. In 539 BC, the Persian King Cyrus destroyed the Babylonian Empire. He solidified the Persian Empire's dominance in a region that extended from modern-day Greece to modern-day India.

Cyrus demonstrated tolerance of the religious practices of his subjects. A notable decree in this regard was written on a clay cylinder and is known as the Cyrus Cylinder. This decree detailed Cyrus's conquest of Babylon and the favor he sought from Marduk, the patron god of Babylon. The decree culminated with the command to repatriate exiled peoples and rebuild their houses of worship. Isaiah prophesied that Cyrus, commissioned by the Lord, would provide an opportunity for the Jewish exiles to return to their homeland (Isaiah 44:28).

Cyrus's decree fulfilled a promise made earlier by the prophet Jeremiah (Jeremiah 29:10, 14). However, the prophecy's fulfillment did not necessitate the return of all exiles, only a "remnant" (Isaiah 10:22).

I. Persian Decree
(Ezra 1:1-4)
A. The Author (v. 1)

1a. In the first year of Cyrus king of Persia, in order to fulfill the word of the Lord spoken by Jeremiah,

That the decree was announced *in the first year* of the reign *of Cyrus king of Persia* indicates the year 538 BC. As the author of 2 Chronicles indicated, the results of Cyrus's actions were foretold *by Jeremiah* (2 Chronicles 36:22; see Lesson Context).

1b. the Lord moved the heart of Cyrus king of Persia to make a proclamation throughout his realm and also to put it in writing:

While the *proclamation* came from *Cyrus*, it was only because *the Lord* anointed Cyrus as a tool for his will (see Isaiah 45:1, 13). Cyrus was just one of many rulers throughout history whom God *moved* and used to work out his divine plan (2 Chronicles 36:22; see 1 Chronicles 5:26; 2 Chronicles 21:16; Jeremiah 51:11).

> *What Do You Think?*
> How do you recognize the Lord's call to action?
> *Digging Deeper*
> What questions will you ask to test that you are hearing from the Lord? How might Romans 12:2 and 1 John 4:1 support your answer?

In 1944 the Soviet government accused the Tatars, an ethnic minority located around the Black Sea in a region known as Crimea, of traitorous actions against the government. The Soviets ordered that the Tatars be removed from their homes and sent to distant regions of Asia. With little warning thousands of Tatars were detained and sent away from their homeland.

The surviving Tatars told their descendants about their homeland of Crimea. Generations of Tatars developed a love for a homeland they never experienced. After the fall of the Soviet Union, the exiled Tatars slowly returned to Crimea. Their longing for home had been fulfilled.

Followers of Jesus experience a similar longing for home as they await the day when the kingdom of God will be fully realized over all creation. Are you ready to settle yourself in the kingdom that is "not of this world" (John 18:36)? While you may be a foreigner in this world (1 Peter 2:11), remember your true citizenship (see Philippians 3:20)!
—L. M.-W.

B. The Proclamation (vv. 2-4)

2. "This is what Cyrus king of Persia says:
"'The Lord, the God of heaven, has given me all the kingdoms of the earth and he has appointed me to build a temple for him at Jerusalem in Judah.

While *Cyrus* recognized the role of *the Lord* in ordaining his leadership (see 2 Chronicles 36:23), Cyrus's decree was also politically motivated. He wanted to honor the many gods of the people of his empire. Ultimately, the exiles' good fortune

HOW TO SAY IT

Babylon	*Bab*-uh-lun.
Babylonian	Bab-ih-*low*-nee-un.
Cyrus	*Sigh*-russ.
Diaspora	Dee-*as*-puh-ruh.
Marduk	*Mar*-duke.
Mithredath	*Mith*-re-dath.
Nebuchadnezzar	*Neb*-yuh-kud-**nez**-er.
Nippur	Nih-*poor*.
Sheshbazzar	Shesh-*baz*-ar.

did not come from a human ruler, but from the gracious God who oversaw the political movements of *all the kingdoms of the earth* (see 2 Kings 19:15; Isaiah 37:16).

The title *God of heaven* is a distinctive of the text of Ezra, where 9 of its 22 Old Testament occurrences are found (here and Ezra 5:11, 12; 6:9, 10; 7:12, 21, 23 [twice]). The title combined with the phrase *has given me* recognized God's sovereignty as the creator of both the heavens and the earth. While God is all-powerful as creator, he is active in his creation (see Genesis 24:7; Nehemiah 1:4-5; 2:20; Daniel 2:19).

Cyrus proclaimed new building plans, as Cyrus himself would help the exiles build God's *temple*. That the temple would be rebuilt *at Jerusalem in Judah* reflects certain importance. Ancient Israel had illegitimate worship sites at other locations (1 Kings 12:28-33; Amos 4:4). However, because of God's declaration and King David's leadership, Jerusalem became the political and religious center for Israel (2 Samuel 5:6-9; 6:1-17; 1 Kings 11:36; 2 Chronicles 6:6; 7:12; see Psalm 78:67-72).

3. "Any of his people among you may go up to Jerusalem in Judah and build the temple of the LORD, the God of Israel, the God who is in Jerusalem, and may their God be with them

The decree did more than provide orders for the exiled *people*. It oriented their perspective of *God*. God had not abandoned them, but his presence was *with them* as they rebuilt the temple.

That God was *in Jerusalem* did not imply that the presence of God was limited to this city alone (1 Kings 8:27; Isaiah 66:1; compare Acts 17:24). Instead, it indicated that God was present to his people in a special way in Jerusalem, especially in his *temple* (Deuteronomy 12:5; 14:23).

4. "And in any locality where survivors may now be living, the people are to provide them with silver and gold, with goods and livestock, and with freewill offerings for the temple of God in Jerusalem."'

Two major interpretations exist as to the identity of the *survivors* who *may now be living* and *the people*. One interpretation describes these people as non-Jewish individuals living in Persia. The other interpretation recognized them as Jews who

decided against returning to Jerusalem. That these individuals were asked *to provide* for the returning exiles reinforces the second interpretation.

Recent archaeological discoveries also support the second interpretation. Clay cuneiform tablets from the fifth century BC describe business dealings of a non-Persian family in the city of Nippur. Some of the family names were Hebrew in origin, leading scholars to believe that many Jews stayed in Persia and continued their already established livelihood. The Jews who stayed behind were known as the Diaspora. This title is an English transliteration of a Greek noun meaning "scattering" (see Isaiah 11:12; James 1:1).

The gifts included *silver* and *gold*, important resources for the economy and the establishment of the place of worship (compare Ezra 2:69; 6:5; 8:26-27). *Goods* implied necessary resources for community building. And the *livestock* were necessary as flocks and herds. *Freewill offerings* were an additional gift for the people of God (see Leviticus 22:23; 23:38; Deuteronomy 12:6). The offerings provided for proper worship at *the temple of God in Jerusalem* (Ezra 7:16-17).

> *What Do You Think?*
> What are some ways Christians might live as exiles in the world?
> *Digging Deeper*
> How, if at all, would this reality shape your interactions with your neighbors and coworkers?

II. Preparation for Travels
(EZRA 1:5-8, 11)
A. Assembling Leaders (v. 5)

5. Then the family heads of Judah and Benjamin, and the priests and Levites—everyone whose heart God had moved—prepared to go up and build the house of the LORD in Jerusalem.

In this patriarchal culture, the *heads* of the tribes consisted of the fathers of the *family*. Therefore, tribal decisions were made by the tribal chief. Tribal leadership was intact, even in the midst of exile. The specification of *Judah* and *Benjamin* is notable because these tribes made up the southern kingdom of Judah (1 Kings 12:17, 21-24; 2 Chronicles 11:1) and were the specific tribes taken into exile by the Babylonians (2 Kings 24:2).

Levites were members of the tribe of Levi. They were tasked with overseeing Israel's worship, holy places, and holy objects (Numbers 1:47-53; 3:6-16; Deuteronomy 10:8; 1 Chronicles 15:2). The author of Ezra often listed Levites alongside *the priests* and lay people to clarify the scope of all the exiles (see Ezra 3:8, 12; 6:16; 8:29; 9:1; 10:5).

While Cyrus issued the decree to rebuild the temple, it was ultimately God's plan that those *whose heart God had moved* would return to *build the house of the Lord* (compare Psalm 127:1). That the text mentions *Jerusalem* seven times in these early verses indicates the importance of that city (Ezra 1:2, 3 [twice], 4, 5, 7, 11). That city, not others, would be a location of importance for the exiles.

B. Accepting Resources (vv. 6-8, 11)

6. All their neighbors assisted them with articles of silver and gold, with goods and livestock, and with valuable gifts, in addition to all the freewill offerings.

Cyrus's previous commands came to fruition (see commentary on Ezra 1:4, above). A similar example of unselfish support occurred when people gave generously and willingly *assisted* with the construction of the temple (1 Chronicles 29:9).

7. Moreover, King Cyrus brought out the articles belonging to the temple of the LORD, which Nebuchadnezzar had carried away from Jerusalem and had placed in the temple of his god.

After he conquered Babylon, *King Cyrus* took control of the royal treasury. The treasury contained *the articles belonging to the temple of the Lord* from the campaign of *Nebuchadnezzar* against *Jerusalem* (2 Kings 24:13; 25:13-15; 2 Chronicles 36:10, 18; Jeremiah 52:17-20). Apparently, Cyrus had not melted down the articles into valuable bullion. Instead, the articles were kept and placed *in the temple of his god*, perhaps at the temple of Marduk (see Lesson Context).

Ancient texts describe other instances when

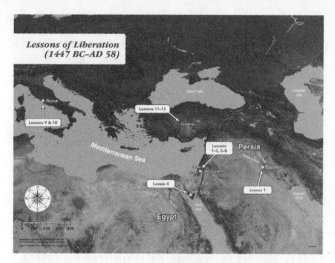

Visual for Lesson 1. *Keep this map posted throughout the quarter to give participants a geographic perspective.*

Cyrus returned sacred artifacts to sacred cities. By concerning himself with the sacred artifacts of his subjects, Cyrus acted as a pious king who honored all gods of his empire. However, his actions did not necessitate a particular attachment to those gods, including the God of Israel.

8. Cyrus king of Persia had them brought by Mithredath the treasurer, who counted them out to Sheshbazzar the prince of Judah.

Cyrus needed *Mithredath the treasurer* to release the artifacts from the treasury. Ezra mentions another individual by the same name (Ezra 4:7). It's unclear whether these are the same person, since several years have passed between the two events.

In a report to King Darius, *Sheshbazzar* was described as the "governor" (Ezra 5:14). His only mention in Scripture is found in the book of Ezra (1:8, 11; 5:14, 16).

11. In all, there were 5,400 articles of gold and of silver. Sheshbazzar brought all these along with the exiles when they came up from Babylon to Jerusalem.

The *articles . . . brought* from the treasury consisted of utensils and resources made *of gold and of silver* (see Ezra 1:9-10, not in this lesson's printed Scripture text). The book of Ezra shows interest in numbers that detail the return to Judah (see 2:2-61, 64-67, 69, 6:17; 7:21-22; 8:1-14, 26-27, 35). These numbers reflect a desire to tell precisely the story of Israel's return.

Like many ancient temples, Israel's temple served as the treasury in which royalty and priests stored valuable materials. That *there were 5,400 vessels* describes the relative wealth to be housed in the rebuilt temple. Temples were considered to be safe because ancient peoples believed theft would offend the temple's divine occupants.

III. People Returning
(Ezra 2:64-70)
A. Their Composition (vv. 64-67)
64. The whole company numbered 42,360,

The second chapter of Ezra begins by listing the family groups of exiles that returned to Judah and Jerusalem (Ezra 2:1-62). A close inspection of those lists determines that they do not add up to the *company numbered 42,360* (compare Nehemiah 7:66).

Perhaps some family units were left off the list (compare Ezra 2:59; Nehemiah 7:8-62) or the list included men of a certain age (compare Numbers 1:19-46).

The list highlighted three observations about the returning people: (1) the exiles formed a family of the people of God, (2) the exiles preserved family relationships during the exile, and (3) the exiles returned to their homeland in sufficient numbers to rebuild.

> *What Do You Think?*
> How can you build relational unity with other believers, especially where unity may be lacking? Does Paul's appeal in 1 Corinthians 1:10-17 affect your answer in this regard?
> *Digging Deeper*
> Under what circumstances should you avoid working for unity? Why?

65. besides their 7,337 male and female slaves; and they also had 200 male and female singers.

The included *male and female slaves* might refer to indebted Israelites (Leviticus 25:39-40) or to foreigners (Exodus 12:44; Deuteronomy 20:14). The prophet Isaiah called on Israel to accept foreigners (Gentiles) who loved God, kept the Sab-

bath, and adhered to God's covenant stipulations (Isaiah 56:3, 6-8).

> *What Do You Think?*
> How might you serve neighbors who have worldviews different from yours?
> *Digging Deeper*
> How does love and hospitality inform your answer (see Hebrews 13:1-2)?

❧ *A Socially Distant Melody* ❧

The soft melody of a flute, accompanied by the bright timbre of an oboe, wafted through the streets of Rio de Janeiro, Brazil. The husband-and-wife duo of Simon and Sofia sat on their balcony and serenaded neighbors with pleasant melodies. Their musical performance united the neighborhood.

Neighbors playing music for their neighborhood is not uncommon, but the practice took a new meaning for Simon and Sofia. Stay-at-home orders for the COVID-19 pandemic had been established, and people around the world found themselves confined to their homes. Amid the fear and anxiety, talented (and even not-so-talented) musicians used their skills to bless their now homebound neighbors.

The singers who returned to Jerusalem were invaluable. Their talent reminded the exiles of the beauty and enjoyment of God's creation. What talents has God given you to build his kingdom? Are you following the psalmist by worshipping the Lord with gladness (see Psalm 100:1-2)?

—L. M.-W.

66-67. They had 736 horses, 245 mules, 435 camels and 6,720 donkeys.

The *horses, . . . mules, . . . camels and . . . donkeys* the exiles needed for their return was surely a reminder of their ancestors' exodus from Egypt (Exodus 3:21-22). As those Israelites left Egypt, they requisitioned the necessary wealth (11:2; 12:35) and livestock (12:38) for the journey. The exodus defined Israel and its relationship with God (see Deuteronomy 5:6; compare Nehemiah 9:9-15, 24-25). God repeated history for Israel's benefit, providing the exiles with sufficient resources for their return home.

B. Their Offerings (vv. 68-70)

68. When they arrived at the house of the LORD in Jerusalem, some of the heads of the families gave freewill offerings toward the rebuilding of the house of God on its site.

Although the temple had not been rebuilt, its ruins were likely accessible and its altar would be rebuilt (Ezra 3:2). *The heads of the families* took on the responsibility to encourage their household to give toward the reconstruction. That the people *gave freewill offerings* was reminiscent of giving for the construction of the tabernacle (see Exodus 35:5).

69. According to their ability they gave to the treasury for this work 61,000 darics of gold, 5,000 minas of silver and 100 priestly garments.

The *gold* and *silver* formed an endowment for the *work* of reconstructing the temple and for the work of the priests. The elaborate *priestly garments* were made of gold, fine linen, and precious stones (Exodus 39:1-31). Because of the garments' value, they were counted as part of the temple treasury. The book of Nehemiah describes the same event, but gives further detail on the families' contributions (Nehemiah 7:70-72).

> *What Do You Think?*
> What are one or two ways you can ensure a generous heart when giving?
> *Digging Deeper*
> How do Matthew 6:1-4 and 2 Corinthians 9:7 shape your answer?

70. The priests, the Levites, the musicians, the gatekeepers and the temple servants settled in their own towns, along with some of the other people, and the rest of the Israelites settled in their towns.

The repatriation efforts would not occur at one time but would take time as *some of the other people* began to settle throughout the *towns* of Israel. The leaders of Israel's religious practice would stay near the soon-to-be rebuilt temple, but the others would begin to build a new life in the land.

The temple servants were individuals who had given their lives to work in the temple in a non-priestly capacity (see 1 Chronicles 9:2; Ezra 8:20). Their specific roles are unclear.

Conclusion

A. Rebuilding for the Future

After a 2019 fire destroyed parts of the cathedral of Notre-Dame, an international competition redesigned the building's destroyed rooftop and spiral. Architects had to keep in mind a variety of concerns: rebuilding costs, the cathedral's history, and the relationship between the cathedral and the city.

Similar concerns are present in the narrative surrounding the return of Jewish exiles to their homeland. This week's lesson speaks of the exiles' history, their promised return, their relationships, and even their economic needs. While their return could have been disastrous, God provided direction through a decree of Persia's King Cyrus.

Modern readers of Ezra may face major rebuilding efforts. These may be physical buildings, like a house, business, or church. However, the rebuilding effort may be less tangible, like relationships. These rebuilding projects invite the participants to envision a new reality, something wholly different from what was before. In those moments, we have to be available for God's provision and work.

B. Prayer

God, we have seen our dreams shattered and our relationships lost. Restore us and give us courage to rebuild in your name so that we can celebrate your grace. In Jesus' name. Amen.

C. Thought to Remember

Rebuilding requires courage and envisioning a new reality.

VISUALS FOR THESE LESSONS

The visual pictured in each lesson (example: page 237) is a small reproduction of a large, full-color poster included in the *Adult Resources* packet for the Spring Quarter. That packet also contains the very useful *Presentation Tools* CD for teacher use. Order No. 3629122 from your supplier.

INVOLVEMENT LEARNING

Enhance your lesson with NIV Bible Student *(from your curriculum supplier) and the reproducible activity page (at www.standardlesson.com or in the back of the* NIV Standard Lesson Commentary Deluxe Edition*).*

Into the Lesson

Divide the class into four groups to design a dream home for a hypothetical couple in their mid-30s who have three pre-teenage children. The designs can include floor plan sketches, ideal appliances, storage ideas, etc. After several minutes, have groups share their designs. With the help of the whole class, award the following superlatives: Most Expensive, Most Creative, Most Attractive, and Most Frugal.

Alternative. Distribute copies of the "Famous Projects" exercise from the activity page, which you can download. Have learners work individually or in pairs to complete as indicated in less than one minute.

After either activity, lead into Bible study by saying, "Today's lesson from the Old Testament repeats itself in the New Testament in certain ways. See if you can remember passages as we go."

Into the Word

Ask a volunteer to read Ezra 1:1-4. Then divide the class into four groups: **"Who?" Group / "What?" Group / "Where?" Group / "Why?" Group**. Ask each group to write down three questions that start with their group name that can be answered from these verses. (Example: The "Who?" Group might ask, "*Who* prompted Cyrus that the Jerusalem temple should be rebuilt?")

After no more than 10 minutes, have each group pass its list to another group. Each group is to write the answer to one of the questions on the paper it receives. Repeat this process until all four papers include three answers each.

Ask a volunteer to read Ezra 1:5-8, 11. With the help of the whole class, make a list of the materials described in these verses. Ask a volunteer to read 1 Kings 6:7, 14-36 and make a list of materials that were used in the construction of the first temple, then lead the class in comparing and contrasting the lists.

Follow the compare and contrast by discussing implications.

Alternative. Extend the discussion by focusing on spiritual elements as you distribute copies of Parts A and B of the "Construction Proposal" exercise from the activity page. Depending on the size and nature of your group, the questions can be discussed in small groups or as a whole class.

Follow by asking a volunteer to read Ezra 2:64-70. Divide the class into four groups: **People Group** (vv. 64-65) / **Livestock Group** (vv. 66-67) / **Riches Group** (vv. 68-69) / **Specialists Group** (v. 70). Have each group make a list of the people or resources described in their verse(s) and identify in ensuing whole-class discussion the purpose(s) fulfilled by each.

Alternative. If you used Parts A and B of the "Construction Proposal" exercise above, distribute Part C now. As above, the questions can be discussed in small groups or as a whole class, depending on the size of your group. **Important**: be sure to come prepared with answers of your own. Your preparations should include a readiness to give an example if learners seem stumped as well as additional responses to those of the learners.

Into Life

Return to your earlier statement that today's lesson repeats itself in the New Testament in certain ways. Ask if anyone has a passage in mind in that respect (*example*: Luke 14:28 in a physical sense). Then distribute handouts (you prepare) that feature the following questions, all questions on every handout.

1–From what bondage have you been freed that you might do God's will more fully?
2–What caused that bondage in the first place?
3–How will you keep from reentering that bondage?

Due to the personal nature of these questions, you may wish to distribute these as a take-home.

Free to Worship

Devotional Reading: Ezra 6:1-12
Background Scripture: Ezra 5; 6:1-12; 10:1-5

Ezra 6:1-12

1 King Darius then issued an order, and they searched in the archives stored in the treasury at Babylon. 2 A scroll was found in the citadel of Ecbatana in the province of Media, and this was written on it:

Memorandum:

3 In the first year of King Cyrus, the king issued a decree concerning the temple of God in Jerusalem:

Let the temple be rebuilt as a place to present sacrifices, and let its foundations be laid. It is to be sixty cubits high and sixty cubits wide, 4 with three courses of large stones and one of timbers. The costs are to be paid by the royal treasury. 5 Also, the gold and silver articles of the house of God, which Nebuchadnezzar took from the temple in Jerusalem and brought to Babylon, are to be returned to their places in the temple in Jerusalem; they are to be deposited in the house of God.

6 Now then, Tattenai, governor of Trans-Euphrates, and Shethar-Bozenai and you other officials of that province, stay away from there. 7 Do not interfere with the work on this temple of God. Let the governor of the Jews and the Jewish elders rebuild this house of God on its site.

8 Moreover, I hereby decree what you are to do for these elders of the Jews in the construction of this house of God:

Their expenses are to be fully paid out of the royal treasury, from the revenues of Trans-Euphrates, so that the work will not stop. 9 Whatever is needed—young bulls, rams, male lambs for burnt offerings to the God of heaven, and wheat, salt, wine and olive oil, as requested by the priests in Jerusalem—must be given them daily without fail, 10 so that they may offer sacrifices pleasing to the God of heaven and pray for the well-being of the king and his sons.

11 Furthermore, I decree that if anyone defies this edict, a beam is to be pulled from their house and they are to be impaled on it. And for this crime their house is to be made a pile of rubble. 12 May God, who has caused his Name to dwell there, overthrow any king or people who lifts a hand to change this decree or to destroy this temple in Jerusalem.

I Darius have decreed it. Let it be carried out with diligence.

KEY TEXT

May God, who has caused his Name to dwell there, overthrow any king or people who lifts a hand to change this decree or to destroy this temple in Jerusalem. —**Ezra 6:12a**

GOD FREES AND REDEEMS

Unit 1: Liberating Passover
LESSONS 1–4

LESSON AIMS

After participating in this lesson, each learner will be able to:

1. List the main points of the decree.

2. Compare and contrast the decree of Darius with that of Cyrus (last week's lesson).

3. Commit to praying for opportunities to practice faithfulness in the tasks that God has assigned.

LESSON OUTLINE

Introduction

A. Worcester v. Georgia

Samuel Worcester (1798–1859) was aware that it was against Georgia state law for a white person to live among the Cherokee Indians. But in 1825 he and his wife did so anyway because his mission work required it; he was translating Scripture into the Cherokee language. Additionally, he advocated for the sovereignty of the Cherokee Nation.

At the same time, the state of Georgia prohibited non-Cherokees from being present or doing business on native lands without the state's approval. Worcester did not have the state's approval to live and work on the Cherokee lands. For this violation, Worcester was found guilty by the state. An appeal was heard before the US Supreme Court. *Worcester v. Georgia* ruled in favor of the Cherokee Nation. The ruling stated that Georgia's laws interfered with the federal government's authority. Therefore, the state had no force over the Cherokee Nation. While not always honored by the US government, *Worcester v. Georgia* allowed the Cherokee Nation to self-rule.

The once exiled residents of Judah and Jerusalem tried to exert their sovereignty in their homeland as they reconstructed the temple. However, certain forces delayed and prevented the construction. Instead of giving up on construction or acting violently against their opposition, the resettled Jews found support for their construction efforts from a surprising place.

B. Lesson Context

This lesson contains the text of a decree of Persian King Darius I (reigned 522–486 BC). He came to power after several years of internal strife. Darius strengthened the Persian government, established a new method of taxation, and further organized the empire. The decree continued a policy established by Cyrus (reigned 539–530 BC). His policy allowed for the return of Jewish exiles to Jerusalem and the reconstruction of the Jewish temple (Ezra 1:2-5, last week's lesson).

Under the leadership of Zerubbabel, the exiles

returned to Jerusalem and Judah (Ezra 2:1-2; see Zechariah 4:9). Two years after the exiles returned, reconstruction began on the temple in Jerusalem, in 535 BC (Ezra 3:8-9). However, the reconstruction was delayed several times by local opposition and regional authorities (4:1-5, 24).

Today's Scripture text comes as a response to questioning from Persian officials Tattenai and Shethar-Bozenai. After seeing the efforts at reconstruction, they questioned Zerubbabel and the local leaders concerning whose authority granted them rebuilding rights (Ezra 5:3, 9). The builders noted that their authority came from God and Cyrus. A letter was sent to Darius to inquire on the nature and authority of Cyrus's decree (5:5-17). Today's lesson concerns Cyrus's decree and Darius's response to the Persian officials.

While Darius was concerned with following Cyrus's decree, he also had a pragmatic reason to support the temple's reconstruction. By allowing agreeable Israelites to return to their homeland, Darius would have loyal subjects located in a geographically expedient place near Egypt, a region known for its rebellions and insurrections. Additionally, Darius would be able to institute a new tax system among the repatriated Jews in the regions of Judah, thus increasing his coffers.

Ezra 4:8–6:18 is written in the Aramaic language (unlike the Hebrew of Ezra 1; compare 4:7). Aramaic was used for business and government dealings of the Persian Empire. As our lesson text records official government documentation, the use of Aramaic is understandable.

I. The Conduct of a Search
(Ezra 6:1-2)
A. Regarding the Archives (v. 1)

1. King Darius then issued an order, and they searched in the archives stored in the treasury at Babylon.

Archaeological remains of Persian *archives* reveal detailed reports of taxes, expenditures, and local government occurrences throughout the empire. However, not all official records were stored *at Babylon*. Other cities held local and national records and treasures. Therefore, a search

for Cyrus's records would extend outside the capital (next verse).

What Do You Think?
How will you ensure thoroughness when following the tasks God has placed before you?
Digging Deeper
How might you respond differently if you were met with opposition?

B. Retrieving the Scroll (v. 2)

2. A scroll was found in the citadel of Ecbatana in the province of Media, and this was written on it: Memorandum:

The search for Cyrus's decree took investigators to *Ecbatana*, a city located about 285 miles northeast of Babylon. The city served as the summer palace for Persian royalty, so it is possible that Cyrus issued his decree there during the summer of 538 BC (see Ezra 1:1).

II. The Content of the Decree
(Ezra 6:3-12)
A. Reestablishing the Temple (vv. 3-5)

3a. In the first year of King Cyrus, the king issued a decree concerning the temple of God in Jerusalem:

The focus of Cyrus's decree expands on a directive given in previous text (see Ezra 1:2-4). *King Cyrus* had given permission for the Jewish exiles to return to their homeland. Now the text elaborates on a key detail of their return: the reconstruction of *the temple of God in Jerusalem*.

3b. Let the temple be rebuilt as a place to present sacrifices, and let its foundations be laid. It is to be sixty cubits high and sixty cubits wide,

Prior to Darius's decree, the altar, the *place to present sacrifices*, had been reconstructed (Ezra 3:2-3). Now *the temple* would *be rebuilt* to provide a space for worship . The temple's height and width were to be *sixty cubits*, or approximately 90 feet each way. (A cubit equals about 18 inches.) These dimensions differ from those of Solomon's temple. That temple had a length of 60 cubits, a width of 20 cubits, and a height of 30 cubits (1 Kings 6:2).

The decree did not include the temple's length. One might assume that its length would match its height and width. If this assumption is correct, then the building would form a perfect cube. This shape would echo the dimensions of the Most Holy Place of Solomon's temple (1 Kings 6:20).

4a. with three courses of large stones and one of timbers.

Archaeological discoveries in modern-day Syria have shown that the use of *timbers* after several rows of *large stones* helped buildings survive earthquakes. This practice was utilized in the construction of the inner courtyard of Solomon's temple (1 Kings 6:36) and the courtyard of Solomon's palace (7:12). Both mention the use of cedar wood, but Cyrus's decree does not elaborate in that regard.

4b. The costs are to be paid by the royal treasury.

Those remaining in exile contributed to the temple's reconstruction (Ezra 1:4, 6). But in an act of goodwill, the decree placed part of the financial burden on *the royal treasury*. These funds came to the treasury via new taxation practices (see 6:8, below).

5. Also, the gold and silver articles of the house of God, which Nebuchadnezzar took from the temple in Jerusalem and brought to Babylon, are to be returned to their places in the temple in Jerusalem; they are to be deposited in the house of God.

The centrality of the sacred *articles*, their removal from *the house of God*, and their eventual return to the temple is again made evident by Cyrus's repetition (compare Ezra 1:7-11). These articles were made by Solomon and were used at *the temple* for worship (see 1 Kings 7:48-51). However, *Nebuchadnezzar* confiscated them and took them to *Babylon* following the destruction of Judah and *Jerusalem* (2 Kings 25:13-17; 2 Chronicles 36:18).

These articles had been used in unholy ways during the exile (see Daniel 5:1-4). Therefore, they would need to be reconsecrated before they were *returned* and *deposited* into the temple. The restorative act required sacred anointing oil (see Exodus 30:22-29; 40:9). The presence of these items in the newly restored temple represented the restoration of Israelite life as the holy people of God.

> *What Do You Think?*
> How can Christians show the new life and restoration found in Christ Jesus?
> *Digging Deeper*
> How can Isaiah 58:1-14 and Luke 4:14-21 inform your answer?

B. Restraining Local Leadership (vv. 6-7)

6. Now then, Tattenai, governor of Trans-Euphrates, and Shethar-Bozenai and you other officials of that province, stay away from there.

What follows are the direct words of Darius to his officials, *Tattenai* and *Shethar-Bozenai* (see Lesson Context). The Trans-Euphrates refers to the area west of the Euphrates River and east of the Mediterranean Sea. This area was a satrapy, or province, of the Persian Empire, of which Tattenai was *governor* (see Ezra 5:3).

The identity and role of the *other officials of that province* is unclear. The underlying Aramaic text gives little insight to their identity. They were either an ethnic group from Samaria, the region north of Judah, or Persian officials who accompanied the governor of the satrapy. Perhaps the same officials are mentioned elsewhere in the text (see Ezra 4:9).

> *What Do You Think?*
> How can Christians make sure they are not hindering the work of God?
> *Digging Deeper*
> In what ways, if any, can God's work be hindered? How does Genesis 37:12-36 and 50:15-20 inform your answer?

7. Do not interfere with the work on this temple of God. Let the governor of the Jews and the Jewish elders rebuild this house of God on its site.

Zerubbabel served as *the governor of the Jews* who had returned from exile (see Ezra 5:2). The governor coordinated local affairs with the Persian authorities. Another group of localized leadership consisted of *the Jewish elders.* These were leaders who handled local affairs like family disputes or village conflicts (see Deuteronomy 21:1-9; 25:7-10).

This division allowed the leaders to respond to the internal challenges of the community and maintain good relationships with the Persians. Additionally, it allowed the Persians to maintain control over the satrapy without overt concern in all local matters.

> **What Do You Think?**
> How might the government use its authority for the good of the governed?
> *Digging Deeper*
> How do Luke 3:14 and Romans 13:3-4 shape your answer in this regard?

C. Releasing the Royal Treasury (vv. 8-10)

8. Moreover, I hereby decree what you are to do for these elders of the Jews in the construction of this house of God: Their expenses are to be fully paid out of the royal treasury, from the revenues of Trans-Euphrates, so that the work will not stop.

Darius's *decree* concerned the financial burden of rebuilding the *house of God.* The Persians provided space for its reconstruction. They also provided a financial backing, following Cyrus's precedent (see commentary on Ezra 6:4, above).

Specifically, Darius committed to funding part of the temple's construction *expenses* from taxes and *revenues* from the *Trans-Euphrates* satrapy. This action reflects a larger policy to restore and provide for local temples and cults in the empire. Darius's financial generosity highlighted his desire to honor the temple, whether or not he believed in the temple's God.

❧ *EFFECTIVE INCENTIVES* ❧

On the morning of January 17, 1994, the heavily trafficked Santa Monica Freeway lay in ruins. That morning an earthquake had rocked Los Angeles and the surrounding region. A portion of the freeway, known for its heavy traffic, was no longer passable. As a result, traffic delays and congestion increased throughout Los Angeles.

Because the freeway was crucial for the livelihood of the region, local officials offered a financial incentive for the freeway's rapid reconstruction. As a result, the project was completed two months ahead of schedule. The financial backing encouraged workers to rebuild rapidly. Without a restored freeway, the livelihood of Los Angeles was at stake.

As unexpected as that financial backing was, the backing by Darius was all the more so. A pagan king who offered to help subsidize Israel's temple! Through what unexpected measures has God provided for you to do his work? How can you cut through opposition in order to continue toward the goal God has set for you? —L. M.-W.

9. Whatever is needed—young bulls, rams, male lambs for burnt offerings to the God of heaven, and wheat, salt, wine and olive oil, as requested by the priests in Jerusalem—must be given them daily without fail,

In addition to financial backing, Darius ordered officials to provide the necessary resources for regular sacrifices in the temple. *Young bulls, rams,* and *male lambs* were valuable livestock *for* the *burnt offerings* required of Israel (see Leviticus 1:2-13; 22:27; Numbers 7:87-88; 1 Chronicles 29:21). With these animals the returning exiles would eventually offer sacrifices (Ezra 8:35).

Flour made of *wheat* was used alongside daily sacrifices and burnt offerings (see Exodus 29:40; Leviticus 2:1-2; 5:11; 6:20; etc.). *Salt* accompanied grain offerings (2:13) and burnt offerings (Ezekiel 43:24). The preservative properties of salt served as a reminder of the preserving nature of God's covenant (Numbers 18:19; 2 Chronicles 13:5). *Oil* accompanied the sacrifices, and *wine* was presented as a drink offering (Exodus 29:40; Leviticus 23:13).

Darius's use of the title *God of heaven* acknowledged the power and scope of the exiles' God (see Ezra 1:2; 5:11-12; 6:10; 7:12, 21, 23). This God is the creator of all things and omnipotent (all-powerful) over all creation, even the Persian Empire (see Genesis 14:19; Isaiah 37:16; Daniel 2:44).

10. so that they may offer sacrifices pleasing to the God of heaven and pray for the well-being of the king and his sons.

Visual for Lessons 2 & 3. *Start a discussion by pointing to this visual as you ask, "How do God's acts of goodness surprise you?"*

Darius's motives for backing the reconstruction became evident. He desired that the returning exiles have a location where they might *offer sacrifices* rightly. Darius hoped that the *God* of the Jews would be content and would hear their prayers, specifically those for *the king and his sons.*

When Israel offered sacrifices in the way God desired, those sacrifices were considered to be a *pleasing* aroma to God (Numbers 28:24; contrast with Isaiah 1:11; Jeremiah 6:20; Hosea 8:13). Considering the rich ingredients included in these sacrifices (see commentary on Ezra 6:9, above), a pleasing aroma was likely

Leaders asking that their constituents *pray* to their gods was not inconceivable. Greek historian Herodotus (c. 484–425 BC) described how Persians would offer a prayer for the king while offering sacrifices to their pagan gods. The practice continued through the New Testament era (see 1 Timothy 2:1-2). Sometimes rulers recognized Israel's God as a supreme God (Daniel 2:47; 6:26-27). As a result, Israel fulfilled the promise that they would be a blessing to Gentiles (Genesis 12:3).

> **What Do You Think?**
> What prayer can you offer for leaders of your local, state, and national governments?
> *Digging Deeper*
> How can Jeremiah 29:7 and 1 Timothy 2:1-4 inform your prayers?

D. Risking the Curse (vv. 11-12)

11. Furthermore, I decree that if anyone defies this edict, a beam is to be pulled from their house and they are to be impaled on it. And for this crime their house is to be made a pile of rubble.

As with an ancient covenant or a royal inscription, the *decree* ended with a warning or curse for anyone who might disregard and defy the *edict* of the king. The dramatic and violent conclusion would not have shocked ancient audiences. Worshippers and leaders would have thought it appropriate that anyone not honoring the temple of a god should have *their* own *house* destroyed and turned to *rubble* (compare Jeremiah 26:1-6).

As for the form of punishment, the underlying Aramaic text is unclear whether the punishment referred to being hanged, crucified, or *impaled.* While gruesome, the act of impaling an individual as punishment would not be unprecedented for a Jewish audience (see Genesis 40:22; Joshua 8:29). However, the Law of Moses restricted the practice of impaling (Deuteronomy 21:22-23). Persian audiences would be familiar with the punishment of impalement, as Persian officials suffered a similar gruesome fate after a failed assassination attempt of the king (Esther 2:21-23). Further, Haman, a high-ranking Persian official, was impaled after he attempted to massacre Jews in Persia (5:14; 7:10).

❧ *UNHOLY INTERFERENCE* ❧

"Ouch!" My husband let out a shriek as I investigated a small blemish on his forehead. The surrounding skin was hot to the touch. He thought it was infected, but I was unsure. Maybe he was overreacting? I was skeptical that it was anything serious. I told him to take some ibuprofen. Maybe the blemish would improve in the morning.

The next morning, the blemish had not improved. In fact, his face was so swollen that his eye was almost shut. A few hours passed and the swelling only got worse. Finally, I admitted concern and took him to the emergency room. The doctors diagnosed him with a staph infection! Contrary to my skepticism, my husband had been right; the blemish was serious. I had to apologize for not taking his concerns to heart sooner.

While others expressed doubt and opposition to the rebuilding of the Jerusalem temple, Darius confirmed the project's legitimacy. When have you let doubt or opposition interfere with the work God has for you? Or might you be opposing God's work in someone else's life? If so, why?

—L. M.-W.

12. May God, who has caused his Name to dwell there, overthrow any king or people who lifts a hand to change this decree or to destroy this temple in Jerusalem. I Darius have decreed it. Let it be carried out with diligence.

Following the format of a curse, the decree's final line acknowledges the presence of *God* and the protection of all under his domain. This is the same God who promised to choose a place where he would cause *his Name to dwell* (Deuteronomy 12:11; see Exodus 20:24). This promise referred to the unique place where God met his people, the *temple in Jerusalem* (1 Kings 8:29; 9:3; 2 Chronicles 6:2).

Darius anticipated that Israel's God would protect his holy place and all within its premises. By calling a curse to *overthrow any king or people*, Darius followed an ancient Near Eastern tradition that taught that the gods would protect that which was considered precious and divine. This protection was notable for all people and items located within holy places.

While unlikely that Darius was influenced by ancient Hebrew literature, the psalmist warned against the "kings of the earth . . . and the rulers" who "band together against the Lord and against his anointed" (Psalm 2:2). The Lord would "break them" and "dash them to pieces" (2:9). Those who would go against the Lord and the his intentions

would be destroyed. Those who would stand against and defile the temple of God would suffer destruction.

While the temple of God that Darius envisioned no longer stands, God's promises to watch over his "temple" remain true (see 1 Corinthians 3:16-17).

Conclusion

A. Surprising Circumstances

The ruling of *Worcester v. Georgia* did not improve the sovereignty of the Cherokee Nation. Seven years after the decision, US President Andrew Jackson oversaw the forced removal of the Cherokees from their homelands through the Trail of Tears. Even as the U.S. Supreme Court (surprisingly) ruled in favor of the Cherokees, the sovereignty they won was short-lived.

The sovereignty the Jews gained under Cyrus and maintained under Darius was short-lived. In the centuries that followed, the Jewish people experienced many years of occupation. However, in that specific season under the reign of and support from Darius, the Jews survived and even flourished as they resettled their homeland.

Especially in difficult circumstances and trying situations, God calls his people to be faithful to his purpose for their lives. That Cyrus and Darius, two Gentile leaders, allowed for the resettlement of Jerusalem and the reconstruction of the temple showed the surprising ways God provides for his people. How has God called you to obey him? Through what unexpected circumstances is he calling you to obey?

B. Prayer

God of Heaven, you are the creator of all good things. You bring life and joy, laughter and healing, peace and plenty. You provide for your people in unimaginable ways. Surprise us! Show us how we might follow you in ways unimaginable. In Jesus' name. Amen.

C. Thought to Remember

God can work through surprising circumstances to bring restoration and renewal.

HOW TO SAY IT

Ecbatana	Ek-buh-*tahn*-uh.
Darius	Duh-*rye*-us.
Herodotus	Heh-*rod*-uh-tus.
Shethar-bozenai	*She*-thar-**boz**-nye.
Tattenai	*Tat*-nye or *Tat*-eh-nye.
omnipotent	ahm-*nih*-poh-tent.
Zerubbabel	Zeh-*rub*-uh-bul.

INVOLVEMENT LEARNING

Enhance your lesson with NIV Bible Student (from your curriculum supplier) and the reproducible activity page (at www.standardlesson.com or in the back of the NIV Standard Lesson Commentary Deluxe Edition).

Into the Lesson

Before the lesson, write three different creative projects on three different notecards (examples: "Grow an orchard," "Install a shower," "Restain an outdoor deck"). Divide the class into three equal groups. Give each group a pen, paper, and a creative project notecard. Instruct the groups to discuss the creative project and make a list of the challenges they might face if they were to complete the project. After each group completes their list, have them pass their notecard and list to another group. Instruct groups to consider the challenges listed and write a solution to each challenge. When complete, have groups return the cards and lists to the original groups for review.

Make a transition to the Bible study by saying, "It's easy to become overwhelmed when all we see are problems and obstacles in front of us. But we serve a creative God who is all-powerful and provides for his people. Today's lesson will show us one example of how God provides for his people in circumstances that seem impossible."

Into the Word

Divide the whole group into six equal groups. Assign each group one of the following sets of verses from 2 Kings to read: 24:8-13; 24:14-20; 25:1-7; 25:8-12; 25:13-17; 25:18-21. While the groups are reading, write "What Nebuchadnezzar Did" at the top left of the board. Ask each group to report on the damage that Nebuchadnezzar did as indicated in their verses. List responses on the board.

Ask a volunteer to read Ezra 6:1-7. Write "What God Did" at the top right of the board. Ask, "In what ways did God use the decree of Ezra 6 to redeem what was lost or destroyed in 2 Kings 24–25?" Invite the class to offer responses.

Before class, put together a box full of items to symbolize the resources mentioned in Darius's decree: money ("revenues"), bulls, rams, lambs, wheat, salt, wine, and oil. Provide multiples of some items to ensure that all learners will have at least one item. Ask a volunteer to read Ezra 6:8-10. Pass the box around to all learners and ask them to take an item at random until the box is empty.

Ask a volunteer to read Ezra 6:8-10 again slowly. Set aside a space (like a podium, basket, or chair) where items could be collected. Invite learners to come forward with their item(s) as they are mentioned in the verses. Say, "This represents the abundant generosity required by the decree."

Have one volunteer represent the "people of God." After all items have been brought forward, have the volunteer stand up and collect the items. Say, "This person represents the people of God who have received the abundance of gifts from God."

Alternative. Distribute copies of the "Rebuild and Redeem" exercise from the activity page, which you can download. Have learners complete the activity as indicated.

Into Life

Give each learner a notecard. Have them write on it one task they believe God is asking them to do. Then have learners write challenges that prevent them from obeying.

Read Ephesians 3:20. Ask learners to get in small groups with one or two others and share their notecards. Have group members offer encouragement in the tasks God has for the other group members. Close class by asking group members to pray for each other regarding their faithfulness in the tasks that God has given them.

Alternative. Distribute copies of the "God's Resources" exercise from the activity page. Have learners work in pairs to complete Part 1 but work independently on Part 2. Ask learners to consider sharing their responses to Part 3 at the beginning of the next lesson. Conclude class by praying for opportunities to grow in trust of God's faithfulness and promises.

FREE TO CELEBRATE

DEVOTIONAL READING: Ezra 6:13-22
BACKGROUND SCRIPTURE: Ezra 6:13-22; Leviticus 23:4-8

EZRA 6:13-22

¹³ Then, because of the decree King Darius had sent, Tattenai, governor of Trans-Euphrates, and Shethar-Bozenai and their associates carried it out with diligence. ¹⁴ So the elders of the Jews continued to build and prosper under the preaching of Haggai the prophet and Zechariah, a descendant of Iddo. They finished building the temple according to the command of the God of Israel and the decrees of Cyrus, Darius and Artaxerxes, kings of Persia. ¹⁵ The temple was completed on the third day of the month Adar, in the sixth year of the reign of King Darius.

¹⁶ Then the people of Israel—the priests, the Levites and the rest of the exiles—celebrated the dedication of the house of God with joy. ¹⁷ For the dedication of this house of God they offered a hundred bulls, two hundred rams, four hundred male lambs and, as a sin offering for all Israel, twelve male goats, one for each of the tribes of Israel. ¹⁸ And they installed the priests in their divisions and the Levites in their groups for the service of God at Jerusalem, according to what is written in the Book of Moses.

¹⁹ On the fourteenth day of the first month, the exiles celebrated the Passover. ²⁰ The priests and Levites had purified themselves and were all ceremonially clean. The Levites slaughtered the Passover lamb for all the exiles, for their relatives the priests and for themselves. ²¹ So the Israelites who had returned from the exile ate it, together with all who had separated themselves from the unclean practices of their Gentile neighbors in order to seek the LORD, the God of Israel. ²² For seven days they celebrated with joy the Festival of Unleavened Bread, because the LORD had filled them with joy by changing the attitude of the king of Assyria so that he assisted them in the work on the house of God, the God of Israel.

KEY TEXT

The people of Israel—the priests, the Levites and the rest of the exiles—celebrated the dedication of the house of God with joy. —**Ezra 6:16**

Photo © Getty Images

GOD FREES AND REDEEMS

Unit 1: Liberating Passover

LESSONS 1–4

LESSON AIMS

After participating in this lesson, each learner will be able to:

1. State the emotion that characterized the celebrations of Passover and Unleavened Bread.

2. Compare and contrast the dedication of the second temple with that of the first (1 Kings 8:62-66).

3. Suggest and help plan a church-wide celebration to commemorate an occasion of God's provision and faithfulness.

LESSON OUTLINE

Introduction
    A. The Challenge of Joy
    B. Lesson Context
I. Obedient Dedication (Ezra 6:13-18)
    A. Leaders and Associates (v. 13)
    B. Elders and Prophets (vv. 14-15)
    Exceptional Examples
    C. Priests and Exiles (vv. 16-18)
    Dedication and Celebration!
II. Celebratory Fellowship (Ezra 6:19-22)
    A. Passover (vv. 19-21)
    B. Unleavened Bread (v. 22)
Conclusion
    A. Building a Joyful Community
    B. Prayer
    C. Thought to Remember

Introduction

A. The Challenge of Joy

In 1936 the German theologian Dietrich Bonhoeffer established and taught at a secret seminary in Finkenwalde, located in modern-day Poland. Establishing a seminary that ran against the state-supported church was risky. At any time, the German secret police could close the seminary. Even worse, they could put its leaders in prison. Despite the risk, Bonhoeffer held to his convictions that the seminary was crucial. On the verge of a worldwide crisis, the seminary developed church leaders.

At the seminary Bonhoeffer taught on the Old Testament text of Ezra. He thought that the text offered a model for faithfulness to God during times of crisis. During difficult times, God's people must maintain hope that the promises of God will remain true. This hope is evident no matter the time period, whether post-exilic Israel or prewar Europe—or today.

B. Lesson Context

Today's lesson continues the narrative of Ezra 6:1-12 (see lesson 2). The resettled Jewish exiles, under Zerubbabel's leadership, rebuilt the foundation of the Jerusalem temple (Ezra 3:8). After the work began, Persian officials questioned under whose authority they rebuilt (5:3-5). Persian King Darius responded and reiterated a declaration of King Cyrus. Only then were the exiles free to rebuild without fear of interference (6:1-5). Further, King Darius made allowances to financially support the reconstruction (6:8-9). The exiles were able to rebuild a place fit for the Lord's worship.

Humans often attach importance and significance to specific places. So it should be of no surprise that the exiles would value the temple and celebrate its reconstruction. The temple marked the place where God's presence was with his people (1 Kings 8:27-30). But if Israel were to disobey God, then his presence would leave the temple (Ezekiel 10:1-18). The temple (and its predecessor the tabernacle) allowed the Israelites to experience God's presence in their midst. It even allowed Israel to rightly follow the commands of God (see Deuteronomy 12:11).

Construction of the temple was just the first step. The building had to be dedicated to signify its holiness before God. Previously, the temple of Solomon's time underwent the same. Sacrifices were offered and God's people celebrated his goodness (1 Kings 8:62-66; 2 Chronicles 7:4-11).

In numerous instances the temple had undergone changes. For example, the unfaithful King Ahaz removed certain parts (2 Kings 16:17-18). In response, faithful leaders reinstituted certain practices (23:21-23). It was important for the temple to be ritually purified (see 2 Chronicles 29). Even when used improperly, the temple's importance was not lost. It stood as a holy place where the presence of God was declared to Israel.

I. Obedient Dedication
(Ezra 6:13-18)

A. Leaders and Associates (v. 13)

13. Then, because of the decree King Darius had sent, Tattenai, governor of Trans-Euphrates, and Shethar-Bozenai and their associates carried it out with diligence.

Tattenai, the *governor*, oversaw the region on the west side of the Euphrates River, a region known as the *Trans-Euphrates*. His patience is notable. He waited until *the decree* of *King Darius* before responding to the reconstruction (see Ezra 5:5).

Little is known about the *associates* who joined Tattenai and *Shethar-Bozenai*. They likely consisted of numerous groups of people (see Ezra 4:9). The leaders inquired of the Jews, reported to Darius, and received his support (see 5:6; 6:6-12). Previous opposition to the exiles dissipated because of the patronage shown by the king (see 4:1-5).

Patronage was a socioeconomic relationship between a benefactor and a client. The benefactor provided materials and financial support for the client's needs. In return, the client pledged loyalty to the benefactor. In this example, Darius served as the benefactor for the temple and provided for its reconstruction. In return, he hoped to quell any possible uprising among the exiles.

B. Elders and Prophets (vv. 14-15)

14a. So the elders of the Jews continued to build and prosper under the preaching of Haggai the prophet and Zechariah, a descendant of Iddo.

Work on the temple's reconstruction began in 536 BC (Ezra 3:8). For a time, work did stop due to opposition. However, it began again in the second year of Darius, 520 BC (4:24). The repatriated exiles and *the elders of the Jews continued* in their rebuilding efforts. However, they would *prosper* in their efforts only as they followed *the preaching* of prophets (5:1).

Decades after the events of Ezra 6, Jerusalem's population was sparse (see Nehemiah 7:4). Eventually 10 percent of the repatriated population moved to Jerusalem (11:1-2). Still, the city was not a massive metropolis like other major cities. Therefore, the prophets were likely familiar with each other and each other's teachings.

For a time, the exiles avoided work on rebuilding the temple (Haggai 1:2). However, in August of 520 BC, *Haggai the prophet* urged rebuilding efforts, which soon occurred (1:1, 8, 14-15). Haggai's exhortation was not a one-time occurrence. Over the months that followed, he appealed to the people of Judah. He was most concerned with the glory of the temple and the actions of its priests (2:1-23).

The first address of *Zechariah* came two months later, in November of 520 BC (Zechariah 1:1). He warned the exiles of repeating the past mistakes of their people (1:4). The mercy of the Lord was emphasized among the people (1:16; 3:1-10). In response, they were to seek just and compassionate treatment of the community's vulnerable members (7:8-10).

HOW TO SAY IT

Aviv	*A-viv.*
Adar	*Ay*-dar.
Ahaz	*Ay*-haz.
Artaxerxes	Are-tuh-*zerk*-seez.
Haggai	*Hag*-eye or *Hag*-ay-eye.
Nisan	*Nye*-san.
Pentateuch	*Pen*-ta-teuk.
Purim	*Pew*-rim.
Zechariah	*Zek*-uh-**rye**-uh.

What Do You Think?
How can you build relationships with your
neighbors that lead to their prospering?
Digging Deeper
How do Romans 15:1-7; Galatians 5:13; 6:2
inform your answer?

❧ EXCEPTIONAL EXAMPLES ❧

Millard Fuller (1935–2009) wanted something more from life. The self-made millionaire found life lacking. Millard and his wife, Linda, sold their possessions and began the search for something meaningful. After spending five years in the international mission field, the Fullers returned to the United States. They were led to help create a housing ministry. The ministry sought to solve housing disparities by building houses on a profit-and-interest-free basis. From that foundation, Habitat for Humanity began its work in 1976. Through the Fullers' exceptional example, others have participated in the vision of Habitat for Humanity.

The prophetic voices of Haggai and Zechariah encouraged the exiles to continue their reconstruction work. When the exiles followed, they were filled with hope. The glory of God would soon fill the temple! How can you serve as an example to others for God's work? Is your vision of God's work clear so that you might become an exceptional example?　　　　　—A. S.

14b. They finished building the temple according to the command of the God of Israel and the decrees of Cyrus, Darius and Artaxerxes, kings of Persia.

The decrees of Cyrus and *Darius* commanded that the Jerusalem temple be rebuilt (Ezra 1:2-3; 6:7). Their decrees came to fruition as the exiles *finished building the temple*. While there were several rulers with the name *Artaxerxes*, this one was Artaxerxes I (reigned 464–423 BC). In 457 BC Artaxerxes paused the reconstruction efforts of Jerusalem (4:7-23). He tasked Ezra with visiting the city on his behalf (7:1, 8, 11-26).

Artaxerxes's inclusion with the others *kings of Persia* shows that Ezra 6 was written at a later time than the events it described. Persian support for Jerusalem and its temple did not stop with Darius. Artaxerxes's inclusion with Cyrus and Darius showed the continuation of Persian patronage toward the Jewish temple.

15. The temple was completed on the third day of the month Adar, in the sixth year of the reign of King Darius

The year 516 BC marked *the sixth year of the reign of King Darius* (522–486 BC). *The month Adar* marks the final month of the Jewish religious calendar. This month corresponds to late February or early March. Seventy years after the temple was destroyed by the Babylonians, it was rebuilt.

Furthermore, Adar marked an important time for exiles remaining in Persia. The festival of Purim was celebrated during this month. That festival was established around 470 BC; therefore, it did not exist during the reign of Darius I. Purim commemorated the deliverance of the Jews from their enemies (Esther 9:20-32).

C. Priests and Exiles (vv. 16-18)

16. Then the people of Israel—the priests, the Levites and the rest of the exiles—celebrated the dedication of the house of God with joy.

Acts of dedication were central throughout Israel's history. Large crowds of *the people of Israel* joyously dedicated Solomon's temple (1 Kings 8).

In a similar manner, a crowd gathered for *the dedication* of the rebuilt temple. All involved— *the priests, the Levites and the rest of the exiles*— acknowledged that "the Lord builds up Jerusalem; he gathers the exiles of Israel" (Psalm 147:2).

What Do You Think?
How will you joyously celebrate God's work in
the lives of other believers?
Digging Deeper
What prevents believers from experiencing the
joy of the Lord?

17a. For the dedication of this house of God they offered a hundred bulls, two hundred rams, four hundred male lambs,

The *offered* sacrifices were much smaller in number than those offered at *the dedication* of Solomon's temple (see 1 Kings 8:62-63). The discrepancy could be due to the fewer number of people. Or, perhaps the exiles' poverty prohibited them from amassing larger numbers of sacrifices.

Their offerings were not chosen randomly but were consistent with the people's history. The law required *bulls* to be offered during the burnt offering (Leviticus 1:3, 5). In addition, bulls were offered as a part of the sin offering (4:3, 13-14). A sacrifice of *rams* was required during the guilt offerings (5:14-15; 6:6). The fellowship offering (3:6-8) and the sin offering (4:32) made allowance for the use of *lambs*. The text of Ezra does not indicate whether these specific offerings were made at the dedication.

These animals were offered as Israel celebrated the Festival of Trumpets (see Numbers 29:1, 13, 17-18, etc.). Also, when Israel dedicated the tabernacle altar (7:10), these animals were offered (7:87-88).

That the animals were offered at the dedication of the rebuilt temple reflects two major points. First, it showed a concern to uphold the stipulations God required of the people. Second, the offering followed precedent made by previous generations.

Ritual purification and repentance were prerequisites for Israel to offer proper worship to God. Furthermore, Israel saw no contradiction between repentance and joyfulness before the Lord (see also Nehemiah 8:9-12). The repatriated tribes experienced joy as they offered sacrifices before God.

17b. and, as a sin offering for all Israel, twelve male goats, one for each of the tribes of Israel.

A *sin offering* of *male goats* purified the people of their sins or ritual violations (see Leviticus 4:22-26; 5:6; 9:3, 15). That *twelve* were offered represented the split nation as a unified 12 *tribes of Israel*. As not all tribes had returned from exile, the offerings anticipated a reunited nation. During exile, the Jews had been without proper accommodations to make sin offerings. Their act of purification acknowledged decades of impure and sinful acts. As a new temple was dedicated, the people had a new start before God.

Visual for Lessons 2 & 3. *Have this visual on display as you pose the discussion question that is associated with Ezra 6:16.*

❧ DEDICATION AND CELEBRATION! ❧

My senses were tingling that morning. I can remember the sight of the new sanctuary, the smell of new carpet, and the feeling of new pews. That day marked the dedication of our church's new building. The anticipation of planning, building, and moving into a new building had come to its grand conclusion. I was excited for the work that the Lord would do in that building.

Our church community was filled with joy and gratitude as the dedication ceremony proceeded. We were eager to see God's work in that building. However, we were most excited for how God would work among us.

For ancient Israel, God's presence was made known in the temple. However, that presence now resides in a different temple: his people (see 1 Corinthians 3:16-17; 6:19; 2 Corinthians 6:16; Ephesians 2:21). Are you filled with joy and hope for how God might work? Are you living in a way that will show God's presence to others? —A. S.

18. And they installed the priests in their divisions and the Levites in their groups for the service of God at Jerusalem, according to what is written in the Book of Moses.

A rebuilt temple required a new labor force. *The priests* and *Levites* were tasked with care for the building and overseeing the sacrificial rituals in *service of God*. The prescriptions for their labor are found in parts of *the Book of Moses*, the

Pentateuch. There Moses described the consecration and duties of Israel's leadership (Exodus 29; Leviticus 8; Numbers 3:5-13; 18).

The Law of Moses set the boundaries for the priests and the Levites. However, *their divisions* and *groups* were established by King David (1 Chronicles 24; compare Ezra 2:36-40). The renewed focus on worship highlighted the importance of the priesthood for Israel. Even in regard to physical health and well-being, the priests served God and Israel (Leviticus 13:2-44).

> **What Do You Think?**
> How can your church become more effective in service through the use of organized groups for specific ministries?
>
> *Digging Deeper*
> How does the church's ministry depend on the whole "body of Christ" (1 Corinthians 12:27)?

II. Celebratory Fellowship
(Ezra 6:19-22)
A. Passover (vv. 19-21)

19. On the fourteenth day of the first month, the exiles celebrated the Passover.

Beginning with this verse, the language of the text switches from Aramaic to Hebrew. This marks a transition and a new focus. Previously the text was concerned with the dedication of the rebuilt temple. Now the text focuses on the religious practices of *the exiles* once in captivity. A new focus reinforced Israel's distinctiveness, one that diminished during their time in exile (see Nehemiah 13:24).

The observation of *the Passover* gave space for remembrance. Israel was to remember God's deliverance of their nation from oppression in Egypt (Exodus 12:1-14; Leviticus 23:4-8). Proper observation required that it begin *on the fourteenth day* of the month of Aviv (Leviticus 23:5; Numbers 28:16; Deuteronomy 16:1-2).

Aviv was the Canaanite name *of the first month* of the Hebrew religious calendar. During the exile, Israel adopted the Babylonian calendar system. As a result, the name of that month changed to Nisan (Nehemiah 2:1).

20. The priests and Levites had purified themselves and were all ceremonially clean. The Levites slaughtered the Passover lamb for all the exiles, for their relatives the priests and for themselves.

Earlier descriptions of the observance of Passover do not mention *the priests and Levites*. Instead, the elders of the community of Israel selected and killed the Passover sacrifice (Exodus 12:21). However, depictions from the time of Kings Hezekiah (reigned 715–687 BC) and Josiah (reigned 640–609 BC) describe a different story. In those cases, the Levites *slaughtered the Passover lamb* for the people because of their uncleanness (2 Chronicles 30:17; 35:3-6, 10-11). The practice of having the Levites kill the sacrifice seems to have continued into postexilic Israel.

> **What Do You Think?**
> How can believers live lives of purity in regard to their daily actions?
>
> *Digging Deeper*
> How do Psalm 24:3-6; Galatians 5:16-25; 1 Thessalonians 4:1-12; 2 Timothy 2:22-25; and James 1:27 inform your answer?

21. So the Israelites who had returned from the exile ate it, together with all who had separated themselves from the unclean practices of their Gentile neighbors in order to seek the Lord, the God of Israel.

Proper observance of Passover required eating roasted lamb, seasoned with bitter herbs, and bread made without yeast (Exodus 12:8-9; Numbers 9:11). Some of the meal's participants were those *who had separated themselves*. This identification might refer to members of the northern kingdom of Israel or Israelites who did not experience exile. More likely, however, they were non-Israelites who chose to renounce idolatry and turned away *from the unclean practices* of the surrounding nations *to seek the Lord, the God of Israel* (compare Nehemiah 9:2).

As long as they followed God's requirements, these individuals could eat (Exodus 12:44, 48). Distinctiveness as the people of God was most important to Israel. However, that did not imply blind patriotism or nationalistic fervor. Non-Jews, or Gentiles, could participate in Israel's blessing. This occurred if they followed the stipulations God had for his people (see exceptions in Deuteronomy 23:1, 3-6). The prophet Isaiah envisioned a future where this occurred. Gentiles were admitted as God's people when they observed the Sabbath and followed his requirements (see Isaiah 56:3, 6-8).

B. Unleavened Bread (v. 22)

22a. For seven days they celebrated with joy the Festival of Unleavened Bread, because the LORD had filled them with joy

The one-day celebration of Passover preceded a week long observance of *The Festival of Unleavened Bread*. During this week participants ate bread that was unleavened, or without yeast. This act served as a reminder of Israel's salvation and rescue out of Egypt (Exodus 12:14-20; 13:3-10; 23:15; Leviticus 23:6; Numbers 28:17-25; Deuteronomy 16:3-4). The feast was not to be somber but, rather, one of *joy* (see 2 Chronicles 30:21). It reminded Israel of the ways *the Lord had* provided. For the exiles, the festival was even more timely. It reminded them of his provision as he brought them out of exile.

22b. by changing the attitude of the king of Assyria so that he assisted them in the work on the house of God, the God of Israel.

This portion of the narrative reaches its dramatic conclusion as the Lord *changed the attitude of the king.* As a result, new life would emerge in Israel. The once exiled people would increase in number, fulfilling the promises made to Abraham (Genesis 12:2; 15:5; compare Isaiah 54:1-3).

The mention of *Assyria* is a puzzling inclusion. The reign of Assyrians ended almost a century prior to the described events of this text. While the Persians adopted aspects of Assyrian government and culture, they were a different force altogether. The best explanation is that the text describes the king in this regard to remind readers of their history. Exile had begun with Assyria and the rule of its king (see Nehemiah 9:32). However, *the God of Israel* showed concern toward his people as he worked through pagan rulers.

What Do You Think?
What attitude of your heart needs to change for God to work through you?
Digging Deeper
Who will you ask to help you in this regard?

Conclusion

A. Building a Joyful Community

By 1942 the gestapo had shut down numerous underground seminaries, including Finkenwalde. War was in full swing in Europe. Bonhoeffer's former students were scattered around the continent. However, they were still faithful to their calling to serve the underground church. In an effort to encourage the leaders, Bonhoeffer wrote a series of letters calling the leaders to embrace joy. As suffering and indifference had become prevalent, finding joy was a challenge for these leaders.

The rebuilt temple was a result of God's provision and faithfulness toward his people. As a result, the exiles expressed their joyous worship and gratitude to God. These expressions took the form that had been prescribed to them centuries before. The temple's dedication and the celebratory feasts invited the exiles to express proper joy toward God. Once again the people could experience right relationship with God, a true cause for joy and celebration.

Our community of faith may be driven to build new buildings and establish new programs. But our primary challenge when building is to respond joyfully. God's faithfulness to us demands such a response! From that foundation we are called to build ministries as an outpouring of God's faithfulness. Ultimately, these become a sign for the world to see.

B. Prayer

God, during difficult times, finding joy is a challenge. Fill us with the joy that comes only from you. May we be a people who celebrate your work in our lives in a joyous manner. In the name of Jesus. Amen.

C. Thought to Remember

God's people live in joyous and celebratory hope!

INVOLVEMENT LEARNING

Enhance your lesson with NIV Bible Student *(from your curriculum supplier) and the reproducible activity page (at www.standardlesson.com or in the back of the* NIV Standard Lesson Commentary Deluxe Edition*).*

Into the Lesson

Invite the class to create a new holiday for the country to recognize. Suggest that it can be serious and honor a significant person or moment, or it can be silly and highlight something they think is special. Once the class decides on the holiday, ask the following questions of the group: 1–On what date will it fall? 2–How it will be celebrated? 3–What traditions will this holiday introduce?

Alternative. Distribute copies of the "Holiday Matching" exercise from the activity page, which you can download. Have learners complete the activity as indicated.

Lead into the Bible study by saying, "Significant moments are worth remembering and celebrating. Today we will look at a long-awaited moment in the history of God's people, and how they responded in celebration."

Into the Word

Ask a volunteer to read aloud Ezra 6:13-15. Divide the whole class into three equal groups. Each group will then assign each group member a character role to act out. Group members will come up with a prop for each character to wear or hold, a statement for each character to say, and an action for each character to demonstrate their role.

The Governors Group: Tattenai, Shethar-Bozenai, and their associates

The Prophets and Builders Group: Haggai, Zechariah, and the elders of the Jews

The Commanders Group: Cyrus, Darius, Artaxerxes

Invite group members to act out their parts as they interact with other groups. Encourage every character to participate. After no more than 10 minutes, ask participants the following questions: 1–Which group seemed to have the most work? 2–Which group seemed to have the most power? 3–In what ways did each group need the other two?

Ask a volunteer to read aloud Ezra 6:16-22

and 1 Kings 8:62-66 to compare the two temple dedication ceremonies. Divide the class into two groups: **Similarities Group** and **Differences Group**.

Ask the **Similarities Group** to list all the similarities between the dedication ceremonies. Ask the **Differences Group** to list all the differences between the dedication ceremonies. Give no more than five minutes for each group to make their list. Have a representative from each group read their list to the whole class.

After each representative speaks, challenge the groups to discuss within their teams why there were these particular similarities and differences. Then ask a representative from each group to share their conclusions with the whole group.

Alternative. Divide the whole class into small groups of two or three people. Distribute copies of the "Compare and Contrast" exercise from the activity page. Ask groups to complete the activity as indicated. After a few minutes, invite groups to share what they found.

Into Life

Ask the whole class, "How have we witnessed God's provision and faithfulness in the history of our church?" Discuss this as a group, letting learners share stories and experiences. After a few minutes, focus on one story or experience that stands out as significant to a majority of the class. Ask the group to develop a plan for a church-wide celebration to commemorate the significant experience.

Ask the group to consider questions: 1–When would be the best time to have this celebration? 2–Where is the best location to have this celebration? 3–What offerings of praise and worship to God could people bring to this celebration? 4–What kind of food (feast) would best celebrate this occasion? Close class by making a plan to bring these ideas to the church leadership for consideration.

FREE BECAUSE OF THE LORD

DEVOTIONAL READING: Deuteronomy 8:1-11
BACKGROUND SCRIPTURE: Deuteronomy 8

DEUTERONOMY 8:1-11

¹ Be careful to follow every command I am giving you today, so that you may live and increase and may enter and possess the land the LORD promised on oath to your ancestors. ² Remember how the LORD your God led you all the way in the wilderness these forty years, to humble and test you in order to know what was in your heart, whether or not you would keep his commands. ³ He humbled you, causing you to hunger and then feeding you with manna, which neither you nor your ancestors had known, to teach you that man does not live on bread alone but on every word that comes from the mouth of the LORD. ⁴ Your clothes did not wear out and your feet did not swell during these forty years. ⁵ Know then in your heart that as a man disciplines his son, so the LORD your God disciplines you.

⁶ Observe the commands of the LORD your God, walking in obedience to him and revering him. ⁷ For the LORD your God is bringing you into a good land—a land with brooks, streams, and deep springs gushing out into the valleys and hills; ⁸ a land with wheat and barley, vines and fig trees, pomegranates, olive oil and honey; ⁹ a land where bread will not be scarce and you will lack nothing; a land where the rocks are iron and you can dig copper out of the hills. ¹⁰ When you have eaten and are satisfied, praise the LORD your God for the good land he has given you. ¹¹ Be careful that you do not forget the LORD your God, failing to observe his commands, his laws and his decrees that I am giving you this day.

KEY TEXT

Be careful that you do not forget the LORD your God, failing to observe his commands, his laws and his decrees that I am giving you this day. —**Deuteronomy 8:11**

Photo © Getty Images

GOD FREES AND REDEEMS

Unit 1: Liberating Passover
LESSONS 1–4

LESSON AIMS

After participating in this lesson, each learner will be able to:

1. List the imperatives in Deuteronomy 8:1-11.
2. Explain the nature of those commandments.
3. Make a plan to practice greater humility in serving the Lord in one particular area.

LESSON OUTLINE

Introduction

A. Negligent Plant Slaughter

How hard is it to water a plant? As it turns out, very difficult—at least for me. I was home from college for summer break. When my mother had to leave on a business trip, she instructed me to water *one* outside plant. If I didn't and the plant died, I would have to buy a new one. I was confident I could not forget. After all, it was clearly visible through the large window behind the TV!

Not once did I water the plant. Worse yet, it rained very little while my mother was gone. By the time she returned, the plant was a dried husk, and the leaves crumbled to dust at a mere touch.

It wasn't out of rebellion that I didn't water the plant, or even that I didn't care for my mom. The problem was that I never wrote it down, nor did I make a point to include watering the plant in my daily habits. Her instructions just slipped my mind. I still wish I had guarded myself against forgetting—that was an expensive plant!

Through my failure I learned that even *forgetting* to obey has consequences! But would Israel learn this lesson the easy way?

B. Lesson Context

The setting for today's lesson is "near Beth Peor east of the Jordan, in the land of Sihon king of the Amorites" (Deuteronomy 4:46) in about 1406 BC. The recipients were the Israelites of a new generation who were about to enter the promised land. Moses would soon die on Mount Nebo, located in Moab (chapter 34), having been barred from entering the promised land because of his disobedience at Meribah (Numbers 20:7-12).

Deuteronomy is a covenant renewal treaty, delivered by Moses in a series of speeches (Deuteronomy 1:1–4:43; 4:44–28:68; etc.). In these speeches, he recounted the covenant God had made with Israel at Mount Sinai some four decades previously. This covenant is very similar to a specific kind of ancient Near Eastern treaty called a suzerainty covenant. In such covenants, a sovereign king (the suzerain) would write out terms of an agreement with a weaker king (the vassal). This generally required obedience from the lesser king in exchange for certain protections and benefits from the greater king. Typical suzerainty covenants contained at least six parts: (1) an introduction, (2) a historical basis for the treaty, (3) general stipulations followed by (4) specific stipulations, (5) divine witness, and finally (6) curses for disobedience and blessings for faithfulness.

Deuteronomy 5–11 is the high point of the book. Here the Ten Commandments are recounted (chapter 5; compare Exodus 20:1-17 and Deuteronomy 4:13; 10:4). This is followed by an exposition of how to love and obey the Lord (chapters 6–11). Our text today, from Deuteronomy 8:1-11, falls under general stipulations in the second speech.

One helpful way to categorize laws in the Bible is to distinguish between conditional and unconditional laws. Unconditional laws are what we have with the Ten Commandments. They are foundation principles for Israel's covenant relationship. Covenant recognizes a relationship, and adherence to the rules maintains the relationship. Conditional laws rightly begin with a conditional clause (beginning with "if" or "when," either expressed or implied), followed by a declarative judgment (beginning with "then," either expressed or implied; examples: Exodus 21:28-29; 22:26-27).

I. Remember
(DEUTERONOMY 8:1-5)
A. Who Holds the Future (v. 1)

1. Be careful to follow every command I am giving you today, so that you may live and increase and may enter and possess the land the LORD promised on oath to your ancestors.

This week's passage continues the call to observe *every command* God gave Israel (compare: Deuteronomy 4:1-2; 5:1; 6:1-2; 7:11-12). What follows are positive reminders of God's work and the blessings that will follow from continuing to obey *the Lord*. Deuteronomy 8:12-20 (not in our printed text) presents the negative flipside. Curses can and will result from failure to follow the Lord's ways.

Obeying God's commands results in experiencing fulfillment of God's promises (compare John 10:10b). To *increase* is both a command from the Garden of Eden (Genesis 1:28) and a blessing given by God (Deuteronomy 7:13). Israel had multiplied in Egypt, but their growth resulted in a perceived threat to the Egyptians. They resolved this danger by enslaving the Israelites (Exodus 1:6-13). Possessing the promised *land* would allow the people to multiply in peace. Fulfillment of all these promises was predicated on obedience; the people's failure to obey accounted for their exile in Babylon (2 Chronicles 36:11-21).

Your ancestors refers to Abraham, Isaac, and Jacob (Exodus 3:15). God had made a promise of the land of Canaan to Abraham (Genesis 12:6-7). God then formalized his promise with a covenant in Genesis 15 and 17. He renewed the covenant with both Isaac (26:3-5) and Jacob (35:9-12).

B. Who Provided in the Past (vv. 2-5)

2. Remember how the LORD your God led you all the way in the wilderness these forty years, to humble and test you in order to know what was in your heart, whether or not you would keep his commands.

Though we may not think of *remember* as an enforceable command, it is often given this power in Deuteronomy (examples: 7:18; 15:15; 16:12; 24:22). Festivals, sacrifices, Sabbath rest, and other rhythms of life were meant to help the people keep this command (examples: Exodus 13:2-3; 20:8). In a similar way, the Lord's Supper and baptism remind us of what *the Lord* has done for us, especially through Christ.

Future generations would be well served to learn lessons from the hardships faced *in the wilderness these forty years* without repeating the same sins. Proud people believe they have earned everything they have through their own power; humble people recognize that without the Lord, they would have nothing. Experiencing uncertainty about resources in the wilderness was meant to humble the Israelites, reminding them not only

HOW TO SAY IT

Sinai	*Sigh*-nye or *Sigh*-nay-eye.
suzerainty	*soo*-zuh-ruhn-tee.

of their need but of God's ability and trustworthiness to care for them. Though the next generation was going into a land rich with resources, forgetting humility before God would be a dire misstep.

God was able to see the hearts of his people and *test* their faithfulness. Though God's seeking evidence of faith may seem to contradict the fact that he knows everything, the story of Abraham and Isaac on Mount Moriah provides precedent for God's proving the people's faith (Genesis 22:1-18). There as here, God wants to be sure that his people remain faithful to him by keeping *his commands*. And perhaps as importantly, the people were reassured that God saw their efforts and valued their devotion to him.

> **What Do You Think?**
> What have humbling experiences revealed about your character?
> *Digging Deeper*
> How does remembering these experiences reveal growth areas and God's faithfulness?

3a. He humbled you, causing you to hunger and then feeding you with manna, which neither you nor your ancestors had known,

Immediately after leaving Egypt, the Israelites moaned that Moses was leading them to their deaths (Exodus 14:10-12). They also spoke against him twice more when they were thirsty (15:22-24; 17:1-3), as well as when they didn't have food (16:2-3). This is an example of how God used their circumstances in an effort to humble them (see Deuteronomy 8:2-4).

Although Israel feared a lack of provision, God provided *manna*, "bread from heaven" (Exodus 16:4, 14-15). This bread "was white like coriander seed and tasted like wafers made with honey" (16:31; compare Numbers 11:7-9). In naming it, the people threw up their hands and said in essence, "Manna—we don't know what this is!" But they didn't need to recognize the food—only that God's provision was a concrete example of his care and capability. The intended effect of humbling the people and teaching them to trust God with a grateful heart, however, does not seem to have taken (see Exodus 16:19-20).

3b. to teach you that man does not live on bread alone but on every word that comes from the mouth of the LORD.

This explanation falls in the middle of the list of things that the Lord provided for the Israelites while they were in the wilderness. Any time a list is interrupted with explanation, the reader should pay close attention. The interruption is important to understanding what surrounds it.

God's response to Israel's hardships was meant to inspire the people to trust him. It's not that the people didn't need bread; rather, it's that heeding *every word that comes from the mouth of the Lord* is the only path to life (see Psalm 119:9-16). What good is a healthy body if the soul languishes? Or as Jesus said, "What good is it for someone to gain the whole world, yet forfeit their soul?" (Mark 8:36). If Israel wanted to live, they needed not only food and water, but to obey God and find life in him (see Isaiah 45:22-25).

Jesus quoted this Scripture when Satan tempted him to create bread (Matthew 4:1-4). Though Israel struggled with the truth that the Father sought to teach them, Jesus knew it well. Hunger lasts for a time, and God's provision comes when he wills it. But seeking after God's words—his laws, his promises, and his other proclamations of love—ensures life, whether one's stomach rumbles or not. Jesus would wait for God's time. And if we are to heed the wisdom of Jesus' words, we will wait too (compare 6:25-33).

> **What Do You Think?**
> What evidence of faithfulness to God's commands do outsiders see in your life? What contradictory evidence might they see?
> *Digging Deeper*
> What practices can you begin or strengthen to live by every word that comes from God?

4. Your clothes did not wear out and your feet did not swell during these forty years.

The list of God's provision continues. These two preventative measures kept Israel in good health and ensured they could continue the journey, even for *forty years*. Having *clothes* not wear out was important, given the scarce resources to make new clothing along the way. Swelling in the *feet* often results from injury or disease, though exercise (like lots of walking) can also cause it. Prolonged exposure to heat—a reality in the Sinai peninsula where summer highs hover in the high 90s Fahrenheit—can have the same effect.

❧ ALL WHO WANDER ❧

One summer I hiked in the Rocky Mountains for several months with a single pair of hiking boots. This range boasts peaks that rise more than 14,000 feet above sea level. Oxygen is precious, and trees do not grow above about 11,000 feet. The rocky crags above the tree line are exposed to the sun, high winds, and violent thunderstorms.

This unforgiving landscape chewed up my hiking boots. The laces broke, the soles thinned and then tore away from the toe box, the threaded stitching disintegrated, the leather wore through until my toes stuck out. When I retired them, those boots were a stark image of what happens to hard-used footwear.

The Israelites wandered in the wilderness for 40 years, traversing many miles of unforgiving land. But their clothes never wore out. God protected them. And he still protects us, no matter how challenging our environment. How does God provide for you in your current hostile environment?

—W. L.

5. Know then in your heart that as a man disciplines his son, so the LORD your God disciplines you.

The *heart* in the Hebrew language represented the origin of will, or volition. (The same Hebrew word is translated "conscience" in Genesis 20:5-6 and "minds" in Exodus 14:5.) The command here is not about an emotional reaction but, instead, one of considering the facts of what God has done.

Though the people may have felt sorely used, it benefited them to consider their hardships as instruction to make them wise and capable of living well (Hebrews 12:5-11; compare James 1:2-5). The familial imagery—God as Father, Israel as *his son*—speaks to the love behind God's actions. Even the curses contained in the covenant were meant to lead the people back to him (Deuteron-

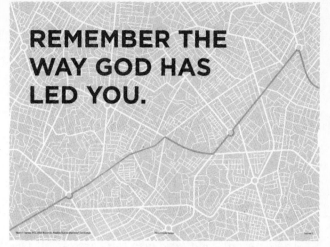

Visual for Lesson 4. *While discussing the questions with verse 7a, ask the class for examples from the congregation as well as personal experience.*

omy 30:1-10). And when Israel called out, God delighted in delivering his children (examples: Judges 3:7-9, 12-15; 4:1-7; compare Jonah 3:5-10; Revelation 3:19).

II. Anticipate
(DEUTERONOMY 8:6-11)
A. The Walk to Take (v. 6)

6a. Observe the commands of the LORD your God, walking in obedience to him

"Therefore" (*KJV*; not translated in the NIV) transitions from what God did in the past to what he would do in the near future (see Deuteronomy 8:7a and following, below; contrast 8:2). When we think of *the commands*, we may think specifically of the Ten Commandments. But the instruction to *observe* God's commands by *walking in obedience* refers to the instruction contained within the entire covenant (contrast Psalm 1:1; see Deuteronomy 8:11, below). The Ten Commandments serve as a summary in many ways, but the rest of the legal code gives Israel further direction in *how* to carry out those fundamental commands. Israel was required to keep God's commandments by living lives that reflected his ways.

6b. and revering him.

Elsewhere the Hebrew word rendered *revering* is translated "fear" (Genesis 22:12; Exodus 9:30; Leviticus 19:14; etc.). This phrase called the people to a proper, humble respect of God. Even so, the word *revere* in this context does not lose the connotation of terror. When people have a fuller understanding of God's power and authority, fear is an entirely appropriate response. The righteous do not need to fear God's wrath; their respectful fear of the Lord motivates them to keep his laws and continue to live rightly (Psalms 34:9; 52:5-7; etc.).

B. The Land to Take (vv. 7-10)

7a. For the LORD your God is bringing you into a good land—

The original *good land* was the earth itself (see Genesis 1:10, 12, 25). Canaan was the specific land God promised to Abraham and his descendants hundreds of years before (Genesis 15; 17; 26:1-5; 28:12-15). "Good" is repeated in verse 10 (below) and to describe the houses the people would build for themselves ("fine" in Deuteronomy 8:12, not in our printed text). In declaring the work of their own hands "good," they would risk not appreciating that *everything* comes from the Lord (compare Daniel 4:28-37). God is not in the habit of giving mediocre gifts (compare John 2:6-10; 3:16; James 1:17), and the place he set apart for the people's promised home was no exception (Deuteronomy 6:3; 11:9; 26:9; etc.). To forget this was to invite dire consequences.

> *What Do You Think?*
> In what ways do you see that God has brought you into a "good land"?
> *Digging Deeper*
> How can you be better satisfied with God's provision?

7b. a land with brooks, streams, and deep springs gushing out into the valleys and hills;

After wandering in a wilderness where water was not easily found (Exodus 17:1; Numbers 20:2-4), abundance of water would seem like an appropriate litmus test for answering the question "Is the *land* good?" Flowing water from *brooks*, *streams*, and *deep springs* ensured that disease wouldn't flourish in stagnant water.

8-9a. a land with wheat and barley, vines and fig trees, pomegranates, olive oil and honey; a land where bread will not be scarce and you will lack nothing;

The northern portions of Canaan were ideal for fields of *wheat* and *barley*. These grains were used to make bread and other food. The southern mountains yielded a more temperate environment that could sustain *fig trees* and *pomegranates* along with *olive* groves. Some students propose that *honey* refers to the syrup from fruits rather than to what bees produce.

While this list should not be taken as comprehensive, the elements named illustrate that the people would eat *bread* without scarceness and find nothing lacking in the land (see commentary on Deuteronomy 8:3b, above). This once again reversed the scarcity the Israelites had experienced in the wilderness (see 8:3a, above). The 12 Israelite spies had brought back a report of abundance in the land, coupled with information concerning the people who lived there. When the Israelites disobeyed the Lord and gave in to fear, the first generation out of Egypt was barred from entering the land (Numbers 13:17–14:25).

9b. a land where the rocks are iron and you can dig copper out of the hills.

Here the focus shifts to materials for crafting tools and weapons. *Iron* was known during the Bronze Age (about 3300–1200 BC) but not widely used (compare Deuteronomy 3:11). As the Israelites were soon to enter the promised land, the year was about 1406 BC, around 200 years before the beginning of the Iron Age (about 1200–550 BC), when iron's value would be better appreciated. *Copper* when alloyed with tin resulted in bronze, the metal that defined the Bronze Age. This metal was still widely used as societies were learning how to work with iron.

10. When you have eaten and are satisfied, praise the LORD your God for the good land he has given you.

God's provision was meant to teach the people to depend on him, to live by faith and not by sight (2 Corinthians 5:7; see Deuteronomy 8:3b, above). Such abundance might lure the people into believing they were self-sufficient or that the "gods" who were already worshipped in the land had helped them. The people would labor in the fields and vineyards, but God gave them *the good land* and then the conditions to benefit from his bounty. The only appropriate response to his provision is always to *praise the Lord*.

What Do You Think?
What ordinary blessings do you tend to take for granted?
Digging Deeper
How will your life change when you take time to thank God for *all* your daily provision?

❧ GRATITUDE AND GREEN THUMBS ❧

I once knew a delighted, delightful gardener. Her yard was a riot of teal lamb's ear, hollyhock, yellow and white daisies, soft purple columbines, pale catmint, bone white aspen roots, and snow-in-summer. She kept a golden peach tree and an orchard of bright green apple trees. An enormous grapevine scaled the east-facing side of her house. In late fall the vine grew plump clusters of vivid wine-colored grapes that hung down and touched the ground. The garden vibrated with iridescent hummingbirds that shimmered green and pink and silver, fat bumblebees, ladybugs, robins, and great orange monarch butterflies.

I imagine the good land as an alpine garden overflowing with fruit, bursting with color, teeming with life. Just as we are to rely on God in times of trouble, we are also called to praise him when blessed to sit and eat in a bountiful garden. Give praise today for your own "good land"! —W. L.

C. The Failure to Avoid (v. 11)

11. Be careful that you do not forget the LORD your God, failing to observe his commands, his laws and his decrees that I am giving you this day.

Memory is the beginning of obedience (see Deuteronomy 8:2, above). If the people failed to remember, it would be seen in their disobedience to all that *God* commanded them. The repetition of this command makes clear its importance and even models how to remember.

Too fine a distinction can be made between *commands*, *laws*, and *decrees*. When used in quick succession this way, the three are meant to give a sense of the weightiness of all the covenant ordinances Israel had been given to obey. God's people were responsible not for the pieces they liked or whatever was easy but for the entire law (Deuteronomy 6; Luke 11:42; James 2:10-11).

What Do You Think?
Which of God's expectations do you most struggle to adhere to on a daily basis?
Digging Deeper
What memory aids can you use to remember God's commands and seek to keep them?

Conclusion
A. Credit Where Credit Is Due

God has given us words to remember, laws to live by. Our peace depends on remembering what God has commanded and then acting faithfully on that memory (see John 14:21).

Though much has changed between when Israel stood at the boundary of the promised land and the time of the global church, we too are called to remember all that the Lord has done for us. We are not self-sufficient—God has given us all that we have. We must look to him in times of both need and plenty. Only when we honor and fear him like this can we call others to the same respect.

And, of course, we bring not only knowledge of God's law but also the peace of God's forgiveness through Jesus' sacrifice. His love has been shown to us; let us show it also to the watching world. Only then will we experience life in our own good land—the world God created—and beyond, in his Heaven.

B. Prayer

Thank you, Lord, for all the ways that you bless us daily. Help us to remember you in hard times and in times of bounty. Show us opportunities to tell the stories of your faithfulness to everyone we meet. In Jesus' name we pray. Amen.

C. Thought to Remember

The Lord's faithfulness to us calls for our faithfulness to him.

INVOLVEMENT LEARNING

Enhance your lesson with NIV Bible Student (from your curriculum supplier) and the reproducible activity page (at www.standardlesson.com or in the back of the NIV Standard Lesson Commentary Deluxe Edition).

Into the Lesson

Invite the class to play a memory game called Going on a Picnic. Explain that participants will take turns saying, "We're going on a picnic and we're taking…" and add a word. The first person's word begins with the letter A (example: apples). The second person repeats the A word and adds a B word (example: apples and bananas). The third person will need to remember the A and B words and add a C word (example: apples, bananas, and cheese). The goal is to have a list of items from A to Z, without forgetting any of them! Make this activity competitive (if a participant forgets an item, that person is out) *or* cooperative (everyone can help each person remember all the items).

After this activity say, "Sometimes it's a challenge to remember things, even things that are important to us. We'll see in today's lesson some things God commands his people to remember and why."

Into the Word

Ask a volunteer to read Deuteronomy 8:1-5. Divide the whole group into three smaller groups and give each group a poster board. Assign different focuses to each group: **Command Group**, **Reason Group**, and **Lesson Group**. Instruct the **Command Group** to write down the command words and phrases in this passage (example: *remember*), the **Reason Group** to write down the reasons the people should obey the commands (example: *that you may live*), and the **Lesson Group** to write down the lessons the people learn about the character of God through the reasons (example: *to know what was in your heart*).

Alternative. Distribute the "Looking Backward/ Looking Forward" exercise from the activity page, which you can download, to pairs of participants. Instruct them to only complete Part A.

Ask a volunteer to read Deuteronomy 8:6-10. Continue the previous activity of listing the commands, reasons, and lessons in the three groups. Then post the three posters on a wall, in a triangle pattern: the **Command Group** and **Reason Group** posters side by side, and the **Lesson Group** poster centered below. Give a handful of 24-inch lengths of yarn and a roll of tape to each group. Instruct them to tape the yarn on the wall, connecting the words they listed on their poster to the related words on the next poster. When they are finished, have the whole group study the visual effect and give feedback on what they notice.

Alternative. Instruct pairs to complete Part B of the "Looking Backward/Looking Forward" exercise from the activity page. When they are finished, ask them to discuss the results as a whole class and summarize what they notice about God's character—in both the past and the future. (Possible conclusions may be: God always provides what is needed; God's provision is abundant and gracious; God cares about the physical well-being and prosperity of his people.)

Ask a volunteer to read Deuteronomy 8:11. Ask the whole group to discuss: If the people did not heed this warning, how would it change their understanding of who God is? Invite participants to cite examples from the Old Testament, as well as the consequences the people faced.

Into Life

Give participants one minute to write down some of the blessings they have. Allow time to share these things in their previous groups and discuss how counting their blessings can help them practice humility when they serve the Lord. Allow one more minute for participants to write a reminder to serve God humbly.

Alternative. Distribute the "Remember" activity page to each participant as a take-home to be completed as indicated.

Close class with a prayer of thanks for all that God has done and will do for his people.

TRIUMPHAL ENTRY OF THE KING

DEVOTIONAL READING: Matthew 21:1-11
BACKGROUND SCRIPTURE: Matthew 20:25-28; 21:1-11

MATTHEW 21:1-11

¹ As they approached Jerusalem and came to Bethphage on the Mount of Olives, Jesus sent two disciples, ² saying to them, "Go to the village ahead of you, and at once you will find a donkey tied there, with her colt by her. Untie them and bring them to me. ³ If anyone says anything to you, say that the Lord needs them, and he will send them right away."

⁴ This took place to fulfill what was spoken through the prophet:

⁵ "Say to Daughter Zion,
    'See, your king comes to you,
gentle and riding on a donkey,
    and on a colt, the foal of a donkey.'"

⁶ The disciples went and did as Jesus had instructed them. ⁷ They brought the donkey and the colt and placed their cloaks on them for Jesus to sit on. ⁸ A very large crowd spread their cloaks on the road, while others cut branches from the trees and spread them on the road. ⁹ The crowds that went ahead of him and those that followed shouted,

"Hosanna to the Son of David!"

"Blessed is he who comes in the name of the Lord!"
"Hosanna in the highest heaven!"

¹⁰ When Jesus entered Jerusalem, the whole city was stirred and asked, "Who is this?"
¹¹ The crowds answered, "This is Jesus, the prophet from Nazareth in Galilee."

KEY TEXT

"Say to Daughter Zion, 'See, your king comes to you, gentle and riding on a donkey, and on a colt, the foal of a donkey.'" —**Matthew 21:5**

Photo © Getty Images

GOD FREES AND REDEEMS

Unit 2: Liberating Gospels

LESSONS 5–8

LESSON AIMS

After participating in this lesson, each learner will be able to:

1. List the details of the triumphal entry.

2. Explain Matthew's use of Zechariah 9:9.

3. Express worship to the Lord by writing a poem, prayer, or devotional thought.

LESSON OUTLINE

Introduction
    A. Columbo
    B. Lesson Context
 I. The Preparation (Matthew 21:1-5)
    A. Setting (v. 1a)
    B. Instructions (vv. 1b-3)
       Planning the Journey
    C. Fulfillment (vv. 4-5)
 II. The Procession (Matthew 21:6-11)
    A. Obedience (vv. 6-7)
    B. Reaction (vv. 8-9)
    C. Identity (vv. 10-11)
       Cheering for . . . Him?
Conclusion
    A. Faith on Parade
    B. Prayer
    C. Thought to Remember

Introduction

A. Columbo

In most mysteries the reader or viewer tries to figure out "who done it" along with the detective in the story. The best stories always have a surprising ending. But the 1970s show *Columbo* turned this formula on its head. The viewer saw the murder and knew the perpetrator from the very beginning, so the tension came from the uncertainty of whether the case could be solved. Inspector Columbo, the detective played by Peter Falk, appears to be bumbling and dull-witted. However, he is actually quite a good sleuth. Each episode followed how the inspector cracked the case. At the end, Columbo revealed proof of the perpetrator's identity.

The proof of Jesus' identity is clear to us because we have all the evidence of history at our disposal. To his disciples and the crowds, however, the mystery was intact: Who was Jesus? What was he going to do in Jerusalem? The triumphal entry was one twist in the plot on his way to the cross.

B. Lesson Context

Matthew 21–28 is devoted to the final week of Jesus' life through the resurrection and post-resurrection appearances. That week left the world changed forever.

Today's text comes from Monday of that fateful week and covers the triumphal entry. This event is recounted in all four Gospels (see Mark 11:1-11; Luke 19:28-44; John 12:12-19). Matthew, Mark, and Luke frequently overlap in their presentations, so we do not find ourselves surprised by the shared information. But to have an event shared also in John is less expected. Inclusion in all four Gospels speaks to the importance of the triumphal entry.

Several months before, Jesus had warned his disciples that he must go to Jerusalem and suffer many things, including his own death, at the hands of the elders, chief priests, and scribes (Matthew 16:21-28). Peter strongly resisted such an idea. He even rebuked Jesus. The idea of Jesus' dying was completely foreign to what Peter and the other disciples understood Jesus' mission to be. When Jesus entered Jerusalem, the disciples must have believed that their hopes of establishing Jesus as an earthly Messiah were about to be realized.

Though the disciples did not yet understand, Jesus' death would fulfill the Scriptures—just not as they had expected. The theme of fulfillment of Scripture permeates Matthew's Gospel. From Jesus' birth, Matthew both alluded to prophecy (Matthew 1:1; compare Isaiah 9:7; Jeremiah 23:5; etc.) and outright quoted it (Matthew 1:22-23). Matthew spells out in his account of the triumphal entry that this event fulfilled prophecy once again and paved the way for other fulfillments to come.

I. The Preparation
(MATTHEW 21:1-5)
A. Setting (v. 1a)

1a. As they approached Jerusalem and came to Bethphage on the Mount of Olives,

Jesus and his disciples were traveling with many other pilgrims to *Jerusalem* to celebrate Passover (see lesson 6). The people who lived in Jerusalem also were preparing for the festival and the influx of religious visitors. Jesus arrived "six days" before the Passover, spending time in the home of Mary, Martha, and Lazarus in Bethany (see John 12:1-3). The two small villages of Bethany and Bethphage are on the eastern side of Jerusalem. Bethany served as Jesus' normal base of operation when in Judea. The village was located about two miles southeast of Jerusalem.

The arrival was late Friday afternoon, for Jesus and his fellow Jews would not travel all the way from Jericho on a Sabbath Day, which begins at sundown Friday night. The group arrived at *Bethphage* (meaning "house of unripe figs"), which is near Bethany (see Mark 11:1). *The Mount of Olives* is a north-south ridge that flanks the eastern side of Jerusalem. Bethany and Bethphage were on the far side of this mount, somewhat isolated from the city, yet conveniently close to it.

B. Instructions (vv. 1b-3)

1b-2. Jesus sent two disciples, saying to them, "Go to the village ahead of you, and at once you will find a donkey tied there, with her colt by her. Untie them and bring them to me.

The *two disciples* Jesus sent are not named. The expectation that the female *donkey* (a jenny) was *tied* with *her colt* indicated that the donkey was not out grazing or involved in work, but ready and waiting for Jesus' purposes. She may have been fitted with some type of halter that allowed her to be tied to a post, readily available for being led back to Jesus. All four of the Gospels mention the younger donkey (compare Mark 11:2; Luke 19:30; John 12:14), but only Matthew includes the detail that there was an older female donkey as well.

Jesus' knowledge of the availability of the colt may have come supernaturally. On the other hand, it is entirely possible that the Lord made prior arrangements for the use of the animal.

3. "If anyone says anything to you, say that the Lord needs them, and he will send them right away."

Jesus anticipated the disciples' being asked about taking the donkeys, and told his followers how to answer. *The Lord needs them* functioned as a password or code. This gives us the impression that Jesus had prearranged the availability of the two animals. Many commentators believe that the owner of the colt was quietly making a contribution to Jesus' ministry in his own way. There may have been thousands of such followers in Palestine at that time. The Lord needed some to serve publicly out in front, but he also used many whose ministries were performed quietly behind the scenes.

❧ PLANNING THE JOURNEY ❧

After months of quarantine, my wife and I were delighted to attend a family wedding 2,000 miles from home. And planning was part of the fun! Do we drive or fly? We decided to drive. Do we use our camping trailer or stay in motels? We decided on "hoteling." That settled the "Which car?" question, since my wife's car pulls the trailer and my car gets better gas mileage.

Reservations were made, routes were decided, and the car was given a thorough safety check.

With all that done, all that was left was to pack: travel clothes, wedding clothes, and masks.

Perhaps Jesus had been envisioning this short journey from Bethphage to Jerusalem for a while. When the day of the triumphal entry arrived, his plans were complete and in keeping with the Father's will. How do you seek or recognize God's guidance for your own life's journey? —C. R. B.

C. Fulfillment (vv. 4-5)

4. This took place to fulfill what was spoken through the prophet:

Jesus alluded to *the prophet* Zechariah, who prophesied concerning the "king" coming into Jerusalem (Zechariah 9:9). His prophecies and others were not fulfilled by random chance. The events they foresaw were pieces of God's deliberate plan, a plan carried out by Jesus.

A key verse in understanding this is Matthew 5:17, which sets the tone for the entire book in the area of prophecy: Jesus did not come "to abolish the Law or the Prophets . . . but to fulfill them." There is perfect convergence between the prophets—who were given a glimpse of God's plan—and the Messiah, who enacted the plan centuries later (examples: Matthew 1:22-23; 2:5-6; 8:14-17).

> *What Do You Think?*
> Does your knowledge of the Old Testament bolster your faith? Why or why not?
> *Digging Deeper*
> How would the apostles answer this question? Give scriptural examples.

5. "Say to Daughter Zion, 'See, your king comes to you, gentle and riding on a donkey, and on a colt, the foal of a donkey.'"

So there would be no mistake or ambiguity, Matthew recorded an abbreviated version of Zechariah's prophecy. We noted earlier that *Zion* is equivalent to Jerusalem. (The *Daughter* part comes from Isaiah 62:11.) Though some claim that Jesus never saw himself as the prophesied Messiah, or Christ, Scripture shows otherwise (examples: Matthew 16:17; Luke 24:25-27; John 4:25-26).

Jerusalem was overflowing with Passover pilgrims at this time. This feast temporarily would nearly double Jerusalem's normal population of perhaps 50,000.

Here was their king, entering the royal city. Even though Jesus rode on an animal and was the object of such praise, his humility was actually on display. He was not riding a giant stallion with flaring nostrils, but a lowly donkey. The animal was used primarily for plowing or as a beast of burden, not to announce the presence of royalty. We easily imagine Jesus' legs sticking out from the donkey's round belly, with Jesus' feet barely clearing the ground. He is the humble king—a contradiction of terms in the ancient world, but perfect in God's plan.

> *What Do You Think?*
> How do you practice humility?
> *Digging Deeper*
> When boldness is called for, what continued role does humility play in your actions?

II. The Procession
(Matthew 21:6-11)
A. Obedience (vv. 6-7)

6-7. The disciples went and did as Jesus had instructed them. They brought the donkey and the colt and placed their cloaks on them for Jesus to sit on.

A triumphal procession in the city of Rome could take weeks to prepare. The Roman general or emperor receiving "the triumph" rode in a ceremonial chariot specially crafted for the event. The Roman triumphs consisted of long parades of dignitaries, captured enemy soldiers and kings, and wagons heavy with the spoils of war. Such carefully planned spectacles sometimes included the erection of a new triumphal arch. In contrast, Jesus' entry was much more impromptu.

Saddles as we know them were not commonly used in the ancient Near East. Instead, *the disciples* laid some of their clothing on the back of the animal to cushion Jesus' ride. Without a saddle or stirrups, *Jesus* probably had to be lifted onto the back of the animal. It doesn't seem like a given that *the colt* would remain docile as Jesus rode it. Perhaps this animal recognized Jesus as the ruler of the universe and behaved accordingly.

B. Reaction (vv. 8-9)

8. A very large crowd spread their cloaks on the road, while others cut branches from the trees and spread them on the road.

The description *a very large crowd* can be understood as "the largest of crowds." Matthew knows of a crowd of 5,000 men (not counting women and children) that came to hear Jesus in Galilee (Matthew 14:21), and this Passover crowd seems to be even larger. This is the biggest thing happening in Jerusalem that day, with perhaps 10,000 or more people lining Jesus' path to the city. It is likely that many were from the Galilee region.

Speculation was buzzing about if and when Jesus would come (John 11:55-57). Jesus did not stir up the crowd; their celebration was a spontaneous act by the people who had been anticipating his arrival. The nature of this event was contagious, and the crowd responded by paving the triumphal path of Jesus with their own *cloaks* and with freshly cut *branches*. John identifies those as coming from palm trees (John 12:13). The phrase *spread them* brings to mind the strewing of fresh, clean straw in a stable or in a house that has a dirt floor.

John tells us that the crowd also *cut* palm branches or fronds and waved these as they went out to meet Jesus (John 12:13). Normally this behavior was reserved to honor nobility. Crowds of people had welcomed the Jewish hero Simon

HOW TO SAY IT

Bethany	*Beth*-uh-nee.
Bethphage	*Beth*-fuh-gee.
Galilee	*Gal*-uh-lee.
Hosanna	Ho-*za*-nuh.
Jerusalem	Juh-*roo*-suh-lem.
Maccabees	*Mack*-uh-bees.
Messiah	Meh-*sigh*-uh.
Nazareth	*Naz*-uh-reth.
Zechariah	Zek-uh-*rye*-uh.
Zion	*Zi*-un.

Maccabeus in a similar manner some 110 years before (see the nonbiblical 1 Maccabees 13:51). The people demonstrated their belief that Jesus was more than just another prophet or rabbi.

Since palm fronds grow at the very top of the trees, the people must have gone to considerable effort to cut them for this occasion. This action is the basis for observing the day of Jesus' triumphal entry as Palm Sunday.

What Do You Think?
How does it encourage you to be with a crowd of people who are praising Jesus?
Digging Deeper
What pitfalls do you see if the *only* time you worship is with others?

9a. The crowds that went ahead of him and those that followed shouted,

The acclamation of the multitudes has three parts (see Matthew 21:9b-c, below), all pointing to Jesus as the promised Messiah. All four Gospel accounts record Jesus' triumphal entry into Jerusalem (see Lesson Context), and these accounts present some interesting variations. Both Matthew and Mark indicate that two groups made up the crowd that accompanied Jesus: those *that went ahead* came out from Jerusalem to meet him (John 12:12-13), while *those that followed* had come from Bethany with him.

9b. "Hosanna to the Son of David!" "Blessed is he who comes in the name of the Lord!"

The word *Hosanna*, a Hebrew term that means "save," is associated with the Hallel ("praise") psalms (113–118), especially Psalm 118:25-26. These particular psalms were associated with the Festival of Tabernacles, which celebrated the Lord's delivering Israel from Egypt. Echoes of deliverance permeated the people's celebrating Jesus as he entered Jerusalem. They hoped that he would save them from Rome in a way similar to their historic deliverance from Egypt.

The people's acclamation of Jesus as *the Son of David* was a clear reference to God's promise to David and his lineage (see 2 Samuel 7; Psalm 89:3-4). The crowd seemed to know that Jesus was in the line of David (Matthew see 1:1, 6;

Visual for Lessons 5. *Before closing the class with prayer, allow the learners one minute to consider how they continue to seek after Jesus.*

contrast the uncertainty of a previous occasion in John 7:41-42). The Gospel of John makes this knowledge even more explicit, recording that the crowd also hailed Jesus as "king of Israel" (12:13).

The people at the triumphal entry clearly anticipated great things from a king who *comes in the name of the Lord*. But they did not yet realize or appreciate how Jesus' kingship would differ from every monarch they had ever known. Nor did they know Jesus' absolute worthiness to receive such praise and worship. The Pharisees understood the threat of the people's adoration, however, and regarded their behavior as worthy of rebuke (Luke 19:37-44).

> *What Do You Think?*
> What situations cause you to cry out for God's deliverance?
> *Digging Deeper*
> How do you react when God responds to your petition differently than you had wanted?

9c. "Hosanna in the highest heaven!"

The highest heaven refers to God's dwelling place (example: Luke 2:14). The people were asking God to hear them from his home and to act on their behalf. Little did they know that Immanuel was with them, not far removed.

Luke tells us that some of the religious leaders demanded that Jesus silence the enthusias-

tic crowd. Jesus responded, "If they keep quiet, the stones will cry out" (Luke 19:40). Luke also informs us that Jesus stopped before he entered the city and wept as he predicted the tragic future that awaited Jerusalem (19:41-44).

Jesus did not silence the people, but neither did he take time to explain to them everything they didn't understand about him. Then as now, Jesus can truly be known only when we accept the truth that he was crucified, died, and then rose from the grave (1 Corinthians 1:22-25). He brought God's kingdom close, and he showed through his life, death, and resurrection that citizenship in his kingdom is different from that of any earthly nation. (Consider Jesus' teaching in Matthew 5–7.) No amount of preaching to the people would be as persuasive concerning Jesus' identity and purpose as would the way he died and the miracle of his rising back to life.

C. Identity (vv. 10-11)

10. When Jesus entered Jerusalem, the whole city was stirred and asked, "Who is this?"

The Jewish pilgrims who found lodging outside the city for the holiday (as Jesus and his disciples had) would walk into *Jerusalem* each day of the weeklong celebration. On this day, many such pilgrims accompanied Jesus into the city (Matthew 21:9a, above), and the commotion was so great that *the whole city* noticed. The question of the day, though, was not "What's happening?" but *"Who is this?"*

That question is profound and has lasting consequences for faith and discipleship. In order to give his disciples greater insight into his identity, Jesus had asked them who people said he was (Matthew 16:13-14). The disciples mentioned various prophets (see 21:11, below). When Jesus asked the disciples who *they* believed he was, Peter confessed, "You are the Messiah, the Son of the living God" (16:15-16). Even so, Peter did not understand what this meant or how dangerous this confession would prove to be. Still, Jesus declared that on the truth of this great confession the church would be built. Only by accepting Jesus as he disclosed himself—not just as a prophet or teacher but as Savior and Messiah—can a person truly follow Jesus and the church remain faithful to him.

11. The crowds answered, "This is Jesus, the prophet from Nazareth in Galilee."

Despite the previous acclamation of Jesus as "Son of David," *the crowds* gave a somewhat tamer answer to the question of Matthew 21:10, above. The crowd identified him by name (*Jesus*), by hometown (*Nazareth in.0 Galilee*), and by special vocation (*prophet*), but there is no language of Jesus as Messiah or king. Even so, the designation of Jesus as a prophet seems to have had a powerful effect on the city; it is the reason the Jewish leaders plotted carefully and secretly to have Jesus arrested (Matthew 21:46).

What Do You Think?
What opportunities does incomplete understanding of Jesus' identity offer in evangelization?
Digging Deeper
What challenges are presented by the same incomplete knowledge?

❧ CHEERING FOR . . . HIM? ❧

P. T. Barnum (1810–1891) of Barnum & Bailey Circus fame was a master showman who entertained Americans for many decades in the nineteenth and twentieth centuries. His hometown of Bridgeport, Connecticut, has held an annual Barnum festival and parade for the last 75 years to honor their native son.

My friend Len was a banker in the Bridgeport area before he retired. While I was in Bridgeport one year, the grand marshal—Len—invited me to ride with him on the grand marshal's float. No one in the crowd knew me, but they cheered anyway. I was riding with the grand marshal, so I basked in their acclaim as if I deserved it.

Many joined Jesus' "parade" to Jerusalem. And when the crowd cheered, I suspect that, like the crowd in Bridgeport, many were caught up in the spirit of the celebration. But Jesus deserved their praise, even though many didn't know who he really was. So celebrate Jesus, whatever you know of him—but also seek to know him better. You'll find even more reason to cheer.   —C. R. B.

Conclusion
A. Faith on Parade

Hearing the story of Jesus always leaves us with a question: Who is he? Just a good teacher, basing his lessons on God's laws? No more than a prophet, given insight from the Lord? Or is he the Son of God, the promised Messiah, sent to save the world from sin and death? Based on our answer, we also have a decision to make: Will we follow?

On days like the one described in this lesson, following Jesus is not just the right thing to do; it's the joyful thing! We want to follow Christ when he is being celebrated by everyone we know. And indeed, following Jesus is the path of life to the fullest (John 10:10b; 14:6).

But we must not forget that Jesus was heading to the cross. All of us experience great happiness, but sorrow, pain, betrayal, and loss will still befall us, as they did Jesus. This is not an exception to a good life; it is a fact of living in a world marred by sin. Will we still follow when we know that Jesus might be leading us to more pain than if we simply watched him pass by? What gives us staying power when others lay down their palm branches and reach instead for stones (John 8:59)?

Growing in our knowledge of Jesus and our relationship with him helps us choose to follow his lead every day. Our preparation for extraordinary struggle begins in ordinary preparations: spending time in the Word and in prayer, seeking the Spirit's guidance; worshipping with the body of Christ, and lamenting too; serving our brothers and sisters, our neighbors, and our enemies. May we celebrate Jesus in all circumstances and follow him, even to death.

B. Prayer

Dear Lord, thank you for sending Jesus, your Son, to save us from our sins. May we always praise him. In Jesus' name we pray. Amen.

C. Thought to Remember
Hosanna in the highest!
Jesus has come.

INVOLVEMENT LEARNING

Enhance your lesson with NIV Bible Student *(from your curriculum supplier) and the reproducible activity page (at www.standardlesson.com or in the back of the* NIV Standard Lesson Commentary Deluxe Edition*).*

Into the Lesson

Set up a scenario in which a celebrity comes to your town and your class is in charge of hosting that person for a weekend. Divide learners into groups of five. Ask each group to decide on a specific reason the visitor is a celebrity. Examples include all-star athletes, award-winning actors, best-selling writers, etc. Each group needs to create an agenda, plan meals, provide lodging, reserve spaces for events, and supply transportation. Give a 10-minute limit for them to come up with a basic weekend plan. Allow time to discuss the plans with the whole class, especially any differences based on the kind of celebrity who was hosted.

Alternative. Distribute the "Monarch for a Day" exercise from the activity page, which you can download. Allow learners one minute to work individually before pairing up to complete the activity and discuss.

After either of these activities, say, "Important people often are given special treatment. Today we will look closely at a story about how Jesus chose to present himself and the way others received him."

Into the Word

Ask a volunteer to read Matthew 21:1-11. Tell the class that they will develop a full issue of a daily newspaper in Jerusalem, based on the events of today's passage. Invite the learners to brainstorm ideas for the paper's title.

Once a title is chosen, divide the class into pairs or small groups. Give each group one of these assignments plus a possible article title to get them started:

Advice Column Group: "How to Plan Your Royal Entrance"

Celebrity Profile Group: "The Prophet from Nazareth"

Police Report Group: "Not-Quite-Stolen Livestock"

Public Survey Group: "False Prophet or Prophecy Fulfilled?"

Political Analysis Group: "Son of David: New King in Town?"

Traffic Report Group: "Crowds, Cloaks, Colts, and Cut Branches Create Chaos"

Option: If there are any artists in the class, a **Comic Strip** or **Feature Photo Group** can be formed.

Suggest that quotes or statistics can be created as long as they do not contradict the facts in the passage. Allow 15–20 minutes for the learners to create their pieces and submit them to the editorial team (the whole class) for review.

Into Life

To wrap up the newspaper issue, ask each pair or small group to write a letter to the editor in the form of a poem, prayer, or devotional thought, reflecting on what was seen and reported. The content should be from the learners' own points of view, as people reading the account of the triumphal entry from many years in the future and who know what happened in the following week. Allow 10 minutes for them to create their pieces before discussing these briefly as a class.

Option. Compile all the pieces into an official format (examples: in a binder, folder, or pasted on larger pieces of paper), and invite the whole group to reflect on this creative project.

Alternative. Distribute the "Who Is This?" exercise from the activity page to be completed according to the instructions. Encourage participants to take the exercise home this week, pray over it, and write down their responses. Also ask them to bring it back to share with the whole group next week.

Close the class by playing "All Glory, Laud, and Honor" (available on the internet) or another appropriate song. Give thanks in prayer for Jesus' saving work on the cross.

PASSOVER WITH THE KING

DEVOTIONAL READING: Matthew 26:17-30
BACKGROUND SCRIPTURE: Matthew 26:17-30

MATTHEW 26:17-30

¹⁷ On the first day of the Festival of Unleavened Bread, the disciples came to Jesus and asked, "Where do you want us to make preparations for you to eat the Passover?"

¹⁸ He replied, "Go into the city to a certain man and tell him, 'The Teacher says: My appointed time is near. I am going to celebrate the Passover with my disciples at your house.'"

¹⁹ So the disciples did as Jesus had directed them and prepared the Passover.

²⁰ When evening came, Jesus was reclining at the table with the Twelve. ²¹ And while they were eating, he said, "Truly I tell you, one of you will betray me."

²² They were very sad and began to say to him one after the other, "Surely you don't mean me, Lord?"

²³ Jesus replied, "The one who has dipped his hand into the bowl with me will betray me. ²⁴ The Son of Man will go just as it is written about him. But woe to that man who betrays the Son of Man! It would be better for him if he had not been born."

²⁵ Then Judas, the one who would betray him, said, "Surely you don't mean me, Rabbi?"

Jesus answered, "You have said so."

²⁶ While they were eating, Jesus took bread, and when he had given thanks, he broke it and gave it to his disciples, saying, "Take and eat; this is my body."

²⁷ Then he took a cup, and when he had given thanks, he gave it to them, saying, "Drink from it, all of you. ²⁸ This is my blood of the covenant, which is poured out for many for the forgiveness of sins. ²⁹ I tell you, I will not drink from this fruit of the vine from now on until that day when I drink it new with you in my Father's kingdom."

³⁰ When they had sung a hymn, they went out to the Mount of Olives.

KEY TEXT

I tell you, I will not drink from this fruit of the vine from now on until that day when I drink it new with you in my Father's kingdom. —**Matthew 26:29**

Photo © Getty Images

GOD FREES AND REDEEMS

Unit 2: Liberating Gospels
LESSONS 5–8

LESSON AIMS

After participating in this lesson, each learner will be able to:

1. Summarize what Jesus said at the last supper.

2. Explain the historic significance of the Feast of Unleavened Bread and Passover.

3. Suggest a way to improve his or her church's observance of the Lord's Supper.

LESSON OUTLINE

Introduction

A. Memory Food

What makes a great chef? Training is often required—to acquire excellent knife skills and other techniques, knowledge of flavor profiles and world cuisine, and so on. But one episode of each season of *Top Chef* highlights the passion behind a meal as the real genius of fantastic food. The episode in question is always a variation on creating a meal based on memory: a traditional holiday menu, the favorite dish of a deceased parent, the national food of one's home country. . . . Those who succeed in this challenge allow their memories to build the meal, and the love they feel translates onto the plate. Both chefs and judges might cry, because a meal is an opportunity to show one's self, celebrate one's heritage, and draw others into friendship.

The Passover meal commemorates the struggles that began in Egypt. When eating it together Jesus and his disciples not only remembered what had happened to their people but also anticipated what was to come.

B. Lesson Context

Our lesson takes us about midway into the week of Passover, after Jesus and many others had arrived in Jerusalem for the feast. (Other accounts of the meal are found in Matthew 26:26-29; Mark 14:22-24; Luke 22:17-20; John 13:1-30; compare 1 Corinthians 11:17-34). God commanded the Jewish people to observe the Passover Feast in memory of their dramatic deliverance from bondage in Egypt (Exodus 12). Passover became a national spiritual holiday. God had commanded it to be celebrated in Jerusalem on the 14th day of the first month (Leviticus 23:5; Numbers 28:16). This was the month of Nisan (formerly called Aviv in the Hebrew religious calendar), which is late March and early April.

During Jesus' time, groups of pilgrims slew their lambs at the Jerusalem temple, where the blood would be sprinkled on the altar. Then they went to celebrate the meal with their families or other companions in groups of at least 10 people. Despite the lamb's centrality to this feast, the bread and fruit of the vine play much larger roles in the accounts of Jesus' last supper (see Mark 14:12-26; Luke 22:7-38; contrast John 13:1-30). The symbolism of the animal's absence from the story should not be lost on us. As our lesson begins, the sacrifice was already present.

I. Readying the Passover
(MATTHEW 26:17-19)
A. Preparations (v. 17)

17. On the first day of the Festival of Unleavened Bread, the disciples came to Jesus and asked, "Where do you want us to make preparations for you to eat the Passover?"

Jewish tradition made Jerusalem the ideal destination for passover celebrations. The number of pilgrims arriving to celebrate *Passover* in Jerusalem in Jesus' time likely exceeded 85,000, or several thousand more Jews than lived in Jerusalem. In this severely overcrowded environment, finding a room in which to observe the meal could be difficult.

Because of the long journey, pilgrims had taken to purchasing sacrificial animals in Jerusalem instead of traveling with the beasts. This was not considered problematic until the merchants moved inside the temple, making the prayerful space into a commercial market (see Matthew 21:12-13). *Jesus* did not own a house or livestock (8:20), so his disciples would have purchased a lamb.

The Festival of Unleavened Bread lasted a full week immediately following the night of the Passover meal (Deuteronomy 16:1-8). Baking bread with yeast was a slow process. A piece of dough was set aside and allowed to rise; before the next meal, the leavened dough was worked into a new batch of dough so that it too would rise. The speed of unleavened bread's preparation reminded Jews of the haste of the flight from Egypt (Exodus 12:39).

What Do You Think?
How do you prepare yourself to eat the Lord's Supper?
Digging Deeper
How does your preparation honor Jesus?

Visual for Lesson 6. *Before closing with prayer, encourage the class to reflect on this promise throughout the week.*

B. Instructions (vv. 18-19)

18-19. He replied, "Go into the city to a certain man and tell him, 'The Teacher says: My appointed time is near. I am going to celebrate the Passover with my disciples at your house.'" So the disciples did as Jesus had directed them and prepared the Passover.

The city refers to Jerusalem. Jesus and his disciples approached from the neighboring village of Bethany (see lesson 5 commentary on Matthew 21:1a). It seems that Jesus had made arrangements with *a certain man* before the festival was upon them. Mark and Luke specify that the disciples were meant to find a man carrying "a jar of water" (Mark 14:13; Luke 22:10). Fetching water was typically woman's work, so his carrying the pitcher would make the man easy to spot.

Jesus was called *Teacher* throughout the Gospel of Matthew (8:19; 12:38; 22:16; etc.). In the mouths of those who respected him, the term acknowledged Jesus' wise teaching. Others called him this with sneering contempt. In either case, the term was appropriate of Jesus, but any speaker using it didn't necessarily have a full understanding of Jesus or his ministry and mission.

A form of the word here translated *time* echoes Judas's search for an "opportunity [appropriate time] to hand [Jesus] over" (Matthew 26:16). The Greek word is not uncommon. Still, the linguistic echo hints that God would use Judas's betrayal to bring about his purposes in Christ.

Mark 14:13 tells us that Jesus sent two *disciples*. Luke 22:8 reveals that they were Peter and John.

> *What Do You Think?*
> How does your congregation honor believers who serve behind the scenes?
> *Digging Deeper*
> What does this recognition (or lack thereof) communicate about the importance of many different ways to serve?

II. The Passover Plot
(MATTHEW 26:20-25)
A. Fellowship (v. 20)

20. When evening came, Jesus was reclining at the table with the Twelve.

Judas already had agreed to the contract on Jesus' life (Matthew 26:14-16), but none of the other disciples knew that. Therefore, *when evening came* for them to share the Passover, it was easy for Judas to join as one of *the Twelve* with his plan undetected.

In Jesus' time, the seating for special meals like this involved reclining on low couches. Participants leaned on the left elbow with their heads toward *the table* and their feet away from it, and they would eat with their right hands.

B. Betrayal (vv. 21-25)

21. And while they were eating, he said, "Truly I tell you, one of you will betray me."

Prophets introduced what they heard from the Lord with "this is what the Lord says" and close variations (examples: Joshua 7:13; Isaiah 28:16; Zechariah 8:2), while apostles often grounded similar statements with "it is written" (examples: Acts 1:20; 13:33; 15:13-18). Jesus did not appeal to any authority but his own whenever he said *truly I tell you* (examples: Matthew 5:18, 26; 6:2, 5, 16). In this subtle difference, Jesus asserted his place as God's Messiah, not just a prophet or teacher.

After Peter's confession of Jesus as the Son of God, the Lord had begun to reveal that he would be rejected by the Jewish leaders, suffer, and be killed (Matthew 16:21; Luke 9:22). This is the first time, however, that they had heard him say *one of you will betray me*.

22. They were very sad and began to say to him one after the other, "Surely you don't mean me, Lord?"

Jesus' comments hit the group with maximum force. They were extremely distressed. They never dreamed that the cancer of betrayal could infiltrate their group. Judas conducted his charade so flawlessly that no one suspected him.

Out of emotional anguish and with personal urgency, each asked, *Surely you don't mean me, Lord?* Judas had already arranged to betray Jesus (Matthew 26:14-16), but none of the other disciples suspected him. Each man trusted the others, so the only place to look was inward. Each one wondered if some fatal character flaw would be exposed to his own shame and disgrace. Still, each one worded the question with the expectation that Jesus would answer in the negative.

23. Jesus replied, "The one who has dipped his hand into the bowl with me will betray me.

As with many cultures still today, the custom was for food to be shared by everyone out of large serving dishes rather than individual place settings. *The one who has dipped his hand into the bowl with me* could refer to anyone in the room, for all of them were sharing in that activity during the evening meal. In Matthew's telling, Jesus did not narrow down the list of suspects (contrast John 13:26-28). This emphasized a sentiment expressed by the psalmist's lament, "Even my close friend, someone I trusted, one who shared my bread, has turned against me" (Psalm 41:9). Jesus knew that the betrayal would indeed come from within their group.

24. "The Son of Man will go just as it is written about him. But woe to that man who betrays the Son of Man! It would be better for him if he had not been born."

The phrase *Son of Man* evokes Jesus' connection with fragile humans as well as with Daniel's prophesied messianic figure. This one received authority and glory from God, and all nations worship him forever (Daniel 7:13-14). In using the title of himself, Jesus chose a phrase that was known but did not have the expectations of *king* or *messiah*. Thus the phrase was more enigmatic, not something that people immediately associated with earthly rule or authority.

Jesus acknowledged his willing intent to fulfill God's plan *as it is written about him* in the Old Testament (example: Isaiah 53). He never dodged the work of giving his life to pay sin's price for our eternal salvation.

But Jesus sternly warned that his betrayer would not be allowed to dodge the consequences of his rebellion either. (See also Acts 1:15-20.) In the terrible judgment he would face, Judas could not argue, "I wasn't warned!" Jesus lamented Judas's choice and the loss of his beloved friend.

> **What Do You Think?**
> What scriptural warnings do you find difficult to remember or obey?
> *Digging Deeper*
> In what situations would remembering these warnings change your actions?

25. Then Judas, the one who would betray him, said, "Surely you don't mean me, Rabbi?" Jesus answered, "You have said so."

Judas addressed Jesus with the same form of question as the other disciples, except that he used the title *Rabbi* rather than Lord (see Matthew 26:22, above). While this was an honorary title for exceptional teachers of the law (23:7-8), when applied to Jesus it missed the heart of his identity. Judas is the only disciple in the Gospel of Matthew to refer to Jesus this way (see also 26:49). Judas may have believed that Jesus was a wise teacher, but there is no record that he confessed Jesus as Lord.

Judas maintained his charade of loyalty to the very end. Knowing full well that he was the one, he still asked, *Surely you don't mean me?* In true prophetic fashion, Jesus threw off the cover to reveal Judas's wicked betrayal. If Judas thought he had successfully hidden his evil work, he found out what he should have known all along: nothing can be hidden from the Lord.

But the Lord's reply fell on deaf ears. Although Jesus made it clear to Judas that he knew about the nefarious plan, Judas would betray him any-

way. The chief priests and elders had previously planned to wait until after the weeklong feast in order to avoid any riots (Matthew 26:5). Perhaps Judas, feeling exposed, accelerated his plans to betray Jesus that very night (26:45-47).

> **What Do You Think?**
> Who knows you well enough to point out your spiritual blindspots that can become sinful action?
> *Digging Deeper*
> What heart changes are required for you to better heed your wise friend's warnings?

❧ *DINNER PARTY* ❧

What ingredients are required for a dinner party? Although many items could be included—background music, table linens and silverware, lighting, flower arrangements, and so on—only two things are really necessary: food and people. And a *successful* dinner party combines good food and great company.

Imagine your ideal dinner party. Who is around your table? What food do you prepare to share with them? Your group might mirror mine, with best friends who have stuck by your side in the hills and the valleys. We might both include family, spiritual mentors, friends of friends, out-of-town visitors, and so on.

Christ's final dinner party included those who walked with him and learned from him. The success of the party was in question, though, once Jesus revealed that he would be betrayed. And yet we celebrate this meal and remember him. How might Judas's presence at Jesus' last supper cause you to reevaluate who a dinner party should include?
—L. P.

III. Passover and the Kingdom
(MATTHEW 26:26-30)
A. Bread and Body (v. 26)

26a. While they were eating, Jesus took bread, and when he had given thanks, he broke it

Traditionally in the Passover meal, God was

blessed (gave *thanks* to) as the one who delivered Israel from Egypt and provided their bread. The original Greek is less clear about whether *Jesus* blessed the *bread* or the Father here. (A similar issue comes up in Matthew 14:19.) Giving thanks for the meal comes closer to later Christian practice of blessing the bread and the fruit of the vine in their own Lord's Supper remembrances (example: 1 Corinthians 10:16).

26b. and gave it to his disciples, saying, "Take and eat; this is my body."

The Passover meal was infused with symbolic significance. Eating the bread called for the explicit reminder of God's deliverance. This encouraged feelings of continuity with ancestors —with Jewish participants' knowing that they were part of that same people God had saved.

Jesus didn't do away with that ancient symbolism. He magnified and expanded it, bringing God's salvation to fulfillment. The broken bread took on new significance as the *body* of Christ, a new symbol of God's miraculous salvation to be remembered and shared by the community of believers. Though the *disciples* apparently obeyed Jesus, this symbolism would lead to horrifying rumors in the Roman world that Christians were cannibals.

B. Cup and Blood (vv. 27-29)

27a. Then he took a cup, and when he had given thanks,

It's unclear which *cup* of four drunk at Passover Jesus referred to here. The regulations regarding these cups are found in the Mishnah, an ancient rabbinic text that was finalized around AD 200. Each cup is associated with promises God made in Exodus 6:6-7: "I will bring you out . . . I will free you from being slaves to [the Egyptians] . . . I will redeem you . . . I will take you as my own people."

The third cup (associated with "I will redeem you") was typically a benediction. Jesus likely offered his own *thanks* in place of a more traditional blessing with the third. The "cup of thanksgiving" named in 1 Corinthians 10:16 further suggests that the third cup is in view.

27b-28. he gave it to them, saying, "Drink from it, all of you. This is my blood of the cove-

nant, which is poured out for many for the forgiveness of sins.**

The blood of the Passover lamb had protected the Israelites from God's final plague (Exodus 12:13), and blood was later sprinkled on the people as they entered a new relationship with God (24:5-8). However, nowhere was it suggested that the people should drink the blood; quite the contrary, this practice was explicitly forbidden for *any* animal (Leviticus 17:10-14). The command to *drink from it, all of you* intensified the jarring symbolism of eating Jesus' body (compare Matthew 20:22-28).

While symbolism of being covered in the blood of the Lamb persists, ingesting the *blood of the covenant, which is poured out for many for the forgiveness of sins* speaks to an inner change, not only an outer show (compare Isaiah 53:11-12; Romans 5:15). This may remind the reader of God's promise to "remove from them their heart of stone and give them a heart of flesh" (Ezekiel 11:19; compare 36:26)—a promise of spiritual renewal, which is fulfilled through faith in Christ. The covenant in Exodus required obedience to God and strict loyalty to him alone (Exodus 20:1-6), which the Israelites proved unable to do. The prophesied new covenant would be different from the one their ancestors entered into at Sinai (see Jeremiah 31:31-34). This new covenant was enacted by the shedding of Jesus' blood.

29. "I tell you, I will not drink from this fruit of the vine from now on until that day when I drink it new with you in my Father's kingdom."

The fourth Passover cup traditionally looked forward to the coming kingdom, which differed greatly from earthly kingdoms (consider descriptions from Jesus' Sermon on the Mount in Matthew 5–7 regarding his Father's kingdom ethics). Jesus either abstained from the final cup or declared that this was his last time drinking it . . . for now. In doing so he declared by word and deed that the *Father's kingdom* was coming, and Jesus would celebrate in that kingdom with the disciples. This was in keeping with various depictions of God's kingdom being or centering around a feast (examples: Isaiah 24:23; 25:6-8; Matthew 22:1-14; Luke 13:29; Revelation 19:7-9).

> *What Do You Think?*
> What memories of Christ do you focus on when eating the Lord's Supper?
> *Digging Deeper*
> What promises come to mind as you anticipate drinking the cup with Jesus?

❧ REMEMBER AND DO ❧

As a young child I knew I could count on Grandpa Ray. He taught me what love is by demonstrating the importance of building and keeping trust, acting humbly, and caring deeply for others.

One day we were downtown together. Grandpa Ray saw a man curled up across the street. This man seemed very distressed. I remember vividly my grandpa going out of his way to get this man some food and pray with him. Grandpa stated afterward, "The best way to remember Christ's love for us is to be Christ's love for others." To this day, Grandpa Ray's words call me to demonstrate that I remember Jesus' love for me through my service to others in obedience to him.

When we participate in the Lord's Supper, we remember Jesus' sacrifice for us. But we also look forward to sharing the cup with Jesus. Our lives must reflect this expectation. How does your daily life demonstrate your memory of Jesus' work and your hope in his promises? —L. P.

C. Closing Song (v. 30)

30. When they had sung a hymn, they went out to the Mount of Olives.

The Passover meal ended with singing, traditionally from the Hallel, Psalms 113–118. These songs extol the Lord as the one true God of all the nations, among other praises.

The Mount of Olives lay to the east of Jerusalem. Its elevation gave an excellent view of the city, including the temple. It was here, specifically at Gethsemane, that Jesus would be betrayed and his disciples scattered (Matthew 26:36, 47-56, not in our printed text); he then faced the trials that sent him to his death on the cross (26:57-68; 27:11-26).

Conclusion
A. The Lord's Supper

Jesus knew that his whole life pointed to a final Passover that would be an act of ultimate obedience. He would be preparing himself to fulfill his mission as the perfect Passover Lamb (see John 1:29; 1 Corinthians 5:7; Revelation 5:12; 13:8). His life was given in sacrifice for the sins of humanity, washing us clean in his blood so that our sins are forgiven, never to be brought against us. One last Passover with his closest friends would mark the beginning of a new Lord's Supper that galvanizes Christian worship to this day.

Themes of remembrance and thanksgiving have united Christians worldwide for nearly 2,000 years in a practice that honors our crucified Lord. All Christians are given opportunity to remember God's miraculous salvation—with a new ceremonial meal shared by a new family. We participate together, knowing that we are part of a body in a new covenant with God, forgiven of sins through the body and blood of Jesus. What the prophets dreamed of is the life that we today have been given in Christ.

At the same time, we long for the ultimate coming of the Father's kingdom when we will sit at the table with Jesus himself. We live in anticipation of this joy. Every bite of bread or sip of the fruit of the vine connects us to the past, present, and future of God's story.

B. Prayer

Father, thank you for sending Jesus as our perfect sacrificial Lamb and for inviting us to your table. Let the anticipation of sharing the feast with Jesus guide us daily. In Jesus' name we pray. Amen.

C. Thought to Remember

The Lord's Supper reminds us that we are part of God's past, present, and future story.

HOW TO SAY IT

Aviv	*A*-bib.
Hallel (Hebrew)	Ha-*layl*.
Nisan	*Nye*-san.

INVOLVEMENT LEARNING

Enhance your lesson with NIV Bible Student (from your curriculum supplier) and the reproducible activity page (at www.standardlesson.com or in the back of the NIV Standard Lesson Commentary Deluxe Edition).

Into the Lesson

Bring a favorite snack that has special significance to you to share with the class. As the learners eat, tell the memory attached to that food. Ask volunteers to share what tastes trigger memories for them. *Option.* In the week before class, ask for volunteers to supplement your snack with their own and to be prepared to share their own memories.

Alternative. Ask for volunteers to share a memory of a special meal they ate, including the occasion, who was present, and what was eaten. After allowing time for responses, ask what tastes (whether entire dishes, combinations of spices, etc.) can bring this memory to mind without other prompting.

Say, "Our sense of taste is a powerful link to our memories and emotions. In today's passage, we will see how Jesus takes a traditional meal and gives new significance to it."

Into the Word

Ask a volunteer to read Matthew 26:17-19 aloud. Divide the whole group into pairs (or small groups). Have the pairs look up the following passages for more context regarding Old Testament regulations and accounts of Passovers: Exodus 12:1-27; Deuteronomy 16:1-8; 2 Chronicles 30; 35:1-19; Ezra 6:19-22. Ask each pair to jot down notes about preparation, celebration, historical context, and anything else they find interesting. After about 10 minutes, ask the pairs to share their responses with the whole class. Supplement with information from the lesson 6 Lesson Context and any pertinent commentary.

Ask a volunteer to read Matthew 26:20-25. Have the pairs jot down any connections they hear in this second reading. Tell the pairs they are going to role-play the reactions of Judas and the apostles to Jesus' declaration; both parties will take a turn as the apostles and as Judas. The pairs should consider how the emotional reaction differs between the apostles and Judas.

Ask a volunteer to read Matthew 26:26-30. Have the pairs once again role-play, this time focusing on how the apostles and Judas would experience the meal, having *already* been told that one of them would betray Jesus. Following this exercise, bring the class together to discuss what they've found.

Alternative. Distribute to pairs "The Passover Lamb" exercise from the activity page, which you can download. Have them complete as directed before allowing groups to share their responses.

Into Life

Allow one minute for personal, private reflection on any sins Jesus would want learners to repent of in order to experience the joy of the Lord's Supper more fully.

Ask a volunteer to read 1 Corinthians 11:17-34. As the class listens, have them jot down ideas that are important for Christians to keep in mind when eating the Lord's Supper. Ask specifically for ideas to help both individuals and the congregation be better prepared to eat the meal together. Then discuss these observations.

Next, allow one minute for personal reflection on aspects of joy and gratitude to consider whenever they're preparing to take the Lord's Supper. Ask volunteers to share, but do not put anyone on the spot. Discuss the effect of remembering the future feast in which we will see Jesus face-to-face.

Alternative. Distribute the "Remember!" exercise from the activity page. Encourage learners to complete the activity at home, as directed, and be prepared to share with the class at the start of next week's time.

Close the class with a prayer of thanksgiving for Jesus' sacrifice and for the meal that we still eat in his memory.

RESURRECTION OF THE KING!

DEVOTIONAL READING: Matthew 28:1-10
BACKGROUND SCRIPTURE: Matthew 27; 28:1-10

MATTHEW 28:1-10

¹ After the Sabbath, at dawn on the first day of the week, Mary Magdalene and the other Mary went to look at the tomb.

² There was a violent earthquake, for an angel of the Lord came down from heaven and, going to the tomb, rolled back the stone and sat on it. ³ His appearance was like lightning, and his clothes were white as snow. ⁴ The guards were so afraid of him that they shook and became like dead men.

⁵ The angel said to the women, "Do not be afraid, for I know that you are looking for Jesus, who was crucified. ⁶ He is not here; he has risen, just as he said. Come and see the place where he lay. ⁷ Then go quickly and tell his disciples: 'He has risen from the dead and is going ahead of you into Galilee. There you will see him.' Now I have told you."

⁸ So the women hurried away from the tomb, afraid yet filled with joy, and ran to tell his disciples. ⁹ Suddenly Jesus met them. "Greetings," he said. They came to him, clasped his feet and worshiped him. ¹⁰ Then Jesus said to them, "Do not be afraid. Go and tell my brothers to go to Galilee; there they will see me."

KEY TEXT

Jesus said to them, "Do not be afraid. Go and tell my brothers to go to Galilee; there they will see me."
—Matthew 28:10

Photo © Getty Images

GOD FREES AND REDEEMS

Unit 2: Liberating Gospels
LESSONS 5–8

LESSON AIMS

After participating in this lesson, each learner will be able to:

1. List facts of Jesus' first post-resurrection appearance in Matthew's account.

2. Compare and contrast that account with those of the other Gospels.

3. Sing with fellow classmates "Because He Lives" as an act of communal worship.

LESSON OUTLINE

Introduction

A. When Everything Changed

"Rome wasn't built in a day" expresses the foolishness of expecting change to happen immediately and completely. But people frequently characterize events like the dropping of the atomic bomb, the Apollo 11 moon landing, the fall of the Berlin Wall, and 9/11 as having changed everything. And to some extent, they are right. Events that have worldwide repercussions, test the limits of human ingenuity and technological prowess, and/or expose great hatred or capacity for unity—these often do mark the *beginning* of a shift in how we think of ourselves and our world.

Today is Resurrection Sunday, when Christians around the world focus attention on a Sunday two millennia ago. On that day *everything* actually did change, and the world has never been the same.

B. Lesson Context

Jesus' followers had hoped he was the one who would redeem Israel (Luke 24:19-21), but he had been brutally executed at the hands of the Jewish leaders and Roman officials (Matthew 26:47–27:50). Ominous events had accompanied his death. A deep darkness covered the land (27:45). The curtain of the temple was torn from top to bottom, and an earthquake had split rocks and opened graves in the area (27:51-53). The manner in which Jesus died led a Roman centurion and other guards to acclaim Jesus as the Son of God (27:54).

Matthew 28:1-10 is the first of four resurrection narratives in the Gospels (see Mark 16; Luke 24; John 20). These all paint the same picture in broad strokes: Jesus Christ was crucified, buried, and rose from the dead. The overarching truth of these three events guides each writer, even when they differ on details. And the differences in emphasis and detail among the resurrection narratives should comfort us. They indicate that the accounts are not the product of a conspiracy created by a group focused on getting their stories straight. The resurrection narratives complement one another as they affirm that witnesses saw an empty grave and the risen Savior.

Every Gospel account counters the disinformation and lies of the chief priests and Pharisees that resulted after Jesus' resurrection. Many Jews anticipated that God would inaugurate his kingdom in its fullness at the end of history. At that time, the righteous would be raised bodily to eternal life (Daniel 12:1-2; John 11:23-26). Because the Jewish leaders feared that Jesus' disciples would steal the body from the grave and then claim Jesus was alive, the religious leaders had convinced Pilate to authorize guards to be placed at the tomb (Matthew 27:62-66).

I. The Empty Tomb
(Matthew 28:1-7)
A. The Women Arrive (v. 1)

1. After the Sabbath, at dawn on the first day of the week, Mary Magdalene and the other Mary went to look at the tomb.

Sunset marked the end of *the Sabbath*. Dawn of *the first day of the week* (Sunday) was the first opportunity to go to the tomb to care for Jesus' body. *The tomb* and the stone to close it had been provided by a wealthy disciple named Joseph of Arimathea (Matthew 27:57-60). Nicodemus had aided Joseph in placing Jesus in the tomb on Friday, though without any ceremony—the Sabbath and its rest fast approached with sunset Friday (John 19:38-42). The women arrived on Sunday, not out of a sense of morbid curiosity or even simple mourning, but with spices to continue preparation of Jesus' body for burial (Mark 16:1; Luke 24:1).

Mary Magdalene and the other Mary have key roles in Matthew's passion narrative. In contrast to the apostles, the women were present at Jesus' crucifixion (Matthew 27:50-56) and saw where he was buried (27:57-61). Mary Magdalene was a follower of Jesus from the early days of his ministry. Jesus had delivered her from a terrifying case of demon possession (Luke 8:2). We remind ourselves that Magdalene is not a surname in the modern sense. Rather, it designates this particular Mary as being "from Magdala."

The "other" Mary was the mother of James and Joseph (Matthew 27:56) and possibly the wife of Clopas (John 19:25). Though the other Gospels name additional women (see Mark 16:1; Luke 24:10), Matthew may have focused on these two because of their prominence among those of Jewish background who first read his Gospel.

B. The Angel Appears (vv. 2-4)
2a. There was a violent earthquake,

"Behold" (*KJV*; not translated in the NIV) is used to call close attention to what follows. An *earthquake* had also occurred at Jesus' death (Matthew 27:51). God's presence or work was sometimes accompanied by grand disruptions of nature (examples: Exodus 19:16-19; Acts 16:26). Those who did not know that God was present would be terrified in the face of nature's fury without realizing that the far more terrifying Lord of the universe was present.

> *What Do You Think?*
> Do displays of natural destruction cause you to fear God? Why or why not?
> *Digging Deeper*
> What place do calmer natural scenes have in causing you to revere the Lord?

2b. for an angel of the Lord came down from heaven

Angels *of the Lord* had played a pivotal role in Matthew's account of the birth of Jesus, communicating and making clear God's words and intentions (Matthew 1:20; 2:13, 19-20). Even without speaking, the angel's presence here suggests the tomb was emptied by divine agency *from heaven*, not by physical, human activity.

2c. and, going to the tomb, rolled back the stone and sat on it.

Stones used to close tombs were usually disk-shaped and extremely heavy. For added difficulty in accessing *the tomb*, those guarding it had placed a seal on the stone (Matthew 27:65-66). That the angel *rolled* it *back* singlehandedly points to his power.

Interestingly, Jesus had already risen and left the grave before any of the Gospels indicate that *the stone* was moved. The resurrected Lord could

Visual for Lessons 7. *While discussing verse 1, ask learners how they follow the women's example and what effect their own seeking has on others.*

enter or exit a locked room without opening the door (example: John 20:19-20, 26-27). He did not need the stone to be removed in order to exit the tomb.

3-4. His appearance was like lightning, and his clothes were white as snow. The guards were so afraid of him that they shook and became like dead men.

The angel's *appearance* was similar to Jesus' own during the transfiguration (compare Matthew 17:2). The angel's physical appearance clearly marked him as a supernatural being and caused *the guards* great fear (compare 17:5-6). The Greek verb translated *shook* is related to the noun translated "earthquake" (see Matthew 28:2a, above). The echo of this word makes the stated quaking seem more violent than if it stood alone. This was not a shiver; it was a human quake. Revelation 1:17 describes a similar reaction by John to a vision of the ascended Jesus.

Notice the irony: Jesus is alive, but the guards who thought they were guarding a dead body were themselves *like dead men*!

❧ GOD'S FIREWORKS SHOW ❧

I shot awake around 4 a.m. Even with my eyes closed, I kept seeing flashes of light coming in through the windows. Looking out the sliding screen door, I saw not the prowlers I expected but the black sky itself erupting with light!

I had never seen lightning like this—

continuous, with no break in the brightness. There was no rain, no thunder. I gasped when the sky brightened nearly to daylight for a brief moment. It was as if God was putting on a fireworks show.

I wonder if this is how the women felt when they saw the angel at the tomb: dazzled, mesmerized. They sought Jesus, and God sent a stunning sight to greet them. Then as now, those who seek Jesus find him and find themselves in awe. This week seek Jesus without an agenda. Though there probably won't be an angel or a lightning show, know that God is prepared to amaze you when you seek his Son.   —K. D.

C. The Angel Speaks (vv. 5-7)

5a. The angel said to the women, "Do not be afraid,

Earlier in Matthew, an angel had told Joseph not to fear the events around Jesus' conception and birth (Matthew 1:20). Now, even though the guards—whom we would expect to be pinnacles of courage—were incapacitated, *the women* were called to *not be afraid*. This *angel* was potentially a much more frightening presence than the guards. The women's reaction to this exhortation is not immediately revealed (see 28:8, below).

5b-6a. "for I know that you are looking for Jesus, who was crucified. He is not here; he has risen, just as he said.

One would expect a crucified man to both be and remain dead. But in Jesus' case, crucifixion and death were the last barriers to fulfilling the Father's plan. *Jesus* had *said* he would rise from the dead on the third day (Matthew 16:21; 17:9; etc.), although the disciples clearly had not understood what he meant (examples: 17:22-23; John 20:9).

Jesus knew he was not caught up in some tragic accident of history. His death and resurrection confirmed his identity as Lord, Messiah, and Son of God (Acts 2:22-24, 36; Romans 1:4). Death was handily defeated by the Creator, the Lord of life (1 Corinthians 15:54-55). The immediate effects of Jesus' crucifixion—suffering, abuse, humiliation, and painful death—are past (Philippians 2:6-11). The continuing results of that crucifixion—the forgiveness of sins—endure (Hebrews 10:19-23).

This is the first explicit notice that Jesus *has risen*. The New Testament contains no accounts of Jesus' resurrection per se. Instead, there are records of disciples finding the tomb empty and encountering the resurrected Jesus (examples: Matthew 28:9, below; 1 Corinthians 15:3-8). These serve as part of the validation that the event occurred, even though no one was present to observe it.

Paul's letters consistently emphasize the Father's role in raising the Son (examples: Romans 6:4; Galatians 1:1; compare Acts 5:30). The Son had trusted the Father and submitted to the Father's will even to the point of death (Matthew 26:42; Luke 23:46). As a result, the Father had exalted the Son.

6b. "Come and see the place where he lay.

The emphasis on the empty tomb counters any notion that Jesus' followers were only experiencing Christ's spiritual presence. Jesus' resurrection involved the coming to life again of his physical body—even though that body was changed (see Matthew 28:3-4, above; compare 1 Corinthians 15:35-53). Jesus had been dead for three days, but he was alive again. *The place where* Jesus *lay* was vacant!

7a. "Then go quickly and tell his disciples: 'He has risen from the dead

The Old Testament insisted that testimony be confirmed by "two or three witnesses" (Deuteronomy 17:6; 19:15). But women were not considered reliable witnesses and so were normally not called on to bear witness in Jewish courts. No one in the first-century AD world trying to fabricate this story would have made women the lead witnesses to it. How extraordinary that the Lord chose female disciples to be the first witnesses to the resurrection!

Mary Magdalene and the other Mary were not called to testify that Jesus' body was gone, which anyone could see by looking in the tomb as they had. Instead they carried the much more wonderful and astounding message that Jesus *has risen from the dead!* From this point forward, the resurrection of Jesus would be the heart of the church's proclamation (example: 1 Corinthians 15:1-4).

The *disciples* to whom the angel referred may have been the larger group of Jesus' followers that the remaining 11 apostles were a part of (Acts 1:15). However, it is more likely that it was the eleven to whom the women were to *tell* the message (compare Matthew 28:10 with 28:16).

> **What Do You Think?**
> How does your belief in the resurrection of Christ influence your daily life?
> *Digging Deeper*
> What changes might a greater focus on the hope of resurrection make in your routines?

7b. "'and is going ahead of you into Galilee. There you will see him.' Now I have told you."

Galilee was the area of primary focus in Jesus' ministry (Matthew 4:12-25; 9:35–11:1; Luke 8:1-3). The particular city of ministry focus was Jerusalem. The disciples were reminded to leave the *city* of primary focus and return to the *area* of primary focus.

Jesus had earlier told the disciples that he would go before them *into Galilee* after he had risen (Matthew 26:32). Far from Jesus' death throwing off all their hopes and dreams, the disciples would come to know that his death was always part of Jesus' plans. Far from thwarting his intention to meet with them, his death was a necessary step toward that fateful day. Within a few weeks Jesus would commission those who had deserted him, just where he had said he'd find them (28:16-20).

Just as the Old Testament phrases "the Lord has spoken" (Jeremiah 13:15; etc.) or "this is what the Lord . . . says" (Exodus 5:1; etc.) emphasized the need for the hearer to heed what was said, *Now I have told you* lent additional authority and urgency to the angel's message.

HOW TO SAY IT

Arimathea   *Air*-uh-muh-***thee***-uh (*th* as in *thin*).
Clopas   *Klo*-pus.
Magdalene   *Mag*-duh-leen or Mag-duh-*lee*-nee.
Nicodemus   *Nick*-uh-***dee***-mus.

II. The Risen Lord
(MATTHEW 28:8-10)
A. The Women Obey (v. 8)

8. So the women hurried away from the tomb, afraid yet filled with joy, and ran to tell his disciples.

In obedience, *the women hurried away* in a mixture of emotion. Their fear likely stemmed both from awe of their contact with the angel and the magnitude of what they had heard. But they were also *filled with joy* that was sweeping away the grief of previous days. This great joy propelled them to run on their mission *to tell his disciples* about Jesus.

For how surprising it would have been to the first-century church that the women were the first to testify to Jesus' resurrection, Matthew had not hidden the importance of faithful women throughout his Gospel. Jesus' genealogy mentioned four ancestresses (Matthew 1:3, 5-6). Throughout his ministry, Jesus had had significant encounters with women (examples: 15:21-28; 26:6-13; 28:1, above). Though women's voices can be lost in history—especially when most believers were illiterate, and those who were not were usually men—their role in this narrative celebrates the very beginning of faithful women's bearing witness to Jesus' resurrection, which has continued through the centuries.

> **What Do You Think?**
> What prevents you from running to tell others the news of Jesus' resurrection?
>
> *Digging Deeper*
> Is testifying about Christe to other believers a precursor to evangelizing? Why or why not?

❧ FEAR AND JOY ❧

My mother plans carefully, always has an exit strategy, and researches excessively. She packs extra sunscreen, extra napkins, extra everything. And she always has an emergency fund for unexpected bills.

One day this risk-averse woman decided to go skydiving. It was totally against her character! But even though she was scared, she wanted to know what it felt like to be completely out of control, just once. Following her safe, though ungraceful, landing, Mom had the biggest grin on her face! It's one of my most joyous memories of her.

My minister likes to say, "The safest place you can be is living dangerously in the will of God." God doesn't always ask safe things of us—just ask the women who were told to report that Jesus was alive! When we're obeying the Lord, even if we're afraid, He'll be with us. What's one scary thing you can do for the Lord this week? Do it, and rediscover the thrill and joy of obedience.　　—K. D.

B. Jesus Speaks (vv. 9-10)

9a. Suddenly Jesus met them. "Greetings," he said.

As though the honor of announcing the angel's words was not enough, the women were *met* by *Jesus* himself! Their faithfulness to him was rewarded in his faithfulness and care for them.

Greetings can also be translated "rejoice" (example: Matthew 5:12). The astute reader might hear more echoes from Jesus' birth: a form of the Greek greeting here described the reaction of the magi when they saw the star over the place where the Christ child was (2:10). Jesus' greeting also echoes the taunts Jesus suffered as he died (27:29). These women would have heard those taunts. Though the soldiers had not been sincere, giving reverence to Jesus was appropriate from his birth forward, and never more so than on the day of his resurrection.

9b. They came to him, clasped his feet and worshiped him.

The women's actions on encountering Jesus make two very important points. Taking hold of Jesus' *feet* shows that Jesus was present physically, having experienced a bodily resurrection (see Matthew 28:6b, above). He was not a hallucination, vision, or phantom.

Second, they *worshiped* Jesus, and Jesus accepted that worship. The Old Testament Scriptures make clear that worship belongs to God alone (examples: Exodus 34:14; Deuteronomy 8:19). Neither angels nor apostles allowed people to worship them (examples: Acts 10:25-26; 14:11-

15; Revelation 22:8-9). The women's actions signaled that they rightly believed Jesus was God in the flesh.

> *What Do You Think?*
> How do you express your worship of Christ outside of church services?
> *Digging Deeper*
> What Scriptures inform your worship habits?

10. Then Jesus said to them, "Do not be afraid. Go and tell my brothers to go to Galilee; there they will see me."

Jesus' words reinforced the angel's commands to *not be afraid* and to *go and tell* (Matthew 28:5a, 7a, above). The call to fearlessness also parallels earlier commands Jesus gave his disciples when they experienced awesome demonstrations of his identity and power (examples: 14:27; 17:7).

While the angel called the eleven "disciples," *Jesus* emphasized his special familial love for them by calling them *brothers* instead (compare Matthew 12:46-50; 25:40). His command also makes clear that the men's fleeing during Jesus' trial and crucifixion did not result in his abandoning them. All that he had said would happen really would happen.

It appears Jesus spent at least seven days in Jerusalem (John 20:19, 26) before he moved on to *Galilee* for a time of intense teaching with his disciples (John 21; Acts 1:3-11). Isaiah 9:1-2 calls this region "Galilee of the nations," and Matthew 4:15 calls it "Galilee of the Gentiles." Since "Gentiles" simply means "nations," the reference to Galilee here probably alludes to the large numbers of non-Jews who resided in Galilee. It is highly fitting that the resurrected Jesus would launch his program of salvation from Galilee into all nations (Matthew 28:19-20).

> *What Do You Think?*
> What fear do you need to set aside in order to faithfully obey God?
> *Digging Deeper*
> In what ways does Christian fellowship bring you confidence to act without fear?

Conclusion

A. He Is Risen!

At the center of Christian faith is the affirmation that Jesus rose from the dead. This is the testimony of women who saw the empty tomb and who encountered the resurrected Jesus. We can trust their words, and we can live in the light of the message they were given.

Believers have a new start and new life in Christ. We need not fear the grave. The resurrection of Jesus has changed everything, and we have been entrusted with that message. Because we are released from the fear of death, we are free to live for God. The faithful life requires much of us, but all that we do begins with the joy and awe of Jesus' resurrection. From there we go out into the world to announce his resurrection and the invitation to join in his kingdom.

Jesus' resurrection demonstrates that the kingdom of God has broken into history. Its final consummation will come at the return of Christ (1 Corinthians 15:20-24; Revelation 11:15). Believers may be confident that, when Christ returns, the Father will bring with Christ the dead in Christ who also had submitted and entrusted themselves to the Father (1 Thessalonians 4:14; 2 Timothy 1:12). The resurrection of Jesus is the guarantee of the believers' resurrection and transformation at Christ's second coming (example: 2 Corinthians 4:14). As believers, we live between the ages. The kingdom has been inaugurated, but we await its consummation (Colossians 1:12-13; Hebrews 12:28; 2 Peter 1:10-11). May our lives reflect God's kingdom presence on earth in anticipation of the day we will experience it fully with him.

B. Prayer

We praise you, our Father, because you sent your Son, Jesus, to die for our sins. We praise you because you raised him from the dead and you will raise us to eternal life. In Jesus' name we pray. Amen.

C. Thought to Remember

Our king is risen! Everything has changed!

INVOLVEMENT LEARNING

Enhance your lesson with NIV Bible Student *(from your curriculum supplier) and the reproducible activity page (at www.standardlesson.com or in the back of the* NIV Standard Lesson Commentary Deluxe Edition*).*

Into the Lesson

Before the lesson, write "Events That Changed the United States" on the board. Record responses on the board. For any events that occurred within the lifetime of the learners, ask for volunteers to share how they experienced the event and how life seemed changed afterward.

After a few minutes, erase "the United States" and replace it with "My Life." Allow one minute for individual thought about personal events (unlikely to be shared by the larger class) before asking for volunteers to share. *Option.* Instead of sharing with the whole class, learners can be divided into pairs or small groups to facilitate sharing.

After this activity, say, "There are moments that have greatly impacted all our lives. We share some of these, and others are specific to our own lives. But as believers, we can agree that there is one event that changed everything for everyone, everywhere, for all time: the resurrection of Jesus Christ."

Into the Word

Ask a volunteer to read Matthew 27:50-66 and another to read 28:1-10. Give learners a handout (you prepare) with the text from these two passages printed side by side. Have the learners highlight people or events that are similar across the two texts. Examples include an earthquake (v. 51), the presence of guards (vv. 54, 65-66), and feelings of terror (v. 54). After 10 minutes, bring the groups back for class discussion of the parallels they discovered. Consult the lesson 7 commentary for more information.

Break the class in half to explore the theme of fear in Matthew 28:1-10. *Option.* Both of the following groups can be split into smaller groups to facilitate more conversation under these two main ideas. **The Paralyzing Fear Group** will consider the negative effects of fear, starting with the guards at the tomb. **The Faithful Fear Group** will consider the positive effects of rejecting fear, starting with the women at the tomb. Both groups should provide biblical citations of 1) other times people were told not to fear and 2) what resulted when they obeyed or did not obey. Invite each group to share their list with the whole group.

Alternative. Distribute the "Declaration and Command" exercise from the activity page, which you can download, to be completed in pairs as directed.

Into Life

Allow learners one minute of silent reflection on their own experiences of fear that have resulted in paralysis or in faithfulness. Ask for volunteers to share.

Have learners pair up to discuss what fears they have about spreading the gospel. How do Jesus' words encourage them to overcome this fear? After a few minutes of discussion, give learners one minute to write down reminders not to give in to fear but, instead, to call others to meet Jesus. Enourage learners to put these reminders somewhere they can be seen daily.

Alternative. Distribute the "He Arose!" exercise from the activity page. Play a recording of the song "Up from the Grave He Arose" (available on the internet) and encourage participants to sing along with the chorus. Ask learners to jot down any words or phrases in the song lyrics that are most meaningful to them. Allow time for volunteers to share how the words are meaningful in their testimony.

Close the class by playing "Because He Lives" or another resurrection song and encouraging the class to sing along. Offer a prayer of thanksgiving to Jesus for his sacrifice and for all the reasons he has given us to overcome our fears. Ask for his help in faithfully calling others to him.

FREEDOM IN THE KING

DEVOTIONAL READING: John 8:31-38
BACKGROUND SCRIPTURE: John 8:31-38

JOHN 8:31-38

31 To the Jews who had believed him, Jesus said, "If you hold to my teaching, you are really my disciples. 32 Then you will know the truth, and the truth will set you free."

33 They answered him, "We are Abraham's descendants and have never been slaves of anyone. How can you say that we shall be set free?"

34 Jesus replied, "Very truly I tell you, every-one who sins is a slave to sin. 35 Now a slave has no permanent place in the family, but a son belongs to it forever. 36 So if the Son sets you free, you will be free indeed. 37 I know that you are Abraham's descendants. Yet you are look-ing for a way to kill me, because you have no room for my word. 38 I am telling you what I have seen in the Father's presence, and you are doing what you have heard from your father."

KEY TEXT

If the Son sets you free, you will be free indeed. —**John 8:36**

Photo © Getty Images

GOD FREES AND REDEEMS

Unit 2: Liberating Gospels
LESSONS 5–8

LESSON AIMS

After participating in this lesson, each learner will be able to:

1. Identify the two referred to as "Father" and "father."

2. Explain the nature of the freedom available in the Son.

3. Create a list of ways to continue abiding in Jesus.

LESSON OUTLINE

I. Introduction

A. Freedom Day

April 27, 1994. For many South Africans, this date marked a new reality and brought a new expression of freedom. On this date the first post-apartheid national election was held. For the first time in decades, all South Africans of voting age were eligible to vote, regardless of their ethnic heritage or skin color. During the apartheid era, indigenous peoples and people of color lacked the freedom to vote. Further, apartheid placed overt segregationist restrictions on non-white citizens of South Africa. Even in their own country, non-white South Africans were not free to live full and flourishing lives.

By the early 1990s, after 50 years of discriminatory and unjust practices, negotiations between governing parties began the long process of undoing apartheid-era restrictions. One result of the negotiations was free elections. On April 27, 1994, millions of newly enfranchised South Africans voted for a new government and, therefore, a freer vision of life. Freedom Day serves to remind South Africans of the decades-long quest for equality and the desire for all South Africans to experience freedom.

Freedom can be looked at from at least four angles: (1) those who have freedom, and they know it; (2) those who lack freedom, and they know it; (3) those who have freedom, but they don't realize it; and (4) those who lack freedom, but they don't know it. Various forms of the words *freedom, liberty,* and their synonyms occur dozens of times in the New Testament, indicating the importance of the topic. We need to know which of the four categories we're in spiritually.

B. Lesson Context

The Gospels of Matthew, Mark, and Luke are called synoptic. This designation implies that these Gospels tell the story of Jesus from similar perspectives. (For an example of these similarities, compare Matthew 24:4-8; Mark 13:5-8; and Luke 21:8-11.)

However, John's Gospel is different. While telling the same basic story of Jesus, John often includes material not found in the synoptic Gospels (example: Jesus' "Bread of Heaven Discourse" in John 6:25-59). In other instances John omits material found in the synoptic Gospels (example: Jesus' transfiguration in Matthew 17:1-9; Mark 9:2-13; and Luke 9:28-36).

Today's Scripture text is an example of the former. The synoptics Gospels do not mention Jesus' teaching found in John 7–9. That John's Gospel has different emphases than the synoptics does not mean that John cannot be trusted. Just as different observers might have dissimilar yet accurate retellings of the same event, John's depiction provides a different yet complementary perspective on Jesus' person and work.

John's Gospel notes the special relationship he had with Jesus (see John 13:23; 19:26; 21:7, 20). Further John was one of three witnesses to Jesus' transfiguration (see Matthew 17:1-8; Mark 9:2-8; Luke 9:28-36). John was among the closest of Jesus' disciples—he had a front-row seat to Jesus' person and work. Therefore, John's attestation can be trusted (see John 21:24).

Today's Scripture passage is a part of a longer discourse that took place in Jerusalem during the Festival of Tabernacles (see John 7:2, 10, 14). The observance was one of Israel's most important celebrations and dated to the time of Moses (see Leviticus 23:33-36, 39-43; Numbers 29:12-34; Deuteronomy 16:13-17; 31:10).

The festival began on the 15th day of the month of Tishri, which is in late September or early October. Its significance was twofold. First, it celebrated the end of the harvest season. Second, it commemorated God's provision during Israel's wilderness wanderings. After the Israelites left Egypt, but before they entered the promised land, the people lived in tents. The celebration was to remind Israel of this history. Ultimately the festival thanked God for his daily provision.

The festival provided a backdrop for Jesus to express his divine identity by using items common in first-century observation: water and lamp light. During the festival, a priest took water from the Pool of Siloam, carried it to the temple, and poured it over the altar. On the festival's final day the priest marched around the altar without pouring water. This act demonstrated hopeful expectation that the Messiah would provide water as had been promised centuries before (see Joel 3:18). On the festival's seventh day, against this backdrop, Jesus stated, "Let anyone who is thirsty come to me and drink" (John 7:37).

Additionally, on each night of the festival, except on the Sabbath, giant oil lamps were lit in the temple's Court of Women. It was against this backdrop that Jesus proclaimed himself to be "the light of the world" and that whoever followed him "will never walk in darkness, but will have the light of life" (John 8:12). Jesus proclaimed himself to be the fulfillment of Israel's messianic hope, speaking the words of his heavenly Father (see 8:28).

I. Jesus Speaks
(JOHN 8:31-32)
A. Word and Discipleship (v. 31)

31. To the Jews who had believed him, Jesus said, "If you hold to my teaching, you are really my disciples.

The focus of Jesus' teaching was on *the Jews who had* "believed in him" (John 7:31). Their belief was due, in part, to his pointed teaching (7:14, 46) and miraculous healing acts (7:21). However Jesus questioned whether they had true belief of "he who sent me . . . You do not know him" (7:28). Did their belief go no deeper than simple amazement at his miraculous healing acts?

In the verse before us, *Jesus* established the way to distinguish proper belief from improper belief: only those who continued in his *teaching* were to be counted among his *disciples*. Merely to be amazed at and respectful of his miraculous acts and brilliant teaching was not enough. The test of true and lasting belief was to be found in

HOW TO SAY IT

Abrahamic	Ay-bruh-*ham*-ik.
Mishna	*Mish*-nuh.
Siloam	Sigh-*lo*-um.
synoptic	sih-*nawp*-tihk.
Tishri	*Tish*-ree.

persistently following Jesus' words, teachings, and commandments (see John 14:15, 21, 23; 1 John 2:4). Fickle faith in contrast to valid faith is a running theme in this Gospel (compare and contrast John 2:23-25; 4:48; 5:24; 6:60; 10:38; also 2 John 9; Revelation 2:26).

The Old Testament described Moses as Israel's teacher (see Deuteronomy 4:1-2). Therefore, Jesus' opponents claimed to be disciples of Moses (John 9:28-29). Their claim was appropriate—God spoke through Moses, so to be Moses' disciple was to be God's disciple. But now God had revealed himself more fully through Jesus, so to listen to the teachings of Jesus was to listen to God (see 7:16; 12:49-50).

God said that he would hold Israel accountable for ignoring the teachings of his prophet Moses (Deuteronomy 18:19). To reject or ignore Jesus' words was the same as rejecting God's words. As a result God would hold people accountable, just as he did with ancient Israel. If God punished Israel for not listening to Moses, how much more will he judge those who don't listen to the teachings of Jesus?

To *hold* implied the intimate knowledge disciples were to have of Jesus' teaching: they were to dwell on and in it. The Greek word behind this translation is used in the writings of John more than all other New Testament writers combined. It indicates closeness and association with Jesus and God and the fellowship of true disciples (see John 15:1-20; 1 John 3:9). They believed based on Jesus' teaching and, in response, followed him. Such disciples would know his Father (see 2 John 9).

What Do You Think?
How do John 15:11-17 and 1 John 2:3-10 provide a framework for the ways Christians can grow as disciples of Jesus?
Digging Deeper
What prevents Christians from following Jesus' teaching and growing as his disciples?

B. Truth and Freedom (v. 32)

32. "Then you will know the truth, and the truth will set you free."

A discussion on the nature of freedom might lead to different interpretations. For some, an expression of freedom implies unrestrained pursuit of personal desires. For others an expression of freedom may mean nothing more than the ability to refuse to submit to anyone—an attitude of defiance. However, these interpretations do not address the freedom that Jesus implied. The freedom to which Jesus alluded was an eternal freedom, not human expectations of earthly freedom.

As disciples continued to follow Jesus' teaching (see commentary on John 8:31, above), their knowledge of God's *truth* would expand. Old Testament Scriptures describe truth in terms of God's faithfulness and salvation (see Exodus 34:6; 2 Samuel 2:6; Psalms 25:5; 119:142, 151, 160; Isaiah 61:8). John's Gospel continued with this idea and applied truth to the person and work of Jesus, "the way and the truth and the life" (John 14:6; see 1:17; 18:37). As disciples remained in Jesus' teaching, they would know his truth: a life made *free* through salvation found in Christ Jesus.

What Do You Think?
How will you evaluate your habits to make sure you're living in accordance with God's truth?
Digging Deeper
How will you respond to those who see Christianity as merely following "a bunch of rules?"

II. Believers React
(JOHN 8:33)
A. Declaration (v. 33a)

33a. They answered him, "We are Abraham's descendants and have never been slaves of anyone.

Jesus had reminded hearers that he was "not of this world" but was instead "from above" (John 8:23). When he tried teaching on heavenly things, his hearers often misunderstood his point. For example, Jesus taught that a person must be "born again" (3:3), but Nicodemus assumed natural birth (3:4). Jesus had offered "living water" to a Samaritan woman (4:10), but she assumed natural water (4:11). These misunderstandings occurred because people did not recognize that

Jesus spoke concerning spiritual realities. The Jews who *answered* Jesus here fell prey to similar misunderstandings; they assumed Jesus was teaching about physical freedom.

Their response to Jesus acknowledged a particular nationalistic identity but showed disregard for a key part of that identity. Their place as *descendants* of Abraham was a central aspect of Israel's covenant with God (see Genesis 13:15; 17:8). Their identity as a people centered on the promises made by God to Abraham. Therefore, to align with Abraham was an ethnic identification that related Israel to God by means of covenant (see Luke 13:16; 19:9).

However, the declaration that *we . . . have never been slaves of anyone* failed to acknowledge previous commands made to Israel. Moses commanded Israel to "remember that you were slaves in Egypt" (Deuteronomy 5:15; see 15:15; 16:12; 24:18). It was not as if Jesus' audience suddenly suffered amnesia. It is unclear whether they were willfully disregarding their collective history as a people who once lived in bondage, or if they were expressing their own personal status of having never been in bondage themselves. In either case, their declaration showed a failure to follow what Moses had commanded of Israel. But perhaps more significantly, their declaration was a failure to remember their dependence on God.

This narrative includes all 11 references to Abraham in John's Gospel. These references are often an appeal to Abraham as a means to reject the teachings of Jesus (see John 8:39, 52-57). The claim to be of *Abraham's* lineage was true but lacked perspective regarding what was relatively more important (see Luke 3:8-9). An appeal to physical ancestry revealed a failure to grasp the nature of the kingdom of God about which Jesus taught.

> **What Do You Think?**
> What reasons might nonbelievers give to avoid following Jesus' teaching?
> *Digging Deeper*
> What excuses do Christians use to avoid following Jesus' teaching? How might Matthew 16:24 address these excuses?

B. Question (v. 33b)

33b. "How can you say that we shall be set free?"

The Jews questioned Jesus, placing the burden of proof on him. Their question implied that they believed they were currently *free*, which disregarded their current status in the Roman Empire. They also failed to realize that Jesus was concerned with a different kind of freedom.

III. Jesus Responds
(JOHN 8:34-38)
A. Sin and Servitude (v. 34)

34. Jesus replied, "Very truly I tell you, everyone who sins is a slave to sin.

Jesus' response instantly upended the Jewish audience's faulty understandings of bondage and freedom. While they were concerned with an earthly sense of bondage, Jesus spoke of a more important form. Jesus applied the bondage metaphor to *everyone who sins*. Such a person was a *slave to sin*. The ironic aspect was that it was one's own sinful desires that bound a person.

Other New Testament texts continue the bondage theme when discussing the influence of sin. The apostle Paul wrote that the bondage of sin leads to death (Romans 6:6, 16-17). Therefore, to find freedom, people should seek to become "slaves to righteousness" (6:18). The apostle Peter warned against false promises of freedom that led people to become "slaves of depravity" (2 Peter 2:19).

❧ SMOKE AND MIRRORS ❧

The boredom had become too much for sixteen-year-old me to handle. I had to do something to pass the time. "Why not? What's the big deal?" I said to myself as I lit my first cigarette. A practice that I intended to pass the time with grew into something larger. As I got older, smoking had a bigger hold on me. I planned my days around each cigarette and each smoke break. When asked, I was quick to dismiss my habit. Everybody smoked, and I thought I could quit at any time.

In reality, I was addicted to cigarettes. Their influence took over my life and affected my

Visual for Lesson 8. *Have this visual on display as you pose the discussion question that is associated with John 8:36.*

health, my job, and my relationships. Often I would rather be late to work than forgo my cigarettes. I was bound captive to a smoking habit I couldn't drop.

People can be bound captive by unchecked sin. Enticing sin seems innocent. It seduces people into believing it's not a big deal—when in fact it brings death. Sin might seem innocent and justified. But the longer you continue in it, the more likely it will send your freedom up in smoke. Don't deceive yourself! Who will you confess your sins to today (see 1 John 1:8-10)?   —P. L. M.

B. Temporary and Permanent (v. 35)

35. "Now a slave has no permanent place in the family, but a son belongs to it forever.

Jesus continued his response to his Jewish audience through the use of a household metaphor. In a wealthy person's household, a *slave* would work for the master. However, even as a part of *the family*, a servant's presence was uncertain, as he or she could be sold or set free at any time.

By contrast, the master's firstborn *son* and heir received all the safety, security, and economic advantage of the family. No matter the situation, the son was considered a permanent member of the household and received the blessing of the inheritance to future generations (see Genesis 21:10; Ezekiel 46:16). Jesus pointed his hearers to find permanent freedom from sin through the Son of God and the promise of his inheritance.

C. Son and Freedom (v. 36)

36. "So if the Son sets you free, you will be free indeed.

A primary descriptor of Jesus in John's Gospel is *Son* of God. The title highlights the unique relationship Jesus has with his Father, who sent him (John 3:16, 18; 5:19). The title stressed the Son's deity even while he was on earth (5:20-25). As the Son of God, Jesus is the source of eternal life (5:26). The Son and the Father are one (14:10-11), and they give glory to each other (17:1).

Jesus taught that only he can set people *free* from sin. His audience misunderstood the implications of his teaching concerning the Son and his Father (see John 8:19, 27). With the proclamation in the verse before us, Jesus identified himself with the "truth" (see commentary on 8:32, above) who would bring freedom from condemnation and death (3:18; 5:24).

> *What Do You Think?*
> How does the Son's freedom differ from worldly ideas of freedom?
> *Digging Deeper*
> How do Romans 6:22; Galatians 5:1-13; James 1:25-27; and 1 Peter 2:16-17 affect your answer in this regard?

❧ *FIXING STITCHES* ❧

Spending hours crocheting with my mom is one of the fondest (and most frustrating!) memories of my childhood. She sat with me and taught me each stitch. Anytime I missed a stitch, I would unravel the yarn and fix the missed spot. Sometimes I would make another mistake in the process of fixing the original mistake! I spent so much time fixing mistakes that I often didn't fully enjoy the final product!

Constantly fixing mistakes is how I once perceived my life with God: if I didn't make mistakes with my life, then I would be right with God. But it felt like mistakes were unavoidable, one occurring right after another.

Jesus' audience thought their law, their history, and their actions made them free and right with God. However, they were in bondage. The truth that provides freedom is found in Jesus. There are no mistakes that are too much for Jesus. Are you trying to fix the "missed stitches" of your life? Or, instead, have you accepted the freedom that Jesus brings? How will you use your freedom in Christ for the good of others (see Galatians 5:13)?

—P. L. M.

D. What and Why (vv. 37-38)

37a. "I know that you are Abraham's descendants.

Jesus confirmed his audience's earlier assertion that they were *Abraham's descendants* (see commentary on John 8:33, above). However, a valid claim to Abrahamic lineage was not enough. Jesus would remind his audience that "if you were Abraham's children . . . you would do what Abraham did" (8:39). True children of Abraham followed in the faith of Abraham (see Romans 4:3, 12). As a result, the people of God expand beyond the scope of an ethnic identification with Abraham (see 9:6-8).

37b. "Yet you are looking for a way to kill me, because you have no room for my word.

Not only did Jesus' audience refuse to listen to his teaching; they conspired against him. This is not the first time Jesus acknowledged this desire in his audience. Previously, he asked the Jews at the temple courts: "Why are you trying *to kill me*" (John 7:19). In that instance the crowds refused to answer Jesus directly, preferring instead to question the validity of his question, stating that he was possessed (7:20). As a result of their indirect answer, Jesus assumed that they were indeed seeking to kill him. True disciples would make *room for* the *word* of Jesus, which bore witness to the Father who sent the Son (5:36-40).

38. "I am telling you what I have seen in the Father's presence, and you are doing what you have heard from your father."

Jesus pronounced a contrast. On the one hand, Jesus' word gave witness to his heavenly Father who sent him. On the other hand, Jesus observed that his audience was more concerned with what they *have heard from* their *father*, the devil (see John 8:44).

Jesus' audience thought that their freedom was inevitable because of their ancestry. However, Jesus stated that they were deceived. As long as

they refused to listen and adhere to the teaching of Jesus, they would not experience true freedom. They would not know their heavenly Father. By failing to heed Jesus, the audience failed to listen to God.

> *What Do You Think?*
> How might the actions and concerns of Christians change as they follow God the Father?
> *Digging Deeper*
> Do Luke 10:27-28 and John 14:15 give insight to the actions necessary to follow God?

VII. Conclusion

A. True Freedom

Modern discussions regarding the concept of freedom revolve around ideas of personal volition, responsibility, and the ability of people to express themselves without interference. But Jesus was less concerned with freedom in that regard. Instead, Jesus was concerned about freedom and liberation from the insidious grip of sin. Jesus' audience did not realize that they were experiencing this kind of bondage. While they thought their ethnic heritage provided freedom, they were actually experiencing bondage. Their so-called freedom was an illusion based on a lie.

Jesus spoke truth because he spoke the words of his Father—a declaration of true freedom. Freedom that comes from the Father leads to eternal life with the Son. Those who crave this freedom will seek Jesus and his Word and become his disciples. As such, his disciples will know the truth, and the truth will set them free. A new day of freedom has been established.

B. Prayer

Heavenly Father, give us ears to hear your truth and hearts that love your truth. May our attitudes, words, and actions reflect your truth so we can bear witness to your Son. May the world be illuminated by your truth shining in and through us. In Jesus' name. Amen.

C. Thought to Remember.

Freedom is found in the truth of Jesus.

INVOLVEMENT LEARNING

Enhance your lesson with NIV Bible Student (from your curriculum supplier) and the reproducible activity page (at www.standardlesson.com or in the back of the NIV Standard Lesson Commentary Deluxe Edition).

Into the Lesson

Bring a ball of string to class. Before class, write on strips of paper 10 simple tasks that can be done in the classroom. (These tasks might include gathering certain items, cleaning parts of the room, or moving small furniture.) Place the strips of paper in a bowl. Ask for four volunteers from the class. Place the volunteers in two teams of two people. Using the string, tie together team members' legs and arms, as for a three-legged race. Each team will have three "legs" and three "arms."

At your signal, have each team draw a task from the bowl and complete the task. Once a team completes a task, they are to draw another task from the bowl and complete it. The first team to complete five tasks is declared the winner.

After a winner is declared, use scissors to cut everyone free. Ask teams, "How did being tied up limit what your team was able to do?" Invite team members to share their feelings about being entangled and restricted. Of the rest of the class, ask: 1–What made teams successful in completing the tasks? 2–What made teams unsuccessful in completing the tasks? 3–What real-life scenarios might this situation parallel?

After this activity, say, "We have all experienced the bondage of sin—and no matter what we do, we cannot free ourselves from it. Sin's bondage makes it hard for us to follow God's direction for our lives. Today's lesson will direct our focus to the only one who can truly make us free."

Into the Word

Ask a volunteer to read aloud John 8:31-32. Divide the whole class into four equal groups: "Teaching" Group / "Disciples" Group / "Truth" Group / "Free" Group. Give each group a paper and pen. Ask each group to study these verses, focusing on the significance of their word in these verses. Then each group is to write a dictionary entry for their word, based on its usage in these verses. The entry should include its part of speech, its definition, and an example sentence. Allow no more than five minutes to complete.

After the groups complete their entry, invite a representative from each group to share their entry with the class. Write these two verses on the board, but replace these four words with the groups' definitions. Ask the class the following questions: 1–How, if at all, do these definitions add clarity to the original verses? 2–How, if at all, do these definitions change the main point of the original verses? 3–How, if at all, has your understanding of these verses changed, based on these definitions?

Give each group a new term: "**Abraham's descendants**" / "**slave**" / "**Son**" / "**Father**." Ask groups to use the same papers as before and write down answers to the following questions: 1–To whom does this role refer? 2–What are the rights of this role in relation to the others? 3–What are the responsibilities of this role in relation to the others? 4–How, if at all, has your understanding of these verses changed, based on these answers?

Alternative. Distribute to each group a copy of the "Roles and Expectations" exercise from the activity page, which you can download. Have groups complete the activity as indicated.

Into Life

Ask the class to brainstorm ways sin subjugates both Christians and non-Christians, as well as ways Jesus gives freedom from sin. List responses on the board. Ask the class to brainstorm ways that Christians can abide in Jesus and his teaching, and thus better enjoy and exemplify his freedom. Ask learners to write down what steps they will take in their own lives to continually abide in Jesus.

Alternative. Distribute to each learner a copy of the "Word Web" activity page. Encourage everyone to complete the activity at home, as directed, and be prepared to share with the class at the start of next week's time together.

FREEDOM FROM SIN

DEVOTIONAL READING: Romans 6:1-14
BACKGROUND SCRIPTURE: Romans 6:1-14

ROMANS 6:1-14

¹ What shall we say, then? Shall we go on sinning so that grace may increase? ² By no means! We are those who have died to sin; how can we live in it any longer? ³ Or don't you know that all of us who were baptized into Christ Jesus were baptized into his death? ⁴ We were therefore buried with him through baptism into death in order that, just as Christ was raised from the dead through the glory of the Father, we too may live a new life.

⁵ For if we have been united with him in a death like his, we will certainly also be united with him in a resurrection like his. ⁶ For we know that our old self was crucified with him so that the body ruled by sin might be done away with, that we should no longer be slaves to sin— ⁷ because anyone who has died has been set free from sin.

⁸ Now if we died with Christ, we believe that we will also live with him. ⁹ For we know that since Christ was raised from the dead, he cannot die again; death no longer has mastery over him. ¹⁰ The death he died, he died to sin once for all; but the life he lives, he lives to God.

¹¹ In the same way, count yourselves dead to sin but alive to God in Christ Jesus. ¹² Therefore do not let sin reign in your mortal body so that you obey its evil desires. ¹³ Do not offer any part of yourself to sin as an instrument of wickedness, but rather offer yourselves to God as those who have been brought from death to life; and offer every part of yourself to him as an instrument of righteousness. ¹⁴ For sin shall no longer be your master, because you are not under the law, but under grace.

KEY TEXT

If we have been united with him in a death like his, we will certainly also be united with him in a resurrection like his. —**Romans 6:5**

Photo © Getty Images

GOD FREES AND REDEEMS

Unit 3: Liberating Letters
LESSONS 9–13

LESSON AIMS

After participating in this lesson, each learner will be able to:

1. State the result of dying with Christ.

2. Compare and contrast the old self with the new self.

3. Make a plan to be a more effective instrument of righteousness.

LESSON OUTLINE

Introduction
  A. Set Free
  B. Lesson Context
I. Dead to Sin (Romans 6:1-5)
  A. Rhetorical Question (v. 1)
  B. Emphatic Answer (vv. 2-5)
    End-of-Life Care
II. Alive in Christ (Romans 6:6-14)
  A. Freedom from Sin (vv. 6-11)
    Which Adam?
  B. Freedom to Serve God (vv. 12-14)
Conclusion
  A. Who Will You Serve?
  B. Prayer
  C. Thought to Remember

Introduction

A. Set Free

President Abraham Lincoln delivered the Emancipation Proclamation on January 1, 1863. By this time, the Civil War had raged for nearly two years. According to the president's decree, "All persons held as slaves . . . are, and henceforward shall be free." Of course, words without appropriate action—even the words of a president—cannot create change. The proclamation did not immediately end slavery throughout the nation. This speech, however, did fan the flame of liberation, especially in the North. The Civil War ended in 1865 with a Union victory. The battle for freedom was long and bloody, but ultimately victorious.

We still experience echoes of slavery. Though freedom for slaves was declared, the long process of becoming equal citizens under the law is, in many ways, an ongoing struggle. The parallel is imperfect, but some similarities exist between the fight to end slavery in the United States and Jesus' sacrifice to end slavery the world over. The lesson today focuses not on the moment of victory, but, instead, the work that is still to be done in the aftermath.

B. Lesson Context

The letter to the Roman church was probably written during Paul's long stay in Corinth (Acts 18:11), in about AD 58 in the midst of his third missionary journey. The church in Rome had been planted by other, unknown missionaries—possibly people who had been present to hear Peter at Pentecost (2:10). Beyond encouraging the believers there, Paul's letter also sought the Roman believers' support for a planned mission into Spain (Romans 15:23-28).

The nature of the church in Rome was influenced by an edict, issued by Emperor Claudius in about AD 49, that had forced Jews living in the city to leave (Acts 18:2). The Roman historian Suetonius tells us that Claudius "banished from Rome all the Jews, who were continually making disturbances at the instigation of one Chrestus," the word Chrestus likely referring to Christ.

This experience probably fostered a certain division within the Roman church between Gentile and Jewish believers, with each group contending that it had better claim on salvation in Christ than did the other (compare Romans 11:13-24).

The expulsion of Jews from Rome resulted in Gentile Christians being in the majority in the church there, if they had not been the majority already (Romans 1:5-6, 13). Their majority status seems to have continued even after the death of Claudius in AD 54 allowed Jews to return to the imperial city (compare Acts 18:2 with Romans 16:3-5a). Much of Paul's letter is therefore directed specifically to the Gentile believers there (11:13).

Paul used this letter as an opportunity to carefully explain the gospel (and his own teaching on it) to an audience who did not know him and had never heard him preach in person. As a result, this letter contains the most thorough and organized defense of Paul's preaching (Romans 2:16; 16:25). He argued that faith in Jesus is the only way to be justified before God. This justification comes by grace, through faith in Jesus, and not by obedience to the Old Testament law (3:21-26). Both Jew and Gentile are alike in sin, and both can be saved only through the redemption of Jesus (3:23-24). To confirm his point that God has always been concerned about faith, Paul used the example of Abraham. Abraham was declared righteous before God on the basis of his faith, not his obedience to the law (4:13).

In Romans 5 Paul again looked closely at the work of Jesus Christ. Adam was created in the image of God (Genesis 1:26-27) but gave in to temptation (3:6). Through the sin of Adam, death came into the world (3:19; Romans 5:12). Jesus, however, has done what Adam could not. Jesus, God himself in the flesh, was sinless despite temptation (Hebrews 4:15). And his death and resurrection brought grace and life to the world (Romans 5:17). Now, in Romans 6, Paul turns to examine the practical effect of Jesus' work in our lives.

I. Dead to Sin
(ROMANS 6:1-5)
A. Rhetorical Question (v. 1)

1. What shall we say, then? Shall we go on sinning so that grace may increase?

The two questions here are rhetorical (also see Romans 6:2, below). Instead of seeking an answer from the audience, Paul primed the reader for his answer to the question *Shall we go on sinning* (compare 3:8). We can see in the question this flow of logic: (1) Since forgiveness of sin is a sign of God's grace to us and (2) since grace is a good thing, then (3) why not sin all the more so that we may get more *grace* from God?

B. Emphatic Answer (vv. 2-5)

2. By no means! We are those who have died to sin; how can we live in it any longer?

Paul is using a technique known as "reduction to the absurd." In this method, an argument is boiled down to a level at which supporting it seems crazy. Anyone who would argue that continuation of *sin* is a good thing because it results in more opportunities for God to forgive us has missed the point entirely! Do we think we are doing God a favor by increasing his grace business?

3. Or don't you know that all of us who were baptized into Christ Jesus were baptized into his death?

Though we may read this as a rhetorical question, Paul's Roman audience had never heard him preach and so may not have been familiar with the concept of being *baptized into [Jesus'] death*. Baptism was commonly understood as a ritual washing away of sins, which John linked explicitly to genuine repentance (see Matthew 3:1-2, 6, 11a; Luke 3:3). This symbolism was not lost in emerging Christian understandings of baptism but

HOW TO SAY IT

Chrestus	*Crest*-us.
Claudius	*Claw*-dee-us.
Colossians	Kuh-*losh*-unz.
Corinthians	Ko-*rin*-thee-unz (*th* as in *thin*).
Ephesians	Ee-*fee*-zhunz.
Gentile	*Jen*-tile.
Suetonius	Soo-*toe*-nee-us.
Thessalonians	*Thess*-uh-*lo*-nee-unz
	(*th* as in *thin*).

deepened that understanding by tying baptism to faith in Jesus and the gift of the Holy Spirit (Acts 2:38; 19:1-5; 22:16; Titus 3:5; 1 Peter 3:21). Paul connected baptism to a personal identification of the believer with Christ (see Galatians 3:27).

Notice too that Paul appealed to baptism as a shared experience. The believer has not made a commitment to be carried out in a solitary way but, instead, in solidarity with others who have also taken on Christ. The body of Christ is made up of the many who call him Savior.

4a. We were therefore buried with him through baptism into death

Therefore draws a conclusion from Romans 6:2-3. *Baptism* is a fitting analogy for *death*. Churches have practiced baptism in various ways from early centuries, but it is worth noting that the burial analogy works best if we understand baptism as a full immersion of a person under water. As a dead body is *buried* in the ground, so we are lowered into the water of baptism to symbolize our death to sin. There is a sense of death when one is completely under the water, for normal sensory perceptions are suspended.

Through baptism we are brought into Christ so that his death becomes our death. Baptized persons put sin to death and bury it when they believe, repent, and are baptized (see Colossians 2:12).

4b. in order that, just as Christ was raised from the dead through the glory of the Father, we too may live a new life.

Jesus died, but he was *raised* to life by *the Father*. In the same way, our death in *Christ* is not the end but the means for having *new life*. At the point of conversion (symbolized here by baptism), the believer's old life of sin ends and a new life begins (Romans 8:6-7). God's *glory* that has given Jesus new life does the same for us (8:11).

5. For if we have been united with him in a death like his, we will certainly also be united with him in a resurrection like his.

Just as a person goes into the water of baptism and is buried (*KJV:* "planted") with Christ, so a seed is planted into the soil. In both cases, one expects new life to flourish. Our sharing in Christ's *resurrection* depends on our unity with his

death. Christian baptism is a likeness of, or a demonstration or reenactment of, the central facts of the gospel message as defined by Paul in 1 Corinthians 15:1-4 (the death, burial, and resurrection of Jesus). Baptism provides a wonderful opportunity to be like Jesus!

> *What Do You Think?*
> How do you strike a balance between your own efforts to be sinless and God's necessary work in your rebirth?
> *Digging Deeper*
> What other texts inform your thinking?

❧ END-OF-LIFE CARE ❧

Terminal disease brings death to the front of one's mind. Treatments have failed; experimental drugs haven't yielded a miracle cure. For this person, hospice care is a great mercy. The focus is on the alleviation of suffering. A team of doctors, nurses, social workers, and chaplains work with both the patient and her family to relieve physical, emotional, and spiritual pain in the face of death. Such care allows important conversations to happen. Far from giving up on life, this is an opportunity to enjoy the last days of one's life and make the most of the fleeting hours.

Those of us who have accepted Christ are already experiencing end-of-life care. We are released from our sin disease and live without the pain of our guilt or the fear of our death. This frees us to proclaim the good news of Jesus. Let us not choose to live with the pain of a terminal sin; choose instead Jesus' care. How will you make your newness of life a mercy to others? —J. A. K.

II. Alive in Christ
(ROMANS 6:6-14)
A. Freedom from Sin (vv. 6-11)

6-7. For we know that our old self was crucified with him so that the body ruled by sin might be done away with, that we should no longer be slaves to sin—because anyone who has died has been set free from sin.

In the remainder of this chapter and in Romans

7–8, Paul continued to describe the ongoing battle in which Christians are engaged—a battle of which we all are keenly aware. As long as we live in this world, the fleshly part of us (*the body ruled by sin*) will be calling for attention; that will be the part of us through which Satan will work the hardest to capture our allegiance and erode our faith.

Here the apostle insists that we no longer take orders from *sin* or from its headquarters. He uses the term *our old self* to describe the individual under sin's rule (Ephesians 4:22). But now that we are new creatures in Christ Jesus (2 Corinthians 5:17), we live under a new master, or by the "new self" (Ephesians 4:24). By joining with Christ, we no longer *be slaves to sin*. We are not free from temptation, but we are *free from sin* as the controlling factor in our lives. God has also given us his Holy Spirit to equip us for the battle, and the Spirit is stronger than Satan (1 John 4:4). Sin will continue to entice, but now it has met its match.

❧ WHICH ADAM? ❧

My father was a church leader, a positive example in many ways. His great flaw, though, was his temper. I remember vividly an occasion when my brothers and I were fussing in the car's back seat. Dad stopped the car and unleashed a verbal torrent. I heard my mother question his reaction later. He justified himself by saying, "Children need to see their dad hopping mad sometimes."

But when I became a father, I committed not to be controlled by anger. Have I always been successful? No. But my now-adult children are not distressed by memories of my unchecked temper.

All of humankind sins against God, following the example of our parents from Adam on. But we should be following "the last Adam" (1 Corinthians 15:45). Christ Jesus leads us to a new life where sins like out-of-control anger no longer dominate us and ruin our relationships. Which Adam are you following? —M. K.

8. Now if we died with Christ, we believe that we will also live with him.

In a sense, we've already begun to enjoy resurrection life (John 17:3), following our burial *with*

Christ symbolized in baptism. But there is still much more to come. We haven't yet experienced the full resurrection and still experience the temptations of sin. But we hope—not wish—for full life and restoration in faith (Romans 8:29-30; see lesson 10). The sure fact of what Christ has already done for us by his own death and resurrection provides all the confidence we need in order to trust that our own resurrection will follow.

9. For we know that since Christ was raised from the dead, he cannot die again; death no longer has mastery over him.

Although other humans were raised from the dead (examples: 1 Kings 17:17-24; John 11:38-44), their new life was temporary; they died again. *Christ*, however, *was raised from the dead* once and for all, never to *die again*. The Christian faces death knowing that it is a beaten enemy because of Jesus' resurrection. Thus what is true of Jesus is true of the Christian: *death no longer has mastery over him*. With the death and resurrection of Christ, sin and death have been overturned and the new era has begun (Colossians 1:18).

> *What Do You Think?*
> How do you balance a natural fear of death with your faith that death no longer has dominion over you?
> *Digging Deeper*
> How can you face death honestly, confidently, and without fear?

10. The death he died, he died to sin once for all; but the life he lives, he lives to God.

Jesus' singular sacrifice for our sin is sufficient for all time (Hebrews 9:24-28; 10:10). It never will be repeated. While Jesus' *death* was *to sin*, this doesn't mean that Christ ever sinned but, instead, that he submitted to death, which is the consequence of sin. But he now reigns at the right hand of the Father. His *life* is *to God*, as it was before he laid aside his glory to live among us (Ephesians 1:20; Philippians 2:6-8).

11. In the same way, count yourselves dead to sin but alive to God in Christ Jesus.

Because of what Christ has accomplished, we are free from slavery to sin and given the freedom

United in
LIFE.

United in
DEATH.

United in
RESURRECTION.

Visual 9–Spring 2022, Adult Resources, Standard Lesson Quarterly® Curriculum   Photo © Getty Images   Licensed

Visual for Lesson 9. *Direct learners' attention to this visual as they consider the final set of discussion questions in this lesson.*

to choose obedience to God. This is the case even if we don't actually feel *dead to sin*. Because of our new identity *in Christ Jesus*, we can be *alive to God*, choosing his purposes over our former sinful preoccupations.

B. Freedom to Serve God (vv. 12-14)

12. Therefore do not let sin reign in your mortal body so that you obey its evil desires.

Here in the first half of Romans, Paul personifies three spiritual realities as being tyrants; each has dominion as it reigns over us. All this is described with language derived from a king's reigning over his subjects or from a master's ruling over his slaves.

The first of these three is death, introduced as a reigning tyrant in Romans 5:14. The second is *sin*, explicitly seen as the reigning tyrant in the verse before us. The third is the law, spoken of extensively in chapters 2 and 3, but introduced fully as having "authority" in 7:1 (but see 6:14, below). These three oppress us in different ways. We fear death, we suffer because of sin, and we are judged inadequate by the law (see Romans 2:12).

Paul urged his readers not to allow the ominous spiritual tyrant of sin to exercise any sort of authority in their lives. Although we are dead to sin, we will continue to struggle against it. Paul was not talking about abstract sins of the intellect, but about real-world acts that involve

our bodies. Such sins come from yielding to *evil desires*. The underlying Greek reflects language Paul used elsewhere when talking about sexual sins (Romans 1:24; 1 Thessalonians 4:5). Living under Christ's rule, however, we have been given a path to flee from sin and escape its clutches. Resisting sin is not passive. It requires effort (2 Timothy 2:22). We have been set free from sin, but we must also choose to abandon sinful thoughts and behaviors.

> *What Do You Think?*
> How do you typically resist the evil desires and lusts that still tempt you?
> *Digging Deeper*
> What spiritual resources can you employ to fortify yourself against sin?

13. Do not offer any part of yourself to sin as an instrument of wickedness, but rather offer yourselves to God as those who have been brought from death to life; and offer every part of yourself to him as an instrument of righteousness.

This command builds on the previous verse, emphasizing that no part of our bodies should remain *an instrument of wickedness*. Our body is no longer Satan's possession. *Any part of yourself* refers to every member of the human body, such as hands or ears. This use is reflected in English in the word *dismember*, referring to cutting off an arm or leg. We are to use our eyes, our hands, our feet, our minds, and our mouths in ways that show we are people *who have been brought from death to life*. That does not simply mean avoiding wicked uses of those features; it also means putting them to work to serve, to bless, and to draw others to the righteous God. Every part of our bodies is to be used *as an instrument* for God's right purposes (Romans 12:1).

Christians live in the era between the moment that God dealt *sin* a deathblow through Jesus' death and resurrection and the day of the final victory that will occur at Jesus' return. During this interval, we are to live under God's authority, reflecting the *righteousness* that he requires of his people (Ephesians 4:24). We cannot live lives of divided loyalties, serving two masters. We must yield fully every aspect of ourselves to the service of God. We are not partly alive and partly dead. We are completely alive from the dead (2:5). In the new life, we serve only God in acts of righteousness.

> *What Do You Think?*
>   What individual parts of your body do you tend to view as irrelevant to practicing righteousness?
> *Digging Deeper*
>   How could focusing on these deepen your practice of faith?

14. For sin shall no longer be your master, because you are not under the law, but under grace.

Paul returns to his language of *sin* as a tyrant, insisting again that it cannot be our *master*. The reason for this is found in the controlling rule by which we live. If we allow sin to dominate us, then we position ourselves to be subject to the law. Paul certainly had the Jewish law in mind here, but the application is broader if *under the law* is understood to mean "under the old realm." Paul has already argued that if we are under the law, then we are judged guilty (see Romans 3:19-20). Anyone who attempts to be righteous by rule keeping will fail (3:23). Law does not save; it points out sin. Obeying the law to the best of one's ability is an exercise of wisdom and will, but that does not provide the answer for mastering sin. If we allow sin to reign over us, we are putting ourselves right back into slavery, despite the freedom given to us by Christ.

Instead, we are to be ruled by *grace*. It is not about which law or set of rules we try to keep, but about which master we serve. Apart from grace, we cannot overcome sinful desire. By grace, death has been destroyed, sin's hold has been broken, and the law has been fulfilled through the perfect obedience of Jesus. Even when we avoid sinful behavior, we are mastered by sin if we are doing this in an attempt to earn favor with God (the way of law). If our motivation is to serve God, then righteous behavior will follow naturally.

Conclusion
A. Who Will You Serve?

With Jesus' resurrection we see that both the new era of resurrection life and the old era of sin and brokenness exist side by side until Christ's return. This time of both fulfillment of promises and expectation of future perfection can be called the "Already/Not Yet." This phrase captures the tension that exists in this age. Through faith in Jesus, believers have the beginnings of resurrection life in the Holy Spirit right now (Ephesians 1:13-14). This is our spiritual resurrection and new life in Christ (2:1, 6; Colossians 3:1). The fullness of this new life will come with the final resurrection from physical death. For the believer, new life is both present and future.

Our baptism has united us with the death and resurrection of Jesus Christ. With his death, we are set free from slavery to sin. With his resurrection, we are given new life. However, we must make the choice of how we will live in this new freedom. We may continue to live in disobedience, becoming slaves to sin all over again. Or we may choose to live in righteousness, enjoying the new life Christ has purchased for us. Out of our knowledge of, and gratitude for, the grace of God, let us eagerly serve righteousness. It's the best life now—and forever.

B. Prayer

Father, thank you for your grace made clear to us through your Son. May we be encouraged and strengthened to live for you each day. We ask these things in the name of Jesus, by whose blood we have been set free and made new. Amen.

> *What Do You Think?*
>   What areas of your life have you been withholding from Jesus' service?
> *Digging Deeper*
>   What change will you make in the coming week to serve Jesus in *every* aspect of your life?

C. Thought to Remember
Let us live free from sin in the grace of Jesus.

INVOLVEMENT LEARNING

Enhance your lesson with NIV Bible Student *(from your curriculum supplier) and the reproducible activity page (at www.standardlesson.com or in the back of the* NIV Standard Lesson Commentary Deluxe Edition*).*

Into the Lesson

Ask class members to brainstorm a list of signs that require or restrict certain behaviors. Allow 90 seconds for them to shout out as many as they can; write each one on the board. Add some of the following if they do not mention them: Do Not Enter. Stay Off the Grass! Speeders Will Be Ticketed. No Trespassing. Do Not Pick the Flowers. Do Not Tap on Glass.

Then poll the class. For each item on the list, ask for a show of hands from class members who have ever violated that specific rule. Ask volunteers when the existence of a rule made them feel rebellious instead of obedient.

Lead to Bible study by saying, "Today's passage reminds us of the inability of the law to ensure our obedience. The Scripture shows us a better way."

Into the Word

Divide the class into groups of three or four. Distribute a handout (you create) containing each of the following sentences. Ask the groups to examine today's Scripture with these statements in mind. For each one, they are to mark the sentence true or false and indicate the verse(s) supporting their answer.

Note: Other verse references will be possible for some answers.

1. Something important happens at baptism.
2. Accepting Christ gives us new ways to live in our sin.
3. The more we sin, the more we're able to experience God's grace.
4. Freedom follows death.
5. Christ's death on the cross was just the first of many sacrifices for our sins.
6. Our baptism is a picture of the death and resurrection of Christ.
7. The gospel is all about new life, not death.

Answers: 1. True (vv. 3-5); 2. False (vv. 12-14); 3. False (vv. 1-2); 4. True (vv. 6-11); 5. False (vv. 9-10); 6. True (vv. 3-4); 7. False (vv. 8-11).

After about 10 minutes, call the class together and discuss the statements. For the false statements, discuss the best ways to make those statements true. Use this discussion as a framework for discussing today's Scripture. See today's commentary for further insight.

Alternative. Distribute the "Romans Vocabulary Puzzle" exercise from the activity page, which you can download, to be completed in pairs as directed. After 10 minutes, reconvene the class to discuss the concepts raised in the puzzle. *Option.* As learners list the answers from the puzzle, write the words on the board. The completed list will include: sin, grace, baptism, resurrection, once, reign, mortal, law, buried, crucified, old, dead, alive. Have the students work in their pairs to write sentences that each contain at least two of these words, based on today's Scripture. Students should write as many sentences as possible in 10 minutes. Come together as a class and ask for volunteers to read one of their pair's sentences.

After either activity, use this discussion as a framework for exploring today's Scripture. See today's commentary for further insight.

Into Life

Allow one minute for students to reflect silently on how they can be more effective instruments of righteousness (Romans 6:13). Allow a few more minutes for pairs to discuss their plans and write down a simple plan to carry out.

Alternative. Distribute the "His Resurrection and Our New Life" exercise from the activity page. Have the students complete this exercise in pairs according to the instructions. Reconvene the class to discuss.

Close in prayer, thanking God for freedom in Christ.

FREEDOM FOR THE FUTURE

DEVOTIONAL READING: Romans 8:18-30
BACKGROUND SCRIPTURE: Romans 8:18-30

ROMANS 8:18-30

18 I consider that our present sufferings are not worth comparing with the glory that will be revealed in us. 19 For the creation waits in eager expectation for the children of God to be revealed. 20 For the creation was subjected to frustration, not by its own choice, but by the will of the one who subjected it, in hope 21 that the creation itself will be liberated from its bondage to decay and brought into the freedom and glory of the children of God.

22 We know that the whole creation has been groaning as in the pains of childbirth right up to the present time. 23 Not only so, but we ourselves, who have the firstfruits of the Spirit, groan inwardly as we wait eagerly for our adoption to sonship, the redemption of our bodies. 24 For in this hope we were saved. But hope that is seen is no hope at all. Who hopes for what they already have? 25 But if we hope for what we do not yet have, we wait for it patiently.

26 In the same way, the Spirit helps us in our weakness. We do not know what we ought to pray for, but the Spirit himself intercedes for us through wordless groans. 27 And he who searches our hearts knows the mind of the Spirit, because the Spirit intercedes for God's people in accordance with the will of God.

28 And we know that in all things God works for the good of those who love him, who have been called according to his purpose. 29 For those God foreknew he also predestined to be conformed to the image of his Son, that he might be the firstborn among many brothers and sisters. 30 And those he predestined, he also called; those he called, he also justified; those he justified, he also glorified.

KEY TEXT

I consider that our present sufferings are not worth comparing with the glory that will be revealed in us.
—**Romans 8:18**

Photo © Getty Images

GOD FREES AND REDEEMS

Unit 3: Liberating Letters

LESSONS 9–13

LESSON AIMS

After participating in this lesson, each learner will be able to:

1. List ways in which the Holy Spirit is active in the lives of believers.

2. Give an example from Scripture where the Holy Spirit interceded for believers.

3. Write a prayer to thank God for his presence during a difficult time.

LESSON OUTLINE

Introduction

A. Against the Odds

Voyager 1 entered interstellar space on August 25, 2012. Scientists estimate, based on its performance, that the space probe will continue operating and gathering information until 2025. When it runs out of power, *Voyager 1* will drift off into deep space, losing momentum every second until it comes to rest somewhere among the stars.

Included in *Voyager 1*'s payload is a gold-plated audiovisual disc with pictures, audio recordings, and scientific data. Although the odds against encountering intelligent life in deep space are overwhelmingly low, this record was considered important enough to be included. As Carl Sagan said, "The spacecraft will be encountered and the record played only if there are advanced space-faring civilizations in interstellar space. But the launching of this bottle into the cosmic ocean says something very hopeful about life on this planet."

In the midst of suffering, the hope of restoration and glory can feel as miniscule as the odds of *Voyager 1* encountering intelligent alien life. What gives us confidence in hope? Our text today gives us the answer.

B. Lesson Context

The apostle Paul was involved in several important mission trips, the last of which was his trip to Rome for a hearing before the emperor. The book of Acts ends with Paul awaiting this trial (Acts 28:30-31). Rome was a destination he had desired for many years (Romans 1:13), but not necessarily in the status of prisoner!

The letter to the Romans includes Paul's understanding of the Old Testament background for the Christian message, the nature of Christian salvation based on the atoning death of Christ, the centrality of faith as the only path for human salvation, the relationship between Christians of Jewish and Gentile backgrounds in the plan of God, and several other matters.

All this makes Romans both the most challenging of Paul's letters to understand and the richest depository of what he calls "my gospel" (Romans 2:16; 16:25). The basis and reality of being justified by faith is the subject of Romans 1–4 in general and 3:24, 28 in particular. Paul quoted Habakkuk 2:4 in Romans 1:17 to set the tone for the entire book: "the righteous will live by faith."

This means that faith—complete trust in Jesus—is the only way that eternal life may be found. It cannot be earned by obedience, although obedience is important. It is not inherited by ancestry, although this is not unimportant (see Romans 3:1-2; 9:4-5). True life, eternal life, the life of salvation, is only found in trusting God to save us through his Son.

Abraham, the great patriarch of the Jews, was justified by faith (Romans 4:3, quoting Genesis 15:6). Thus the idea of faith in God as the core element of one's life is not a Christian innovation. Such faith is to be the foundation of our relationship with God. This was intended as central in the pre-Israel period (Abraham), in the nation of Israel itself (Habakkuk), and now is so in the church.

In Romans 5–8, Paul lays out the implications of Jesus' death and resurrection. Through Christ, the reign of sin and death has been overthrown by righteousness and grace (Romans 5:21). With the reign of sin and death defeated, believers are free. New life in Christ also means freedom from bondage to the law (7:1-6).

Romans 8 brings these various elements to a climactic resolution. There is "now no condemnation" for those "in Christ Jesus" (Romans 8:1). What the law failed to do, God himself has done through Jesus (8:3). Righteous living is enabled by the Holy Spirit, who dwells in those who have faith in Christ (8:9-10).

All these wonderful truths, however, raise a painful question: Why do suffering and death still wreak havoc? Paul indicated the likelihood

that Christians would suffer for Christ's sake. Paul encouraged the Roman believers to keep the big picture in mind: we are "heirs of God and co-heirs with Christ" (Romans 8:17, not in our printed text).

I. Present Sufferings
(ROMANS 8:18-25)
A. Glory to Be Revealed (v. 18)

18. I consider that our present sufferings are not worth comparing with the glory that will be revealed in us.

Paul was trained by the respected Jewish teacher Gamaliel (Acts 5:34; 22:3). So for Paul to *consider* was for him to draw on both his faith in Christ and his vast knowledge of Scripture. His thoughts are not to be taken lightly.

Paul was careful to put *our present sufferings*—whatever their causes—in proper perspective. Jesus' resurrection initiated a new era of salvation and restoration (see lesson 9). Because God's faithfulness to his salvation promise has been revealed (Hebrews 1:1-3), suffering of any kind pales in comparison to *the glory that will be revealed in us*. Forms of the word *glory* occur here and in Romans 8:21, 30 (see below), further defining what believers have to anticipate. The path of suffering ends with being glorified with Christ and with all who have traveled the same path.

> *What Do You Think?*
> How do you find a faithful balance in dealing with current challenges without losing sight of hope?
> *Digging Deeper*
> What barriers prevent you from maintaining this balanced approach to the present and future?

❧ *PAIN AND REWARD* ❧

The Sistine Chapel nearly defeated Michelangelo (1475–1564). Between 1508 and 1512, the man who considered himself a sculptor faced the frustrating difficulties of painting the Sistine's ceiling. He fought with the pope on concepts, overcame

HOW TO SAY IT

Augustus	Aw-*gus*-tus.
Caesar	*See*-zer.
Gaius Octavius	*Gay*-us Ok-**tey**-vee-*uhs*.
Julius	*Joo*-lee-us.
Michelangelo	Mahy-kuhl-*an*-juh-loh.
Raphael	*Raf*-ee-uhl or Rah-fahy-*el*.
Tiberius	Tie-*beer*-ee-us.

Visual for Lesson 10. *Direct learners' attention to this visual while considering the discussion questions associated with verse 18.*

physical challenges in scaffolding, fussed with his helpers, and spent agonizing hours on his back with brush and paint. Throughout the period, Michelangelo carried on personal feuds with painter Raphael and inventor Leonardo da Vinci. But Michelangelo persevered. The result is considered one of the greatest works of art in all the world.

Michelangelo's years of agony led to triumphal ecstasy. Paul's decades of toil and tribulation would lead to a glorious reward from his Lord Jesus. We, too, deal with pain. This may come from our faith commitments or simply from our life's circumstances. But Paul promises a future in which sufferings will give way to glory with our Lord. Are you paralyzed by personal pain, or encouraged by future reward?   —M. K.

B. Great Expectations (vv. 19-25)

19. For the creation waits in eager expectation for the children of God to be revealed.

Creation includes anything and everything God has made (see Romans 8:22, below; compare its use in 8:39 [not in our printed text]; Colossians 1:15; Revelation 3:14). Here it refers to the entire created world with the exception of *the children of God*. While the adoption of believers is a present reality (Romans 8:14-15, not in our printed text), this fact can be obscured by the troubles of living in a sinful world. The suffering that results from our fallen world can further conceal the reality of redemption that is already present (8:17-18).

20a. For the creation was subjected to frustration, not by its own choice, but by the will of the one who subjected it,

Following Adam and Eve's sin in the Garden of Eden, God cursed the ground as part of the humans' punishment (Genesis 3:17-18). Through no fault of its own, creation was thwarted from flourishing and *subjected to frustration*. (The verb form of the Greek word is translated "became futile" in Romans 1:21.)

The phrase *the one who subjected it* could be taken to refer to Adam as the reason for the curse rather than to the power behind the curse. This would be in error, although the thinking behind the supposition is sound: because humanity was to exercise wise rule over creation (Genesis 1:26-30), the fall revealed that people were not up to the task. As a natural outcome of humanity's foolishness, creation suffers. Its caretakers fell into sin and were no longer capable of exercising proper dominion. However, in context it is clear that God is the one who subjected creation to futility.

20b-21. in hope that the creation itself will be liberated from its bondage to decay and brought into the freedom and glory of the children of God.

In the midst of the curse, God made a promise: "I will put enmity between [the serpent] and the woman, and between your offspring and hers; he will crush your head, and you will strike his heel" (Genesis 3:15; compare Romans 16:20). Creation, despite its suffering, has reason for *hope*! The crushing of Satan's head was good news not only for all who put faith in Jesus but for all of creation.

Bondage to decay further defines the "frustration" of Romans 8:20a (above). Since human sin resulted in creation's fallen state, only when the *freedom and glory of the children of God* is finally and fully gained will *the creation* be released from the curse as well. The Greek word translated *glory* (compare Romans 8:18, 30) can be interpreted in two ways: as an adjective to describe *freedom* or as a noun standing on its own. This second option would explicitly refer to believers' status as being glorious rather than experiencing a glorious liberty. This goes beyond restoration to a fulfillment of God's plan for people. The fate of creation is inextricably tied to God's fulfilling his promises to those who have been adopted into his family (Galatians 4:4-7).

22. We know that the whole creation has been groaning as in the pains of childbirth right up to the present time.

Childbirth is painful (to say the least), but the healthy infant who is born brings immediate joy. The analogy captures a common first-century Jewish belief: that as the salvation of God drew near, conditions on the earth would worsen progressively, like the contractions that get worse and worse until finally the baby is born. Portions of Daniel chapters 7 and 9 helped shape this expectation. Jesus also spoke of the difficulty of the end times, both concerning events that were near at hand and others that would continue until his return (Matthew 24; John 16:1-11, 31-33). His disciples continued to speak of the troubles that would be seen before Jesus' return ended this age (example: 1 Timothy 4:1-3). All that pain, though, is meant to result in joy for the world. It is not a vain struggle.

> *What Do You Think?*
> How do you respond to the fact that creation
>   suffers because of human sinfulness?
> *Digging Deeper*
> How can you intentionally care for God's
>   creation this week?

23. Not only so, but we ourselves, who have the firstfruits of the Spirit, groan inwardly as we wait eagerly for our adoption to sonship, the redemption of our bodies.

Firstfruits as a concept comes from the Festival of Harvest, also called the Festival of Weeks (Exodus 23:16a; 34:22a; Numbers 28:26-31; etc.). The people would make sacrifices to the Lord of the first grains they gathered. This expressed thanks for God's providing the harvest and confidence that God would bless the people with bounty throughout the harvest season. Like the firstfruits of a harvest, the indwelling of *the Spirit* within believers is a kind of down payment, guaranteeing what is still to come (Ephesians 1:13b-14).

Adoption in the Roman world differed from our

laws and customs. One common scenario would involve a wealthy Roman man who had no sons. He would adopt a promising young man from a poor family, paying the natural father for rights to bring the son into the new, adoptive household. This adopted son would be groomed to take over the family business, continue the good name of the adoptive father, and become the adoptive father's heir. Such adoption is seen in the history of the Caesars, who frequently adopted a nephew or other male to inherit their title. Examples include Julius Caesar's adoption of Gaius Octavius, who was later called Caesar Augustus, and Augustus's own adoption of Tiberius. Adoptions such as these were familiar to everyone in the Roman world, but especially to residents of Rome itself.

Although believers are already children of God, we still await *the redemption of our bodies*, victory over physical death (Romans 6:8; see lesson 9).

❧ ADOPTION ❧

I was perplexed by the parents of my childhood friends. The children were my age, but their parents were much older than my own parents. I continued to wonder about this for years, not learning until I was a teenager that these were my friends' grandparents. The couple had adopted their grandchildren as toddlers due to tragedy with the children's natural parents. This godly couple had given them their name, their home, and their love. Other than the ages of those parents, I might never have realized their family was different from mine; my friends were secure in their family, just as though it had never been otherwise.

Paul used adoption imagery to describe our future reward as sons and daughters of God. Christians become "co-heirs" with Christ (Romans 8:17), heirs to the glory of salvation promised to believers. We assume the name of our Lord Jesus Christ, Christian, as our identifying mark to the world. And we continue our Father's business, seeking the lost for salvation. Are you living so that others recognize that your Father is raising you in his image and you are secure in his love?
— M. K.

24-25. For in this hope we were saved. But

hope that is seen is no hope at all. Who hopes for what they already have? But if we hope for what we do not yet have, we wait for it patiently.

Christian *hope* is not wishful thinking or anticipating a probable outcome; rather, it is assured because hope is based not on our own faithfulness but on God's faithfulness to his promises (Titus 1:2-3). Still, we *do not yet have* what *we hope for*, because in that case *we* would no longer require hope. When Paul declares that "faith, hope, and love" remain and the last is the greatest (1 Corinthians 13:13), it is not because faith and hope are of dubious value. Instead, it indicates that when faith and hope are realized in Heaven, we will not need them as we do now, to anticipate our promised future. But love will still be required, even in Heaven. God has given us every reason for confidence, which gives us the patience to *wait for* our hopes to be realized (see Romans 5:3-5).

> ### What Do You Think?
> How does impatience affect your relationship with the Lord?
> ### Digging Deeper
> What opportunities has God placed before you to grow in patience?

II. Present God
(ROMANS 8:26-30)
A. The Spirit's Help (vv. 26-27)

26. In the same way, the Spirit helps us in our weakness. We do not know what we ought to pray for, but the Spirit himself intercedes for us through wordless groans.

The state of the world can leave us so completely horrified that we are left speechless. *Our weakness* includes every piece of evidence that we live in a sin-sick and dying world. But when *we do not know what we ought to pray for,* the Spirit steps in on our behalf. This comes as no surprise since Jesus promised the Spirit would be his disciples' "advocate" (John 14:16, 26; 15:26). Paul built on this, giving believers confidence that *the Spirit himself intercedes for us.* When words fail us, the Spirit does not.

Groans is the noun form of the verb "groan" in Romans 8:23 (above). This context suggests that the Spirit's intercession also happens within ourselves. This is supported by the fact that creation does not speak in language but does groan in brokenness (see 8:22, above).

27. And he who searches our hearts knows the mind of the Spirit, because the Spirit intercedes for God's people in accordance with the will of God.

He who searches our hearts refers to God (1 Samuel 16:7; 1 Chronicles 28:9; Psalms 7:9; 139:23; etc.). Note that, like Jesus, *the Spirit* only speaks *in accordance with the will of God* (John 14:10; 16:13). Though we may not always pray according to God's will—especially since we do not know *the mind of* Father, Son, or Spirit—nevertheless the Spirit will only intercede in keeping with God's plans.

> ### What Do You Think?
> How do your prayer practices reflect that the Spirit intercedes for you?
> ### Digging Deeper
> What changes can you make to remain aware of the Spirit's help when you pray?

B. The Supreme Plan (vv. 28-30)

28. And we know that in all things God works for the good of those who love him, who have been called according to his purpose.

Even the darkest night of the soul does not mean we are cut off from God. Paul had an unshakable faith that all things are under the control of God, that *all things God works for the good of those who love him.* Faith in the sovereign God means believing that he is in control of all things. Even the evil in our world that causes the suffering of righteous people is not beyond his control.

Our problem is that of limited perspective. Only God can see how all things work together for good. The question about suffering, then, is not *why* (compare Judges 6:13), but *how long.* The *why* is because of human decision to turn away from God (Genesis 2:16, 17; 3:19; 6:3; Romans

1:21, 28). The question can only be *how long*—how long will the suffering continue until my soul is flooded again by God's love and comfort (compare Psalms 6:3; 94:3; Revelation 6:10)?

What Do You Think?
    How would you respond to Christians experiencing despair in their circumstances?
Digging Deeper
    What other Scriptures would you cite to bolster faith, hope, and love in your fellow believers?

29. For those God foreknew he also predestined to be conformed to the image of his Son, that he might be the firstborn among many brothers and sisters.

While doctrines of foreknowledge and predestination are important to consider, Paul's letter precedes by centuries debates about these terms and does not address the arguments that future Christians would engage in. Rather, Paul's point is that God is working within a plan, not haphazardly throwing people or events together in some sort of cosmic or salvific experiment (compare Ephesians 1:11-14). Though chaos or chance may seem to rule the day, we take comfort that the Lord knew us long before we accepted the call to join him in his ultimate purpose for people: *to be conformed to the image of his Son* (Psalm 139:13). This is both a new creation and a re-creation, for to be made in the image of Christ is to be restored to our unsullied state of having been created in the image of God (Genesis 1:27).

As the first to rise from the dead into glory, Jesus' bodily resurrection made him *the firstborn* from the dead (Colossians 1:18). Because of his resurrection, we expect to be *among many brothers and sisters* who will also return to life (contrast 1 Corinthians 15:12-19). The promise of our own resurrection is the ultimate hope we have in the midst of our sufferings (compare Acts 23:6; 1 Corinthians 15).

30. And those he predestined, he also called; those he called, he also justified; those he justified, he also glorified.

Although elaborate and confusing doctrines have been offered to explain the concept of pre-

destination, it is a rather straightforward idea as presented by Paul. In this context it means that God has made an earlier decision about our future (see commentary on Romans 8:29, above).

This predetermined plan has three stages. First, God has *called* us, giving us the opportunity to respond to the gospel by faith. Second, a positive response leads to being *justified*, declared righteous through our faith in Christ because of his sacrifice on our behalf (Romans 3:24-26). The final stage is our being *glorified* when our own resurrections take place and we join Christ in Heaven for all eternity (compare 1 Corinthians 15:42-58).

Conclusion
A. Hope for the Future

Christians have a hope that persists through the ordeals of life. Outside of faith in Christ, this hope is not possible. Still, we observe and experience suffering. Focusing on these things makes a person nearsighted. Only with an eye on our future glory can a Christian not only endure hardship but also thrive in the hope of God's promises.

While we hope for the glorious future in Christ, we still have work to do. Though our minds turn to evangelism—and rightly so—these verses remind us that we also have a responsibility to *all* creation. God has made us stewards of his good earth. While people suffer, all creation suffers. Likewise, believers' peace is the peace of the world; our glory will be the glory of creation.

We wait in hope for the ultimate fulfillment of God's promises. May we, as people who have died with Christ and live again in the Spirit, be beacons of God's wonderful intentions for all creatures, great and small.

B. Prayer

Father, help us view suffering through the perspective of faith. Teach us to depend on your Holy Spirit. Thank you for your Son, who has purchased our freedom. In his name we pray. Amen.

C. Thought to Remember

God is working all things together to accomplish his perfect will.

INVOLVEMENT LEARNING

Enhance your lesson with NIV Bible Student (from your curriculum supplier) and the reproducible activity page (at www.standardlesson.com or in the back of the NIV Standard Lesson Commentary Deluxe Edition).

Into the Lesson

Read each of the following statements, asking class members to raise a hand each time they hear a sentence they agree with. Pause after some or all of these and allow volunteers to explain why they raised their hand or, if no one raises a hand, why they did not.

1. I remember a time when life seemed hopeless.
2. The older I become, the more difficult life becomes.
3. This year has been hard for me.
4. I expect to have trouble in this life.
5. Even when things are bad, I have hope.

Alternative. Distribute the "Prayer Requests" exercise from the activity page, which you can download, to be completed as directed. After one minute, ask volunteers to share their responses, especially to the final question.

After either activity, lead into Bible study by saying, "Life can be difficult. But Jesus offers hope in all situations. Today we'll examine one passage that explores this idea."

Into the Word

Ask a volunteer to read Romans 8:18. Divide the class into small groups (or pairs). One half of these groups should find examples of suffering that the New Testament church endured, while the other half should focus on Paul's own life experiences. After a few minutes, list these examples on the board as groups call them out. Be sure to include instances from the Roman Christians' experience (see the Lesson Context sections of lessons 9 and 10 for more information).

Discuss these answers; then ask a volunteer to read Romans 8:19-30. Have the groups discuss what impact Paul's words would have if Paul had *not* suffered or if the Roman Christians had *not* experienced hardships.

Alternative. Distribute the "Patterns in God's Will" exercise from the activity page, to be completed in pairs (or small groups) as directed. Bring the class back together after 15 minutes to discuss what they found. Supplement their answers with information from the lesson commentary as needed.

Following either activity, have volunteers call out ways that creation's suffering is seen, and write their responses on the board. After a few minutes, have the students break into pairs to focus on one of the examples and come up with as many connections as possible between nature's suffering and humans' suffering. After about three minutes, ask them to imagine what a glorified resolution to the suffering might look like. For instance, how do both nature and humanity suffer because of pollution? Answers will vary but could include an end to respiratory diseases, clearer skies, etc.

Allow one minute for learners to reflect on their past and present struggles. Ask volunteers to share. Ask for some answers before discussing as a class how focusing on the Spirit's intercession rather than the struggle itself can change their attitudes. Can they sense the Spirit's presence in these struggles? What practices would help learners find peace and hope in the Spirit's help?

Into Life

Ask volunteers to share examples of their experiences of the Spirit's presence in a challenging situation. After a few minutes, allow one minute for the students to write a prayer of thanks for God's presence during a difficult time. Allow the students to pair up to pray for one another about any current difficult situations or in thanks for God's past care.

Encourage students to reflect on or complete the activity page in the week ahead. Encourage the students to come to class next week prepared to share either what action in addition to prayer they have taken on to address their concerns or how this lesson encouraged them in the struggles they faced.

FREEDOM AND THE LAW

DEVOTIONAL READING: Galatians 3:18-29
BACKGROUND SCRIPTURE: Galatians 3

GALATIANS 3:18-29

¹⁸ For if the inheritance depends on the law, then it no longer depends on the promise; but God in his grace gave it to Abraham through a promise.

¹⁹ Why, then, was the law given at all? It was added because of transgressions until the Seed to whom the promise referred had come. The law was given through angels and entrusted to a mediator. ²⁰ A mediator, however, implies more than one party; but God is one.

²¹ Is the law, therefore, opposed to the promises of God? Absolutely not! For if a law had been given that could impart life, then righteousness would certainly have come by the law. ²² But Scripture has locked up everything under the control of sin, so that what was promised, being given through faith in Jesus Christ, might be given to those who believe.

²³ Before the coming of this faith, we were held in custody under the law, locked up until the faith that was to come would be revealed. ²⁴ So the law was our guardian until Christ came that we might be justified by faith. ²⁵ Now that this faith has come, we are no longer under a guardian.

²⁶ So in Christ Jesus you are all children of God through faith, ²⁷ for all of you who were baptized into Christ have clothed yourselves with Christ. ²⁸ There is neither Jew nor Gentile, neither slave nor free, nor is there male and female, for you are all one in Christ Jesus. ²⁹ If you belong to Christ, then you are Abraham's seed, and heirs according to the promise.

KEY TEXT

If you belong to Christ, then you are Abraham's seed, and heirs according to the promise. —**Galatians 3:29**

Photo © Getty Images

GOD FREES AND REDEEMS

Unit 3: Liberating Letters
LESSONS 9–13

LESSON AIMS

After participating in this lesson, each learner will be able to:

1. Summarize what makes a person a child of God through faith in Christ.

2. Compare and contrast life under the law with a life of faith in Christ.

3. Write out the promises God has made to him or her as an heir.

LESSON OUTLINE

Introduction
  A. All Skate
  B. Lesson Context
I. Inheritance (Galatians 3:18-19a)
  A. Given by Promise (v. 18)
    The Audacity of Faith
  B. Questions of the Law (v. 19a)
II. Law (Galatians 3:19b-21)
  A. Added for Transgressions (vv. 19b-20)
  B. Limitations of the Law (v. 21)
III. Faith (Galatians 3:22-25)
  A. Promised in Christ (vv. 22-23)
  B. Deficiencies of the Law (vv. 24-25)
    Advanced Coaching
IV. Unity (Galatians 3:26-29)
  A. Resulting by Faith (vv. 26-27)
  B. Regardless of the Law (vv. 28-29)
Conclusion
  A. Time to Grow Up
  B. Prayer
  C. Thought to Remember

Introduction

A. All Skate

By putting on roller skates, a person's movement is transformed as he or she glides across the pavement. One of the best settings for roller skating is at a roller-skating rink. In addition to being an easy place to skate, rinks often include colorful lights and engaging music.

Rinks might have times set apart for particular groups of skaters—times designated specifically for boys, girls, parents, grandparents, and so on. There may even be times for couples to skate. After a few minutes of the special skate, the announcer proclaims over the loudspeaker, "It's all-skate time! Everyone, come skate!" No longer does anyone feel left out. All skaters are welcome to participate!

In this week's lesson, the apostle Paul made a sweeping declaration. This declaration invited all people to hear and experience the promises of God's transforming good news.

B. Lesson Context

The Galatian Christians were a community of believers in the region of Galatia, located in modern-day Turkey. Paul's missionary journeys took him through this region and its cities. Depending on whether "Galatia" is understood in a political sense or a demographic sense, it was during either Paul's first missionary journey (Acts 13–14) or his second (16:1–18:22) that he first taught the gospel message to the Galatians (see 4:12-13).

The year Paul wrote the Galatian epistle is unknown. Some research has proposed that it was written as early as AD 48 or as late as AD 57/58. The latter would imply that Paul wrote this epistle after the Jerusalem Council described in Acts 15. If this were the case, part of Galatians includes Paul's retelling of the council's key concerns: circumcision as part of adherence to the Law of Moses (Galatians 2:1-10; see Acts 15:5). These same concerns were of importance among the Galatian churches.

The Galatians had received the gospel message from Paul (Acts 16:6; 18:23; Galatians 1:11-12), but there were some among them who tried to add to the message. These individuals taught that circumcision as part of adherence to the Law of Moses was a requirement for salvation; Paul declared that to be "a different gospel" (1:6; see 2:14). Advocates for this approach were known as Judaizers because they called for Gentile believers to adhere to the distinctions of Jewish law. The Judaizers' beliefs were understandable. From their point of view, Israel was and continued to be the distinct people of God. It was to Israel that God had revealed himself, given his law, and prescribed circumcision as a mark of his covenant (Genesis 17:7-14).

Paul urged the Galatian churches to reject the Judaizers' addition to the gospel message (Galatians 1:7-9). Paul reflected on his own "extremely zealous" experience in Judaism (1:14) as he highlighted his inability to follow the law to the point of justification (2:15-21). Through Christ, the promise of salvation was to be revealed to the whole world (3:6-9). Paul went on to show the unifying nature of that salvation for all who would believe in Christ.

I. Inheritance
(GALATIANS 3:18-19a)
A. Given by Promise (v. 18)

18a. For if the inheritance depends on the law, then it no longer depends on the promise;

That Paul began with *for* indicates a continuation of his preceding discussion on *the inheritance* from God (Galatians 3:15-17). This inheritance implies eternal life and being counted righteous by God—for those having faith in Jesus (see Acts 20:32; Hebrews 9:15). Paul's concern was the means by which the inheritance was received.

If the promised life and righteousness came via *the law*, then God's promises—especially his promises to Abraham—would be of little value (see commentary on Galatians 3:18b, below). The law's role was not to provide entrance into God's *promise*. The law, given to Moses, was introduced long after God's promise (see 3:17). This fact pro-

HOW TO SAY IT

Galatia	Guh-*lay*-shuh.
Galileans	Gal-uh-*lee*-unz.
Judaizers	*Joo*-duh-*ize*-ers.

vided a distinction for God's relationship with his people; he desires relationship, not regulation. If God's inheritance was received by following the law, then his promises would be of no value and faith would be irrelevant (see Romans 4:13-16).

18b. but God in his grace gave it to Abraham through a promise.

The *promise* of *God*, made *to Abraham* centuries prior, designated a blessing (Genesis 12:1-3), a reward and heir (15:1-6), and a guarantee of descendants (17:1-8). In contrast to the demands of the law, God's gracious act was in giving the promise. Ultimately, God's promises would be fulfilled in Christ (Galatians 3:16). This observation led to Paul's essential question, next.

> **What Do You Think?**
> How do God's people live differently in light of God's promises?
> *Digging Deeper*
> How do 2 Corinthians 6:16b–7:1 and 2 Peter 1:3-11 inform your answer in this regard?

❧ THE AUDACITY OF FAITH ❧

Unbeknownst to the girl, her father was quite busy. Little did she know the weight of her request when she asked him, "Do you promise you'll come to my game?" Her father hated breaking promises, so he paused before answering. The demands of his day weighed heavily in his mind, but those demands paled in comparison to supporting his daughter. He didn't make promises lightly. He could not and would not break his word!

The Old Testament tells how the Lord made promises to Abraham, an obscure herdsman in the ancient Middle East. Abraham was promised land, numerous descendants, and the presence of the Lord. The audacity of these promises required Abraham to accept them by faith—an equally audacious act. God's word would come true so long as Abraham faithfully followed God in all circumstances.

Unlike earthly fathers, God never fails on his promises. Have you claimed God's promise of new life? If so, how will you now live? Will the audacity of faith now guide your life?   —M. S. K.

We are *all* 1 in Christ Jesus.

Visual for Lesson 11. *Have this visual on display as you pose the discussion question that is associated with Galatians 3:28.*

B. Questions of the Law (v. 19a)

19a. Why, then, was the law given at all?

By asking this question, Paul anticipated the Galatians' response regarding the promise. If God's inheritance came through his promise, then why should people of God continue to rely on *the law* for salvation? The practice of anticipating the readers' questions is common in Paul's writings (examples: Romans 3:1, 3, 5, 7; 6:15; 7:7). It was his way of addressing their (assumed) concerns since he couldn't be with them in person.

II. Law
(Galatians 3:19b-21)

A. Added for Transgressions (vv. 19b-20)

19b. It was added because of transgressions until the Seed to whom the promise referred had come.

The word *transgressions* indicates a violation of a boundary. In this instance, the boundary transgressed is the law (see Romans 2:23). The law *was added* to reveal the nature and extent of human transgression (4:15; 5:13, 20). As a result, people became conscious of their violations (3:20; 7:12-13). Through the Law of Moses, the Israelites had common language for understanding their transgressions and enforcing discipline. However, the law's application was limited as it served to reveal, rather than heal, transgressions.

The law would apply *until* a specific time

ordained by God. Galatian Judaizers required obedience to the Law of Moses to become an heir of Abraham's *promise* (see Lesson Context). However, Paul nullified their argument by noting a temporal aspect: the law was fulfilled by the coming of Abraham's *Seed*, Christ Jesus (Galatians 3:16).

19c. The law was given through angels and entrusted to a mediator.

The law's inferiority was due, in part, to its mediated nature. While Scripture never calls Moses *a mediator*, God gave him the law and entrusted it to his care (see Exodus 20:19-22; 21:1; 34:29; Leviticus 26:46). Other Scriptures indicate a belief that *angels* served a role in revealing *the law* (see Acts 7:53; Hebrews 2:2). However, God's promise is without angelic mediation. Therefore it is more enduring.

20. A mediator, however, implies more than one party; but God is one.

That the law was given through *a mediator* did not strengthen its influence. In fact, the opposite occurred. The mediated nature of the law differed from God's direct interaction with Abraham (Genesis 12:1). For believers, Christ Jesus serves as the mediator between God and humans (1 Timothy 2:5). As a result, there exists a new relationship between God and humanity, mediated through the "better promises" of Christ Jesus (Hebrews 8:6; see 9:15; 12:24). The law differentiated Jew from Gentile. *But God is one* and his people are one through faith in Christ (Romans 3:29-30; see commentary on Galatians 3:28, below).

B. Limitations of the Law (v. 21)

21a. Is the law, therefore, opposed to the promises of God? Absolutely not!

Paul again anticipated a rebuttal, so he cited a possible concern for the Galatians. *The law* and *the promises* are not against each other. Both are *of God* and both are holy (see Romans 7:12; 1 Timothy 1:8). However, each serves a different purpose.

The Greek phrase behind *absolutely not* is a favorite expression of Paul's (see Romans 3:4, 6, 31; 6:2, 15; 7:7, 13; 9:14; 11:1, 11; 1 Corinthians 6:15; Galatians 2:17; 6:14). It is an expression of emphatic rejection.

21b. For if a law had been given that could

impart life, then righteousness would certainly have come by the law.

The *law* was never intended to give eternal *life*. This is why Paul emphasized that the giving of the law came years after God's covenant and Abraham's faith (Galatians 3:17). If *righteousness* could *come by the law*, then the work of Christ, particularly his death, would be "for nothing" (2:21). As the law shows humans their sinful ways, it follows God's holy intention (see Romans 7:7-10).

> **What Do You Think?**
> In what ways do Christians use good behavior to earn favor with God and with others?
> *Digging Deeper*
> What should be the role of good behavior and good works in the lives of believers?

III. Faith
(Galatians 3:22-25)
A. Promised in Christ (vv. 22-23)

22. But Scripture has locked up everything under the control of sin, so that what was promised, being given through faith in Jesus Christ, might be given to those who believe.

It is unclear which *Scripture* Paul has in mind. Perhaps he recalled the Law of Moses that called "cursed" those people who did not conform to "the words of this law" (Deuteronomy 27:26). The law concluded that both Jews and Gentiles were "all *under . . . sin*" (Romans 3:9), and all people were thereby guilty (3:10-18).

Because Paul declared that all were guilty under the law, all were unfit to receive life on the basis of the law. This serves to contrast the law's condemnation with the life provided by *what was promised*. Only those who believe will be counted righteous. The righteous person will be considered a recipient of the promise (Romans 4:3, 13, 16), conveyed by the "seed" of Abraham, Jesus (Galatians 3:16, 19).

God's plan never depended on the law. Through *faith in Jesus Christ* and his faithfulness to follow the call of his Father, Jew and Gentile can experience the blessed promise of redemption. *Those who believe* become God's children, regardless of their ethnic identity (see John 1:12-13).

23. Before the coming of this faith, we were held in custody under the law, locked up until the faith that was to come would be revealed.

For Paul, *this faith* was more than a person's mental trust or a deep-seated hope. Instead, he attributed faith to God's way of dealing with humanity. Jesus' faithfulness in following his Father was the way God revealed his righteousness to the world (see Romans 1:17; 4:16; Ephesians 3:12).

Before Christ's arrival, *the law* kept humans *in custody*. This might imply that the law served as a restraint, showing the extent of sin through Scripture (see commentary on Galatians 3:22, above).

Paul envisioned a new era of God's working among humanity. This era was one in which God's promise was *revealed* through *faith*. Paul drew demarcations between the era of law and the era of faith, with Christ's faithfulness in his work being the moment of transition.

B. Deficiencies of the Law (vv. 24-25)

24. So the law was our guardian until Christ came that we might be justified by faith.

Paul's next metaphor softened the description as he described *the law* as *our guardian*. The illustration referred to the duties of certain servants in ancient Greco-Roman culture. These servants supervised the education of the household heir, keeping a close eye on the heir's behavior, character formation, and discipline. Eventually the heir would mature and no longer need this guardian.

Similarly, the law was only needed for a time. It served its purpose *until Christ came* and brought an end to the law's power for justification (Romans 10:4). The law could only do so much for humanity in regard to the promises of God. Humans could never be *justified* by the law (see Acts 13:39).

25. Now that this faith has come, we are no longer under a guardian.

Paul's Galatian audience held that justification was a "both-and" construct. Their understanding of justification required both following the law and expressing faith in Christ. To that end, Paul highlighted the superiority and finality of *faith* in bringing justification. Since *this faith has come*, the law—serving as a guide—is *no longer* needed.

This fact is because the law has been fulfilled in

Christ (see Matthew 5:17). Because the law could do only so much, God sent his Son to fulfill the requirements of the law (see Romans 8:1-4). What the law could not accomplish, God accomplished through Jesus.

✂ ADVANCED COACHING ✂

If a visitor came to the Feller family farm in Iowa during the 1920s and '30s, the visitor was likely to see young Bob Feller (1918–2010) throwing a baseball with his father, Bill. While other boys were learning the family farm, Bob was under the focused tutelage of his father. As they played catch, Bob learned to be a skilled pitcher, undoubtedly set for the major leagues.

As a high schooler, Bob's fastball pitch impressed numerous scouts. Before he turned 19, Bob signed a contract to pitch for the Cleveland Indians. As a result, he left his family's farm and his father's unofficial coaching to play in the major leagues. Had he decided to stay home, would Bob have experienced baseball success? Likely not. But because of his decision, Bob found great career success as a pitcher for the Cleveland Indians.

Whether they were fully aware or not, the Galatians had outgrown following every stipulation of the law. Paul taught that the law, while holy, could not bring spiritual life. Are you seeking life by your law abidance—trying to be "good enough" by your own efforts—or are you finding life in the one who fulfills the law (see Matthew 5:17)?   —M. S. K.

IV. Unity
(GALATIANS 3:26-29)
A. Resulting by Faith (vv. 26-27)
26. So in Christ Jesus you are all children of God through faith,

Previously, Paul had been speaking to an audience that would identify with his Jewish background, a collective "we" (see Galatians 3:23-25). Regarding knowledge and observance of the law, Paul was an expert (see Philippians 3:3-7).

Paul's *you . . . all* included every believer in his Galatian audience, Jew or Gentile. The Judaizers' insistence on adherence to the Law of Moses was of great concern for Paul. Regardless of whether a

person followed the law, all people could be considered the *children of God*. This was a phrase first used to describe the biological descendants of Abraham, those who were given the Law of Moses (see Deuteronomy 14:1-2). However, a new era had arrived, one in which God's children were no longer marked by their observance of the law. Instead, they were marked by their expression of *faith* in *Christ Jesus* (see Romans 8:14-16).

> **What Do You Think?**
> How do children of God act in ways that make their status obvious to nonbelievers?
> **Digging Deeper**
> How can children of God support each other and bring about love and good works?

27. for all of you who were baptized into Christ have clothed yourselves with Christ.

So the Galatian Christians might demonstrate their faith in Christ, Paul reminded them that they had been *baptized into Christ.* Paul often stressed the importance of baptism for the believer. Baptism unites the believer with the death of Christ and the glory of his resurrection (Romans 6:3-7). Further, baptism brought unity and a transformation "by one Spirit so as to form one body—whether Jews or Gentiles" (1 Corinthians 12:13).

The result of faith, demonstrated by baptism, was that Jewish and Gentile believers would become unified. To *have clothed yourselves with Christ* implied putting to death the sinful nature and being renewed with a new nature, transformed by Christ (Romans 13:13-14; Colossians 3:5-14). The prophet Isaiah rejoiced when God "clothed me with garments of salvation" (Isaiah 61:10). For Paul the garments of salvation were the work of Christ and the expression of faith in him.

> **What Do You Think?**
> How do people identify with a sports team or a community organization when they wear those parties' logo?
> **Digging Deeper**
> What steps can believers take to ensure that they identify with Christ?

B. Regardless of the Law (vv. 28-29)

28. There is neither Jew nor Gentile, neither slave nor free, nor is there male and female, for you are all one in Christ Jesus.

The result of baptism into Christ is the formation of a new self in Christ (see 2 Corinthians 5:17). This resulted in unity with others also in Christ. To reinforce this reality, Paul upended notable social structures of a first-century audience.

First, Paul addressed concerns of ethnic divisions centered on the Law of Moses. Of main concern for a *Jew* was adherence to the law, most notably the law's prescriptions for circumcision. However, the law would not have been binding for a *Gentile*. As a result of God's new economy of salvation, though, circumcision was no longer applicable for God's people. The identity of God's people expanded to include Gentiles (see 1 Corinthians 7:19; Colossians 3:11).

Second, the structure of the Roman Empire required an economy of slavery. In the structure of God's economy of salvation, though, the *slave* and the *free* person are equal; both find eternal life in Christ Jesus. Under Christ, a slave was counted as "a dear brother" (Philemon 16).

Third, Paul's statement that *nor is there male and female* is not meant to disregard gender distinction or address fully the varied beliefs on the roles of men and women. Given his audience, Paul was likely addressing the limitations of circumcision. Both men and women, created in God's image (Genesis 1:27), are baptized into the unified fellowship of believers.

Regardless of any differences, through faith all can become God's children (Galatians 3:26). The children of God are *one* through the peace of *Christ Jesus* (see Ephesians 2:14-18).

What Do You Think?
How can Christians reconcile disputes that may arise due to differences in economic status, gender, or ethnicity?
Digging Deeper
How do 1 Corinthians 12:4-27; Ephesians 2:11-22; and Colossians 3:1-17 inform your answer in this regard?

---

29. If you belong to Christ, then you are Abraham's seed, and heirs according to the promise.

Having confirmed the diverse yet unified nature of God's people, Paul explored the implications of this diversity. All people who express faith can *belong to* the body of *Christ*.

As a result, the promises made to Christ are applicable to all people who have faith (see Galatians 3:16). The promises made to *Abraham's seed* are fulfilled through those people in Christ as they become heirs with him (Romans 8:17).

Heirs according to the promise will attain more than an earthly heir might attain (see Galatians 4:7). Being in Christ implies having full access to the promise of his blessing. Further, it means his Spirit would be present in the lives of believers (see 2 Corinthians 1:20-22).

Conclusion

A. Time to Grow Up

It was time for the Galatian church to mature. First, they needed to acknowledge that they were no longer under the law as the way to attain God's righteousness. They were heirs of God with full familial rights to God's promises.

Second, they needed to realize that following the Law of Moses no longer marked the children of God. Jew and Gentile, rich and poor, male and female—all could inherit God's blessing.

Is there something in which we place our faith that is other than the good news of the gospel of Jesus Christ? Embrace Christ and live confidently as sons and daughters of God! When it comes down to it, do we stand with Paul on the bedrock that all believers are one in Christ Jesus?

B. Prayer

Our Father, thank you that we are your children through faith in Christ Jesus. Help us to live in the freedom we have as heirs according to the promise of your Son. Show us how to live in unity with all of your children. In Jesus' name. Amen.

C. Thought to Remember

Through Christ we are offered a life that the law could never provide.

INVOLVEMENT LEARNING

Enhance your lesson with NIV Bible Student *(from your curriculum supplier) and the reproducible activity page (at www.standardlesson.com or in the back of the* NIV Standard Lesson Commentary Deluxe Edition*).*

Into the Lesson

Before class recruit two volunteers to participate in an interview concerning their family upbringing. Have each volunteer introduce themselves and describe their family of origin. Then ask the following questions: 1–What were some ways your family expressed its identity? 2–Was there a time when you felt unworthy to be part of your family? 3–As a child, were there any promises made to you by your family? 4–What steps did you take to claim those promises?

Allow 10 minutes for the interview. Then lead to Bible study by saying, "Today's lesson will explore the nature of God's family and the reasons we can rejoice as God's own sons and daughters."

Into the Word

Divide the class into three groups and assign the associated Scripture text: **Added Group (Galatians 3:18-20) / Promised Group (Galatians 3:21-22) / Revealed Group (Galatians 3:23-25)**. At the top of the board, write, "Why the law fails to save." Then say, "In today's Scripture Paul explained the law's limitations for salvation. However, Paul highlighted another, better way."

Give each group a sheet of paper on which they can answer the following questions, based on their assigned verses: 1–How does Paul describe the limitations of the Law of Moses? 2–Using what imagery, if any at all, does Paul describe these limitations? 3–Through what steps has God fulfilled the law through Christ Jesus? 4–Why is faith in Christ not only better, but necessary for salvation?

After no more than 10 minutes, have a representative from each group read aloud the group's assigned Scripture text and explain the group's answers in whole-class discussion.

Option. Divide the class into three groups. To each group distribute copies of the "What About Baptism?" exercise on the activity page, which you can download. Have groups complete the activity

as indicated. Ask a volunteer from each group to share their final definition.

Ask a volunteer to read aloud Galatians 3:26-29. Using the same groups as the previous exercise, distribute a list of believers (you prepare) with the following descriptors:

Added Group: a recovering drug addict, a teenager, a person whose native language is not English

Promised Group: a single parent, a paroled criminal, an affluent business owner

Revealed Group: a senior citizen, a person from an ethnic minority, a college student

Have each group answer the following questions about each individual described on the list: 1–How might this person struggle to feel united in our church congregation? 2–What steps can we take to ensure that this person might be united with other believers?

After no more than 10 minutes, have groups share their insights for how children of God can live unitedly.

Into Life

On the board write, "God has promised _____." Encourage learners to work in small groups to determine possible answers to fill in the blank. After five minutes, ask a representative from each group to offer an answer.

After each group has answered, write, "What promises have been given to us by God as his heirs and children?" Allow no more than five minutes for whole-class responses. As volunteers share their responses, point out the differences between God's timeless promises made to all his heirs and promises that are applicable only generally.

Option: Distribute copies of the "Adopted to a New Life" exercise on the activity page as a take-home. As a motive to complete it, state that you will begin the next class session by reviewing volunteers' results.

FREEDOM, LOVE, AND FAITH

DEVOTIONAL READING: Galatians 5:1-15
BACKGROUND SCRIPTURE: Galatians 5:1-15

GALATIANS 5:1-15

¹ It is for freedom that Christ has set us free. Stand firm, then, and do not let yourselves be burdened again by a yoke of slavery.

² Mark my words! I, Paul, tell you that if you let yourselves be circumcised, Christ will be of no value to you at all. ³ Again I declare to every man who lets himself be circumcised that he is obligated to obey the whole law. ⁴ You who are trying to be justified by the law have been alienated from Christ; you have fallen away from grace. ⁵ For through the Spirit we eagerly await by faith the righteousness for which we hope. ⁶ For in Christ Jesus neither circumcision nor uncircumcision has any value. The only thing that counts is faith expressing itself through love.

⁷ You were running a good race. Who cut in on you to keep you from obeying the truth? ⁸ That kind of persuasion does not come from the one who calls you. ⁹ "A little yeast works through the whole batch of dough." ¹⁰ I am confident in the Lord that you will take no other view. The one who is throwing you into confusion, whoever that may be, will have to pay the penalty. ¹¹ Brothers and sisters, if I am still preaching circumcision, why am I still being persecuted? In that case the offense of the cross has been abolished. ¹² As for those agitators, I wish they would go the whole way and emasculate themselves!

¹³ You, my brothers and sisters, were called to be free. But do not use your freedom to indulge the flesh; rather, serve one another humbly in love. ¹⁴ For the entire law is fulfilled in keeping this one command: "Love your neighbor as yourself." ¹⁵ If you bite and devour each other, watch out or you will be destroyed by each other.

KEY TEXT

The entire law is fulfilled in keeping this one command: "Love your neighbor as yourself."

—**Galatians 5:14**

GOD FREES AND REDEEMS

Unit 3: Liberating Letters

LESSONS 9–13

LESSON AIMS

After participating in this lesson, each learner will be able to:

1. Identify the key tenets of a life free in Christ.

2. Explain the connections between the law, faith, and love.

3. Plan one way to serve his or her neighbors as a practice of living a life of freedom in Christ.

LESSON OUTLINE

Introduction

A. Spiritual Parenting

Teaching a child to seek good for others remains a difficult part of parenting. A child's behavior highlights the intrinsic selfish nature of humanity. A child may fight over toys, demand the last cookie, or balk at household chores. Parenting involves more than telling scriptural truths; it also involves modeling ethical behavior for children.

Yet even mature adults have trouble overcoming selfish practices. Adults are often no better than children regarding love for others. The churches in Galatia were wrestling with the tension of personal freedom and what was required of them as God's children. Divisions had been formed; Paul, like an attentive father, offered a new perspective on the nature of law, liberty, and love.

B. Lesson Context

Today's Scripture text marks a transition in Paul's teaching to the Galatian Christians. To this point, Paul defended the nature of his ministry (Galatians 1:9-11) and offered a new understanding on the nature of the law (3:21-22), especially for God's children (3:26-29).

Among the Galatians were individuals who required Gentile believers' adherence to Jewish religious customs and practices. Paul called out these Judaizers for compelling "Gentiles to follow Jewish customs" (Galatians 2:14). Judaizers emphasized faithfulness to the old covenant—the Law of Moses—for salvation. They taught that Gentiles should show faithfulness to the works of the law to find salvation (1:6; see Acts 15:1-5). The most visible way such faithfulness could be shown was by the act of circumcision (see Genesis 17:7-14). What resulted among the Galatians was a tension between the works of the law and expressions of faith (Galatians 3:1-14).

Prior to today's Scripture text, Paul refers to the story of Abraham's wives, Hagar and Sarah (Galatians 4:21-23; see Genesis 16:15; 17:16-21; 21:2). Paul retells the birth narratives of Isaac (by Sarah) and Ishmael (by Hagar). One might assume that Paul would connect the physical descendants of Isaac and Ishmael to that of Jews and non-Jews, respectively. However, Paul relates the spiritual descendants of Isaac to individuals in freedom from the old covenant, children of God's promises (Galatians 4:28). By contrast, Paul describes the spiritual descendants of Ishmael as those in bondage to the old covenant, never to experience the inheritance of God's children (4:30). The retelling made Paul's point clear: through faith, not law adherence, is God's blessing inherited.

I. Fight for Freedom
(GALATIANS 5:1)
A. Accomplished by Christ (v. 1a)

1a. It is for freedom that Christ has set us free. Stand firm, then,

Paul's previous discussion—concerning freedom and inheritance (Galatians 4:21-31)—has come to its fulfillment. Paul reminded his audience to *stand firm* in light of that *freedom*. Paul's retelling of the story of Sarah and Hagar served to show that individuals who express faith in Christ—whether they be Jew or Gentile—live in freedom (4:31; see Lesson Context).

Freedom in this regard was the result of a believer's life made new in *Christ*. But freedom is not without cost. That Christ *has set* believers *free* indicated the cost: He "gave himself" for humanity's sins (Galatians 1:4; 2:20), "becoming a curse for us" as he hung on the cross (3:13; see Acts 5:30-31).

B. Abandoning the Yoke (v. 1b)

1b. and do not let yourselves be burdened again by a yoke of slavery.

Throughout the letter, Paul emphasized the limitations of the Law of Moses as it related to the children of God (Galatians 2:16-20; 3:10-14, 19-26). Paul's directive to avoid becoming *burdened again* in this regard was due to the teachings of the Judaizers (see Lesson Context).

That Paul described the law as a *yoke* high-

HOW TO SAY IT

amanuensis	uh-man-yoo-*en*-sis.
Hagar	*Hay*-gar.
Judaizers	*Joo*-duh-*ize*-ers.

lighted the law's demands, especially those placed on Galatian Gentiles (Acts 15:10). A yoke indicated the submission of a weaker power to a stronger power (see Genesis 27:40; Leviticus 26:13; Isaiah 9:4; 1 Timothy 6:1).

God desired that his people live freely (Colossians 2:16-23), following Jesus' reminder that "my yoke is easy and my burden is light" (Matthew 11:30). Believers are to be burdened by the needs of others (see Galatians 6:2).

> **What Do You Think?**
> What steps can believers take so they don't become burdened by sin?
> *Digging Deeper*
> How might the armor of God (Ephesians 6:10-18) provide an effective response to sin's burden?

II. Searching for Freedom
(GALATIANS 5:2-6)
A. Looking to Law (vv. 2-4)

2. Mark my words! I, Paul, tell you that if you let yourselves be circumcised, Christ will be of no value to you at all.

In at least one other letter, Paul dictated the letter's contents to an amanuensis. This individual wrote down Paul's dictated words (see Romans 16:22). It is unknown whether the letter to the Galatians was composed in the same manner (compare Galatians 6:11). If it was, we can imagine *Paul* taking over the pen or quill in an effort to stress the importance of the point at hand. The Galatians might have noticed a change of handwriting when they read *mark my words! I . . . tell you.*

The present tense of *if you let yourselves* indicated that some Galatians had not yet been *circumcised*, but they were considering it because of the Judaizers' influence. To that end, Paul warned that their outward practices—circumcision and uncircumcision—were considered nothing of *value* (see 1 Corinthians 7:18-19). Neither practice automatically allowed a person to experience God's promises (see Galatians 3:26-29; 4:28).

When a person depended on the works of the law—including circumcision—for their salvation,

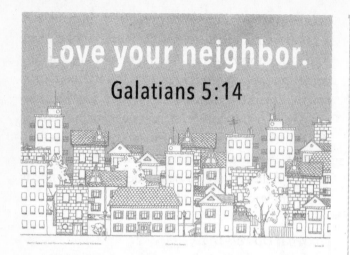

Love your neighbor.
Galatians 5:14

Visual for Lesson 12. *As the class discusses Galatians 5:14, ask them how they might follow this command. In closing, pray for opportunities to do so.*

that act served to "set aside the grace of God" (Galatians 2:21). Paul desired that a person show faith in *Christ*, not righteousness by the law. If the Galatians accepted the requirements of circumcision as mandatory for salvation, Christ's work in freeing people from the curse of the law, sin, and death would provide them no value.

While Paul warned of circumcision to the Galatians, elsewhere he asked Timothy to undergo the practice (Acts 16:1-3). Because of Timothy's Jewish heritage, Paul wanted to remove all possible distractions to their proclamation of the gospel message. (See Galatians 2:1-3 for an example of the opposite scenario.)

3. Again I declare to every man who lets himself be circumcised that he is obligated to obey the whole law.

If the Galatian believers were to *be circumcised*, then they would be required to follow the entirety of the Law of Moses. It was not as though they could pick and choose which parts of the law to observe. They would become like a debtor, giving their life to *the whole law*. Obedience to the law was an all-or-nothing requirement! If people disobeyed the law at one point, they were guilty of disobeying the whole law (Romans 2:25).

4. You who are trying to be justified by the law have been alienated from Christ; you have fallen away from grace.

Paul reiterates a previous point: A person cannot *be justified* by both *Christ* and *the law* (see

Galatians 5:2-4). Only faith can bring justification (Romans 3:28).

The phrase *fallen away from grace* served as a warning: the Galatians' acceptance as children of God was entirely dependent on God's grace. Any attempts to find justification in the law would be equivalent to falling out of grace's realm.

❧ FULLY BINDING AGREEMENTS ❧

If you've ever downloaded a smartphone application or computer software, you've seen (and perhaps ignored) the lengthy End User's License Agreement (EULA). Developers require users to accept the agreement before using the application or software. The text of these agreements is often indecipherable for the average person. As a result, many people fail to read the whole agreement, and they bind themselves (and their device) to the agreement's intricacies. There is no way to opt out of parts of the EULA—acceptance is all or nothing!

Paul reminded the Galatians that trusting in their adherence to the law for salvation was not a matter of preference. If they followed one aspect of the law for salvation (like circumcision), they were bound to the entirety of the law. Even though the law was from God, no one could obey it entirely.

However, God invites people to accept the terms, conditions, and benefits of a new covenant. If you have not accepted this agreement, why not? If you have, how will you live in light of God's eternal terms and conditions to gain the benefit?

—M. S. K.

B. Looking to Love (vv. 5-6)

5. For through the Spirit we eagerly await by faith the righteousness for which we hope.

The identifier *we* introduces a direct contrast to the "you . . . fallen away from grace" of the previous verse. Paul included himself among those who based their *hope* on justification apart from the law. Their hope was instead based on *faith* and *the Spirit*.

The concept of justification refers to believers being declared righteous before God as their sins are forgiven. The concept has roots in the judicial system—as a judge might declare a person righteous or condemned (see Deuteronomy 25:1). Some people argued that justification could only come through following the Law of Moses (Acts 15:1-5).

However, Paul opposed that perspective (Acts 13:38-39; Romans 3:20; Galatians 2:16). Instead, he taught that *righteousness*—for both Jew and Gentile—was attained only through faith in Christ (Romans 3:30; 5:1; compare John 14:6). By a person's faith, God would declare them righteous (Romans 4:5; Philippians 3:8-9).

While justification is a one-time occurrence, believers have hope that the Holy Spirit will transform and sanctify (Romans 12:1-2; 1 Timothy 1:7-11; Titus 3:5). This transformation begins when a believer is justified (1 Corinthians 6:11) and progresses until the end of their life (see Ephesians 4:22-24; 1 Thessalonians 5:23; Hebrews 10:14).

> **What Do You Think?**
> How can believers wait for the fullness of God's righteousness in the midst of daily life?
> **Digging Deeper**
> Whose support will you invite so that waiting can become a daily, proactive practice?

6. For in Christ Jesus neither circumcision nor uncircumcision has any value. The only thing that counts is faith expressing itself through love.

Because Paul had already expressed the failures of *circumcision*, some Galatians might have highlighted their own *uncircumcision*. Paul reminded them that *neither . . . has any value* regarding God's righteousness. By highlighting the limitations of both, Paul reinforced that "there is neither Jew nor Gentile . . . you are all one in Christ Jesus" (see lesson 11 on Galatians 3:28; compare Galatians 6:15).

Instead, what counted was a person's faith in *Christ Jesus* (see Galatians 2:16; 3:11-12, 23-25). This *faith* is not passive; it is not mere believing or hoping. Instead, faith has an active component, *expressing itself* in the lives of believers.

This outward expression is demonstrated *through love*—a love rooted in God's love (1 John 4:19). The element of love highlights faith's superiority over the law. Love is the fulfillment of the law (Romans 13:8, 10; see Matthew 22:38-40). And as a result, it was the crux of the law (see commentary on Galatians 5:14, below).

III. Obstacles to Freedom
(GALATIANS 5:7-12)
A. Persuasion (vv. 7-10)

7. You were running a good race. Who cut in on you to keep you from obeying the truth?

The metaphor of *running* a race is common in Paul's writings (see 1 Corinthians 9:24-25; Philippians 2:16). It described the Galatians' pursuit of Paul's teaching (see Galatians 1:11; 2:2). They had started the *race* well; they had followed what he taught! But Judaizers, teaching a different message, obstructed the Galatians' obedience. That Paul asked *who cut in on you* was likely a rhetorical question; he knew their situation. He wanted them to recognize the problem in their midst (compare 3:1).

8. That kind of persuasion does not come from the one who calls you.

Paul called the *persuasion* of the Galatian Judaizers "a different gospel" (Galatians 1:6), which would "pervert the gospel of Christ" (1:7). Their message distracted other Galatians from following the gospel that *calls* to faith, obedience, and love.

9. "A little yeast works through the whole batch of dough."

This verse could be a part an ancient proverb familiar to many of Paul's audiences (compare 1 Corinthians 5:6). The proverb described the effect *a little yeast* would have on *the whole batch of dough*. The New Testament uses the word *yeast* figuratively elsewhere (example: Matthew 16:6-12). To Paul, the teachings of another "gospel" served as leaven among the Galatian believers. As they allowed a little of opposing persuasive teaching to take hold, specifically the alleged need for circumcision, the rest of the false teachings would take hold. The result would be division among the Galatians.

> **What Do You Think?**
> What small acts can serve as a negative influence on the lives of Christians?
> **Digging Deeper**
> What steps can Christians take to positively influence unbelievers for the advancement of God's kingdom (see Matthew 13:31-35)?

10. I am confident in the Lord that you will take no other view. The one who is throwing you into confusion, whoever that may be, will have to pay the penalty.

Against the influence of the other teachings, Paul was *confident* in the Galatians' mindset toward faith. The resulting positive reinforcement served to motivate the Galatians, like a parent encouraging a child. Paul hoped they would not *take* another *view* of the gospel of Christ Jesus. The individual teacher (*the one . . . throwing you into confusion*) who taught a different gospel than Paul's would face God's judgment and *pay the penalty* (Galatians 1:8-9).

B. Persecution (vv. 11-12)

11. Brothers and sisters, if I am still preaching circumcision, why am I still being persecuted? In that case the offense of the cross has been abolished.

Without further contextual clues, we are left to assume that the Judaizers claimed Paul had continued *preaching circumcision*. Perhaps their claims were based on Paul's former zeal in Judaism (Galatians 1:13-17), or his seemingly casual approach toward the issue (see 5:6).

Before his conversion, Paul had *persecuted* followers of Christ (see Acts 9:4-5; 22:4; 26:11; 1 Corinthians 15:9; etc.). However, Paul was now the one to suffer the hardships he caused others to experience (compare 2 Corinthians 11:24-27).

This is not the only time when Paul wrote on *the offence of the cross*. For messianic expectations, a crucified Messiah was "a stumbling block" (1 Corinthians 1:23). To the Judaizers, salvation without the merit of the law was equally as offensive.

❧ *Offensive!* ❧

While I pursued my graduate degree, my family and I lived in Cambridge, England. On my way home from my studies, I would walk through the Cambridge central square. Street performers known as buskers would usually fill the square. One day a certain busker played a bagpipe. The instrument's drone could be heard from many blocks away. While the performer's skill was evident, I preferred hearing bagpipes from a distance. Apparently, I was not the only person with this

preference. Others complained; the bagpipes were displeasing and offensive to their ears!

In Paul's day, a cross used for crucifixion was an offensive image. It served as a reminder of the shame of a criminal's execution. Advocates of the Law of Moses could not imagine a crucified Messiah. In this sense, the cross was a blatant offense!

However, through Christ's death on a cross and his resurrection, new life by faith was possible. Have you embraced fully the new life brought through the offense of the cross? —M. S. K.

12. As for those agitators, I wish they would go the whole way and emasculate themselves!

The crescendo of Paul's defense hit an unexpected (and graphic) climax. Regarding the teacher(s) who had been pushing for circumcision, Paul wished they would *emasculate themselves*. While this could mean Paul wished their teaching would be cut off, more likely he was referring to a literal cutting off part of one's body! Pagan sects and empires of antiquity sometimes required emasculation, or castration, of certain followers or captives (see 2 Kings 20:18; Matthew 19:12; Acts 8:27). Paul seems to say sarcastically that if the Judaizers are so impressed with circumcision, then they should go even further (see also Philippians 3:2-4).

IV. Paradox of Freedom
(GALATIANS 5:13-15)
A. Denying the Flesh (v. 13)

13a. You, my brothers and sisters, were called to be free.

Paul's Galatian *brothers and sisters*—believers who expressed faith—*were called* from the yoke of the law's demands. They were henceforth to live into the freedom that Christ had given. The Lord had worked in the Galatians, and the time had come for them to move forward in his Spirit (see 2 Corinthians 3:17)!

13b. But do not use your freedom to indulge the flesh; rather, serve one another humbly in love.

But Paul extended a caution. The word *flesh* describes human nature that acts in sinful ways contrary to God's Spirit (Romans 8:1-12; Galatians

6:8; Ephesians 2:3). *Freedom* is not an occasion for believers *to indulge* their personal desires, especially sinful ones. In short, liberty does not mean license.

Christian freedom requires outward-facing action, dealing with a believer's treatment of other people. The remedy for living under the flesh is to *serve* others in *love*. As the Spirit brings freedom, a believer is required to use that freedom responsibly, concerned for the good of others (see Romans 12:3-8; 1 Corinthians 12:7).

If Paul had desired an example of this teaching, he could have referred to the life and ministry of Jesus (see Mark 10:45; John 13:4-16, 34-35; Philippians 2:3-8). Further, Paul's own life and ministry was an application of this verse (see 1 Corinthians 9:19-23).

What Do You Think?
How might an inaccurate understanding of freedom hinder a Christian's witness?
Digging Deeper
How, if at all, does 1 Corinthians 10:23-33 inform your answer?

B. Fulfilling the Law (vv. 14-15)

14. For the entire law is fulfilled in keeping this one command: "Love your neighbor as yourself."

Paul was likely referring to the *law* of Moses and all that it required. The law's teachings did not culminate in customs and rituals like circumcision. Instead, the law was *fulfilled* and found complete through a person's overt concern for others (Romans 13:10).

Paul continued in the tradition of Jesus' ethical teaching, reminding believers of the importance of *love* for *neighbor* (see Matthew 22:36-40; Luke 10:25-28). Both Jesus and Paul expanded on the law's teaching, applying it broadly (see Leviticus 19:18). God is most loved when his children show love toward others (compare Romans 13:8; 1 John 4:19-21).

15. If you bite and devour each other, watch out or you will be destroyed by each other.

A tense conflict might lead a person to say or act in a manner that serves to *bite and devour*

other people, like the actions of a predator toward a weaker animal. If believers are not filled with love (see Galatians 5:14, above), their actions may tear others down.

If the Galatians attacked one another, the result would be mutually assured destruction. They would be *destroyed* by fleshly desires.

What Do You Think?
How might a Christian's response to unfair treatment give testimony to the Spirit?
Digging Deeper
What steps will you take to prevent conflict with a person who you find difficult to love?

Conclusion

A. They Will Know Us by Our Love

As Peter Scholtes (1938–2009) directed his South Side Chicago youth choir in the 1960s, he wanted a song that would unite the varied experiences of his church's youth group. After a day of work, Scholtes composed "They'll Know We Are Christians." The song, now made popular in numerous hymnals, reflected the sentiment of Jesus' teaching that "by this everyone will know that you are my disciples, if you love one another" (John 13:35).

While believers might be free from the demands of the law, Paul taught the Galatians that such freedom requires active love for others. Showing this love is the litmus test for a believer's love for God. Self-examination regarding love is prudent for followers of Jesus. Does anything prevent or distract from your expression of love to God and others? Might your own definition of freedom stand in the way of love?

B. Prayer

Our Father, thank you for the freedom you have given us because of your Son, Jesus Christ. Help us use that freedom to express neighborly love to all people that we encounter. Focus our hearts to love as you have loved us. In Jesus' name. Amen.

C. Thought to Remember

Christian liberty always seeks the good of others.

INVOLVEMENT LEARNING

Enhance your lesson with NIV Bible Student (from your curriculum supplier) and the reproducible activity page (at www.standardlesson.com or in the back of the NIV Standard Lesson Commentary Deluxe Edition).

Into the Lesson

Have the following displayed on the board, and ask for responses as learners arrive:

What are some ways a person might use their freedom for their own good or the good of others?

Jot responses on the board. You may need to come with your own examples to encourage thought. Some examples might include: an athlete (using her freedom to train and practice for their own athletic successes), a musician (using his freedom to perform for the enjoyment of others), or a parent (using her freedom to provide for their children's well-being).

Lead into Bible study by saying, "For several weeks now we've been talking about different kinds of freedom. Today we will look at how people are to use their freedom."

Into the Word

Announce a Bible-marking activity. Provide copies of Galatians 5:1-15 for those who do not want to write in their own Bibles. Provide handouts (you create) with these instructions:

1–Underline everything Paul said about freedom.

2–Put an asterisk beside everything Paul said about the law.

3–Put a heart beside everything Paul said about love.

4–Put an exclamation point beside everything Paul said about faith.

Read the Scripture aloud (or ask volunteers to do so) slowly at least twice and as many as four times. As the Scripture is read, class members are to mark their copies in the ways noted.

After the final reading, divide class members into four equal groups for class discussion. Provide each group a handout with the following questions: 1–How does Paul define freedom? 2–

How are law and faith related? 3–How are the law, faith, and love related? 4–How are faith, freedom, and love related? Have groups discuss the questions, based on their observations from the Bible-marking activity.

After 10 minutes, have a representative from each group answer one of the questions, until all the questions have been answered. Finally, ask for volunteers to share what they find especially helpful and challenging from the text.

Option. Distribute copies of the "Love Your Neighbor" activity from the activity page, which you can download. Have learners divide into pairs and complete the activity as indicated.

Into Life

Write at the top of the board, "Free to Love." Ask the class, "How can a Christian use their freedom to love and serve others?" Jot down answers on the board. You may need to come with your own examples to encourage thought. Some examples might include: loving a person recovering from addiction through sponsorship or loving church members through works of benevolence.

Ask a volunteer to read aloud Galatians 5:13-14. Divide the class into pairs and have each pair make a list of possible "neighbors." (These can include friends, coworkers, or literal next-door neighbors.) Have the pairs write down ways to use their freedom in Christ to serve and love each neighbor in the coming week. Allow no more than five minutes for pairs to complete the task. Without giving away the identity of the neighbor, have each pair give an example of how they might serve and love neighbors. Discuss how a Christian's freedom provides the opportunity to show love and service.

Option. Distribute copies of the "Who's My Neighbor?" exercise from the activity page. Encourage everyone to complete the activity at home, as directed, and be prepared to share their experiences with the class at the start of next week's time.

THE FRUIT OF FREEDOM

DEVOTIONAL READING: Galatians 5:16-26
BACKGROUND SCRIPTURE: Galatians 5:16-26

GALATIANS 5:16-26

16 So I say, walk by the Spirit, and you will not gratify the desires of the flesh. 17 For the flesh desires what is contrary to the Spirit, and the Spirit what is contrary to the flesh. They are in conflict with each other, so that you are not to do whatever you want. 18 But if you are led by the Spirit, you are not under the law.

19 The acts of the flesh are obvious: sexual immorality, impurity and debauchery; 20 idolatry and witchcraft; hatred, discord, jealousy, fits of rage, selfish ambition, dissensions, factions 21 and envy; drunkenness, orgies, and the like. I warn you, as I did before, that those who live like this will not inherit the kingdom of God.

22 But the fruit of the Spirit is love, joy, peace, forbearance, kindness, goodness, faithfulness, 23 gentleness and self-control. Against such things there is no law. 24 Those who belong to Christ Jesus have crucified the flesh with its passions and desires. 25 Since we live by the Spirit, let us keep in step with the Spirit. 26 Let us not become conceited, provoking and envying each other.

KEY TEXT

Since we live by the Spirit, let us keep in step with the Spirit. —**Galatians 5:25**

Photo © Getty Images

GOD FREES AND REDEEMS

Unit 3: Liberating Letters

LESSONS 9–13

LESSON AIMS

After participating in this lesson, each learner will be able to:

1. List characteristics of life in the flesh and life in the Spirit.

2. Explain how elements of "fruit of the Spirit" and "acts of the flesh" can be rank-ordered as to importance or why such an attempt should not be made.

3. Identify a sinful tendency most besetting and commit to developing one specific fruit of the Spirit to counteract it.

LESSON OUTLINE

Introduction

A. Familiar Narrative

Any great story—word or film—will include components of plot development and narrative flow. These components include the beginning, rising action or conflict, a climax, falling action or conflict, and the conclusion.

Yet narrative flow is not enough to hold a story. Gripping stories have engaging, almost lifelike, characters. When conflict exists between such characters, the story's narrative builds toward its breathtaking climax.

A story's narrative conflict and climax usually reflect an inner turmoil we can identify with. Paul understood that his readers experienced spiritual turmoil. In what serves as the dramatic climax (but not the end) of Paul's letter to the Galatians, the conflict between Spirit and flesh comes to a head.

B. Lesson Context

Central to Paul's argument in this lesson is the nature of "the flesh." However, the nature and implications of the flesh are not static in the New Testament. Even the dozens of uses of the word in Paul's writings indicate slight differences and nuances. To claim a singular understanding of "Paul's view of the flesh" would be mistaken.

Paul uses the word to speak of physical matter of living creatures generally (1 Corinthians 15:39) and the human body specifically (6:16). In other instances, flesh is regarded negatively. Paul referred to it in the context of circumcision (Galatians 6:12; Philippians 3:3), rebellious human nature and desires (Romans 8:3-12; Ephesians 2:3), and temporal lineage in contrast to an eternal one (Romans 4:1; Galatians 4:23, 29).

As used in today's Scripture text, flesh refers to the carnal, unredeemed self and its rebellious nature and desires (see Romans 13:13-14). In order for believers to live fully as children of God, the ways of the flesh must die (see Galatians 2:19-21).

The entire epistle to the Galatians has been building to this lesson's Scripture text. With a proper understanding of God's law and promises (Galatians 3:1-22) and true freedom in God's Spirit (4:21–5:14), Paul puts all the pieces together.

I. Stating the Sides

(GALATIANS 5:16-18)

A. Spirit and Flesh (vv. 16-17)

16. So I say, walk by the Spirit, and you will not gratify the desires of the flesh.

Paul envisioned one option for the Galatian believers: to *walk by the Spirit* of God. By using a metaphor, Paul described the kind of life required of disciples as a walk (see Romans 13:13; 2 Corinthians 5:7; Colossians 2:6-7). The metaphor referred to the ways first-century students might follow in the steps of their rabbis (teachers of the Jewish law). As students did so, they would listen to the teaching and allow it to change their hearts and minds. If the Galatians followed Paul's exhortation, their whole way of life would change.

As the Galatians walked in God's Spirit, they would avoid defilement that comes from a heart out of tune with the Spirit. This would consist of *the desires of the flesh* (see Mark 7:18-23; 1 John 2:16). Paul did not suggest that the Galatian believers should invite the Spirit of God into their already established way of life. Rather, he wanted them to allow the Spirit to determine their motivations and behaviors (see Galatians 5:25, below).

> *What Do You Think?*
> How can Christians measure whether they're living in the direction of God's Spirit?
> *Digging Deeper*
> How will you follow another's example of a Spirit-filled walk in the coming weeks?

17a. For the flesh desires what is contrary to the Spirit, and the Spirit what is contrary to the flesh.

The way of *the flesh desires* that the working of *the Spirit* in a believer's life would be thwarted. That Paul described this as a desire alludes to the sinful acts of coveting (see Romans 7:7; 13:9) and lust (Matthew 5:28). Acts of the flesh involve more than these two sins, but all acts of the flesh imply the flesh's sinful desires.

The conflict between the flesh and Spirit was evident to Paul. The desires of the flesh lead to death, but the desires of the Spirit lead to life (Romans 8:5-8). In other letters, Paul described this conflict as being between the old, sinful self and the new, righteous self (Ephesians 4:20-24; Colossians 3:9-10). Without the presence of God's Spirit working against the flesh, a person will act in sinful and selfish ways (see Galatians 5:19-21, below).

17b. They are in conflict with each other, so that you are not to do whatever you want.

A person cannot at the same time embrace fully the ways the flesh and the ways of the Spirit. Their ways *are conflict with each other*. As a result, a believer—while filled with God's Spirit—may experience a spiritual frustration (see Romans 7:17-25). God's Spirit has already provided a way out: freedom from the ways of the flesh (8:10-11, 16).

In this sense, the battle has been won and believers are to follow the Spirit (see Galatians 5:25, below). Therefore Paul's conclusion is clear: believers are not to *do whatever* the flesh desires. Instead, believers follow the Spirit's way of life.

> *What Do You Think?*
> How can Galatians 6:1-5 assist a believer's battle against the desires of the flesh?
> *Digging Deeper*
> What steps will you take to "carry each other's burdens" with a spirit of gentleness (Galatians 6:1-2)?

B. Spirit and Law (v. 18)

18. But if you are led by the Spirit, you are not under the law.

Paul introduced a new point of conflict between *the Spirit* and *the law*. Given the context of the epistle (see Lesson Context, lesson 11), Paul was likely speaking of the demands of the Law of Moses.

Paul previously connected the demands of the law and the ways of the flesh (Galatians 3:2-5). He had reminded the Galatians of their freedom from the law. As a result, they were no longer "under a curse" (3:10) nor "in custody under the law" (3:23). As they followed the Spirit, they would not experience the bondage of the flesh and the law (5:1).

Paul's exhortation was the fulfillment of the words of the prophet Jeremiah. God's people

Visual for Lesson 13. *Have this visual on display as you pose the discussion question that is associated with Galatians 5:22.*

would be marked by their following of God's law on their hearts (Jeremiah 31:33). This promise took hold through a life committed to be in tune "with the Spirit of the living God" (2 Corinthians 3:3).

II. Chasing the Flesh
(GALATIANS 5:19-21)
A. Acts (vv. 19-21a)

19. The acts of the flesh are obvious: sexual immorality, impurity and debauchery;

To provide examples of how *the flesh* might be made *obvious* in people, Paul gave further examples of these kinds of *acts*. What follows are lists of vices (Galatians 5:19-21a) and virtues (5:22-23). Such lists were never intended to be an exhaustive catalog for the readers but were representative (compare Roman 1:29-31; Colossians 3:5-9).

Indulgent and self-gratifying sexual acts with another person outside of a marriage relationship make up *sexual immorality* (see 1 Corinthians 5:1). In addition to hurting others, these acts harm the guilty person (6:18). *Impurity* results from improper sexual acts. This term was also used in conjunction with purity codes of the Law of Moses (Leviticus 5:3; 7:21; etc.). God desires that his people acknowledge the holiness of their bodies and act accordingly (see 1 Corinthians 6:19-20).

Extravagant sexual vice, uncontrolled and

shameless, is *debauchery*. The term implies lack of self-control, even to the point of shocking others without regard for decency (see Ephesians 4:19).

✵ OBSESSION AND DISCIPLINE ✵

With a few quick clicks of the mouse, the internet has made pornography accessible (and frequently, unsolicited) for people. Even church-going people also admit to viewing pornography. All society seems saturated with sexuality.

Paul's cultural context was also obsessed with sexuality. Sites of pagan worship, such as temples to the goddess Aphrodite, utilized practices of sexual exploitation. Religious festivals frequently encouraged public and graphic expressions of sex.

Paul called Christians to a life of self-discipline, contrary to the ways of their culture. Indiscipline and excessiveness were not suitable for a life in God's Spirit. Invite the Spirit to develop in you an attitude of self-discipline, even more than what you might expect (see Matthew 5:28)!   —M. S. K.

20a. idolatry and witchcraft;

Paul's second grouping concerned idolatrous acts of worship. *Idolatry* involves replacing worship of the one true God. In essence, this act exchanged God for a lie (see Exodus 20:3-6; Leviticus 19:4; Isaiah 44:9-20; Jeremiah 10:14; Romans 1:25).

Modern audiences need not think of idolatry strictly in terms of acts of worship to physical images. Rather, idolatry should be considered in terms of what diverts peoples' attention, effort, and resources away from the desires of God (see Isaiah 2:8; Jeremiah 1:16; Micah 5:12-13; Acts 17:29).

Witchcraft is the attempt to use physical objects and rituals to manipulate the spiritual world. Examples would include ancient pagan practices of magic, incantations, and drug use.

20b. hatred, discord, jealousy, fits of rage, selfish ambition, dissensions, factions

Paul's final grouping concerns a person's treatment of others. *Hatred* refers to a spirit of hostility toward another person, God, or both. *Discord* is a general description for the feelings of hostility among people—quarreling and disharmony (see 1 Corinthians 1:11; 3:3). Feelings of *jealousy* speak to the strong feelings that may arise from seeing the success of another person. *Fits of rage* are strong bursts of anger stemming from an impetuous mindset. *Selfish ambition* results when hostile groups advance their own interests. These kinds of acts are the opposite of the self-giving love initiated by God's Spirit. *Dissensions* continue interpersonal strife to the point of causing division (see Romans 16:17-18). *Factions* point to false beliefs that lead to destructive differences within the community.

21a. and envy; drunkenness, orgies, and the like.

The semicolon after the word *envy* indicates that it goes with the previous grouping of selfish behavior. It refers to the desire to deprive others of what they have.

Paul ends the list of vices by describing two public displays of overindulgence and self-destruction. *Drunkenness*—intoxication from alcohol—harms the body and clouds a person's mind. A drunk person might lose control of his or her better judgment and participate in *orgies*. These are public displays of indulgence, gluttony, and immorality (see Romans 13:13; 1 Peter 4:3). The underlying Greek text reflects the name of the mythical Greek god Comus, the god of festivities. The Roman festival Bacchanalia was observed in honor of the gods and celebrated through rampant drunkenness and sexual immorality.

That the vice list concludes with *and the like* confirms that Paul had not compiled a comprehensive list. Rather, he wanted to highlight specific works of the flesh applicable to the Galatians.

B. Warning (v. 21b)

21b. I warn you, as I did before, that those who live like this will not inherit the kingdom of God.

The first two phrases of this partial verse indicate that this was not the first time Paul had taught the Galatians concerning these topics. Perhaps he had instructed their behavior during his initial encounter with them on a missionary journey (Galatians 1:9; see Acts 13:4–14:28; 16:1-3).

To *those* people *who live like this*, the listed vices

of the flesh, a strong warning is evident. People gain their eternal inheritance of life through faith, not ethical behavior (Galatians 3:11-12, 18). But right behavior serves as an indication of the presence of God's Spirit. People who fail to act in accordance with the Spirit *will not inherit the kingdom of God*.

Occasional failure to live in this regard was not Paul's concern. Instead, he was concerned with individuals who mock God's Spirit as they continually live in the flesh (Galatians 6:7-9). Persistent disregard for the Spirit indicates that transforming faith is not present. A life led by the Spirit will not continue the status quo of living apart from God's path.

> **What Do You Think?**
> In what ways is the kingdom of God already established, but not yet fully realized?
> **Digging Deeper**
> How do Mark 1:14-15; 4:26-32; 10:13-15; Luke 11:2-4; 1 Corinthians 15:24-28, 50-54; and Revelation 11:15-19 inform your answer?

III. Showing the Spirit
(GALATIANS 5:22-26)
A. Fruit (vv. 22-23)

22a. But the fruit of the Spirit is love, joy, peace,

Having given his list of vices, Paul now provides an in-depth listing of virtues appropriate to the life of a Spirit-filled believer. Greco-Roman philosophers created virtue lists based on the cardinal values of their culture. However, Paul's virtue list had a different basis: love for others indicative of the presence of God's *Spirit* (Galatians 5:13-16).

Paul described the Spirit-filled life in agricultural terms, calling the attributes of such a life *fruit* (compare his other "fruit" thoughts in Ephesians 5:9; Philippians 1:11, 22; see John 15:1-17). The metaphor alludes to the Spirit's role in producing this harvest—a shift from human striving to the Spirit's supplying. Only through submission to God's Spirit will these fruits be evident in a believer's life (see Matthew 7:16-20).

This list of spiritual fruit begins with the greatest of all Christian virtues: *love* (1 Corinthians 13:13).

This love is different from the feelings of affection between friends, family members, or romantic partners. This kind of love demonstrates itself by sacrificial self-giving (see John 15:13; Romans 5:8). The entire law was fulfilled by this love (Galatians 5:13-14; compare Leviticus 19:18; Matthew 5:43-45a). The destructive ways of the flesh are neutralized by radical, self-giving love.

A Spirit-filled sense of *joy* does not depend on circumstances. Rather, this joy remains steadfast and prevalent during difficult situations (see 2 Corinthians 8:2; 1 Thessalonians 1:6; Hebrews 10:34; James 1:2-3).

Spirit-filled *peace* does not imply the absence of distress. Rather, peace finds its basis in the conviction of God's all-sufficiency. Believers demonstrate peace as they work toward taking part in God's restoration of the world. This begins with the restoration of the relationships within the church (compare 1 Corinthians 14:33; 2 Corinthians 13:11).

22b. forbearance, kindness, goodness, faithfulness,

The next grouping of spiritual fruit describes a person's attitude toward others. *Forbearance* expresses patient treatment of others, even in response to wrongful treatment.

Kindness speaks of a person's loving disposition toward others. People can show this temperament because God's actions toward humanity provide the ultimate example (see Romans 2:4).

Goodness is an attribute that marks the collective people of God (see Romans 15:14). The concept might imply a willingness to do good for others by acts of radical generosity (see Matthew 20:1-16).

Such fruit addressed the difficult work of building right relationships among believers and establishing appropriate witness to unbelievers (Colossians 4:5; 1 Thessalonians 4:12). That Paul's teaching emphasized this work was because of factions that had formed among the churches of Galatia (see Galatians 1:6-9). Therefore, formation by the Holy Spirit was required for the Galatians to become one in Christ.

The underlying Greek word translated as *faithfulness* can also be translated as loyalty. It probably carries that meaning in this verse. Specifically, it refers to the faithfulness required between believers (see Galatians 4:12-16; compare Philemon 5).

> **What Do You Think?**
> How are the Spirit's gifts (Romans 12:6-8; 1 Corinthians 12:4-11) similar to the Spirit's fruit? How are they different?
> **Digging Deeper**
> How is love the means for applying the Spirit's gifts and fruit (see 1 Corinthians 13)?

❧ UNSOCIABLE MEDIA ❧

Many positive interactions have resulted from social media. However, social media's power has also contributed to the spread of division and hate. The perpetrator of a 2019 shooting in Christchurch, New Zealand, spread his radical ideologies through a platform that allowed the gunman to easily (and anonymously) broadcast his ideas.

Shocking cases like this are easy to identify. However, have you seen or engaged in lesser (but still dangerous) forms of contention and strife while online? Scrolling through any social media platform will highlight name-calling, attacks, and harassment. While these may seem innocent and a way to let off steam, why should Christ followers engage with or encourage such behavior?

Paul's antidote to strife is love, a feeling of overt concern for others' good. This feeling applies even to people with whom we have a disagreement. Love presents itself as believers are filled with peace, joy, and patience. Hateful rhetoric springs from a heart out of tune with God's Spirit. Objectively, are your comments and "likes" on social media more like "hates"?   —M. S. K.

23. gentleness and self-control. Against such things there is no law.

While the previous grouping of fruit focused on a person's treatment of others, the final grouping concerns a person's demeanor. *Gentleness* implies self-restraint, even in the midst of a disagreement (see 2 Timothy 2:25; 1 Peter 3:15-16). Paul would encourage the Galatians to put this fruit into practice as they worked to restore their community (see Galatians 6:1). When the fruit of *self-control* is present in a believer's life, desires and passions do not rule that person.

B. Expectations (vv. 24-26)

24. Those who belong to Christ Jesus have crucified the flesh with its passions and desires.

Christians are not to be passive while bearing the Spirit's fruit. While the Spirit has a role in the growth of the fruit, the Christian must end anything that might hinder the growing conditions of the fruit. This requires that Christians put to death selfish desires (see Romans 8:13; Colossians 3:5).

Paul's imagery unites Jesus' followers with his experience on the cross. Following Jesus and expressing faith in him requires believers to *have crucified* the desires and ways of *the flesh*. Doing so does not require that believers experience physical crucifixion. Rather, the language reminds believers to put to death sinful practices so that new life might be found (Romans 6:1-14; Galatians 2:20). Paul wanted the Galatians to live not for themselves, but for the one who died for them (2 Corinthians 5:15). As we live in the Spirit, we avoid all sinful tendencies, including the *passions* and "sinful *desires*, which war against the soul" (1 Peter 2:11).

25. Since we live by the Spirit, let us keep in step with the Spirit.

Considering Paul's similar imperative in Galatians 5:16 (above), this statement serves as the bookend to this section of the letter. By including himself in the subject (*we . . . us*), Paul identified with the situation of the Galatians. What he asked of them applied to himself as well. To *live by the Spirit* necessitates a resulting walk *with the Spirit*. Following the Spirit's lead brings a life of righteousness, demonstrating the transformational fruit of the Spirit (Romans 8:4-5).

26. Let us not become conceited, provoking and envying each other.

Paul's concern for the Galatians' unity is evident. If they lived by the flesh, the Spirit's fruit would be absent and divisions would deepen. The *conceited* glory sought by some Galatians would lead to discord among the whole community. When this provoking occurred, people were diverted away from the ways of the Spirit and resulting good works

(contrast Hebrews 10:24). Selfish acts of our sinful nature are contrary to the humility required of Christ followers, demonstrated by Christ (see Philippians 2:3). A life filled with God's Spirit would show fruit and build unity among believers.

> *What Do You Think?*
> How does Jesus' garden prayer (John 17:6-26) reinforce Paul's exhortation to the Galatians?
> *Digging Deeper*
> What steps will you take to live in peace and unity with other believers?

Conclusion

A. Narrative Conflict

If the Galatian epistle were a narrative, Flesh and Spirit would serve as the main characters. In this scenario, the conflict between the two played out in the lives of the Galatians. However, the Spirit has already won—the resolution of the story has been made complete! Therefore, Paul wants his hearers and readers to act accordingly.

As followers of Jesus live in step with the Spirit, we will bear the Spirit's fruit. When this life is demonstrated in a community of believers, the result is a unified people of God. Mutual submission in love becomes the ultimate example of the Spirit's presence. This narrative is timeless; it is just as applicable for modern audiences as it was for the first-century Galatians!

B. Prayer

Our Father, thank you for your Spirit. We want the Spirit to guide our lives and our interactions. Strengthen us to avoid sinful distractions so that we might live holy lives filled with unrelenting joy and love for others. In Jesus' name. Amen.

C. Thought to Remember

The sweetest fruit comes from walking in God's Spirit!

HOW TO SAY IT

Bacchanalia   Bah-keh-*nail*-yuh.
Greco   *Greck*-oh.

INVOLVEMENT LEARNING

Enhance your lesson with NIV Bible Student *(from your curriculum supplier) and the reproducible activity page (at www.standardlesson.com or in the back of the* NIV Standard Lesson Commentary Deluxe Edition*).*

Into the Lesson

As class members arrive, write "Look out for number one" on the board. Begin today's lesson by asking students to answer the following questions: 1–How often have you seen this philosophy in action? 2–Who do you usually view as being "number one"? 3–In what ways do the implications of this phrase shift if we adjust who we identify as "number one"?

Lead into Bible study by saying, "We might hear that the secret to a person's success is for them to 'look out for number one'—themselves. However, today's Scripture text reevaluates that statement."

Into the Word

Divide the class into five groups. Have a volunteer read aloud Galatians 5:16-26. Distribute handouts (you create) of the following group assignments and questions. Give groups 10 minutes to complete the questions.

Love Group: 1–How can Christian love be an antidote to sexual immorality? 2–How might this love's self-sacrificial nature address sexual immorality? 3–How can Christians develop this love?

Faithfulness Group: 1–How does faithfulness overcome idolatry? 2–What idols take away from our faithfulness to Jesus? 3–How can Christians further develop faithfulness?

Peace and Kindness Group: 1–How do peace and kindness overcome feelings of hatred, hostility, or anger? 2–What causes people to show hatred, hostility, or anger? 3–How can Christians develop peace and kindness?

Goodness, and Gentleness Group: 1–How do goodness and gentleness overcome feelings of envy and strife? 2–What are common reasons a person might experience envy or strife? 3–What steps can Christians take to develop goodness and gentleness?

Self-control and Joy Group: 1–How does an attitude of self-control and joy overcome desires related to debauchery and drunkenness? 2–Why might joy be necessary along with self-control? 3–How can Christians develop self-control and joy?

Option. Distribute copies of the "What Kind of Fruit?" activity from the activity page, which you can download. Have learners work in pairs to complete the activity as indicated

After calling time for either activity, have each group present their findings for whole-class discussion. Use the lesson commentary to correct misconceptions regarding the Spirit's fruit.

Into Life

Before class, recruit two or three class members to prepare two-minute testimonials they will share with the whole class at this time. The testimonies will tell how another Christian displayed a fruit of the Spirit and provided an example for others to "live by" and "keep step with the Spirit" (Galatians 5:25).

After each testimony, ask class members to tell what they found most convicting or helpful about it. Ask how each testimony provided a practical insight for ways Christians might display the Spirit's fruit.

On sheets of paper you provide, have each class member write down a sinful tendency most in need of correction. Then have class members write down a fruit of the Spirit they wish to display in the following week to counteract that tendency. Allow no more than one minute for completion. Because of the personal nature of this assignment, some group members may not wish to share aloud.

Option: Distribute copies of the "Read All About It!" exercise from the activity page. Have learners work in small groups to complete the activity as indicated. After 10 minutes, have each group share their findings.

End class with a prayer asking God to help each class member demonstrate the Spirit's fruit in the coming week.

PARTNERS IN A NEW CREATION

Special Features

Lessons

Unit 1: God Delivers and Restores

Unit 2: The Word: The Agent of Creation

Unit 3: The Great Hope of the Saints

QUARTERLY QUIZ

Use these questions as a pretest or as a review. The answers are on page iv of This Quarter in the Word.

Lesson 1

1. According to Isaiah, Babylon trusted in what? (wickedness, laziness, chariots) *Isaiah 47:10*

2. Isaiah sarcastically told Babylon to consult astrologers for deliverance. T/F. *Isaiah 47:13*

Lesson 2

1. When was Isaiah "called" by the Lord? (as a teenager, after marriage, before birth) *Isaiah 49:1*

2. The Lord made Isaiah's mouth like a sharp _____. *Isaiah 49:2*

Lesson 3

1. The Lord predicted that the Israelites would wear children as what? (ornaments, masks, coats) *Isaiah 49:18*

2. In restored Israel, the queens of the Gentiles would be like what? (nursing mothers, farm oxen, broken pottery) *Isaiah 49:23*

Lesson 4

1. Isaiah predicted Israel's wilderness would become like what? (Eden, Egypt, Edom) *Isaiah 51:3*

2. God's judgments will bring darkness to the nations. T/F. *Isaiah 51:4*

Lesson 5

1. "In the beginning was the _____." *John 1:1*

2. John the Baptist was sent to do what? (be an apostle, bear witness, be the light) *John 1:6-7*

Lesson 6

1. Jesus changed water into wine in the city of _____. *John 4:46*

2. Jesus noted that people wouldn't believe without what? (pick two: signs, wine, myrrh, wonders, money) *John 4:48*

Lesson 7

1. Jesus claimed that he had come to judge the world. T/F. *John 12:47*

2. Judgment occurs when? (never, the last day, when we're good enough) *John 12:48*

Lesson 8

1. Bethany, the town of Lazarus, was close to what city? (Nazareth, Heliopolis, Jerusalem) *John 11:18*

2. Jesus told Martha that he was the resurrection and the _____. *John 11:25*

Lesson 9

1. Jesus said that to love him meant doing what? (keeping his commandments, reaping material blessings, finding peace) *John 14:15, 21*

2. Jesus referred to the Spirit as the Spirit of _____. *John 14:17*

Lesson 10

1. John compares New Jerusalem to a beautifully dressed _____. *Revelation 21:2*

2. The Alpha and Omega is like what? (beginning and end, old and new, hunger and thirst) *Revelation 21:6*

Lesson 11

1. The 12 foundations of New Jerusalem are named for the tribes of Israel. T/F. *Revelation 21:14*

2. The gates of New Jerusalem were made of gigantic _____. *Revelation 21:21*

Lesson 12

1. John saw the tree of life in New Jerusalem. T/F. *Revelation 22:2*

2. What is to bring healing to the nations? (tree leaves, water, aloe vera plants) *Revelation 22:2*

Lesson 13

1. Jesus is likened to the morning _____. *Revelation 22:16*

2. What do the Spirit and the bride say? (come, go, stay) *Revelation 22:17*

QUARTER AT A GLANCE

by Mark S. Krause

THE BOOK OF JUDGES documents a dismal pattern of apostasy, oppression, repentance, and restoration in ancient Israel. But these times of crisis were not unique to the period of the judges (about 1373 to 1043 BC). The two greatest crises Israel faced happened centuries later. These were the exile to Assyria in 722 BC and the destruction of Jerusalem and exile at the hands of the Babylonians in 586 BC.

Back to the Future

The prophet Isaiah lived through the Assyrian crisis, having begun his prophetic ministry in about 740 BC in Jerusalem. He foresaw the coming oppression by Babylon as a time when the land of Israel would be largely emptied of its people (lesson 1). Even so, he offered hope for a future time when "the Lord comforts his people and will have compassion on his afflicted ones" (Isaiah 49:13, lesson 2). This was a promise to the faithful of Israel, for "those who hope in me will not be disappointed" (49:23, lesson 3).

Isaiah also saw a future that would involve more than a restoration of peace. He spoke of the final restoration of humanity, when "[the Lord] will make her deserts like Eden, her wastelands like the garden of the Lord" (Isaiah 51:3, lesson 4). As the passing of some seven centuries would reveal, that restoration would come through Jesus the Christ, the Son of the living God.

Grace and Truth

The Gospel of John pictures the ministry of Jesus as more than his journey to the cross. Jesus came as a light to the world, one that shines brightly for "grace and truth" (John 1:14, lesson 5). John sees this as one key to humanity's return to the state God intended at the beginning.

Grace and truth are evident in Jesus' miracles. One example is the healing of the official's son (lesson 6) when Jesus' statement of truth (John 4:48) was immediately followed by his gracious act of healing. Jesus came not to judge the world, but he told the truth of judgment to come nevertheless (12:44-50, lesson 7). Another powerful example of the grace and truth combination is the resurrection of Lazarus (11:17-27, 38-44, lesson 8). The Holy Spirit Jesus promised to send is "the Spirit of truth" (14:17, lesson 9).

The Future That Awaits

This quarter's lessons climax with John's vision of the New Jerusalem in the book of Revelation. This vision presents the Holy City restored, but much more than that. It is enhanced to a glorious degree (lesson 10). The New Jerusalem has features historical Jerusalem never imagined! Gold, precious gems, and pearls are used as building materials. A life-giving river flows within, and the tree of life reappears, the tree lost in Eden (lesson 11). This fulfills Isaiah's vision, that the desert would become like the garden of the Lord.

> *Jesus came as a light . . . that shines brightly for "grace and truth."*

There is more to this than restoration though. Now the tree has leaves that cause "the healing of the nations" (Revelation 22:2, lesson 12). The new city restores the gardenlike paradise of Genesis. It also signifies the end of international conflict, for believers from all nations will be reconciled.

This will not be a restoration project that returns to some cherished "normal" of the past. The cycle of apostasy/crisis/repentance/restoration will never return. This is the truth of a new creation, and John desires that "the grace of the Lord Jesus" be with us as we await the promise to become reality (Revelation 22:21, lesson 13). It is our hope for the future as we wait expectantly for the return of the Lord.

GET THE SETTING

by Mark S. Krause

RARELY READ TODAY, John Milton's epic poem *Paradise Lost* tells the classic story of Adam and Eve, the first humans. Milton's story includes the fall of Satan, the temptation and sin of Eve and Adam, and their banishment from the Garden of Eden paradise. As they exit, Milton's Eve says, "Though all by me is lost . . . By me the Promised Seed shall all restore."

Milton employed one of the most powerful themes in religion: restoration. In Genesis, humans are removed from the garden and lose access to the tree of life. Daily life becomes a struggle. This is the future for all humans, who are now under the power of the great tyrant, death (Romans 5:12). In the book of Revelation, paradise is recreated in the New Jerusalem, and access to the tree of life is restored to those in the city.

Earthly Jerusalem

Rulers in the ancient world often built or improved their capital cities lavishly. In Egypt, Ramses II (reigned 1279–1213 BC) left the capital of Thebes to a build a new capital to the east, named Pi-Ramesses. This magnificent city displayed the power and wealth of the pharaoh. In Assyria, King Sennacherib (reigned 705–681 BC) did much the same with his capital of Nineveh.

Concerning the city of Rome, some historians believe that its great fire of AD 64 was started by agents working for Emperor Nero (reigned AD 54–68), who allegedly needed some way to clear out the old to make way for the new. Nero ended up building his new city on top of the old one! He followed the precedent of kings before him who built cities to show their glory.

Improvements to ancient Jerusalem followed this path to varying degrees (1 Kings 10:27; 1 Chronicles 11:8; 2 Chronicles 26:9; 27:3; 33:14; etc.). Nowhere was this more apparent than with the building of the temple (2 Chronicles 2–4). Jerusalem's temple was unique and could not be relocated or duplicated. When Jerusalem was destroyed by the Babylonians in 586 BC, the people of Israel did not look for alternative sites for the royal palace or the temple. They wanted Jerusalem to be restored and the temple to be rebuilt on the same mountaintop.

This hope of restoration burned strongly among prophets such as Isaiah, even before the Babylonian conquest. The same was true with Jeremiah after Jerusalem's destruction.

Ultimately, the aggrandizement of capital cities of pagan kings was designed to stroke their own egos in self-proclaimed greatness. By contrast, the magnificence of Jerusalem and its temple were designed to bring glory to God. As the city failed to do that, it ceased to exist. Rebuilding under Ezra and Nehemiah wasn't permanent either. Neither was the 46-year temple rebuilding effort of King Herod's day (John 2:20); destruction at the hands of the Romans in AD 70 saw to that.

Heavenly Jerusalem

John wrote the book of Revelation after Jerusalem was destroyed by the Romans. There was no more temple. As the Jews in Babylon longed for a restoration, so did the Jews of John's day. But John's vision does not present a restored Jerusalem. Rather, he foresaw a New Jerusalem, a city of extraordinary magnificence and permanence. It is the city of the King of kings and Lord of lords—the city of King Jesus. He is the promised seed of Eve who comes not only to restore but to make all things new. The new city is appropriate for its eternal king.

The new, heavenly Jerusalem will also be an appropriate dwelling for us as well—that is, for those who are admitted.

> Blessed are those who wash their robes, that they may . . . go . . . into the city. Outside are the dogs, those who practice magic arts, the sexually immoral, the murderers, the idolaters and everyone who loves and practices falsehood (Revelation 22:14-15).

THIS QUARTER IN THE WORD

Mon, Aug. 15 — My Soul Thirsts for You — Psalm 63
Tue, Aug. 16 — Living Waters Shall Flow — Zechariah 14:6-11
Wed, Aug. 17 — Jesus Promises Living Water — John 4:4-14
Thu, Aug. 18 — Worship God in Spirit and Truth — John 4:15-26
Fri, Aug. 19 — Rivers of Living Water — John 7:37-40
Sat, Aug. 20 — Water on the Thirsty Land — Isaiah 44:1-8
Sun, Aug. 21 — For the Healing of the Nations — Revelation 22:1-9

Mon, Aug. 22 — Invited to the Heavenly Banquet — Luke 14:16-24
Tue, Aug. 23 — Preparing for God to Appear — Exodus 19:9-15
Wed, Aug. 24 — The Alpha and Omega — Revelation 1:3-8
Thu, Aug. 25 — The End Declared from the Beginning — Isaiah 46:8-13
Fri, Aug. 26 — God Is Your Husband — Isaiah 54:1-5
Sat, Aug. 27 — God's Love Never Ceases — Lamentations 3:21-31
Sun, Aug. 28 — Come, Lord Jesus! — Revelation 22:10-21

Mon, May 30 — Babylon's Days Are Numbered — Jeremiah 29:8-14
Tue, May 31 — Let Your Compassion Come Speedily — Psalm 79
Wed, June 1 — Persecution Foretold — Mark 13:1-13
Thu, June 2 — Keep Awake! — Mark 13:28-37
Fri, June 3 — Rise Up, O God! — Psalm 74:10-23
Sat, June 4 — The Humiliation of Babylon — Isaiah 47:1-9
Sun, June 5 — No Security in Wickedness — Isaiah 47:10-15

Mon, June 6 — God's Redemption Defies Human Wisdom — 1 Corinthians 1:18-25
Tue, June 7 — Righteousness, Sanctification, and Redemption — 1 Corinthians 1:26-31

Wed, June 8 — God Sent Redemption to People — Psalm 111
Thu, June 9 — Christ Brings Eternal Redemption — Hebrews 9:11-14
Fri, June 10 — Pardon My Guilt, O Lord — Psalm 25:1-11
Sat, June 11 — Redeem Israel, O God — Psalm 25:12-22
Sun, June 12 — The Lord Will Have Compassion — Isaiah 49:1-17

Mon, June 13 — God Puts Down and Lifts Up — Psalm 75
Tue, June 14 — God Protects a Restored People — Leviticus 26:3-13
Wed, June 15 — Blessings upon God's People — Luke 6:20-26
Thu, June 16 — God Has Turned Mourning into Dancing — Psalm 30
Fri, June 17 — God Gives Good Gifts — James 1:13-18
Sat, June 18 — Blessings for Obedience — Deuteronomy 28:9-14
Sun, June 19 — Wait for the Lord — Isaiah 49:18-23

Answers to the Quarterly Quiz on page 338

Answers to the Quarterly Quiz on page 338

Lesson 1—1. wickedness. 2. true. **Lesson 2**—1. before birth. 2. sword. **Lesson 3**—1. ornaments. 2. nursing mothers. **Lesson 4**—1. Eden. 2. false. **Lesson 5**—1. Word. 2. bear witness. **Lesson 6**—1. Cana. 2. signs, wonders. **Lesson 7**—1. false. 2. the last day. **Lesson 8**—1. Jerusalem. 2. life. **Lesson 9**—1. keeping his commandments. 2. truth. **Lesson 10**—1. bride. 2. beginning and end. **Lesson 11**—1. false. 2. pearls. **Lesson 12**—1. true. 2. tree leaves. **Lesson 13**—1. come. 2. star.

SERVANT SONGS

ISAIAH 42:1-9   Judgment to the Gentiles

49:1-7   A light to the Gentiles

50:4-9   The Lord's promised help

52:13–53:12   The coming Messiah

61:1-4   The Savior's promised renewal

Photo © Getty Images

Lesson 2

Sheet 2—Summer 2022, *Adult Resources, Standard Lesson Quarterly® Curriculum*

TEACHING IS MORE THAN TALKING

Part 4: Get Out of the Classroom   *Teacher Tips by Mark A. Taylor*

EVEN THOUGH you work to prepare excellent lessons, remember this: they are only the beginning. Your most important teaching may happen outside of class time, away from the church building, without formal preparation. In fact, it's not an exaggeration to say your weekly Bible lessons only create the opportunity for you to make your most significant impact later.

This is the example of Jesus. He taught his disciples by living with them. His spoken lessons also hit home as he engaged personally with others. Zacchaeus, Nicodemus, the Samaritan woman . . . we could list person after person whose lives were changed not by sitting in rows inside a classroom but by encountering Jesus in everyday life.

You can follow our master teacher's example by spending time with your class members. Here are some ideas to get you started.

Share a Meal

Invite class members to your home or choose a restaurant to enjoy together. Be strategic about this; keep a list of members and visitors, and schedule times with as many as possible in the next year. After each meal, jot down what you've learned: family and job details, preferences, prayer concerns. Talk to God about them in your prayer times. Remember these friends' experiences as you plan future lessons.

Maximize Teachable Moments

Adults are often most open to change at life's crossroads: a serious illness, deaths in the family, a job loss, etc. Watch for these and seize the opportunity to be present. In these situations, you'll accomplish three things: you will (1) have the chance to speak truth that your friends may never forget, (2) create a bond with those you serve that will make them more open to your formal teaching, and (3) create an example for those who see you or work with you.

Plan an Outing

You need not wait for a crisis. Plan regular ways for class members to get together. Some classes sponsor monthly or quarterly socials. Some host prayer meetings. Some organize service projects at food pantries, crisis pregnancy locations, halfway houses, or hospitals. Be sure to choose based on the level of the need, not just the chance to feel good about serving.

Go on a Retreat

This can be simple. Choose a resort or park or campsite and allow class members (maybe with their families) to enjoy the space in an unstructured way as you gather in the evening for prayer, Bible reading, and personal sharing. A bonfire is always good for a no-pressure, unstructured retreat.

For a more structured approach, use the setting to determine the Bible reading. A cloudless night far from artificial light is ideal for a devotional from Psalm 19; a fishing trip might suggest John 21:7-14 as a study passage. This involves planning a theme and perhaps recruiting someone to lead teaching times. Set up a schedule that combines formal teaching with meals and recreation. Schedule prayer walks; challenge people to spread out for private Bible reading; plan a devotional scavenger hunt with Bible verses, prayer prompts, and directions to the next station at each stop.

Remember the Goal

Whatever you do, remember that your purpose is more than social activity. Your goal is to build relationships so that class members can learn from each other. Your purpose is to know class members better so you can point them to Christ more effectively. Your challenge is to be the person in informal settings that you're encouraging class members to become with your weekly Bible lessons.

GOD FORETELLS DESTRUCTION

DEVOTIONAL READING: Isaiah 47:10-15
BACKGROUND SCRIPTURE: Isaiah 47

ISAIAH 47:10-15

10 "You have trusted in your wickedness
  and have said, 'No one sees me.'
Your wisdom and knowledge mislead you
  when you say to yourself,
  'I am, and there is none besides me.'
11 Disaster will come upon you,
  and you will not know how to conjure
    it away.
A calamity will fall upon you
  that you cannot ward off with a ransom;
a catastrophe you cannot foresee
  will suddenly come upon you.
12 "Keep on, then, with your magic spells
  and with your many sorceries,
  which you have labored at since
    childhood.
Perhaps you will succeed,
  perhaps you will cause terror.

13 All the counsel you have received has only
    worn you out!
  Let your astrologers come forward,
those stargazers who make predictions
    month by month,
  let them save you from what is coming
    upon you.
14 Surely they are like stubble;
  the fire will burn them up.
They cannot even save themselves
  from the power of the flame.
These are not coals for warmth;
  this is not a fire to sit by.
15 That is all they are to you—
  these you have dealt with
  and labored with since childhood.
All of them go on in their error;
  there is not one that can save you.

KEY VERSE

That is all they are to you—these you have dealt with and labored with since childhood. All of them go on in their error; there is not one that can save you. —**Isaiah 47:15**

Photo © Getty Images

Partners in a New Creation

Unit 1: God Delivers and Restores

LESSONS 1–4

LESSON AIMS

After participating in this lesson, each learner will be able to:

1. Identify the object of God's condemnation.
2. Explain the prophet's use of sarcasm.
3. Identify one personal way to avoid repeating a sin of ancient Babylon.

LESSON OUTLINE

Introduction

A. How to Get Away with Murder?

Michelle Martinko was a miracle child. She was born 12 years and five miscarriages after her older sister, when their mother was 44 years old. Friends described her as a kind, smart person. When she was found murdered in her car on December 20, 1979, her family was devastated and the city was stunned.

The killer had come prepared. There were no fingerprints or other usable evidence found; DNA testing was not yet available. The case went cold for years. Michelle's parents died without ever seeing her killer brought to justice.

When DNA testing finally became available, a full profile of the murderer was worked up. In 2005, that profile was tested against a nationwide database, but no matches were found. It wasn't until a relative uploaded her own profile onto a genealogical website that detectives were able to connect the dots and to identify the perpetrator. He had no other connection to Michelle and no apparent motive; in the intervening years he had lived quietly as a family man.

For decades it appeared that justice would never be served in Michelle Martinko's cold case. But God always sees the wickedness of individuals and nations. We may cry out, as did the prophet, "How long, Lord, must I call for help, but you do not listen? Or cry out to you, 'Violence!' but you do not save?" (Habakkuk 1:2). And in crying out, we may feel that God is slow to act. But God's timing is not ours. Though evil in all eras seems to prevail, in the end justice wins.

B. Lesson Context: Isaiah and His Times

The prophet Isaiah had a lengthy ministry in Judah. (The books of Isaiah and 2 Kings contain most of the information we have about the prophet Isaiah.) Isaiah 1:1 places that ministry in the days of "Uzziah, Jotham, Ahaz, and Hezekiah, kings of Judah." The first dated event is the death of Uzziah (also called Azariah; 2 Kings 15:1, 6-8, 17, 23, 27) in about 739 BC (Isaiah 6:1), the same year Isaiah received his call (see time line to the right). The final dated event is the death of

King Sennacherib of Assyria, who died in 681 BC (37:38).

Isaiah had the most direct association with two kings of Judah: Ahaz (Isaiah 7:1-17) and Hezekiah (2 Kings 19–20; Isaiah 38). Isaiah seems to have had free access to the palace. This has caused some to think that he may have been a member of the royal family.

Judah experienced great changes politically, economically, militarily, and spiritually during Isaiah's prophetic ministry. Uzziah in Judah and his contemporary Jeroboam II in Israel did well militarily. The land area under the control of the two nations was similar to what it had been in the days of David and Solomon (2 Kings 14:28).

Jotham succeeded Uzziah as king of Judah and became mighty because of his good life before the Lord. But the people were corrupt spiritually (2 Chronicles 27:1-2). Ahaz followed Jotham on the throne and became the spiritual opposite of his father. Ahaz even practiced child sacrifice (2 Kings 16:3). Ahaz and Judah were attacked by Israel, and Judah suffered greatly.

Hezekiah eventually succeeded Ahaz, and Hezekiah was a faithful follower of the Lord. Judah prospered at first, but then was devastated militarily by a king of Assyria, Sennacherib (2 Kings 18:13-16). The exile that had befallen northern Israel in 722 BC was also to befall Judah, but not at the hands of the Assyrians.

C. Lesson Context: Isaiah and the Future

Isaiah 39:5-6 predicts a captivity in Babylon. (Isaiah 36–39 runs parallel to 2 Kings 18:13–20:19.) Isaiah wrote as though Babylon had already conquered Judah, but his prophecies predated Babylon's existence as an empire by about 150 years!

At the time Isaiah wrote, Babylon was a major city in the Assyrian Empire. Babylon rebelled between 700–689 BC in an attempt to overthrow Assyria, which destroyed the city in retaliation. Even so, the Babylonians ultimately destroyed and replaced the Assyrians. A key event was the destruction of Nineveh, Assyria's capital city, in 612 BC.

God had at least two plans for the Babylonian Empire: to bring about the end of the Assyrian Empire and to punish the people of Judah because of their idolatry (2 Chronicles 24:18; Isaiah 10:3-19; etc.). Babylon would take Judah into captivity in waves. This began in 598 BC (2 Kings 24:10-16) and culminated with the destruction of Jerusalem and its aftermath in 586 BC (2 Kings 25).

I. Failed Confidence
(ISAIAH 47:10-11)
A. God Complex (v. 10)

10a. "You have trusted in your wickedness and have said, 'No one sees me.'

The word *you* refers to Babylon, whom the prophecy concerns (Isaiah 47:1). Babylon's *wickedness* was a show of power, designed to enforce compliance by means of fear. We keep in mind that Isaiah was writing many decades before Babylon's rise as a world power. Yet so certain is Isaiah's prophecy that he writes not only in future tense, but also in past tense!

The phrase *No one sees me* implies that the Babylonian Empire viewed itself as above

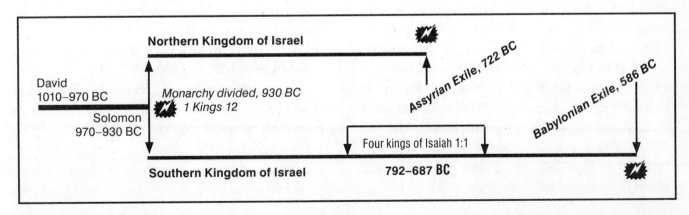

BEWARE THE FIRE OF UNGODLINESS.

Visual for Lesson 1. *While discussing verse 14, point to this visual and ask learners whether this fire can be used as God's refining fire. Why or why not?*

accountability for its actions; the people of Judah and Jerusalem were similarly guilty (see Isaiah 29:15-16). The scope of *no one* can encompass the entirety of the heavens and the earth. The Babylonian Empire had not faced any consequences from either sphere for exercising its enormous power inhumanely, which led to the supposition that unjust treatment was acceptable —a "might makes right" philosophy.

Such a philosophy still permeates many societies: "If my country is the strongest, then surely *everything* my nation does is sanctioned by God." We do well to remember that God uses the nations as he sees fit, not according to our limited understandings of power and influence.

10b. "Your wisdom and knowledge mislead you when you say to yourself, 'I am, and there is none besides me.'

This half verse speaks to an exercise in self-delusion (compare Isaiah 5:21; 44:19-20). All true *wisdom* and *knowledge* begin with "the fear of the Lord" (Proverbs 1:7). Claiming to be wise or knowledgeable apart from God's teaching is foolishness (Isaiah 29:14-15; 1 Corinthians 1:20-21).

Babylon trusted in its military and political might to the degree that it imagined its every move to have been mandated by a god. To put it another way, the empire ended up seeing itself as the god who justified its own actions. Their twisted self-image that *I am, and there is none besides me* was a claim of godhood (contrast Exodus 3:14).

The temptation to set oneself up as a god has proved itself irresistible throughout the generations. Adam and Eve sinned by wanting to be like God (Genesis 3:4-6), and we have all inherited sinful tendencies to put ourselves in God's place (example: Ezekiel 28:2). Phrases like "in their own eyes" often accompany condemnations of self-delusion in this regard (Psalm 36:2; Proverbs 26:12; 28:11; 30:12; Isaiah 5:21; compare 1 Corinthians 3:18-20).

We see extreme examples in modern-day cult leaders claiming divinity. But anytime someone acts as though his or her concerns are the ultimate concerns, danger looms. We all must be wary of our own, personal tendencies to behave as though we are the ultimate authority in our own lives. Nothing good can come of trying to unseat the Creator.

> **What Do You Think?**
> What sources of confidence in secular society tempt you to trust in them for security in place of or in addition to God?
> *Digging Deeper*
> How do you guard against putting your confidence in *anything* or *anyone* other than the Lord?

❧ THE LIMITS OF POWER ❧

King Cnut the Great (also known as Canute; AD 985/995–1035) was simultaneously king of England, Denmark, Norway, and part of Sweden. He was Danish by birth and inherited the throne when his father, Swyen I (Forkbeard), died. Though Cnut conquered England with violence, his rule over the land was characterized by peace and prosperity. After converting to the Christian faith sometime before AD 1027, Cnut maintained important ties with Rome. In all, Cnut administered his kingdoms skillfully.

A story written about a century after Cnut's death posited that the man believed he was so powerful, he could stop the tide from coming in. Such a belief would put Cnut's earthly power on par with (and in opposition to) the Creator's own.

When a nation's leaders focus on their own

power, we cannot be surprised to find citizens following their lead into disaster. How often do you pray for the world's leaders in this regard, that the wisdom of God—and not their own delusions of power—will guide their decisions?   —C. R. B.

B. God's Guarantee (v. 11)

11a. "Disaster will come upon you, and you will not know how to conjure it away.

The Hebrew word translated *disaster* is the same word that was translated "wickedness" in the previous verse. The *KJV* "evil" retains the element of sinfulness that is not necessarily present in the *NIV* translation. This implies that a moral evil is to overtake Babylon. In context, it is clear that this consequence comes from the Lord as punishment for Babylon's deeds.

We should note that God does not inflict moral evil on anyone (see James 1:13). That's on us (1:14). We bring it on ourselves (example: 1 Timothy 6:9). But God does permit both moral and physical evils in allowing natural consequences of our own actions. And although God never inflicts moral evils, he is known to have strengthened the preexisting evil resolve of people (compare Exodus 8:32 with 9:12), in addition to inflicting what are called physical evils or natural disasters (Genesis 19; etc.).

Punishment would come as a shock to the Baby-

lonians. They would neither foresee its coming nor be able to thwart it. Their "sorceries" and "spells" would be powerless to stave off God's wrath (Isaiah 47:9, not in today's text; 47:12, below). They who had been the instrument of God's wrath on Judah would find the tables reversed as they became the object of that same wrath (47:6).

11b. "A calamity will fall upon you that you cannot ward off with a ransom; a catastrophe you cannot foresee will suddenly come upon you.

The Hebrew word translated *calamity* occurs only three times in the Old Testament: here and twice in Ezekiel 7:26. It is used as a parallel description with "disaster" (above) and *catastrophe*. It may be tempting to try and discern the differences among these three words, but it's more likely that the cumulative effect is intended: the punishment is going to be worse than the Babylonians could possibly imagine! Nothing they could do would prevent its coming or mitigate its terrible impact.

> *What Do You Think?*
> How can you talk about difficult passages of the Bible in a way that builds others' faith?
> *Digging Deeper*
> Would you talk about these passages differently with nonbelievers than with believers?

HOW TO SAY IT

Ahaz	*Ay*-haz.
Assyrians	Uh-*sear*-e-unz.
Babylonians	Bab-ih-*low*-nee-unz.
Cnut	*Keh*-nyoot.
Ezekiel	Ee-*zeek*-ee-ul or Ee-*zeek*-yul.
Hezekiah	Hez-ih-*kye*-uh.
Isaiah	Eye-*zay*-uh.
Jeroboam	Jair-uh-*boe*-um.
Jotham	*Jo*-thum.
Judah	*Joo*-duh.
Nebuchadnezzar	*Neb*-yuh-kud-**nez**-er.
Sennacherib	Sen-*nack*-er-ib.
Sweyn	Svehn.
Uzziah	Uh-*zye*-uh.
Zedekiah	Zed-uh-*kye*-uh.

II. Failed Defenses
(Isaiah 47:12-15)

A. Futile Future-Telling (vv. 12-13)

12. "Keep on, then, with your magic spells and with your many sorceries, which you have labored at since childhood. Perhaps you will succeed, perhaps you will cause terror.

Magic spells and *sorceries* were common practices in the ancient Near East, meant to give people insight into their gods' desires and intentions. In fact, Israel's faith was meant to be unique in the ancient Near East for refusing such means to divine God's will, looking instead to his chosen prophets and other leaders.

This is not to say that such works were seen

as useless; the magicians in Egypt were successful up to a point when Moses confronted the pharaoh (Exodus 7:9-12, 22a; 8:7; contrast 8:18), and the medium at Endor called up Samuel's spirit for Saul (1 Samuel 28:3-15a). Refusing to participate in practices that actually *could* affect reality was surely a higher, harder calling than eschewing rituals that never had any discernible impact.

Note that this magic was not meant to be entertainment (as in illusions) but, instead, intended to manipulate their gods into doing what the people wanted or needed (example: 1 Kings 18:26-29). God cannot be manipulated and does not tolerate anyone trying to force his hand. Given the intentions of these magical interventions, it's no surprise that every variety of sorcery or witchcraft was forbidden in Israel (Leviticus 20:6, 27; Deuteronomy 18:9-14; etc.).

Isaiah mocked Babylon by encouraging them to continue in worthless magical practices. Who knew—maybe these would succeed! But Isaiah knew that God would not allow such practices to benefit Babylon any longer. Their days of brutalizing other nations with their might were numbered. Similar sarcastic calls can be found in Job 38:31; Jeremiah 44:25; Amos 4:4; and Matthew 23:32. Various means of future-telling were prevalent in the first century, when the church was being established. Clashes with dark powers always resulted in God's wisdom and power being found greater (Acts 8:9; 13:6-12; 16:16-18; 19:19).

> **What Do You Think?**
> How would you speak to a friend who consults occult practitioners to discover the future?
> **Digging Deeper**
> How could you speak words of truth about this practice in a loving manner?

13a. "All the counsel you have received has only worn you out!

Bad advice is tiring. Though Babylon did not realize it yet, *all the counsel* they sought were useless and would only weary them in trying to discover the truth and prevent disaster (Isaiah 57:10; Jeremiah 51:58; Habakkuk 2:13). And yet their "wisdom" would continue to be sought (see next)!

13b. "Let your astrologers come forward, those stargazers who make predictions month by month, let them save you from what is coming upon you.

The astrologers and the *stargazers* all searched the sky for signs of the gods' doings (compare Daniel 2:2). The practice was especially prevalent in Babylon. Calendars were drawn up based on the movements of heavenly bodies. These calendars were believed to reveal blessed or cursed days so that the people could act appropriately. We should note that there was not a clear distinction between the practices of astrology and astronomy at the time. This distinction is well made today, however, as the scientific study of the universe beyond planet Earth is an opportunity to experience renewed awe at *all* that God created.

In at least one instance, watching the night sky led wise men to a glorious discovery (Matthew 2:1-2, 7, 9-10). This exception only proves God's great mercy and willingness to meet people where they are and *literally* lead them to seek Jesus. In Babylon's case, however, even if these stargazers were correct in their predictions and knew when and *what is coming upon* Babylon, they would not be able to find a way to *save* the nation.

❧ READING THE STARS ❧

On the few occasions in my life when I have read a horoscope column, I have been bemused and befuddled. Advice for people "born under" the various signs of the Zodiac could be conjured up by anyone with some imagination and used interchangeably for everyone. Who could put their trust in what the stars "revealed"?

While staying out of town at a fellow minister's house, I found myself reading the local evening paper and laughing at the day's horoscope. When I shared my amusement with the minister's wife, she turned toward me with a disapproving look and asked, "Do you think Christians should be reading such things?" I responded, "Mockery is the only appropriate reaction to horoscope messages. Our Creator is in control, not the stars."

But she had a point: reading the night sky—or anywhere else in creation—without looking first to the Creator is at best misguided and at worst a sinful pratice. Seek first the Lord (Matthew 6:33)!

—C. R. B.

B. Fiery Fortunes (vv. 14-15)

14. "Surely they are like stubble; the fire will burn them up. They cannot even save themselves from the power of the flame. These are not coals for warmth; this is not a fire to sit by.

They refers to the "wise" men who were trusted to read the sky and guide the people to right actions based on what they saw (see Isaiah 47:13b, above). These learned men were thought to be a source of light in the form of knowledge and thus safety through wise living. But instead, these very counselors would be the *stubble* that feeds *the fire* that blazes dangerously, devouring everything it touches.

15. "That is all they are to you—these you have dealt with and labored with since childhood. All of them go on in their error; there is not one that can save you."

Riches often make a people feel safe. The presence of successful merchants in Babylon was another source of false security. Though Babylon had believed these friends were like a homey fire, keeping them warm and safe, such businessmen were actually the stubble to be burned up. It will turn out that Babylon and all its allies are doomed; *not one* would *save* them.

> **What Do You Think?**
> Do those closest to you encourage you to seek God or, rather, to look to other sources of help?
> *Digging Deeper*
> What changes could you make to encourage them more in seeking God?

Conclusion

A. God's Timing

Israel can be likened to Michelle Martinko's parents—waiting for justice that never seemed to be within reach. Advancements in DNA technology became the antidote to the "magic" of all the circumstances that allowed the killer to go unpun-

ished for so many years. But no amount of luck or skill would prevent Babylon's fall, just as it did not prevent the murderer's conviction.

God is not surprised at what happens among and within the nations of the world. Every group of people falls under God's jurisdiction, and he can use any and all nations to fulfill his purposes. We Christians do well to remember and trust that God sees the injustice and violence around us and has a plan to right all wrongs.

Though our enemies may never see the error of their ways or repent, we know our faith in God is not misplaced and will result in our seeing his plan come to fruition. Faith in anything else results in disappointment and misplaced priorities. May we trust his timing and wait patiently for the day he destroys wickedness once and for all. His promises are steadfast.

> **What Do You Think?**
> In what current situations do you need encouragement to continue waiting on the Lord with patience?
> *Digging Deeper*
> What actions will help you as you wait on the Lord's time?

B. Prayer

Almighty God, thank you that we can be confident in your knowledge about our lives and in your wisdom concerning judgment. We ask for strength to live faithfully even when the present and future seem nothing like we expected. In Jesus' name we pray. Amen.

C. Thought to Remember

Since God's enemies will fall,
don't stand with them!

VISUALS FOR THESE LESSONS

The visual pictured in each lesson (example: page 348) is a small reproduction of a large, full-color poster included in the *Adult Resources* packet for the Summer Quarter. That packet also contains the very useful *Presentation Tools* CD for teacher use. Order No. 4629122 from your supplier.

INVOLVEMENT LEARNING

Enhance your lesson with NIV Bible Student *(from your curriculum supplier) and the reproducible activity page (at www.standardlesson.com or in the back of the* NIV Standard Lesson Commentary Deluxe Edition*).*

Into the Lesson

Begin class by showing a short video or PSA about texting and driving. Discuss it by asking, "What other bad behaviors do people think they can get away with?" (Responses can range from the minor, such as leaving trash at a park, to the major, such as embezzling from an employer.)

Shift the conversation to consequences of those actions. Follow by asking, "Why might people think they can disobey God without consequence?" Encourage deeper reflection by asking, "Have you ever been led astray by listening to bad advice when making a major decision?" Allow volunteers time to answer both questions before moving on.

Alternative. Distribute copies of the "Advice in the Stars?" exercise from the activity page, which you can download. Encourage class members to work in pairs to complete as indicated. Invite volunteers to share their responses with the group.

Option. Allow one minute for learners to think of the sort of future events they would or would *not* like to have foreknowledge concerning. Follow this with small group discussion about their answers and generally why people want to know the future.

Say, "Today we'll consider the prideful sins and consequences of ancient Babylon and what happens when arrogance about our own power leads us away from God."

Into the Word

Have participants form small groups, making sure that each group has access to a concordance (either a hard copy or a digital version on a smart device). Exclude today's text from discussion for the time being. Ask groups to search for references to Babylon throughout the Bible. Allow about 10 minutes for groups to compile lists and summaries of these references. While groups give examples, write their answers on the board. Then ask, "What picture do these verses paint about Babylon?"

Ask a participant to read Isaiah 47:10-15 out loud. In their small groups, ask learners to discuss what new insight they have about Babylon based on this reading. Supplement this discussion with information from the commentary as needed.

Switch up the small groups, and then have learners brainstorm and/or quickly research (using mobile devices) a few modern-day references or parallels to Babylon in songs, movies, and books. Ask, "Do you see any parallels between the ancient empire and its depiction in the present day? Do the messages about living in a modern Babylon agree with the biblical accounts?" Write their responses on the board.

Into Life

In pairs, have learners compare and contrast ancient Babylonian magical practice with any present-day secular practices. Have them specifically consider how such practices are intended to keep the practitioner safe. *Option.* Distribute copies of the "Am I Safe?" exercise on the activity page and allow the pairs to use Part 1 to help them keep track of their answers. Gather the class together to discuss their answers.

Ask, "How does following secular ways of seeking advice or insight into the future lead us away from God's Word?" After allowing time for discussion, ask the learners to brainstorm ways to guard against seeking illicit advice. *Option.* If you used the alternative activity, ask learners to complete Part 2 now.

Pass out notecards to all learners. Give participants one minute to identify one personal way to avoid repeating a sin of ancient Babylon and to write down a few words as a reminder. Close with prayer asking for God's guidance and care in the unknown future.

GOD FORETELLS OF REDEMPTION

DEVOTIONAL READING: Isaiah 49:1-17

BACKGROUND SCRIPTURE: Isaiah 49:1-17

ISAIAH 49:1-13

1 Listen to me, you islands;
    hear this, you distant nations:
Before I was born the LORD called me;
    from my mother's womb he has spoken
        my name.
2 He made my mouth like a sharpened
        sword,
    in the shadow of his hand he hid me;
he made me into a polished arrow
    and concealed me in his quiver.
3 He said to me, "You are my servant,
    Israel, in whom I will display my
        splendor."
4 But I said, "I have labored in vain;
    I have spent my strength for nothing at
        all.
Yet what is due me is in the LORD's hand,
    and my reward is with my God."
5 And now the LORD says—
    he who formed me in the womb to be
        his servant
to bring Jacob back to him
    and gather Israel to himself,
for I am honored in the eyes of the LORD
    and my God has been my strength—
6 he says:
"It is too small a thing for you to be my
        servant
    to restore the tribes of Jacob
    and bring back those of Israel I have
        kept.
I will also make you a light for the
        Gentiles,
    that my salvation may reach to the ends
        of the earth."
7 This is what the LORD says—
    the Redeemer and Holy One of Israel—

to him who was despised and abhorred by
        the nation,
    to the servant of rulers:
"Kings will see you and stand up,
    princes will see and bow down,
because of the LORD, who is faithful,
    the Holy One of Israel, who has cho-
        sen you."
8 This is what the LORD says:
"In the time of my favor I will answer you,
    and in the day of salvation I will help
        you;
I will keep you and will make you
    to be a covenant for the people,
to restore the land
    and to reassign its desolate inheritances,
9 to say to the captives, 'Come out,'
    and to those in darkness, 'Be free!'
"They will feed beside the roads
    and find pasture on every barren hill.
10 They will neither hunger nor thirst,
    nor will the desert heat or the sun beat
        down on them.
He who has compassion on them will
        guide them
    and lead them beside springs of water.
11 I will turn all my mountains into roads,
    and my highways will be raised up.
12 See, they will come from afar—
    some from the north, some from the
        west,
    some from the region of Aswan."
13 Shout for joy, you heavens;
    rejoice, you earth;
    burst into song, you mountains!
For the LORD comforts his people
    and will have compassion on his
        afflicted ones.

KEY VERSE

This is what the LORD says: "In the time of my favor I will answer you, and in the day of salvation I will help you; I will keep you and will make you to be a covenant for the people, to restore the land and to reassign its desolate inheritances, —**Isaiah 49:8**

Partners in a New Creation

Unit 1: God Delivers and Restores

LESSONS 1–4

LESSON AIMS

After participating in this lesson, each learner will be able to:

1. Identify the servant.
2. Describe the function of the text as part of Isaiah's "Servant Songs."
3. Identify one way to be a better servant of the servant.

LESSON OUTLINE

Introduction

A. The Right Time

Young people are constantly in a state of impatiently waiting for "the right time," which often feels like it will never come. They wait with eager anticipation for the day they can attain a learner's permit as a step to having a driver's license and maybe even a car. This taste of freedom may also come with new responsibilities as the new driver begins working and paying for gas and insurance. High school graduation looms large—and with it the need to successfully complete entrance exams, essays, and other prerequisites to begin college, trade school, or a chosen profession. Awaiting the right time (and the right person) to marry is also a source of anxious waiting. In all, young people desire to have the independence and freedom of adults—although whether they still want that when they also receive the responsibilities is open to debate!

Israel was also waiting impatiently, waiting for God to act (1 Peter 1:10-13). And while their freedom in him would certainly come with responsibilities, that day would also be one of great joy. All this would be accomplished through one servant eager to do God's will.

B. Lesson Context

In the book of Isaiah, there are four poems about the Messiah (Isaiah 42:1-9; 49:1-7; 50:4-9 [or through 50:11]; and 52:13–53:12). They are called "Servant Poems" or "Servant Songs." A fifth passage, Isaiah 61:1-4, is sometimes added to the list because its content is very similar to the others, even though the word *servant* is not used in it. Our text today is from the second Servant Song. It is more than a poem about a servant. It is a prophecy about the work of Jesus, the Messiah. It is he who is the servant in the Servant Poems.

This Servant Song begins and ends with an appeal, not only to Israel but also to the nations of the world. The last three verses of Isaiah 48 exhort the people to flee from Babylon, and assurance is given that God will care for them as they travel. What's next?

I. Identity of the Servant
(ISAIAH 49:1-5)
A. Called by God (vv. 1-3)

1a. Listen to me, you islands; hear this, you distant nations:

The speaker—the servant—is not yet identified (see Isaiah 49:3, below). The exhortation to *listen* is a necessary precursor to receiving any news (example: Exodus 23:21-22). Though *hear this* means the same, their use together emphasizes that just hearing words will not be enough; the information must be believed and acted on. Without appropriate action, the act of listening remains unfulfilled. *Islands* and *you distant nations* refer first to scattered Israel but also to nations that are outside of God's covenant people.

1b. Before I was born the LORD called me; from my mother's womb he has spoken my name.

What could give a person more confidence in a calling than to know *the Lord called* that person from the *womb*? God's plan is not haphazard or slapdash; it's not being made up as humanity progresses, without an end in God's mind. Rather, God knows his intentions for the servant even before his mother was aware she was pregnant (see Isaiah 9:6; Matthew 1:21)!

Shakespeare asked, "What's in a name?" In the case of this servant, quite a lot! More important than revealing the *name* itself is the fact that God *has spoken* it. We've all experienced greeting someone who has clearly forgotten our name. It's not an unforgivable error, but it can have the effect of making the unnamed person feel unknown, anonymous. But God knows each of our names, and he cares about each of us personally, intimately, in ways that are not possible for unnamed masses.

2a. He made my mouth like a sharpened sword,

In context, the *sharpened sword* in a prophet's *mouth* likely refers to the words God calls his servant to speak prophetically. God imbues these words with authority (see Ephesians 6:17; Hebrews 4:12). Although Jesus' words bring peace when accepted, they also act to divide the righteous from the unrighteous (Matthew 10:34-39).

2b. in the shadow of his hand he hid me; he made me into a polished arrow and concealed me in his quiver.

The shadow of God—whether *his hand* or his wings—is one way to speak of the safety of being in God's care (examples: Psalms 63:7; 91:1; Isaiah 51:16). Like *a polished arrow* God kept the servant safe and at the ready so that when his task came, the servant would be perfectly able to accomplish his work. In conjunction with the image of the sword, this implies judgment to those who do not accept the words the servant speaks.

❧ SOME POLISHING NEEDED ❧

I was already serving in my first full-time ministry when I realized I didn't know everything. One of the elders, Arnie, was a man of great wisdom and patience. When frustrated by a problem or perplexed by a church member, I went to Arnie for counsel. He would calmly help me look more deeply (and more graciously) at the people I was called to serve. While I had seen myself as an arrow aimed at the target of truth, there was still much work to be done so I could fly true. Arnie was one person who polished and prepared me to faithfully answer God's call.

Isaiah spoke of the servant's preparation. For 30 years Jesus was on the path toward the cross. When the time came, Jesus stayed true to his purpose and the Father's will. The empty tomb proves that Jesus' preparation had been complete. Who (or what) is preparing you to remain true to God's will?

—C. R. B.

3. He said to me, "You are my servant, Israel, in whom I will display my splendor."

The Lord names the speaker his *servant* (see Lesson Context). A few explanations can be given for why *Israel* is named. One view is that Jesus is the true Israel, and this is simply a figure of speech. Because Jesus is the fulfillment of God's plan to bless all nations (Genesis 12:1-3), he represents the pinnacle of all the nation of Israel was meant to be. Another possibility is that God does speak here to the nation as the people *in whom I will display my splendor*. If this is this case, then Israel would be fulfilled in the church, which has taken up Israel's spiritual mantel and carried the good news of the Messiah into all the world. And because the church is Christ's body, empowered by the Spirit, ultimately the servant really *is* Jesus.

B. Confident in God (vv. 4-5)

4. But I said, "I have labored in vain; I have spent my strength for nothing at all. Yet what is due me is in the LORD's hand, and my reward is with my God."

Is there any more discouraging feeling than to look at one's work and feel that you *have labored in vain*? Because God's definition of success is not a conventional, earthly definition, faithful servants can be discouraged. For instance, the prophet Jeremiah faithfully proclaimed what God wanted him to say (2 Chronicles 36:12). But from a human standpoint he failed—because Judah did not repent and went into captivity, and Jerusalem was destroyed by the Babylonians (36:15-21).

Jesus also experienced discouragement: when the disciples experienced fear in place of faith (examples: Matthew 8:26; Luke 12:28), when his friends fled and betrayed him (Mark 14:43-72), and when he hung on a brutal cross to die in excruciating pain (Matthew 27:46; see Psalm 22). But Jesus had even more reason than Jeremiah for confidence that his work and the *reward* for his work were in God's hands. Human understandings of Jesus' work were nothing compared to knowing that the Father would reward his Son for his faithful ministry and sacrifice.

> **What Do You Think?**
> How will you keep your eyes on the big picture of God's plan during times of disappointment?
> **Digging Deeper**
> What biblical promises regarding God's plans for the future help keep you focused?

5. And now the LORD says—he who formed me in the womb to be his servant to bring Jacob back to him and gather Israel to himself, for I am honored in the eyes of the LORD and my God has been my strength—

The womb recalls Isaiah 49:1b, while the servant's future glory points back to 49:3. This repeti-

tion is one way Isaiah expressed the confidence the servant would feel; repetition of this nature is typical in Hebrew poetry. *My God has been my strength* represents a reversal of 49:4. Whereas the servant had felt that his strength was wasted, with God that strength would be renewed and sustained (Isaiah 12:2; 33:2; 40:29-31; etc.).

In this verse the words *Jacob* and *Israel* are used interchangeably, as they were in the book of Genesis. Sometimes the word *Israel* in the book of Isaiah means only the northern kingdom of that name, as distinct from the southern kingdom of Judah. At other times, however, the word *Israel* refers to all the Jewish people in both northern and southern kingdoms together. At this time the servant could only anticipate gathering Israel together, and its redemption would glorify God's name.

II. The Lord's Plan
(ISAIAH 49:6-13)
A. Call to All (vv. 6-7)

6a. he says: "It is too small a thing for you to be my servant to restore the tribes of Jacob and bring back those of Israel I have kept.

The last verses of the printed text primarily concern a gathering of God's people, but which one? Some scholars see this passage as further comments about the return from Babylon that took place after Persia's Cyrus the Great captured Babylon. Others think that the reference to the Gentiles in Isaiah 49:6b (below) is a strong reason to interpret it as referring to believers around the world who come to Christ during the church age. A third option is that this is a prophecy about a return of Jews to Israel in the millennium that is still in the future. These differences may be matters for discussion, but they should not evolve into dissension and division. The main thing is to remember that from Isaiah's perspective this is a prophecy involving the *servant* of the Lord. The fulfillment is certain.

Nothing in the history of *the tribes of Jacob* suggests that restoring the people would be *too small a thing*. The people struggled with faithfulness throughout their days in Egypt, the wilderness, and the promised land. Indeed, though *Israel* had been a united nation, idolatry contributed to their fracturing into the northern 10 tribes and southern 2. The way God speaks to the servant here suggests that not only Judah would be restored, but all the tribes. The 10 had been lost in Assyria or assimilated into people later called Samaritans for generations by this point. This was a huge task, easy only for the Lord to accomplish.

6b. "I will also make you a light for the Gentiles, that my salvation may reach to the ends of the earth."

The affirmation is made that the Lord's plan was for the message of redemption in Christ to include *Gentiles* as well as the Jews (see Isaiah 49:3, above; also lesson 4). Paul and Barnabas cited this verse as a justification for their decision to turn to the Gentiles (Acts 13:46). Later Paul would write in Romans 1:16 that the gospel was to the Jews first, and then to the Gentiles. This salvation has a far reach, including the entire *earth*.

> ### What Do You Think?
> How do you participate in extending to the world the invitation to experience God's blessings?
>
> *Digging Deeper*
> What changes could you make to more faithfully carry out the gospel mission or to amplify the good work you are already doing?

❧ *The Most Segregated Hour?* ❧

Is 11:00 am on Sunday morning still "the most segregated hour of the week" in the United States? When my wife and I moved to a new city, we searched for a congregation that would reflect the racial and ethnic makeup of the diverse community we were joining. And we found it! The American church is making progress.

In Israel's day there was a different kind of "us vs. them" spirit. Israel was to be careful not to mix pagan Gentile practice with the proper worship of the Lord. But that situation would also have made it difficult for Israel to comprehend that the Lord wanted the Gentiles to come to him.

Isaiah said that the Messiah—the Servant—and his people would bring a saving light to all the peoples of the world, uniting them under the banner of the gospel. Jesus did his part to bring humanity together. We can do more toward completing the task. What, specifically, do you need to start doing in order to honor our task?　　　　—C. R. B.

7a. This is what the LORD says—the Redeemer and Holy One of Israel—to him who was despised and abhorred by the nation, to the servant of rulers:

What *the Lord* does flows from his character, and the titles attributed to God result from his actions. *The Redeemer . . . of Israel* acted to free the people from slavery in Egypt (Exodus 6:6; 15:13; etc.). God chose Israel as his special people, but whether they acted in holiness or not, God remained the *Holy One* (2 Kings 19:22).

God's titles here emphasize his power and majesty, fidelity to his promises, and his sole claim of holiness. This is the Lord who addressed *him who was despised and abhorred by the nation*. Being rejected by so many could make the *servant* wonder if God had also rejected him.

7b. "Kings will see you and stand up, princes will see and bow down, because of the LORD, who is faithful, the Holy One of Israel, who has chosen you."

Effectively, the rejection of man and nation (Isaiah 49:7a) is here dismissed. Both *kings* and *princes* will heed the servant's words. As with any success in ministry, it is not based on the charisma or magnetism or leadership qualities of the preacher or missionary. Success is not the result of ironclad apologetics or perfect servant ministry. The reason people respond with worship when hearing the gospel is because *the Lord . . . is faithful*.

B. Day of Salvation (vv. 8-12)

8. This is what the LORD says: "In the time of my favor I will answer you, and in the day

HOW TO SAY IT

Aswan	*Az*-wawn.
Babylon	*Bab*-uh-lun.
Gentiles	*Jen*-tiles.
Isaiah	Eye-*zay*-uh.

SERVANT SONGS

ISAIAH 42:1-9 *Judgment to the Gentiles*

49:1-7 *A light to the Gentiles*

50:4-9 *The Lord's promised help*

52:13–53:12 *The coming Messiah*

61:1-4 *The Savior's promised renewal*

Visual for Lesson 2. *Point to this visual while discussing the Lesson Context. Ask volunteers to read the other songs before entering into the lesson.*

of salvation I will help you; I will keep you and will make you to be a covenant for the people, to restore the land and to reassign its desolate inheritances,

In the time of God's *favor* and *the day of salvation* are parallel terms here. Both denote the time when God would hear his people and act again on their behalf. In the short term, this would be seen in the people's return from Babylon. Ultimately, however, this day is fulfilled in Jesus. Paul quoted this assertion in 2 Corinthians 6:2 in reference to a person's accepting the invitation of salvation in Christ. There is no bad time to accept the gift of salvation!

The promise is primarily to the servant, but it extends beyond that to include *a covenant for the people.* Though we might expect this was a promise made with Israel, context suggests instead that the nations are intended here. God would work in them to bring about his promise of restoring the people. *To restore the land and to reassign its desolate inheritances* once again should be read as parallel terms. This promise recalls the land distributions made by Joshua after Israel had completed the basic conquest of the land (Joshua 14:1). Judah had been left bereft after the exiles went to Babylon, but all that land would be reassigned and renewed.

9a. "to say to the captives, 'Come out,' and to those in darkness, 'Be free!'

This concept directly relates to God's role as

redeemer (see Isaiah 49:7a, above). The imagery continues the idea that those who are oppressed or *in darkness* may shed their fears because God has chosen to rescue them (9:2).

9b. "They will feed beside the roads and find pasture on every barren hill.

The imagery from here through Isaiah 49:11 (below) is of herds coming home. A shepherd would expect to find greener pastures in valleys, near flowing streams of waters. But the abundance God promises through the servant is so great that vegetation would grow even beside the busiest of *roads* and *on every barren hill* that otherwise might be desolate, rocky, and too harsh for pastureland. This last phrase is also noteworthy because idolatry was frequently associated with high places (examples: Leviticus 26:30; Numbers 33:52; Deuteronomy 12:2). But God's promise is that his own faithful people will be able to eat safely in places that had previously been polluted by idolatrous practices. The entire creation is God's, and he will reclaim it from the evil that has invaded it.

10. "They will neither hunger nor thirst, nor will the desert heat or the sun beat down on them. He who has compassion on them will guide them and lead them beside springs of water.

It's easy to read these promises from a spiritual point of view, assuming that *hunger* and *thirst* are metaphors for the longing for God. Isaiah's original audience, however, would have looked forward to security against scarcity, especially following exile in Babylon. Protection from *heat* and *sun* might suggest that the people would not need to work through the noon hour, when conditions like heatstroke are more likely to occur. And there would be no search for water because the servant guides them *beside springs of water* (compare Psalm 23). Keeping with the imagery of herds returning home, there would be plenty to graze on and the heat would not sap their energy. Water would run plentifully.

Jesus fulfilled this verse both literally and figuratively (Luke 4:16-21; John 6:35). His encounter with the Samaritan woman speaks to his power over spiritual thirst (4:10, 13-14). And one need only look to the feeding of the 5,000 to realize that Jesus is more than capable of alleviating hunger (Matthew 14:13-21).

What Do You Think?
What relationship do you see between having your physical and your spiritual needs met?
Digging Deeper
What encourages you to trust in God even when you feel you lack what you need?

11. "I will turn all my mountains into roads, and my highways will be raised up.

A traveler approaching a mountain in ancient times had three options: go over it, go around it, or turn around. Going over might be the most direct route, but all sorts of dangers are found on the heights. But when the servant led the people, even in the *mountains* there would be a safe way across. The *highways* here likely refer to desert roads that would have been sunken; raising them made them less treacherous to follow.

12. "See, they will come from afar—some from the north, some from the west, some from the region of Aswan."

Two directions are given as starting points for the pilgrims who make this journey *from afar*. This could imply the return of the 10 tribes of Israel that disappeared *north* into Assyria and the arrival of Gentiles from the Mediterranean to *the west*. The exiles in Babylon would return from the east. *The region of Aswan* likely refers to land near the southern border of Egypt, as suggested by a copy of Isaiah found in the Dead Sea Scrolls. So by explicit citation and by implication, all directions are covered; people will come from everywhere.

C. Call to Joy (v. 13)

13. Shout for joy, you heavens; rejoice, you earth; burst into song, you mountains! For the LORD comforts his people and will have compassion on his afflicted ones.

Shout, rejoice, and *burst into song* are parallel terms here. The repetition once again emphasizes that joyful song is the correct impulse following God's works. In Hebrew thinking, the sky contained several layers of *heavens* (Deuteronomy 10:14; 1 Kings 8:27; etc.). These heavens rested on

the *mountains* as a ceiling is supported by firm pillars; the *earth* sat beneath. Isaiah calls all creation to enter into praise when *the Lord* announces his intentions to comfort *his people* and *have compassion on his afflicted ones*. Paul picks up this theme, declaring that creation still suffers until God's people are revealed (Romans 8:18-22).

What Do You Think?
What role does worship in song have in your personal devotional time?
Digging Deeper
How can God's creation inspire you to worship, even if you find yourself away from nature?

Conclusion
A. Speak and Sing

At the right time, God sent Jesus to earth to offer salvation to all who accept him as Lord and Savior (Romans 5:6-8; Galatians 4:4-5). The call is to those who are in our families and communities and also in far distant villages we will never visit or even know exist. Our responsibility in the time of salvation is twofold: to proclaim the good news to all (Matthew 28:18-20) and to worship God with all creation. We are comforted, and we experience mercy. Therefore sing to God! And spread the good news throughout the earth.

What Do You Think?
What in today's lesson encouraged you? How will you share that encouragement?
Digging Deeper
What challenged you? How will you meet that challenge in the week ahead?

B. Prayer

Lord, thank you for Isaiah's prophecies and the ways that your Son, Jesus, fulfilled them. Make us people who call captives to freedom in Christ and whose faith in his care is unwavering. In Jesus' name we pray. Amen.

C. Thought to Remember

The day of salvation is *now!*

INVOLVEMENT LEARNING

Enhance your lesson with NIV Bible Student *(from your curriculum supplier) and the reproducible activity page (at www.standardlesson.com or in the back of the* NIV Standard Lesson Commentary Deluxe Edition*).*

Into the Lesson

Ask learners to pair off and respond to the following: "Describe a boss you've had (without naming names) who either managed as a servant leader or did not. What characteristics put that boss in one category or the other?" After a few minutes of discussion, ask for volunteers to share their examples of both types of bosses as you write their responses on the board. Pay special attention to any characteristics that could describe either boss.

Alternative. In small groups, ask learners to think of fictional examples of good or bad servants. Then have each group choose one example they brainstormed and imagine that their imaginary servant is elevated to a position of power (for instance, if Cinderella was in charge of her father's home instead of her stepmother). Ask volunteers to share whether the servant they talked about would make a good leader based on the characteristics they exhibited as a servant. *Option.* Depending on the temperament of your class, have a few groups act out their scenarios.

After either activity, say, "We have expectations of the qualities that make a good servant and a good leader, and how sometimes these qualities are appropriate for both. In today's lesson, we will see how a godly servant is also a godly leader."

Into the Word

Divide the whole group into three groups and assign each group an image from the text: **The Womb Group**—verse 1, **The Sharp Sword Group**—verse 2a, **The Polished Arrow Group**—verse 2b. Ask a volunteer to read Isaiah 49:1-13. Have each group discuss: "What is the significance or meaning of this imagery? How is the characteristic evoked by the imagery reinforced throughout this prophecy?" After about 10 minutes, ask groups to briefly summarize their responses for the whole group.

Reassign groups as follows: **The Inheritance Group**—verses 8-9a and Luke 4:16-21, **The Satisfied Group**—verses 9b-10 and John 10:11-16, **The Joyful Group**—verses 11-13 and John 14:2-6. Have each group discuss: "How is Jesus the fulfillment of this prophecy, in his earthly ministry and his ongoing work in the world?" The learners should be encouraged to supply additional citations to back up their assertions.

Alternative. Distribute the "Acceptance Speech" exercise from the activity page, which you can download. Ask pairs to complete only the "Servant's Speech" column for now.

After either activity, ask groups to briefly summarize their responses for the whole group. Allow time for discussion.

Into Life

Ask a volunteer to read John 13:3-17. Invite the whole group to discuss: "How is Jesus' example in this passage one of a leader and a servant?"

Option. Have the pairs who worked togther on the "Servant's Speech" exercise come together to talk through the "Personal Speech" column based on the texts in Isaiah and John. After a few minutes, ask volunteers to share their ideas.

Alternative. Distribute one "Servant Leader" exercise from the activity page to all the learners. Give them one minute to consider the activity before pairing up. Tell them their new partner is their accountability partner for the week to encourage them to do what they have brainstormed. *Option.* Assign this activity as an individual take-home. Encourage participation by stating that the class will discuss this activity at the start of the next lesson.

Ask participants to identify one way they can be a better servant of the Servant this week in thought, word, and action. Close class with prayer that God will bless his servants as they strive to follow Jesus' example.

GOD'S PEOPLE SHALL PROSPER

DEVOTIONAL READING: Isaiah 49:18-23
BACKGROUND SCRIPTURE: Isaiah 49:18-26

ISAIAH 49:18-23

18 "Lift up your eyes and look around;
    all your children gather and come to you.
As surely as I live," declares the LORD,
    "you will wear them all as ornaments;
    you will put them on, like a bride.
19 "Though you were ruined and made desolate
    and your land laid waste,
now you will be too small for your people,
    and those who devoured you will be far away.
20 The children born during your bereavement
    will yet say in your hearing,
'This place is too small for us;
    give us more space to live in.'
21 Then you will say in your heart,
    'Who bore me these?
I was bereaved and barren;
    I was exiled and rejected.
    Who brought these up?
I was left all alone,
    but these—where have they come from?'"

22 This is what the Sovereign LORD says:
"See, I will beckon to the nations,
    I will lift up my banner to the peoples;
they will bring your sons in their arms
    and carry your daughters on their hips.
23 Kings will be your foster fathers,
    and their queens your nursing mothers.
They will bow down before you with their faces to the ground;
    they will lick the dust at your feet.
Then you will know that I am the LORD;
    those who hope in me will not be disappointed."

KEY VERSE

Then you will know that I am the LORD; those who hope in me will not be disappointed."

—Isaiah 49:23c

Photo © Getty Images

PARTNERS IN A NEW CREATION

Unit 1: God Delivers and Restores

LESSONS 1–4

LESSON AIMS

After participating in this lesson, each learner will be able to:

1. List one or more ways by which people will know that God is the Lord.

2. Tell how the meanings of one or more lines of the text are clarified by a parallel thought(s) that follows.

3. Identify and share with others an aspect of your testimony that reveals your hope in the Lord.

LESSON OUTLINE

Introduction

A. Reversal of Fortune

Reversal of fortune has long been a popular topic for story plots. For instance, in the movie *The Princess Diaries* Mia Thermopolis finds out that she is the crown princess of Genovia. This information causes upheaval in her world, as she must decide whether to accept this role. In considering her duties, Mia receives the requisite makeover, etiquette training, and so on. Her reversal of fortune from the daughter of a single mother to the heir of an entire nation causes friction with her mother, newly discovered grandmother, friends, and classmates.

Change in fortune often results in a change in identity. From being an artist's only daughter, Mia became a princess. While it was an exciting change, it also came with great challenges that made Mia ask, Is it worth it?

God's people faced a reversal of fortune, as did the nations of the world. God's servant would offer a change of identity to all. There were great challenges for the servant, Israel, and the nations. So the question remained: Is it worth it to be part of God's great reversal?

B. Lesson Context: Historical

The first readers of the prophecy in today's text understood it as concerning a return from Babylon, for Isaiah had earlier given the dire prophecy about being taken into exile there (Isaiah 39:6-7; see lesson 1 Lesson Context). When Babylon fell, the Jews would return to Judah and Jerusalem (Isaiah 40–48; Ezra 1:5). At that time Jerusalem would be rebuilt, and the foundation of the temple laid.

Jerusalem lost its inhabitants when the Babylonians destroyed the city in 586 BC. Jeremiah wrote that there were only 832 who were taken from the city at that time (Jeremiah 52:29), compared with 10,000 who had been taken earlier (2 Kings 24:14). Those who remained had endured the deprivations and starvation that occurred during the siege. This small remnant was taken away to join others already in Babylon. The city was a desolate ruin for almost 50 years.

On the night in 539 BC that soldiers of Darius the Mede captured Babylon, the Babylonian King Belshazzar was having a gigantic banquet that featured vessels from the temple in Jerusalem. The king was a co-regent with his father, Nabonidus, who was frequently absent from the capital. Belshazzar and his guests at the banquet were startled when fingers appeared and began to write on a wall (Daniel 5). Daniel was finally called to interpret the message. The last part of Daniel's message was that the kingdom was given over to the Medes and Persians—that night! Babylon had been considered impregnable, and a large food supply was always maintained in case there was a siege.

The Babylonian Empire came to an end following its capture by the Persians and Medes under Cyrus. Cyrus the Great established the Persian Empire, which lasted about 200 years. The famous Cyrus Cylinder contains the decree that all captive peoples could return to their homelands and that they were to take their gods with them. The Jewish people were not specifically mentioned in Cyrus's own edict, though his attention to Jerusalem is recorded in the Bible (2 Chronicles 36:23; Ezra 1:2-3). The biblical account later refers to a separate proclamation that was made for them, and it became very important in the days of Darius the Great when opposition arose to the building of the temple (6:2-3). The Jews did not have gods to take, but they did have many items from the temple (1:6-11).

The first wave of exiles returned in 538 BC. It is assumed that the 50,000 people who returned first went to Jerusalem. Then they scattered to find their ancestral homes throughout Judah, as stated in Ezra 2:1.

C. Lesson Context: Literary

The previous lesson ended with Isaiah 49:13, and great joy was predicted to be expressed (compare 51:3). Gentiles in all directions would rejoice as the Lord comforted his people. Five verses later is where this study begins.

Isaiah prophesied that a virgin would conceive and bear a son (Isaiah 7:14). That passage is cited in Matthew 1:22-23 as fulfilled in the birth of Jesus. The fulfillment was 700 years away. That same child would grow up to fulfill many other prophecies of Isaiah, not least the prophetic expectations linked to a person referred to as the suffering servant. Our text comes from the second Servant Song, the same discussed last week (see lesson 2 Lesson Context). The servant is the one who is the speaker for the text of this lesson. The servant is understood to be the Son of God. Some have suggested that the speaker is Isaiah, but the context indicates that the speaker is more than a prophet.

The mood changed from exuberance (Isaiah 49:1-13; see lesson 2) to a lamentation that the Lord had forgotten his people and Jerusalem. It is easy to imagine Jerusalem stating that God had forgotten the city and the people (see lesson 1 Lesson Context). Metaphorically, Jerusalem sat in the dust wearing torn clothes or sackcloth and ashes, head bowed with sorrow and hopelessness (compare Lamentations 2:10).

The Lord asked rhetorically whether a woman can forget the child she gave birth to and nursed (Isaiah 49:15). Though an unhealthy mother might forget that child, even a mediocre mother cannot. In the same way, the Lord could not forget the people or Zion. To show his attention he assured Zion that the ones who had mistreated his people by taking them away were leaving. This provided opportunity for God's children to hurry to return (49:14-17).

God had promised a return, and he also said that Jerusalem and the cities of Judah would be rebuilt (Isaiah 44:26). At least some of the people in captivity were aware of the passages in Isaiah about a deliverer named Cyrus, and that the captivity would last about 70 years (Jeremiah 25:12; 29:10). It is definite that Daniel was aware of the prophecy of Jeremiah (Daniel 9:2).

I. Promise of Restoration
(ISAIAH 49:18-21)
A. Ornamentation (vv. 18-20)

18a. "Lift up your eyes and look around; all your children gather and come to you.

The command to *lift up your eyes* is a call to a

God restores joy!

Visual for Lesson 3. *Have learners pair up while discussing verse 20 and each take one minute to share a time when God has restored their joy.*

new posture, one of hope rather than desperation. Upon obeying the command, Lady Zion would *look around* and see to her *children* (Isaiah 49:17, not in our printed text) returning to her.

18b. "As surely as I live," declares the LORD, "you will wear them all as ornaments; you will put them on, like a bride.

Once again the image is one of extreme reversal. In contrast to the mourning clothing Zion had been wearing (see Lesson Context), *the Lord* promised that she would have reason to dress *like a bride* (compare Jeremiah 2:32). Brides then as now dressed to impress. In the modern Western world, it's easy to forget how important marriage was in the ancient world. This was not the result of two independent adults choosing to pledge themselves to one another. Women had very little opportunity to care for themselves economically and usually left their father's home *only* when they married. Their wedding day marked the day their economic fortune became their husband's concern, not their father's. It was also the day they could begin trying to fulfill one of the, if not *the*, most important roles for women: becoming a mother and raising her children. The end of a marriage—whether in divorce or widowhood—was a grave hardship on a woman, especially if her children were not grown and in a position to care for her.

Dressing as a bride, then, is another analogy for turning toward joy instead of sorrow (com-

pare Jeremiah 33:11). The appropriate "attire" for a bridal city is a thriving human population. Those who returned would be Zion's ornamentation, the source and sign of her newfound joy.

> **What Do You Think?**
> What insight can embracing our shared identity as God's "bride" give us regarding how to remain faithful to him?
> *Digging Deeper*
> What are some cultural expectations of brides that can serve as a warning?

19a. "Though you were ruined and made desolate and your land laid waste, now you will be too small for your people,

The people who returned would find desolation and ruins. Zion would be plowed, and Jerusalem would become heaps (Micah 3:12). The image of *waste* encourages the reader to think of the utter destruction of not only Jerusalem but all the *land*. Once-cultivated fields would be wild and overgrown, having reverted to their own natural state. Stones that had been walls would be strewn within and without the city limits (compare Nehemiah 4:2). The population would have dwindled to the point that the whole land was *desolate*.

Further evidence of the reversal of fortune would be in regard to the land that had been suffering with too few people. But the happy issue would instead be that the land was *too small* for all those who would return. Rather than emphasizing the current scarcity of the land, the prophecy instead focuses on its future when it will teem with life, be revitalized, and experience all the joys and thriving of human life within its borders.

> **What Do You Think?**
> How would you encourage someone who is going through a time of spiritual darkness?
> *Digging Deeper*
> What Scriptures speak to the sound wisdom of hoping in the Lord?

19b. "and those who devoured you will be far away.

The city and the returned exiles were assured

that *those who devoured you*, the Babylonians, would *be far away* and thus unable to cause them further pain and terror. Even more important than actual geographical distance was to be the absolute loss of power Babylon experienced, positioning it as far as could be from causing any more sorrow in Judah.

❧ DESOLATION AND RUIN ❧

We who live in the western United States are feeling the growing threat of wildfires. Wilderness areas are most in danger, but wildfires often blow into inhabited areas, destroying towns and cities in the process. We have our "go bags" packed with irreplaceable possessions—family pictures, computers and backups with data that can't be replaced, and the clothes we would need while displaced and awaiting the "you can go home now" announcement.

Following fires in residential areas, homeowners return to find widespread devastation, with whole communities reduced to a wasteland of ash and twisted metal. Rebuilding can take months or years, and sometimes the destruction is so complete that a community is simply abandoned. Those who do rebuild feel the happiness of restoration but do not forget the terror and grief of losing their homes.

The Jews returning to ruined Jerusalem must have felt similarly when they got the "you can go home now" news. But the Judeans could trust in God's help in rebuilding Jerusalem. How does your faith help you when events in life destroy what you have built? —C. R. B.

20. "The children born during your bereavement will yet say in your hearing, 'This place is too small for us; give us more space to live in.'

The growth in the Jewish population during the captivity was significant. It is reminiscent of the growth that the Hebrews experienced when they were in bondage in Egypt for 430 years (Exodus 12:40-41). They went into Egypt as 70 people (Genesis 46:26-27); as the family of Jacob, and they left as a nation of about 600,000 men (Exodus 12:37), or more than two million people.

The ones who return to Zion are portrayed as her *children*. In the short term, these are primarily a new generation born in exile. Though some elders would return, many other returning exiles had never seen Jerusalem in its heyday, when the temple was standing (Ezra 3:10-13). As in Egypt, the population of the people expanded so that the land was *too small* to contain them all (Exodus 1:6-7). But unlike then, the people would not be oppressed because of their flourishing (1:8-14).

Although the temple would be rebuilt in Jerusalem (Ezra 6:12-18), the exiles in Babylon were dedicated to maintaining their faith while far from their center of worship. And some exiles stayed in Babylon, even after the way was opened to return to Judah. This paved the way for the rise of synagogues and religious leaders called rabbis. Jews scattered throughout the Mediterranean region during the second temple period (around 538 BC–AD 70), taking their faith with them. That Diaspora ("dispersing") resulted in more territory experiencing Jewish influence (example: Acts 2:9-11).

This became highly important in the long term, when Gentiles would be welcomed into God's family, regardless of religious or ethnic background or their geographical relationship to Jerusalem. The *place* where Zion's children could *live* would turn out to be throughout the world, to its most remote locations (Revelation 15:4).

> *What Do You Think?*
>   How might Isaiah 49:20 encourage a church that appears to be declining?
> *Digging Deeper*
>   What measures beyond numerical growth are important in order to gauge the spiritual health of a congregation?

B. Disorientation (v. 21)

21. "Then you will say in your heart, 'Who bore me these? I was bereaved and barren; I was exiled and rejected. Who brought these up? I was left all alone, but these—where have they come from?'"

The change of fortune promised to Zion is so extreme that she will experience extreme disorientation when hearing it. Her reaction is not described as disbelieving exactly but incredulous or bewildered, afraid to hope that this can be true. Zion will have lost her children and become *bereaved and barren; . . . exiled and rejected*, without a safe home to settle into. She will not be aware that any of her children had survived. Her experience would soon be that of Babylon, who had brought all this evil on Zion; Babylon would experience widowhood and the loss of her children in one day (Isaiah 47:10-11; see lesson 1).

> *What Do You Think?*
> Is being surprised by God's blessing a faithful reaction? Why or why not?
> *Digging Deeper*
> How would you encourage a friend who struggles to accept God's blessings?

II. Explanation of Restoration
(Isaiah 49:22-23)
A. Foreigners Called (vv. 22-23a)

22a. This is what the Sovereign Lord says: "See, I will beckon to the nations, I will lift up my banner to the peoples;

Zion is once again called to *see* (see Isaiah 49:18, above). God's beckoning *to the nations* and lifting *up* his *banner to the peoples* reveals that God will use foreign nations to accomplish his will for Zion. It could also be that God was warning any people who would stand against his people. Language like lifting God's hand and setting up his standard is used throughout Isaiah to emphasize how the Lord chose to communicate with foreigners to draw them to him and to his will (Isaiah 5:26; 11:12; 18:3; etc.). We might think of the Magis' reading the sky to learn of Jesus' birth and where to go to praise him as an example of this (Matthew 2:1-2).

22b. "they will bring your sons in their arms and carry your daughters on their hips.

The Gentiles will provide help for the *sons* and *daughters* who make the return trip to Judah (Ezra 1:7-11; Nehemiah 2:8-9). The image is of parental care, unexpected from foreign nations but in keeping with what God required of them. The exiles would not be kicked out of their exilic homes and left defenseless to fend for themselves.

23a. "Kings will be your foster fathers, and their queens your nursing mothers. They will bow down before you with their faces to the ground; they will lick the dust at your feet.

The image here is one of both care and humility. Being provided for by *kings* and *queens* as *foster* parents reveals how important the people are to God—that the most powerful royals are to be called to nurture them. It also suggests the abundance of worldly resources that God will muster for the sake of his people. The image might remind us of how the daughter of Pharaoh cared for Moses (Exodus 2:1-10).

Darius, as well as Cyrus, arranged for several types of provisions for the Jews to be supplied from the royal revenues collected in that area (Ezra 6:8-10). This would have been about 520 BC. Later, Artaxerxes and his seven counselors gave silver and gold to the people who returned with Ezra in 458 BC (7:14-15).

The language of Gentiles being in submission points to the future when people from all nations will acknowledge that the God of Israel is the only God. Although in the past powerful people had set themselves up as gods, those who heed God's call will humble themselves to him and be glad to serve his people.

B. Hopeful, Not Shamed (v. 23b)

23b. "Then you will know that I am the Lord; those who hope in me will not be disappointed."

The phrase *you will know that I am the Lord* is used frequently in the book of Ezekiel (6:7; 7:4, 9; 11:10; etc.). Knowing starts with accepting the facts but requires much more. Then as now, knowing the Lord requires obeying him, first of all by rejecting all others who claim the same status (Exodus 6:2; Isaiah 42:8; etc.). Following closely after this is living in accordance with God's revealed laws, not choosing for ourselves what seems good or simply justifiable (Psalm 22:23; etc.). And although knowing the Lord requires faith, he also supplies plenty of evidence to give us confidence in who he is.

Waiting on the Lord is rarely easy, but it is *always* worthwhile (examples: Psalm 130:5-8; Luke 2:25-32, 36-38). Though his good plans may not be revealed in our lifetimes, "we know that in all things God works for the good of those who love him" (Romans 8:28). Between his past deeds, his demonstrated faithfulness to his promises, and his assurances regarding our future with him, we have every reason to *hope* patiently and know that he will vindicate our faith (8:24, 38-39).

❧ NUMBLE PIE ❧

Back in the 1300s, *numbles* was the term for the heart, liver, and entrails of an animal. These were fed to servants and the lower class, usually in a savory pie to make the servings go further. In time, *numbles* became *umbles,* a word that has a different etymology from *humble.* But the similar sound of the words and the fact that umble pie was eaten by those of humble station in life probably accounts for the shift.

Over the centuries, the phrase has become a figure of speech; eating humble pie today describes a person having to publicly admit to some past wrongdoing or failure. Isaiah might have described the Gentiles' predicament similarly. After all, they offered assistance to the Jews as they returned to Jerusalem.

Whether current society should try to atone for the sins of past generations is a bigger issue than any of us can resolve by ourselves. But perhaps there are ways to say our ancestors were wrong. How do you think it should be done?

—C. R. B.

Conclusion

A. Change of Address

Jesus' coming results in a change of fortune: though we were condemned, we are now promised eternal life when we choose to follow him as our Lord and Savior (Romans 8:1-2). And this change of fortune results in a change of identity: we who were once far away are now part of God's family (8:14-17; Ephesians 2:13). Essentially our address has changed from being in this world to residing in the kingdom of Heaven (John 3:3-5; Acts 28:31; Revelation 12:10-12).

This Servant Song is one of great hope for Israel and all others. Though Isaiah's audience couldn't know, the redemption promised here goes well beyond an end to exile in Babylon. It encompasses an end to exile *in sin.* Through Jesus we have abundant life; he can be trusted with *all* our needs.

What Do You Think?
What in today's lesson encouraged you? How will you share that encouragement?
Digging Deeper
What challenged you? How will you meet that challenge in the week ahead?

B. Prayer

Almighty God, we are thankful for the promises that you made to your people. In Jesus' name we pray. Amen.

C. Thought to Remember

Wait for the Lord,
who does not disappoint.

HOW TO SAY IT

Artaxerxes	Are-tuh-*zerk*-seez.
Babylon	*Bab*-uh-lun.
Belshazzar	Bel-*shazz*-er.
Cyrus	*Sigh*-russ.
Darius	Duh-*rye*-us.
Diaspora	Dee-*as*-puh-ruh.
Ezra	*Ez*-ruh.
Gentiles	*Jen*-tiles.
Isaiah	Eye-*zay*-uh.
Jeremiah	Jair-uh-*my*-uh.
Jerusalem	Juh-*roo*-suh-lem.
Judah	*Joo*-duh.
Medes	Meeds.
Micah	*My*-kuh.
Nabonidus	Nab-uh-*nye*-dus.
Persians	*Per*-zhens.
Zion	*Zi*-un.

INVOLVEMENT LEARNING

Enhance your lesson with NIV Bible Student *(from your curriculum supplier) and the reproducible activity page (at www.standardlesson.com or in the back of the* NIV Standard Lesson Commentary Deluxe Edition*).*

Into the Lesson

Begin class by inviting pairs to share a personal experience involving a reunion or homecoming event they attended. Have them respond to the following questions: 1–What emotions did you have when you saw all the people who came together? 2–What memories did the gathering bring up for you? 3–What evidence of change did you see in the group since the last time you were together? After a few minutes, ask volunteer pairs to share what their partners told them.

Alternative. Distribute copies of the "Bedtime Story" exercise from the activity page, which you can download, to be completed as directed alone or in pairs. Bring the class together and allow volunteers to read their completed stories before discussing the questions together as a class.

After either activity say, "In today's lesson we'll explore the promises God made to his people and how they responded."

Into the Word

Ask a volunteer to read Isaiah 49:18-21. Divide the whole group into small groups (or pairs). Give each pair a Scripture reference from this list: Genesis 15:1-6; Genesis 37:2-8; Exodus 3:1-10; 1 Kings 5:1-11; Jeremiah 29:10-14; Matthew 16:15-19; Luke 1:26-38; Acts 9:10-16. *Option.* Allow all the pairs to review as many of these citations as possible in a certain amount of time.

Ask partners or groups to read their passage(s) and discuss: 1–What promise was made or assurance given? 2–Why did fulfillment seem impossible to those involved? 3–How did God fulfill his promise?

Ask a volunteer to read Isaiah 49:22-23. Hand out blank paper to the pairs. Ask the learners to look back through the passages above and identify at least one thing that the people would see or experience that could remind them that God is the Lord. Ask the pairs to sketch an image that stood out to them in particular from Isaiah 49:18-23. *Option.* Assure participants that their sketches will not be shared with the class unless they so volunteer. Have the pairs write down the significance of the image they chose before asking volunteers to discuss the images they sketched and talked about.

Ask the whole group to discuss: 1–How do the things mentioned in this passage help people know that God is Lord? 2–Why is it important to God that his people know that he is the Lord? Allow time for several participants to respond.

Into Life

If you used the first activity in the **Into the Lesson** section, bring the original pairs back together. Ask them to discuss what evidence of the Lord's faithfulness and redemption they saw in the reunion they described. If none, ask them to imagine how the experience would have been different if God's work had been more evident in that gathering. Allow volunteers to share with the class.

Alternative. Read aloud the following statement from the last verse of the text: "Those who hope in me will not be disappointed." Then hand out copies of the "Waiting and Hoping" exercise from the activity page. Allow individuals one minute to jot down answers before they pair up to discuss their answers together. Invite participants to share these responses with a partner, and then pray for each other.

Encourage partners to consider and discuss ways they can share this testimony with others this week. Ask each learner to note any time they share their faith and how their testimony helped them connect with the person they were speaking to. End class with a prayer that each person would seek ways to testify to God's gracious promise keeping this week and be renewed in their own hope in his promises.

GOD OFFERS DELIVERANCE

DEVOTIONAL READING: Isaiah 51:1-8
BACKGROUND SCRIPTURE: Isaiah 51

ISAIAH 51:1-8

1 "Listen to me, you who pursue
  righteousness
  and who seek the LORD:
Look to the rock from which you were cut
  and to the quarry from which you were
  hewn;
2 look to Abraham, your father,
  and to Sarah, who gave you birth.
When I called him he was only one man,
  and I blessed him and made him many.
3 The LORD will surely comfort Zion
  and will look with compassion on all
  her ruins;
he will make her deserts like Eden,
  her wastelands like the garden of the
  LORD.
Joy and gladness will be found in her,
  thanksgiving and the sound of singing.
4 "Listen to me, my people;
  hear me, my nation:
Instruction will go out from me;
  my justice will become a light to the
  nations.

5 My righteousness draws near speedily,
  my salvation is on the way,
  and my arm will bring justice to the
  nations.
The islands will look to me
  and wait in hope for my arm.
6 Lift up your eyes to the heavens,
  look at the earth beneath;
the heavens will vanish like smoke,
  the earth will wear out like a garment
  and its inhabitants die like flies.
But my salvation will last forever,
  my righteousness will never fail.
7 "Hear me, you who know what is right,
  you people who have taken my instruction to heart:
Do not fear the reproach of mere mortals
  or be terrified by their insults.
8 For the moth will eat them up like a
  garment;
  the worm will devour them like wool.
But my righteousness will last forever,
  my salvation through all generations."

KEY VERSE

Listen to me, you who pursue righteousness and who seek the LORD: Look to the rock from which you were cut and to the quarry from which you were hewn. —**Isaiah 51:1**

PARTNERS IN A NEW CREATION

Unit 1: God Delivers and Restores

LESSONS 1–4

LESSON AIMS

After participating in this lesson, each learner will be able to:

1. Identify what endures and what does not.

2. Explain the connection between seeking righteousness and seeking the Lord.

3. State one way he or she will better pursue both righteousness and the Lord in the coming week.

LESSON OUTLINE

Introduction

A. Look Both Ways?

We've heard this since we were small children: "Look both ways before crossing a street, and then cross when it's safe." That's still good advice, but it is not adequate for the present culture. Why? One reason is that there are so many more ways to be distracted than in the past.

The distractions take place for those who walk, for drivers of automobiles, and those who ride bicycles. At intersections it sometimes appears as if nobody looks. The pedestrians seem oblivious to traffic lights, stop signs, and walkways. They are focused on things such as making calls, reading text messages or e-books, or listening to a podcast or music. Those on wheels are also seen looking at a device instead of at the road. The "look both ways" admonition is no longer enough. People also need to stay aware of their surroundings. The result is that the old saying could be changed to "Look up, and then look both ways before crossing a street."

This lesson will develop three "looks" that were given to the people of Judah: to look to the past, the future, and straight into the present.

B. Lesson Context

The opening lines of Charles Dickens's *A Tale of Two Cities* are easily recognized by many readers: "It was the best of times, it was the worst of times." The same words could be used to describe Judah during Isaiah's ministry (see lesson 3 Lesson Context). The best of times were reflected in Judah's economic and military prowess (Isaiah 2:7); the worst of times were marked by the sin of idolatry and consequent exile in Babylon (39:6-7).

In many ways, Judah's punishment was an indictment of their false gods and of the sins those "gods" condoned. The people had turned from the true God in spite of the great acts of deliverance they had experienced as a nation, and the admonitions in the Ten Commandments to have no other gods or graven images (Exodus 20:3-6). And the exile did have a purifying effect. Following the Babylonian captivity, Jewish idolatry was never a serious problem again (though of course other issues arose). The Jews who returned stood firm on their faithful foundation (see Isaiah 51:1b-2, below), no matter what foreign invaders tried to tempt them with new gods. Though they had suffered through the worst of times, even better than their previous best times were still ahead.

We can also assert that Babylon was punished for following their false gods. Had their worship been rendered to God and concerned with justice and righteousness instead of acquisition and power, the story of the Babylonian Empire would have been very different. In Isaiah 46–47 God mocked the Babylonians' idolatry and its associated practices (see lesson 1). The idols have to be carried, but God's judgment would have them carried *away* (Isaiah 46:1). Though the people bowed to gods that they made, the God of the heavens had declared their end (46:10). Their "best of times" was about to come to a permanent close.

I. Look to the Past
(Isaiah 51:1-3)

A. The Follower, the Seeker (v. 1a)

1a. "Listen to me, you who pursue righteousness and who seek the LORD:

Our text contains three calls to *listen* (see Isaiah 51:4, 7, below; compare 51:21; 52:8; see also lesson 3). Each call in our text is followed by a two-part description of the people who are being addressed. In each instance, the two phrases augment each other, adding depth to the portrait of the listener.

Undoubtedly *you who pursue righteousness* are the same as *who seek the Lord*. Those who strive to be righteous want to live according to God's laws and his will. In the case of Abraham, even before the laws were revealed or the prophets had spoken, faith was declared to be the basis of righteousness before God (Genesis 15:6; compare Romans 3:21-26; see Isaiah 51:1b-2, below). To seek is to have a goal and to search diligently to reach it. God is near those who look for him (Deuteronomy 4:29; Matthew 7:7-8; Acts 17:24-28).

We can note the many philosophers who have sought to define the good life without feeling the need to include God's will in the equation. And we can think of people who say they seek God

but do not seem inclined to obey his law, choosing instead a "god" of their own making. Any attempts that do not seek God *and* also strive to obey him will be lacking; these do not lead to true or eternal life (John 14:5-17).

> *What Do You Think?*
> What circumstances distract or discourage you from seeking righteousness?
> *Digging Deeper*
> How can you prepare for those times now in order to continue seeking the Lord faithfully?

B. Remember Origins (vv. 1b-2)

1b-2. "Look to the rock from which you were cut and to the quarry from which you were hewn; look to Abraham, your father, and to Sarah, who gave you birth. When I called him he was only one man, and I blessed him and made him many.

We might expect *the rock* to refer to God here, and for good reason. This image of origin, deliverance, and safety in the Lord occurs with some frequency in the Old Testament (examples: 1 Samuel 2:2; Psalms 18:2, 31; 62:2, 6-7; Isaiah 17:10). In his farewell address Moses charged that Israel had become unmindful of the "Rock" that had begotten them and had forgotten that God had formed them (Deuteronomy 32:15, 18, 30-31). Isaiah might charge the people of his day with the same. It would be entirely appropriate for Isaiah then to call the righteous person to *look* to God as the one who formed and blessed the nation of Israel.

In context, *Abraham* actually seems to be referred to as the rock *from which you were cut*. This is appropriate for the faithful to whom Isaiah speaks, since all who put their faith in God and later in Christ are declared to be true children of Abraham (Galatians 3:7-9). In this way, Abraham is the *father* because God *called him* and

HOW TO SAY IT

Sela   *See*-luh.

wadi   *wah*-dee.

blessed him and *made him many* (see Genesis 12:1-3; Romans 4:16; 9:8).

Sarah then is likened to *the quarry from which you were hewn.* This unusual parallelism would be a reference to her womb, which had to be emptied through birth in order for descendants to be brought forth. Though Hagar bore Abraham a son who was blessed by association with his father, Isaac was the child of promise through whom the promise of a nation would be fulfilled (Genesis 17:19-21; Galatians 4:21-31).

The rock imagery eventually extends to Christ himself (Luke 20:17; 1 Peter 2:4, 7; compare 1 Corinthians 10:4). In Christ God's people expanded beyond the boundaries of Abraham's family, just as God always intended. So it is appropriate to speak of being called in Christ alone, of his blessing in ministry and blessing to us through his resurrected life, and of the expansion of the church into all places. Remember the joy of salvation when you became a Christian? Look back to the beginning of your walk with Christ for a refresher.

What Do You Think?

How does recounting your spiritual heritage strengthen your confidence in the Lord's faithfulness?

Digging Deeper

What are some areas from earlier in your walk with Christ that you would like to make a bigger part of your life today?

❧ *THE ROCK* ❧

Petra, in western Jordan, is the red-rock city carved out of "living stone." It is believed by many to be Sela (2 Kings 14:7; Isaiah 16:1; possibly also referenced in Judges 1:36; Isaiah 42:11). Especially interesting to me when I visited was the eastern entrance. A narrow, half-mile pathway down a wadi took us through a crevice in a wall of rock. At the end of the wadi, an unforgettable view of the solid-rock city presented itself to us. Tradition says that wall is the stone that Moses struck to get water for the people of Israel and the cleft in the rock is the fissure through which water poured out (Exodus 17:1-7).

Remembering one's solid foundation sets the tone for growth throughout life. Abraham served as the solid foundation and example of faithful, righteous living for Israel. Today we look to the one Abraham waited for—Jesus Christ. How will you honor your solid foundation?   —C. R. B.

C. Expect Comfort (v. 3)

3. "The LORD will surely comfort Zion and will look with compassion on all her ruins; he will make her deserts like Eden, her wastelands like the garden of the LORD. Joy and gladness will be found in her, thanksgiving and the sound of singing.

The destruction of *Zion* was complete and completely devastating—so much so that Judah broadly and Jerusalem specifically were *ruins* (Nehemiah 1:3; 2:3, 17; Lamentations 1:1; 2:8-9, 13). We might consider images we've seen of contemporary war zones to get an idea about the complete annihilation of Jerusalem. It was not simply left empty-but-intact when the people went into exile; the city was left in chaos, stones overthrown, buildings burned to the ground, and likely even unburied human remains in the streets.

Only by imagining how complete and brutal the Babylonians' conquest of Jerusalem was can we imagine how good this news is. *Deserts* where a city once was is a lonesome, haunting image; but a thriving *Eden*—a paradise—in its place is a hopeful, joyful image. In Eden, Adam and Eve had worked, but easily; the ground was not yet cursed and God provided every good thing they needed. They lived free of sin; they enjoyed each other's company and even walked with God (Genesis 2:15-25; 3:8). Nothing could be better for Jerusalem than for *her wastelands* to become *like the garden of the Lord.* Add to that people who had experienced life outside of such a paradise; the *thanksgiving* and *sound of singing* of returned exiles to such a place would surely be a symphony of *joy and gladness.*

Joy is one characteristic of Christians (Galatians 5:22-23). Philippians 4:4 gives a double command to rejoice, and in 1 Thessalonians 5:16 the admonition is to rejoice always. When our life or our world seems like devastated Zion, our joy comes from the knowledge that God has a greater plan. The destruction is not the end; and knowing that, we can experience joy, no matter our temporary situation.

❧ *A Thriving City* ❧

Are urban dwellers entitled to green space in their cities? The Parks for All nonprofit is dedicated to "the creation, maintenance and beautification of public parks, playgrounds & green space throughout New Orleans." The organization holds that well-planned and maintained parks are key to thriving in a city. More city planners and other officials agree. And a growing body of research asserts that green spaces are good for health—mental and physical—and overall well-being of a city's population.

God is well ahead of this urban trend, describing the newly rebuilt Jerusalem as an Eden; even the New Jerusalem centers on a life-giving tree and river (Revelation 22:1-5; see lesson 12). The reconstructed Jerusalem would not be a perfect city on earth, but in both human thriving and natural bounty, it would be a beautiful place and a sign of what God has in store for his faithful people. Challenge yourself this week to go to one of your local parks and consider the many and varied ways that God provides for you and your community.

—J. A. K.

II. Look to the Future
(Isaiah 51:4-6)
A. "My People, My Nation" (v. 4a)

4a. "Listen to me, my people; hear me, my nation:

Listen and *hear* constitute one call to pay attention (see Isaiah 51:1, above). *My people* and *my nation* continues to address the Jews, specifically the exiles in Babylon. In 51:1b-2 (above) it's clear that this call is to the descendants of Abraham; Isaiah does not need to be so explicit here because of the specificity before.

B. Coming Light (vv. 4b-5)

4b. "Instruction will go out from me; my justice will become a light to the nations.

God creates life everywhere.

Visual for Lesson 4. *Ask learners to consider this visual before answering the questions associated with verse 5.*

This verse has parallels to a prophecy made in Isaiah 2:3—that God's *instruction* would go forth from Zion (see Micah 4:2). The servant was previously identified as the one to "bring forth justice" and "[establish] justice on earth" (Isaiah 42:3-4). This is once again an indication that the Lord does not intend to hide the *light* from the nations but instead to draw them to himself (compare Matthew 5:13-16).

5. "My righteousness draws near speedily, my salvation is on the way, and my arm will bring justice to the nations. The islands will look to me and wait in hope for my arm.

The pursuit of *righteousness* (Isaiah 51:1, above) is about to be rewarded. *Salvation* in the Old Testament frequently refers to a very physical, earthy deliverance from evil and harm (examples: 1 Chronicles 16:35; Psalm 27:1-9; Habakkuk 3:13). For this reason, many misunderstood Jesus' mission of salvation as being one of political liberation in the vein of other rebellious "messiahs" before him (example: Acts 5:36-37). In hindsight, however, we see that this salvation is essentially spiritual in nature, given how Jesus would call people from all nations—here *the islands* (compare Isaiah 11:11)—to come to him for deliverance from sin (Acts 13:38-48). Only through spiritual wholeness can any other kind of thriving be anticipated.

Elsewhere the Lord directs the people to "Maintain justice and do what is right, for my salvation is close at hand and my righteousness will soon be revealed" (Isaiah 56:1). There he explicitly welcomes both strangers and eunuchs—people typically excluded from being part of Israel—to be integral members of his people when they keep his law. One of Jesus' final commissions to the apostles shows a fulfillment of what had been prophesied by Isaiah. Just before his ascension, Jesus said that the apostles were to be his witnesses to Jerusalem, Judea, Samaria, and to the entire world (Acts 1:8). In Romans 1:16 Paul summarized these concepts when he wrote that the gospel was for everyone who believes, to Jews and also to Gentiles.

The *arm* of the Lord is often associated with deliverance and justice (examples: Isaiah 30:30; 59:15b-16; Jeremiah 21:5; Ezekiel 20:33-34). Here his judgment is linked to the people's *hope*. Without the Lord's promise to judge, it would be impossible to trust him. After all, how could a good God who loves righteousness simply ignore evil? And if he did not have the power to judge, that would be another reason for mistrust. But this God has the authority, the will, and the power to judge the wicked and will protect all who place their trust in him.

> **What Do You Think?**
> How do you demonstrate God's love for people in distant lands?
> *Digging Deeper*
> What opportunities does your community offer to show God's love for *all* people?

C. Everlasting Reign (v. 6)

6a. "Lift up your eyes to the heavens, look at the earth beneath; the heavens will vanish like smoke, the earth will wear out like a garment and its inhabitants die like flies.

To the casual observer *the heavens* and *the earth* seem permanent. But *smoke* drifts on the wind and then dissipates. Wearing out *like a garment* suggests hard use, tearing, ripping, outgrowing. These analogies suggest that, far from lasting forever, both heavens and earth are quick to fall apart. Other passages also describe heaven and earth as being temporary (Psalm 102:25-26; Matthew 24:35; 2 Peter 3:10). All creation only lasts as long as God chooses to sustain it (Colossians 1:15-18).

Life is also described as fleeting (Job 7:7; Psalm 39:5, 11). Like the speed with which smoke disappears or an old garment falls to shreds, so will *its inhabitants die* (Ecclesiastes 3:19). In context, this refers to all living creations—death is the end. There's no doubt it will happen; there's no preventing it.

> **What Do You Think?**
> In what ways is the impermanence of this world a comfort to you rather than a threat?
> *Digging Deeper*
> How does God's sustaining our fragile world give you reassurance about his love?

6b. "But my salvation will last forever, my righteousness will never fail.

In contrast to creatures, the earth, and even the heavens (Isaiah 51:6a, above), God's *salvation* and *righteousness will never fail.* The purpose of the coming of the Messiah was to grant these things to the ones who come to Jesus through faith. In the end, no more will death or sorrow afflict his people, because all of that will pass away with all else that is temporary (Revelation 21:1-4; see lesson 10). And though sin has an end, righteousness will be the law of the heavenly land where the saints live with God (2 Peter 3:13).

The Bible uses the figure of a walk or road to refer to the journey of life (examples: Psalm 1; John 14:6). In the spiritual realms there are only two ways. The "wide" gate and "broad" road lead to destruction, and that is the easy way of life. It is the "small" gate and "narrow" road that lead to true life (Matthew 7:13-14). It requires serious dedication and effort to walk in God's way, but it's worth it.

III. Look Straight Ahead
(ISAIAH 51:7-8)

A. The Righteous at Heart (v. 7a)

7a. "Hear me, you who know what is right, you people who have taken my instruction to heart:

For the final time in this lesson, the audience is commanded to *hear*. As before, *you who know what is right* are the very same *people who have taken* God's *instruction to heart*. In Hebrew thought, the heart was not only (or not primarily) the seat of emotions but, instead, of reason and insight (examples: "conscience-stricken" 1 Samuel 24:5; 2 Samuel 24:10; "mind" Nehemiah 5:7). This is not to say that those who had the law in their hearts did not love it; plenty of poetry exists extolling God's Word and its great benefit for those who learn from it (examples: Psalms 37:30-31; 40:8-10; 119). From the time the law was given, God instructed the people to hide it in their hearts and even gave them instructions on how to do so (Deuteronomy 6:4-9; Jeremiah 31:31-34). And those who took their studies of the law seriously spoke of the joy of a heart turned toward God (example: Psalm 119:2-3, 7, 10-11).

But for many generations, the people struggled to observe God's laws the way they were meant to. This is what got them into exile in the first place! To hear that God was speaking to the righteous who loved his law would be heartening to them. God had not abandoned them forever but had provided a way for them to return not only home but, more importantly, to him (2 Chronicles 6:36-39). When God spoke to the prophet Ezekiel, the Lord explicitly promised to give the people open hearts that would be disposed to hearing his word and obeying it (Ezekiel 11:19-20; 14:4-5; 18:31; etc.).

B. Do Not Fear (vv. 7b-8)

7b-8a. "Do not fear the reproach of mere mortals or be terrified by their insults. For the moth will eat them up like a garment; the worm will devour them like wool.

Just like the earth and the heavens, *the reproach of mere mortals* and *their insults* last but a moment before inevitably coming to nothing (see Isaiah 51:6a, above). The scorn of people who do not seek righteousness, do not love God's words, and do not care to follow the Lord is fleeting indeed. It won't even take a ferocious bear or fire or other massive force to destroy them; *the moth* and *the worm* will suffice to judge those who speak against God's people.

8b. "But my righteousness will last forever, my salvation through all generations."

Righteousness and *salvation* are once again declared to last *forever* (see Isaiah 51:6b, above). *Through all generations* is another way to express this unending time line. But the phrase might bring to mind God's faithfulness from generation to generation (example: Genesis 9:12-16). Though he brings judgment, he forgives too (example: Exodus 20:4-6). This salvation is the last plan; there is no next salvation to come. Each generation is given the opportunity to accept the gift.

> *What Do You Think?*
> How do you manage feelings of fear when you feel threatened or unsafe?
> *Digging Deeper*
> How would redirecting your thoughts to seeking God help you react faithfully in that moment?

Conclusion
A. Which Way?

Looking to our past offers important insights: about faithfulness, examples to follow or deviate from, the people and events that have shaped us. Isaiah prepared the nation to look forward to Jesus, but we look to the past, present, *and* future when we look to him. The salvation work Jesus has done is the reason for our joy in the present and our hope in the future. So when you think about whether to look to the past, present, or future, the answer is: all three! Look to Christ and his ministry, his sacrifice, his death and resurrection. Look to the body of Christ that continues to call the world to repent of sins and be reconciled to God. And look to the glorious future when God's promises of eternal life will no longer be a hope but our present, eternal reality.

B. Prayer

Thank you, Lord, for these reminders that you have always loved and admonished your people. As we leave class now, we ask for wisdom in making the tough decisions that are ahead of us this week. In Jesus' name we pray. Amen.

C. Thought to Remember

Hear that? God is calling.

INVOLVEMENT LEARNING

Enhance your lesson with NIV Bible Student (from your curriculum supplier) and the reproducible activity page (at www.standardlesson.com or in the back of the NIV Standard Lesson Commentary Deluxe Edition).

Into the Lesson

Have learners pretend they are 12 years old again. Ask volunteers to use one word to describe life before they turned 12. Then ask for one word that describes life *while* they were 12. Then have them imagine what word their 12-year-old self would supply for what they thought the future would be like. How far off would that word be from where the learner is today? *Option.* Instead of discussing as a class, break learners into pairs or small groups.

Alternative. Distribute the "What Are You Searching For?" exercise from the activity page, which you can download. Allow learners one minute to individually find as many words related to today's lesson as they can before allowing them to work in pairs for a few minutes longer. Allow time briefly to discuss the final answer together.

After either activity, say, "In today's lesson, we will see how God turns his people's focus in different directions to help them become oriented to who he is and who he has called them to be."

Into the Word

Say, "This passage is addressed to those who follow after or pursue righteousness and seek the Lord. How are these two things connected?" Give participants an opportunity to share and discuss. Ask them to share verses that speak to this connection. Examples may include 2 Samuel 23:3; Psalms 5:8; 35:28; Jeremiah 9:24; Romans 4:24; contrast Isaiah 26:10.

Then ask a volunteer to read Isaiah 51:1-8. Divide the class into three groups. Ask each group to consider this passage from one of these points of view: **The Past Group** will offer insight into how the past would offer *Isaiah's original audience* confidence in God's promises; **The Present Group** will explore how the *original audience's* present circumstances might impede their believing what Isaiah said; **The Future Group** will consider how to interpret this passage and its fulfillment—both for Isaiah and for the future—in light of what we know about Jesus and his fulfillment of Scripture. Each group should offer other verses that back up their thinking. Consult the commentary text as needed to help inform the groups' work.

After they discuss, have each group report their conclusions to the whole group. Consider what benefits and drawbacks, if any, these three perspectives have when hearing this prophecy or others like it.

Alternative. Divide the class into four small groups. Distribute to each group the "Look Around!" exercise from the activity page. Ask the groups to study and discuss the verses together, completing as directed. Then bring the class back together to discuss further.

Into Life

If the class participated in the original **Into the Word** activity, ask them to remain in their groups to consider how the past, present, and future perspectives can also aid or hinder spiritual growth in the church. They should consider how using these three perspectives might give them different insight in Sunday school class, while listening to a sermon, or in their individual devotional time.

Ask a volunteer to read Matthew 6:31-33. Ask, "How can we seek the Lord and pursue righteousness this week?" Discuss this in broad terms as a class before dividing into pairs (or small groups).

Invite the pairs to discuss further and come up with practical, actionable ways they can seek the Lord and pursue righteousness this week in thought, word, and deed. Pass out notecards and ask each individual to write down one of their ideas to pursue in the week ahead. Encourage them by adding that volunteers will be asked to share their experience or any aha moments they had at the beginning of class next week.

THE WORD BECOMES FLESH

DEVOTIONAL READING: John 1:1-14
BACKGROUND SCRIPTURE: John 1:1-14

JOHN 1:1-14

¹ In the beginning was the Word, and the Word was with God, and the Word was God. ² He was with God in the beginning. ³ Through him all things were made; without him nothing was made that has been made. ⁴ In him was life, and that life was the light of all mankind. ⁵ The light shines in the darkness, and the darkness has not overcome it.

⁶ There was a man sent from God whose name was John. ⁷ He came as a witness to testify concerning that light, so that through him all might believe. ⁸ He himself was not the light; he came only as a witness to the light.

⁹ The true light that gives light to everyone was coming into the world. ¹⁰ He was in the world, and though the world was made through him, the world did not recognize him. ¹¹ He came to that which was his own, but his own did not receive him. ¹² Yet to all who did receive him, to those who believed in his name, he gave the right to become children of God— ¹³ children born not of natural descent, nor of human decision or a husband's will, but born of God.

¹⁴ The Word became flesh and made his dwelling among us. We have seen his glory, the glory of the one and only Son, who came from the Father, full of grace and truth.

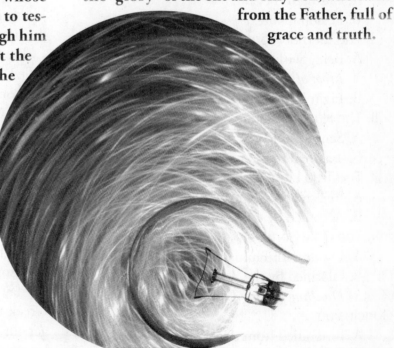

KEY VERSE

Through him all things were made; without him nothing was made that has been made. —**John 1:3**

PARTNERS IN A NEW CREATION

Unit 2: The Word: The Agent of Creation

LESSONS 5–9

LESSON AIMS

After participating in this lesson, each learner will be able to:

1. Identify "the Word."

2. Explain the respective missions of John the Baptist and "the Word."

3. Identify one way he or she can continue the mission of John the Baptist—and make a plan to commit to it.

LESSON OUTLINE

Introduction

A. Caring in Person

I enjoy nearly every aspect of ministering in local churches. Visiting church members remains a special task. During some visits, I might drink tea with a longtime church member as I ask about the person's walk with Christ. Other visits might be during less than happy circumstances—I might visit a church member in the hospital and pray for his or her healing. A church member once told me, "I didn't fully understand how much you cared, until you came."

My in-person ministry to the individuals in my church demonstrated my love for them. Scripture tells of God's love for his people. The extent of his love has been and still is being demonstrated for the world to see.

B. Lesson Context

The beginning of John's Gospel is unlike that of the three other New Testament Gospels. Matthew's Gospel begins with a genealogy and the birth narrative of Jesus (Matthew 1:1-24), Luke's Gospel begins with two birth narratives (Luke 1:1–2:21), and Mark's Gospel skips straight to Jesus' adult ministry (Mark 1:1-20). But the introduction to John's Gospel differs dramatically.

The Gospels of Matthew, Mark, and Luke are called "synoptic" because of their similar perspectives on recounting the person and work of Jesus. John's Gospel stands apart from the others as the writer stresses Jesus' divine identity as the Son of God and Messiah (John 20:31). The introduction to John's Gospel draws the reader's attention in referring to the eternality of the Word of God.

Throughout this week's Scripture text, John makes reference to "the Word" (John 1:1, 14). By using this designation, John is actually reflecting philosophical and rhetorical concepts common in his day. Specifically, John's use of the underlying Greek word for "Word"—*logos*, from which we get our English word *logic*—reflects the ways philosophers tried to make sense of the world. Pagan philosophers used the term to address the ways the pagan gods communicated with the cosmos and the created order. For pagans, the concept of "the

Word" was an attempt to make sense of the world and the animating forces therein.

However, John upends the pagan expectations. Instead of a distant animating life force or an obscure connection to supernatural "reason," John applies the concept of the Word to the eternal God of Israel. This God is the one through whom all creation came into being. This God has revealed himself specifically to his creation.

That John would repurpose a concept used by pagan philosophers makes sense considering the context and audience of John's Gospel. The Gospel was likely composed in the second half of the first century by Jesus' own disciple John—"the disciple whom Jesus loved" (John 21:20). This was "the disciple who testifies to these things and who wrote them down" in the Gospel (21:24).

In addition to this Gospel, John the apostle —not to be confused with John the Baptist (see commentary on John 1:6-8, below)—also wrote the New Testament epistles of 1, 2, and 3 John and the text of Revelation. We might assume that John wrote his Gospel to appeal to a broad audience, Jew and Gentile. If these were the collective audience of his Gospel, then John's emphasis on repurposing pagan philosophical concepts would be understandable; these communities would be familiar with such ideas.

I. The Eternal Word
(JOHN 1:1-5)
A. Being with God (vv. 1-3)
1a. In the beginning was the Word,

John begins his Gospel with the same words that introduce the Hebrew Scriptures: *"In the beginning"* (Genesis 1:1). In both accounts, this phrase highlights that God is eternal—he exists beyond our limited understanding of space and time. The concept of the eternal God, who existed before creation, needed no further introduction for John's audience (see Hebrews 1:10; Revelation 4:11).

1b. and the Word was with God,

Not only is the Word eternal, but *the Word* also coexists *with God*. In this sense, the Word shares in God's nature in a distinct way (compare John 1:1c). John highlights the close relationship between the Word and God (10:30; see also Matthew 3:17).

1c. and the Word was God.

While *God* the Father and the eternal Word are of one and the same nature, they are also two distinct persons. The Word shares the same nature as God the Father (Colossians 2:9) but operates in unique ways (see Hebrews 1:1-3; 1 John 4:14).

John had to stress that *the Word* is equal to the eternal God of Israel. Therefore, the Word has the same attributes as God, specifically eternality and divinity (see John 8:58).

2. He was with God in the beginning.

John concluded the introductory text by again referring to the eternal nature of the Word (see John 1:1a, above). The nature that characterizes *God* the Father also has characterized the Word since *the beginning*.

3. Through him all things were made; without him nothing was made that has been made.

John transitions from a discussion on the nature of the Word to a discussion on the work of the Word. The Word is creative and personal. Genesis tells how God created by his word (see Genesis 1:1-31; Psalm 33:6). John applies the idea to the work of the eternal Word in *him* making *all things*. As the Word coexisted with the Father, the Word is the source of life; and through the Word, all things came into existence (see 1 Corinthians 8:6; Colossians 1:15-20; Hebrews 1:2-3).

❧ *PROOF OF IDENTITY* ❧

After years of saving, my wife planned to take our children to Europe. In the weeks leading up to the trip, I helped ensure that all important details of the trip were addressed. Among the most important was the location of our children's passports. Before the trip, I placed the passports in a safe location—or so I thought.

From the second airport, where my family was to connect for their international departure, I received

HOW TO SAY IT

Incarnation	In-kahr-*ney*-shuhn.
logos (Greek)	*law*-goss.
synoptic	sih-*nawp*-tihk.

Seek the Light.
Find LIFE.

Visual for Lessons 5 & 7. *Have learners pair up and each take one minute to discuss the relationship between the light and life.*

a panicked phone call from my wife. During check-in for that flight, she realized that she held my passport rather than our son's. We spent the next 24 hours scrambling to prove our son's identity. Since my wife and our kids were already halfway across the country, we needed an expedited passport for our son! Because we could quickly prove our son's identity, the trip continued as planned.

John's Gospel begins with a proof of identity. The Jesus who would teach people and do miraculous works was also eternal with God because he was (and *is*) God. We can trust his teaching because his identity tells us he speaks the words of his heavenly Father. What prevents you from declaring Jesus' divine identity to others?   —R. O.

B. Light in Darkness (vv. 4-5)

4. In him was life, and that life was the light of all mankind.

The Word of God did not simply create *life*, but life preexisted *in him* by nature of the Word's relationship with God the Father (John 5:26). The substance of life is more than physical, for in the Word is found eternal life (see 1 John 1:2; 5:11-12).

In bringing *light* into the world, the Word contrasts with the world's darkness. In this regard, John speaks of spiritual light (see John 3:19-20). Jesus connects himself with the nature of this light (see 8:12; 12:35-36). The spiritual light is available to the whole world (see commentary on 1:9,

below), but not all people would receive the light (3:19-20).

5. The light shines in the darkness, and the darkness has not overcome it.

The Word became a spiritual *light* for all people who would receive the Word. Again, John expands on the creation account and God's creation of light by the power of his word (see Genesis 1:3).

Darkness might specifically refer to people who have resisted the Word. They experience spiritual blindness as they willfully live in the darkness of their evil (see John 3:19). However, darkness could also refer generally to the status of the world as a whole (compare 12:46; 1 John 2:8; 17). John could be referring to both possibilities. The two types of darkness could occur simultaneously but would not diminish the role of God's light.

The darkness *has not overcome* the scope of God's light. This phrase might allude to the way the light is overtaking the darkness, in the same way that darkness might overtake a person (John 12:35). As God's light overtakes darkness, the darkness is unable to overpower the brilliance and power of the light.

What Do You Think?
What areas of a believer's life might especially need God's light to shine?
Digging Deeper
How might darkness affect the relationships between believers (see 1 John 2:7-11)?

II. The Human Witness
(JOHN 1:6-8)

A. Sent by God (vv. 6-7)

6. There was a man sent from God whose name was John.

John transitioned to describe the *man* who would turn out to be the earthly forerunner to the Word. As this forerunner was *sent from God*, this man served as a prophet to the ministry of God. Old Testament prophets served a similar role as they proclaimed God's will to his people—even when the people refused to listen (see 2 Chronicles 24:19; Jeremiah 7:25-26; 35:15).

This prophet, *whose name was John,* is not the apostle who wrote the Gospel, but John the Baptist (compare Matthew 3:1; Luke 7:20). As a witness to all who would hear, John the Baptist came before the incarnate Word of God to prepare the hearts of all people for the Word's arrival (see Luke 1:15-17).

7. He came as a witness to testify concerning that light, so that through him all might believe.

John the Baptist *came* into the world with a God-given commission: to bear *witness* and *testify* to Jesus Christ, the *light* of the world (see John 1:19-34). Before John the Baptist was tragically murdered (Matthew 14:1-12), he served as a herald declaring the coming of the Messiah. Many of Jesus' own disciples came to follow Jesus and *believe* after hearing John's witness (John 1:35-42).

> *What Do You Think?*
> How might you bear witness to your neighbors of God's light of salvation?
>
> *Digging Deeper*
> How can believers maintain a faithful witness when God's light is rejected by others?

B. Testified to the Light (v. 8)

8. He himself was not the light; he came only as a witness to the light.

As John the Baptist spoke regarding *the light* of God, some people thought that he might be the promised Messiah (see Luke 3:15-18). At the time of the composition of John's Gospel, some people apparently still held to that belief. However, the Gospel dispelled that misunderstanding. John the Baptist only gave *witness* to that eternal *light* (see John 3:28).

III. The True Light
(JOHN 1:9-13)
A. Rejected by Some (vv. 9-11)

9. The true light that gives light to everyone was coming into the world.

Even though John the Baptist's witness illuminated the hearts of his audiences, the Word of God is the *light* for humanity. Truth implies accu-

racy and veracity (see John 19:35). However, as the Gospel uses the word in this specific instance, *true* emphasizes the light's authentic nature as being from God. (Compare the usage of the same word in John 4:23, 6:32; 15:1; 17:3.)

The true light has come *into the world* and has been revealed to *everyone.* Those people who receive the gift of Jesus Christ will live in the light of his salvation (see John 12:46).

10. He was in the world, and though the world was made through him, the world did not recognize him.

John described a sad irony related to the coming of the true light. While that light *made* the world and dwelled *in the world,* not all people accepted him. In John's Gospel, "the world" can refer to the entirety of planet Earth (see John 21:25). However, it can also refer to the world's rebellion in hostility to God and his Son (see 7:7; 15:18-19; 16:20; 17:14; also 1 John 2:15). Either possibility could be understood as the object of John's observation. Despite the creation of the world by the Son of God (Colossians 1:16), many people *did not recognize him.*

> *What Do You Think?*
> How might believers recognize and know God's presence in their lives?
>
> *Digging Deeper*
> To what extent does creation reveal God to the world (see Psalm 19:1-6; Romans 1:20)?

11. He came to that which was his own, but his own did not receive him.

Since the true light, the Word of God, created the world and was in the world, the world and the people therein are considered *his own.* Therefore, when he came to the world, it was as its originator and possessor. However, the reception was less than welcoming, even from the people most intended to accept him.

In this verse, John's Gospel looks at the totality of Jesus' earthly ministry. From the standpoint of several decades after Jesus' ascension, John reflects on the nature of that ministry. The reality was that Jesus' *own* people—the children of Israel—*did not receive him;* nor did they receive his message of salvation. In this sense, the words of Isaiah were fulfilled: Jesus was "despised and rejected" (Isaiah 53:3) and he became like "the stone the builders rejected" (Psalm 118:22; see Matthew 21:42-44).

B. Accepted by Children (vv. 12-13)

12. Yet to all who did receive him, to those who believed in his name, he gave the right to become children of God—

Despite the sad reality that many people rejected Jesus as God's Son, many others *did receive* Jesus and his testimony to God's eternal life. As a result, these people received God's grace (see John 1:16-18). Further, they came to know God the Father all the more clearly as they received his Son (see Matthew 10:40).

The underlying Greek text translated as *right* (compare Hebrews 13:10; Revelation 22:14) can also be translated as "power" (see John 19:10-11). God gives the power (see commentary on John 1:13, below) for believers to claim the right to a new identity.

This new identity that believers claim is that of sons and daughters—the *children of God*. As people accept Jesus, believe in him, and follow his teachings, they experience new birth into the family of God (see John 3:3-8; 20:31).

13. children born not of natural descent, nor of human decision or a husband's will, but born of God.

The new family identity happens by virtue of birth, but not a physical birth. John uses three negative phrases to stress that being *born* as *children* of God cannot be attained through physical procreative acts (compare John 3:3-7). No physical reality—a person's *descent*, the human desires, or human *will*—can result in this new birth. Only through faith in "the word of truth" can a person be *born* into the family *of God* (James 1:18).

IV. The Only Son
(JOHN 1:14)

A. Dwelt with Humanity (v. 14a-b)
14a. The Word became flesh

John previously stated that *the Word*—the true light—had come into the world (John 1:9, above). The nature of that coming into the world is now

evident. The Word took on human *flesh*. This identifies the eternal, preexistent Word as the Son of God—Jesus Christ. Eternal life comes by salvation through Jesus Christ, the Son of God (11:25; 17:3).

In the scope of John's New Testament writings, the concept of flesh can refer to fallen human nature in contrast to the ways of God's Spirit (see John 6:63; 1 John 2:16). However, it can also refer to a physical human body (examples: John 3:6; Revelation 19:18, 21). John's usage in this instance regarding the Word refers to the latter. In ways mysterious yet glorious, the Word of God *became* human and entered his creation (see 1 John 4:2).

This reality is the central component of the Incarnation, a doctrine that describes the Word of God becoming a human man in Jesus Christ. The details of the Incarnation are a paradox: the Word of God humbled himself to live among his creation (Philippians 2:6-8). This occurred as God sent his Son, born of a virgin (Galatians 4:4), conceived by God's Spirit (Matthew 1:20). The *how* of the Incarnation is a mystery to the human mind. Despite this mystery, the result of the Incarnation is clear: salvation for humanity through God's incarnate Son.

14b. and made his dwelling among us.

In the Incarnation, the Word of God did more than just come to earth. In Jesus Christ, the Word *made his dwelling* within creation. By describing the incarnate Word in this manner, John alludes to God's presence—his dwelling place—in the tabernacle in the camp of ancient Israel (see Exodus 40:34-38; Ezekiel 37:27).

The same God who made his presence known in a particular way to ancient Israel has revealed his presence through Jesus Christ. God took up residence in the midst of his creation by taking on the same flesh and blood as humanity (Hebrews 2:14). As a result of this intimacy of relationship, God will be a Father, and his people will be his children.

B. Glorified by the Father (v. 14c)
14c. We have seen his glory, the glory of the one and only Son, who came from the Father, full of grace and truth.

John includes himself as among *we* who *have seen* the *glory* of the incarnate Word of God. John had seen firsthand the person and work of Jesus Christ (1 John 1:1-4). He had also been among the closest of Jesus' disciples who saw his glory firsthand (see Matthew 17:1-8; Mark 9:2-13; Luke 9:28-36).

In addition to providing proof of Jesus' divine nature, *the glory* observed by John could only be ascribed to God *the Father*. The incarnate *Son* was able to receive (and show) this because he was the unique and *only* Son of God (see John 1:18; 3:16, 28; 1 John 4:9). There is no other like Jesus!

As the unique and only Son of God, Jesus demonstrated the attributes of his Father for the world (see John 1:16-17). Through the Incarnation, God's *grace* was made available to the world (Romans 3:21-24; Ephesians 2:7-8). Furthermore, Jesus embodied God's *truth* (John 14:6). Through the incarnate Word, God's truth has been revealed to all humanity (John 8:31-32; see Ephesians 2:15-17).

> *What Do You Think?*
> How might believers live in a way that reflects to other people the grace and truth of Jesus?
> *Digging Deeper*
> How do Ephesians 4:15 and 1 Peter 3:15-16 inform your answer in this regard?

⁂ DWELLING AMONG US ⁂

My graduate school professor and his family sensed God's call to begin a new ministry in Memphis, Tennessee. Unfortunately, they faced trials during the transition. For example, they could not find housing in the new city. Their ministry would not last if they could not find a dwelling place.

When they did eventually find housing, the family could not help but worship God. They asked God to use their home as a place of peace in their new neighborhood. The family wanted to share in the same experiences of the community they were called to serve. They desired to show God's love toward their neighbors. And they did.

The Son of God made the earth his temporary dwelling place; he moved into the neighborhood of humanity. He understands the human experience—even our weaknesses (see Hebrews 4:15)! As a result, humans have direct access to God

through the Son. How will you live differently in light of Jesus' having dwelt among us?   —R. O.

Conclusion

A. Embodied from the Start

So much of the work of ministering and leading a church requires in-person work. Meeting church members for fellowship, praying for them in the hospital, visiting families with newborns. These and other occurrences are commonplace in ministry and require physical presence. The central theme of the Christian faith required a similar kind of physical, embodied presence.

God extended his love and grace to humanity in an extraordinary way—the Word of God became flesh and dwelt within his creation. This act, beyond human comprehension, was an extraordinary gift of God's embodied presence. In response, people can accept his gift with humility, gratitude, and faith. As a result of this gift, there is a change of identity to becoming the children of God!

God's children are tasked with extending his love to others. In an increasingly "disembodied" human experience—demonstrated by the frequent use of smartphones and social media—God's children can intentionally chose to love others by their physical presence! How will you love others by your presence in the days to come?

> *What Do You Think?*
> How does this lesson provide a deeper understanding of the basis of your faith in Jesus?
> *Digging Deeper*
> Who can you tell in the coming weeks the ways the Word of God has changed your life?

B. Prayer

Heavenly Father, you demonstrated your love for us when you sent your Son to live among us and be our light. Help us be attentive to the light of your Son. Show us how we might reflect that light to our community. In Jesus' name. Amen.

C. Thought to Remember

God's salvation has dwelt among us.

INVOLVEMENT LEARNING

Enhance your lesson with NIV Bible Student *(from your curriculum supplier) and the reproducible activity page (at www.standardlesson.com or in the back of the* NIV Standard Lesson Commentary Deluxe Edition*).*

Into the Lesson

Ask a volunteer for the name of a familiar celebrity. Ask volunteers to share information they may know about the celebrity. After no more than 3 minutes, ask the class, "Suppose this celebrity invited you to lunch. What questions would you ask of them concerning their life?" Allow no more than 5 minutes for whole-class discussion.

Lead into Bible study by saying, "After that lunch, you will know the celebrity better than you did before. Today's lesson shows us the extent of God's self-disclosure to humanity."

Into the Word

Ask a volunteer to read aloud John 1:1-5. Divide the class into three groups with the following assignments to interpret this passage.

Filmmaker Group. Write the outline of a movie trailer using this Scripture passage as its narrative text. Include details for voice-overs, background music, and camera shots.

Broadcaster Group. Write a script for a radio retelling of this Scripture passage. Include details for the genre, the script, sound effects, and the local radio station where this would be played.

Graphic Designer Group. Write a four panel comic strip to depict the message of this Scripture passage. Include details for the dialogue, captions, sound effects, and the title of the comic strip.

Allow groups no more than 10 minutes to design their production. Allow each group to present their work to the whole class.

Alternative. Distribute copies of the "Word/ Creator/Light" exercise from the activity page, which you can download. Have learners complete it individually before discussing conclusions in small groups.

Ask a volunteer to read aloud John 1:6-8. Divide the class into three groups and distribute to each group handouts (you create) with the text of John 1:19-34. Have each group read Scrip-

ture text on the handout and discuss the following questions which you will write on the board.

Identity Group. 1–Who was John the Baptist? 2–What did he consider his purpose and work?

Mission Group. 1–How did John the Baptist live out his mission? 2–What did he consider to be the limitations of his mission?

Testimony Group. 1–How did Jesus' person and work fulfill the witness of John the Baptist? 2–How did his testimony differ from the testimony of Jesus?

Alternative. Divide the class into pairs and distribute copies of the "A Witness to the Light" activity from the activity page. Have learners work in pairs to complete as indicated. After calling time under either activity, have groups or pairs present their findings in whole class discussion.

Ask a volunteer to read aloud John 1:9-14. Ask class members to give answers in whole class discussion to the following questions, which you will write on the board: 1–Where do you have authority? 2–How, if at all, did you earn that authority? 3–How does that authority provide certain powers? 4–How do we receive the right to become God's children? 5–What does this right entail?

Into Life

Say, "John the Baptist was *not* the light for which people had been waiting and searching. But he gave witness to the incarnate light of God: Jesus."

Divide the class into pairs and have them answer the following questions which you will write on the board: 1–If John the Baptist lived in our cultural context, how might his mission look different? 2–How can you continue the mission of John the Baptist in your specific context? 3–What challenges might arise to prevent you from continuing that mission and how will you address those challenges?

Close class by asking each pair to pray that they might continue the mission of John the Baptist and bear witness to the incarnate Word of God.

THE WORD HEALS

DEVOTIONAL READING: John 4:46-54
BACKGROUND SCRIPTURE: John 4:46-54

JOHN 4:46-54

⁴⁶ Once more he visited Cana in Galilee, where he had turned the water into wine. And there was a certain royal official whose son lay sick at Capernaum. ⁴⁷ When this man heard that Jesus had arrived in Galilee from Judea, he went to him and begged him to come and heal his son, who was close to death.

⁴⁸ "Unless you people see signs and wonders," Jesus told him, "you will never believe."

⁴⁹ The royal official said, "Sir, come down before my child dies."

⁵⁰ "Go," Jesus replied, "your son will live."

The man took Jesus at his word and departed. ⁵¹ While he was still on the way, his servants met him with the news that his boy was living. ⁵² When he inquired as to the time when his son got better, they said to him, "Yesterday, at one in the afternoon, the fever left him."

⁵³ Then the father realized that this was the exact time at which Jesus had said to him, "Your son will live." So he and his whole household believed.

⁵⁴ This was the second sign Jesus performed after coming from Judea to Galilee.

KEY VERSE

The father realized that this was the exact time at which Jesus had said to him, "Your son will live." So he and his whole household believed. —**John 4:53**

PARTNERS IN A NEW CREATION

Unit 2: The Word: The Agent of Creation

LESSONS 5–9

LESSON AIMS

After participating in this lesson, each learner will be able to:

1. Summarize the account of the healing.

2. Compare and contrast the concepts of faith and belief.

3. Suggest an appropriate action that follows right belief in Jesus.

LESSON OUTLINE

Introduction
  A. Epidemics and Pandemics
  B. Lesson Context
I. Request of a Father (John 4:46-50a)
  A. Certain Official (v. 46)
  B. Confident Interaction (vv. 47-50a)
    Signs of the Times
II. Responses of Faith (John 4:50b-54)
  A. Trusting Departure (vv. 50b-52)
  B. Resulting Belief (v. 53)
    Perfect Timing
  C. Documented Miracle (v. 54)
Conclusion
  A. True Healing
  B. Prayer
  C. Thought to Remember

Introduction

A. Epidemics and Pandemics

Epidemics and pandemics are often associated with centuries past. Generally, a disease is considered an epidemic if the disease rapidly affects a large group of people in a specific region. An epidemic becomes a pandemic when the disease rapidly spreads across many countries and regions. The Black Death (bubonic plague) of the fourteenth century is a prime example of a pandemic.

Because of medical advances, sanitation, and a forgetting of history, we might assume that the age of epidemics and pandemics is over. However, the events of recent history tell a different story.

Since the end of the nineteenth century, the world has faced numerous health crises. Epidemics and pandemics are still a harsh reality. For example, a cholera pandemic originated in India and spread throughout the global west in the first years of the twentieth century. To this day, cholera epidemics continue throughout parts of Asia, Africa, and the Middle East.

Even the first decades of the twenty-first century have seen multiple outbreaks of illness. Severe Acute Respiratory Syndrome (SARS), HIV/AIDS, H1N1 influenza ("Swine Flu"), Middle East Respiratory Syndrome (MERS), Ebola, Zika fever, and COVID-19 are among notable outbreaks of illness since the year 2000. These illnesses serve as harsh reminders for the prevalence of sickness and, ultimately, death. Despite wondrous medical advances, sickness and ailments still fill the world.

The complete healing of all physical maladies will not be achieved on earth—no matter the extent of modern medicine. In today's Scripture text, Jesus provides a sign to something greater than physical healing.

B. Lesson Context

John's Gospel can be divided into four major movements: an introduction (John 1:1-51, see lesson 5), Jesus' earthly ministry (2:1–11:57), the events of Passion Week (12:1–20:31), and an afterword (21:1-25). Today's Scripture text comes from the second movement.

This movement tells of Jesus' earthly ministry through seven miraculous works (John 2:1-11; 4:43-54; 5:1-15; 6:1-15; 6:16-24; 9:1-41; 11:1-57) and seven teaching discourses (see 2:12–3:36; 4:1-42; 5:16-47; 6:25-71; 7:1–8:59; 10:1-21; 10:22-42). Presented together, these moments flesh out the nature of Jesus' ministry and provide evidence "that this is God's Chosen One" (1:34).

This lesson's Scripture text comes as Jesus returns to Galilee, the region of his first public miracle at Cana (see John 2:1-11). Following that miracle, Jesus traveled to Jerusalem in Judea for the Passover (2:13). While in Jerusalem, Jesus corrected unholy occurrences at the temple area (see 2:14-24) and addressed a religious leader (see 3:1-21).

The text does not give insight for how long Jesus stayed in Judea. Realizing the Pharisees were noticing his popularity, Jesus returned to Galilee via Samaria (John 4:1-4). After a two-day stop in Samaria (4:43), Jesus arrived in Galilee. The miracle worker of Galilee had returned!

The way John presents Jesus' teachings and miraculous works highlights their continuity and gives evidence that Jesus is more than a Galilean miracle worker. Jesus quenched the thirst of the wedding party in Cana (John 2:7-10), then taught a Samaritan woman how to quench her spiritual thirst (4:10-15). Similarly, Jesus taught how he could provide eternal life and backed up that claim by restoring physical life to a young child (4:43-54). John's inclusion of Jesus' teachings reveals that Jesus is more than a miracle worker. Jesus is the Son of God, who brings eternal life (3:14-15) and living water (4:13-14).

John's Gospel places a high emphasis on Jesus' miraculous works. These works serve as signs of Jesus' identity as the Son of God (John 20:30-31). Despite these miraculous signs, John's Gospel acknowledges that many people would not accept or listen to Jesus (examples: 1:11; 2:18).

I. Request of a Father
(JOHN 4:46-50a)
A. Certain Official (v. 46)

46a. Once more he visited Cana in Galilee, where he had turned the water into wine.

His journey from Judea was completed when Jesus *visited* his final destination: *Galilee*. This was a region north of Samaria and Judah. The central geographic feature of the region is the Sea of Galilee. This so-called sea (in actuality, a lake) is the source for the Jordan River. Further, it was the backdrop and the site for many of Jesus' miracles (see Matthew 15:29-39; Luke 8:22-25; John 6:16-21). The town of *Cana* was located in the mountains west of the Sea of Galilee. Jesus' disciple Nathanael came from this community (John 21:2).

John's inclusion in his Gospel account of this Galilean community was not by chance—Jesus' adult public ministry was inaugurated in Cana. While attending a wedding banquet, Jesus miraculously *turned* jars of *water into wine* after the banquet ran dry (John 2:1-12). John referred to this event as the "first of the signs" (2:11), the first of many miracles to come from Jesus (see Lesson Context).

46b. And there was a certain royal official whose son lay sick at Capernaum.

This *royal official* likely worked in service to the regional ruler to this area: Herod Antipas. Herod was the tetrarch (that is, administrator) of Galilee (Luke 3:1). This *certain* official could have served Herod through a variety of administrative, political, or military contexts. Further, the official could have been Jew or Gentile. Other healing accounts in the Gospels provide clear details of all characters involved (see 7:1-2). However, John's account of this healing narrative does not give the same level of detail.

The only other identifying marker of the official is that his ailing *son* was not in Cana with his father. Instead, the *sick* son was in *Capernaum*, another Galilean town. Capernaum sat on the

HOW TO SAY IT

Cana	*Kay*-nuh.
Capernaum	Kuh-*per*-nay-um.
Galilee	*Gal*-uh-lee.
Galileans	Gal-uh-*lee*-unz.
Herod Antipas	*Hair*-ud *An*-tih-pus.
Judea	Joo-*dee*-uh.
Nazareth	*Naz*-uh-reth.

northwestern shore of the Sea of Galilee, about 16 miles directly northeast of Cana. The town served as Jesus' base of operations (see Mark 1:21; Luke 4:31; John 6:59).

B. Confident Interaction (vv. 47-50a)

47. When this man heard that Jesus had arrived in Galilee from Judea, he went to him and begged him to come and heal his son, who was close to death.

News likely had reached the official concerning Jesus' interactions in *Judea* and his claims of divine authority and power (see John 2:14-21). Hearing of Jesus' claims (and perhaps having a recollection of his miraculous act at the wedding banquet), the official apparently saw no other option than to plead to Jesus for healing on behalf of his ailing *son*. Since *Jesus* had returned to *Galilee*, the time had come for the official to act. The official *went* from Capernaum to Cana to find Jesus.

John's narrative does not provide further detail on the nature of the boy's sickness. Whatever it was, it had advanced to where the boy's life was at stake; he *was close to death*. Some level of medical knowledge existed in the first century, and physicians worked to heal people of their afflictions (see Matthew 9:12; Colossians 4:14). However, many people still lived with incurable ailments (see John 5:5). As Jesus' earthly ministry grew in notoriety, he frequently was approached by people desperate for physical healing. These people had sought the help of a physician, but were unable to find workable remedies and healing (see Mark 5:26).

> *What Do You Think?*
> How often should believers turn to God in prayer regarding physical healing?
> *Digging Deeper*
> How do our prayers, whether concerning small or large requests, give honor to God?

48. "Unless you people see signs and wonders," Jesus told him, "you will never believe."

Jesus responded to the official's request for healing in an unexpected manner. Instead of addressing the sick child, Jesus questioned the spiritual status of the official's countrymen. They were *you people* who required miraculous acts from Jesus. The underlying Greek text indicates that Jesus' declaration was directed to a collective group. The official came seeking help, but Jesus responded to his request with particular criticism.

Many of Jesus' own countrymen demanded that he produce *signs and wonders* to justify the validity of his actions and teachings (see John 2:18; 6:30). Through these signs, some people came to *believe* in and follow him (see 2:11, 23). The desire for evidence and tangible signs is understandable, especially regarding the claims of Jesus (see 1 Corinthians 1:22). The ultimate goal of these signs was belief in the Messiah and the life that he provides (see John 20:31).

However, not all people accepted Jesus' miracles. This reflected their stubbornness and the hardness of their hearts. Time and time again Jesus' claims were backed by his actions—a sign of who he is. Despite this reality, many people refused to listen to Jesus (see John 12:37).

Jesus used this interaction with the official to critique the lack of faith of the Galileans. Rather than receive the gift of Jesus, they demanded signs. It would be easy to read Jesus' words as an angry indictment toward his countrymen. However, it's possible that Jesus spoke this as a lament regarding their spiritual blindness. Jesus came to his own people, yet they did not receive him (see John 1:11). Not only was Jesus frustrated, but he was also grieved by their lack of faith. Perhaps this official would change the tide and provide an example for how a person might properly believe.

While Jesus knows each person's heart (John 2:25), the official's level of faith at this point is unknown. Did his heart question Jesus' claims, or was he like the apostle Thomas, who desired tangible evidence for authentic faith (see 20:25)?

> *What Do You Think?*
> How can believers faithfully follow Jesus even when they do not immediately observe evidence of God's work?
> *Digging Deeper*
> How do 2 Corinthians 4:16-18 and Hebrews 11:13 affect your response in this regard?

While driving through a small town in Ohio, I noticed a street sign that read, "Tom, Dick & Harry Road." The sign commemorated an infamous local trio. Because of the sign's novelty or originality, I imagine many people try to steal the sign as a keepsake!

In my travels, I've seen other amusing, eye-catching signs. A local tire store advertised "Free Air." (I thought air was always free!) A souvenir shop in Turkey proudly sells "Authentic Fake Watches." A chain of mortuaries in upstate New York is named "Amigone Funeral Home." A sign on a flower shop in Ohio bears the name of its owners: "Swindler & Sons." (You'd better count your change!)

Jesus' miraculous acts were not meant for the amusement and amazement of the gathered crowds. Instead, these acts serve as signs and guideposts to God's eternal truth in Christ Jesus. The miraculous signs presented in the Gospel accounts confirm Jesus' identity as the Messiah. Have you opened your eyes and softened your heart to see Jesus' work in your life (see John 12:37-40)?   —D. F.

49. The royal official said, "Sir, come down before my child dies."

The royal official begged Jesus to see the urgency of the situation. Here was a father dealing with the worst tragedy a parent could experience: his son was about to die. The official had no sharp retort to Jesus' previous declaration on the nature of signs, wonders, and belief. Instead, the man wanted healing for his son. (Compare and contrast the request of Jairus for his daughter in Mark 5:23.)

Stories from ancient Israel describe how God's prophets healed children or raised them from the dead (see 1 Kings 17:17-24; 2 Kings 4:32-37). In these cases, the prophet would visit the ailing child and be in their presence before healing. Perhaps the official thought Jesus' physical presence was a prerequisite for healing. If Jesus would *come down* to his house, then he thought that his *child* would live.

50a. "Go," Jesus replied, "your son will live."

Instead of accompanying the official to Capernaum, *Jesus* told him to *go* on his way home and return to the child. Unlike ancient Israel's prophets, Jesus is the Son of God and one with God the Father (John 1:18; Hebrews 3:5-6). He has the power of life in himself (John 1:3-4). Therefore, he merely had to speak the word and the official's *son* would *live* (compare Matthew 8:13).

> **What Do You Think?**
>   How should believers respond when God's timing does not align with their expectations?
> **Digging Deeper**
>   How do Ecclesiastes 3:1-22; Isaiah 40:27-31; and 2 Peter 3:8-9 inform your answer in this regard?

II. Responses of Faith
(JOHN 4:50b-54)

A. Trusting Departure (vv. 50b-52)

50b. The man took Jesus at his word and departed.

The official took *Jesus at his word* and believed in its validity. Because of his belief and trust, the official *departed* and returned to Capernaum. This moment provides a critical contrast in John's Gospel. Whereas the crowds looked for a sign in order to believe Jesus (see John 4:48), this official trusted Jesus without seeing the results of Jesus' word. He showed genuine faith in Jesus without the confirmation of an immediate sign.

In this sense, the official fulfilled Jesus' proclamation: "Blessed are those who have not seen and yet have believed" (John 20:29). By believing the word of Jesus, the official's response provided an example for the kind of faith necessary for disciples of Jesus.

51. While he was still on the way, his servants met him with the news that his boy was living.

The official's journey *on the way* from Cana to his home in Capernaum would have been a literal walk downhill. Capernaum is located on the Sea of Galilee and, therefore, at a lower elevation than Cana.

Since most people traveled on foot, even a trip

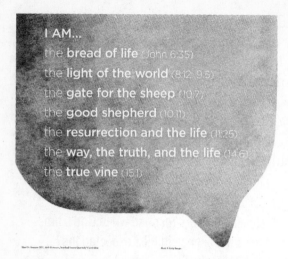

I AM...

the **bread of life** (John 6:35)

the **light of the world** (8:12; 9:5)

the **gate for the sheep** (10:7)

the **good shepherd** (10:11)

the **resurrection and the life** (11:25)

the **way, the truth, and the life** (14:6)

the **true vine** (15:1)

Visual for Lesson 6. *Show this chart as you ask students how Jesus fulfills one of these claims through the events of this week's Scripture text.*

between the Galilean villages could take several hours or most of the day. We can only imagine that this man's emotional and physical states were likely pushed to the breaking point. Like any father, his only concern was to see his son healthy. He surely went to great lengths in order to see and plead with Jesus. As *he* rushed home to see his son, he likely pushed himself to the limit as well.

Before the man reached home, he heard the good news. His *servants* were so amazed at the dramatic change in the *boy* that they *met* the official on his way home. Likely, the servants had known the reason for and destination of the man's journey. Therefore, they could anticipate the direction and route by which he would return. Knowing the extent of the father's anxiety, the servants wanted to bring him relief and peace as they declared that the son *was living*. Despair had changed to relief, and grief had turned to rejoicing!

52. When he inquired as to the time when his son got better, they said to him, "Yesterday, at one in the afternoon, the fever left him."

Until this point in the narrative, John has not provided a critical detail—the exact time at which Jesus declared "your *son* will live" (John 4:50, above). Therefore, at this point readers of the Gospel are left to conclude that the man's interaction with Jesus was held on the previous afternoon at 1:00 p.m. (*yesterday*). At the point at which Jesus declared it, the child experienced healing from his illness—his *fever left him*. Jesus' power in healing

did not require him to be physically present with the ailing child.

B. Resulting Belief (v. 53)

53a. Then the father realized that this was the exact time at which Jesus had said to him, "Your son will live."

The text confirms what the previous verse anticipated but never explicitly stated. Jesus' declaration of healing—*your son will live*—and its fulfillment occurred at *the exact* same *time*. This *father* had demonstrated faith that *Jesus* would heal his son. As a result of his faith, the man rejoined his healthy son. But even as the father celebrated the healing, something greater had been occurring for the man and his household.

53b. So he and his whole household believed.

The official had already shown faith concerning Jesus' healing word. His expression of faith, as a result, affected others in his household beyond his son. Upon seeing the fulfillment of Jesus' word, the official, his family, and all people in *his whole household* demonstrated belief in Jesus. The text does not include the object of their belief, but we can assume they believed in the messianic claims of Jesus. Like the Samaritan woman, they *believed* that "this man really is the Savior of the world" (John 4:42).

The official's whole house likely included any immediate and extended family members and any servants in the household. Accounts of the growth of the church in the years immediately following Jesus' ascension describe how whole households would express belief in Christ (see Acts 11:14; 16:15, 31; 18:8). The official and his family believed in Jesus upon seeing the ways he changed their lives.

❧ PERFECT TIMING ❧

The timing of a joke will make or break a comedian's routine. If the comedian rushes to the punch line or pauses in the middle of the joke's setup, the joke may be ruined.

Issues of timing aren't just related to comedic performances. Professional athletes require exact timing for peak performance. (Next time you watch an American football game, observe the timing required for a placekick!) Without perfect timing, photographers will snap unbecoming and awkward photos. I'm sure you know the importance of perfect timing in your daily activities!

Even when Jesus' timing is different from ours, his is always perfect! Following Jesus' timing might prove challenging. He may act when you least expect! Are you willing to adapt your ways to Jesus' timing? What obstacles stand in the way of your following his perfect timing?
—D. F.

C. Documented Miracle (v. 54)

54. This was the second sign Jesus performed after coming from Judea to Galilee.

John casts this, *the second sign,* against the backdrop of Jesus' previous miracle in Cana (see John 2:11). In so doing, John does not include in the miracle count those performed in Judea (2:23). The early travel narrative of John's Gospel came full circle. Jesus had traveled to Jerusalem in *Judea* (2:13) and, shortly after, had decided to return to his homeland in *Galilee* (4:3, see Lesson Context). Although this was only the second miracle done in Galilee, the Galileans had seen other miracles while in Jerusalem for Passover (2:23; 4:45).

Older translations of the Bible translate the underlying Greek text, here translated "sign" (compare John 2:18; 4:48; 6:30), as "miracle."

In John's Gospel, Jesus' miracles served as signs so that people "may believe that Jesus is the Messiah, the Son of God" (20:31). Jesus used miracles and signs to reveal his glory (see 6:2; 7:31; 9:16; 11:47). Jesus was not interested primarily in providing physical life; he came to bring spiritual, eternal life to all who would believe.

What Do You Think?
How might periods of lament and celebration each provide opportunities to glorify God?
Digging Deeper
Who will you recruit to encourage your walk with God during times of lament?

Conclusion
A. True Healing

Beyond the detail of the son's fever (John 4:52), we are left wondering about the son's ailment. Perhaps it was a respiratory illness similar to the modern outbreaks of MERS or SARS. Whatever the ailment, it was not more than Jesus could handle —even from a distance!

In addition to leading to humanity's belief (see John 20:30-31), Jesus' repeated acts of healing show us God's concern for humanity's ailments. Human suffering is unavoidable—just watch the nightly news! Only God has the power to heal every illness, hurt, and pain.

Ultimately, Jesus' physical healings testify to God's ultimate healing project—the spiritual healing of all who believe. As Jesus' disciples today, we set our eyes on this ultimate healing that is available only through faith in the Son of God. True disciples live for the promise of Jesus that he will someday raise believers from the dead and give them eternal life. Only by faith can people become disciples of Jesus and experience the complete and final healing he brings. Even when Jesus *feels* far away, does your life reflect your belief that he's never too far way to provide healing—in this life or in the life to come?

What Do You Think?
In what ways has God worked in your life to lead you to saving belief in Jesus Christ?
Digging Deeper
How might you be used by God to help lead others to saving belief in Jesus Christ?

B. Prayer

Heavenly Father, we pray for our family, friends, and neighbors who need your healing. May your acts of physical healing serve as a testimony to your ultimate and final healing. Fill us with faith so that we might believe, even when we can't always see your work. In Jesus' name. Amen.

C. Thought to Remember

Our God can heal—in every way!

INVOLVEMENT LEARNING

Enhance your lesson with NIV Bible Student (from your curriculum supplier) and the reproducible activity page (at www.standardlesson.com or in the back of the NIV Standard Lesson Commentary Deluxe Edition).

Into the Lesson

Before class begins, write the following prompts on the board:

- The farthest I traveled to see a doctor.
- The farthest I traveled to see a sports team.
- The farthest I traveled to see a performance or concert.
- The farthest I traveled on a vacation.

As class begins, point class members to the written prompts. Give them one minute to decide on which of the prompts suggests a story they'd be willing to share. Divide the class into four groups and have each group member share with their group a story based on one of the prompts.

After 5 minutes of discussion, reconvene the class. Ask which class member reported the farthest trip. Have them speak briefly regarding their travel and the reasons for their travels.

Lead into Bible study by saying, "At one time or another, many of us have traveled—out of necessity or for pleasure. Today we'll learn about a man who traveled to see Jesus because only Jesus could provide what the man's family needed."

Into the Word

Divide the class into groups of three. To each group member, assign one of the following people from this lesson's Scripture text: **Jesus, the royal official, a servant of the royal official**. Ask a volunteer to read aloud John 4:46-54 while group members focus on the statements and reactions of their assigned role in the story.

Distribute a handout (you create) to each group member with the following headings across the top: **Thoughts, Actions**. Down the left side of the handout, list every verse in today's Scripture. Ask each triad to complete the chart for their assigned person. Where the Scripture text does not specify, class members should imagine how their character might think or act based on scriptural context.

After 10 minutes, reconvene the class. Read aloud each verse from today's Scripture text, pausing after each verse. Ask volunteers to share what they wrote under each verse. Allow time for class members to discuss the statements of others.

Option. Distribute copies of "Significant Miracles" exercise from the activity page, which you can download. Have learners work in pairs to complete as indicated. After 10 minutes, ask volunteers to share their findings.

Into Life

Write "What do we believe about God, Jesus, the Bible, and Christianity?" on the board. Ask class members to respond to this prompt through whole class discussion. Don't edit or correct the responses—write down the responses on the board as they are stated. After three minutes, ask the class which of the statements are most important for faith. Draw a circle around those statements.

Divide the class into four groups. Ask the groups to discuss the following questions (which you will write out on a handout): 1–What are the sources and standards to inform right belief? 2–What is the connection between right *belief* and right *action*? 3–How should believers act in response to the circled statements?

After 5 minutes, ask class members to reconvene and discuss their answers in whole class discussion. Point to circled statements on the board and have a volunteer from each group read the suggested action step regarding that belief.

End class by saying, "Today's lesson shows us that right belief and right action are connected. Let's pray that we will be a people marked by belief and resulting right action."

Option. Distribute copies of the "Seeking God's Power" activity from the activity page. Have learners work in pairs to complete the activity as indicated.

THE WORD SAVES

DEVOTIONAL READING: John 12:44-50
BACKGROUND SCRIPTURE: John 12:27-50

JOHN 12:44-50

⁴⁴ Then Jesus cried out, "Whoever believes in me does not believe in me only, but in the one who sent me. ⁴⁵ The one who looks at me is seeing the one who sent me. ⁴⁶ I have come into the world as a light, so that no one who believes in me should stay in darkness.

⁴⁷ "If anyone hears my words but does not keep them, I do not judge that person. For I did not come to judge the world, but to save the world. ⁴⁸ There is a judge for the one who rejects me and does not accept my words; the very words I have spoken will condemn them at the last day. ⁴⁹ For I did not speak on my own, but the Father who sent me commanded me to say all that I have spoken. ⁵⁰ I know that his command leads to eternal life. So whatever I say is just what the Father has told me to say."

KEY VERSE

I have come into the world as a light, so that no one who believes in me should stay in darkness.
—**John 12:46**

Photo © Getty Images

PARTNERS IN A NEW CREATION

Unit 2: The Word: The Agent of Creation

LESSONS 5–9

LESSON AIMS

After participating in this lesson, each learner will be able to:

1. Summarize the relationship between the Son and the Father as Jesus explained it.

2. Explain the interrelationship between salvation and divine judgment, as far as Jesus presented it.

3. Recruit an accountability partner for greater action on the commands of Jesus.

LESSON OUTLINE

Introduction

A. Standing Before the Judge

I walked into the police station so they could take my fingerprints. The process was intimidating, but necessary for the legal proceedings. Police officers on duty asked for all my personal information, shot several photographs of me, and took detailed prints of my fingers.

My interactions with the law continued over the next year. I was required to attend court hearings where I would stand before a judge and plead the particulars of my case. Some courtrooms were larger than others; but in each one, crowds of people heard me and heard the details of my case. Each hearing was a nerve-racking ordeal.

My family was active in each appearance, and I hoped that someday we would all be united. Lest you misunderstand, I wasn't accused of any crime. My wife and I were going through the tedious process of adopting a child born in a different country.

Throughout the whole process, we followed the guidance of the family court judges and our lawyers. Even if we didn't understand the *why* behind something (like getting our fingerprints), we followed through because we wanted our family to be united. Ultimately our patience and resolve paid off! Our growing family now includes a new child.

The whole experience served as a reminder to the importance of belief and faith. We had to believe the adoption process would be resolved so long as we faithfully followed the directives of the authorities. If we disregarded their directives, the entire process might end abruptly without the completion. Jesus had strong words regarding belief and faithfulness. His words have eternal consequences, more serious than from any judge or lawyer.

B. Lesson Context

After a notable introduction (John 1:1-50, see lesson 5), John's Gospel focuses on the bulk of Jesus' public ministry: his miraculous works and teaching (2:1–11:57, see lesson 6). In this section of the Gospel, John recorded seven accounts of

Jesus' miraculous acts and seven accounts of Jesus' teachings. Together they highlight the way Jesus showed his mission to the world, a mission given by his heavenly Father.

But throughout this section of the Gospel, Jesus' audiences were unable and unwilling to accept his teachings. They saw his miracles and enthusiastically received him. However, far too often they failed to rightly understand his teaching (see John 6:14-15, 42, 52). Jesus did not fulfill the hopes and wishes they desired from a savior or messiah. As a result, many stopped following Jesus (6:60-66). Despite seeing and hearing Jesus, belief was not always present.

Today's Scripture text marks a transition to a third section of the Gospel. This section tells of the events surrounding Jesus' death and resurrection (John 12:1–20:31). Given that half of John's Gospel is dedicated to the events of Jesus' final week, there can be no doubt of John's focus. A Savior who does miraculous acts and provides eternal teaching is nothing without the events of the Passion Week.

This lesson's Scripture text serves as Jesus' final public discourse to his generally unbelieving audience. Immediately prior to this text, John provides some editorial context surrounding the teaching. John cites the words of the ancient prophet Isaiah in order to frame the situation Jesus faced (John 12:37-38; see Isaiah 53:1). Even as Jesus performed many miraculous acts, there were people who failed to believe and follow him.

This reality was highlighted in the nature of Jesus' coming into Jerusalem. Many people celebrated his entry (John 12:12-19), but there would be other people who would call for his crucifixion several days later (19:1-6). As a result of their unbelief, many people would experience certain consequences and judgment (12:40; see Isaiah 6:10).

I. On Belief
(JOHN 12:44-46)
A. Seeing (vv. 44-45)
44. Then Jesus cried out, "Whoever believes in me does not believe in me only, but in the one who sent me.

Having gone into hiding (see John 12:36), *Jesus* reappeared and *cried out*. Perhaps his urgent statement was directed to the "many even among the leaders [who] believed in him" (12:42).

John's Gospel details two other instances when Jesus cried out in exhortation (John 7:28, 37). With this language, John evokes an image of a town herald declaring the latest news of the kingdom and the intentions of the king (compare Daniel 3:4; Habakkuk 2:2). In a sense, today's Scripture marks the final exhortation for an unbelieving audience. For this audience, Jesus spoke out—as with the proclamation of a herald—on the importance of proper belief.

Further, by describing Jesus' declaration in this manner, John may have been drawing from ancient wisdom texts as a framework to describe Jesus' proclamation. The book of Proverbs describes Wisdom, embodied as a woman, crying out to any person who might hear her words (see Proverbs 1:20-21).

The message that Jesus brings is greater than the message of Wisdom as described in Proverbs. John reminds his audience that Jesus has brought the greatest news of human history. Jesus cries out, yet few people listen or understand (see John 12:40).

The concepts of belief and resulting action from belief serve as Jesus' main point. If a person *believes in* him, then that person also believes in God the Father. This statement equates Jesus with God the Father. To believe in Jesus means to *believe* in *the one who sent* Jesus: God the Father (John 14:1, 6-7). As a result of proper belief, a person would experience life change.

To be sent by God speaks of Jesus' authority, power, and honor (John 5:23). Jesus' words are the same words as of the Father. Therefore, Jesus' words carry the authority of the Father (7:16; 8:28). Since God sent Jesus, the world must listen to Jesus. His teachings point to the life in God because "whoever continues in the teaching has both the Father and the Son" (2 John 9).

The concept of belief is a central theme of John's Gospel. John wrote so that people would believe that Jesus is the Son of God and, thereby, receive life (John 20:31). One cannot reject Jesus' teachings but claim to follow God. If a person rejects Jesus, they also reject God (compare 14:24).

45. "The one who looks at me is seeing the one who sent me.

The Old Testament describes Moses' unique relationship with God. The Lord God "knew" Moses as if they were "face to face" (Deuteronomy 34:10). However, Moses could not see God directly (Exodus 33:20). God permitted Moses to see only part of him (33:23). Despite Moses' unique relationship with God, no person would dare claim that to see the face of Moses was the same as seeing God himself.

However, in Jesus, God had come and was present among humanity. The glory of the Son was the same glory as of the Father (John 1:14). When a person looked at Jesus, they were also seeing God—*the one who sent* Jesus to earth (see 14:9). But mere physical vision is not enough; a person must believe. Seeing *and* believing in the Son of God must occur for the future resurrection and eternal life (see 6:40)!

> **What Do You Think?**
> What things prevent people from seeing God and his work in the world?
>
> **Digging Deeper**
> How might Jesus' teaching found in Matthew 5:3-14 inform believers on the ways they can show God to the world?

B. Abiding (v. 46)

46. "I have come into the world as a light, so that no one who believes in me should stay in darkness.

For people to see clearly and know the direction they are headed, they must have light. Jesus declares himself to be the one who will cast spiritual *light* for *the world*. The totality of his person and work has been to provide spiritual light to each person *who believes in* him. As a result, the spiritual lives of his followers are illuminated. Following the will of God is doable as the light of Jesus shines on his disciples.

The binary of light and darkness is a dominant theme in the writings of the apostle John. He describes the Son of God as being the Word of God that gives witness to God's light (see lesson 5 on John 1:7-9). Additionally, Jesus refers to himself as the light of the world (8:12; 9:5; 12:35-36, 46). Jesus bears God's light and is light in himself. John desired that his audience believe in the light and live in a manner that reflects this spiritual light (see 1 John 1:5-9).

The spiritual light of Jesus exposes the dark ways of the world. Further, spiritual darkness is unable to overcome this spiritual light (John 1:5). People who *stay in darkness* and embrace the evil of the world are unable to believe in Jesus (see 3:19; 1 John 2:9-11). Only Jesus can provide the light of spiritual life for people to see their dark ways (John 8:12).

Jesus has the power to give light to all people who wish to see clearly. This includes physical and spiritual vision (see John 9:1-41). While some people wander in spiritual darkness, people who believe in Jesus and his words receive spiritual light. As a result, their lives are illuminated by Jesus' teachings, and they align with God's intentions for the world. When disciples experience the spiritual light of Jesus' teaching, they can guide others to glorify the Father (see Matthew 5:16).

The process of growing as a disciple of Jesus, known as discipleship, is predicated on remaining in and keeping Jesus' teaching (John 8:31). When disciples follow him and his teachings, they show their love for him (14:23-24).

Further, Jesus' words bring spiritual renewal and cleansing (John 15:3). Ultimately, discipleship in the way of Jesus leads to eternal life (8:51). This hope finds its basis on the words of Jesus, words that bring life (6:68)! Discipleship and the words of Jesus go hand in hand (14:15). Disciples follow the way of their heavenly master!

> **What Do You Think?**
> What approaches to evangelism have you found to be most effective for calling people from spiritual darkness into the light of Jesus Christ?
>
> **Digging Deeper**
> Who will you next invite to accept the light that only Jesus Christ can bring?

Flip a light switch in your kitchen, and the overhead light will come on automatically. Open your refrigerator door, and its light will illuminate the contents therein. Step outside during a midsummer afternoon, and the summer sunlight will beat down on your skin. The presence of light is so commonplace that we take it for granted in our daily lives.

Light's illuminating nature grows more powerful when many smaller lights are combined. On a clear summer night at my childhood home, the glow of the nearby large city—located 50 miles away—was evident on the horizon. The many lights of the city combined to cast an ethereal glow in the sky surrounding my home.

Scripture uses the concept of light as a metaphor for the ways of God. The Word of God is described as a light that illuminates the psalmist's spiritual walk (Psalm 119:105). God's people are described as being like light, serving as a beacon for a spiritually dark world (see Matthew 5:14-16; 1 Thessalonians 5:5). Even God and his salvation serve as light for the world (see Psalm 27:1; John 1:4; 1 John 1:5). How are you letting the light of God shine forth to your family, friends, and neighbors?   —D. F.

II. On Judgment
(John 12:47-50)
A. Timing (vv. 47-48)

47. "If anyone hears my words but does not keep them, I do not judge that person. For I did not come to judge the world, but to save the world.

Early in Jesus' adult ministry, he interacted with Nicodemus the Pharisee. Nicodemus was confused regarding the nature of Jesus' ministry. Nicodemus could only suppose that Jesus was merely a teacher from God (John 3:2).

However, Jesus was more than a mere teacher. In fact, Jesus declared his purpose on earth as God's Son. He came not to "condemn the world" but to provide salvation for the world (John 3:17-18). In this sense, Jesus' task while on earth was to declare the *words* of his heavenly Father so that all people might hear him, believe in him, and have everlasting life (3:16).

Further, Jesus made clear that in this moment he would not *judge* a person who failed to believe in Jesus and *keep* his commands (see John 8:15). God's purpose for Jesus is to bring salvation to the world. The opportunity remains for people to repent and receive forgiveness.

However, this statement does not mean that Jesus will never render judgment. As the Son of Man, he has the authority to do so (John 5:27; 9:39). Is Jesus so confused about his mission that he contradicted himself regarding his acts of judgment?

On further investigation, this difference can be resolved by thinking about the varied kinds of judgments. At God's appointed time, all humanity will face judgment (Acts 17:31; Romans 2:16; 1 Corinthians 4:5). Jesus' first coming to earth was not the time for that. Then (and now!) Jesus desires *to save the world*. This salvation will occur as people repent of sin, believe in him, and follow the plan of salvation as the New Testament expresses it. There will be a time for eternal judgment. But in this moment, Jesus had come to bring the light of eternal life.

> **What Do You Think?**
> How might believers be not only hearers of God's Word but also doers of his Word?
> *Digging Deeper*
> What obstacles prevent you from following God's Word?

48. "There is a judge for the one who rejects me and does not accept my words; the very words I have spoken will condemn them at the last day.

Jesus acknowledged that not all people will follow him as a disciple. Some will reject him and will *not accept* his *words* of teaching (see Luke 10:16). For those who have rejected him, Jesus' *words* will be their judge and *will condemn them* (see John 5:30; 8:16).

The themes of Jesus and the Word have a heavy emphasis in John's Gospel. In the famous introduction, John identifies Jesus as the Word (John 1:1-5, 14; see lesson 5). Further, Jesus is portrayed as emphasizing the importance of hearing and believing his words (5:24). While some people

Visual for Lessons 5 & 7. *Show this image as you discuss the Digging Deeper question associated with John 12:46.*

followed Jesus after they saw his power on display, many people turned away from Jesus because of the demanding nature of his words (6:60).

The timing of the final judgment is unknown. In John's Gospel, *the last day* refers to the future bodily resurrection of believers (see John 6:39-40, 54; 11:24). In this instance, Jesus speaks of the last day as a day of judgment for unbelievers. But he also spoke of a day when all people would be judged—believers and unbelievers (see 5:28-30). How a person regards the words of Jesus will dictate their eventual judgment.

Discipleship is predicated on remaining in Jesus' word (John 8:31). Love for Jesus is demonstrated by keeping his word (14:23-24). Cleansing is effected by means of Jesus' word (15:3). Eternal life is contingent upon keeping Jesus' word (8:51-52). Jesus' word is, in fact, the point of division between those who follow him and those who don't, those who are in Christ and those who are not (6:60-66; 10:19). Jesus' true disciples are those who confess and believe that he has the words of eternal life (6:68).

> **What Do You Think?**
> How are the concepts of hearing, belief, and judgment connected as represented in John 12:44-48?
>
> **Digging Deeper**
> How might James 1:22-25 inform the importance of your obedience to God's commands?

B. Declaring (vv. 49-50)

49. "For I did not speak on my own, but the Father who sent me commanded me to say all that I have spoken.

The words that bring life and judgment are *not* only spoken by Jesus, but come from his heavenly *Father who sent* him (see John 6:38-40; 8:26). The Father sent Jesus with a particular task, part of which included that he should *speak* and teach the Word of God (7:16-17).

The exact nature of that which the Father *commanded* Jesus *to say* is not immediately evident from this text (compare John 14:31). However, Jesus previously spoke of his authority—given to him by his heavenly Father—to "lay down [his] life—only to take it up again" (10:17). Jesus' words would eventually lead to this unavoidable fact. As Jesus willingly declared his Father's intentions for the world (see 5:18; 18:19-23; 33-37), his death would become a reality.

Jesus' time on earth is a perfect example of humble submission and obedience to his heavenly Father (see Philippians 2:8; Hebrews 5:7-8). Through his obedience, Jesus was faithful to his Father—he spoke only what his Father commanded of him. Therefore, he calls his disciples to follow him with love and faithfulness (John 14:21; 15:10).

This background reinforces the urgency in needing to respond to Jesus' teaching. To reject Jesus' Word is the same as rejecting the entirety of the Word of God. The Father sent his Son to the world and provided a specific task: speaking the words concerning salvation for the world.

50. "I know that his command leads to eternal life. So whatever I say is just what the Father has told me to say."

All of Jesus' work, as well as John's purpose in writing his Gospel, has eternal life as its ultimate objective. Jesus did not only come to bring physical healing, but also spiritual life. By obeying the Father's *command*, Jesus made *eternal life*—physical and spiritual—available to humanity.

Jesus' faithfulness in following the command of his heavenly *Father* gives opportunity for humanity to receive this life. The reception of this life starts with and requires belief that Jesus is the Son of God and the only way to the Father (John 14:6-7). For disciples who adhere to this belief and follow the New Testament plan of salvation, a new life will result (see 3:15; 5:24, 39-40; 6:40; Acts 2:38; Ephesians 2:8-9; James 2:14-26; etc.).

Jesus bears light to all who would believe. Belief in Jesus leads to spiritual cleansing and renewal (John 15:3-4). A person can't claim to be a disciple of Jesus and not obey him and his Word. Disciples of Jesus "live in him" and so they "must live as Jesus did" (1 John 2:6).

> *What Do You Think?*
> What is an example of God's commandment from Scripture that you will recommit to following in the coming week?
> *Digging Deeper*
> How might a particular fruit of the Spirit (Galatians 5:22-23) provide the necessary mindset so that you can follow God's commands?

❧ GLOVES OFF! ❧

The final buzzer sounded, and Indianapolis Colts linebacker Darius Leonard was elated. His superb defense had helped his team win a victory against the Minnesota Vikings. As he left the field, Darius removed his game gloves and haphazardly tossed the gloves to a young Colts fan in the stands.

Once in the locker room, Darius realized that his wedding ring was missing from his hand. Concurrently, the young Colts fan realized he had received something much more valuable than mere football gloves; he had inadvertently received gloves *and* a wedding ring! With the help of his family, the young fan returned the wedding ring, much to the relief of Darius and his wife.

Some items are too precious for us to lose—or so we think. The truth, however, is that nothing of this earth can be retained forever. The ultimate (and only) "item" that's too precious to lose is the Word: Jesus Christ. Through God's revelation in him, the world has been given the ultimate gift. His words lead to eternal life. What earthly thing are you tempted to replace him with?
—D. F.

Conclusion
A. The Word Saves

After this teaching, Jesus' public interactions would be greatly limited. He would celebrate Passover with his disciples (John 13:1-30) and give them his final teaching (13:31–16:33) before his trial and crucifixion. Therefore, we can look at Jesus' teaching as his final public teaching (and warning) on the saving nature of his Word.

True belief requires confession that Jesus is Lord and a life change resulting from that confession. Disciples of Jesus prioritize obedience as his light directs their actions. In Jesus' time, many people saw God's miraculous power at work in him. But when time came to listen and obey his words, many people stopped following him. For this reason, Jesus taught of the necessity of belief and of judgment.

Later in John's Gospel Jesus said, "If you love me, keep my commands" (John 14:15). Love is demonstrated by right belief and hearing and obeying Jesus' words. All believers must faithfully abide in Jesus' words. In the future, his words will judge all humanity. Disciples love and follow him!

Jesus' words will transform us and lead us into a life that bears the fruit of obedience (see James 2:14). Jesus has brought spiritual light into the world. Will you receive it?

B. Prayer

Heavenly Father, we want to faithfully listen to and follow the words of your Son. Show us how to make his word primary in our lives so that it will transform us. Remove any distractions that prevent us from faithfully obeying your Son. Reveal to us how we might live as a witness to your salvation. In the name of your Son, Jesus. Amen.

C. Thought to Remember
Jesus brings spiritual light!

HOW TO SAY IT

Habakkuk	Huh-*back*-kuk.
Nicodemus	*Nick*-uh-dee-mus.
Philippians	Fih-*lip*-ee-unz.

INVOLVEMENT LEARNING

Enhance your lesson with NIV Bible Student *(from your curriculum supplier) and the reproducible activity page (at www.standardlesson.com or in the back of the* NIV Standard Lesson Commentary Deluxe Edition*).*

Into the Lesson

Before class, find four recipes from a cookbook. Rewrite the recipes on their own handouts, but omit or substitute a key ingredient or procedure. (Make sure that the omission or substitution is obvious for even the most unskilled cooks!)

Divide the class into four groups and distribute a recipe handout to each group. Have each group evaluate their recipe and look for omissions or substitutions. After five minutes, ask each group to state their recipe title, any omissions or substitutions, and how they might correct the recipe.

Lead into Bible study by saying, "Many people have so-called recipes for a flourishing life. Yet too many of these recipes miss the most important ingredient. As a result, their life is lacking."

Into the Word

Announce a Bible-marking activity. Provide copies of John 12:44-50 for those who do not want to write in their own Bibles. Provide handouts (you create) with these instructions:

- Write an equal sign above every phrase that affirms that Jesus is equal to God.
- Draw a star above every phrase regarding belief.
- Write an exclamation point above every phrase that deals with judgment.
- Underline any word or phrase that you find difficult to understand.

Read the Scripture aloud (or ask volunteers to do so) slowly at least twice and as many as four times. As the Scripture is read, class members are to mark their copies in the ways noted.

After the final reading, divide class members into four groups for class discussion. Provide each group a handout with the following possible statements from an unbeliever:

- There's no way for humans to know God, including learning more about Jesus.
- Jesus was only a man and, therefore, he is not an adequate substitute for God himself.

- People should be afraid of Jesus because he is the ultimate judge.
- Jesus' words may reflect God's will, but we can't assume his words are sufficient for life and faith.

Based on the findings from the Bible-marking activity, have groups respond to each statement, referring to a specific verse from the lesson Scripture text. After 10 minutes have a representative from each group provide a response to one of the statements, until all the statements have been addressed. Finally, ask volunteers to share what they find especially helpful or challenging from the text.

Option. Distribute copies of the "Light and Dark" activity from the activity page, which you can download. Have learners work in pairs to complete the activity as indicated.

Into Life

Divide the class into pairs to answer these questions which you will write on the board: 1–Why do you think some people acknowledge that Jesus was a good man, but do not acknowledge that he is God? 2–What commands of Jesus do you think are most difficult for believers to follow?

After several minutes, ask volunteers to share their responses to each question. After no more than 10 minutes, say, "Following the commands of Jesus is how we can live a life that reflects God's light for the world to see."

Have students work in the same pairs to develop a plan of action for how they each might better follow the commands of Jesus. This plan should include how each student will recruit an accountability partner to encourage their obedience.

Alternative. Distribute copies of the "Light Meter" activity from the activity page. Have learners work in pairs to complete the activity as indicated. After no more than five minutes, have volunteers give their answers to the third question on the handout.

THE WORD RESURRECTS

DEVOTIONAL READING: John 11:20-27, 38-44
BACKGROUND SCRIPTURE: John 11:17-44

JOHN 11:17-27, 38-44

¹⁷ On his arrival, Jesus found that Lazarus had already been in the tomb for four days. ¹⁸ Now Bethany was less than two miles from Jerusalem, ¹⁹ and many Jews had come to Martha and Mary to comfort them in the loss of their brother. ²⁰ When Martha heard that Jesus was coming, she went out to meet him, but Mary stayed at home.

²¹ "Lord," Martha said to Jesus, "if you had been here, my brother would not have died. ²² But I know that even now God will give you whatever you ask."

²³ Jesus said to her, "Your brother will rise again."

²⁴ Martha answered, "I know he will rise again in the resurrection at the last day."

²⁵ Jesus said to her, "I am the resurrection and the life. The one who believes in me will live, even though they die; ²⁶ and whoever lives by believing in me will never die. Do you believe this?"

²⁷ "Yes, Lord," she replied, "I believe that you are the Messiah, the Son of God, who is to come into the world."

. . . .

³⁸ Jesus, once more deeply moved, came to the tomb. It was a cave with a stone laid across the entrance. ³⁹ "Take away the stone," he said.

"But, Lord," said Martha, the sister of the dead man, "by this time there is a bad odor, for he has been there four days."

⁴⁰ Then Jesus said, "Did I not tell you that if you believe, you will see the glory of God?"

⁴¹ So they took away the stone. Then Jesus looked up and said, "Father, I thank you that you have heard me. ⁴² I knew that you always hear me, but I said this for the benefit of the people standing here, that they may believe that you sent me."

⁴³ When he had said this, Jesus called in a loud voice, "Lazarus, come out!" ⁴⁴ The dead man came out, his hands and feet wrapped with strips of linen, and a cloth around his face.

Jesus said to them, "Take off the grave clothes and let him go."

KEY VERSES

Jesus said to her, "I am the resurrection and the life. The one who believes in me will live, even though they die; and whoever lives by believing in me will never die. Do you believe this?" —**John 11:25-26**

PARTNERS IN A NEW CREATION

Unit 2: The Word: The Agent of Creation

LESSONS 5–9

LESSON AIMS

After participating in this lesson, each learner will be able to:

1. Recount the sequence of events in the raising of Lazarus from the dead.

2. Explain how Jesus' raising of Lazarus proves the truth of Jesus' claim in John 11:25.

3. Contrast his or her life as now lived in confidence that Jesus is "the resurrection, and the life" with his or her prior life.

LESSON OUTLINE

Introduction
A. The Point of No Return
B. Lesson Context
I. Faith at a Funeral (John 11:17-27)
A. Status (vv. 17-19)
B. Frustration (vv. 20-22)
   Not What I Expected
C. Life (vv. 23-26)
   The Final Mile
D. Belief (v. 27)
II. Freed from the Grave (John 11:38-44)
A. Emotion, Cave, Stone (v. 38)
B. Request, Objection, Response (vv. 39-40)
C. Prayer, Belief, Command (vv. 41-44)
Conclusion
A. Pleasant Surprises
B. Prayer
C. Thought to Remember

Introduction

A. The Point of No Return

The phrase *the point of no return* originated in the early days of powered flight. Technically, it is that place on a flight path where the amount of fuel remaining makes it impossible to return to the airfield of takeoff. When we use that phrase in other contexts, we usually mean that we've reached a point where it is impractical or even impossible to turn back and start over.

Our Bible story today is about a person named Lazarus who seemingly had reached the ultimate point of no return: death. Death is the last stop for all our hopes and dreams in this world, the final and unavoidable end to every plan and purpose. As we've all been told, the only two things that are certain in this life are death and taxes. While we theoretically can avoid taxes, there's simply no coming back from the grave.

Or is there?

B. Lesson Context

This week's lesson finds Jesus back in Judea after having withdrawn to minister in Perea, on the eastern side of the Jordan River (John 10:40).

Often noted is the fact that there are seven famous "I am the [something]" sayings of Jesus in the Gospel of John. These are found in John 6:35; 8:12; 10:7, 9; 10:11, 14; 11:25; 14:6; and 15:1, 5. Today's lesson concerns the fifth of those seven, uttered by Jesus' in the third year of his ministry as a preface to the raising of Lazarus.

I. Faith at a Funeral

(JOHN 11:17-27)

As today's text opens, Jesus was already aware of the death of Lazarus (John 11:1-6, 14).

A. Status (vv. 17-19)

17-18. On his arrival, Jesus found that Lazarus had already been in the tomb for four days. Now Bethany was less than two miles from Jerusalem,

The *Lazarus* of this account appears in the Gospels only here and in the story that immediately follows in John 12. The fact that Lazarus *had already been in the tomb for four days* is significant. Ancient Jews believed that the souls of the dead hovered near their bodies for three days, after which time they departed. Therefore, the Jews in this account likely assumed that Lazarus had passed the point of no return, with no hope of recovery. For reasons to be seen, Jesus had been in no hurry to travel to Bethany after hearing of Lazarus's illness (John 11:6-7).

Before moving on, we note that this particular *Bethany* is the one that is *less than two miles* distant from *Jerusalem*—1.72 miles to be more precise, based on converting the *King James Version's* "about fifteen furlongs." John's note on distance thus serves to distinguish this particular town from the Bethany that is on the other side of the Jordan River (see John 1:28).

19. and many Jews had come to Martha and Mary to comfort them in the loss of their brother.

John 11:1-2 also establishes Lazarus, *Martha*, and *Mary* to be siblings. The sisters are known from the famous story in Luke 10:38-42. In another well-known episode, this Mary was the one who would later anoint Jesus' feet with expensive perfume (Mark 14:3-9; John 11:2; 12:1-8). The presence of *many Jews* who *came* to mourn Lazarus's death indicates that the family was well established in the community. It appears that the entire village of Bethany, and perhaps also some residents of Jerusalem (compare 11:45-46), had come to pay their respects.

> **What Do You Think?**
> What lessons have you learned from occasions when others tried to comfort you in a time of loss?
> *Digging Deeper*
> Which Scriptures support your conclusions?

B. Frustration (vv. 20-22)

20. When Martha heard that Jesus was coming, she went out to meet him, but Mary stayed at home.

This verse allows us a peek at the personal-ity differences between *Mary* and *Martha*. As in Luke 10:38-42, Martha seems to have been the more assertive of the two. The fact that Martha met *Jesus* on the road, before he got to the house, allowed for a time of private discussion.

21. "Lord," Martha said to Jesus, "if you had been here, my brother would not have died.

Martha's words are a little difficult to interpret. Some see them as an accusation (as in, "Why weren't you here to help?"). Others see them as a statement of faith (as in, "If you had been able to come, I know you could have helped").

We note that the sisters had sent word to *Jesus* when Lazarus fell ill, but Jesus purposefully delayed his return by two days (John 11:3-6). Yet the fact that Lazarus had been dead for four days by this time (11:17, above) means that he still would have been dead for two days even if Jesus had not delayed.

Of course, Jesus could have healed Lazarus from a distance (as in Matthew 8:5-13). But Jesus allowed Lazarus to die because Jesus was planning to raise him from the dead (see John 11:4, 11). Naturally, Martha did not know this. Thus as is so often the case, emotions can overwhelm us before God reveals his larger plan.

> **What Do You Think?**
> Without giving directive advice, how would you counsel a friend who is distressed that the Lord does not answer her prayers as quickly as she would like?
> *Digging Deeper*
> How would insights from Job 2:13; 16:1-5; and 26:1-4 improve your counseling technique?

❧ Not What I Expected ❧

I was leading a new church near New York City. At first we met in a rented facility, but we soon we found a building to purchase—a former funeral home that was for sale at a price our young congregation could afford. We mused about how God would bring new life to a place previously devoted to death. We dreamed about how our ministry would grow in this new location. But just days before we finalized the deal, another buyer made a better offer, and we lost the opportunity to buy the building.

Congregation members were disappointed, and I felt like a failure as a leader. We had invested a lot of effort into the failed purchase, and I wondered why God hadn't answered our prayers. I asked, "Lord, if you love our church, why didn't you help us get this building?"

Looking for solace, I met with an older, experienced church leader who had served in the area for many years. I expected him to comfort me, but instead he challenged me, saying, "A leader's character shows in the way you handle adversity." That counsel wasn't what I expected—but it was what I needed.

We persevered. Eventually, God led us to purchase a wonderful facility. This time it wasn't a funeral home; it was a church building. We bought it for half the asking price, and the church thrived there. What God had in mind wasn't what I expected. It was better. Will you trust him when you don't understand him? —D. F.

22. "But I know that even now God will give you whatever you ask."

At first glance, this statement may look like a veiled request: "Jesus, you can still save Lazarus if you want to." But John 11:39 (below) indicates that Martha was not thinking along that line. Thus Martha's statement here should be taken as a general expression of confidence in Jesus rather than as a particular expectation regarding Lazarus. Martha still respected and believed in Jesus. Her faith during a time of loss is noteworthy.

What Do You Think?
Which of the psalms are good models for you of how to express faith during frustration?
Digging Deeper
How can you ensure that your frustration doesn't end up as seen in Job 38:1-2; 40:1-5?

C. Life (vv. 23-26)

23. Jesus said to her, "Your brother will rise again."

In the Gospel of John, *Jesus* often says things that are subject to more than one interpretation. The ambiguity may have been intentional on Jesus' part to test peoples' levels of faith and understanding (example: John 3:3-4). Jesus could take the discussion to a deeper level if the person latched onto the wrong meaning.

24. Martha answered, "I know he will rise again in the resurrection at the last day."

Some first-century Jews did not believe in *resurrection* (Mark 12:18; Acts 23:8). But many did believe that the righteous are to rise to eternal life *at the last day* (Daniel 12:2), and *Martha* was one who so believed. Thus Jesus' words "Your brother will rise again" of the previous verse was a comfort in that regard. But Martha's faith affirmation in the verse at hand reveals that she did not detect that Jesus had something else in mind.

25a. Jesus said to her, "I am the resurrection and the life.

Here we see the fifth of Jesus' seven "I am the [something]" sayings in the Gospel of John (see the Lesson Context). *Jesus* was attempting to push Martha's understanding to a deeper level. Earlier he had affirmed himself to be the one who raises the dead (John 5:25). But Jesus not only had the ability to *perform* resurrections; he is *the resurrection*.

The phrase *and the life* adds even more. Whereas many may think of eternal life as something that begins after we leave this world, John's Gospel insists that eternal life begins when a person is reborn spiritually. That being the case, Jesus told people that eternal life was immediately available through him (John 5:24).

❧ THE FINAL MILE ❧

While driving to work I noticed a semi emblazoned with the words *Final Mile*. Underneath those words was a slogan stressing that the customer's last mile was the company's top priority. In the transportation industry, "the last mile" refers to the final leg of the supply chain as products reach their intended destinations.

We encounter many bumps, potholes, and detours as we journey through life. The road takes many twists and turns. But in the end, death cannot confine a follower of Christ to the grave. The

Lord will see to it that those who trust in him will arrive at their destination, making it home safely —for eternity. Our final mile is Jesus' highest priority. Is it ours as well?   —D. F.

25b-26a. "The one who believes in me will live, even though they die; and whoever lives by believing in me will never die.

Jesus pressed harder. In the phrases *even though they die* and *will live,* he used the word *dead* in a literal, physical sense and the word *live* in a spiritual sense: even if a person died physically (as was the case with Lazarus), he or she would live forever spiritually, based on belief in Christ.

The phrases that follow state the same things in reverse: anyone who believes in Jesus while physically alive, as Lazarus had believed in him, *will never die* spiritually. In other words, the person of faith has an eternal hope that goes beyond the grave.

All this makes sense to us in hindsight. But for Martha, full of grief over her loss, the entire matter may have seemed hopelessly confusing. Perhaps she wondered why Jesus was waxing philosophical when what she really needed was a sympathetic ear and a shoulder to cry on. Little did she realize that Jesus would soon provide a source of comfort beyond her wildest dreams!

26b. "Do you believe this?"

This is not a question about Martha's belief in resurrection. She had already affirmed belief in that. This is, rather, a question about her personal trust in Jesus. Her answer follows.

D. Belief (v. 27)

27. "Yes, Lord," she replied, "I believe that you are the Messiah, the Son of God, who is to come into the world."

The Gospel of John is filled with situations where people responded in varying ways to something that Jesus said or did. Sometimes the response was in faith, but sometimes the response was that of confusion or downright disbelief. These give us a chance to think about our own response to Jesus.

In this particular case, Martha serves as a model of faith in the face of loss. Despite her grief

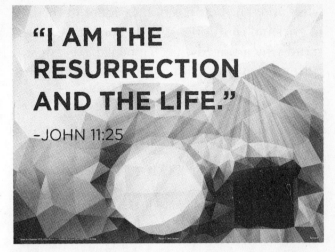

Visual for Lesson 8. *Give learners one minute to reflect on a situation in which confessing Jesus would reinforce their faith.*

and confusion, she seems to have come closer to a genuine understanding of Christ's identity than any other character in John's story at any point before Jesus' resurrection. John 20:30-31 indicates that this Gospel was written to lead the reader to believe that "Jesus is the Messiah, the Son of God"; Martha's words here closely echo John's stated objective, although it seems doubtful that she fully understood all the implications of her own words.

As a faithful Jew of her day, Martha probably believed that *the Messiah* would come to deliver Israel from political bondage (compare Acts 1:6). She may also have thought that the Christ would be *the Son of God* in the same sense that the great Jewish kings were sometimes called sons of God in the Old Testament (example: 2 Samuel 7:13-14). The Jews as a whole were certainly not expecting a Messiah who would actually be God in the flesh (John 1:11, 14)!

Some may find fault with Martha for not sorting through Jesus' intentionally ambiguous words to answer in a deeper way. But sometimes a simple affirmation of trust that Jesus is the promised

HOW TO SAY IT

Bethany	*Beth*-uh-nee.
Judea	Joo-*dee*-uh.
Lazarus	*Laz*-uh-rus.
Perea	Peh-*ree*-uh.

Messiah is the best position to adopt in the face of grief and confusion. Whether or not we understand why a tragedy has happened, we can still turn to God with faith and trust, believing that he has everything under control.

> **What Do You Think?**
> What situations in your life are most in need of a faith response right now?
> *Digging Deeper*
> How do you decide when to rest in childlike faith vs. when to probe deeper for "answers"?

II. Freed from the Grave
(JOHN 11:38-44)

John 11:28-37 (not in today's text) deals primarily with Jesus' interaction with Mary, sister of Martha. This interaction and certain comments by others who were present (11:36-37) set the stage for the resurrection of Lazarus.

A. Emotion, Cave, Stone (v. 38)

38. Jesus, once more deeply moved, came to the tomb. It was a cave with a stone laid across the entrance.

Jesus was experiencing heavy emotions, described as being *deeply moved*. We should remember that even though Jesus was God, he was also a human (John 1:14). So he experienced human emotions.

The place of interment *was a cave* that was probably located in a stone outcropping on the lower eastern side of the Mount of Olives. Other family tombs were likely there as well, tombs that were caves—having been prepared to be suitable as underground rooms for the remains of the dead.

Such tombs were sealed with heavy stones, and the tomb of Lazarus was no exception. Ancient family tombs have been found having disk-like stones that are three or four feet in diameter. Such stones would often be on a track across the entrance.

However, the language here indicates *a stone* laid over the entrance. Not all tomb-caves have upright entrances. Sometimes such caves descend

vertically rather than extend back horizontally. This may be the case here. Artists sometimes portray Lazarus's subsequent exit from the tomb as coming up a stairway that has been chiseled out of the stony ground.

B. Request, Objection, Response (vv. 39-40)

39. "Take away the stone," he said. "But, Lord," said Martha, the sister of the dead man, "by this time there is a bad odor, for he has been there four days."

To open a tomb is a serious matter. Such action can be construed as a desecration of the grave, so it must be ordered by a family member. That may be why *Martha* rather than Mary was the one to respond when Jesus told them to *take away the stone*. She seems to have been the older of the sisters, in charge of the family's business following the death of her brother.

Martha was not eager to agree to Jesus' request. *Four days* had passed since the death of Lazarus, and she assumed that his body was in its smelliest phase of decomposition. What we see are the limits of faith. Martha fully believed that Jesus could have healed Lazarus of his sickness and prevented his death (John 11:21, above), as did her sister (11:32). But their faith could not imagine what was about to happen. For them, resurrection was a future event, a promised time when all of God's righteous people would be raised from the dead (11:24). Had the two sisters not heard of the raising of the widow's son at Nain (Luke 7:11-17) or that of Jairus's daughter (8:40-56)?

40. Then Jesus said, "Did I not tell you that if you believe, you will see the glory of God?"

In response, *Jesus* reminded Martha of their earlier conversation. His challenge to her was that a person who believed in him would never die (John 11:26). Death is sad, but it is not the end for those who trust in Jesus. This was a crucial moment, for the tomb might not have been opened if Martha's faith faltered. Her faith was challenged by the trauma of being asked to have a beloved relative's grave disturbed—and the smell that would accompany it.

We are reminded of John's later conversation with the risen Christ, who declared himself to hold "the keys of death and Hades" (Revelation 1:18); he is capable of breaking the hold that death has over humanity. To believe in and understand Jesus' power over death is to be aware of *the glory of God*, and this glory was about to be revealed to Martha in the resurrection of her dead brother.

In the Old Testament, "the glory of the Lord" is synonymous with God's presence, something that was observed at Sinai (Exodus 24:17), at the tabernacle (40:34), and in the temple (2 Chronicles 7:1). God was present in the person of Jesus, and this was revealed earlier in glorious fashion at the transfiguration (see Matthew 17:2; compare 2 Peter 1:16-17). Although what has unfolded thus far in our text may seem little more than a humble human drama witnessed by a few dozen people in an insignificant village, no one present there should doubt the power of the Lord after what would happen next.

C. Prayer, Belief, Command (vv. 41-44)

41-42. So they took away the stone. Then Jesus looked up and said, "Father, I thank you that you have heard me. I knew that you always hear me, but I said this for the benefit of the people standing here, that they may believe that you sent me."

Jesus uttered a prayer that revealed the ultimate purpose of the miracle that followed: *that they may believe you sent me*. While many of Jesus' miracles demonstrated compassion, all are intended to point people to God through Christ. There can be no doubt about the source of Jesus' power, as he directed all credit to the *Father* for what was about to happen.

> *What Do You Think?*
> In what ways should you change your prayers so that God is more likely to honor them?
> *Digging Deeper*
> To what extent will James 4:3 apply to those needed changes?

43. When he had said this, Jesus called in a loud voice, "Lazarus, come out!"

This verse is a graphic illustration of what John envisions happening at the end of time, when Christ will call all the faithful to him at his return. In John 5:25-28, *Jesus* promised that a time is coming when the dead will hear the *voice* of the Son of God and be raised to eternal life. Lazarus's resurrection (next verse) was thus a foreshadowing of what will happen to all who believe.

44. The dead man came out, his hands and feet wrapped with strips of linen, and a cloth around his face. Jesus said to them, "Take off the grave clothes and let him go."

In ancient times, dead bodies were wrapped in strips of cloth with spices before burial to control the odor of decay. Many comparisons have been drawn between the *grave clothes* and *cloth* of Lazarus and Jesus (John 20:6-7). We can only wonder how the crowd reacted while watching Lazarus emerge from the tomb, wrapped in these items! The fact that *his hands and feet* were *wrapped* brings a comical image to mind: Lazarus, unable to remove the wrappings, perhaps was able only to hop as he emerged. Clearly, when Jesus calls, you come!

Conclusion

A. Pleasant Surprises

While it's always nice to get what you've worked for, sometimes a pleasant surprise goes a long way. Things we don't expect—like a bonus at work or a letter from an old friend—make us feel appreciated. Martha received the ultimate pleasant surprise as she saw something unfold that was humanly impossible.

Since Jesus really does have power over death, why should we fear anything? Since he secures our eternal destiny, can he not also provide everything else we need in this world now?

B. Prayer

Heavenly Father, help us to trust you more in the face of death. We pray in the name of the one who conquered death, Jesus. Amen.

C. Thought to Remember

The grave is not the end.

INVOLVEMENT LEARNING

Enhance your lesson with NIV Bible Student *(from your curriculum supplier) and the reproducible activity page (at www.standardlesson.com or in the back of the* NIV Standard Lesson Commentary Deluxe Edition*).*

Into the Lesson

Create three slips of paper having the following prompts, one each:

- The saddest funeral I ever attended was . . .
- The funeral I attended that had the best message of hope was . . .
- What I want my funeral to include is . . .

Give one slip of paper to each of three class members. Ask that the prompts be read aloud in turn, followed by your asking who in the class would tell a story indicated by the prompt.

Alternative. Distribute copies of the "(Mis) conceptions About Death" exercise on the activity page, which you can download. Have participants work in pairs to complete as indicated. After five minutes, reconvene for whole-class sharing of insights regarding the stages of life. Do not discuss the compare/contrast with 1 Corinthians 15 at this point; save that for **Into the Word.**

After either of the above, lead into Bible study by saying, "Even though we may not want to think about it, death is a regular part of life. But that won't always be the case. Let's see why."

Into the Word

Distribute the following on handouts (you create) as a closed-Bible pretest. Assure participants that they will score their own results; you will not collect them.

1. Martha addressed Jesus with this word: _____.
2. Mary and Martha's brother: _____.
3. The first sister to greet Jesus: _____.
4. Martha and Jesus agreed that her brother would do this: _____.
5. What Jesus promised Martha would see: _____.
6. Used as a grave: _____.
7. How Jesus addressed God: _____.
8. What Martha was commanded to do: _____.
9. The number of days Lazarus was in the tomb: _____.
10. Where the friends of Jesus lived: _____.

(*Answers* according to John 11: 1–Lord [v. 21]; 2–Lazarus [vv. 19, 21, 43]; 3–Martha [v. 20]; 4–rise [vv. 23-24]; 5–glory [v. 40]; 6–cave [v. 38]; 7–Father [v. 41]; 8–believe [v. 40]; 9–four [vv. 17, 39]; 10–Bethany [v. 18].)

Option. Depending on the nature of your class, you may find it useful to convert the above from fill-in-blanks to a matching quiz. If you do, it's best to provide more possible answers than there are questions so that correct answers cannot be arrived at by process of elimination.

After your class studies the lesson, surprise them by administering the same quiz again to see what has stuck with them. (*Option.* If you gave the quiz in matching format the first time, switch to fill-in-blanks this time.)

Option 1. If you used the alternative activity "(Mis)conceptions About Death" in the Into the Lesson segment, return to that exercise to compare and contrast the stages-of-life views of death with what Paul says in 1 Corinthians 15.

Option 2. If you desire to focus on the one who has conquered death, Jesus, distribute copies of the "Right Thoughts About Jesus" exercise from the activity page. Announce a speed drill to see how fast participants can finish the seven statements under the "What's So" header (only). Call time after one minute in any case. Then move to whole-class discussion or small group consideration of the significance ("So What?") for each "I am . . ." statement. Skip number five, saving its consideration for the Into Life segment.

Into Life

Form participants into study pairs. Everyone has the same assignment: compare and contrast his or her life now in Jesus, who is "the resurrection, and the life," with life before believing in him. (Explain that "compare" means how the two were the same; "contrast" means how the two were different.)

THE WORD GIVES PEACE

DEVOTIONAL READING: John 14:15-29
BACKGROUND SCRIPTURE: John 14:15-31

JOHN 14:15-29

15 "If you love me, keep my commands. 16 And I will ask the Father, and he will give you another advocate to help you and be with you forever— 17 the Spirit of truth. The world cannot accept him, because it neither sees him nor knows him. But you know him, for he lives with you and will be in you. 18 I will not leave you as orphans; I will come to you. 19 Before long, the world will not see me anymore, but you will see me. Because I live, you also will live. 20 On that day you will realize that I am in my Father, and you are in me, and I am in you. 21 Whoever has my commands and keeps them is the one who loves me. The one who loves me will be loved by my Father, and I too will love them and show myself to them."

22 Then Judas (not Judas Iscariot) said, "But, Lord, why do you intend to show yourself to us and not to the world?"

23 Jesus replied, "Anyone who loves me will obey my teaching. My Father will love them, and we will come to them and make our home with them. 24 Anyone who does not love me will not obey my teaching. These words you hear are not my own; they belong to the Father who sent me.

25 "All this I have spoken while still with you. 26 But the Advocate, the Holy Spirit, whom the Father will send in my name, will teach you all things and will remind you of everything I have said to you. 27 Peace I leave with you; my peace I give you. I do not give to you as the world gives. Do not let your hearts be troubled and do not be afraid.

28 "You heard me say, 'I am going away and I am coming back to you.' If you loved me, you would be glad that I am going to the Father, for the Father is greater than I. 29 I have told you now before it happens, so that when it does happen you will believe.

KEY VERSE

I will ask the Father, and he will give you another advocate to help you and be with you forever.

—**John 14:16**

Photo © Getty Images

PARTNERS IN A NEW CREATION

Unit 2: The Word: The Agent of Creation

LESSONS 5–9

LESSON AIMS

After participating in this lesson, each learner will be able to:

1. Summarize Jesus' promise regarding the Holy Spirit.

2. Explain the link between the presence of the Holy Spirit and living in obedience to Christ.

3. Write a prayer of thanks to God for the presence of the Holy Spirit in his or her life.

LESSON OUTLINE

Introduction

A. Abandoned!

"Sorry, I have to leave now." Words like these have broken many hearts. Someone goes off to war, a dear friend moves far away, an elderly loved one passes on. There is likely a sad embrace, a final farewell, and thoughts of being abandoned.

By one estimate, there are over 100 million people in the world who face the harsh reality of being orphans. War, famine, and disease have no respect for the plight of children stripped of their parents. Such children have little hope unless someone steps in to help. They feel—and often literally are—abandoned (Lamentations 5:3).

For most of three years, Jesus had been the constant companion of his chosen 12. They had left everything to follow him. But he was about to leave. What would the sheep do if they were abandoned by their shepherd?

B. Lesson Context

Jesus revealed God to humanity. Jesus was the Word who "was God"; he was the Word who "became flesh" (John 1:1, 14; lesson 5). He was the Lamb of God who came to take away the sins of the world (1:29). As the Gospel of John progresses, we see an increasing emphasis on Jesus' divine nature. He was accused of "making himself equal with God" (5:18). He exhibited power to raise the dead and authority to pronounce judgment (5:21-22). He said, "I and the Father are one" (10:30). His miracles proved the truth of his claims (10:36-38).

The climax of Jesus' claims came in an upper room in the week before his death. There Jesus told his disciples that no one could come to the Father except through him (John 14:6). More stunningly, he declared, "Anyone who has seen me has seen the Father" (14:9). Truly God was present with his people! But Jesus also had an unpleasant shock for his disciples that night: he was leaving. Just when they were realizing that they had God's presence in their midst, it seemed that they were about to lose it!

It was in this setting that Jesus promised to send another: the Holy Spirit. From the very beginning of Jesus' ministry, the Spirit had had an active role (see John 1:32; 3:5; 4:24; etc.), and Jesus promised that one day the Spirit would be granted to all believers (7:39). On that Thursday night in the upper room, Jesus made final preparations for that to be possible.

I. Promise of the Spirit
(JOHN 14:15-17)
A. Initial Requirement (v. 15)
15. "If you love me, keep my commands.

Interwoven with promises of the coming Spirit was this insistence of Jesus. Love for him must be more than a fickle emotion. The Bible meaning of love includes loyalty and commitment. That is the kind of love Jesus meant when he declared that the greatest commandment is to love God with all one's heart, soul, and mind (Matthew 22:37). We owe this kind of love to Jesus; nothing less will do. Genuine Christians don't just *believe*; they *obey*.

> *What Do You Think?*
> Name some of Jesus' commandments right now. (After all, if we can't name them, how can we keep them?)
> *Digging Deeper*
> What would be a passing score on naming them?

A tragic footnote must be added to the words of the verse before us. When Jesus said *if you love me*, he was keenly aware that not all his disciples did, in fact, love him. Only minutes before, Jesus had dismissed Judas Iscariot out into the night to do what that traitor was determined to do—betray his Lord to the temple authorities (see John 13:21-30). We will always show by our actions our response to Jesus' fateful words "if you love me."

B. Firm Promise (vv. 16-17)
16. "And I will ask the Father, and he will give you another advocate to help you and be with you forever—

Jesus had already told his disciples that he would be with them only a little while longer (John 13:33). As they puzzled over the significance of those alarming words, Jesus made the promise we see in the verse before us. The Father always heard the Son (see 11:41-42), and this prayer would be honored. By Jesus' personal request, *another advocate* would soon be given.

But who was this Advocate and what would he do? The main difficulty with the word *advocate* is its potentially wide range of meanings. Older translations of the Bible render this word as "Comforter" (*King James Version*) and "Helper" (*New American Standard Bible*). The Greek word being translated is often found in legal settings to refer to someone who goes to court with another to help plead a case. (The same Greek word is translated "advocate" in 1 John 2:1, where it refers to Jesus himself.) In a more general sense, such an individual might promise, "If you're ever in trouble, I'll be there for you."

So as Jesus announced his pending departure, he also promised that someone would take his place. That replacement was going to *be with* the disciples *forever*. In the Old Testament, the Spirit of God came upon individuals somewhat sporadically and temporarily (examples: Judges 14:6, 19; 15:14). But for Christians, the indwelling Spirit abides continually (see Acts 2:38; Ephesians 1:13-14).

❧ IN OUR CORNER ❧

My best friend was frantic. She had been summoned to court by her ex-husband, who was seeking sole custody of their children. The reasons he declared for wanting sole custody weren't exactly true. My friend was scared and intimidated due to the manipulation she was used to receiving at his hands.

I wrote a character letter for her, outlining how hard she worked with each of her children. But it turned out she needed something else more. She needed a friend. She needed a comforter and advocate to stand with her during that stressful time.

I immediately booked a flight. And for an entire week, we battled the weight of oppression that threatened to bury her. When the court date came, I stood by her. I was waiting to be called to the stand to bear witness of my friend's character. Thankfully, the truth was discerned, and the judge ruled in my friend's favor.

Life's biggest storms don't seem so bad when we have someone in our corner to walk through the storm with us. How tragic it would be if we ignored the Comforter and Advocate we have. Look for him in your storms!   —P. M.

17a. "the Spirit of truth. The world cannot accept him, because it neither sees him nor knows him.

The Holy Spirit is *the Spirit of truth* (also John 15:26; 16:13) because God himself is always true (17:17; Hebrews 6:18). This same Spirit moved those who wrote the prophecies of the Old Testament to write infallible truth (2 Peter 1:21). It was time for the Spirit to come to the disciples and to the church (compare John 15:26; 16:13).

But the Spirit would not indwell those of *the world*—they *cannot accept* him (compare 1 Corinthians 2:14). God sends the Spirit only into the hearts of those who are redeemed (Galatians 4:6). Only the children of God have the Spirit of God, and only those who are led by the Spirit are his children (see Romans 8:14).

17b. "But you know him, for he lives with you and will be in you.

Although the Spirit wouldn't be poured out until the Day of Pentecost (Acts 2), the disciples already *know him* in the sense that they were already aware of various ways he had worked so far (Luke 1:41, 67; 2:25; 3:22; etc.). The Spirit both *lives with* (present tense) and *will be in* (future tense) the disciples.

II. Assurance by the Son
(John 14:18-24)
A. Presence (v. 18)

18a. "I will not leave you as orphans;

Jesus fully understands that his disciples may feel like *orphans*, forlorn and alone, after he departs, so he is preparing for this. Just as God the Father had promised that he would never leave or forsake the children of Israel (see Deuteronomy 31:6), now God the Son makes a similar promise to his disciples. The children (see John 13:33) are not being abandoned.

18b. "I will come to you.

This promise has drawn three interpretations: it refers to (1) Jesus' second coming (John 14:3), (2) the gift of the Holy Spirit (14:16-17, 26), or (3) Jesus' resurrection (20:19, 26). Based on what Jesus said in John 14:20 (below), the third proposal is probably the best.

B. Life (v. 19)

19. "Before long, the world will not see me anymore, but you will see me. Because I live, you also will live.

On the very next day, which we now call Good Friday, Jesus would be crucified and buried. After his resurrection, Jesus appeared repeatedly to his disciples, in both small and large groups (see also John 16:16). But never again would the unbelieving world see him alive. (Individual exceptions to this statement included appearances to his half brother James, who previously did not believe in him, and to Saul. Compare Mark 3:21; 6:3; John 7:5; 1 Corinthians 15:5-8.)

Jesus' resurrection would give new hope to disciples: *because I live, you also will live.* His forthcoming victory over death will mean victory for all who follow him.

C. Knowledge (v. 20)

20a. "On that day you will realize that I am in my Father,

Jesus had already discussed his relationship with his Father (John 14:7-11). However, the disciples' understanding of that relationship was not yet what it should be. The greater understanding would come on a certain day when they *will realize that I am in my Father*.

But when exactly is *that day*? Bible students have proposed three possibilities: (1) the day Jesus rose from the dead (John 2:22), (2) the day when Jesus was glorified (12:16), or (3) the day when the Holy Spirit came (16:12-15). The strongest case probably can be made for the day of Jesus' res-

HOW TO SAY IT

Judas Iscariot	*Joo*-dus Iss-*care*-ee-ut.
Pentecost	*Pent*-ih-kost.
Thaddaeus	Tha-*dee*-us.

urrection, given the last part of John 14:19, just considered.

20b. "and you are in me, and I am in you.

The forthcoming transformation of the relationship between Jesus and his disciples seems to be the intent of this phrase. Jesus addressed the significance of this more fully in John 14:23-24 (below) and in John 17.

D. Obedience (v. 21)

21a. "Whoever has my commands and keeps them is the one who loves me.

Jesus repeated the importance of keeping of his *commands* (John 14:15, above; compare 15:10). His teachings are not mere suggestions or general guidelines for an improved life; they are, rather, directives from the Lord to his servants. It is by keeping the Lord's commands that his servants show that they love him (compare 1 John 5:3; 2 John 6). True discipleship must be more than mere lip service (see Luke 6:46).

❧ *"If You Really Loved Me, You'd . . ."* ❧

People have used the phrase above to manipulate others for as long as anyone can remember. Such manipulators fill in the blank with requests that are often illegal, immoral, and/or unethical. There was even a true-crime book written about a father who used that expression to get his daughter to commit a horrendous crime. Sadly, the manipulation worked, ruining a whole family in the process.

John 14:21a is not at all similar because Jesus' motivation was different from that of a manipulator. In showing our love by keeping his commandments, we end up doing what is in our best interests too, not only his. When we get this straight, we may just find ourselves less susceptible to becoming one of the world's manipulators—or being victimized by one.   —P. M.

21b. "The one who loves me will be loved by my Father, and I too will love them and show myself to them."

True love is to be modeled on the Father's own love for us: always loyal and committed. The harmonious oneness between *Father* and Son is so

profound that to *be loved* by one is to be loved by the other. The result for the disciples in being so loved was that Jesus planned to *show* himself to them. This certainly happened after Jesus' resurrection (John 20:19-29; 21:1-14).

E. Clarification (vv. 22-24)

22. Then Judas (not Judas Iscariot) said, "But, Lord, why do you intend to show yourself to us and not to the world?"

Judas *Iscariot* had already departed to betray Jesus at this point (John 13:26-30). But there was another man named *Judas* among the 12 apostles (Luke 6:16; Acts 1:13); this Judas was also known as Thaddaeus (Matthew 10:3; Mark 3:18). He was struggling to understand what Jesus meant by his statement in John 14:19, above. Judas wasn't asking *how* in terms of methods or procedures; rather, he was asking *why*.

> **What Do You Think?**
> When in a crisis situation, how do you know when it's better to voice your concerns and when it's better to remain quiet?
> *Digging Deeper*
> Don't just answer that with "it depends on the situation." Dig deeper!

23. Jesus replied, "Anyone who loves me will obey my teaching. My Father will love them, and we will come to them and make our home with them.

For the third time (see John 14:15, 21, above), *Jesus* emphasized that those who love him must *obey* his *teaching*. This time it is stated not as a command but as a simple fact.

When followers do obey their Lord, two things are promised to follow. First, the *Father will love* that person. Second, both the Father and the Son *will come* to that person and will *make* their *home with* him or her. The word translated "home" is the same that is translated "rooms" in John 14:2. In both places the emphasis is on the intended permanence of the dwelling place. Therefore, when Jesus departed to prepare the place of John 14:2, he was also making the believer to be a dwelling place for him. The role

Visual for Lesson 9. *Have learners pair up to discuss what reasons they have for confidence that the Spirit is at work in their lives and in the church.*

of the Holy Spirit in this is addressed in 14:25-26, below.

24. "Anyone who does not love me will not obey my teaching. These words you hear are not my own; they belong to the Father who sent me.

After saying that those who love him will keep his commands, Jesus then stated the flip side of this same truth: whoever *does not love* him does *not obey* his *teaching*. After all, how can someone truly love Jesus but ignore what he says?

These commands/sayings were not just from Jesus; they were in fact those of the Father (compare John 7:16; 14:10). God *sent* his Son to deliver the Father's message and to show the Father's love. Therefore, to disregard Jesus is to disregard God.

> *What Do You Think?*
> When is it not wrongly "judgmental" to point out someone's disobedience to Jesus?
> *Digging Deeper*
> Consider Matthew 7:1, 20; Romans 14:4, 10, 13; 1 Corinthians 4:4-5; 5:12-13; James 5:20; etc.

III. Purpose of the Spirit
(JOHN 14:25-26)
A. Son's Present Message (v. 25)

25. "All this I have spoken while still with you.

Jesus said many things to his disciples that

night. He had instituted the Lord's Supper, demonstrated a servant spirit by washing their feet, and taught them about the coming of the Advocate. While Jesus was *still with* them, he had yet more to teach. But their minds were able to absorb only so much (compare John 20:9). Even so, there was more to come, as the next verse shows.

B. Spirit's Future Ministry (v. 26)

26. "But the Advocate, the Holy Spirit, whom the Father will send in my name, will teach you all things and will remind you of everything I have said to you.

Jesus now summarizes the forthcoming ministry of *the Advocate* (see on John 14:16, above), who is also known as *the Holy Spirit*. This is God's own Spirit, who was soon to be sent to the apostles in the name of Jesus.

Jesus also added information about what the apostles were to expect the Holy Spirit to do. First, he *will teach you all things*. This would become the basis of the inspiration of the men who wrote the New Testament. Things that they did not know would be taught to them by the Holy Spirit. Like the prophets of old, they would be moved by the Spirit to write Scripture.

> *What Do You Think?*
> How do you know when a promise of Scripture applies to all Christians rather than just to those to whom it was originally given?
> *Digging Deeper*
> What Scripture passages support your answer?

The Spirit would also remind the disciples of things previously seen and heard. Since two of those present, namely Matthew and John, would later write Gospels of Jesus' life, it would be vital for them to be able to recall accurate details of what they had witnessed. Even as they wrote decades later, their thoughts on the life of Jesus would be clear and correct.

In an indirect way, the work of the Spirit to teach and to remind is a promise to all of us. First through Scripture and then through his indwelling presence, the Spirit leads us toward the truth and to recall it (example: Mark 13:11). The Spirit is our helper indeed!

> *What Do You Think?*
> How do you respond to someone who claims to have had a revelation from the Holy Spirit?
>
> *Digging Deeper*
> When would you cite Scripture passages in your response and when would you not?

IV. Insight of Jesus
(JOHN 14:27-29)
A. Peace Bestowed (v. 27)

27. "Peace I leave with you; my peace I give you. I do not give to you as the world gives. Do not let your hearts be troubled and do not be afraid.

Jews of the era customarily used *peace* as a word of greeting and farewell (examples: 2 Corinthians 1:2; 13:11). Given the context, Jesus' use of that word was a farewell bequest. But this farewell word was to become again a word of greeting, after the resurrection (see John 20:19, 21, 26).

B. Failure Rebuked (vv. 28-29)

28a. "You heard me say, 'I am going away and I am coming back to you.' If you loved me, you would be glad

The disciples hadn't fully comprehended Jesus' repeated announcement of his pending departure (John 14:2-4, 12, 18-19). This failure drew a rebuke from Jesus: if they truly *loved* him, they *would be glad* for him. The reason they didn't rejoice was because they were focused on their own grief at their forthcoming loss of Jesus' companionship.

28b-29. "that I am going to the Father, for the Father is greater than I. I have told you now before it happens, so that when it does happen you will believe."

Many verses make clear that Jesus was and is equally divine with God the Father (John 1:1, 18; 5:16-18; 10:30; 20:28). Therefore, Jesus' declaration *the Father is greater than I* cannot mean that Jesus played second fiddle to the Father in the core nature of their being. Throughout Christian history, this belief has been roundly condemned as a heresy referred to as subordinationism.

The solution is to understand the role that Jesus had accepted: in his then-current role as God incarnate, Jesus had subordinated himself to the Father's desires (John 4:34; 5:19-30; 8:29; 12:48-50). It is in comparison with those two roles as sender-from-Heaven and sent-to-earth that the Son declared the Father to be the greater. But when Jesus returned to his eternal home, his role of subordination was completed. Thus Jesus' statement here was part of his rebuke of the disciples. In their self-centered grief, they were unwilling to see what Jesus would regain by returning to Heaven.

Conclusion
A. Abandoned? Never!

The disciples in the upper room were startled, even frightened, to hear that their shepherd was going to leave them. Their lack of understanding was still evident at the empty tomb (John 20:9) and again at the ascension (Acts 1:6). But was their Lord going to abandon them? Never!

One of the most precious promises in the Bible, stated in both the Old and New Testaments, is God's promise not to abandon his people (see Joshua 1:5; Hebrews 13:5). Even though we "walk through the darkest valley," our shepherd is with us (Psalm 23:4). We are not forsaken.

As we are reminded each Christmas season, one of the names of Jesus is Immanuel, which means "God with us" (Isaiah 7:14; 8:8; Matthew 1:23). That truth becomes real for believers in every generation. Because we have the divine presence of the Holy Spirit, we are never abandoned.

B. Prayer

Father, help us sense the presence of your Spirit as he dwells within us. May we draw on his strength to show your Son's love daily through our obedience. Give us peace in him. In his name we pray. Amen.

C. Thought to Remember

We have the promised Spirit of God.

INVOLVEMENT LEARNING

Enhance your lesson with NIV Bible Student (from your curriculum supplier) and the reproducible activity page (at www.standardlesson.com or in the back of the NIV Standard Lesson Commentary Deluxe Edition).

Into the Lesson

Distribute handouts (you prepare) that feature these scrambled words:

nabker   eidrfn   crootd

Allow one minute for participants to unscramble as the three words and note what they have in common. (*Answers*: banker, friend, doctor; all are people to whom we might go for counsel or advice with a project.)

After a brief time of sharing and discussion, say, "Such advisors aren't always available, and their counsel is subject to error." (*Option*. At this point, encourage learners to share bad experiences in that regard.) Make a transition by saying "Let's see what the Bible has to say about someone who is the opposite with regard to both availability and infallibility."

Into the Word

Display the following sayings on the board to appear as bumper stickers:

Love Is Something You Do

Just Be Nice

Be Yourself

Assign sayings to groups of three or four. Challenge them to search today's text to answer the following question, also written on the board:

In what way(s) are these sentiments congenial with or opposed to the message of today's text of John 14:15-29?

Use the size and nature of your class to guide you in determining how many "bumper stickers" to have each group to evaluate, whether to add more of your own, etc. Allow no more than eight minutes for groups to reach conclusions. As groups report during whole-class discussion, add commentary to affirm or correct as needed.

Alternative or *Option*. Distribute copies of the two exercises on the activity page, which you can download. There are many ways to connect these studies with the bumper-sticker exercise just considered. You could have some groups could do the two exercises on the activity page while other groups do the bumper-sticker activity. Or all groups could do all activities in sequence, etc. Evaluate which approach to take according to the nature of your class and the time that is available.

Option. Another possibility is to recruit volunteers to present two-minute mini-lectures. Give them access to the lesson commentary, and ask each of the two volunteers to answer one of the following questions for the whole class:

- What's the best method to use to determine what the word *Advocate* means and signifies?
- How do we determine which promises of Jesus are for all believers in all eras or just specifically for the original apostles?
- Has Jesus' promise, "I will come to you" (John 15:18) been fulfilled? Why, or why not?
- When is "that day" when Jesus will be fully known (15:20)? What is the evidence for your conclusion?

Into Life

Give to each participant a slip of paper on which you have printed these two questions (or just write them on the board—but don't write the second before the first in answered, etc.):

1–Which saying of Jesus in today's text encourages you the most?
2–Which saying presents the biggest challenge?
3–Which makes you want to study the Holy Spirit more?

Close by having participants write a prayer of thanks to God for the presence of the Holy Spirit in his or her life. *Option*. As they write, have playing a video of "There's a Sweet, Sweet Spirit in This Place" being sung as part of a meditative close to your session.

A NEW HOME

DEVOTIONAL READING: Revelation 21:1-9
BACKGROUND SCRIPTURE: Revelation 21:1-9

REVELATION 21:1-9

[1] Then I saw "a new heaven and a new earth," for the first heaven and the first earth had passed away, and there was no longer any sea. [2] I saw the Holy City, the new Jerusalem, coming down out of heaven from God, prepared as a bride beautifully dressed for her husband. [3] And I heard a loud voice from the throne saying, "Look! God's dwelling place is now among the people, and he will dwell with them. They will be his people, and God himself will be with them and be their God. [4] 'He will wipe every tear from their eyes. There will be no more death' or mourning or crying or pain, for the old order of things has passed away."

[5] He who was seated on the throne said, "I am making everything new!" Then he said, "Write this down, for these words are trustworthy and true."

[6] He said to me: "It is done. I am the Alpha and the Omega, the Beginning and the End. To the thirsty I will give water without cost from the spring of the water of life. [7] Those who are victorious will inherit all this, and I will be their God and they will be my children. [8] But the cowardly, the unbelieving, the vile, the murderers, the sexually immoral, those who practice magic arts, the idolaters and all liars—they will be consigned to the fiery lake of burning sulfur. This is the second death."

[9] One of the seven angels who had the seven bowls full of the seven last plagues came and said to me, "Come, I will show you the bride, the wife of the Lamb."

KEY VERSE

He will wipe every tear from their eyes. There will be no more death or mourning or crying or pain, for the old order of things has passed away. —**Revelation 21:4**

Photo © Getty Images

PARTNERS IN A NEW CREATION

Unit 3: The Great Hope of the Saints

LESSONS 10–13

LESSON AIMS

After participating in this lesson, each learner will be able to:

1. Classify those who escape "the second death" and those who do not.

2. Contrast aspects of the old creation with counterparts or other aspects of the new creation.

3. Identify one way to shift his or her focus from the current world to the new heaven and earth, and make a plan to do so.

LESSON OUTLINE

Introduction
  A. New City
  B. Lesson Context
I. United (Revelation 21:1-4)
  A. Heaven and Earth (vv. 1-2)
  B. God and His People (vv. 3-4)
    Happily Ever After—or Not?
II. Separated (Revelation 21:5-8)
  A. New Creation (vv. 5-6a)
  B. Life Water (vv. 6b-7)
  C. Fire Lake (v. 8)
    Dangerous Fiction
III. Transition (Revelation 21:9)
  A. Angelic Messenger (v. 9a)
  B. Lamb's Wife (v. 9b)
Conclusion
  A. One Life
  B. Prayer
  C. Thought to Remember

Introduction

A. New City

My family and I have lived in several different cities. But a few years ago, we took a trip to interview for a job in a new city. We were excited to visit a city of which we knew nothing.

We arrived at night. Our host drove us past a shimmering lake, gleaming tall buildings, a new ballpark, and other intriguing sights. We were impressed. The city seemed clean and vibrant.

But living there for several years—in the daylight—exposed us to other sights as well: the scruffy neighborhoods of substandard housing; the once-proud mall that was nearly abandoned; the vacant lots of former gas stations that awaited environmental cleanup. The city, like many others, is a mix of the new and the old, the shining and the tarnished, the well-maintained and the dilapidated.

Also like many other cities, it is home to many strong churches and faithful Christians. But it's not without its share of gangs, prostitution, domestic violence, and corruption. Were someone able to establish a new city that had just the good parts, it wouldn't stay that way for long. An internet search on the subject of utopian movements is telling in this regard. Such a topic is great fodder for science-fiction stories. But the utopianism of today's study is not in that category.

B. Lesson Context

The book of Revelation (not "Revelations") is fittingly the last book in the Bible. It is likely the final book that was written, penned by the apostle John near the end of his life. A very early tradition places the writing in about AD 96. That was the final year of Roman Emperor Domitian's 15-year reign, the year he was assassinated.

John was on the island of Patmos in the Aegean Sea (Revelation 1:9a). The island was a barren, rocky place of fewer than 14 square miles in area. It is generally believed that John had been exiled there as punishment for conducting forbidden evangelistic work in the city of Ephesus (see 1:9b).

The book of Revelation has three parts. The first chapter relates an appearance of the risen

Christ to John on Patmos. Christ told John that he (John) was to receive visions of glorious and mysterious things. John was to write them down for sending to the churches of seven nearby cities (1:11).

The second part of the book consists of personalized messages to those churches (Revelation 2–3). We sometimes refer to these messages as "letters to the seven churches," but they are more than that. Each serves as an introduction to the book as a whole for the named congregations.

The third part, Revelation 4–22, is John's record of the series of visions he experienced. These are visions of Heaven and its activities, along with prophetic words delivered to John by angels who served as his guides.

The book of Revelation features a type of literature known as apocalyptic. The root word *apocalypse* does not mean "worldwide catastrophe" (as the word is often used in popular media today), but "uncovering of the hidden" and thus "revelation." This book reveals the hidden workings and plans of the Lord God Almighty in the midst of the church's trials and tribulations, to give hope to the persecuted. It has been serving this function for nearly 2,000 years, showing readers that evil will not triumph. God has a plan for ending the power of evil emperors and of Satan and his allies.

I. United
(Revelation 21:1-4)
A. Heaven and Earth (vv. 1-2)

1a. Then I saw "a new heaven and a new earth," for the first heaven and the first earth had passed away,

Sin has spoiled creation, and God's promised solution is to re-create. This is not simply a "makeover," for the current *heaven* and *earth* are to be *passed away* to make way for the *new*. For more detail regarding how that is to happen, see 2 Peter 3:5-7, 10.

1b. and there was no longer any sea.

John's vision of a new creation differs from the first creation story in Genesis 1 in a way we see here. The seas were hostile places to ancient peoples, as they often are today. But there will be no

such terror in the new creation. The prediction of *no more sea* symbolizes not just the absence of chaos and horror in the depth, but also the complete impossibility of such sorrow reaching into the New Jerusalem.

2. I saw the Holy City, the new Jerusalem, coming down out of heaven from God, prepared as a bride beautifully dressed for her husband.

The descent of *the new Jerusalem* indicates that *heaven* and earth are to be linked in a way that is analogous to *bride* and *husband* being joined in a wedding ceremony. This is another major feature of the new heaven and earth.

Jerusalem is referred to as *the Holy City* six times outside the book of Revelation (see Nehemiah 11:1, 18; Isaiah 48:2; 52:1; Matthew 4:5; 27:53). Those are idealized descriptions since there always seemed to be unholiness present (examples: 2 Kings 21:16; Lamentations 1:8; Micah 1:5). By contrast, the New Jerusalem is holy in all ways and at all times because of the very presence of God.

Isaiah foresaw a time when many would desire to "go up to the mountain of the Lord" to worship him (Isaiah 2:3). "Go up" is a natural thing to say since earthly Jerusalem is at a higher elevation than the surrounding terrain (compare: 1 Kings 12:27-28; Psalm 24:3; Zechariah 14:16-17; Matthew 20:17-18). How surprised Isaiah might be with John's clarifying vision as Isaiah's "mountain of the Lord" becomes a city that is coming to meet us! This is further clarified in Revelation 21:10 (not in today's text), where we are given the impression that the holy city is descending to rest on top of a mountain. Isaiah 52:1 and 61:10 prefigure the images of the phrase *as a bride beautifully dressed for her husband.*

> ### What Do You Think?
> Which practice in 1 Peter 4:7-11 should you focus on to help prepare the church for Christ's return?
> ### Digging Deeper
> How would you rank-order the practices in 1 Peter 4:7-11 in terms of importance for the last day? Or is that even possible? Explain.

B. God and His People (vv. 3-4)

3a. And I heard a loud voice from the throne saying,

A *voice from the throne* speaks at least twice in John's visions (Revelation 16:17; 19:5; compare 10:4; 11:12; etc.). The source of the voice in the verse before us is unspecified, but we should probably understand it as the voice of an angel. Elsewhere in this book (especially in chapter 14), angels speak in *loud* voices to make great pronouncements.

3b. "Look! God's dwelling place is now among the people, and he will dwell with them. They will be his people, and God himself will be with them and be their God.

The voice announced the significance of the new city. In Old Testament times, God's *dwelling place* was the portable tabernacle (2 Samuel 7:6), which was used before the temple was built. The tabernacle was actually a tent; the Hebrew word is translated that way in hundreds of places (example: Genesis 4:20).

We may struggle to comprehend God as dwelling in a tent inside a city, no matter how perfect and glorious either might be (see Acts 17:24)! But that is not the point here. John's vision is revealing a time when all the things that separate us from perfect fellowship with God will be removed.

Will that seem like city dwelling to us? Perhaps (see Revelation 21:10-27). The important thing is that we will *be his people* and he will *be [our] God.* There will be no physical or spiritual barrier separating us. This is an absolute and eternal future, not a temporary situation like the current separation of Heaven and earth. "So we will be with the Lord forever" (1 Thessalonians 4:17).

4. "'He will wipe every tear from their eyes. There will be no more death' or mourning or crying or pain, for the old order of things has passed away."

The heavenly voice went on to describe some of the spiritual and emotional aspects of this situation to come: *death* and every other cause of *pain* and *mourning* will be *no more.* This is surely one of the greatest promises in the Bible, a verse that we can hold dearly (compare Isaiah 25:8; 35:10; 65:19; Revelation 7:17). Life brings us sor-row, sometimes unrelentingly. We tell ourselves "It can't get any worse," and then it does. Sometimes it is the headline news of great tragedies. Often it is the personal news of our families. Christians are not immune from pain and tears.

But try to imagine no more causes for weeping! The emotional body blows we now suffer will cease forever! Just as the old creation is passed away, so will be our lives of pain and hardship. How can this be? Won't we remember the past and its pain? John goes on to explain some of the aspects of this in the remainder of Revelation.

> **What Do You Think?**
> What are some ways to use pain to grow spiritually?
> *Digging Deeper*
> Does your answer differ depending on whether the pain is physical or spiritual? Explain.

❧ *Happily Ever After—or Not?* ❧

A friend of mine made some very bad choices and ended up in a coma. After about a year, the coma gave way to death. He woke once from the coma during that year, but he was not the same man. He couldn't speak, and diminished capacity was evident.

We visited often and held prayer circles around his hospital bed. During one particular prayer time, I happened to look up and see his face twisted in what could only be described as revealing anguish, sorrow, and regret. Did he at that moment realize wasted opportunity because of bad decisions?

Here on this earth, we cannot escape coming face-to-face with the death of loved ones. We will see and experience the resulting sorrow. There's no avoiding it.

What we *can* avoid while on this earth is the pain of regret for having wasted life on ungodly pursuits and unholy lifestyles. And if repentance has occurred before Christ returns, even the tears of having wasted one's life can pass away (compare 2 Chronicles 33; Luke 7:36-48).

This might be a good time to give some thought to what constitutes "happily ever after." —P. M.

II. Separated

(REVELATION 21:5-8)

A. New Creation (vv. 5-6a)

5. He who was seated on the throne said, "I am making everything new!" Then he said, "Write this down, for these words are trustworthy and true."

Whereas an angel seems to have been speaking in our previous verses, the phrase *he who was seated on the throne* indicates that John then heard directly from God himself (see also Revelation 4:9; 20:11). Twelve times in this book John is told to *write*, and this is the final one.

The *trustworthy and true* fact that the Lord will make *everything new* is certainly a commentary on all that John saw. But there is more here. This is a promise for the readers, a promise so important that John is reminded he must write it down.

This promise was needed in John's day as his readers dealt with the dark specter of persecution and martyrdom. This promise is also needed today for believers struggling to live faithfully for Christ.

The pain and heartaches we experience are not the final chapter of our stories. There is an eternal future that has no more pain or tears, a time when all is new and perfect, a time when nothing grows old or corrupt.

6a. He said to me: "It is done. I am the Alpha and the Omega, the Beginning and the End.

Combining the image of a throne of authority (above) with the self-designation *the Alpha and the Omega*, we must again conclude that the voice is that of "the Lord God . . . the Almighty" (Revelation 1:8). Alpha and omega are the first and last letters of the Greek alphabet (also 22:13, lesson 13). So in English, this is like the voice saying, "I am A and Z." This concept is reinforced as the voice from the throne self-identified as *the Beginning and the End*. We take care to note that this is not an attempt to establish beginning and ending points for God's existence or reign. It is saying, rather, that he is both the source and the goal of all things.

God was there at the beginning of history with the first creation, and he will there at the end of history as well—at the re-creation of heaven and earth.

Visual for Lesson 10. *Before closing with prayer, listen to and/or sing a hymn together that celebrates the Alpha and Omega.*

He is "the Lord God Almighty" who reigns forever (Revelation 19:6; compare Isaiah 44:6; 48:12).

B. Life Water (vv. 6b-7)

6b. To the thirsty I will give water without cost from the spring of the water of life.

We are not to understand this promise merely to mean that the New Jerusalem will have a safe and abundant water supply. Rather, this is a fulfillment of a promise from the prophet Isaiah, who prophesied spiritual satisfaction for those who seek the Lord (Isaiah 55:1).

We rightly understand this image to be that of eternal *life* (John 4:10-14). But there is more here. In the language of John, the living *water* is also the Holy Spirit (7:38-39). No spiritual thirst will go unquenched in the new Heaven and earth. Just as there is direct access to the Lord God and to Christ the Lamb, there will be a lavish abundance of the Holy Spirit to all residents of the New Jerusalem (compare Revelation 22:17).

> *What Do You Think?*
> Considering any of the other four "What Do You Think?" questions in this lesson, what are some ways you can better avail yourself of the Holy Spirit's life-giving support?
> *Digging Deeper*
> What are some wrong or questionable practices you've seen in this regard?

7. "Those who are victorious will inherit all this, and I will be their God and they will be my children.

The theme of overcoming, or being victorious, is pervasive in the book of Revelation and elsewhere in John's writings (see John 16:33; 1 John 2:13-14; 4:4; 5:4-5). This is based on the Greek word *nike* which derives from Nike, the name of the Greek goddess of victory. (The same word is trademarked today as a line of athletic apparel.) To overcome is to conquer and be *victorious*.

Each of the greetings to the seven churches in Revelation 2 and 3 ends with a promise to the one who overcomes: permission to eat from the tree of life (2:7), immunity from the second death (2:11), a new name (2:17), authority to rule the nations (2:26), a white robe (3:5), a part in the New Jerusalem (3:12), and even an invitation to share the great throne of authority (3:21; compare 2:26). All these are summed up in the verse before us, for the one who overcomes is promised to *inherit all things*.

This is a climactic, all-inclusive promise to the readers, to us. God promises to be our God, and we can consider ourselves his sons and daughters. In this we are "co-heirs with Christ" (Romans 8:17).

> *What Do You Think?*
> What spiritual practice helps you most in being an overcomer?
> *Digging Deeper*
> Which element of the armor of God in Ephesians 6 do you associate with that response?

C. Fire Lake (v. 8)

8a. "But the cowardly, the unbelieving,

The picture here is that of a cosmic housecleaning. Those listed are the opposite of the overcomers of the previous verse, the antithesis of the victorious who have lived faithfully. *The cowardly* are those who have been afraid to commit fully to Jesus and thereby overcome. Similarly, *the unbelieving* are those who refuse to trust Jesus and follow him.

8b. "the vile, the murderers,

The word translated *vile* includes the sense of stench, those who stink of sin. It also has the sense of being polluted and may be inclusive of those who live hypocritically (example: Romans 2:17-29). *Murderers* is a category especially pointed to those who have killed the faithful, the victims who cry "How long, Sovereign Lord, holy and true, until you judge the inhabitants of the earth and avenge our blood?" (Revelation 6:10). Martyrs (those who die for the faith) will not share eternity with their unrepentant killers.

8c. "the sexually immoral, those who practice magic arts,

The sexually immoral is a general category including various sins, in particular those who engage in prostitution. These violate God's standards for sexual purity. The word being translated occurs as part of a wider word group, members of which appear 56 times in the New Testament, with 19 of those in Revelation. *Those who practice magic arts* seek power through the spiritual forces of evil and are thus completely opposed to God.

8d. "the idolaters and all liars—

Idolaters constitute an ongoing threat to the church. This problem is underlined by this book's connection with Ephesus (Revelation 2:1-7); that city was the home of the great temple of the pagan goddess Artemis, also known as Diana (Acts 19:23-41).

The list concludes with a group we might think would be a lesser threat: *liars*. The idea behind this designation is only partly covered by saying that these are people who tell lies. More directly, these are false believers, imposters in the church (see 2 Corinthians 11:13; Galatians 2:4; 2 Peter 2:1; Jude 4; Revelation 2:2). God, who knows the hearts of all, will see through any pretense.

❧ DANGEROUS FICTION ❧

Truthiness. Popularized by satirist Stephen Colbert in 2005, that word is defined as a

> seemingly truthful quality that is claimed for something not because of supporting facts or evidence but because of a feeling that it is true or a desire for it to be true.

The rise of "truthiness" tag-teams with the misuse of social media to make it close to impossible to discern truth from fiction. Certain algorithms built into social media platforms and internet search engines make it easier to access information that reaffirms our own beliefs, sometimes regardless of any basis in fact. To distinguish between truth and falsehood becomes increasingly difficult as a result.

But there is hope in the God who both speaks truth and is truth. A focus on him and his Word is what will keep us from becoming liars, whether in the general sense or the specific sense of false believers. Is he indeed your primary source for truth? —P. M.

8e. "they will be consigned to the fiery lake of burning sulfur. This is the second death."

Rather than be admitted into the city, those listed go to their just punishment. There they will join their true masters: the devil and his associates (Revelation 19:20; 20:10). To be consigned to *the fiery lake of burning sulfur* is to be cut off from God and Christ for eternity.

III. Transition
(Revelation 21:9)
A. Angelic Messenger (v. 9a)

9a. One of the seven angels who had the seven bowls full of the seven last plagues came

The angel referred to here is first noted in Revelation 15:1, 6-7 (see also 17:1). The number *seven*, which often signifies completion or perfection, occurs about 90 times in the New Testament. The book of Revelation features more than half of those!

B. Lamb's Wife (v. 9b)

9b. and said to me, "Come, I will show you the bride, the wife of the Lamb."

What the angel is about to show John is further discussed in Revelation 18:23; 19:7-8; 21:2 (above); and 22:17 (see lesson 13).

Conclusion
A. One Life

Life seems to gallop by at ever-increasing speed as we age. We cannot slow it down. I have a plaque in my office to remind me of this. It reads:

Only one life, 'twill soon be past,

Only what's done for Christ will last.
To me to live is Christ.

What does the future hold for us then? John's vision is that of a genuine, eternal utopia. The New Jerusalem will be the perfect place, for it is the dwelling place of God and of the Lamb. It will be a place of spiritual wholeness, where there will be no more tears and where those who despise God are denied entrance. It will be the ultimate, eternally new city, the city of God for all time.

We have confidence, for we believe that the promises of Revelation "are trustworthy and true" (Revelation 21:5). We have a reward, for we are heirs of the riches of God (21:7a). Most of all we have an assured hope, for we will have perfect, eternal fellowship with him (21:7b).

> **What Do You Think?**
> Considering this quarter's title "Partners in a New Creation," what's the most important thing you can do to prepare yourself for your role in that partnership?
> *Digging Deeper*
> How should your head, hands, and heart interact in that regard?

B. Prayer

Eternal God, may we never forget your promises! May we not fear death, for we that your Son has conquered death. In his name we pray. Amen.

C. Thought to Remember

Trust the promises of Revelation!

HOW TO SAY IT

Aegean	A-*jee*-un.
Alpha	*Al*-fa.
apocalypse	uh-*pock*-uh-lips.
Artemis	*Ar*-teh-miss.
Domitian	Duh-*mish*-un.
Ephesus	*Ef*-uh-sus.
Omega	O-*may*-guh or O-*mee*-guh.
Patmos	*Pat*-muss.
utopian	you-*toe*-pea-un.
Zechariah	Zek-uh-**rye**-uh.

INVOLVEMENT LEARNING

Enhance your lesson with NIV Bible Student *(from your curriculum supplier) and the reproducible activity page (at www.standardlesson.com or in the back of the* NIV Standard Lesson Commentary Deluxe Edition*).*

Into the Lesson

Divide your class into three equal groups. The **Wonderful Group** will brainstorm a list of why your community is a wonderful place to live. The **Difficult Group** will brainstorm a list of why your community is a difficult place to live. The **Prediction Group** will try to anticipate what each of the other two groups will say by making lists under each of those two categories. Distribute handouts (you create) that state the groups' assignments.

After five minutes, have the first two groups report their conclusions in a back and forth manner. As they do, members of **The Prediction Group** should listen to decide which of the other two groups is more convincing.

After discussion, lead into Bible study by saying, "No matter how much we appreciate life in this community, the Bible describes a place that will be better. Let's see why and how."

Into the Word

Distribute printed copies (you prepare) of Revelation 21:1-9, one handout per person. Include on the handout the following tasks:

1–Underline every promise.
2–Circle every symbol.
3–Star everything that gives you hope.
4–Put a question mark beside what you don't understand or makes you somewhat afraid.

Have participants complete the tasks as you read the text aloud twice.

Then have participants pair off to compare and contrast their conclusions. As they do so, write the following questions on the board:

1–Which verses did you and your study partner mark the same? Why?
2–Which verses did you and your study partner mark differently? Why?
3–What surprised you most in this exercise? Why?

After a few minutes, reconvene for whole-class discussion.

Option 1. To focus on the "symbol" aspect of the first set of tasks, distribute copies of the "Words as Depictions" exercise from the reproducible page, which you can download. Learners can work on this in study pairs, or they can use it as a note-taker as you work through the text. It should not be used for individual in-class study.

Option 2. To explore symbolic language further, also distribute copies of the "Here Comes the Bride" exercise from the activity page, to be completed as Option 1, above.

Into Life

Form learners into groups of three or four; distribute to them paper, markers, and appropriate art supplies to create "real-estate brochures" for Heaven. Each brochure should help a person looking at it to shift focus from his or her current residence to a future residence in the new heaven and earth. Challenge participants to sketch a biblical picture as well as list reasons someone should want to move there.

Encourage your "artists" to use as many descriptions as possible from today's text, couching them in terms today's adults would understand. The brochures should communicate with those outside the church as well as with longtime believers.

Option 1. Have groups do the above, but make separate brochures for believers and unbelievers.

Option 2. After the above exercise, time allowing, give each participant a slip of paper and have them write on one side to all class members. On one side they are to complete the first sentence below; on the other side, the second sentence:

The best thing about my life is . . .
The most difficult thing about my life is . . .

Allow no more than a minute before asking for volunteers to share (don't put anyone on the spot). Discuss how both will change in eternity.

A NEW CITY

DEVOTIONAL READING: Revelation 21:10-21
BACKGROUND SCRIPTURE: Revelation 21:10-27

REVELATION 21:10-21

[10] And he carried me away in the Spirit to a mountain great and high, and showed me the Holy City, Jerusalem, coming down out of heaven from God. [11] It shone with the glory of God, and its brilliance was like that of a very precious jewel, like a jasper, clear as crystal. [12] It had a great, high wall with twelve gates, and with twelve angels at the gates. On the gates were written the names of the twelve tribes of Israel. [13] There were three gates on the east, three on the north, three on the south and three on the west. [14] The wall of the city had twelve foundations, and on them were the names of the twelve apostles of the Lamb.

[15] The angel who talked with me had a measuring rod of gold to measure the city, its gates and its walls. [16] The city was laid out like a square, as long as it was wide. He measured the city with the rod and found it to be 12,000 stadia in length, and as wide and high as it is long. [17] The angel measured the wall using human measurement, and it was 144 cubits thick. [18] The wall was made of jasper, and the city of pure gold, as pure as glass. [19] The foundations of the city walls were decorated with every kind of precious stone. The first foundation was jasper, the second sapphire, the third agate, the fourth emerald, [20] the fifth onyx, the sixth ruby, the seventh chrysolite, the eighth beryl, the ninth topaz, the tenth turquoise, the eleventh jacinth, and the twelfth amethyst. [21] The twelve gates were twelve pearls, each gate made of a single pearl. The great street of the city was of gold, as pure as transparent glass.

KEY VERSE

The wall of the city had twelve foundations, and on them were the names of the twelve apostles of the Lamb. —**Revelation 21:14**

PARTNERS IN A NEW CREATION

Unit 3: The Great Hope of the Saints

LESSONS 10–13

LESSON AIMS

After participating in this lesson, each learner will be able to:

1. Summarize the importance of vivid imagery in John's account of the New Jerusalem.

2. Explain the danger of misinterpreting that imagery.

3. Describe one way this passage should influence his or her behavior.

LESSON OUTLINE

Introduction

A. Beauty in the Irish Countryside

I lost my breath when visiting the St. Colman's Cathedral in Cobh, Ireland. As I explored the historic building, heard the cathedral's bells, and gazed through the cathedral's windows, its beauty overwhelmed me.

Even the cathedral's surroundings stunned me. One side of the cathedral overlooked the sea and brilliantly colored trees. On the other side, multicolored houses and the buildings of the town surrounded the cathedral. The sight of this cathedral and its surroundings was a glimpse of God's glory revealed in and through the Irish countryside.

While beautiful and stunning, St. Colman's Cathedral is only a pale reflection of the place God has prepared for his people. The apostle John was shown a vision of this heavenly place—one more eternal and more beautiful than an Irish cathedral.

B. Lesson Context

First century Greco-Roman cities—such as Rome, Athens, and Corinth—were often spoken of in high regard by ancient philosophers and writers. They would go to great lengths to laud a city's accomplishments, while providing stirring descriptions of the city for unfamiliar readers. In today's Scripture text, John sees a great city coming from the heavens. He describes it in a manner that stirs the hearts of believers for what they can expect.

Prophetic visions of a city of God were not uncommon in biblical and Jewish texts. The psalmist described the beauty of the city of God, forever made secure by the presence of God (Psalm 48). The prophet Isaiah envisioned the centrality of God's city, Jerusalem, in the last days (Isaiah 2:2-3). This New Jerusalem would be the source of joy for all God's people (65:17-19).

Tobit, a Jewish text written in the intertestamental period, describes a heavenly Jerusalem, very similar to John's. The city would be rebuilt with precious stones and gold; it would become a place where the God of Israel would be worshipped (Tobit 13:16-18).

A vision of the prophet Ezekiel provides the most notable Old Testament comparison to John's vision. Ezekiel was taken to a mountain and shown a vision of what appeared to be a city (Ezekiel 40:2). The bulk of Ezekiel's vision includes the dimensions of a heavenly temple and its courts to reflect God's glory (40:5–43:12). The vision includes a life-giving river flowing from the temple (47:1-12), and the boundaries and divisions of a reestablished Israel (47:13–48:29). The vision culminates as Ezekiel sees the gates and dimensions of the city (48:30-35).

A close comparison between the visions of Ezekiel and John will reveal differences. However, John's vision is in fundamental harmony with the theological tradition that was at the heart of Ezekiel's. Throughout history, God's people have held firmly to the truth that God will provide for his people at the end of time. These visions, while not necessarily depicting a physical location, nevertheless point to God's faithfulness to his people.

I. The City's Descent
(Revelation 21:10-14)
A. Eternal Glory (vv. 10-11)

10a. And he carried me away in the Spirit to a mountain great and high,

John describes how *he* was *carried* by "one of the seven angels" (Revelation 21:9). Since he asserts that this experience took place *in the Spirit*, we can infer that this was a vision (compare 1:10; 4:2; 17:3).

Throughout Israel's history, mountains had great significance. At Mount Sinai, Moses received the law from God (Exodus 19:2-25) and the stipulations for proper worship (24:15–31:18). On Mount Nebo, God showed a dying Moses the promised land (Deuteronomy 34:1-4). Ezekiel described being taken to a *mountain* where he saw a heavenly city and a rebuilt temple (Ezekiel 40:2-4; see Lesson Context).

10b. and showed me the Holy City, Jerusalem, coming down out of heaven from God.

From his vantage point, John saw *the Holy City* of *Jerusalem*. But this city shared only its name with the terrestrial Jerusalem. God will establish this New Jerusalem. It will be the place where he will dwell with his people—his bride (Revelation 21:2).

Many prophets held expectant hope for a New

Jerusalem. Zechariah anticipated the manifestation of the Lord's glory in this city (Zechariah 2:4-5, 10-13). God's people would gather in peace among the nations (8:3-6, 20-23). Isaiah highlighted the city's splendor in God's new creation (Isaiah 65:17-19), a city adorned with jewels (54:11-12).

The vision of the city *coming down out of heaven* serves as a representation of God's relationship with humanity. God's city, his dwelling place, will come down to be among his people. Mediation between God and humanity will no longer be needed. God will be present with his people in the city.

That the city is *from God* reminds people of the focus of their worship: it is directed to "the Alpha and the Omega, the Beginning and the End" (Revelation 21:6). He is worthy of the highest praise and honor from the city's citizens, the bride of Christ (21:9).

> **What Do You Think?**
> How can believers live like citizens of New Jerusalem during their lives here and now?
> **Digging Deeper**
> How does Revelation 22:3-5, 12-17 offer an encouragement in this regard?

❦ *THE DAWN WALL* ❦

In the main valley of Yosemite National Park sits El Capitan, a 3,000-foot granite monolith. The Dawn Wall is the name given to the highest and most vertical part of the rock face. As the morning sun rises on El Capitan, quartz in the Dawn Wall catches the sun's rays. The little bits of colorful rock shimmer like the embers of a fire.

During my first visit, El Capitan's size dizzied me. As I looked up toward the face of the Dawn Wall, I felt small and insignificant. A rock of this size—so awesome and staggering—could come only from the creative hand of the eternal, all-powerful God.

As the apostle John envisioned the grandeur of New Jerusalem descending from Heaven, I imagine he felt small and insignificant. However, as he saw God's glory evident in the holy city, John fell down in worship (see Revelation 22:8). Are you ready to respond with worship to the God who declares, "I am making everything new!" (21:5)? —W. L.

11. It shone with the glory of God, and its brilliance was like that of a very precious jewel, like a jasper, clear as crystal.

The glory of God was unmistakable as John looked at the New Jerusalem. He noted that celestial bodies were not needed as sources of light; God's glory lit up the city (Revelation 21:23). Regarding the brilliance of God's glory, the language of John's vision agrees with that of earlier heavenly visions (see Isaiah 60:1; Ezekiel 43:1-2).

John referred to *a very precious jewel* to provide a tangible parallel to the radiance of God's glory. Previously John had described God on his throne as having the appearance of *jasper* (Revelation 4:3).

John's poetic language obscures whether this jewel is the same as what we know as jasper today: a stone that is opaque, not *clear*. Perhaps a fuller understanding of the underlying Greek text would highlight the stone's radiance, like that of a *crystal*.

> *What Do You Think?*
> How can you realistically help your earthly city of residence reflect God's presence and glory?
> *Digging Deeper*
> How can Christians respond to obstacles that might hinder their seeking peace in their city (see Jeremiah 29:7)?

B. External Perspective (vv. 12-14)

12. It had a great, high wall with twelve gates, and with twelve angels at the gates. On the gates were written the names of the twelve tribes of Israel.

A city's walls were a symbol of its strength and unity. A city without walls signaled weakness and disgrace (see Nehemiah 1:3-4; Proverbs 25:28).

However, the *wall* of New Jerusalem served a different purpose than an earthly wall. In John's vision, the heavenly city's enemies have been destroyed (Revelation 20:7-10, 13-15). Therefore, this wall does not serve to keep out adversaries. Rather, the *great* and *high* nature of the wall holds God's glory and purity (see 21:26-27).

The inclusion of *twelve gates* parallels Ezekiel's vision (Ezekiel 48:30-34). In Ezekiel's vision, each gate is named for a tribe of Israel. However, John's vision does not connect a particular tribe to a particular gate. All *the names of the twelve tribes of Israel* seem to be listed at each gate.

The 12 tribes of Israel were the foundation for God's people and, therefore, for New Jerusalem. The vision reassures all who would hear: all of God's people will be included in that city (compare Hebrews 11:39-40).

13. There were three gates on the east, three on the north, three on the south and three on the west.

As opposed to a singular city gate open for certain times (see Joshua 2:5), the multiple *gates* of New Jerusalem never close (Revelation 21:25). All the people of God, from all parts of the earth, are invited to enter the New Jerusalem. Individuals from every nation, tribe, and language will worship God in this city (see 7:9-10).

14. The wall of the city had twelve foundations, and on them were the names of the twelve apostles of the Lamb.

An ancient city's foundations were often laid on bedrock with only the upper foundation levels visible. As the New Jerusalem descended from Heaven (Revelation 3:12), every foundation was visible.

Twelve foundations, named for *the twelve apostles,* highlight the heavenly city's fundamental origin and source. The earliest Christians considered the apostles and ancient prophets to be the foundation of the church, with Christ—*the Lamb*—as the cornerstone (see Ephesians 2:19-21).

John highlights God's work in salvation history. The presence of both Israel and the church emphasize the scope of God's covenant people. In the New Jerusalem all God's people will be united so that God's glory might be on display.

> *What Do You Think?*
> What steps will you take to ensure that your actions are based on Scripture?
> *Digging Deeper*
> Who will you recruit to help you follow through in this regard?

II. The City's Detail
(REVELATION 21:15-21)

A. The Measurements (vv. 15-17)

15. The angel who talked with me had a measuring rod of gold to measure the city, its gates and its walls.

The *angel who talked with* John used a *measuring rod* in order *to measure* the dimensions of New Jerusalem. The length of this rod likely ranged from 8 to 10 feet. However, modern equivalents to ancient measures are not always exact.

John had previously used a rod to measure "the temple of God and the altar, with its worshipers" (Revelation 11:1). However, in this instance, the angel provided a rod made *of gold*—appropriate for a golden city—to measure *the city, its gates and its walls*.

The image is reminiscent of Ezekiel's vision. At that time Ezekiel saw "a man whose appearance was like bronze" holding "a measuring rod" (Ezekiel 40:3). The man proceeded to measure the dimensions of the house of Israel (40:4–42:20). In both visions, Ezekiel's and John's, the act of measuring revealed the perfection of God's handiwork.

16. The city was laid out like a square, as long as it was wide. He measured the city with the rod and found it to be 12,000 stadia in length, and as wide and high as it is long.

Each dimension of New Jerusalem—its *length*, width, and height—is identical. Therefore, *the city* measures as a cube, a three dimensional *square*. The temple of Ezekiel's vision measured equally in two dimensions: its length and height (Ezekiel 42:15-20; 45:2). However, the dimensions of the New Jerusalem demonstrate the city's holiness. It is a visual representation of the statement, "The Lord is there" (48:35).

New Jerusalem resembles the dimensions of the inner sanctuary of the temple—the Most Holy Place where God's glory dwelt among Israel (1 Kings 6:20; 2 Chronicles 3:8-9). God in his glory will live with his people in New Jerusalem (Revelation 21:3). The city's dimensions draw attention to the holiness of the temple. In this heavenly city there is no need for the Most Holy Place. The whole city is, in essence, the Most Holy Place.

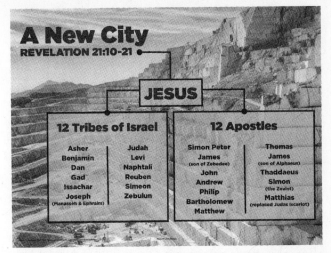

Visual for Lesson 11. *Display this visual while discussing the parts of the heavenly city as described in the commentary on Revelation 21:12-14.*

One stadion is the length of an ancient Greek racetrack, approximately 200 yards. Therefore, *12,000 stadia* would be approximately 1,300 miles. The estimated volume of this city is a staggering 2 billion square miles! This fact has led some people to question the validity of John's vision. We can't imagine how John "saw" such vastness. But he was conveying what the Lord wanted to show him regarding the expanse and role of the city. It will be a place where God's glory is evident. God's saints from every era can worship him in this city (see Revelation 5:9; 7:9; 21:24-26).

17. The angel measured the wall using human measurement, and it was 144 cubits thick.

The *measurement* of *144 cubits* is equivalent to 72 yards. The underlying Greek text is unclear whether this dimension applied equally to the wall's thickness and height. Based on the city's dimensions, a *wall* of this size seems meager and not appropriate for the city. However, the wall's purpose is not to exclude his people.

Rather, the wall's dimensions possibly represent the 144,000 redeemed people noted in Revelation 7:4 and 14:1-3. Their inclusion in the city's design, along with the 12 tribes of Israel, the apostles, and the prophets, acknowledge the totality of God's people in this holy city.

B. The Materials (vv. 18-21)

18a. The wall was made of jasper,

John described God, sitting on his throne, as

appearing "like a *jasper*" (Revelation 4:3). It is no coincidence that John envisioned the city's *wall* as of the same material. The radiance of God's presence surrounds the city (see 21:19).

18b. and the city of pure gold, as pure as glass.

The inclusion of *gold* in the eternal city might be making a reference to the original garden paradise (see Genesis 2:11-12). Once used to indicate a person's beauty or wealth (1 Peter 3:3; Revelation 3:18), gold now indicated the presence of God. The rare element has now become common, the material for constructing a whole *city*. Further, the city's purity was unparalleled, making it *pure as glass*, more refined than human hands can produce.

> *What Do You Think?*
> How does God test the hearts of believers (Proverbs 17:3) so that they might be refined and offer praise (1 Peter 1:7)?
>
> *Digging Deeper*
> How might Hebrews 6:1-20 inform believers' response to times of testing and refining?

19-20. The foundations of the city walls were decorated with every kind of precious stone. The first foundation was jasper, the second sapphire, the third agate, the fourth emerald, the fifth onyx, the sixth ruby, the seventh chrysolite, the eighth beryl, the ninth topaz, the tenth turquoise, the eleventh jacinth, and the twelfth amethyst.

For *the foundations of the city walls* to be built and *decorated with every kind of precious stone* was unusual and indicative of the city's heavenly nature. In the construction of ancient cities, the usage of gems and precious stones was reserved for the higher parts of the structure. However, God does not reserve splendor or grandeur in the construction of his cities. The prophet Isaiah foresaw that Jerusalem would be rebuilt with precious stones and gems (see Isaiah 54:11-12). The beauty of New Jerusalem stands in direct contrast to earthly beauty (see Revelation 17:4) and temporary wealth (see 18:12).

This specific listing of precious stones is found only in this passage. However, specific stones are cited throughout Scripture. God on his throne and the glory of God are both imagined with the appearance of *jasper* and *ruby*—a stone older translations of Scripture might call sardius (see Revelation 4:3). The deep-blue shade of *sapphire* invites comparisons to lapis lazuli, another precious stone known for its blue shade (see Exodus 24:10). Modern understandings of *agate*—sometimes called chalcedony—view it as a type of quartz, although its meaning here is unclear. Previously, "a rainbow that shone like an *emerald*" surrounded God's throne (Revelation 4:3). This passage is the only mention of *chrysolite, beryl, topaz, turquoise, jacinth,* and *amethyst* in the New Testament.

This listing of precious stones invites comparison to another listing of precious stones: those included in the high priest's breastplate (Exodus 28:15-20). While a comparison between the listings would highlight dissimilarities, these could be explained by differences of original language. The mention of different stones in the Old and New Testament (and in various Bible versions) assigns different names for some stones. Therefore, the stones cannot be indentified with absolute certainty.

The New Jerusalem is without a temple because the mediatory work of the priests is no longer needed. God dwells with his people as among a kingdom of priests (Exodus 19:6; Revelation 1:6; 5:10; 20:6). The foundation stones serve as an "outerwear" for the heavenly city, just as stones were utilized for the outerwear of Israel's high priests.

Further, John previously heard the declaration of "the wedding of the Lamb" to his bride (Revelation 19:7). The bride—God's chosen and redeemed people—has readied herself for the union with the bridegroom. The heavenly city is described as "the bride, the wife of the Lamb" (21:9; see 21:2). Its

HOW TO SAY IT

beryl	*ber*-ul.
chalcedony	kal-*sed*-uh-nee.
chrysolite	*kris*-uh-lite.
jacinth	*jay*-sinth.
sardius	*sard*-ee-us.
onyx	*ahn*-iks.

ornate and precious jewels are like those worn by a bride on her wedding day (see Isaiah 61:10).

❦ FRACTALS: PRECISION AND BEAUTY ❦

Fractals are the visual representations of complex and infinitely repetitive mathematical equations. Fractals describe things that seem to be random or chaotic. Some of the most mysterious (and beautiful) patterns in nature can be described by fractals. The growth patterns of crystals, the division of lightning bolts, and the spiral nature of some galaxies are among some examples of fractals. Each unique fractal highlights the precision and beauty of God's creation.

The precious stones inlaid in the foundations of New Jerusalem highlight the precision and beauty of God's creative acts. Each unique stone shows us that God is not a God of chaos, but of beauty and purpose. The psalmist declared, "From Zion, perfect in beauty, God shines forth" (Psalm 50:2). If the idea of fractals blows your mind, how much more wow is the thought of worshipping the creator God in the heavenly city?   —W. L.

21a. The twelve gates were twelve pearls, each gate made of a single pearl.

John previously described two details of *the twelve gates* of the heavenly city. The gates included 12 angels and the names of the tribes of Israel (see Revelation 21:12, above). In ancient times, *pearls* were extremely valuable and enormously costly (see Matthew 13:45-46). Further, given the size of the wall (144 cubits), these pearls would have been unnaturally large and unfathomably valuable.

21b. The great street of the city was of gold, as pure as transparent glass.

Even behind its walls, the city displays incredible beauty. John speaks only of a singular *street* made of *gold*. However, *the city* may include other roads besides this "Main Street." Like the jasper of the city's walls (Revelation 21:18), the *pure gold* is as *transparent* as *glass*. Even the city's road is more refined and more valuable than human equivalents.

God's glory and the idea of life are represented by this refined street. John would describe a "river of the water of life, as clear as crystal, flowing from the throne of God" and flowing down the middle of this golden street (Revelation 22:1). Like trees lining a boulevard, the tree of life stood on both sides of the street, somehow (22:2).

God displays beauty for his people. But more importantly, God will bring new life. Ultimately, he will restore his creation for his glory.

> *What Do You Think?*
> How does John's heavenly vision provide a peace and hope for a follower of Christ?
> *Digging Deeper*
> How can this heavenly hope fuel your current toiling on earth?

Conclusion

A. There Will Be No Place Like It!

Approximately 500 miles southeast from St. Colman's Cathedral sits the royal chapel of Sainte-Chapelle in Paris, France. While the 700-year-old chapel is small and unassuming, its size is not its main draw. Instead, the chapel's massive and delicate stained glass features are its claim to fame.

Over 1,000 individual biblical and historical scenes are depicted in stained glass, arranged across 15 windows, each approximately 50 feet high. As the sun shines across Paris and pours through the stained-glass, the chapel's nave lights up with hues of blues, reds, and greens.

The apostle John used vivid language to describe a glorious and splendid heavenly city. Unlike earthly cities, the heavenly city glows with the brightness of God's glory. God's glory shines through the city, more vivid and illuminating than sunlight. Our hope as believers is that we will someday worship God in that beautiful, heavenly city. There will be no place like it!

B. Prayer

Creator God, you are a God of beauty. Thank you for glimpses of your glory that we see through your creation. Help us to share with others what you have done for us. In Jesus' name. Amen.

C. Thought to Remember

God's glory is evident for all to see.

INVOLVEMENT LEARNING

Enhance your lesson with NIV Bible Student (from your curriculum supplier) and the reproducible activity page (at www.standardlesson.com or in the back of the NIV Standard Lesson Commentary Deluxe Edition).

Into the Lesson

Option. Place in chairs before learners arrive the "Gems" word-search puzzle from the activity page, which you can download. Your early arrivers can work on this before class begins.

Begin class proper by displaying the following discussion prompt:

The city I'd most like to visit again in North America is . . .

Pair up class members (but not husbands with wives) to share responses. Display a large map of North America as they do so.

After no more than two minutes, ask volunteers to come to the front, locate their chosen city on the map, and share what they told their partner. After each person shares briefly (don't let this drag out), ask what are some common attributes of the favorite places mentioned.

Lead into Bible study by saying, "Let's compare and contrast those ideas and ideals with the Christian's final and ultimate destination—not a place merely to visit, but a place to live permanently."

Into the Word

Form learners into triads. Provide each with a large sheet of posterboard or blank newsprint and colored pencils. Using the description in today's text, ask triads to draw an illustration of the new Jerusalem. As participants work, draw this spectrum on the board:

|—————————————————————————|
Blueprint   **Artist's Conception**

After triads finish, have them post their illustrations on the wall or board with painter's masking tape. Then have triads individually place an X on the spectrum to reflect whether the text depicts a blueprint (exact details), an artist's conception (impressionistic), or somewhere inbetween.

Alternative. Distribute handouts (you create) of a chart featuring these three column headings:

Today's Text / Other Scriptures / Echoes

Have printed under *Today's Text* the following seven references vertically as row stubs: verse 10a / verse 11a / verse 11b / verse 11c / verses 12-13 / verses 16-17 / verses 19-21. For each of the seven references from today's text, class members should match one the following passages (which you have printed at the bottom of the handout) to the best counterpart among the seven. The suggested best matches are in italics—*do not print these italicized answers on the handout!* To match: Exodus 28:21 *[vv. 12-13]*; Isaiah 54:11-12 *[vv. 19-21]*; Isaiah 60:1-2, 19 *[v. 11a]*; Ezekiel 40:2 *[v. 10a]*; Ezekiel 48:16-17 *[vv. 16-17]*; Revelation 4:3 *[v. 11b]*; Revelation 4:6 *[v. 11c]*.

After participants working in triads finish, reconvene for whole-class discussion of the third column—how the texts in the second column echo those in the first column, line by line. Be sure to discuss the significance of the connections for best teaching value.

Option. For extra study on meaning and significance (and the difference between those two terms), distribute copies of the "Meaning and Significance" exercise from the activity page to your triads, to be completed as indicated. After several minutes, reconvene for whole-class discussion.

Into Life

Distribute to your triads handouts (you create) on which are printed the following:

1–How today's text displays God's power.
2–How today's text displays God's provision.
3–How today's text displays God's protection.

For each response, learners should also note how the items on their listings meet needs for believers today. In light of their conclusions, discuss how God's power, provision, and protection should result in changed behavior on the part of Christians. (*Option.* This can be a session of writing private challenges in that regard to themselves.)

THE RIVER OF LIFE

DEVOTIONAL READING: Revelation 22:1-9
BACKGROUND SCRIPTURE: Revelation 22:1-7

REVELATION 22:1-7

¹ Then the angel showed me the river of the water of life, as clear as crystal, flowing from the throne of God and of the Lamb ² down the middle of the great street of the city. On each side of the river stood the tree of life, bearing twelve crops of fruit, yielding its fruit every month. And the leaves of the tree are for the healing of the nations. ³ No longer will there be any curse. The throne of God and of the Lamb will be in the city, and his servants will serve him. ⁴ They will see his face, and his name will be on their foreheads. ⁵ There will be no more night. They will not need the light of a lamp or the light of the sun, for the Lord God will give them light. And they will reign for ever and ever.

⁶ The angel said to me, "These words are trustworthy and true. The Lord, the God who inspires the prophets, sent his angel to show his servants the things that must soon take place."

⁷ "Look, I am coming soon! Blessed is the one who keeps the words of the prophecy written in this scroll."

KEY VERSE

Then the angel showed me the river of the water of life, as clear as crystal, flowing from the throne of God and of the Lamb —**Revelation 22:1**

Photo © Getty Images

PARTNERS IN A NEW CREATION

Unit 3: The Great Hope of the Saints

LESSONS 10–13

LESSON AIMS

After participating in this lesson, each learner will be able to:

1. State characteristics and function of the river of life.

2. Compare and contrast Revelation 22:1-7 with Genesis 2:8-10 and Ezekiel 47:1-12.

3. Draft a devotional of hope based on Revelation 22:1-7, such as would be suitable for publication in his or her church's newsletter.

LESSON OUTLINE

Introduction

A. Life Extenders

How long do you expect to live? A person born in 1850 in America had an average life expectancy of fewer than 40 years. That statistic is skewed, however, by a high infant mortality rate. Those born in 1850 who managed to live to be 5 years old (thus avoiding the many deadly illnesses that claimed young children) could expect to live to their mid-50s.

Today's US life expectancy is about 78.6 years, but it varies depending on race, gender, location, and other factors. The sharp increase is due to better medical treatment, chlorination of drinking water, etc. Yet some people want to extend their lives even further. They work hard to eat healthy food and maintain high fitness levels. Predictions are that we will continue to see a greater percentage of our fellow citizens live to their 90s and 100s than ever before.

The Bible tells the story of the paradise of Eden that was lost to humanity because of sin. In that garden was the tree of life, and the eating of its fruit would allow people to live forever (Genesis 2:9; 3:22). When Adam and Eve sinned, they were expelled from the garden and denied access to this tree (2:17; 3:22-24). Death has been a certainty for every child born ever since (with the two exceptions in Genesis 5:24 and 2 Kings 2:11). What if we could have that life-giving fruit? Today's lesson offers truth in that regard.

B. Lesson Context

A feature of the New Jerusalem drawn from the Old Testament is the tree of life. This mysterious tree is referred to in three books in the Bible. It first appears as an important part of the Garden of Eden (Genesis 2:9; see above).

A tree of life is also mentioned four times in the book of Proverbs as a metaphor for divine wisdom (Proverbs 3:18), the fruit of righteousness (11:30), desire fulfilled (13:12), and a properly used tongue (15:4). We should note that this is *a* tree of life, not *the* tree of life.

The tree of life mentioned in Revelation is a primary feature of "the paradise of God" (Revelation 2:7). Some have referred to this paradise as Eden restored, as people eat the fruit of the tree with God's blessing.

Water is closely associated with this tree in today's lesson. The image of water is used in both physical and spiritual senses in the Bible. In a physical sense, fresh (sweet) water has as its opposite water that is brackish (bitter). Fresh water sustains life (Judges 15:18-19; Job 38:25-27); brackish water—or lack of water altogether—yields the opposite (Deuteronomy 8:15; 2 Kings 2:19-22). The ultra-salty Dead Sea is aptly named!

The prophets Ezekiel and Zechariah had visions that bear similarities to John's vision of the New Jerusalem. A feature of the city foreseen by Ezekiel and Zechariah was a river flowing out of it. The water of this river is so refreshing that it not only nourishes life; it changes the ultra-salty Dead Sea into a freshwater lake (Ezekiel 47:8; Zechariah 14:8; compare Joel 3:18).

In Revelation, the concept of spiritual water includes the property of eternal life. Such water is seen as a divine gift, an ever-flowing fountain that provides life to those who drink from it (Revelation 7:17; 22:17).

I. What John Saw
(REVELATION 22:1-5)
A. Water of Life (v. 1)

1a. Then the angel showed me the river of the water of life, as clear as crystal,

As we pick up where last week's lesson ended, we see John still inside the holy city, the New Jerusalem, of his vision. He is still being guided by an *angel* of the seven bowls of Revelation 21:9.

As John beheld *the river*, his descriptions of it signify two things. First, the river's purity and clarity indicate that anything that might pollute

HOW TO SAY IT

Alpha	*Al*-fa.
Ezekiel	Ee-*zeek*-ee-ul or Ee-*zeek*-yul.
Galatians	Guh-*lay*-shunz.
Omega	O-*may*-guh or O-*mee*-guh.
Zechariah	Zek-uh-*rye*-uh.

it had been banished from the city. The water was not muddy or cloudy. It did not have the greenish tinge of algae, as stagnant water might have. We can imagine that it gave off no bad smell (contrast Exodus 7:21). The city of pure gold streets (Revelation 21:21) featured a river of pure water.

Second, the river's designation as *water of life* implies much more than a refreshing source of water for a parched throat. The water featured divine qualities, and we do not sense that John was surprised by this. He seemed to expect to find this river of life in the new city. His vision was that of a great urban complex combined with a garden paradise. No garden would be lush and inviting without an appropriate quantity and high quality of water.

> **What Do You Think?**
> How can you be a blessing to someone this week in a way that involves the living water that's already in you, per Jesus' assurance in John 7:38?
> **Digging Deeper**
> What if the other person isn't thirsty for living water? What do you do then?

1b. flowing from the throne of God and of the Lamb

Looking upstream, John saw the river streaming from the central feature of the city. As such, the vision again defies our expectations that are grounded in the daily experiences of life. A cube-shaped city is hard to imagine (Revelation 21:16). Pearls large enough to be carved as city gates are unknown to us (21:21a). Streets of transparent gold have never been seen (21:21b). Likewise, a spring on a mountaintop city, which results in a river that flows from a seat of authority, is something we can only wonder at. As we do, we acknowledge that in the New Jerusalem there may be new laws of physics that will defy current textbook science.

B. Tree of Life (v. 2)

2a. down the middle of the great street of the city. On each side of the river stood the tree of life,

Celebrate on the banks of the river of life!

Visual for Lesson 12. *At the close of the lesson, ask volunteers to share how they want to celebrate at the river of life and with whom.*

This verse also describes something difficult for us to visualize: *the river* of life, which comes from the throne, flowing in the middle of the main street of the city. We need to imagine an immense street, a boulevard or parkway so broad that a river with lush, fertile banks divides its lanes.

To propose dimensions is speculative. But perhaps we can imagine a street that is 200 yards wide (double football-field length) with a tree-lined river taking up the middle 100 yards of it (single football field), and golden lanes (Revelation 21:21) that are 50 yards wide each on each side of the river. This may give an idea of proportions, but it is likely that the scene John witnessed was much grander than this.

This river of living water leads to *the tree of life*, known to us from Genesis 2:9 (see the Lesson Context). This is similar to Ezekiel's vision of a great river flowing from a restored Jerusalem temple to transform the Dead Sea (Ezekiel 47:1-12). The prophet saw this river lined on both sides with many trees (47:7, 12). Some scholars believe that is what John saw here, and that we should take *tree* in a plural sense as being a forest or grove of trees. But that is not what John describes.

Somehow, the tree of life is on both sides of the river, perhaps spanning it and towering over it. This is a gigantic tree, not a dwarf variety. Its powerful roots spring up from each side of the river and support a mighty trunk with branches that droop to the banks on each side of the river.

This makes its fruit and leaves easily accessible to the residents of the city. No tree can grow like this naturally, and we do not need to expect such growth in the here and now. This is a supernatural tree, planted by the Lord.

🎋 A TUNNEL OF TREES 🎋

Have you ever seen a tunnel of trees? There's one in northern Michigan along a 20-mile stretch of Highway 119. This "tunnel" consists of trees that grow right to the edges of the roadway, with limbs reaching across the road overhead and meeting in the middle. Driving through this kind of a tunnel is a unique experience for many.

Revelation 22:2 describes an even more spectacular tree formation. This tree somehow grows on both sides of the water, forming an impressive sight. But do you believe it will become reality? If not, why not?
—L. M. W.

2b. bearing twelve crops of fruit, yielding its fruit every month.

The tree John saw was fruit-bearing, but in a way unlike that of any fruit tree of our experience. We know of different months for picking various fruits (cherries in June, peaches in July, apples in September, etc.), but we know of no tree that bears 12 varieties of fruit with a different one ripening each month!

Even so, an ever-bearing multi-fruit tree is one more feature of the New Jerusalem that exceeds anything in our experience. The practical aspect of this is that the life-giving *fruit* will be available to citizens of the city daily, without interruption or times of shortage. The eternal city will have an eternal tree that provides eternal life.

> *What Do You Think?*
> Which have you found to be most helpful in your spiritual growth: receiving from God just what you need at just the right time, or receiving an "over and above" abundance at a seemingly random time?
> *Digging Deeper*
> What Scripture passages can you cite as one or more examples of each?

C. Leaves of Healing (v. 2c)

2c. And the leaves of the tree are for the healing of the nations.

In modern city life, we do not associate tree leaves with healing. The closest we may come is using the gel of aloe vera leaves to treat burns. But aloe vera is a plant, not a tree.

Yet consider that tea leaves are dried and boiled to obtain a liquid with healthful properties. Tea leaves come from the tea shrub, which is considered by some to be a small tree. The idea presented in the verse before us seems to be that *the leaves of the* wondrous *tree* of life can be used to produce a healing elixir of some sort.

This healing is not stated to be for the curing of individual wounds, viruses, etc. Rather, it is *for the healing of the nations.* A key idea is that of spiritual healing for all the peoples from many nations, for Revelation 21:24 depicts the kings of the earth streaming into the new city. This indicates, among other things, a final and lasting peace among all nations. In this light, the city is truly the New Jerusalem, given that the word *salem* means "peace."

D. Absence of Curse (v. 3a)

3a. No longer will there be any curse. The throne of God and of the Lamb will be in the city,

The holy city is just that—utterly holy. It admits neither anything that is accursed nor anything that needs to be cursed (compare 1 Corinthians 12:3; 16:22; Galatians 1:8-9). The curses of humanity are gone.

We often think that the first *curse* resulting from the first sin was the cursing of Adam and Eve. But the first two curses were on the serpent (Genesis 3:14) and on the ground itself (3:17; compare 5:29; 8:21). There will be no Satan-serpent in this city, for he will have been consigned to the lake of fire (see Revelation 20:2, 10). There will be no cursed ground, for the fertile soil and water of life allow the tree of life to thrive with its year-round fruit and healing leaves.

Proverbs 3:33 tells us that "The Lord's curse is on the house of the wicked, but he blesses the home of the righteous." Yet there will be no wicked people in this city! Any and all things that would bring divine condemnation will be absent, for the city will be overwhelmed by God's *throne* and inhabited by His righteous servants. At long last, humanity will be freed from the stain of sin that ended residence in the original Garden of Eden.

> *What Do You Think?*
> Which practices would work best in helping you live above the sin-curse now: practices for achieving a positive outcome or practices for avoiding a negative outcome? Why?
> *Digging Deeper*
> Give an example of each.

E. Servants of God (vv. 3b-5)

3b-4. and his servants will serve him. They will see his face, and his name will be on their foreheads.

The psalmist asks, "My soul thirsts for God, for the living God. When can I go and meet with God?" (Psalm 42:2). The answer is right here! Everyone living in the city will have access to the throne. All residents of the city are God's *servants*, and John describes them in three ways: what they do, what they see, and how they are marked.

What they do is *serve him.* The Greek verb behind this is sometimes translated "worship" (Acts 24:14; Philippians 3:3; compare Revelation 7:15). The servants are engaged in acts of worship before the throne of God.

What they see is *his face*, which John does not describe. (We will have to wait to see for ourselves; 1 John 3:2.) To see the face of a king in the ancient world was a gift of fellowship (compare Esther 1:13-14; contrast Exodus 10:28). This will be a fulfillment of Jesus' promise to those with pure hearts (Matthew 5:8; compare Psalm 17:14-15).

How they are marked is with God's *name . . . on their foreheads.* This is a divine marking placed by either Jesus (Revelation 3:12) or God's angels (7:1-3). It is a beautiful image of acceptance and possession by God. It is the opposite of the mark of the beast that is placed on unbelievers (see 13:15-17; 14:9-11; 16:2; 19:20; 20:4).

What Do You Think?

Christianized bumper stickers, clothing, work areas . . . Is there a single, best way to "mark" ourselves as Christians? Why, or why not?

Digging Deeper

Rank-order these passages from 1 (most helpful in framing the question above) to 6 (least helpful in that regard): 1 Corinthians 6:6; Colossians 4:5-6; 1 Thessalonians 4:11-12; 1 Timothy 3:7; Titus 2:7-8; 1 Peter 3:3-4.

5. There will be no more night. They will not need the light of a lamp or the light of the sun, for the Lord God will give them light. And they will reign for ever and ever.

We encounter this *no more night* description also in Revelation 21:23, 25. There as here, *light* given off by *God* himself illuminates the city.

But now we see an important addition: the never-ending light is accompanied by the never-ending *reign* of God's people. This fulfills the prophecies and promises of Daniel 7:18, 27 and Revelation 1:6; 5:10. As Christ will "reign for ever and ever" (11:15), so shall we with him!

⅍ POWER LATER = POWER NOW? ⅍

My life as a missionary in Ukraine of the '90s featured many uncertainties. One was unreliable electrical power, which was rationed. Power went off every night across the city, plunging everyone into darkness. People lamented that they would be in the middle of cooking dinner when everything suddenly went dark.

Make no mistake: that darkness was not the partial darkness that Westerners experience when turning off lights at home. When electricity went off in Ukraine, no street lamps shone, no store signs blazed, no path was lit. For a few hours each night, people lived in silent, pitch-black darkness. One could only light candles, hunker down, and wait for the power to come back on.

I remember going out to walk my dog in such darkness. She sometimes torpedoed down the front steps, too excited to wait for the flashlight. I would then hear her scrambling because she had tripped. One time the lights went out as I walked up the stairs to a friend's apartment. I realized halfway up that I had lost count of what floor I was on. I then heard another person coming down the stairs toward me. We both stopped, hoping not to collide as we inched our ways along by listening to each other's breathing.

There will be no power outages, no darkness in the city of God! But what about now? Do you live and pray as if God's power is unreliable or limited? What are the telltale characteristics of a person who does so?   —L. M. W.

II. What John Heard
(REVELATION 22:6-7)
A. Angel Speaks (v. 6)

6. The angel said to me, "These words are trustworthy and true. The Lord, the God who inspires the prophets, sent his angel to show his servants the things that must soon take place."

The speaker is still *the angel* of the bowls (Revelation 21:9), John's guide to the holy city. The angel's statement touched on several things we have read previously. First is the emphasis that what John heard as being *trustworthy and true* are the same two affirmations made by him "who was seated on the throne" at the beginning of the vision of New Jerusalem (21:5; compare 3:14; 19:11).

Second, the reliability and importance of *these words* are underlined by reference to their source as being *the Lord, the God who inspires the prophets.* This fact serves to (1) include John in the ranks of earlier prophets and (2) emphasize the nature of the book of Revelation as prophecy (Revelation 1:3; see 19:10; 22:19).

The third concerns visions described as God's showing *his servants the things that must soon take place.* The wording in the Greek is precisely the same as that found in the book's opening lines (Revelation 1:1). There are 15 verses left in the book as we come to the verse before us, but the final mention of showing—which is about the holy city—is right here. Thus the initial showing of Revelation 1:1 and the final showing of Revelation 22:6 serve as bookends to the showings in between them (compare 4:1; 17:1; 21:9-10).

We may wonder why the angel promised that *the things* would happen shortly when, from our perspective of some 2,000 years later, they are yet to occur. Many explanations have been proposed. One idea is that all the events of Revelation happen invisibly and are known only to a spiritually elite group. Another theory is that these events are symbolic ways of describing the destruction of Jerusalem in AD 70 as the new era of the church began.

A more likely explanation is that these events will happen quickly when they do come, but they are being delayed for reasons we understand only partially (compare 2 Peter 3:9). God is not controlled by time in the ways we are (3:8), and we are wise to use that reality to temper our desire to know details of the future.

The message of Revelation is faithful and true even if we are inadequate to comprehend all of it. Let us believe that when these events do take place, those who are witnesses and have read Revelation will think, "Of course! Now it all makes sense."

B. Jesus Speaks (v. 7)

7. "Look, I am coming soon! Blessed is the one who keeps the words of the prophecy written in this scroll."

The voice of the Lamb breaks through to deliver a promise and a blessing. He will return. He has not abandoned his people. In the midst of suffering, whether from the ancient Roman government or modern persecutors, he is with us. The initial blessing of Revelation 1:3 is repeated—directed to those who keep *the words of the prophecy.* That leads to the great question prompted by Revelation: What does keeping these sayings entail?

The book does not hide the answers to this question. Faithfulness is the primary answer, and that concept includes repentance (Revelation 2:5, 16; 3:3, 19; 9:20-21; 16:9-11) and patient endurance in the face of opposition (2:10; 13:10; 14:12).

To be faithful is to keep the words of the prophecy!
To repent is to keep the words of the prophecy!
To endure is to keep the words of the prophecy!

There is an abiding message here that transcends any confusion we might have about the details of Christ's second coming. When he comes, may he find us faithful (compare Luke 18:8).

What Do You Think?
Which of *faithfulness, repentance,* and *endurance* gives you the most problems? What will you do about it?
Digging Deeper
Which of Revelation 2:3; 3:3, 10, 19; 13:10; and 14:12 convicts you most in this regard? Why?

Conclusion

A. The Beginning and the End

Many things have clearly defined beginnings and ends. We begin reading a book, then finish it. We buy a house, then sell it. We begin a job, and then the job ends. Transcending all our starts and stops of life is the timelessness of God, who was there at all the beginnings and will be there at all the endings. He is the Alpha and Omega, the A and Z, but with an enduring nature that stretches beyond the range of any human alphabet.

All this is illustrated by the New Jerusalem, a city to feature a physical size that is beyond our comprehension. It will be a city with unending day, an ever-flowing river of life, an ever-bearing tree of life, ceaseless worship, and priceless building materials. It will be ever new.

Such will be our relationship with the Lord. That relationship will be eternally consistent, pure, and true. Yet this description fails to describe the relationship fully, for there is a limitlessness on God's side. Nonetheless, we are blessed by John's revelation to us of his visions. May we be faithful in keeping the lessons we learn.

B. Prayer

Father, we barely understand the marvels of your promised holy city, a place where you will provide all the light we need for our eyes and hearts. May we hold these promises tightly so that when your Son returns, he will find us faithful and ready. We pray this in his name. Amen.

C. Thought to Remember

Seek and share the living water now!

INVOLVEMENT LEARNING

Enhance your lesson with NIV Bible Student (from your curriculum supplier) and the reproducible activity page (at www.standardlesson.com or in the back of the NIV Standard Lesson Commentary Deluxe Edition).

Into the Lesson

Alternative 1. Read a series of opposite choices and ask class members to raise their hands to indicate which they prefer. Some possibilities (add to or draw up your own list): chocolate or vanilla? hot beverages or cold beverages? summer or winter? daytime or nighttime? *[Keep this one last.]*

Lead into Bible study by saying, "Can you imagine a place where 'opposite choices' are severely limited or are absent altogether? Such a place is real—let's find out about it."

Alternative 2. Play a slideshow of lush landscapes. Have the pictures being displayed in a timed sequence as class members arrive. Ask, "Why are we drawn to scenes like these?" Lead to Bible study by saying, "If you have ever thought you would like to live in such a paradise, today's lesson is the place to start planning!"

Alternative 3. Form study pairs, participants not being paired with their own spouses. Ask each person to share with the partner memories of his or her best vacation ever. To keep this from dragging out, announce a two-minute time limit—one minute for each person. Ask the class as a whole, "What makes a vacation enjoyable?" Jot responses on the board. Lead into Bible study by saying, "Anything we can receive from pleasant experiences on earth will be dwarfed by the beauty and satisfaction we'll experience in our eternal home. Today's Bible study explains." (Do not erase the list; you may use it for *Option 2* in the **Into Life** segment.)

Into the Word

Distribute handouts (you prepare) featuring two charts. The first chart has two columns with the headings *Present in Heaven but Impossible on Earth* and *So What?* Form groups of four (quads) to read today's text then list items in the first column from descriptions therein. For each item they should jot the possible significance for believers today.

The second chart features three columns headed *Doing / Seeing / Marked.* Underneath the headings should be blank areas for students to explain each item as it is revealed in Revelation 22:3b-4.

After whole-class discussion of discoveries, have participants form eight groups or study pairs that you designate as **Law / OT History / Wisdom / Prophets / Gospels / NT History / Paul's Epistles / Other Epistles**. Have groups use concordances and/or smartphone Bible apps to find passages that deal with the theme of light within the Bible books their names imply. [*Law:* first five books of the Bible; *OT History:* Joshua through Esther; *Wisdom:* Job through Song of Solomon; *Prophets:* the 18 books written by prophets; *Gospels:* first four books of the New Testament; *NT History* is Acts; *Paul's Epistles:* Romans through Philemon; *Other Epistles:* Hebrews through Revelation.]

Option. For cross-passage comparison, distribute copies of the "The Source of Life" exercise on the activity page, which you can download. Have groups work to complete as indicated. After groups finish, discuss conclusions as a class.

Into Life

Have learners work in pairs to draft a devotional of hope based on today's text such as would be suitable for publication in his or her church's newsletter. Allow time for whole-class sharing.

Time allowing, choose one or both of the following activities:

Option 1. Distribute copies of the exercise "The Promise of Hope" from the activity page for participants to complete in pairs as indicated.

Option 2. Direct participants to reconsider the list of qualities they made under *Alternative 3* in the **Into the Lesson** segment (if you used that alternative). For as many of the items you left on the board as possible, brainstorm how the new Jerusalem will offer more than we can experience on earth.

A WELCOMING INVITATION

DEVOTIONAL READING: Revelation 22:10-21
BACKGROUND SCRIPTURE: Revelation 22:8-21

REVELATION 22:10-21

¹⁰ Then he told me, "Do not seal up the words of the prophecy of this scroll, because the time is near. ¹¹ Let the one who does wrong continue to do wrong; let the vile person continue to be vile; let the one who does right continue to do right; and let the holy person continue to be holy."

¹² "Look, I am coming soon! My reward is with me, and I will give to each person according to what they have done. ¹³ I am the Alpha and the Omega, the First and the Last, the Beginning and the End.

¹⁴ "Blessed are those who wash their robes, that they may have the right to the tree of life and may go through the gates into the city. ¹⁵ Outside are the dogs, those who practice magic arts, the sexually immoral, the murderers, the idolaters and everyone who loves and practices falsehood.

¹⁶ "I, Jesus, have sent my angel to give you this testimony for the churches. I am the Root and the Offspring of David, and the bright Morning Star."

¹⁷ The Spirit and the bride say, "Come!" And let the one who hears say, "Come!" Let the one who is thirsty come; and let the one who wishes take the free gift of the water of life.

¹⁸ I warn everyone who hears the words of the prophecy of this scroll: If anyone adds anything to them, God will add to that person the plagues described in this scroll. ¹⁹ And if anyone takes words away from this scroll of prophecy, God will take away from that person any share in the tree of life and in the Holy City, which are described in this scroll.

²⁰ He who testifies to these things says, "Yes, I am coming soon."

Amen. Come, Lord Jesus.

²¹ The grace of the Lord Jesus be with God's people. Amen.

KEY VERSES

I warn everyone who hears the words of the prophecy of this scroll: If anyone adds anything to them, God will add to that person the plagues described in this scroll. And if anyone takes words away from this scroll of prophecy, God will take away from that person any share in the tree of life and in the Holy City, which are described in this scroll. —**Revelation 22:18-19**

PARTNERS IN A NEW CREATION

Unit 3: The Great Hope of the Saints

LESSONS 10–13

LESSON AIMS

After participating in this lesson, each learner will be able to:

1. Identify the descriptions that apply to Jesus.
2. Explain those descriptions.
3. Sing a praise chorus or hymn that expresses the hope of Jesus' promised return.

LESSON OUTLINE

Introduction
  A. Oh, Those Delays!
  B. Lesson Context
I. Paths, Advent, Separation
               (Revelation 22:10-15)
  A. Two Types (vv. 10-11)
    When God Gives Up
  B. Second Coming (vv. 12-13)
  C. Two Outcomes (vv. 14-15)
II. Testimony, Offer, Warning
               (Revelation 22:16-19)
  A. Jesus (v. 16)
    Twice-Removed (from) Literalism
  B. Water (v. 17)
  C. Tampering (vv. 18-19)
III. Promising, Longing, Closing
               (Revelation 22:20-21)
  A. Reaffirmation (v. 20a)
  B. Desire (v. 20b)
  C. Benediction (v. 21)
Conclusion
  A. Praying Maranatha
  B. Prayer
  C. Thought to Remember

Introduction

A. Oh, Those Delays!

"Your flight has been delayed." These words are distressing to the air traveler. In an environment of tight connections and few direct flights, a departure delay can result in disrupted plans and great inconvenience.

It is a mark of our impatience as a society that a few hours' delay can be so traumatic. Our everyday schedules are thrown into chaos when car repairs take longer than expected, and when a promised two-day delivery actually takes three, when our food at the restaurant takes 10 minutes longer than we think it should. Delays are a frustratingly common element of life.

But what if the delay is for hundreds of years? Thousands? Christians must balance their expectation of Christ's "could be at anytime" return with the awareness that his return has yet to happen after some 2,000 years. How do we live expectantly for Christ's return while simultaneously being in an "expect delays" mode? This quandary has faced the church since the first generation of believers.

B. Lesson Context

In effect, the entire Bible serves as the context to today's lesson. The Old Testament teaches in many places that God will send a deliverer for his people. First-century Jews thought that such a person would be a political and military rescuer. God's anointed leader, they believed, would be empowered to defeat their nation's enemies, bringing peace and independence in the process (compare Acts 1:6; etc.). Jerusalem and its temple would be freed from Gentile influence, and pure worship of the Lord could then take place.

But two things happened to challenge this thinking. First, the Messiah that God sent did not come to be a leader of armies (see John 6:15). He came, rather, to save people from their sins (Matthew 1:21). His mission ultimately was for all humanity, for all are sinners. His death was a sacrifice for sins, intended to be effective for all people for all time. He was the sacrificial Lamb who took away the sin of the world (John 1:29).

Second, the Jerusalem temple was destroyed by the Romans in AD 70 during the horrific War of the Jews. This was something that no Jew of the time expected. Jewish faith, based as it was on the sacrifices of the temple, went into a downward spiral. Expectations of a military messiah to defeat the Romans were crushed.

Some, perhaps most, Christians of the same century found their own hopes being challenged when Jesus' return did not materialize as they thought it should (compare 2 Peter 3:3-4). But Jesus himself promised that he would indeed return. His return will be "with power and great glory" (Matthew 24:30). His return will usher in the final judgment of both the living and the dead (Acts 10:42; 2 Thessalonians 1:5-10). Christians and some Jews both look for the Messiah to come, but their expectations are very different.

I. Paths, Advent, Separation
(REVELATION 22:11-15)
A. Two Types (vv. 10-11)

10. Then he told me, "Do not seal up the words of the prophecy of this scroll, because the time is near.

As today's text opens, the apostle John was still being addressed by the angel of the bowls of plagues (Revelation 21:9). This angel was John's guide to the New Jerusalem (22:1, 8-10). The fact that *the time is near* gives a heightened sense of the necessary fulfillment of *prophecy*. This should cause us to focus anew on the greatest of all Revelation's prophecies: Christ will indeed return.

11. "Let the one who does wrong continue to do wrong; let the vile person continue to be vile; let the one who does right continue to do right; and let the holy person continue to be holy."

The angel sums up the state of things by noting the paths that people take. There are really just two categories here, and the contrast is strong: the path of the unrepentant (who continue to walk the wide way of sin) vs. the path of the repentant (who take the narrow way; see Matthew 7:13-14).

In contrast with Revelation 2:5, 16; 3:3, 19, there is no call for repentance here. It is as if the judgment has already been determined. The obe-

dient will continue to obey; the disobedient are not listening (see also 9:20-21; 16:8-11). Only those with ears to hear will heed (2:7); they are the ones whose hearts are attuned to God's word.

❧ WHEN GOD GIVES UP ❧

A youth minister I once knew was counseling a grieving mother regarding the death of her adult daughter in an automobile accident. At one point the woman cried out in desperation, "Please tell me my daughter didn't go to Hell!" The youth minister did just that, in spite of evidence that the daughter's life was like that of a seedy character in Matthew 13:5-7.

The fact is that we don't always know whether a person makes a last-second admission of sin and repentants, nor precisely how God responds in those circumstances (but see Luke 23:39-43). We may find it more comfortable merely to believe that God never gives up on allowing chances to repent, even after death. But that just isn't true. There comes a time when God determines that there are no more chances. One notable example is Jeremiah 44:1-25a, where God's final warning is once again met with irresolute stubbornness. The prophet, speaking for God, gives up, saying, "Go ahead then, do what you promised! Keep your vows!" (44:25b).

We are to witness for Christ on the assumption that no one is beyond repentance as long as he or she is alive (compare Luke 23:40-43). How should this motivate your own witness?   —R. L. N.

> *What Do You Think?*
> How can you find motivation to continue being a faithful witness even when (or especially when) nonbelievers refuse to repent?
> *Digging Deeper*
> What blessings can you anticipate from your efforts to share Christ, even if they seem ineffective?

B. Second Coming (vv. 12-13)

12. "Look, I am coming soon! My reward is with me, and I will give to each person according to what they have done.

Visual for Lesson 13. *Ask volunteers to share how this quarter's lessons have encouraged them to "stay the course to holiness."*

As in Revelation 22:7 (last week's lesson), the voice of the Lamb (Jesus) breaks through. He does so to restate his promise to come *soon* (see Revelation 2:16; 3:11). Previously a blessing was given to the ones who kept the words of the prophecy (1:3). Here, however, we might interpret the Lamb's pronouncement as both a blessing and a curse, for he promises *to give to each person according to what they have done.* The two sets of rewards are set forth in 22:14, below.

13a. "I am the Alpha and the Omega,

For the final time in Revelation, we hear a voice asserting the speaker to be *Alpha and Omega* (compare Revelation 1:8; 21:6). The first time we heard this self-designation, it was clearly "the Lord . . . the Almighty" speaking (1:8). Now the speaker is the one who is coming, namely Jesus the Lamb.

We should not be troubled by this apparent blurring of the distinction between the Lord God Almighty and the conquering Lamb; this is a feature of this book. They are seated on the throne together (Revelation 22:1) to rule the New Jerusalem as one. While the Bible teaches that there are three persons in the Trinity—Father, Son, and Holy Spirit (and all three are in Revelation)—we should not forget that there is only one God (Deuteronomy 6:4). We do not worship three gods, but one God. While this unity of persons might be mysterious, it is true (Matthew 28:19; Colossians 2:9; 2 Thessalonians 2:13-14; 1 Peter 1:2; etc.).

13b. "the First and the Last, the Beginning and the End.

In this final case of Alpha and Omega self-designation, the two letters of the Greek alphabet are doubly explained. That alphabet has 24 letters, with alpha standing at the beginning and omega at the end. To be Alpha and Omega is, therefore, another way of saying *the Beginning and the End* and *the First and the Last* of all things (compare Isaiah 44:6; 48:12; Revelation 1:17; 2:8; see also the discussion of typological language in the illustration on the next page).

C. Two Outcomes (vv. 14-15)

14. "Blessed are those who wash their robes, that they may have the right to the tree of life and may go through the gates into the city.

The only way to enter the city is *through the gates* of pearl (Revelation 21:21). There is no secret passageway. No one can sneak over the walls at night, because there is no night (21:25; 22:5). The gates are guarded by powerful angels (21:12), and only those who have lived victorious, obedient lives will be allowed *into the city.* These are granted eternal life, as signified by their access *to the tree of life* (compare 22:2, last week's lesson). They have overcome (2:7).

15. "Outside are the dogs, those who practice magic arts, the sexually immoral, the murderers, the idolaters and everyone who loves and practices falsehood.

Comparing this listing with the one in Revelation 21:8 (see lesson 10), we note that the latter designates eight categories of evildoers, while the verse before us has six. Five of these six are duplicates of those in 21:8, while one is new: *dogs.* It is unlikely that John would include a literal reference to an animal group in listing categories of human transgressors, so something else must be meant here.

There are several possibilities. The word *dog,* in singular or plural, serves as a metaphor for a male prostitute (Deuteronomy 23:18), for those who mocked Jesus at his crucifixion (Psalm 22:16-18; Matthew 27:35-44), for the enemies of David (Psalm 59:1-7, 14), for Israel's greedy watchmen (Isaiah 56:9-12), for profane people who are incapable of receiving what is holy (Matthew 7:6), for Gentiles (15:21-26), for Judaizers (Philippians 3:2), and for false teachers (2 Peter 2:1-22).

There seems to be no decisive textual basis for selecting any one of these as the single reference over all the others. But a common thread is that the above categories refer to people who reject God's authority. As seen in lesson 10, those to be denied access to "the water of life" (Revelation 21:6) are designated for housing in the lake of fire (21:8). These are the evildoers who are left *outside* the city in the text before us.

> **What Do You Think?**
>   Which method of motivation to repent should you use in your witness: promise of reward or fear of punishment? Why?
> **Digging Deeper**
>   What examples of each can you cite from Scripture?

II. Testimony, Offer, Warning
(REVELATION 22:16-19)
A. Jesus (v. 16)

16a. "I, Jesus, have sent my angel to give you this testimony for the churches. I am the Root and the Offspring of David,

Jesus includes more self-designations that help us understand the importance of the book of Revelation. To be *the Offspring of David* is easy to grasp: Jesus is from that line by the earthly genealogy traced to Joseph (Matthew 1:1-17; Romans 1:3).

The imagery of *the Root* is a little more complicated. Prophecy spoke of the coming Messiah as a "Branch" to grow from "roots" (see Isaiah 11:1; compare Jeremiah 23:5; 33:15; Zechariah 6:12). For Jesus himself to be that root in an ultimate sense is quite a strong claim! He is Messiah in all fullness. Any status that David had ultimately flowed from Jesus, not the other way around.

16b. "and the bright Morning Star."

Jesus' final self-identifier has resulted in Bible students searching the Old Testament for various "star prophecies" or tie-ins to the star of Bethle-

hem (Matthew 2:2, 7, 10). But that is unnecessary. Most of us have seen the phenomenon called the morning star, which is a reference to the planet Venus as it is visible shortly before sunrise.

❧ TWICE-REMOVED (FROM) LITERALISM ❧

The word *phenomenon* above is more important than you may think. Here, that word is actually shorthand for the longer term *phenomenological language*, a literary feature of the Bible and of language in general. The phrase refers to the way things appear from the point of view of an observer.

For example, when we speak of the sun's rising, we are referring to the sun's *apparent* movement in the sky (Ecclesiastes 1:5; etc.). What is actually, literally happening, as we moderns know, is that the earth is rotating on its axis.

Another literary feature we see in the verse at hand is *typological language*, which deals with symbolic meaning or representation. This feature is often present where someone or something serves as an "example" (1 Corinthians 10:6; 1 Timothy 4:12) or "pattern" (Hebrews 8:5) of someone or something else.

Phenomenological and typological language work together here. The "morning star" isn't literally a star, although to the naked eye it

HOW TO SAY IT

Alpha	*Al*-fa.
Bethlehem	*Beth*-lih-hem.
Gentile	*Jen*-tile.
Deuteronomy	Due-ter-*ahn*-uh-me.
Ecclesiastes	Ik-*leez*-ee-**as**-teez.
Isaiah	Eye-*zay*-uh.
Judaizers	**Joo**-duh-*ize*-ers.
Maranatha (Aramaic)	Mare-ah-*nath*-ah (*nath* as in *math*).
Messiah	Meh-*sigh*-uh.
Omega	O-*may*-guh or O-*mee*-guh.
phenomenological	*fih*-naw-meh-neh-**law**-jih-kuhl.
Thessalonians	*Thess*-uh-**lo**-nee-unz (*th* as in *thin*).
Zechariah	Zek-uh-**rye**-uh.

appears to be. And Jesus isn't literally that "star." Infinitely better, he is an example or pattern of how that "star" functions: night is almost over, he is coming soon with his light. The eternal day of the holy city and of the everlasting reign of the Lord and the Lamb is near (compare 2 Peter 1:19).

The next time you see bright Venus, will that fact come to mind?   —R. L. N.

B. Water (v. 17)

17. The Spirit and the bride say, "Come!" And let the one who hears say, "Come!" Let the one who is thirsty come; and let the one who wishes take the free gift of the water of life.

The Spirit is the Holy Spirit, the promised divine presence on earth after Christ's ascension (see John 16:7-13). *The bride* is the church, the embodiment of Christ in his followers on earth (see lesson 10). Their invitation to *come* and drink of the eternal *water of life* is a call to faith and obedience, a call to join Christ before he comes again. It is a choice available to all!

> *What Do You Think?*
> How can you help your church identify things that hinder its invitation to unbelievers to "come"?
>
> *Digging Deeper*
> If you find yourself in a minority of one in identifying one or more such things, what should you do next?

C. Tampering (vv. 18-19)

18. I warn everyone who hears the words of the prophecy of this scroll: If anyone adds anything to them, God will add to that person the plagues described in this scroll.

The voice now switches to that of the one who records it, John himself. Two stern warnings are in order at this point, and the first one is that hearers *of this scroll* must not add content. The penalty of *plagues* on anyone foolish enough to do so is described in Revelation 16.

19. And if anyone takes words away from this scroll of prophecy, God will take away from that person any share in the tree of life

and in the Holy City, which are described in this scroll.

Deletions *from this scroll* are also warned against. All the book's messages are to be taken to heart! Ignoring or removing parts we don't like will have eternal consequences. Persons unwise to the point of making such subtractions will not be part of the citizenry of the New Jerusalem. Deuteronomy 4:2, 12:32 inform us that neither this prohibition nor the one just before it is anything new!

All this should give us something to think about in studying Revelation because we tend to be selective. We avoid chapters that seem too disturbing, too hard to understand, or that don't fit our image of what God "should" do.

A good strategy is to read the entire book in one sitting to allow its full message to speak to our minds and hearts. This is how we will gain the full blessings of Revelation's prophecies. This will be true even if we do not comprehend everything. This book promises blessings for the future but also for today (Revelation 1:3). It is the grandest story of all time. It is the promise that God will defeat the forces of evil and will reign in victory forever from his golden, eternal city.

> *What Do You Think?*
> What can you do to ensure that you neither add to nor subtract from the prophecies and promises of the book of Revelation?
>
> *Digging Deeper*
> Could failing to read the book of Revelation amount to violating 22:19? Why, or why not?

III. Promising, Longing, Closing
(REVELATION 22:20-21)
A. Reaffirmation (v. 20a)

20a. He who testifies to these things says, "Yes, I am coming soon."

One last time John reminds us of Jesus' promise to come *soon*. This promise embraces both the presence of Christ in his church today (compare Revelation 2:5, 16; 3:11) and the promise of Christ's return in the future (compare 22:7, 12).

There will be only two reactions when Christ returns: joy and fear. Christ is coming the second time—a time of glory and judgment. He will vanquish all the evil that seems so powerful now. Who can stand before the wrath of the Lamb? No one (Revelation 6:17). The intent of this book as a whole is to bring readers to repentance, faithfulness, and endurance so that we will greet the return of Christ with joy.

B. Desire (v. 20b)

20b. Amen. Come, Lord Jesus.

Lack of fear is the position of John as he ends the book with a short prayer. The word *Amen* means "It is true." This is a loaded, powerful word in this context, for John is in effect saying, "Everything I just told you—all the visions, all the prophecies, all the warnings, all the blessings—is absolutely true." If this were not the case, then John would not dare express a desire for Jesus to return, lest John's falsehood be exposed!

But John is telling the truth, and his *come, Lord Jesus* is similar to Paul's "Maranatha" in 1 Corinthians 16:22. That is an Aramaic word meaning "Come, Lord." Perhaps the greatest faith prayer a Christian can utter is to ask sincerely for Christ to come, for that means the one praying is ready to meet the Lord, master, and judge face-to-face (compare 2 Timothy 4:8).

> *What Do You Think?*
> Could you pray for Jesus to return *right now* without fear that he actually would? If not, why not?
> *Digging Deeper*
> How does 2 Peter 3:7-12 affect your willingness to pray this prayer?

C. Benediction (v. 21)

21. The grace of the Lord Jesus be with God's people. Amen.

John offers a final blessing to the readers. This is comforting for the persecuted and fearful readers of the seven churches of Revelation 2 and 3, for they are in dire need of God's grace and mercy in their difficult situations. Likewise for us, this is a blessed word of calming peace. It assures us that God's marvelous *grace* toward us is not just past or future. It is present and available *now*.

Conclusion

A. Praying Maranatha

The return of Christ is a key theme of the book of Revelation. We joyously celebrate his first coming, his first "advent," in the Christmas season. But daily we should also anticipate and pray for his return, his second "advent," to take us home to be with him forever.

Today I did so by praying "Maranatha." I am ready for Christ to come again. When I read the news of another mass shooting, another terrorist attack, or another outrage to my Christian conscience, I am ready for Christ to come again. Despite the efforts of people of good faith, the dark side of humanity seems an unquenchable source of evil. I am ready for Christ to return.

I don't know exactly how his coming or our residence in the New Jerusalem will work. The closing chapters of Revelation give answers, but in all honesty, they raise questions as well. Yet I don't need to know everything, and I am at peace with that. I am ready for Christ to come again.

Are you ready as well, or does part of your heart fear that you will be among those excluded from the holy city? Being able and willing to pray for Christ to return right now is a great test of one's spiritual health, a test of one's relationship with the Lord Jesus.

Practice the Maranatha prayer for a week. Pray it sincerely, in true faith. If you take this seriously, it will make a difference.

B. Prayer

Father, thank you for promises both fulfilled and yet to be fulfilled. In this light, we pray, "Maranatha! Come, Lord Jesus!" Amen.

C. Thought to Remember

Make the Alpha and Omega
first and last in your life.

INVOLVEMENT LEARNING

Enhance your lesson with NIV Bible Student *(from your curriculum supplier) and the reproducible activity page (at www.standardlesson.com or in the back of the* NIV Standard Lesson Commentary Deluxe Edition*).*

Into the Lesson

Form learners into three groups. Give each a handout (you create) on which is printed one of the following scenarios, a different scenario per handout:

1–He asked her to marry him even though he didn't have much money, and her parents were against it. This is how she responded:

2–She lost her passport and her credit cards traveling in a foreign country. Here's what she did:

3–When he came home at dinner time, his wife and kids were gone, but her car was in the garage. His worry turned to relief when:

Ask each group to finish its story. As they do, write the three scenarios on the board. After five minutes, let someone from each group share its story ending. Discuss what makes us want to know how a story ends. Lead into Bible study by saying, "Today we come to one of the grandest passages of Scripture where the Bible tells us how its story ends. Be looking for what it tells us about how our story will end too."

Into the Word

Distribute handouts (you create) on which are printed all the following on each, to groups of no more than four.

1–Why not seal up the prophecies (v. 10)?

2–Why exhort sinners to continue sinning (v. 11)?

3–What will happen when Jesus returns (v. 12)?

4–What does Jesus claim about himself (vv. 13, 16)?

5–How are people classified (vv. 14-15)?

6–What's the invitation, and who offers it (v. 17)?

7–Why not replace some of Revelation with current understanding (vv. 18-19)?

8–Why does John pray the way he does (vv. 20-21)?

Give groups several minutes, and then discuss as a whole class. Note that questions having answers that are readily apparent in the text tend to be *knowledge-level questions*. But questions that

require putting two or more facts together to draw a conclusion tend to be *comprehension-level questions*. As the list of questions stand, at least six of the eight are worded at the knowledge level. If you wish to focus on the comprehension level, a general way to do so (with exceptions) is to change questions that begin with *what* to begin instead with *why*.

Option. For deeper study on the titles of Jesus, distribute copies of the "Who Was/Is Jesus?" exercise from the activity page, which you can download. Digging into the distinction between "meaning" and "significance" (as in lesson 11) will result in a much deeper study.

Into Life

Give each group one or two of the following words to unscramble, each word on a separate sheet of paper, with printing large enough to be seen from the front of the class:

EW WKON OWH HET YRSOT NESD

Ask a volunteer from each group to bring its sheet of paper, with the word(s) now unscrambled, to the front of the class and hold it up. Then permit seated class members voice how the sheets should be arranged to make a proper sentence (*expected result:* "We know how the story ends").

Ask, "What does this sentence have to do with today's Scripture?" Allow about five minutes of free discussion. Guide the discussion into discovering how participants are motivated or encouraged by today's lesson.

To close, ask participants to name praise choruses or hymns that expresses the hope of Jesus' promised return. Be sure to research these yourself ahead of time in case the class members seem stumped. Pick one for the class to sing.

Option. As class wraps up, distribute copies of the "Come, Lord Jesus" exercise from the activity page as a take-home.

Activity Pages

·

Fall Quarter
2021
Celebrating God

THESE ACTIVITY PAGES ARE DESIGNED TO:
- Engage students in a way that lecture and open-ended discussion don't.
- Gain insight on what has been learned and what hasn't.
- Encourage students to learn from one another and build vital relationships, in keeping with Proverbs 27:17 and Galatians 6:2.

TIPS FOR USING ACTIVITY PAGES:
- Instructions are on each lesson's "Involvement Learning" page (for teachers) and Activity Page (for students).
- Use these pages as optional alternatives for "Involvement Learning" activities.
- Limit individual work time and focus on facilitating discussion among learners.
- Encourage students to complete take-home work by discussing their results in the next class session.

MAXIMIZE GROUP ACTIVITY TIME!
- Instead of viewing group activities as empty time for you as the teacher, look for opportunities to encourage and challenge your students.
- Pray silently during the activity for the participants' spiritual growth! Pray for them by name, calling on the Lord to bless each person.
- Circulate among the groups of learners and observe their interactions to discover your learners' level of spiritual maturity.
- Pray that the Spirit will fall on your classroom, equipping your students with knowledge and filling them with passion to boldly proclaim the good news.

PRAISE WITH MUSIC

THE PROBLEMS BEFORE THE PRAISE

The praise in today's text came only after God's people were terrified for their lives! In the spaces below, work with a partner to list the events that caused confusion or fear before the praise.

A. Exodus 14:1-4 _____

B. Exodus 14:5-9 _____

C. Exodus 14:10-14 _____

D. Exodus 14:15-20 _____

E. Exodus 14:21-31 _____

In the space below, jot down one problem that caused you to fear until God helped you with the problem—and then you praised him for it. Share this with your study partner.

_____

_____

In the space below, jot down one problem you're facing today. How does the above study, combined with your own experience with God, strengthen your courage to praise him even though the problem is not yet solved?

_____

_____

HIS LOVE LASTS MY WHOLE LIFE

After describing each mighty act of God in Psalm 136, the psalmist uses the phrase "His love endures forever." What has God done that causes you to say the same thing? Write your own psalm of praise by filling in the three blanks below. Time limit of one minute.

God gave me _____.
   His love endures forever.
God rescued me from _____.
   His love endures forever.
God sustained me when _____.
   His love endures forever.

Copyright © 2021 by Standard Publishing, part of the David C Cook family. Permission is granted to reproduce this page for ministry purposes only. Not for resale.

PRAISE IN DANCE

NEW TESTAMENT WORSHIP

Work with classmates to complete this listing. The "other" entries at the bottom offer you opportunities to include additional texts not listed.

<u>Scripture</u>	<u>What the Text Implies About Worship Today</u>
John 4:23-24	_____
	_____
Romans 12:1	_____
	_____
1 Corinthians 14:26	_____
	_____
Hebrews 12:28	_____
	_____
Revelation 14:7	_____
	_____
[Other?]	_____
	_____
[Other?]	_____
	_____

Would you describe the above in terms of an "artist's conception" (general principles) or more in terms of a "blueprint" (exact details)? Why?

_____

_____

_____

_____

_____

_____

_____

_____

Copyright © 2021 by Standard Publishing, part of the David C Cook family. Permission is granted to reproduce this page for ministry purposes only. Not for resale.

Praise by Expecting and Following

Lesson 3, Mark 10:46-52, NIV

One Story, Three Versions

Underline in <u>brown</u> the wording that is common to all three accounts.
Underline in <u>blue</u> the wording that is common to Matthew and Mark but not Luke.
Underline in <u>green</u> the wording that is common to Matthew and Luke but not Mark.
Underline in <u>orange</u> wording that is common to Luke and Mark but not Matthew.
Underline in <u>red</u> any wording that is unique to one of Matthew, Mark, or Luke.

Matthew 20:29-34	Mark 10:46-52	Luke 18:35-43
As Jesus and his disciples were leaving Jericho, a large crowd followed him. Two blind men were sitting by the roadside, and when they heard that Jesus was going by, they shouted, "Lord, Son of David, have mercy on us!"	Then they came to Jericho. As Jesus and his disciples, together with a large crowd, were leaving the city, a blind man, Bartimaeus (which means "son of Timaeus"), was sitting by the roadside begging. When he heard that it was Jesus of Nazareth, he began to shout, "Jesus, Son of David, have mercy on me!"	As Jesus approached Jericho, a blind man was sitting by the roadside begging. When he heard the crowd going by, he asked what was happening. They told him, "Jesus of Nazareth is passing by." He called out, "Jesus, Son of David, have mercy on me!"
The crowd rebuked them and told them to be quiet, but they shouted all the louder, "Lord, Son of David, have mercy on us!"	Many rebuked him and told him to be quiet, but he shouted all the more, "Son of David, have mercy on me!"	Those who led the way rebuked him and told him to be quiet, but he shouted all the more, "Son of David, have mercy on me!"
Jesus stopped and called them.	Jesus stopped and said, "Call him." So they called to the blind man, "Cheer up! On your feet! He's calling you."	Jesus stopped and ordered the man to be brought to him.
	Throwing his cloak aside, he jumped to his feet and came to Jesus.	When he came near, Jesus asked him,
"What do you want me to do for you?" he asked. "Lord," they answered, "we want our sight.	"What do you want me to do for you?" Jesus asked him. The blind man said, "Rabbi, I want to see."	"What do you want me to do for you?" "Lord, I want to see," he replied.
Jesus had compassion on them and touched their eyes. Immediately they received their sight and followed him.	"Go," said Jesus, "your faith has healed you." Immediately he received his sight and followed Jesus along the road.	Jesus said to him, "Receive your sight; your faith has healed you." Immediately he received his sight and followed Jesus, praising God. When all the people saw it, they also praised God.

What do you learn from this exercise? _____

_____

Why might Mark's account be longer than the other two, even though his is the shortest of the Gospels?

_____

Copyright © 2021 by Standard Publishing, part of the David C Cook family. Permission is granted to reproduce this page for ministry purposes only. Not for resale.

PRAISE FOR SALVATION

MORE ON BAPTISM

Work with a partner to summarize what each of these passages says about Christian baptism. You can add additional passages if you think others should be included.

Matthew 28:19-20 _____

_____

Acts 2:38-39 _____

_____

Acts 19:1-7 _____

_____

Romans 6:1-7 _____

_____

Galatians 3:27 _____

_____

Ephesians 4:5 _____

_____

Colossians 2:9-12 _____

_____

Titus 3:4-7 _____

_____

1 Peter 3:20-22 _____

_____

[Other?] _____

_____

[Other?] _____

_____

Based on your study above, summarize baptism in these terms:

Who? _____   What? _____   Where? _____

When? _____   Why? _____   How? _____

Copyright © 2021 by Standard Publishing, part of the David C Cook family. Permission is granted to reproduce this page for ministry purposes only. Not for resale.

IMPORTANT IDEAS FROM PSALM 100

Find each of the words listed below in this word-search puzzle. Then find the words in Psalm 100. Why is each significant?

```
G  I  I  U  Q  H  W  S  C  Z  P  S  H  A  W
H  N  N  R  N  W  S  E  F  P  Q  N  T  A  X
P  V  I  J  U  E  U  N  D  O  G  O  S  G  D
H  R  A  V  N  G  I  T  J  G  L  I  H  Z  D
W  A  A  D  I  Y  T  E  R  E  I  T  P  M  S
T  F  A  I  F  G  H  R  K  S  R  A  F  V  W
Z  L  I  L  S  E  S  U  U  U  N  R  Z  X  M
G  P  P  T  D  E  D  K  V  S  Q  E  Y  Q  A
T  J  D  H  U  B  T  L  N  Q  Y  N  D  M  B
H  S  I  D  H  E  W  E  S  A  N  E  E  O  X
P  A  S  T  U  R  E  L  C  G  H  G  E  X  A
U  S  Z  W  G  R  O  I  L  D  G  T  W  B  S
Q  T  U  R  L  R  N  G  I  P  Y  K  W  J  Z
R  Y  K  Z  D  M  Q  P  A  Q  H  N  W  M  Z
S  O  Y  F  R  Z  U  L  R  C  N  M  H  Q  B
```

WORD BOX

ENTER

LORD

GENERATIONS

PASTURE

GLADNESS

PRAISE

GOD

THANKSGIVING

GOD IS KING

Psalms 95–100 are sometimes grouped as "kingship psalms" because of the way they focus on God as ruler of all. List reasons God deserves to be called king, according to each of the following.

Psalm 95:1-7 _____

Psalm 96:8-10 _____

Psalm 97:1-9 _____

Psalm 98:1-3, 9 _____

Psalm 99 _____

Psalm 100 _____

Copyright © 2021 by Standard Publishing, part of the David C Cook family. Permission is granted to reproduce this page for ministry purposes only. Not for resale.

PRAISE FOR GOD'S ULTIMATE JUSTICE

Lesson 6, Psalm 9:1-12, NIV

WHAT'S THE TRUTH ABOUT POVERTY?

Do internet searches to discover answers to the questions below.

How is poverty defined? _____

_____

What percentage of the world's population lives in poverty? _____

_____

What are major causes of poverty? _____

_____

What are some widely held myths about poverty? _____

_____

Why is poverty an important issue? _____

_____

In what ways, if at all, is poverty linked to oppression? _____

_____

_____

_____

TALKING ABOUT POVERTY

Based on your Scripture and internet studies today, how would you respond to someone who made any of the following statements?

"Really, there's nothing we can do about poverty. No matter how we try to help, poverty won't go away."

"It's terrible that people suffer from poverty. But our biggest concern should be the eternal salvation of people, not their earthly troubles."

"I've worked hard to earn my blessings. Why don't all these poor people work as hard as I do?"

"I don't understand why God is so concerned about poverty when this world will all come to an end someday anyway."

Copyright © 2021 by Standard Publishing, part of the David C Cook family. Permission is granted to reproduce this page for ministry purposes only. Not for resale.

PRAISE GOD FOR PAST DELIVERANCE

Lesson 7, Psalm 107:1-9, 39-43, NIV

TO CRY FOR HELP

Look at all of Psalm 107 to discern a pattern of crying for help in times of trouble and the ways God answered. Describe them below:

Psalm 107:6-7 _____

Psalm 107:13-14 _____

Psalm 107:19-20 _____

Psalm 107:28-30 _____

Examine Psalm 107:8, 15, 21, and 31, which are all worded identically. Describe how the psalmist desired people to respond to God's help.

_____

_____

_____

PSALM 107 REFLECTED IN SCRIPTURE

Read each of the following passages and jot down the words or themes present in both places.

Reference	Repeated Words or Themes	Psalm 107 verse
Isaiah 62:12		
Psalm 38:6		
Psalm 50:15		
Psalm 99:3		
Hosea 14:9		
Luke 1:53		
Luke 13:29		

Copyright © 2021 by Standard Publishing, part of the David C Cook family. Permission is granted to reproduce this page for ministry purposes only. Not for resale.

PRAISE GOD FOR HIS PRESENCE

Lesson 8, Psalm 84, NIV

WHERE GOD DWELLS

Consider the following passages to discover what the Bible says about God's heavenly and earthly dwelling places. What new concept is present in the New Testament era?

Exodus 15:13, 17 _____

Exodus 25:8 _____

Exodus 29:45-46 _____

Leviticus 26:11 _____

Deuteronomy 12:5 _____

Psalm 43:3-4 _____

Psalm 74:2 _____

Psalm 135:21 _____

Isaiah 66:1 _____

Ephesians 2:19-22; 3:16-18 _____

2 Timothy 1:1 _____

James 4:5 _____

HEART TEST

Take a moment three times daily in the week ahead to jot down ways you know God is in your heart and/or steps you're taking to welcome him to stay there.

	Monday	Tuesday	Wednesday	Thursday	Friday	Saturday	Sunday
Morning							
Afternoon							
Evening							

Copyright © 2021 by Standard Publishing, part of the David C Cook family. Permission is granted to reproduce this page for ministry purposes only. Not for resale.

Praise God for His Greatness

Lesson 9, Psalms 149:1-5; 150:1-6, NIV

Praise God Anyway!

Consider these quotes from men and women who have discovered the value of praise in difficult times as well as in easy situations. Put an X next to the quote that most speaks to you; write a sentence at the bottom to explain why.

_____ "The point is not to completely understand God but to worship him. Let the very fact that you cannot know him fully lead you to praise him for his infiniteness and grandeur."
—Francis Chan

_____ "When we complain about our current situation, we remain in it; when we praise God in the midst of difficulty, he raises us out of it." —Joyce Meyer

_____ "Praise is declaration, a victory cry, proclaiming faith to stand firm in the place God has given you. Praise is a proclamation that the enemy's intent to plunder you will not rock you. Praise declares that you will not be moved by the enemy's attempt to snatch you away." —Darlene Zschech

_____ "We can always find a reason to praise. Situations change for better and for worse, but God's worth never changes." —Matt Redman

_____ "Satan's aim is to destroy our joy and trust and delight in God, and to make God look worthless in the world's eyes. Every time someone forsakes God for the world, gets angry at God when part of the world is taken away from them, they highlight the world as valuable . . . and every time someone stays with God, when the world is taken away, and praises God, they highlight the value and glory of God."—John Piper

_____ "The deepest level of worship is praising God in spite of pain, trusting him during a trial, surrendering while suffering, and loving him when he seems distant." —Rick Warren

_____ "In a sense, we are better prepared to praise God than the angels are, for angels have never known the joy of redemption." —David Jeremiah

Reasons for my choices:

_____

_____

_____

_____

Copyright © 2021 by Standard Publishing, part of the David C Cook family. Permission is granted to reproduce this page for ministry purposes only. Not for resale.

POWER AND AUTHORITY

Not everyone who has *the power* (the ability) to do something has *the authority* (the right) to do it, and vice versa. In the two boxes on the left, put some examples of each. Then enter facts in the two boxes on the right as indicated.

Has Power but Not Authority	Power Words in Today's Text
Has Authority but Not Power	**Authority Words in Today's Text**

Complete this sentence: God's power and authority are complete because _____

_____

NOTHING BUT THE BLOOD

The song "Nothing but the Blood of Jesus" has been sung by generations of Christians. How well do you know it? Find out by seeing if you can unscramble its lyrics below.

W R O N G	Flow precious the is O Snow me white makes that as Fount know I other no, Jesus blood of nothing but the	my see for this pardon I Jesus blood of nothing but the my cleansing for this plea my Jesus blood of nothing but the
R I G H T		

Copyright © 2021 by Standard Publishing, part of the David C Cook family. Permission is granted to reproduce this page for ministry purposes only. Not for resale.

GOD OF POWER

THE PERFECT NUMBER

Using the text of Revelation alone, take no more than one minute to put an X under chapters that have one or more occurrences of the perfect number. No concordances or Bible-search apps allowed!

Chapters in Revelation featuring the words *seven* or *seventh*

1	2	3	4	5	6	7	8	9	10	11	12	13	14	15	16	17	18	19	20	21	22

(Hint: you should have 14 or 15 chapters marked with an X.)

HOW LONG?

In what single way does each of the following reflect the conclusion of Revelation 11:15?

Exodus 15:18 _____   Daniel 7:14 _____

Psalm 10:16 _____   Micah 4:5 _____

Daniel 2:44 _____   Zechariah 14:9 _____

TODAY AND TOMORROW

How does the text's picture of future reality encourage you to deal with your present reality?

The most pressing issue I'm facing this week is _____.

_____

Today's Scripture encourages me to deal with today because of this that it says about the future:

_____

_____

Copyright © 2021 by Standard Publishing, part of the David C Cook family. Permission is granted to reproduce this page for ministry purposes only. Not for resale.

MARRIAGE OF THE LAMB

Lesson 12, Revelation 19:1-8, NIV

WEDDINGS

Circulate among your classmates and have each person put his or her initials beside **one** of the affirmations below.

_____ 1. I am married.

_____ 2. I have been married 10 years or more.

_____ 3. I have given a wedding toast.

_____ 4. I have a child who is married.

_____ 5. I have been a best man or maid of honor.

_____ 6. We eloped.

_____ 7. I have a grandchild who is married.

_____ 8. We were married in a church.

Photo: © Getty Images

OT IN NT

Match the verse from the Old Testament with the verse in Revelation 19 that best reflects it.

_____ 1. Revelation 19:2   A. Deuteronomy 32:43

_____ 2. Revelation 19:3   B. Psalm 134:1

_____ 3. Revelation 19:5   C. Isaiah 34:9-10

_____ 4. Revelation 19:6   D. Ezekiel 1:24

Photos: © Getty Images

Copyright © 2021 by Standard Publishing, part of the David C Cook family. Permission is granted to reproduce this page for ministry purposes only. Not for resale.

Lesson 13, Acts 10:34-47, NIV

WHO IS MY GENTILE?

In the spaces below, write down the name of three nonbelievers and a way you'll demonstrate God's love to at least one of them this week.

Name	Loving Action

BROKEN BARRIERS

In the spaces below, write down places or relationships—ones you're very familiar with—where barriers need to be broken.

1. _____
2. _____
3. _____
4. _____
5. _____
6. _____
7. _____

Photos: © Getty Images

In what way can you bring the love of Christ into one of these situations in the week ahead?

Copyright © 2021 by Standard Publishing, part of the David C Cook family. Permission is granted to reproduce this page for ministry purposes only. Not for resale.

Lesson 1

The Problems Before the Praise:
A–Pharaoh would chase after the Israelites.
B–Pharaoh chased after them with his army and chariots and overtook them by the Red Sea.
C–The Israelites were extremely afraid and cried out to God.
D–God told Moses to lift up his rod and part the sea so the people could go through on dry land.
E–The Israelites passed through safely, but all the Egyptians were drowned when the sea returned to its place.

His Love Lasts My Whole Life: *responses may vary*

Lesson 2

New Testament Worship: *responses may vary*

Lesson 3

One Story, Three Versions: *responses may vary*

Lesson 4

More on Baptism: *responses may vary*

Lesson 5

Important Ideas From Psalm 100:

God Is King: *responses may vary*

Lesson 6

What's The Truth About Poverty?: *responses may vary*

Talking About Poverty: *responses may vary*

Lesson 7

To Cry For Help: *responses may vary*

Psalm 107 Reflected In Scripture:
Isaiah 62:12, "the Redeemed of the Lord" (compare Psalm 107:2); Psalm 38:6, "bowed down" (compare Psalm 107:39); Psalm 50:15, "call on me in the day of trouble" (compare Psalm 107:6); Psalm 99:3, "Let them praise" (compare Psalm 107:8); Hosea 14:9, "Who is wise? Let them realize these things" (compare Psalm 107:43); Luke 1:53, "filled the hungry with good things" (compare Psalm 107:9); Luke 13:29, "from the east and west and north and south" (compare Psalm 107:3)

Lesson 8

Where God Dwells: *responses may vary*

Heart Test: *responses may vary*

Lesson 9

Praise God Anyway!: *responses may vary*

Lesson 10

Power and Authority: Several answers are possible. But at least, the word *throne* should be categorized as an authority word; the words *feed them, lead them,* and *might* are power words.

Nothing but the Blood:
O precious is the flow
that makes me white as snow;
no other fount I know;
nothing but the blood of Jesus.

For my pardon this I see:
nothing but the blood of Jesus.
For my cleansing this my plea:
nothing but the blood of Jesus.

lesson 11

The Perfect Number:

Chapters in Revelation featuring the words *seven* or *seventh*

1	2	3	4	5	6	7	8	9	10	11	12	13	14	15	16	17	18	19	20	21	22
X	X	X	X	X	X*		X		X	X	X	X		X	X	X				X	

*Note: Some versions of the Bible don't have the number in chapter 6.

How Long?: They all stress the eternal nature of the reign of God.

Today and Tomorrow: *responses may vary*

Lesson 12

Weddings: *responses may vary*

OT in NT: 1–A; 2–C; 3–B; 4–D

Lesson 13

Who Is My Gentile?: *responses may vary*

Broken Barriers: *responses may vary*

Copyright © 2021 by Standard Publishing, part of the David C Cook family. Permission is granted to reproduce this page for ministry purposes only. Not for resale.

Activity Pages

·

Winter Quarter
2021–2022
Justice, Law, History

THESE ACTIVITY PAGES ARE DESIGNED TO:
- Engage students in a way that lecture and open-ended discussion don't.
- Gain insight on what has been learned and what hasn't.
- Encourage students to learn from one another and build vital relationships, in keeping with Proverbs 27:17 and Galatians 6:2.

TIPS FOR USING ACTIVITY PAGES:
- Instructions are on each lesson's "Involvement Learning" page (for teachers) and Activity Page (for students).
- Use these pages as optional alternatives for "Involvement Learning" activities.
- Limit individual work time and focus on facilitating discussion among learners.
- Encourage students to complete take-home work by discussing their results in the next class session.

MAXIMIZE GROUP ACTIVITY TIME!
- Instead of viewing group activities as empty time for you as the teacher, look for opportunities to encourage and challenge your students.
- Pray silently during the activity for the participants' spiritual growth! Pray for them by name, calling on the Lord to bless each person.
- Circulate among the groups of learners and observe their interactions to discover your learners' level of spiritual maturity.
- Pray for the Spirit to lead as your students grow in their knowledge of the Word—that they may be filled with passion to boldly proclaim the good news.

JUSTICE AND OBEDIENCE
Lesson 1, Deuteronomy 5:1b-3; 10:12-13; 27:1-10, NIV

HEAR HERE

More than once in the book of Deuteronomy we read the admonition for God's people to listen and heed. Use the following chart to examine some instances. How might each of these commands serve as a message for Christians today?

Text	The Command's Intent	Application for Today
5:1		
6:4-5		
9:1		
20:3		
27:9		

DOING WHAT GOD WANTS

Think prayerfully about each of the five admonitions in Deuteronomy 10:12-13. List at least two specific ways you could heed each of them this week.

WHAT GOD WANTS

_____ _____

_____ _____

_____

WHAT I CAN DO

_____ _____

_____ _____

_____

Copyright © 2021 by Standard Publishing, part of the David C Cook family. Permission is granted to reproduce this page for ministry purposes only. Not for resale.

Justice and Kindness

Lesson 2, 2 Samuel 9:1-7, 9-12, NIV

Why Be Kind?

Find six synonyms or near-synonyms to the word *kindness* in the puzzle below. Then rank-order those six words in the blanks to the right in terms of how close they are to the biblical idea of kindness.

```
Q T S Z U O E D T R A Q K F R
B K N V K M L V N G R Z E L R
J G V E Z Q E E E T W Z K J P
L H B N L V B E C I E U D F M
G E N E R O U S I I F Y P K E
E V W V G Q V N F F P Q U L Q
N G V H Y N S E E K W E B W B
E T A R E D I S N O C A S I O
Q E U B T L I Z E E T Q U D Z
Q B W T R A P Z B I B T B D E
P K R V C V V F R K P X C K L
G Z K Q D W J A U D O B I U L
J A B W P C H T B L L N Z F R
Y M Q P R C D K N T R T U F T
I W T E G S L L P N X O A M Q
```

1. _____ (closest to biblical idea of kindness)

2. _____

3. _____

4. _____

5. _____

6. _____

(most distant from the biblical idea of kindness)

WWW.ZIBA&MEPHIBOSHETH.EDU?

Imagine that Ziba and Mephibosheth wrote blogs. Considering today's Scripture text, which social-media shorthand below would Ziba use but Mephibosheth would not? How about the reverse?

		Z. would use but M. wouldn't	M. would use but Z. wouldn't	Why?
BFF	best friends forever.	☐	☐	_____
F2F	face-to-face	☐	☐	_____
FTW	for the win!	☐	☐	_____
FUTAB	feet up, take a break.	☐	☐	_____
IMHO	in my humble opinion	☐	☐	_____
IRL	in real life	☐	☐	_____
LMS	like my status.	☐	☐	_____
LOL	laughing out loud	☐	☐	_____
TBH	to be honest	☐	☐	_____
TIL	today I learned.	☐	☐	_____
TMI	too much information	☐	☐	_____

Copyright © 2021 by Standard Publishing, part of the David C Cook family. Permission is granted to reproduce this page for ministry purposes only. Not for resale.

JUSTICE AND RIGHTEOUSNESS

LOOKING AT THE LIGHT

Fill in this chart to discover more of what Isaiah says about light.

Isaiah	Paraphrase	Application for Today
5:20		
8:20		
9:2		
42:6		
45:7		
50:10		
58:10		
60:19		

NO SANTA

The truth of today's Scripture offers a welcome sentiment for a Christmas greeting that doesn't include fictions, such as Santa Claus.

On the blank card to the right, sketch an image and include a greeting that offers the light and hope promised by Isaiah 9.

Photo © Getty Images

Copyright © 2021 by Standard Publishing, part of the David C Cook family. Permission is granted to reproduce this page for ministry purposes only. Not for resale.

JUSTICE AND DELIVERANCE

OUR JUST GOD

As you read today's Scripture, notice stark contrasts between God's promise to punish the wicked and his promise to restore fellowship with his people. Jot the specifics of those contrasts by making lists under both of the following headings.

Behaviors that call forth God's wrath

_____

_____

_____

_____

_____

_____

Behaviors that ensure God's deliverance

_____

_____

_____

_____

_____

_____

GOOD NEWS

Other Scriptures reflect ideas contained in today's text. In the space below, summarize each verse listed, then answer the questions at the end.

Psalm 101:8 _____

_____

Isaiah 52:7 _____

_____

Romans 10:15 _____

_____

What do these verses suggest about God's view of evangelism? obedience? those who don't know him?

Copyright © 2021 by Standard Publishing, part of the David C Cook family. Permission is granted to reproduce this page for ministry purposes only. Not for resale.

JUSTICE, VENGEANCE, AND MERCY
Lesson 5, Genesis 4:1-15, NIV

CROSSROADS

In the two blank boxes, propose different outcomes if Cain had adopted a different attitude.

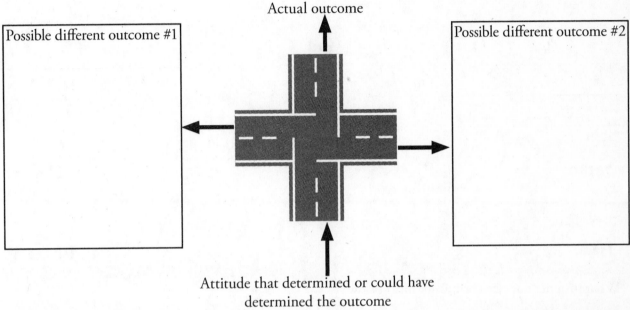

Actual outcome

Possible different outcome #1

Possible different outcome #2

Attitude that determined or could have
determined the outcome

Photo © Getty Images

ANGER TWO WAYS

Describe a time when you allowed anger to control your actions and lead you into sin. What were the consequences of your anger and sin?

_____

Recall a time when you ruled over anger and chose to do the right thing. How did those consequences differ from when you allowed anger to take over?

_____

Write a prayer of repentance for the first instance and a prayer for strength to continue to learn to control your anger as in the second.

_____

_____

Copyright © 2021 by Standard Publishing, part of the David C Cook family. Permission is granted to reproduce this page for ministry purposes only. Not for resale.

RELATIONSHIP DYNAMICS

Read Genesis 21:8-20. Then draw 15 relationship lines, 1 each between every individual below. Make the line (1) straight to indicate a congenial relationship or (2) jagged line for a tense relationship or (3) dotted for an unknown relationship.

God

Abraham

Sarah   **Hagar**

Isaac   **Ishmael**

What insights does this bring? Jot ideas below.

_____

HAGAR AND GOD

The book of Genesis records two encounters between Hagar and God. Read both accounts and answer the questions to compare and contrast.

	Genesis 16:7-15	Genesis 21:14-20
1. Where did God meet Hagar?	_____	_____
2. What did God ask Hagar?	_____	_____
3. What did God command Hagar to do? . .	_____	_____
4. What did God promise to Hagar?	_____	_____

5. What do you learn about God based on his interactions with Hagar?

Copyright © 2021 by Standard Publishing, part of the David C Cook family. Permission is granted to reproduce this page for ministry purposes only. Not for resale.

Justice and Fairness

To Do or Not to Do

Restate each "Do not" command in Exodus 23:1-9 with at least one possible "Instead, do" alternative.

Do not...	Instead, do...
1. Spread false reports.	
2. Be a malicious witness.	
3. Follow a crowd to do evil.	
4. Be biased.	
5. Be automatically favorable to the poor.	
6. Deny justice to the poor.	
7. Put the innocent and righteous to death.	
8. Accept a bribe.	
9. Oppress a foreigner.	

Who Is My Neighbor?

What people come to mind when you hear those words? Fill in as many boxes as you can.

Exodus 23:1-12 →	POOR	INNOCENT	ENEMY	FOREIGNER
Globally				
In my country				
Locally				

Which single area of the 12 could you have the most influence in for promoting fair treatment? Why?

What will you do to get started?

Copyright © 2021 by Standard Publishing, part of the David C Cook family. Permission is granted to reproduce this page for ministry purposes only. Not for resale.

Justice, Judges, and Priests

Job Description

Use Deuteronomy 16:18-20; 17:8-13 as a guide to create a job description for an ideal judge today.

Job Title and Purpose: _____

Accountable to: _____

Oversee these functions: _____

Primary Duties: _____

Secondary Duties: _____

Prerequisite Qualifications: _____

Preferred Character Qualities: _____

Personal Statement

In the space below, list your own credentials for the position described above.

_____

_____

_____

What evidence could you provide of your fitness for the office?

What areas require further education or experience on your part?

How do 1 Timothy 3:1-7; 2 Timothy 2:15-26; and Titus 2 inform your conclusions?

Copyright © 2021 by Standard Publishing, part of the David C Cook family. Permission is granted to reproduce this page for ministry purposes only. Not for resale.

JUSTICE AND THE MARGINALIZED
Lesson 9, Deuteronomy 24:10-21, NIV

COLOR CODING

Color-code Deuteronomy 24:10-21 based on the key below:

Red–What *not* to do.   Green–What to do.   Blue–Reason for action.

¹⁰ When you make a loan of any kind to your neighbor, do not go into their house to get what is offered to you as a pledge. ¹¹ Stay outside and let the neighbor to whom you are making the loan bring the pledge out to you. ¹² If the neighbor is poor, do not go to sleep with their pledge in your possession. ¹³ Return their cloak by sunset so that your neighbor may sleep in it. Then they will thank you, and it will be regarded as a righteous act in the sight of the LORD your God.

¹⁴ Do not take advantage of a hired worker who is poor and needy, whether that worker is a fellow Israelite or a foreigner residing in one of your towns. ¹⁵ Pay them their wages each day before sunset, because they are poor and are counting on it. Otherwise they may cry to the LORD against you, and you will be guilty of sin.

¹⁶ Parents are not to be put to death for their children, nor children put to death for their parents; each will die for their own sin.

¹⁷ Do not deprive the foreigner or the fatherless of justice,or take the cloak of the widow as a pledge. ¹⁸ Remember that you were slaves in Egypt and the LORD your God redeemed you from there. That is why I command you to do this.

¹⁹ When you are harvesting in your field and you overlook a sheaf, do not go back to get it. Leave it for the foreigner,the fatherless and the widow,so that the LORD your God may bless you in all the work of your hands. ²⁰ When you beat the olives from your trees, do not go over the branches a second time. Leave what remains for the foreigner, the fatherless and the widow. ²¹ When you harvest the grapes in your vineyard, do not go over the vines again. Leave what remains for the foreigner, the fatherless and the widow.

EXAMPLES TO FOLLOW

Answer these three questions after reading each passage listed below:

1. Who was marginalized and why?
2. Who was generous and compassionate and why?
3. How can you apply the passage in becoming more compassionate?

Day 1	Day 2	Day 3	Day 4	Day 5
2 Samuel 9:1-13	Ruth 2:1-16	Luke 10:30-37	Acts 9:36-43	Ephesians 2:1-7

Copyright © 2021 by Standard Publishing, part of the David C Cook family. Permission is granted to reproduce this page for ministry purposes only. Not for resale.

NATHAN CONDEMNS DAVID

SAUL VIS-À-VIS DAVID

Compare and contrast these two accounts, especially their outcomes.

	SAUL (1 Samuel 15:13-29)	DAVID (2 Samuel 12:1-15)
1. What sins are named in these passages?		
2. What was the initial response to the prophet's confrontation?		
3. What was God's response to these two?		
4. What were the consequences for the kings' sins?		
5. How did all this affect the kings' relationship with God?		

What were the key differences between the heart attitudes of Saul and David?

How might Saul's life have been different if he had responded as David did?

PSALM 51

Read Psalm 51 daily for five days. Focus on a different aspect of the psalm each day in your prayer time.

DAY 1, verses 1-4: What sin do you need to confess to God? Take some time to consider the nature of this sin and ask him to have mercy on you.

DAY 2, verses 5-6: What temptations and weaknesses do you struggle with? Consider the person God desires for you to be. How is he working to recreate and redeem you?

DAY 3, verses 7-14: What did David desire for God to do for him? Which words resonate with you? Make them your prayer today, for life change and renewal.

DAY 4, verses 15-19: Think about the ways that you can present your heart and body to God as a living sacrifice (Romans 12:1); spend time practicing this today.

DAY 5, write your own psalm of confession to God, using Psalm 51 as a guide.

_____

_____

_____

Copyright © 2021 by Standard Publishing, part of the David C Cook family. Permission is granted to reproduce this page for ministry purposes only. Not for resale.

EZRA AND THE LAW

THE EFFECTS OF GOD'S WORD

As you read Psalm 19:7-11, fill out the chart below.

Verse	Description of the Effect	Modern-Day Result
7a		
7b		
8a		
8b		
9a		
9b		
10a		
10b		
11		

LOOKING FORWARD

What are some ways that you personally can pass a spiritual inheritance to someone of the next generation?

_____

_____

How will you intentionally begin to do so this week? Write your ideas.

_____

_____

What part will prayer play in this?

_____

_____

Copyright © 2021 by Standard Publishing, part of the David C Cook family. Permission is granted to reproduce this page for ministry purposes only. Not for resale.

BILDAD MISSPEAKS GOD'S JUSTICE

Lesson 12, Job 8:1-10, 20-22, NIV

FACT-CHECK THE SPEECH

There is one word wrong in each verse below. Actually, there are a lot of words wrong because Bildad didn't speak rightly about God (Job 42:7). But what we're interested in is one word in each verse that a reporter on the scene would have heard wrong. Find that wrong word, cross it out, and put in the word that Bildad actually said. You score 1 point for each wrong word identified and 1 point for each correct word substituted—24 points total possible.

2 "How long will you say such things? Your words are a weak wind.

3 Does Satan pervert justice? Does the Almighty pervert what is right?

4 When your parents sinned against him, he gave them over to the penalty of their sin.

5 But if you will seek God earnestly and plead with the Angels,

6 if you are impure and upright, even now he will rouse himself on your behalf and restore you to your prosperous state.

7 Your beginnings will seem humble, so impoverished will your future be.

8 "Ask the former generation and find out what their successors learned,

9 for we were born only today and know nothing, and our days on earth are but a shadow.

10 Will they not instruct you and tell you? Will they not bring forth words from their experience?"

....

20 "Surely God does not reject one who is blameless or strengthen the feet of evildoers.

21 She will yet fill your mouth with laughter and your lips with shouts of joy.

22 Your enemies will be clothed in rags, and the tents of the wicked will be no more."

SAY WHAT?

Consider these popular—but superficial, or even downright wrong—beliefs held by Christians. What Scriptures and/or logic would you use to point out problems with them?

1. There is no place for mourning in the Christian life.

2. Cleanliness is next to godliness.

3. Everything happens for a reason.

4. God loves the sinner but hates the sin.

Copyright © 2021 by Standard Publishing, part of the David C Cook family. Permission is granted to reproduce this page for ministry purposes only. Not for resale.

JOB AND THE JUST GOD

NEW PERSPECTIVE

Page 224 of the teacher guide explains the use of these images.

Image 2

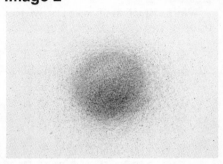

Image 1

Image 3

Photos © Getty Images

A SINCERE PRAYER

Read Job 42:1-6. Write down the words in Job's response to God that relate to each category below.

PRAYER RESPONSE	JOB'S WORDS
1. Confessing the truth	_____
2. Admitting personal wrong	_____
3. Reflecting on relationship	_____
4. Acknowledging understanding	_____
5. Responding with action	_____
6. Reflecting Job's "head knowledge"	_____
7. Reflecting Job's "heart knowledge"	_____

Copyright © 2021 by Standard Publishing, part of the David C Cook family. Permission is granted to reproduce this page for ministry purposes only. Not for resale.

Lesson 1

Hear Here: responses and applications will vary.

Doing What God Wants: responses and applications will vary.

Lesson 2

Why Be Kind? Words to find are *beneficent, benevolent, charitable, considerate, generous, helpful*.

```
Q T S Z U O E D T R A Q K F R
B K N V K M L V N G R Z E L R
J G V E Z Q E E T W Z K J P
L H B N L V B E C I E U D F M
G E N E R O U S I I F Y P K E
E V W V G Q V N F F P Q U L Q
N G V H Y N S E E K W E B W B
E T A R E D I S N O C A S I O
Q E U B T L I Z E E T Q U D Z
Q B W T R A P Z B I R T B D E
P K R V C V V R K P X C K L
G Z K Q D W J A U D O B I U L
J A B W P C H T B L L N Z F R
Y M Q P R O D K N T R T U F T
I W T E G S L L P N X O A M Q
```

[*Option*: to make the puzzle less time-consuming, you can give students a list of the six words to be found.]

www.Ziba&Mephibosheth.edu? responses and applications will vary.

Lesson 3

Both activities: responses and applications will vary.

Lesson 4

Our Just God: responses expected per the lesson's Scripture text.
Good News: responses will vary.

Lesson 5

Both activities: responses will vary.

Lesson 6

Relationship Dynamics: responses will vary.

Hagar and God
1–Near a spring in the desert / In the Desert of Beersheba. 2–"Where have you come from, and where are you going?" / "What is the matter, Hagar?" 3–"Go back to your mistress and submit to her." / "Do not be afraid; … Lift the boy up and take him by the hand." 4–"I will increase your descendants so much that they will be too numerous to count." / "I will make him into a great nation." 5–[Various answers possible.]

Lesson 7

To Do or Not to Do: possible responses among others are 1–Tell the truth; 2–Be a trustworthy and righteous witness; 3–Do what is good; 4–Speak up for what is right; 5 and 6–Make judgements based on facts and the law; 7–Advocate for the life of an innocent person; 8–Refuse bribes and expose the practice of bribery; 9–Extend hospitality to those who need it.

Who Is My Neighbor? responses will vary.

Lesson 8

Both activities: responses will vary.

Lesson 9

Examples to Follow:

	Day 1	Day 2	Day 3	Day 4	Day 5
Marginalized:	Meph.	Ruth	Samaritan	widows	us
Generous:	David	Boaz	Samaritan	Tabitha	God
Result:	[responses per the text]				

Lesson 10

Saul vis-à-vis David: 1–Saul did not destroy everything as God commanded; David committed adultery and murder. 2–Saul denied and excused his disobedience; David repented. 3–Saul was rejected as king; David received forgiveness along with consequences. 4–Saul experienced God's tearing the kingdom from him; David's family would experience conflict and death of a child. 5–Saul had a broken relationship; David's relationship was restored.

Lesson 11

The Effects of God's Word: Responses in the "Description of Effect" column are to be drawn directly from the text of Psalm 19. Responses in the "Modern-Day Result" column will be individualized and therefore highly variable.

Lesson 12

Fact-Check the Speech.
2–*weak* should be *blustering*; 3–*Satan* should be *God*; 4–*parents* should be *children*; 5–*Angels* should be *Almighty*; 6–*impure* should be *pure*; 7–*impoverished* should be *prosperous*; 8–*successors* should be *ancestors*; 9–*today* should be *yesterday*; 10–*experience* should be *understanding*; 20–*feet* should be *hands*; 21–*She* should be *He*; 22–*rags* should be *shame*.

Say What?
1–The ability to express grief or to mourn is a God-given emotion. It can't be a sin because Jesus himself wept (John 11:35); 2–Not in the Bible; 3–See Luke 13:1-5; 4–See Proverbs 6:16-19; 12:22.

Lesson 13

New Perspective: *Image 1*–microscopic grain of sand; *Image 2*–pile of sand; *Image 3*–sand in a desert.

Copyright © 2021 by Standard Publishing, part of the David C Cook family. Permission is granted to reproduce this page for ministry purposes only. Not for resale.

Activity Pages

—————— • ——————

Spring Quarter
2022
God Frees and Redeems

THESE ACTIVITY PAGES ARE DESIGNED TO:
- Engage students in a way that lecture and open-ended discussion don't.
- Gain insight on what has been learned and what hasn't.
- Encourage students to learn from one another and build vital relationships, in keeping with Proverbs 27:17 and Galatians 6:2.

TIPS FOR USING ACTIVITY PAGES:
- Instructions are on each lesson's "Involvement Learning" page (for teachers) and Activity Page (for students).
- Use these pages as optional alternatives for "Involvement Learning" activities.
- Limit individual work time and focus on facilitating discussion among learners.
- Encourage students to complete take-home work by discussing their results in the next class session.

MAXIMIZE GROUP ACTIVITY TIME!
- Instead of viewing group activities as empty time for you as the teacher, look for opportunities to encourage and challenge your students.
- Pray silently during the activity for the participants' spiritual growth! Pray for them by name, calling on the Lord to bless each person.
- Circulate among the groups of learners and observe their interactions to discover your learners' level of spiritual maturity.
- Pray that the Spirit will fall on your classroom, equipping your students with knowledge and filling them with passion to boldly proclaim the good news.

FREED FROM CAPTIVITY

FAMOUS PROJECTS

Match each historical American construction project with the correct duration of its construction, the modern cost of its construction, and the amount of resources needed.

CONSTRUCTION	DURATION	COST	RESOURCES
Golden Gate Bridge			
Hoover Dam			
Mount Rushmore			
Washington Monument			
Willis (Sears) Tower			

DURATION:	COST:	RESOURCES:
3 years	$990,000	400 laborers
4 years	$5.4 million	36,000 stones
9 years	$514 million	74,000 tons of steel
14 years	$750 million	88,000 tons of steel
16 years	$860 million	6,600,000 tons of concrete

CONSTRUCTION PROPOSAL

Using the verses in today's lesson from Ezra 1–2, create an outline for the temple construction project.

PART A
About the Project (Ezra 1:1-4)

- What will be built?
- Where will it be built?
- Who are the overseers of the project?
- Who are the investors of the project?
- How will it be financed/resourced?

PART B
Materials (Ezra 1:5-8, 11)

- What materials are needed to accomplish this project?
- How can these materials contribute to the success of the project (to purchase supplies, construct, pay laborers, or furnish the final product)?

PART C
Participants (Ezra 2:64-70)

- What kinds of people and animals are required?
- How can each contribute to the work and the success of the project?

Copyright © 2021 by Standard Publishing, part of the David C Cook family. Permission is granted to reproduce this page for ministry purposes only. Not for resale.

FREE TO WORSHIP

REBUILD AND REDEEM

Create half of a box by following the instructions below. Then flip the box over so it resembles a brick. Write a blessing for the returned exiles on the outside of Side D. Then work with other participants to stack the "bricks" into a wall or building, to demonstrate how the decree piled more and more blessings on God's people for the temple project.

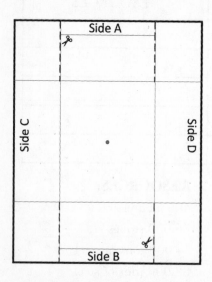

Instructions:

1. Cut out the rectangle.
2. Fold Sides A and B so the edges meet at the dot in the middle. Crease, then unfold.
3. Fold Sides C and D so the edges meet at the dot in the middle. Crease, then unfold.
4. Cut along the four dotted lines, to the intersection of the creases.

5. Refold Sides C and D so they stand up, and fold in the cut wings so they meet in the middle on Sides A and B.
6. Refold Side A up and fold its top over the cut wings and tape the edge of Side A to the inside of the box.
7. Repeat step 6 for Side B.
8. Flip the box over. On the outside of Side D, write your assigned word or phrase.

GOD'S RESOURCES

Draw lines to match the problems on the left with solutions from Scripture on the right.

PROBLEM	SOLUTION
I can't sustain my basic needs.	Exodus 4:11-12
I don't have enough skills.	1 Samuel 17:45-47
I don't have proper tools.	Isaiah 41:10
I don't have enough strength.	Luke 12:24
I don't have enough education or training.	Acts 4:13

Write down one challenging thing that God is asking you to do:

_____

Spend some time researching Scripture references to God's promises or assurances. Write the references down as a reminder and encouragement to yourself:

_____

Copyright © 2021 by Standard Publishing, part of the David C Cook family. Permission is granted to reproduce this page for ministry purposes only. Not for resale.

FREE TO CELEBRATE

HOLIDAY MATCHING

Complete the puzzle using the clues provided.

Across

4. Saint _____ Day is named in honor of a fifth century A.D. missionary to the Irish people.
5. _____ Day comes from Germanic roots and was originally celebrated using a badger.

Down

1. _____ Day is observed with jokes and pranks.
2. _____ Day was established in 1970 and was inspired as a response to the 1969 Santa Barbara oil spill.
3. _____Day is named in honor of a fifth century A.D. martyr in Rome.

After completion reflect on ways you can celebrate the following holidays in a God-honoring manner with a community of believers.

COMPARE AND CONTRAST

Read and compare 1 Kings 8:62-66 and Ezra 6:16-22. In the Venn diagram, write down the items unique to each temple dedication in the outer sections of the circles. Then write the things that both temple dedications have in common in the middle section where the circles overlap.

What do you think was significant about similarities between the dedications? _____

_____

_____

Ezra's Temple

Both Temples

Solomon's Temple

Copyright © 2021 by Standard Publishing, part of the David C Cook family. Permission is granted to reproduce this page for ministry purposes only. Not for resale.

FREE BECAUSE OF THE LORD

NaN*Lesson 4, Deuteronomy 8:1-11, NIV*

LOOKING BACKWARD/LOOKING FORWARD

Part A. Study Deuteronomy 8:1-5 and write down the phrases that indicate what God did in the past for his people.

Part B. Study Deuteronomy 8:6-11 and write down the phrases that indicate what God promised to do in the future for his people.

LOOKING BACKWARD

_____
_____
_____
_____
_____
_____
_____

LOOKING FORWARD

_____
_____
_____
_____
_____
_____
_____
_____

REMEMBER

Fill in the blanks, rewriting parts of the passage to reflect your personal experience with the Lord. Refer to the original verses to help guide you.

Observe the commands of the Lord your God, walking in obedience to him and revering him. For the Lord your God _____
_____
_____.

When you have _____, praise the Lord your God for _____ he has given you. Be careful that you do not forget the Lord your God, failing to observe his commands, his laws and his decrees that I am giving you this day.

Copyright © 2021 by Standard Publishing, part of the David C Cook family. Permission is granted to reproduce this page for ministry purposes only. Not for resale.

Triumphal Entry of the King

Lesson 5, Matthew 21:1-11, NIV

Monarch for a Day

Imagine that you get to be king or queen for one day. What preferences and special treatments would you expect in deference to your new position? Fill in the blanks and then share your plan with the group.

Mode of transportation: _____

Royal costume/outfit: _____

Entourage (top 3 fans/servants): _____

Title (what people would call you): _____

Outing (where you would go): _____

Activity (what you would do): _____

Gifts (what people would give you): _____

Who Is This?

Many people today have incomplete understandings about who Jesus is. If someone said the following to you, how would you respond? Who do you say that he is?

"Jesus was a good teacher but nothing more."

_____

_____

"He was a prophet but not the Messiah."

_____

_____

"I'm not even sure Jesus was a real man."

_____

_____

Copyright © 2021 by Standard Publishing, part of the David C Cook family. Permission is granted to reproduce this page for ministry purposes only. Not for resale.

PASSOVER WITH THE KING

THE PASSOVER LAMB

Write a one-sentence summary of the significance of the lamb from each passage.

John 1:29-30 _____

_____

1 Corinthians 5:7-8 _____

_____

Revelation 5:6-10 _____

_____

REMEMBER

Jesus commanded that we remember him when we partake in the Lord's Supper. We can remember in two ways: recalling what Jesus did, especially the sacrifice he made; and recalling how Jesus' sacrifice has changed us.

Write down key aspects of your salvation testimony that help you remember Jesus while eating the Lord's Supper.

_____

_____

_____

_____

_____

_____

_____

Copyright © 2021 by Standard Publishing, part of the David C Cook family. Permission is granted to reproduce this page for ministry purposes only. Not for resale.

RESURRECTION OF THE KING

DECLARATION AND COMMAND

Use Matthew 28:5-7 and write down the words of the angel in the appropriate box below. If what the angel said was a statement of fact, put it in the "Declaration" box; if what the angel said was instructions for what the women should do, put it in the "Command" box.

DECLARATION	COMMAND
_____	_____
_____	_____
_____	_____
_____	_____
_____	_____
_____	_____
_____	_____

In what ways did Jesus' appearance and words to the women confirm everything the angel said?

HE AROSE!

Sing along with the chorus. Jot down any words or phrases in the song lyrics that are most meaningful to you.

_____
_____
_____
_____
_____
_____

Up from the grave He arose
With a mighty triumph o'er His foes
He arose a Victor from the dark domain
And He lives forever with His saints to reign
He arose! (He arose)
He arose! (He arose)
Hallelujah! Christ arose!

Copyright © 2021 by Standard Publishing, part of the David C Cook family. Permission is granted to reproduce this page for ministry purposes only. Not for resale.

FREEDOM IN THE KING

ROLES AND EXPECTATIONS

For each of the following roles make a list of expectations that society would have for each one. Then, write down how Jesus and His teaching upends those expectations.

Abraham's descendants: _____

_____

_____

A slave: _____

_____

_____

A son: _____

_____

_____

A father: _____

_____

_____

WORD WEB

Choose one of the following words and write it in the center bubble: ***teaching, disciples, truth, free.*** Then brainstorm associated words and write those words in the surrounding bubbles.

How do the associated words help you understand the main word?

In what ways do the associated words deepen your interpretation of the main word?

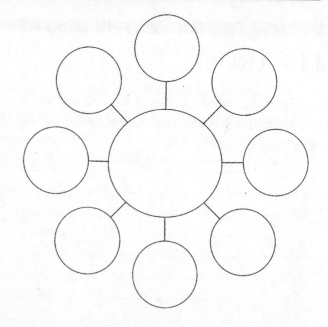

Copyright © 2021 by Standard Publishing, part of the David C Cook family. Permission is granted to reproduce this page for ministry purposes only. Not for resale.

FREEDOM FROM SIN

ROMANS VOCABULARY PUZZLE

Fill in the puzzle by answering the clues below. What importance do these words have in Romans 6:1-14?

Across

2. Describes our current body.
4. Sin no longer _____ in believers' lives.
7. Does not save us from sin.
9. How often Jesus died to sin.
11. We are _____ with Christ.

Down

1. What sin should be in believers' lives.
3. Experience of Christ pictured when a believer rises out of the waters of baptism.
5. The quality that allows us to be reconciled to God.
6. The act that represents our new life in Christ.
8. Consider yourselves _____ to God.
9. Describes our previous self.
10. Experience of Christ pictured when a believer is lowered into the water of baptism.

HIS RESURRECTION AND OUR NEW LIFE

As you read Ephesians 2:1-10 and Colossians 3:1-14, write down the verses that correspond with the text in Romans. Make note of any additional information provided in Ephesians and Colossians. Then answer the question below based on these texts.

Romans 6:1-4 _____

Romans 6:5-7 _____

Romans 6:8-10 _____

Romans 6:11-14 _____

What can I commit to change in my life to experience new life in Christ more fully?

Copyright © 2021 by Standard Publishing, part of the David C Cook family. Permission is granted to reproduce this page for ministry purposes only. Not for resale.

FREEDOM FOR THE FUTURE

PRAYER REQUESTS

Take one minute to jot down prayer concerns you have in the following areas:

Internationally _____

Nationally _____

Locally _____

In my church _____

In my family _____

In me _____

What common thread do you see in these concerns?

PATTERNS IN GOD'S WILL

With a partner, fill in the chart below with appropriate information for each term. Cite verses to back up your answers.

	Definition	Example(s) from Jesus' Life	Example(s) from Believers' Experiences
Foreknowledge			
Predestination			
Calling			
Justification			
Glorification			

Copyright © 2021 by Standard Publishing, part of the David C Cook family. Permission is granted to reproduce this page for ministry purposes only. Not for resale.

FREEDOM AND THE LAW

WHAT ABOUT BAPTISM?

Suppose a non-Christian or a new believer asked, "Why is baptism important?"

How would you answer? _____
_____

Now look at the following Scriptures and jot down what each says about this question:

Acts 2:38 _____
Romans 6:1-14 _____
Galatians 3:26-27 _____
Colossians 2:9-12 _____
1 Peter 3:20-21 _____

Based on these Scripture texts, edit your above answer and rewrite it below:
_____

ADOPTED TO A NEW LIFE

Using a smartphone or computer, research the story of a famous adoptee (some possibilities include Steve Jobs, Dave Thomas, or Simone Biles). Based on that person's story of adoption, answer the left column in the below chart. Then, based on Paul's writing on spiritual adoption in Galatians 3:18-29, answer the right column in the below chart.

	Concerning Physical Adoption	Concerning Spiritual Adoption
Who?		
What?		
Where?		
When?		
How?		
Why?		

Summarize the major differences between physical adoption and spiritual adoption.

As a spiritually adopted child of God, what promises are made to you as his heir?

Copyright © 2021 by Standard Publishing, part of the David C Cook family. Permission is granted to reproduce this page for ministry purposes only. Not for resale.

FREEDOM, LOVE, AND FAITH

LOVE YOUR NEIGHBOR

The command to love one's neighbors is repeated throughout Scripture. Read the following passages from Scripture and answer: Who is speaking? Who is the audience? How does the audience respond? Why does this passage say a person should love their neighbor?

Leviticus 19:18

Mark 12:28-34

Matthew 5:43-48

Romans 13:8-10

Matthew 19:16-30

James 2:1-13

WHO'S MY NEIGHBOR?

Imagine this chart is a map of your neighborhood and the homes surrounding yours. Your home is represented by the center image. In the blank space, write down the names of those neighbors who live around you. If you don't know a neighbor's name, commit to meeting them. When complete, place this chart in a location that you see daily. It will serve as a reminder to remember and pray for your neighbors.

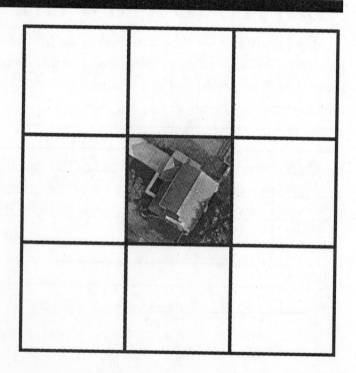

Copyright © 2021 by Standard Publishing, part of the David C Cook family. Permission is granted to reproduce this page for ministry purposes only. Not for resale.

THE FRUIT OF FREEDOM

Lesson 13, Galatians 5:16-26, NIV

WHAT KIND OF FRUIT?

Label each fruit as a different fruit of the Spirit as listed in today's text. Under each label, write a sentence to describe the meaning of this fruit and a practical way this fruit can be demonstrated in the coming days.

READ ALL ABOUT IT!

With the help of a smartphone or computer, go to the website of a local news outlet. Choose three news headlines and write the headlines below. Quickly read through the news story to determine the story's main points. Below each headline, write a sentence telling how the news story might be different if the fruit of the Spirit were evident in the lives of those reported in the story.

Headline: _____

If the Spirit's fruit were evident: _____

Headline: _____

If the Spirit's fruit were evident: _____

Headline: _____

If the Spirit's fruit were evident: _____

Copyright © 2021 by Standard Publishing, part of the David C Cook family. Permission is granted to reproduce this page for ministry purposes only. Not for resale.

Lesson 1

Famous Projects:

Golden Gate Bridge: 4 years/$514 million/88,000 tons of steel
Hoover Dam: 5 years/$750 million/6,600,000 tons of concrete
Mount Rushmore: 14 years/$990,000/400 laborers
Washington Monument: 16 years/$28.4 million/36,000 stones
Willis (Sears) Tower: 3 years/$860 million/74,000 tons of steel

Construction Proposal:

Part A – a temple; in Jerusalem; God or Cyrus; Cyrus and the family heads of Judah and Benjamin, the priests, the Levites, and "survivors"; financed by gifts from the people of God

Part B – silver, gold, goods, livestock, valuable gifts, freewill offerings, vessels from the original temple; answers to the second part may vary, no specific correct answers

Part C – 7,337 slaves, 200 singers, 736 horses, 245 mules, 435 camels, 6,720 donkeys, 61,000 darics of gold, 5,000 minas of silver and 100 priestly garments; answers to the second part may vary, no specific correct answers

Lesson 2

God's Resources: I can't sustain my basic needs – Luke 12:24; I don't have enough skills – Exodus 4:11-12; I don't have proper tools – 1 Samuel 17:45-47; I don't have enough strength – Isaiah 41:10; I don't have enough education or training – Acts 4:13

Lesson 3

Holiday Matching:

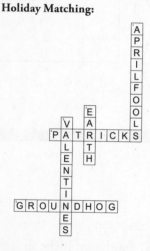

Compare and Contrast: Solomon's Temple – offering included 22,000 cattle, 120,000 sheep and goats; consecrated the middle of the courtyard for offerings; king held a feast for 14 days. Ezra's Temple – offering included 100 bulls, 200 rams, 400 male lambs, 12 male goats; established the priests and Levites; celebrated the Passover; Celebrated the Festival of Unleavened Bread. Both Temples– Gave offerings to God; celebrated feasts, the people had joy for what the Lord had done.

Lesson 4

Looking Backward/Looking Forward: Looking Backward – led them for 40 years in wilderness, fed them with manna, preserved raiment/clothing, kept their feet from swelling; Looking Forward – bring them into a good land, provide plenty (not scarce or lacking)

Lesson 6

The Passover Lamb: Possible answers include: John called Jesus the Lamb who would take our sins away. Christ is called the Passover Lamb. The Lamb was slain but is now alive, victorious, and worthy

Lesson 7

Declaration and Command: Declaration – I know that you are looking for Jesus, who was crucified; He is not here; he has risen, just as he said; he is going ahead of you into Galilee; there you will see him / Command – Do not be afraid; Come and see the place where he lay; then go quickly; tell his disciples he is risen from the dead. His physical appearance confirmed that he was alive; He also said the disciples would see him in Galilee

Lesson 9

Romans Vocabulary Puzzle:

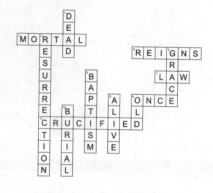

Copyright © 2021 by Standard Publishing, part of the David C Cook family. Permission is granted to reproduce this page for ministry purposes only. Not for resale.

Activity Pages

•

Summer Quarter 2022
Partners in a New Creation

THESE ACTIVITY PAGES ARE DESIGNED TO:

- Engage students in a way that lecture and open-ended discussion don't.
- Gain insight on what has been learned and what hasn't.
- Encourage students to learn from one another and build vital relationships, in keeping with Proverbs 27:17 and Galatians 6:2.

TIPS FOR USING ACTIVITY PAGES:

- Instructions are on each lesson's "Involvement Learning" page (for teachers) and Activity Page (for students).
- Use these pages as optional alternatives for "Involvement Learning" activities.
- Limit individual work time and focus on facilitating discussion among learners.
- Encourage students to complete take-home work by discussing their results in the next class session.

MAXIMIZE GROUP ACTIVITY TIME!

- Instead of viewing group activities as empty time for you as the teacher, look for opportunities to encourage and challenge your students.
- Pray silently during the activity for the participants' spiritual growth! Pray for them by name, calling on the Lord to bless each person.
- Circulate among the groups of learners and observe their interactions to discover your learners' level of spiritual maturity.
- Pray for the Spirit to lead as your students grow in their knowledge of the Word—that they may be filled with passion to proclaim the good news boldly.

GOD FORETELLS DESTRUCTION

Lesson 1, Isaiah 47:10-15, NIV

ADVICE IN THE STARS?

A rough analysis of 22,000 horoscopes revealed that approximately 90 percent of the words were the same. Use this list of the most common words to see how easy it is to make up a false guide for a person's choices for the day.

Word Bank:

able	best	better	careful	change	comes	else
energy	everything	exactly	expect	family	feel	friend
fun	hard	help	important	keep	life	like
love	matter	maybe	mind	moment	mood	others
plans	possible	ready	secret	share	situation	soon
sure	taking	turn	universe	usual	whatever	worry

How does God's advice differ from astrology?

_____

What are other harmful ways people seek reassurance about their decisions?

_____

AM I SAFE?

Summarize the places, people, or exercises the Babylonians trusted to keep them safe.

_____

What similar places, people, or exercises might people in your community wrongly trust instead of the Lord?

_____

Look up what the Bible says about where to put your trust and write it below.

Psalm 56:3-4 _____

_____

Isaiah 12:2 _____

_____

Romans 15:13 _____

_____

Copyright © 2021 by Standard Publishing, part of the David C Cook family. Permission is granted to reproduce this page for ministry purposes only. Not for resale.

GOD FORETELLS REDEMPTION

Lesson 2, Isaiah 49:1-13, NIV

ACCEPTANCE SPEECH

Imagine you have been elected or nominated for a position in civic leadership. In the center column, identify verses from Isaiah 49:1-13 that match with the left column. Complete the activity by jotting down ideas about information you could include in your own acceptance speech that mirror the servant.

	Servant's Speech	Personal Speech
Greet Audience		
Source of Authority		
Qualifications for Leadership		
Purpose and Mandate		
Measure of Success		
Reward/Result for Leadership		

SERVANT LEADER

Brainstorm some ways you can serve God and participate in his mission this week. Choose at least one thing to put into action this week.

Hear/Answer (Respond) Help Preserve/Keep

Establish/Restore Shine Light Relieve Hunger and Thirst

Have Mercy/Protect Guide/Lead Comfort/Have Compassion

_____

_____

_____

_____

_____

Copyright © 2021 by Standard Publishing, part of the David C Cook family. Permission is granted to reproduce this page for ministry purposes only. Not for resale.
Activity Page 500

God's People Shall Prosper

Bedtime Story

Cover the paragraph below before choosing a word for each part of speech specified. If you are working as a pair, make sure you both choose your words before reading the paragraph. Fill in your answers and read your completed bedtime story!

1. girl's name: _____
2. occupation: _____
3. family member: _____

4. color: _____
5. animal: _____
6. number: _____

7. occupation: _____
8. country: _____
9. kind of building: _____

10. -ly adverb: _____

1. _____ always dreamed that she was a 2. _____. When she had chores to do, she would imagine that her real 3. _____ rode up on a 4. _____ 5. _____ to tell her that she was going home! When 1. _____ turned 6. _____, guess who showed up? The 7. _____ of 8. _____! And she learned she really was a 2. _____! 1. _____ went to live in a 9. _____. 1. _____ lived 17. _____ ever after.

How might this silly story relate to how God's people felt about his promise that they would prosper again?

_____

_____

_____

Waiting and Hoping

Answer the following questions and share your responses with one other person.

1. What is it that you are waiting on or hoping for that you've been praying about?

_____

_____

2. What promise of God have you been holding on to that you have not yet seen fulfilled?

_____

_____

Copyright © 2021 by Standard Publishing, part of the David C Cook family. Permission is granted to reproduce this page for ministry purposes only. Not for resale.

GOD OFFERS DELIVERANCE

WHAT ARE YOU SEARCHING FOR?

Find as many words as possible in the puzzle that relate to today's lesson. Solve the anagrams to reveal the letters for the final message. Use the circled letters from the words in the top part to complete the final word or phrase at the bottom. Each circled letter is used just once.

YSEE

ETGAHR

RIDNCLEH

LEIEX

CPALE

ORLD

OENMANTR

RIBED

WEATS

HERAT

SKGIN

QESEUN

TSEHFAR

EHTORSM

SDUT

LOOK AROUND

In Isaiah 51:1-8, the speaker calls the people to turn their focus to the past, future, and present.

Fill in the chart as appropriate from today's text.

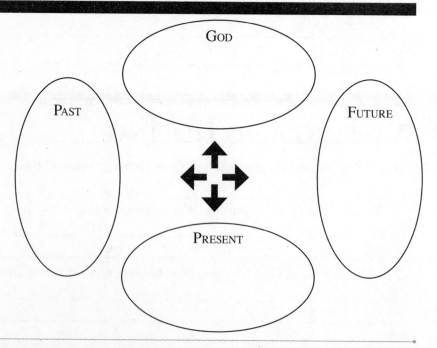

GOD

PAST

FUTURE

PRESENT

Copyright © 2021 by Standard Publishing, part of the David C Cook family. Permission is granted to reproduce this page for ministry purposes only. Not for resale.

THE WORD BECOMES FLESH

WORD/CREATOR/LIGHT

John 1:1-5 attributes these identities to the Son of God. Based on your reading in John 1:1-14, fill out the following chart.

	Word	Creator	Light
Draw an icon to represent this identity.			
Write a definition for the identity.			
List any synonyms or related phrases to the identity.			
How did Jesus demonstrate this identity?			

A WITNESS TO THE LIGHT

Read John 1:19-34 and write down the verses that correspond with the printed text in John 1:6-9. Make note of any additional information provided in John 1:19-34. Then answer the questions below based on these texts.

John 1:6 _____

John 1:7 _____

John 1:8 _____

John 1:9 _____

How would you define the witness of John the Baptist?

How would John's witness look similarly and differently if he gave witness in your current context?

Copyright © 2021 by Standard Publishing, part of the David C Cook family. Permission is granted to reproduce this page for ministry purposes only. Not for resale.

THE WORD HEALS

Lesson 6, John 4:46-54, NIV

SIGNIFICANT MIRACLES

The Scripture texts in the first column each tell of a different miracle of Jesus. Read the Scripture texts and complete the chart.

Scripture	What did Jesus do?	How did people react?	What was the significance for the original audience?	What is the significance for us?
John 2:1-11				
John 5:1-15				
John 6:1-15				
John 6:16-24				
John 9:1-12				
John 11:1-45				

SEEKING GOD'S POWER

With the help of a classmate, consider the needs of your class, church, neighborhood, and nation. Complete the following statements as petitions for God's power to be present in these areas. After completing the statements, spend time in prayer with a classmate.

Lord, our class needs your power to . . . _____

_____

Lord, our church needs your power to . . . _____

_____

Lord, our neighborhood needs your power to . . . _____

_____

Lord, our nation needs your power to . . . _____

_____

Copyright © 2021 by Standard Publishing, part of the David C Cook family. Permission is granted to reproduce this page for ministry purposes only. Not for resale.
Activity Page 504

THE WORD SAVES

Lesson 7, John 12:44-50, NIV

LIGHT AND DARK

In one or two sentences, paraphrase the message of these verses regarding spiritual light and darkness.

Reference	Paraphrase
Isaiah 42:6-7, 16	_____
Isaiah 50:10	_____
John 8:12	_____
Acts 26:15-19	_____
1 John 1:5-7	_____

Based on these verses, how would you summarize Scripture's teaching on light and darkness?

LIGHT METER

How brightly does the light of Jesus shine in your life? Put a mark on the light meter to indicate your answer.

Total Darkness   **Brightest Light**

What factors might cause the light of Jesus to become dimmer in a believer's life?
_____
_____

What factors might cause the light of Jesus to become brighter in a believer's life?
_____
_____

What steps will you take to better follow Jesus and let his light shine in your life?
_____
_____

Copyright © 2021 by Standard Publishing, part of the David C Cook family. Permission is granted to reproduce this page for ministry purposes only. Not for resale.

WORD RESURRECTS

Lesson 8, John 11:17-27, 38-44, NIV

(MIS)CONCEPTIONS ABOUT DEATH

Choose at least two stages of life below and write a sentence for each describing how someone in that stage of life would describe or define death.

Early Childhood (ages 3–6): _____

Middle Childhood (ages 6–8): _____

Late Childhood (ages 9–11): _____

Adolescence (ages 12–20): _____

Early Adulthood (ages 20–35): _____

Midlife (ages 35–50): _____

Mature Adulthood (ages 50+): _____

How do those viewpoints compare and contrast with that of 1 Corinthians 15?

_____

RIGHT THOUGHTS ABOUT JESUS

For each reference, look up the rest of the "I am" statement and write it under "What's So." Fill in the blanks under "So What?" during the ensuing class discussion.

Text	What's So	So What?
1. John 6:35 . . . . I am _____		_____
2. John 8:12 . . . . I am _____		_____
3. John 10:7, 9 . . . . . I am _____		_____
4. John 10:11, 14 . . . . I am _____		_____
5. John 11:25 . . . . . . I am _____		_____
6. John 14:6 . . . . I am _____		_____
7. John 15:1, 5 . . . . . I am _____		_____

Copyright © 2021 by Standard Publishing, part of the David C Cook family. Permission is granted to reproduce this page for ministry purposes only. Not for resale.

THE WORD GIVES PEACE

Lesson 9, John 14:15-29, NIV

INDUCTIVE STUDY, PART 1

The best way to discover what a writer means by a certain word is to look at how that writer actually uses that word.

Text	**Meaning** *(mental image for original audience)*	**Significance** *(implications for us today)*
John 14:16		
John 14:26		
John 15:26		
John 16:7		
1 John 2:1		

For an extended study, also consider these three texts—the only places where the same word for Advocate appears in the Greek version of the Old Testament.

Text	**Meaning** *(mental image for original audience)*	**Significance** *(implications for us today)*
Job 16:2		
Job 21:2		
Psalm 94:19		

INDUCTIVE STUDY, PART 2

Perhaps surprisingly, the designation *Holy Spirit* occurs in the Old Testament in only three verses. Complete the chart below as you did in the "Inductive Study, Part 1."

Text	**Meaning** *(mental image for original audience)*	**Significance** *(implications for us today)*
Psalm 51:11		
Isaiah 63:10		
Job 21:2		

Copyright © 2021 by Standard Publishing, part of the David C Cook family. Permission is granted to reproduce this page for ministry purposes only. Not for resale.

A NEW HOME

Lesson 10, Revelation 21:1-9, NIV

WORDS AS DEPICTIONS

Today's text is full of word-pictures. Some are symbolic, depicting a future reality in present-day terms. For each of the following, jot down what it teaches you about the nature of Heaven.

Sea (v. 1) _____

Jerusalem (v. 2) _____

Bride (v. 2) _____

Throne (v. 5) _____

Alpha and Omega (v. 6) _____

Water of life (v. 6) _____

Lake (v. 8) _____

METAPHOR (*meh*-tuh-four)
→ noun, definition:
A figure of speech in which a word or phrase literally denoting one kind of object or idea is used in place of another to suggest a likeness or analogy between them.

FIGURATIVE (*fih*-geh-reh-tiv)
→ adjective, definition:
Expressing one thing in terms normally denoting another with which it may be regarded as analogous.

HERE COMES THE BRIDE

Read the following passages to get a fuller picture of what the bride imagery signifies. Jot conclusions.

What this passage implies about God's relationship with his people:

Matthew 25:1-10 _____

Mark 2:19-20 _____

John 3:29 _____

[other:_____] _____

Copyright © 2021 by Standard Publishing, part of the David C Cook family. Permission is granted to reproduce this page for ministry purposes only. Not for resale.

A New City

Gems

Find eight gems listed to the right in the puzzle below.

```
S R T L B K E H H P
C M Z F I S M D T E
D N H J X R E N N A
S A P P H I R E I R
O O L K R R A V C L
S T U F E B L Z A M
S R M P E U D E J A
S G S R Z A P O T Y
K A Y G X S N R Y F
J L A M E T H Y S T
```

Amethyst

Beryl

Emerald

Jacinth

Jasper

Pearl

Sapphire

Topaz

Photo: © Getty Images

Meaning and Significance

How should we interpret the following words in terms of the meaning and significance of today's text?

Symbol	Meaning[1]	Significance[2]
High mountain		
12 tribes		
12 apostles		
Perfect square		
144 cubits		
Precious stones		
Gold as transparent glass		

Notes:

[1] *Meaning* deals with mental images—what comes to mind when one hears a word.
   Example: Hearing the word *table* brings to mind an item of furniture having a flat top and four legs.

[2] *Significance* deals with implications.
   Example: When a child hears his mother say "It's time to come to the table," the implication is that it's time for dinner.

Copyright © 2021 by Standard Publishing, part of the David C Cook family. Permission is granted to reproduce this page for ministry purposes only. Not for resale.

THE RIVER OF LIFE

THE SOURCE OF LIFE

Compare and contrast the imagery in today's text with that of other passages.

The River of Life (Revelation 22:1)

Ezekiel 47:1-12 _____

Zechariah 14:8 _____

Revelation 7:17 _____

Revelation 22:17 _____

The Tree of Life (Revelation 22:2)

Genesis 2:9, 17 _____

Genesis 3:22-24 _____

Ezekiel 47:7, 13 _____

What conclusions do you draw?

THE PROMISE OF HOPE

How might truth indicated by today's Scripture encourage someone who makes the following statements? Jot thoughts under each picture.

"Life seems hopeless."

Photo: © Getty Images

"The evil all around almost overwhelms me."

Photo: © Getty Images

"Sometimes I just feel empty."

Photo: © Ron Nickelson

_____

_____

_____

_____

_____

Copyright © 2021 by Standard Publishing, part of the David C Cook family. Permission is granted to reproduce this page for ministry purposes only. Not for resale.

A Welcoming Invitation

Who Was/Is Jesus?

For each title below from today's text, explain the meaning and significance. Other passages with the same title are listed for reference.

Title and Scriptures	Meaning[1]	Significance[2]
Alpha and Omega • Revelation 1:8, 11; 21:6	_____	_____
First and Last • Isaiah 41:4; 44:6; 48:12; Revelation 1:11, 17; 2:8	_____	_____
Beginning and End • Revelation 1:8; 21:6	_____	_____
Root/Offspring of David • Isaiah 11:1; Jeremiah 23:5; 33:15; Matthew 1:1; Romans 1:3	_____	_____
Bright, Morning Star • 2 Peter 1:19; Revelation 2:28	_____	_____

Notes (also see lesson 11):

[1] *Meaning* deals with mental images—what comes to mind when one hears a word.
    Example: Hearing the word *table* brings to mind an item of furniture having a flat top and four legs.

[2] *Significance* deals with implications.
    Example: When a child hears his mother say "It's time to come to the table," the implication is that it's time for dinner.

"Come, Lord Jesus"

Under what circumstances would you reluctantly utter the three words above as a prayer? How about enthusiastically (see Revelation 22:20)? Write a key event for you for each month in the left-hand column. Then answer the two questions above in the other two columns.

Key Event	I would have prayed this reluctantly because	I would have prayed this enthusiastically because
In August		
_____	_____	_____
In July		
_____	_____	_____
In June		
_____	_____	_____

What do you conclude after completing this self-reflection?

Copyright © 2021 by Standard Publishing, part of the David C Cook family. Permission is granted to reproduce this page for ministry purposes only. Not for resale.

Lesson 1

Advice in the Stars?: Answers will vary.

Am I Safe?: Babylonians trusted wickedness, their own wisdom and knowledge, magic spells and sorceries. Answers will vary for the second question. God is the only appropriate "place" for our trust.

Lesson 2

Acceptance Speech: Greet Audience: verse 1a; Source of Authority: verse 1b; Qualifications for Leadership: verse 2; Purpose and Mandate: verse 3; Measure of Success: verse 4a; Reward/Result for Leadership: 4b.

Servant Leader: Answers will vary.

Lesson 3

Both activities: Answers will vary.

Lesson 4

What Are You Searching For?:

Look Around: *God*—law, judgment, righteousness, salvation, trust, salvation forever; *Past*—Abraham, Sarah, God called him, blessed him, and increased; *Present*—righteousness, law, no fear, salvation; *Future*—comfort Zion and all her ruins, make her deserts like Eden, make her wastelands like a garden, there will be joy, gladness, thanksgiving, and the sound of singing.

Lesson 5

Word/Creator/Light: Answers will vary. Consult the lesson commentary for additional guidance.

A Witness to the Light: John 1:6—v. 19; John 1:7—vv. 19, 23; John 1:8—vv. 20, 26-27, 30-31; John 1:9—vv. 29, 34

Lesson 6

Significant Miracles: John 2:1-11: Jesus changed water to wine; the master of the banquet was surprised and Jesus' disciples reacted with faith in Jesus; the original audience recognized Jesus' power over creation. 5:1-15: Jesus healed a man with a disability; the Jewish leaders were concerned that he was healed on the Sabbath; the original audience recognized that the Sabbath was no barrier to Jesus' ministry. 6:1-15: Jesus fed 5000; the people thought Jesus was a prophet and wanted to make him king; the original audience recognized that the Bread of Life provides for his followers. 6:16-24: Jesus walked on water; his disciples were afraid; the original audience saw Jesus' mastery of all nature, even the violent bits. 9:1-12: Jesus healed a man with blindness; some believed the man was healed, while others did not; the original audience understood that only those with eyes to see could recognize Jesus as the promised Messiah. 11:1-45: Jesus raised Lazarus from the dead; many believed in Jesus; the original audience understood that Jesus' power was not limited to nature but also to life and death.

Seeking God's Power: Answers will vary.

Lesson 7

Both activities: Answers will vary.

Lesson 8

(Mis)conceptions About Death: Answers will vary.

Right Thoughts About Jesus: *What's So:* 1–the bread of life; 2–the light of the world; 3–the gate; 4–the good shepherd; 5–the resurrection and the life; 6–the way and the truth and the life; 7–the vine. *So What:* Many responses are possible.

Lesson 9

Both activities: More than one answer is plausible for each line. See teacher-guide commentary.

Lesson 10

Both activities: More than one answer is plausible for each line. See teacher-guide commentary.

Lesson 11

Gems:

Meaning and Significance: More than one defensible conclusion is possible is several cases. Consult the lesson commentary for additional guidance.

Lesson 12

The Source of Life: Answers will vary. See lesson commentary for additional guidance.

The Promise of Hope: Answers will vary.

Lesson 13

Who Was/Is Jesus?: Consult the lesson commentary on Revelation 22:13, 16 for insight.

"Come, Lord Jesus": Responses will be highly individual and variable.

Copyright © 2021 by Standard Publishing, part of the David C Cook family. Permission is granted to reproduce this page for ministry purposes only. Not for resale.